The Blackwell Handbook of Mediation

THE BLACKWELL HANDBOOK OF MEDIATION

Bridging Theory, Research, and Practice

Edited by

MARGARET S. HERRMAN

BLACKWELL PUBLISHING
350 Main Street, Malden, MA 02148-5020, USA
9600 Garsington Road, Oxford OX4 2DQ, UK
550 Swanston Street, Carlton, Victoria 3053, Australia

First published 2006 by Blackwell Publishing Ltd

1   2006

Library of Congress Cataloging-in-Publication Data

The Blackwell handbook of mediation : a guide to effective negotiation / edited by
Margaret S. Herrman.
   p. cm.
  Includes bibliographical references and index.
  ISBN-13: 978-1-4051- 2742-4 (hardback : alk. paper)
   ISBN-10: 1-4051- 2742-2 (hardback : alk. paper)   1. Mediation—Handbooks, manuals, etc.
2. Negotiation—Handbooks, manuals, etc.   3. Conflict management—Handbooks,
manuals, etc.   I. Herrman, Margaret S., 1944–

  HM1126.B53 2006
  303.6′9—dc22

                        2005015462

A catalogue record for this title is available from the British Library.

Set in 10/12pt Baskerville
by Graphicraft Limited, Hong Kong
Printed and bound in Great Britain
by TJ International Ltd, Padstow, Cornwall.

The publisher's policy is to use permanent paper from mills that operate a
sustainable forestry policy, and which has been manufactured from pulp processed
using acid-free and elementary chlorine-free practices. Furthermore, the publisher
ensures that the text paper and cover board used have met acceptable
environmental accreditation standards.

For further information on
Blackwell Publishing, visit our website:
www.blackwellpublishing.com

Contents

Acknowledgments

Decades ago, the late Jim Laue nurtured my fascination with conflict and a love of justice. His encouragement shaped my career, and set the stage for this handbook. Trish Jones, a dear friend and colleague, encouraged me to build what is now chapter 2 of this volume into this handbook. Nancy Hollett, Jerry Gale (my co-authors for the second chapter), and I deliberated for so many hours as we explored the meaning of each measure we could find relating to mediation effectiveness, what a model or organizing theme might look like, and ultimately where a measure might fit into the model we offer in this handbook. The effort was fun and very much in the spirit of creating clarity that might start conversations. Finally, there are so many visionaries and caring activists in the field of negotiation and, more specifically, in mediation. Like Jim, many sustain us through shared values and their wisdom. So many icons contributed to this handbook. I am grateful to all.

M.S.H.

Notes on Contributors

Kevin Avruch is Professor of Conflict Resolution and Anthropology at the Institute for Conflict Analysis and Resolution, and Senior Fellow and faculty in the Peace Operations Policy Program, School of Public Policy, at George Mason University. He is the author of numerous articles and essays on culture and conflict analysis and resolution, negotiation, political violence, and ethnonationalism, and the author or editor of five books, most recently *Culture and Conflict Resolution* (1998) and *Information Campaigns for Peace Operations* (2000). He has lectured widely in the United States and abroad. In 1996–97 he was a Senior Fellow in the Jennings Randolph Program for International Peace at the United States Institute of Peace.

Robert B. Coates is currently part-time Senior Research Associate with the Center for Restorative Justice and Peacemaking. He has held positions of Associate Director, Harvard Center for Criminal Justice; Associate Professor, University of Chicago School of Social Service Administration; and Professor of Social Work, University of Utah Graduate School of Social Work. Dr. Coates has also spent a dozen years serving churches as a pastor. He has authored numerous publications on deinstitutionalization, community-based services, system change, and restorative justice.

Donald E. Conlon is a Professor in the Department of Management, Eli Broad Graduate School of Management, Michigan State University. He received his Ph.D. in business administration from the organizational behavior group at the University of Illinois. Professor Conlon's research examines perceptions of fairness in a wide variety of situations, including interorganizational disputes, person–organization disputes, and interpersonal disputes. Other research interests include intragroup conflict, negotiation, and managerial decision-making. His work has been published in journals such as the *Academy of Management Journal, Academy of Management Review, Administrative Science Quarterly, Organizational Behavior and Human Decision Processes*, and the *Journal of Applied Psychology*. He has also served as Chair of the Conflict Management Division of the Academy of Management, and as President of the International Association for Conflict Management.

Morton Deutsch is Professor Emeritus and Director Emeritus of the International Center for Cooperation and Conflict Resolution at Teachers College, Columbia University. He studied with Kurt Lewin at MIT's Research Center for Group Dynamics, where he obtained his Ph.D. in 1948. He has published extensively and is well known for his pioneering studies in intergroup relations, cooperation–competition, conflict resolution, social conformity, and the social psychology of justice. His books include *Interracial Housing* (1951); *Research Methods in Social Relations* (1951, 1959); *Preventing World War III: Some Proposals* (1962); *Theories in Social Psychology* (1965); *The Resolution of Conflict* (1973); *Applying Social Psychology* (1975); *Distributive Justice* (1985); and *The Handbook of Conflict Resolution* (2000). His work has been widely honored with such awards as the Kurt Lewin Memorial Award, the G. W. Allport Prize, the Carl Hovland Memorial Award, the AAAS Socio-Psychological Prize, the Samuel Flowerman Award, APA's Distinguished Scientific Contribution Award, SESP's Distinguished Research Scientist Award, the Nevitt Sanford Award, and the Harry Levinson Award, and he is a William James Fellow of APS. He has also received several lifetime achievement awards, from the relevant professional associations, for his work on conflict management, cooperative learning, peace psychology, and the applications of psychology to social issues. In addition, he has received the Teachers College Medal for his contributions to education, the Helsinki University Medal for his contributions to psychology, and the Doctorate of Humane Letters from the City University of New York. He has been president of the Society for the Psychological Study of Social Issues; the International Society of Political Psychology; the Eastern Psychological Association; the New York State Psychological Association; and the Society for the Study of Peace, Conflict and Violence, as well as several divisions of the American Psychological Associations.

Kathy Domenici received her Master's degree in communication from the University of New Mexico. She is author of *Engaging Communication in Conflict: Systemic Practice* (2001) and *Mediation: Empowerment in Conflict Management* (2001). She helped establish Prosperity Game methodology, designing, directing, and facilitating high-level strategy and leadership games for such clients as the White House Initiative on Tribal Colleges and Universities, Eastman Kodak, the President's Commission on Critical Infrastructure, Sandia National Laboratories, Lockheed Martin, the Kellogg Foundation, and the Electronic Industries Alliance. She regularly facilitates large-scale change initiatives, such as the design and facilitation of Integrated Planning at Sandia National Laboratories, and facilitating the collaborative effort of land use agency leaders from the Southwest (Southwest Strategy) in developing creative paths for environmental issues and crises in water, fire, borders, and endangered species. With 10 years' academic work in conflict and communication and 20 years' experience in mediation, strategic planning, and public issue management, Ms. Domenici concentrates on conflict system design and innovative methods of planning and decision-making.

Jerry Gale is the Director of the Marriage and Family Therapy Doctoral Program in the Department of Child and Family Development at The University of Georgia. He is the author of *Conversation Analysis of Therapeutic Discourse: Pursuit of a Therapeutic Agenda* (1991), and co-editor of the book *Constructivism in Education* (1995). He is the co-principal investigator, working with Dr. Margaret Herrman, of the Mediator Skills Project (MSP). Dr. Gale is also a Research Fellow for the Institute of Behavioral Research at UGA. He has published many papers and book chapters on family therapy, mediation, and qualitative research, and he has presented at numerous national and international conferences.

Barbara Gray is Professor of Organizational Behavior and Director of the Center for Research in Conflict and Negotiation at the Pennsylvania State University. She has studied environmental conflict, mediation, and collaborative processes for over 25 years and has published three books, including *Collaborating: Finding Common Ground for Multiparty Problems* and *Making Sense of Intractable Environmental Conflict: Concepts and Cases*. She has over 60 other publications dealing with multiparty collaboration, conflict, and dispute resolution. Professor Gray has served on the editorial boards of *Academy of Management Journal*, *Organization Science*, and the *International Journal of Conflict Management* and as an associate editor of the *Journal of Applied Behavioral Science*. She is also a trainer and mediator and has acted as consultant to numerous organizations including the US Fish & Wildlife Service, the National Park Service, the Federal Highway Administration, and the PA departments of Environmental Protection and Agriculture, Union Carbide, Phillips (the Netherlands), the Children's Hospital (Pittsburgh), US Steel, and many others. She organized and led the Inter-University Consortium on the Framing of Intractable Environmental Disputes (<www.environmentalframing.org>). She has held several visiting appointments in the US and Europe, including the Boer & Croon Visiting Chair at TIAS Business School (Tilburg University, the Netherlands) in the fall of 2004.

Sherrill Hayes is currently a Child Custody and Visitation Mediator for the North Carolina 18th District Court and an adjunct faculty member in Human Development and Family Studies at the University of North Carolina at Greensboro. He completed his Ph.D. in Social Policy at the University of Newcastle upon Tyne, England, under the direction of Professor Janet Walker. He used questionnaires, observations, and participant observation to examine the relationships between personal and contextual characteristics and the strategies, techniques, and interventions used by mediators when working with clients. Dr. Hayes is a charter member and former Secretary of the NC Chapter of the Association for Conflict Resolution.

Margaret S. Herrman directs activities of the Herrman Group, LLC, a consulting firm devoted to helping government agencies and programs, corporations, and not-for-profits with dispute resolution, facilitation, problem-solving, and program evaluation. She also assists government and academic programs to develop and maintain quality assurance programs to support effective third party work. She has over 30 years' experience mediating public policy and employment disputes, as well as disputes in other contexts and substantive areas. Dr. Herrman is the founding co-principal investigator, working with Dr. Jerry Gale, of the Mediator Skills Project (MSP). As a Senior Associate (retired) at the Carl Vinson Institute of Government, University of Georgia, she directed the Institute's Dispute Resolution Services, and received the Georgia Sociological Association's "Sociologist of the Year" award in 2002 as well as the Walter B. Hill Award from the University of Georgia in 1996 for outstanding achievements. Dr. Herrman frequently speaks to professional mediators, often as a keynoter. She continues speaking, writing, and publishing on effective mediation. Her publications can be found in *Conflict Resolution Quarterly*, *The Negotiation Journal*, *The Justice System Journal*, and *Peace and Conflict Studies*.

Nancy Hollett is an educator at the University of Georgia in the Department of Child and Family Development. She teaches classes on conflict resolution, merging related theories with the communication and conflict resolution skills training of children as well as young adults. She also directs practicum experiences for professionals and undergraduate students, administering conflict resolution training with children aged 3–18 years. In the area of mediation, she has been involved with the integration of theory and applied research. As a researcher, she has investigated mediator skills and techniques related to the resolution of interpersonal conflict. The measurement of successful mediation outcome is an area in which she has presented at national conferences and in which she has also published.

Tricia Jones received her doctorate from Ohio State University in 1985. She is a Professor in the Department of Psychological Studies in the College of Education, Temple University, Philadelphia. Her teaching and research interests are in interpersonal, group, and organizational conflict processes with special emphasis on emotion in conflict. She has published over 40 articles and book chapters on conflict, and co-edited the volumes *New Directions on Mediation* (1994), *Does It Work? The Case for Conflict Resolution Education in our Nations Schools* (2000), and *Kids Working It Out: Stories and Strategies for Making Peace in Our Schools* (2003). Her research in conflict resolution has been funded by the William and Flora Hewlett Foundation, the Packard Foundation, the Surdna Foundation, the Pennsylvania Commission on Crime and Delinquency, the George Gund Foundation, and the United States Information Agency. Her current funded research from the US Department of Education's FIPSE program (Fund for the Improvement of Postsecondary Education) is the Conflict Resolution Education in Teacher Education program, educating pre-service teacher and counselor candidates in urban education environments about conflict resolution education. Dr. Jones currently serves as the editor-in-chief of *Conflict Resolution Quarterly*, the scholarly journal of the Association for Conflict Resolution. She is the recipient of the 2004 Jeffrey Z. Rubin Theory to Practice Award from the International Association for Conflict Management.

Neil H. Katz After a 30-year career as a professor, author, and director of several programs in the field of conflict resolution at the Maxwell School of Citizenship and Public Affairs at Syracuse University, Dr. Katz currently serves as the Director of Training and Organizational Development for the Executive Education Programs at the Maxwell School, and as a Distinguished Visiting Professor of Practice at the Department of Conflict Analysis and Resolution at Nova Southeastern University in Fort Lauderdale. In these capacities, and as president of his own consulting firm, *Dr. Neil Katz and Associates*, he consults with a variety of prestigious private and public sector organizations throughout the United States.

Stephen Littlejohn received his Ph.D. in communication from the University of Utah. He has written widely on topics related to communication, conflict, and dialog, including *Moral Conflict: When Social Worlds Collide* (1997), *Engaging Communication in Conflict: Systemic Practice* (2001), and *Mediation: Empowerment in Conflict Management* (2001). He works internationally and has recently facilitated peace dialogs in Indonesia and Sri Lanka. He has facilitated planning processes on such topics as problems of the urban interface, teacher licensing, offshore outsourcing, information technology, customer service, college and university strategic planning, and endangered species. He has done mediations for such agencies as the Postal Service, the EEOC, New Mexico Human Rights, and the University of New Mexico. His clients include the International Catholic Migration Commission, Sandia National Laboratories, the New Mexico Commission on Higher Education, American Indian Higher Education Consortium, the Waco Youth Summit, the City of Cupertino, Columbia Basin College, and the Washington State University, among many others.

E. Patrick McDermott is an Associate Professor in the Departments of Accounting and Legal Studies and Management and Marketing at the Franklin P. Perdue School of Business and Director of Research and Evaluation at the Center for Conflict Resolution at Salisbury University. He holds a Ph.D. in Human Resources Management from the George Washington University, an LL.M from New York University School of Law, a J.D. from Rutgers Newark School of Law, an M.S. in Collective Bargaining from the New York State School of Industrial and Labor Relations at Cornell University and a BS in Industrial and Labor Relations from the ILR School at Cornell. Professor McDermott has extensive corporate and law firm experience in employment law and labor relations. He has written extensively on employment law and conflict resolution in the workplace.

Craig McEwen is the Daniel B. Fayerweather Professor of Political Economy and Sociology at Bowdoin College, where he has taught since 1975. A graduate of Oberlin College in 1967, he earned his M.A. (1969) and Ph.D. (1975) from Harvard University. For the past 25 years he has done empirical research and written about mediation and dispute resolution in varied settings: small claims, community, environmental, divorce, civil courts, corporations, administrative agencies, public policy, and appellate courts. He has worked as a mediator for small claims and family cases. With Nancy Rogers and Sarah Cole, he is the co-author of *Mediation: Law, Policy and Practice*. His most recent book, *Divorce Lawyers at Work: Varieties of Professionalism in Practice*, co-authored with Lynn Mather and Richard Maiman, examines issues of the legal profession.

Gerald D. Monk is a Professor at San Diego State University and teaches courses in conflict resolution and counseling interventions. He has worked as a mediator in a successful practice over the last 20 years. His specialty areas focus upon family mediation and divorce mediation utilizing narrative mediation approaches. Professor Monk is a trainer in conflict resolution and mediation for the Training Institute of the National Conflict Resolution Center (NCRC). He is internationally known for his work on the development and application of narrative approaches to mediation and conflict resolution, and he has taught numerous workshops on this subject in Canada, New Zealand, Austria, Iceland, Mexico, and the United States. He has co-authored three texts on narrative mediation and therapy. He lives in San Diego and can be contacted at gmonk@mail.sdsu.edu.

Brian Polkinghorn is an Associate Professor of Conflict Resolution and Executive Director of the Center for Conflict Resolution at Salisbury University (<www.conflict-resolution.org>). He is a mediator, arbitrator, and ombudsman with more than 20 years' experience and has worked as a conflict resolution consultant in 30 countries. He has authored articles, book chapters, and an edited book on applied conflict intervention research applications in a variety of conflict settings. He holds an M.S. in conflict resolution from the ICAR program at George Mason University, as well as an M.A., and a Ph.D. through the PARC program, Maxwell School of Citizenship, Syracuse University. He was also a visiting scholar at the Program on Negotiation (PON), Harvard University Law School, a Research Fellow with the United States Environmental Protection Agency, and a Presidential Management Fellow.

Dean G. Pruitt is Visiting Scholar at the Institute for Conflict Analysis and Resolution at George Mason University and SUNY Distinguished Professor Emeritus at the University at Buffalo: State University of New York. He received his Ph.D. in psychology from Yale University and did postdoctoral work in psychology at the University of Michigan and in international relations at Northwestern University. His specialties are social conflict, negotiation, and mediation. He is a fellow of the American Psychological Association and the American Psychological Society and has received the Harold D. Lasswell Award for Distinguished Scientific Contribution to Political Psychology from the International Society of Political Psychology and the Lifetime Achievement Award from the International Association for Conflict Management. He is author or co-author of five books – *Theory and Research on the Causes of War*; *Negotiation Behavior*; *Mediation Research*; *Negotiation in Social Conflict*; *and Social Conflict: Escalation, Stalemate, and Settlement* (now in its third edition) – and more than a hundred published chapters and research-based articles. He has recently published a chapter on "Social Conflict" in the *Handbook of Social Psychology*, a special issue on the 1993 Oslo negotiations between Israelis and Palestinians in International Negotiation, and a monograph on "Communication Chains in Negotiation between Organizations" in the Occasional Paper series of the Sabanci University Program on Conflict Analysis and Resolution.

Donald T. Saposnek is a clinical child psychologist, child custody mediator, and family therapist, and is on the psychology faculty at the University of California at Santa Cruz. Dr. Saposnek has worked both within the family court system and the private sector, and is a national and international trainer of mediation and child development. Author of the classic, *Mediating Child Custody Disputes* (1983; revised edn. 1998), he has published extensively on child custody, mediation, and child psychology and is on the editorial boards of the *Conflict Resolution Quarterly* and *Family Court Review* journals. He is editor of the Association for Conflict Resolution's *Family Mediation News* and is the *Family Section* editor of the online <www.mediate.com>. Dr. Saposnek is the 2002 recipient of the Association for Conflict Resolution's John M. Haynes Distinguished Mediator Award, the 2002 recipient of the Monterey Bay Psychological Association's Outstanding Psychologist Award, and the 2003 recipient of the California Psychological Association's Award for Distinguished Contribution to Psychology as a Profession.

Sandra Schruijer is Professor of Organizational Psychology, and works for Tias Business School (University of Tilburg) and the Utrecht School of Governance (University of Utrecht), both in the Netherlands. She conducts research into the psychological dynamics of multiparty collaboration, and leadership and organizational change. She is editor of the *Journal of Community and Applied Social Psychology*. Together with Leopold Vansina, she organizes the International Professional Development Programme: Leading Meaningful Change. She carries out her consulting, training, and action research activities through Professional Development International BV, of which she is the director.

Daniel Shapiro, Associate Director of the Harvard Negotiation Project, is on the faculty at Harvard Law School and in the psychiatry department at Harvard Medical School/McLean Hospital. He holds a doctorate in clinical psychology and specializes in the psychology of negotiation. His newest book, co-authored with Professor Roger Fisher, is called *Beyond Reason: Using Emotions as You Negotiate* (2005). Dr. Shapiro directs the International Negotiation Initiative, a Harvard-based project that develops psychologically focused theory and strategies to reduce ethnopolitical violence. He has extensive international experience as a negotiation consultant and has trained political officials, teachers, students, and mental health specialists. Through funding from the Soros Foundation, he developed a conflict management program that now reaches nearly one million people across 25 countries.

Fang Su gained her M.A. at the University of Electronic Science and Technology of China in 1999 and her Ph.D. at the Shanghai University of Finance and Economics in 2002. She is an Associate Professor in the Finance School at Shanghai University of Finance and Economy. Her major research is in insurance and risk management, with an interest in cooperation and competition. She has published 50 articles in international journals and four books in China. She is also dedicated to improving education and developing cooperative learning on the Chinese mainland.

Dean Tjosvold gained his Ph.D. at the University of Minnesota and his B.A. at Princeton University. He is Chair Professor of Management at Lingnan University, Hong Kong, and Director of the Cooperative Learning Center. Simon Fraser University has awarded him a University Professorship for his research contributions. He has published over 200 articles and 20 books on cooperation and competition, managing conflict, leadership, and power. He is a member of the Academy of Management's Board of Governors and is past President of the International Association of Conflict Management. He was elected to the Academy of Management Board of Governors in 2004. He is the Asia regional editor for the *Journal of World Business* and has served on several editorial boards, including the *Academy of Management Review, Journal of Management*, and *Journal of Organizational Behavior*. He is a partner in his family health-care business in Minnesota.

Mark Umbreit is a Professor and Founding Director of the Center for Restorative Justice and Peacemaking at the University of Minnesota, School of Social Work. He also serves as a Fellow at the International Center for Healing and the Law in Kalamazoo, Michigan. Professor Umbreit is the author of six books and more than 130 journal articles, book chapters, and research reports. He has served as a consultant and trainer for the US Department of Justice for the past 23 years. He has lectured and provided mediation training throughout North America and Europe, as well as in China, Japan, Ukraine, and Israel/Palestine.

Leopold S. Vansina is Professor Emeritus at the Catholic University of Leuven and l'Université Catholique de Louvain-la-Neuve, Belgium, and founder of the Professional Development Institute in Belgium (<www. pro-dev.be>). He studied psychology at Yale University and the University of Michigan, where he prepared his doctoral dissertation. After obtaining his Ph.D. from the University of Leuven, he became interested in organizational consulting and action research, activities that he combined with his part-time university teaching assignments. At present, he continues his professional activities from his institute, with a focus on the professional development of organizational consultants and of those in leading positions.

Janet Walker is Professor of Family Policy and Director of the Newcastle Centre for Family Studies at the University of Newcastle upon Tyne, England. During the last 25 years she has directed over 40 studies relating to marriage and divorce and family relationships, including major evaluations of family mediation for the British government. Between 1996 and 1998 she was expert consultant on family mediation at the Council of Europe and she has advised ministers of justice throughout the world on mediation and divorce policy. She has trained and practiced as a family therapist and family mediator.

John M. Winslade is a professor in the College of Education at California State University San Bernardino. He also teaches mediation classes at the University of Waikato in Hamilton, New Zealand, at California State University Dominguez Hills, and at the University of Waterloo in Canada. With Gerald Monk, he is the author of *Narrative Mediation: A New Approach in Conflict Resolution* (2000), and of a number of articles and book chapters outlining the ideas of narrative mediation. He is committed to the development of usable professional practices from the ideas of social constructionism and poststructuralism, and has also written extensively on narrative approaches in counseling. His own professional background is in school counseling and family therapy and mediation work. He is an experienced presenter of numerous workshops on narrative mediation and narrative therapy in New Zealand and Australia, the USA and Canada, and in Britain and Europe. He lives in Redlands, California, and can be contacted at jwinslad@csusb.edu.

Roselle L. Wissler is Director of Research of the Lodestar Dispute Resolution Program at the Arizona State University College of Law. She also serves as a research consultant to courts, conducting empirical research to assess the effectiveness of mediation and arbitration programs and to answer questions about program policy and design. Dr. Wissler is one of the consultants in the Federal Judicial Center's Program for Consultations in Dispute Resolution, which provides federal courts with technical assistance on designing and evaluating ADR programs. She has authored numerous articles reporting empirical research on mediation and arbitration and on attorneys' use of ADR that appear in dispute resolution journals and law reviews.

Zena D. Zumeta J.D. directs activities of the Mediation Training and Consultation Institute, and the Collaborative Workplace, a mediation, training, and consulting firm devoted to helping public, private, and not-for-profits with dispute resolution, facilitation, problem-solving, mediation, and training, based in Ann Arbor, Michigan. She has over 20 years' experience mediating family and employment disputes, as well as disputes in other contexts and substantive areas. Ms. Zumeta is the founding co-principal of the Ann Arbor Mediation Center, and received the State Bar of Michigan ADR Section's Distinguished Service award in 2003 and the Association for Conflict Resolution's John Haynes Distinguished Mediator Award in 2004. She trains volunteer and professional mediators nationally, and frequently trains and speaks to professional mediators at their state and regional conferences. She has been an Adjunct Clinical Professor of Law at the University of Michigan Law School. She writes for *Conflict Resolution Quarterly, Family Mediation News*, and other publications.

Part I

Setting the Stage for a Dialog

Chapter 1

Introduction

MARGARET S. HERRMAN

INTRODUCTION

People who are passionate about their work are lucky beyond words, and many mediators and scholars of various forms of negotiation, including mediation, are passionate about this work. That passion speaks with a loud voice in the chapters of this handbook. Without knowing for sure, I assume the passion reflects, as in my case, a long-standing fascination with conflict between individuals and a desire to be a part of interventions that heal rather than either suppress conflict or wound further. In the 1960s, my fascination propelled me onto an evolving path that began when I was an undergraduate, then a graduate, student in sociology at Emory University in Atlanta, Georgia. My intellectual curiosity was captured by social theorists and philosophers writing about change and conflict, as well as by social activists using conflict in the streets of the United States and Europe to demand change. The juxtaposition spoke volumes about the complexity of conflict and the roles people take during interpersonal conflict scenarios.

This path has always been stimulating and exciting, but the ultimate challenge for most of us is to hone intervention skills that weave theory seamlessly into increasingly effective intervention techniques. This introduction invites prospective readers, who are either following a similar path or who want to know more about what the path means, into a collection of writings by people who love exploring conflict as it relates to various forms of third party work, but especially mediation. In addition to being scholars, many of the contributors are well known mediators, trainers, and negotiators.

EVOLUTION

Like all books, this one began a long time before any of us sat down to write, and it is influenced by a historic as well as a present professional context. This field has evolved most noticeably over a span of at least 40 years – a span consistent with the majority of references in this handbook – and several transitions have influenced themes and tensions evident in it. First, the mental models or theories that captured my imagination decades ago invite continual testing, verification, retesting, and adaptation. Readers familiar with foundational theories will see an evolution and restatement in this handbook. They will also see challenges and new statements about theories currently under consideration.

My first memory of foundational models was of grand predictions about societies, or complex organizations or communities – in the genera of: "After observing my unit of analysis (a society, complex organization, or community), I postulate this is how things work." A simple example of these theoretical roots dates from the nineteenth century, when a social philosopher, Georg Simmel, introduced the idea of "third parties" (i.e. people involved in a conflict, but someone not aligned to an outcome and possibly not to the protagonists) and how "thirds" function to reduce tension and increase the potential for an effective solution to a problem (Simmel 1950).

In time, grand predictions gave ground to descriptions of interactions – in the genera of: "Let me describe patterns." Many descriptions sketched reality – provided by naturalistic data collected at one point in time and, thus, as a static state. Also, many focused on data relevant to the administration and budgetary justification of emerging mediation programs associated with courts or businesses. A few tested conflict interactions including mediations – typically based on data provided by laboratory experiments. Being a new area of study, especially in natural settings, descriptions far outnumbered theory testing or theory evolution. Even so, over the past 20 years or so descriptions evolved into sophisticated and detailed observations of mediated conversations. This cutting edge not only assumes conflict to be a natural component of human interaction, but also that the interactions *per se* produce new understandings of self and reality among the protagonists – including mediators. These descriptions assume changing frames, changing lives – a clear comparison to data that capture static snapshots. These new studies generate fresh knowledge, debates over theory, and suggestions for more sensitive forms of intervention by third parties. The evolution of research, coupled with a co-mingling of descriptive, theoretical, and practical applications, excites me for the future of this work. Readers will quickly see that this handbook exemplifies the co-mingling as well as the best of static and dynamic research. To remain a vibrant field, we need both, and we need to appreciate the strengths of both.

Second, a shift occurred in the way some social scientists define or frame conflict and society's conflict-handling mechanisms. From the 1940s to today, numerous anthropologists have studied conflict-handling mechanisms within societies around the globe. Early sociologists and political scientists explored conflict, in complex organizations such as corporations and the military. In most cases the prevailing assumption was or is of conflict as a signal of a malfunction, a form of deviance that required corrective steps, perhaps the development of correcting or conflict-handling institutions.

By the 1950s, a small cadre of social scientists tossed this core assumption out (or, more correctly, returned to the European roots of the social sciences as exemplified by Weber 1949). For example, Coser (1956) explored functional conflict byproducts observable in simple as well as complex networks of social interactions. Since Coser's writings, others have followed to reframe the role and function of conflict. Likewise, I assume that conflict is inevitable in any repetitive social exchange of even minimal duration (Herrman 1987: 61–62). Conflict is also necessary for an ongoing social interaction to flourish. When handled skillfully, conflict leads to innovation and often more functional social exchanges. But given a marked potential for miserable outcomes, as demonstrated by any news outlet on any given day, what predisposes a functional byproduct? How do "thirds" figure into the equation? Perhaps, without knowing it, I have been having a conversation with Georg Simmel all this time.

Experience tells me that answers to these questions are numerous. During the 1980s, I started and ran an international conference for mediators and peacemakers. The conference exposed me to the work of third parties from across the United States and around the globe. In addition, I have over 30 years of experience as a mediator and facilitator and have trained hundreds of mediators. As a result, I am convinced that effective third parties must exhibit malleability that sensitively adjusts to the needs of clients and self. Most veterans know that various skills produce positive outcomes. No single skill set or style of intervention helps everyone, and in some situations a narrowly defined skill set clearly exacerbates negative consequences of a conflict. Mediator trainers as well as our clients hear and experience a continuum of skills anchored by good and bad practices, and by interventions that are timed well or poorly. What determines? Readers will find that numerous authors of chapters in this handbook exemplify the sophistication of scholars and practitioners who are able to say what might work, when, how, and most of all why.

Finally, values driving the development of the field of mediation are not static. Mediation took root in the United States during the 1930s as one means of addressing violent strikes associated with emerging labor unions (Herrman 1993). Mediation provided an instrumental response (i.e. a way to stop or divert a conflict) designed to reduce and prevent bloodshed by offering non-violent settings hospitable to dialog and resolution of worker grievances and contract disputes. Organizations like the Federal Mediation and Conciliation Service represent institutional embodiments of this effort. Given this impetus, it is logical that some of the first courses in conflict and conflict resolution as well as scholarly writings were supported by graduate business schools (Lewicki 1997).

By the 1960s, a burgeoning civil rights movement exposed two glaring imperfections in the social fabric of the United States. The first involved imperfections in judicial administration, especially inadequate resources to process cases and inflexibility when responding to the needs of litigants (Hofrichter 1982; Sander & Goldberg 1994). During the 1960s and early 1970s, local and state law enforcement and judicial agencies across the United States were overwhelmed by large numbers of cases generated by arrests of civil rights protestors and by significant, related civil unrest. Plus, tort reforms dating to the early 1970s stimulated large numbers of "no-fault" filings to settle divorce and auto accident claims (a phenomenon labeled "hyperlexis," see Galanter 1983). The crush of cases, coupled with new types of cases,

generated administrative reforms in docket management as well as in the development of less costly alternative programs that offered remedies not typically associated
with litigation (cf. Herrman 1989–90: 36–42).[1]

These judicial reforms embraced mediation in much the same way and in the same
instrumental spirit as earlier responses to labor violence. The value placed on instrumental reforms continues to influence how mediation programming develops in the
United States (e.g. the development of courses on negotiation and mediation in law
schools, a proliferation of mediation services as an adjunct to more traditional court
services, and the development of mediation services in employment settings in both
private and government sectors. See chapters 3, 5, and 6 in this handbook). The
value also influences which professionals join the ranks of new mediators. In some
ways this value has overshadowed other values for at least the last two decades.

Discrimination, characterized by disparate access to even basic social resources
(e.g. education, commerce, housing, etc.) represents an even more fundamental
imperfection in the social fabric of the United States. In comparison to support
for instrumentally driven innovations, the development of some mediation programming dating to the early 1960s directly expressed the justice values of the civil
rights and then the anti-war movements in the United States (Herrman 1989–90,
1993). Some mediation proponents advocated the use of mediation to address power
and resource inequities. Mediators, like Jim Laue and Dick Salem, created community-
wide problem-solving conversations that typically forced powerful and powerless
people to talk face to face. These mediated conversations highlighted inequities
and may have contributed to significant changes in law and how communities
did business. In addition, some early mediation program advocates suggested that
teaching community members to conduct their own mediations would return
decision-making to the people directly affected by decisions and avoid decision-
making by strangers such as judges (Danzig 1982; Merry 1982; Harrington & Merry
1988; Herrman 1989–90, 1993; see also chapters 3 and 7 of this handbook for a
glimpse of these values).[2]

Social justice values are very different from instrumental efficiency values. By
the twenty-first century, the efficiency value far outweighed the social justice value
as a driving force behind mediation program development and program legitim-
ization. But the justice value is reemerging in some community-wide facilitations
(see chapter 8 of this handbook) and among mediators working with diversity and
oppression (Wing 1998). Neither justice nor instrumental values should be dis-
counted (Schoeny & Warfield 2000). Voices of both are represented in the pages
of this handbook.

The Mediator Skills Project (MSP)

The researcher/mediator team involved in the MSP wanted to explore the meaning
and behavioral manifestations of effective mediation, and although we did not know
it at the time, this handbook began when we started struggling with definitions.
We talked at length about the difference between skill and skillfulness, between

effectiveness and skill. We asked about skills essential to effectiveness. In the end, we decided to concentrate on the constructs of *effectiveness* and *skill*, thinking that both were foundational. We set the construct of *skillfulness* aside for the moment, thinking that the construct was too complex, layered, harder to pin down (Riskin's 1996 and 2003 articles are good examples of the complexity facing us). Our idea was to build our understanding of core ideas before working with more complex constructs.

We began with a literature review, but quickly found that it increased our confusion. We were caught up in an inconsistent nomenclature, coupled with a plethora of tantalizing themes and ideas about effectiveness and skill. Nothing stood out as definitive, and we also could not find a solid empirical rationale for existing definitions of important skills. Labels for skills existed, but not empirically derived definitions. So, we regrouped. We organized the literature around themes and constructs, and found that organizing helped clarify our thinking. Chapter 2 of this handbook evolved from this effort. We also completed and published a job analysis for mediators working with small groups (Herrman, Hollett, Eaker, Gale & Foster 2002). This second step is atypical within mediation circles, but very typical for other professions. Our job analysis produced an empirically grounded set of essential skill and knowledge definitions that we and others can use in training, practice, and research (Herrman, Hollett, Gale & Foster 2001).

This Handbook

The organization of this handbook illustrates what Mnookin and Ross (1999: 7) considered inherent to a full understanding of the negotiation of conflicts, namely an interdisciplinary approach. It also mimics the Mnookin and Ross (1999: 6) emphasis on both external and internal factors as important sources of influence when negotiating conflicts. Mnookin and Ross defined external factors as including organizational, institutional, and structural factors including, but not limited to, policies, restrictions on the flow of information, constituencies, politics, leadership priorities, and styles. This handbook explores this category of influences under the heading *Contextual Frames* (part II). Factors labeled *Internal Dynamics* in this handbook (part III) encompass two types of factors defined by Mnookin and Ross (1999), namely: (1) logically based, strategic factors including negotiator efforts to make the most of short- and long-term gains, and (2) psychological factors such as cognitive and motivational frames inherent in interactive and social processes.

Part I: Setting the Stage for a Dialog

This section includes this introduction and chapter 2. These two chapters frame the remainder of this handbook. Chapter 2 in particular elucidates both external frames and internal dynamics the MSP team identified in the existing mediation literature. Our analysis and organization of the literature categorizes and labels constructs and their operational definitions in order to provide readers with immediate access to resource material. By cataloging source materials for operational definitions, readers can quickly ground abstract ideas in specific measures including specific language. By naming and defining constructs we also hope to enhance mediator awareness of the dynamics of a mediation, including precursor factors as well as those typical and unexpected riptides that emerge during problem-solving interactions. Our goal is to intensify alertness, perhaps even suggest lines of inquiry, for practitioners and trainers to use to help practitioners and their clients identify how they arrived at a mediation and assumptions that might unlock problem-solving capacities or spin a conflict in negative directions (see Lang & Taylor 2000 for a treatise on our need for deeper awareness).

Chapter 2 steps beyond cataloging by organizing information into a proposed model. The model is similar to, but more extensive than, models presented by Wall (1981), Wall and Lynn (1993), and Weitzman and Weitzman (2000). Like previous models, this one, in the best of all worlds, represents a conversation waiting to happen. I hope every reader considers remaining chapters as episodes in a number of conversations, and will extend all of this text into productive and insightful conversations in the future.

The proposed model is atheoretical. While we make our assumptions transparent, we do not prefer one paradigm over another. In fact, our hope is for a flexible model that suggests numerous ways of exploring many theories and numerous assumptions. We offer some exemplars in the discussion of chapter 2 that are consistent with our assumptions, but we are not advocating one means of framing or understanding effective mediation. In that spirit, the proposed model is not prescriptive. Our intent is not to say: "This is how it is or ought to be." The model does not even say: "This is effective mediation." Instead we say, and following chapters affirm: "Many factors influence mediation. Many markers distinguish mediation." We encourage scholars and practitioners to read, reread, question, explore, test, and stretch our collective understanding of effective mediation.

At first blush, the model proposed in chapter 2 privileges quantitative research. Just the appearance of the model on paper, with operational definitions and paths that connect phases, affirms the collection of quantitative data and multivariate analysis. But, we do not assume that is all or even the "only" approach. Especially within the mediation phase of the model, many things can and do happen. Loops and feedback occur, and only qualitative research methods can explore in depth how people actually engage in problem-solving.

This handbook is offered in a spirit of openness. MSP does not have all the answers. We don't assume that the materials we compiled represent a static literature or a static view of mediation and third party intervention, just the opposite. Authors of chapters other than chapter 2 were invited to move into and beyond our proposals. They did so, beautifully. You are now a part of a living dialog about research and mediation practice.

Part II: Mediation and Negotiation in their Contextual Frames

If all mediation or negotiated intervention occurs in a context, then cultural and institutional frameworks shape any intervention process. They help define the thinking of anyone involved in a conflict well before they sit down to problem-solve. Several chapters in this section explore the model and research in institutional contexts, especially in relation to court environments and in relation to business settings. These chapters are especially important since these settings house or support a vast array of both mediation and negotiation practices, and because this vast array institutionalizes mediation and negotiation practices to a large extent more than other settings in the United States and Europe. Section 2 consists of five chapters. Chapter 3, "Examining Mediation in Context: Toward Understanding Variation in Mediation Programs," is written by Craig McEwen. McEwen notes the institutional embeddedness of mediation programs in courts, agencies, and business organizations. Mediation occurs daily, in the United States and Europe, thanks to the largesse of traditional institutions or in the shadow of legal rules and various corporate or government policies. McEwen starts with a premise of vast variation in program design and implementation and then asks how context (including policy and law, but not limited to these two factors) influences how mediation unfolds, how parties approach the process, and how they use and respond to mediation. McEwen also extends the proposed model in two ways, by: (1) adding variables and constructs, and (2) exploring bi-directional influences not anticipated in the model. Here contextual influence is reversed by acknowledging the power of mediation programming to change settings in which it exists (at some level the idea is similar to the social justice value placed on neighborhood change).

Chapter 4, "Policy, Practice, and Politics: Bargaining in the Shadow of Whitehall," is written by Janet Walker and Sherrill Hayes. This chapter clearly demonstrates how changing contextual frames, in the form of government policies and social norms, influence service delivery and public responses. A chronological account notes how policy articulated at the highest levels of government impacts the delivery of mediation and which professionals hang out a shingle. According to Walker and Hayes, parliament and other policymakers in the UK have been fascinated with the potential benefits of family mediation for 30 years. The fascination continues, even though actual use is sparse, prompting policymakers and practitioners to look for ways to promote family mediation and encourage couples to settle their differences through mediation not litigation. This chapter applies the proposed model to a European setting where evolving political norms created a "family values" backdrop that supported the development and redevelopment of mediation programming.

Chapter 5, "The Role of Antecedent and Procedural Characteristics in Mediation: A Review of the Research," is written by Roselle L. Wissler. This chapter details how existing research answers questions important to mediation program designers and administrators operating as an adjunct to court services or within the shadow of courts. Wissler explores whether the same or different factors contribute to effective mediation in domestic relations, community, small claims, general jurisdiction civil, and appellate civil mediation settings. The chapter covers the following questions: What types of disputes and disputants should be eligible for or referred to mediation? What characteristics should the mediators possess? What approach should the mediators use during mediation? What type of mediation process should the program provide for disputants? What dispute and disputant characteristics should be matched with what mediator characteristics or approach? By clarifying which research findings have been fairly consistent, which present a mixed picture, and which questions remain unanswered, Wissler not only demonstrates one application of the proposed model, but also identifies issues for future research that add constructs beyond those envisioned by the proposed model.

Chapter 6, "Applying the Comprehensive Model to Workplace Mediation Research," is written by Brian Polkinghorn and E. Patrick McDermott. This chapter examines how the model proposed in chapter 2 intersects with and enhances the analysis of an existing, comprehensive analysis of workplace conflict – specifically research on the United States Equal Employment Opportunity Commission's (EEOC's) mediation program. The research described was conducted before the comprehensive model was developed, and yet there is a good deal of congruence. This chapter also demonstrates a variety of ways to examine the model and, as a result, add new information, constructs, and theoretical ideas to an existing analysis. In return, an application of these quantitative data sets to the proposed model suggests further areas of exploration, including what may appear to some researchers and practitioners to be a linear (deterministic) or static (fixed) set of qualities, but which is really a rather flexible framework and functionally dynamic model.

Chapter 7, "Restorative Justice Mediated Dialog," is written by Mark S. Umbreit and Robert B. Coates. This chapter clearly contextualizes the proposed model in a social justice frame – namely that of restorative justice dialogs. Restorative justice mediated dialog evolved out of face-to-face conflict resolution processes between victims and criminal offenders. This approach impacts courts as well as communities across North America. This chapter speaks to how an intersection of court programming and mediation might consciously address social justice and instrumental values, by (1) reducing or preventing offenses including acts of hate; (2) diverting offenders from the formal justice system at several points in the system; (3) reintegrating offenders into a community; (4) resolving conflicts that never come to the attention of formal social control bodies; and (5) following extensive preparation over many months, responding to requests of people who have survived an act of severe violence.

Part III: Exploring Powerful Internal Dynamics

Each chapter in this section explores the potency of select interactional dynamics to enhance or degrade mediated or negotiated interactions. The handbook could not cover all such constructs, but most, such as power (e.g. as control, self-efficacy, self-determination), accountability, emotional distress/pleasure, self-esteem, justice, and satisfaction, are not only described in chapter 2 but also by experts who worked with specific constructs on an ongoing basis. The result is just the type of dialog or conversation the authors of chapter 2 hoped to produce. For example, in the context of highly emotional conflicts (such as those described by Gray, Saposnek, Conlon, or Jones) how do dynamics associated with power, self-esteem, and identity function and shape problem-solving interactions? These chapters beautifully illustrate common threads and unique aspects of conflict, illustrating nuanced differences important to both sophisticated scholarship and practice.

Chapter 8, "Mediation as Framing and Framing within Mediation," is written by Barbara Gray. This chapter explores two important ways that framing and mediation link, affecting both internal problem-solving dynamics and whether protagonists frame the situation as suitable for mediation. First, mediators use framing as an essential tool to perform their tasks as a third party – an activity proposed during the T_m phase of the model described in chapter 2. Gray notes that mediators use framing as a social accounting process to help establish interactional fairness and increase chances for a resolution. Gray argues that different frames offer different social accounts of a conflict. The mediator's role, then, is to help frame the conflict and its potential resolution in a way that all parties perceive to be fair. This form of framing links to procedural factors and several framing tasks conducive to resolution. Second, Gray enhances the constructs noted in the model, especially assumptions and antecedent conditions. She discusses mediation itself as a frame, noting that disputants might invoke a wide variety of frames in conflict situations – examples are social control frames, power frames, and conflict-handling frames. Within this constellation of frames, mediation is positioned as one of several possible conflict-handling frames that disputants could, but often don't, adopt. This chapter explores why and how disputants' framing of the conflict makes them leery of mediation.

Chapter 9, "Does the Model Overarch the Narrative Stream?" is written by John M. Winslade and Gerald D. Monk. Readers might contrast Lang and Taylor's (2000) description of mediators who typically intervene from foggy operational paradigms (this author's words not those of Lang and Taylor) with the Winslade and Monk declaration of a philosophical position that frames their thinking, namely social constructionist writing, narrative practice in mediation, family therapy, poststructuralist discourse theory, and aspects of the postmodern challenge to a modernist worldview.[3] Given their point of reference, it is refreshing that the authors challenge easily formulated perceptions of the proposed model. They pose and answer a number of important questions: Is an overarching model possible? Is it desirable? What might be the consequences for a field of knowledge or practice of such a development? Their critique and concern flow from a perspective that highlights the capacity of models to shape thinking, including whole fields of study (consider Skinner or Freud). This chapter cautions that any model privileges a point of view – which the authors of chapter 2 lay bare in the form of assumptions. This chapter suggests that readers interpret the model with a lower-case "m" rather than an upper-case "M" (implying that the proposed model may or may not encompass all other models). Winslade and Monk point out numerous ways scholars and practitioners might consider the strengths and weaknesses of the proposed model, and conclude with an inviting metaphor. If one envisions the field of mediation practice as a river composed of a variety of streams flowing in a common direction, the model in chapter 2 arches nicely over some of the streams in this river. It also serves as a useful vantage point for viewing the waters flowing beneath it. The authors of this chapter note that the proposed model might not span all the streams in the river; however, people standing on the bridge created by this arch may now see and distinguish one stream from another.

Chapter 10, "A Facework Frame for Mediation," is written by Stephen Littlejohn and Kathy Domenici. This chapter defines facework as an effort that participants and mediators put into managing face. Such work goes beyond managing the image of disputants, as it can also address others who may not be present at the mediation session, as well as relationships among participants and non-participants. Littlejohn and Domenici expand the concept of facework considerably and position it at the center of mediation communication. They argue that facework is an overriding context for understanding disputant behavior and mediator interventions. They first survey the literature on facework. They then expand the concept of face-work by constructing a meta-frame in which mediation practice can be understood. Finally, they use this framework to support and enhance the model presented in chapter 2.

Chapter 11, "Mediation and the Fourfold Model of Justice," is written by Donald E. Conlon. This chapter bridges the literature that underpins the justice field and the model of justice described from the mediation literature noted in the model proposed in chapter 2. Conlon hopes readers of this chapter will come away with a more thorough understanding of how justice is conceived and how this broader view of justice research might inform mediation scholarship and interventions.

Chapter 12, "The Dynamics of Power in Child Custody Mediation," is written by Donald T. Saposnek. The construct of power is highly salient throughout all the dynamics of custody mediation. Saposnek deconstructs the various assumptions under-lying the proposed model of mediation as well as each stage of the model from his vantage point of seasoned practitioner and scholar. The chapter notes that two people enter informal negotiations with each attempting to persuade the other to adopt his or her point of view. The stakes for exercising such persuasive personal power are much higher in a more formal, restrained context of mediation, and even more intense during child custody mediation. The chapter applies the proposed model in a context not unlike a tug-of-war, where each spouse feels overpowered by the other although in fact neither has moved an inch, and where a primary task of the mediator is to get the spouses apart when they feel stuck together.

Chapter 13, "Emotion in Mediation: Implications, Applications, Opportunities and Challenges," is written by Tricia S. Jones. This chapter argues for a commun-ication perspective on emotion in mediation to extend the more psychological orientation of the recent advances in emotion and negotiation theory and research. Implications of emotion for mediation are discussed in a brief overview of the nature of emotion and the centrality of emotion in conflict and mediation. Applications and opportunities are addressed by detailing ways in which mediators can improve their ability to identify disputants' critical identity-based emotions, use elicitive questioning to help disputants achieve a better understanding of their emotional experience underlying the conflict, and help disputants formulate reappraisals that help them past the emotional experience of the conflict. Opportunities come with challenges, and those challenges are introduced in the last section of the chapter, including the complexity of assessing emotional experience, consideration of strategic or manipulative emotional expression, and cultural differences in emotional experience and expression.

Part IV: Extensions

Most of the chapters in this handbook to this point explore mediation within a fairly narrow frame. But as the chapters in part IV attest, ideas and concepts discussed in earlier chapters need not be rigidly limited to that frame. There is relevance to negotiation in general and to more complex settings. At the same time, the constructs and dynamics previously discussed may not be appropriately applied to all conflicts in a wide variety of settings. Authors contributing to this section draw important lines by pointing out limitations and dynamics not previously covered.

Chapter 14, "Preempting Disaster: Pre-Mediation Strategies to Deal with Strong Emotions," is written by Daniel L. Shapiro. Shapiro begins this chapter with an excellent example of how quickly strong negative emotions ignited a destructive conflict. In his illustration, a small dispute over tree-trimming mushroomed into armed conflict, multiple deaths, and a heightened risk of international war. The chapter answers the question of how this tense conflict might have been more effectively defused. While mediation provides one alternative, the chapter explores how a mediator might approach problem-solving discussions when disputants' emotions are inflamed. This chapter advises mediators on how to identify and deal with strong negative emotions before they hijack either party's ability to problem-solve their differences. The chapter argues that the pre-mediation phase as described in chapter 2 – before face-to-face meetings occur – is an opportune time to reduce strong emotions and strengthen problem-solving capacities of all parties.

Chapter 15, "The Meaning of 'Social' in Interpersonal Conflict and its Resolution," is written by Sandra Schruijer and Leopold S. Vansina. Since mediation is a social interaction process between a minimum of three individuals, two of whom are involved in the conflict with a third acting as a mediator, this chapter adds a social-psychological perspective to the mix. This chapter not only adds this dimension, but looks at how the social identities of people involved in both small group and complex interventions impact the dynamics of an intervention no matter how simple or complex. The authors of this chapter work on multiparty collaborations, as researchers, consultants and trainers. Their chapter "reframes" the domain of mediation by: (1) pointing to the role of social identities and social contexts in interpersonal and intergroup interactions; (2) exploring the complex interplay of conflict, collaboration, and collusion; and (3) enriching the concept of mediating by relating it to the way multiparty interactions can be facilitated successfully. This chapter expands the model while creating additional sensitivity to the dynamics of small group and complex interventions ranging from facilitation to mediation.

Chapter 16, "Manager as Mediator: Developing a Conflict-Positive Organization," is written by Dean Tjosvold and Fang Su. Complex organizations such as corporate,

medical, or government complexes are developing formal structures, such as grievance committees and ombudsman's offices, to mediate conflicts between employees
(see, for example, chapter 6 of this handbook). They are also hiring mediators to
cope with escalated labor–management conflict and sharp divisions between units.
While constructs and ideas developed in other chapters of this handbook are highly
relevant and useful for guiding these formal efforts, readers are encouraged to expand
their concept of applications from formal to informal approaches. This chapter
notes that mediation can be much more prevalent in organizations than formal
approaches. Employees continually disagree over issues, interpersonal treatment,
and attitudes. Rather than hire third party specialists, managers are expected to
handle conflicts as they make decisions and resolve differences among employees.
However, most managers have little formal training in conflict and are unprepared
to meet the demands of mediation. This chapter applies the constructs and ideas
of mediation more broadly to organizations. It proposes that mediation needs
to be built into the everyday activities of organizations. The organization's culture
and methods should support managers and employees so that they are able and
willing to mediate and manage their conflicts successfully.

Chapter 17, "Mediation and Difficult Conflicts," is written by Morton Deutsch.
This chapter starts at the end, rather than at the beginning, of the model proposed
in chapter 2. Deutsch is concerned with conflicts that do not typically end up with
people feeling satisfied with their outcomes. In this chapter, he identifies some of
the major factors that obstruct or facilitate the successful mediation of conflict using
four situations: (1) a conflict between a terrorist group and a state; (2) a hostage
situation where the hostage-taker is surrounded by the police; (3) a conflict between
worldviews or deeply held moral values; and (4) a competitive conflict, involving
opposed interests, which is not already embittered. The discussion considers not
only some of the characteristics of the parties in conflict and the institutional contexts which affect the possibility of conflict transformation (antecedent conditions
in the proposed model), but also the skills required of the mediator in facilitating
such a transformation (also antecedent and process considerations in the proposed
model).

Chapter 18, "Enhancing Mediator Artistry: Multiple Frames, Spirit, and Reflection-
in-Action," is written by Neil H. Katz. Katz reveals that sometimes he comes across
a body of knowledge that alters his worldview, describes how he interprets people
and events, and outlines his actions as a professional. This chapter details the
personal impact of a workshop derived from two books: *Reframing Organizations:
Artistry, Choice and Leadership* and *The Wisdom of Solomon at Work: Ancient Virtues for
Living and Leading Today*. While the books focus on organizations and their leadership, this chapter relates the materials to mediation practice and scholarship, for
example: (1) how mediators assess their own and disputant frames of reference;
(2) the structural, human, and political factors that prime procedural clarity,
mediator empathy, feeling heard and understood, the ability to talk about perceptions
and feelings, and global and interactional fairness; and (3) the relative importance of reaching agreement, distributive justice, and relationship change. Katz also
notes how these resources suggest omissions in the proposed model, especially for

constructs that describe mediators who exhibit flexible cognitive dispositions and a reflection-in-action mindset when analyzing complex situations, and deciding upon and delivering interventions.

Chapter 19, "Of Time and the River: Notes on the Herrman, Hollett, and Gale Model of Mediation," is written by Kevin Avruch. This chapter, like the chapters that follow, scans the entire handbook to make the implicit dialog across chapters explicit. It considers prototypes of mediation and mediators. Everyone relies on prototypes to make sense of a complex world. For example, we might describe mediators and mediation thus: mediators are neutral or impartial "outsiders," lacking the power and authority to stipulate decisions or settlements. Likewise a mediation is a one-off "session" even if separated in two or more parts by some days, where a mediator mainly "facilitates" negotiations and any agreement "owned" by the parties. But, remembering that prototypes are constructed cognitive entities, it is important to note that prototypes are never comprehensive or stable constructions. Sometimes within a culture or a professional community, agreement on a prototype is high. Since mediators with extensive cross-cultural experience were the first to question the prototype of mediators and mediation, limiting cultural variation in the proposed model also limits recognition of the complexity of the role. In reality, no single and unique actor called mediator exists for all conditions and contexts in a conflict or dispute, and this chapter relishes considering the proposed model alongside the fine chapters that comprise this handbook. The light they collectively shed on the complexity of the nature of the mediator as "the vessel" traveling intentionally down the mediation "stream" is most intriguing.

Chapter 20, "Mediation at the Start of a New Millennium," is written by Dean G. Pruitt. Mediation practice, theory, and research have traditionally stressed the goal of settling the present conflict and offers problem-solving as the preferred methodology; examples include chapters 2 and 5 in this handbook. But, many other chapters present amendments and challenges to this tradition. That means that the field is growing conceptually and that this handbook is an excellent place to learn about this growth. This chapter begins with a summary of the problem-solving-to-settlement tradition and then moves to a summary of what Pruitt sees as key amendments and challenges to this tradition, drawing on chapters of this handbook along with other sources. He concludes by suggesting links between these models and an ongoing need for empirical examinations that compare traditional to non-traditional models, as a means of "sort[ing] out the lilies from the dandelions and to add to the luster of the lilies."

Chapter 21, "A Trainer Responds to the Model," is written by Zena D. Zumeta. This chapter begins with an observation that a lot of mediation training has functioned in the past as a loose collection of techniques hung on often unspecified theory. For Zumeta the proposed model provides a helpful and flexible contextual frame that allows, even encourages, trainers to expand and specify training modules, thus enhancing clarity for both basic and advanced mediator training. While tracking stages of the proposed model and specific constructs within each stage, the chapter highlights where and how trainers might adapt training modules on the basis of research noted in the model and accompanying definitions of constructs. The chapter concludes with suggestions for a research–training collaboration that would potentially serve as an even greater future resource for trainers and mediators.

Chapter 22, "Conclusion," is written by Margaret S. Herrman. This concluding chapter makes a case for wrapping our arms and minds around opposing ends of a spectrum that runs from simplicity to complexity and back again. Holding rigidly to binary frames – either/or, black/white, research/practice, theory/applied, quantitative/qualitative – might provide comfort to some readers, scholars, and practitioners, as in: "I can understand and perhaps master mediation." But, when it comes to mediation and the more basic form of negotiation, binary reductions misrepresent the complexity and nuances of both mediation and negotiation processes. This could be dangerous to clients and stultifying to the practitioner. The juxtaposition of chapters highlights tensions and a potential for dialog about the complexities of mediation and negotiation. Herrman reframes tension to suggest that different orientations open fissures that prompt questioning: now how does this work? What if we look in a descriptive way at global patterns, how might they inform more specific and interactive/fluid analyses (and vice versa)? This handbook affirms that studies of mediation, negotiation, and dispute resolution have moved well out of the closet of experimental studies and descriptive analyses. We are at least on the brink, if not well over the lip of the cliff, of a capacity to look at mediation and negotiation in increasingly sophisticated and interesting ways.

NOTES

1   Nader (1988) notes, in a review of Greenhouse's *Praying for Justice: Faith, Order, and Community in an American Town,* that ethnographic evidence of a litigious society is questionable. This is not to say that hyperlexis was a figment. Perhaps is was less a value at the level of individual Americans and more an inability of the judicial structure to cope effectively with changing laws.

2   The power of justice claims to force social change is beautifully detailed in Polletta (2000) as well as by Belknap (1989) in his review of two of Carol Brauer's books on the civil rights era in the United States. It might also be interesting to some that American sociologists during the early 1900s viewed themselves and their work in a social justice frame that espoused major social reform (Coser 1956: 16–20). This was perhaps a root for later sociologists to grasp, including Jim Laue, who both understood major social dynamics and helped communities achieve social change.

3   The ability to declare lies at the heart of Schön's (1990) concept of reflective practice.

REFERENCES

Belknap, M. (1989) Civil rights during the Kennedy administration. *Law and Society Review* 23(5), 921–928.

Coser, L. A. (1956) *The Functions of Social Conflict.* The Free Press, Glencoe, pp. 151–156.

Danzig, R. (1982) Towards the creation of a complementary, decentralized system of criminal justice. In R. Tomasic & M. M. Feeley (eds.), *Neighborhood Justice: Assessment of an Emerging Idea*. Longman, New York, pp. 2–24.

Galanter, M. (1983) Reading the landscape of disputes: what we know and don't know (and think we know) about our allegedly contentious and litigious society. *UCLA Law Review* 31(1, October), 4–71.

Harrington, C. B. & Merry, S. E. (1988) Ideological production: the making of community mediation. *Law and Society Review* 22(4), 709–733.

Herrman, M. S. (1987) In support of variety: on the need for refined matching of dispute resolution processes and cases. *International Journal of Group Tensions* 17(1–4), 61–83.

Herrman, M. S. (1989–90) ADR in context: linking our past, present, and a possible future. *Journal of Contemporary Legal Issues* 3, 35–55.

Herrman, M. S. (1993) On balance: promoting integrity under conflicted mandates. *Mediation Quarterly* 11(2, Winter), 123–138.

Herrman, M. S. (1999) Exploring deeper wisdoms of mediation: notes from the edge. *Peace and Conflict Studies* 6(1, November), 67–77.

Herrman, M. S., Hollett, N., Gale, J. & Foster, M. (2001) Defining mediator knowledge and skills. *Negotiation Journal* 17(2, April), 139–153.

Herrman, M. S., Hollett, N., Eaker, D. G., Gale, J. & Foster, M. (2002) Supporting accountability in the field of mediation. *Negotiation Journal* 18(1, January), 29–49.

Hofrichter, R. (1982) Justice centers raise basic questions. In R. Tomasic & M. M. Feeley (eds.), *Neighborhood Justice: Assessment of an Emerging Idea*. Longman, New York, pp. 193–202.

Lang, M. D. & Taylor, A. (2000) *The Making of a Mediator: Developing Artistry in Practice*. Jossey-Bass, San Francisco.

Lewicki, R. J. (1997) Teaching negotiation and dispute resolution in colleges of business: the state of the practice. *Negotiation Journal* 13(3, July), 253–269.

Merry, S. E. (1982) Defining "success" in the neighborhood justice movement. In R. Tomasic & M. M. Feeley (eds.), *Neighborhood Justice: Assessment of an Emerging Idea*. Longman, New York, pp. 172–192.

Mnookin, R. H. & Ross, L. (1999) Introduction, In K. J. Arrow, R. H. Mnookin, L. Ross, A. Tversky & R. B. Wilson (eds.), *Barriers to Conflict Resolution*. PON Books, Cambridge, pp. 3–24.

Nader, L. (1988) A litigious people? *Law and Society Review* 22(5), 1017–1022.

Polletta, F. (2000) The structural context of novel rights claims: southern civil rights organizing, 1961–1966. *Law and Society Review* 34(2), 367–406.

Riskin, L. L. (1996) Understanding mediators' orientations, strategies, and techniques: a grid for the perplexed. *Harvard Negotiation Law Review* 7(Spring), 1–34.

Riskin, L. L. (2003) Decision making in mediation: the new old grid and the new grid system. *Notre Dame Law Review* 79, 1–53.

Sander, F. E. A. & Goldberg, S. B. (1994) Fitting the forum to the fuss: a user-friendly guide to selecting an ADR procedure. *Negotiation Journal* 10(1, January), 49–67.

Schoeny, M. & Warfield, W. (2000) Reconnecting systems maintenance with social justice: a critical role for conflict resolution. *Negotiation Journal* 16(3, July), 253–268.

Schön, D. A. (1990) *The Reflective Practitioner: How Professionals Think in Action*. Basic Books, New York.

Simmel, G. (1950) *The Sociology of Georg Simmel*, ed. K. H. Wolff. Free Press, New York.

Wall, J. A., Jr. (1981) Mediation: an analysis, review, and proposed research. *Journal of Conflict Resolution* 25(1, March), 157–180.

Wall, J. A., Jr. & Lynn, A. (1993) Mediation: a current review. *Journal of Conflict Resolution* 37(1, March), 160–194.

Weber, M. (1949) *The Methodology of the Social Sciences*, trans. and ed. E. A. Shils & H. A. Finch. Free Press, Glencoe.

Weitzman, E. A. & Weitzman, P. F. (2000) Problem solving and decision making in conflict resolution. In M. Deutsch & P. T. Coleman (eds.), *The Handbook of Conflict Resolution: Theory and Practice*. Jossey-Bass, San Francisco, pp. 185–209.

Wing, L. (1998) Multicultural mediation: a new approach to conflict involving difference and dominance. *26th Annual Society for Professionals in Dispute Resolution Conference*, Portland, OR (October).

Chapter 2

Mediation from Beginning to End: A Testable Model

MARGARET S. HERRMAN, NANCY HOLLETT,
AND JERRY GALE

INTRODUCTION

In theory, constructive interpersonal problem-solving emerges when people set aside destructive emotions like anger or a desire to exact revenge, or when they shift from being passive victims to active participants in a search for mutual solutions to mutual problems (Weitzman & Weitzman 2000: 188). Ideally, formal mediation cultivates problem-solving capacities, and given the growing popularity of formal mediation within court programs as elsewhere (Herrman 1993), it is logical to assume that mediation achieves that goal. In many respects, mediation may be superior to giving in, adversarial sparring, or compromise (cf. Brett & Goldberg 1983a: 165–166; Shapiro & Brett 1993; Rubin, Pruitt & Kim 1994: ch. 10; Brett, Barsness & Goldberg 1996; Kressel 2000: 523; Menkel-Meadow 2001).[1]

Perhaps because of methodological difficulties inherent in formal comparisons of distinct types of dispute resolution (i.e. litigation to arbitration to mediation), there are few rigorous tests of the assumption of mediation superiority.[2] At the same time, a voluminous literature on negotiation and mediation exists where numerous authors offer intriguing ways of thinking about mediation (cf. Riskin 1996, 2003; Lang & Taylor 2000). This chapter draws from that literature, a literature that demonstrates a sustained interest in components of effective mediation.

The literature unfortunately lacks consensus with respect to definitions of key concepts and variables. A panoply of conceptual and operational definitions acts as a rich resource and a source of confusion for scholars and mediation practitioners. The array of scholars and practitioners writing about conflict resolution and mediation from so many disciplinary backgrounds and experiences produces a sense of fragmentation (cf. Deutsch 1991: 26, see also McEwen 1999). In addition:

> [While] the large body of conflict research is an advantage because it provides a vast knowledge base on which to build . . . It is also a disadvantage . . . out of the mass of available research, few theories cover the conflict process as a whole. Research has

instead tended to focus on specialized contexts such as games, and on only a few variables at a time. As a result, the "big picture" is often missing. There are dozens of separate explanations and findings, yet it is difficult to integrate them into a whole. (Folger, Poole & Stutman 1997: 13)[3]

Because big-picture models of mediation remain elusive, this chapter proposes a model that: (1) synthesizes a large segment of the mediation literature; (2) operationally defines and distinguishes between antecedent and process components of mediation; (3) operationally defines indicators of effectiveness; (4) offers a model for scholars to use in whole or in part to test numerous hypotheses and theories pertaining to the mediation of interpersonal disputes; and (5) offers the same model to mediation practitioners and trainers as an organizing framework for understanding mediation processes, the things that might influence mediations, the phases and dynamics, and potential results, short- and long-term.[4] The proposed model, and all the resources that go into the description of the model, are not offered as an immutable "word." We offer the model as a resource, not a box. Indeed, our hope is that the model intrigues scholars and practitioners alike, challenges and clarifies thinking, and most of all encourages readers to create new knowledge and more reflective practices in mediation and allied helping interventions.

CREATING A CONTEXTUAL FRAMEWORK

Much of the initial research on dispute resolution in natural settings focused on complex organizations and labor negotiations. While research has jumped far beyond these traces, mediation remains a relatively new platform for formal theory-testing.[5]

Joining Theory and Measurement

Formal mediation of interpersonal disputes is informed by negotiation and problem-solving theory such as Dewey's (1938) problem-solving progression. The progression serves almost as a prescriptive protocol in many standard negotiation and mediation texts (cf. Fisher & Ury 1981; Moore 1986; Weeks 1992).[6] But, just as a complex literature may obfuscate, prescriptive approaches oversimplify. Mnookin and Ross (1999: 7) reflect on a defining feature of studies of conflict resolution, namely a need to explore conflict resolution using a variety of frames of reference and models.

Legal scholar Menkel-Meadow (1984) offers an alternative to prevailing theory by suggesting that: (1) people problem-solve when they are unable to accomplish a goal alone; (2) the social science and legal literature, typically frame problem-solving as a zero-sum, win-lose, adversarial game; (3) a win-lose strategy "maximizes individual victory;" (4) cooperative approaches expand the scope of problem-solving to include institutional, individual, and relational needs; and (5) incorporating a variety of needs into a negotiation allows people to succeed while helping others do likewise.[7]

The proposed model takes advantage of select theories from psychology (cf. Rogers 1975, 1980), social psychology (cf. Deutsch 1991, 2000, 2002), and problem-solving (cf. Dewey 1938; Moore 1986; Johnson, Johnson & Tjosvold 2000). Sources of variation antecedent to a mediation and resulting from a mediation were suggested in the descriptive literature. In essence, the model fosters analysis created from an interplay between select theories and variables drawn from studies published between the mid-1960s and the early 2000s.[8] Even though the literature referenced here spans almost forty years, our search focuses primarily on studies of the following.

Disputes in natural settings

The review focuses on research involving mediator-assisted problem-solving where the dispute occurs in a natural setting.[9]

Interpersonal disputes

Since, it is not clear how negotiation processes and results are affected by the context in which they occur,[10] our review limits this source of variation somewhat by concentrating on research relevant to interpersonal disputes – defined as conflicts that involve at least two people in a direct way. These types of conflicts typically involve personal rather than institutional, macro-economic, or political issues.[11] Thus, the review and reported measures generally cover research on disputes within families (e.g. parent–child, divorce, adult siblings, etc.), within neighborhoods (e.g. between neighbors, landlord–tenant, dry-cleaning, a minor affray between people who know each other, etc.), or involving individuals in disputes that are shadowed by the potential of civil litigation (see below). The review follows in the tradition of Wall (1981) as well as Wall and Lynn (1993) while updating those resources. By including studies beyond the context of divorce, the review is more expansive than reviews by Menzel (1991) as well as Benjamin and Irving (1995).

Mediation that shadows courts

The review includes studies of mediation processes occurring either within court programs or in private settings that operate in the shadow of future litigation (Mnookin & Kornhauser 1979). The implication is that legal/factual concerns along with emotional issues are salient in discussions and in the resolution of a dispute.[12] The review was not limited to court-based studies because many disputes invoke mediation well before a legal petition. An effective mediation has a capacity to prevent litigation, but the shadow still exists.[13]

CAVEATS AND ASSUMPTIONS BEHIND THE MODEL

The model described here falls in between generic discussions of negotiation or mediation processes (cf. Fisher 1983; Menkel-Meadow 1984, 1993) and highly detailed descriptions of actual mediations (cf. Donohue, Lyles & Rogan 1989; Greatbatch & Dingwall 1989; Cobb 1993, 1994; Donohue, Drake & Roberto 1994; Winslade & Monk 2000). It is similar in its level of specificity to a model proposed by Wall (1981). But it goes beyond previous models in that specific measures suggested in the existing literature are matched to proposed constructs and variables. For the most part, measures incorporated into the proposed model represent self-report data. However, a few studies rely on observations of transactions. Finally, just as our review is grounded in a limited sector of research, the model is grounded in several assumptions we need to make explicit.

1   Any form of conflict resolution occurs in a social context – within a family, a group, a community, a nation – that encompasses techniques, symbols, categories, rules, and values relating to conflict and conflict resolution. To understand effective conflict resolution, research on the interplay between interactions designed to resolve a specific dispute and the broader socio-cultural context would be ideal (cf. Deutsch 1991: 28).[14] But an ideal is an ideal. In order to manage our research agenda, we acknowledge that the broader socio-cultural context affects all problem-solving, but omit relevant variables in the proposed model.

2   People prefer harmony to discord.[15] Given a conducive problem-solving environment and in order to create harmony, people will act on their abilities for mature, independent, and responsible interactions (Rogers 1975: 5, but see Putnam & Holmer 1992; Mnookin & Ross 1999).

3   If someone experiences competitive interactions, the experience typically evokes competitive responses. Likewise, experiences of cooperation evoke cooperative responses (Deutsch 2000: 29).

4   Referral to formal mediation signals that people are experiencing a conflict characterized by a lack of cooperation (or poor communication, misunderstanding, etc.)

5   The goal of formal mediation is to change a competitive conflict to a co-operative interaction characterized by: (a) effective communication, (b) less obstruction, (c) orderly discussion, (d) confidence in one's ideas coupled with support for the ideas and concerns of other participants, (e) coordinated efforts to resolve the conflict, (f) high productivity, (g) power-sharing and mutual power enhancement, and (h) acceptance that the problem is a mutual problem that can be overcome (Deutsch 2000: 25).

6   When confronted with a conflict, people express a great deal of attachment to their initial position – often a position based on preliminary and incomplete information (Johnson et al. 2000: 68–69; see also Janis & Mann 1977: 22–25, 45).

7   Verbalizing individual positions and stories provides the speaker and listener with an opportunity to develop a greater understanding of underlying needs and to stimulate higher-level reasoning (Rogers 1975, 1980; Fisher & Ury 1981; Johnson et al. 2000: 69).

8   Exposure to different opinions, information, and interpretations of life experiences can arouse a state of cognitive disequilibrium that helps to thaw positions (Johnson et al. 2000: 69).

9   Uncertainty motivates an active search for more information (Janis & Mann 1977: 36; Johnson et al. 2000: 69).

10   At the same time, people continuously attribute and redefine the meaning of actions, purposes, agreements, even personal and social identities (cf. Gergen 1985; Deutsch 1991: 28; Folger et al. 1997: 114–115). So, there is usually no objective or even representational "truth" to be discovered with regard to past events or experiences. Therefore, in mediation, the goal is not to discover the truth but to achieve a socially constructed, consensual agreement of terms and future actions.[16] Our perspective, even considering the second point above, does not define harmony as precluding the possibility that some people might prefer confrontation as the basis for ongoing interaction. Specifically, two or more people might consciously or subconsciously agree to maintain conflict. They may even find comfort in their apparently (from an outside perspective) dysfunctional behavior.

THE PROPOSED MODEL

Menkel-Meadow (1984) describes dispute resolution as encompassing: (1) the negotiator's mindset, (2) the process used, and (3) the goal or end product. The model proposed in this chapter follows a similar time sequence,[17] and is displayed in figure 2.1. From figure 2.1, T_0 variables (listed in the first column) refer to sources of variation occurring before a mediation begins such as characteristics of the parties and the mediator, various attitudes and beliefs, characteristics of the dispute, and the institutional context in which the case is mediated. T_m variables (listed in column 2) pertain to dynamics of the mediation process including factors that prime people to be able to negotiate effectively, the conditions of the mediation, problem-solving dynamics, and the dynamics of decision-making. T_1 and T_2 variables (listed in columns 3 and 4) constitute short-term and long-term end products such as disputant beliefs and attitudes, characteristics of the resolution, and various institutional indicators of outcomes.[18]

The Negotiator's Mindset

While much of the mediation and negotiation literature focuses on constructs and variables relevant to the bargaining process, research by Kakalik et al. (1996) and Kruk (1998) suggests a need to consider antecedent sources of variation.[19] McEwen (1999) considers knowledge of the context to be vital. Constructs and variables listed for T_0 in figure 2.2 reference important characteristics antedating a mediation.[20] Proposed constructs include personal characteristics of disputants and mediators; disputant beliefs and attitudes (and the variables: willingness to participate, perceptions of voluntariness, expectations/feelings about the mediation, and motivations to resolve the dispute); dispute characteristics (and the variables: legal characteristics, conflict characteristics, and the interpersonal dynamics between disputants); and institutional context including the variables: program context, process access,

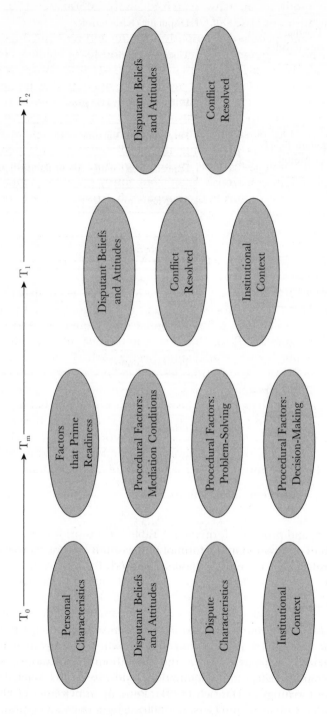

FIGURE 2.1 Comprehensive model

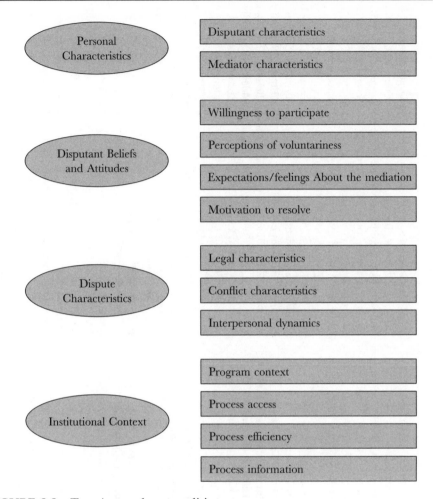

FIGURE 2.2 T_0 = Antecedent conditions

process efficiency, and process information.[21] Table 2.1 lists prior literature exploring antecedent sources of variation in the form of unmeasured constructs, operationalized variables, and references for each variable proposed.

Personal characteristics

Two variables, *disputant characteristics* and *mediator characteristics*, define the construct personal characteristics. In 1975, Rubin and Brown, focusing on experimental studies, summarized what was known at the time about the relationships between demographic characteristics and negotiation styles (see also Macfarlane 2001: 670–678). Recent writings by Deutsch (1991), Putnam and Holmer (1992), Kressel (2000), and Raider, Coleman, and Gerson (2000) suggest non-demographic personal

TABLE 2.1   Antecedent variables (T_0)

Personal characteristics	Disputant beliefs/attitudes	Dispute characteristics	Institutional context
Disputant characteristics Rubin & Brown 1975; Deutsch 1991; Putnam & Holmer 1992; Kressel 2000; Raider et al. 2000; Sandy et al. 2000; Macfarlane 2001 *Archival data* Bridenback et al. 1980; Wyrick & Costanzo 1999; Umbreit & Greenwood 1999; *Client data* Kelly & Gigy 1989; Kelly & Duryee 1992; Pearson et al. 1982; Wissler 2002 **Mediator characteristics** Thoennes & Pearson 1985; Deutsch 1991; Umbreit & Greenwood 1999 *Archival data* Zubek et al. 1992 *Mediator data* Kakalik et al. 1996; Kruk 1998; Herrman et al. 2001; Herrman et al. 2002; Wissler 2002; Herrman et al. 2003; Herrman under review	Mnookin & Ross 1999; Macfarlane 2001 **Willingness to participate** Harrington 1985; Kressel 2000 *Archival data* Bridenback et al. 1980; Gehm 1990 *Client data* Donnelly & Ebron 2000; Umbreit et al. 2001 *Mediator data* Carnevale et al. 1989 **Perceptions of voluntariness** *Archival data* Kelly & Duryee 1992 *Client data* Coates & Gehm 1989; Marshall & Merry 1990; Irving & Benjamin 1992; Kelly & Duryee 1992; Umbreit & Coates 1993; Flaten 1996; Wissler 1999; Donnelly & Ebron 2000 *Mediator data* Kruk 1998 **Expectations/feelings about the mediation** Kressel 2000 *Client data* Bridenback et al. 1980; Pearson et al. 1982; Thoennes & Pearson 1985; Coates & Gehm 1989; Umbreit 1991: Wissler 1999 *Attorney data* McEwen & Wissler 2002: 138–139 **Motivation to resolve** Kressel 2000 *Archival data* McGillicuddy et al. 1987 *Client data* Van Slyck et al. 1992; Umbreit & Coates 1993 *Mediator data* Carnevale et al. 1989	**Legal characteristics** *Archival data* Bridenback et al. 1980; Vidmar 1984; McGillicuddy et al. 1987; Umbreit & Greenwood 1999; Wyrick & Costanzo 1999 *Client data* Vidmar 1985 *Mediator/attorney data* Kakalik et al. 1996; Wissler 1999, 2002 **Conflict characteristics** Whiting 1994; Kressel 2000 *Archival data* McGillicuddy et al. 1987; Zubek et al. 1992; Whiting 1994 *Client data* Van Slyck et al. 1992; Wissler 1999 *Mediator data* Carnevale et al. 1989; Irving & Benjamin 1992; Wissler 1999, 2002; GAODR 2000 *Mediator/attorney data* Kakalik et al. 1996 **Interpersonal dynamics** Irving & Benjamin 1992; Kressel 2000 *Archival data* Bridenback et al. 1980; McGillicuddy et al. 1987; Zubek et al. 1992; Whiting 1994; Donnelly & Ebron 2000 *Client data* Thoennes & Pearson 1985; Van Slyck et al. 1992; Irving & Benjamin 1992; Kakalik et al. 1996 *Mediator data* Carnevale et al. 1989	**Program context** McEwen 1999; Umbreit & Greenwood 1999; McEwen & Wissler 2002; Wissler 2002 **Process access** Harrington 1985 *Archival data* Bridenback et al. 1980; Crosson & Christian 1990; Umbreit & Coates 1993; Kakalik et al. 1996; Donnelly & Ebron 2000; Wissler 2002 **Process efficiency** *Archival data* Roehl & Cook 1989; Kelly & Duryee 1992; Kakalik et al. 1996; Wyrick & Costanzo 1999; *Mediator data* Kakalik et al. 1996 **Process information** *Client data* Coates & Gehm 1989; Umbreit et al. 2001

characteristics and skills each author feels contribute to effective problem-solving. For example, Deutsch (1991) and Raider et al. (2000) refer to abilities to: think about a problem abstractly, analyze problems objectively, use communication skills that foster cooperative dialog, avoid alienating other negotiators, and deal with anger constructively. Putnam and Holmer (1992: 130–135), while discussing theories of "cognitive heuristics," describe possible frames or points of view that influence problem-solving interactions even before they happen. Examples include: a mediator's or client's perceptions of risks associated with loss and gain, aversion to risk or risk-seeking preferences, reference points like bottom lines or best alternatives to negotiated settlements, overconfidence, and judgment. These characteristics tend to be static, yet are extremely important indicators of a person's field of vision. By comparison, "frame categories," also as interpreted by Putnam and Holmer (1992: 135–137), constitute dynamic, not static, categories that might contribute to both antecedent characteristics and procedural dynamics.[22] They include: definitions of the conflict, perceptions of the costs and benefits of various outcomes, expectations of how other people will act and think during negotiations, expectations about the process of mediation, aspirations for meeting needs and interests, and preferred outcomes. Kressel (2000) notes an ability to take responsibility for past deeds. But according to Sandy, Boardman, and Deutsch (2000: 289): "Although conflict resolution practitioners and theorists recognize the potentially important effects that individual differences have on the negotiation process and its outcome, research in this area has been piecemeal and few guidelines exist for practical application."

Research on *disputant characteristics* includes demographic as well as other measures. Wyrick and Costanzo (1999) use archival data (as case records) to study client participation in victim–offender mediation programs. They looked at the type of victim (i.e. institutional, organizational, or individual; see also Wissler 2002: 653) as well as the ethnicity of the offender and victim. Umbreit and Greenwood (1999: 239) looked at whether clients were adults or youth. Pines, Gat, and Tal (2002) analyzed recordings of mediations to see how the gender of disputants influences the style and content of arguments. Bridenback, Bales, and Planchard (1980: 16–17) and Donnelly and Ebron (2000: 15) also rely on archival data to study the demographic characteristics of clients of several dispute settlement centers in their respective states. In addition, they include questions on prior contact with courts, questions that might be surrogate measures for familiarity, and comfort with legal dispute resolution forums. Pearson, Thoennes, and Vanderkooi (1982: 23–25) use client surveys to capture demographic data, as do Kelly and Gigy (1989: 266–267), Kelly and Duryee (1992), and Wissler (2002: 653–654). Kelly and Duryee (1992) also ask about the presence of minor children in a household. While not referring to Galanter's (1974) ideas about repeat players, one study (Wissler 2002: 654) asks parties if they have had prior experience with mediation and how well they were prepared by their attorneys. This study highlights an area where future research might lift the horizon when constructing measures of disputant characteristics and pursue an important experiential dimension.[23]

Mediator characteristics. In a review article, Deutsch (1991: 49) suggests the skills that third parties need to help people resolve their disputes constructively. They include skill in: (1) building rapport (to create trust, open communication, and an environment where disputants listen to suggestions about the process of dispute resolution; see also Thoennes & Pearson 1985: 117);[24] (2) establishing a cooperative, problem-solving attitude between people; (3) facilitating the development of a creative group process that supports exploration of issues and options as well as non-judgmental assessments of potential outcomes; and (4) communicating substantive knowledge in ways that expand information and support evaluation of outcomes.[25] Umbreit and Greenwood (1999: 241) collected information from program administrators that produced a list of tasks that mediators are expected to perform. Some tasks duplicate other lists, such as rapport-building, and facilitating negotiation overlap. Tasks such as active listening, paraphrasing, reframing, getting out of the way so people can talk directly to each other, leading, and efficient process management define tasks in more detail.

In order to define the skills and knowledge mediators need to perform effectively, Herrman, Hollett, Gale, and Foster (2001) and Herrman, Hollett, Eaker, Gale, and Foster (2002) conducted a job analysis that is unique in the field of mediation. This study gathered data nationwide from practitioners who mediate interpersonal disputes. The analysis produced empirically grounded skills and knowledge categories along with detailed descriptions of each. Examples of the 18 knowledge areas include knowledge of: personal limitations as a mediator, various models and techniques of mediation, problem-solving techniques, the dynamics of power and control, and knowledge of various cultural issues. Examples of the 13 skills include skill in: correcting your own errors, managing the intervention process and problem-solving, managing the relational dynamics, dealing with information, and educating.

Kakalik et al. (1996); Kruk (1998); and Wissler (2002: 654–655) gather data from mediators. These studies rely on personal descriptors rather than skills or knowledge areas. Variables such as the age, professional background, mediation training, litigation and mediation experience, how often someone mediates, practice setting, and content knowledge are used.[26] Herrman, Hollett, Eaker, and Gale (2003) and Herrman (under review) analyze two types of variables pertaining to mediators: select demographics (i.e. sex and age) and descriptors of a mediator's professional niche (i.e. experience, professional background, organizational context, etc.) in relation to their attitudes about process dynamics (i.e. goals and focus within the process, preferred outcome, reliance on dialog or caucus, etc.). Finally, Zubek, Pruitt, Peirce, McGillicuddy and Syna (1992: 556) rely on archival data to measure mediator experience (i.e. the number of prior mediations).

Disputant beliefs and attitudes

Two people generally don't remember or interpret the past the same way. It is also highly unlikely that they would interpret the context and the content of their dispute the same way (cf. Macfarlane 2001). Mnookin and Ross (1999) describe a number of cognitive and motivational biases that could produce such differences. So if we suspect that people generally approach a mediation from different perceptual realms, it would be useful to know something about those differences

before a mediation. The second category of variables listed in table 2.1 operational-
izes the construct *disputant beliefs/attitudes*. Kressel (2000: 525) generally discusses
the first variable, *willingness to participate*, in reference to factors that encourage
or discourage participation in a mediation. Several studies infer willingness from
archival data, primarily from case records that show if a mediation occurred (cf.
Bridenback et al. 1980; Gehm 1990). Umbreit, Coates, and Vos (2001: 126–128)
review a number of studies of victim–offender mediation programs to see if victims
were willing to sit down with offenders. Several of the studies rely on survey data
(one survey presented a hypothetical situation), and several rely on secondary
data to track whether a mediation occurred. Using a *post hoc* measure, Donnelly
and Ebron (2000: 37) asked disputants if they had attended their mediation.
Carnevale, Lim, and McLaughlin (1989: 224–228) asked mediators if disputants
were "unreceptive to mediation."[27]

Next, early proponents of mediation championed voluntary participation as
a hallmark of the process. But as early as 1985, Harrington (1985: 112, 123–126)
suggests that people are subtly or not so subtly coerced into participation.
Agencies that refer cases to mediation (i.e. courts and the police) undermine true
voluntariness because the institutional power embodied in the referring institution overshadows individual volition.[28] Studies that explore this second variable,
perceptions of voluntariness, stem from both client and mediator data. Coates and
Gehm (1989) and Umbreit and Coates (1993) ask participants if they felt their
involvement was voluntary. Marshall and Merry (1990) also rely on survey data
and make a distinction between victims and offenders (see also Flaten 1996, who
studied victims of serious crime). Wissler (1999: 64) asked participants if a judge,
the police, or a prosecutor pressured them into attending their mediation (see
also Irving & Benjamin 1992: 41; Kelly & Duryee 1992: 41; Donnelly & Ebron
2000: 37–38). Kruk (1998: 199) asked mediators if the cases being studied were
voluntary or mandated by a court.[29]

Expectations/feelings about the mediation. Kressel (2000: 527), speaking as both
a researcher and practitioner, suggests that participant predispositions to use
alternatives to litigation merit research, as does information participants may
have about a mediator's previous dealings with the other side.[30] Actual measures
of expectations/feelings about a mediation are found in several studies based on
client data. Bridenback et al. (1980) ask people if they were satisfied with the time
and place of the mediation. Pearson et al. (1982: 29) analyzed questions about dissatisfaction with courts, perceptions of judicial bias, and expectations of winning
in court. Thoennes and Pearson (1985: 120) asked clients if they anticipated that
their mediation would produce the desired custody/visitation arrangements or
if litigation would produce the desired outcome. This second study also asked
clients if they had expected more legal advice. Coates and Gehm (1989), as well
as Umbreit (1991), measure levels of anxiety prior to the mediation. Wissler (1999:
92) follows the same line of thinking by asking people if they were concerned about
the mediation, and if they gathered information about the mediation, including talking to court personnel, before beginning their mediation. McEwen and
Wissler (2002: 138–139) cite several studies that rely on attorney reports relating

to a client's choosing mediation: who initiates discussions about using mediation and whether clients are willing to use mediation.

Kressel (2000: 524) underscores the need for analysis of the final variable of this set, *motivation to resolve* the case. Operational definitions derive from archival and mediator data. McGillicuddy, Welton, and Pruitt (1987: 107–108) coded observations of mediations according to whether participants were motivated to resolve the dispute.[31] Van Slyck, Stern, and Newland (1992: 80) surveyed clients prior to their mediation and asked about their motivation to resolve the dispute. Umbreit and Coates (1993: 570–571) defined the variable in the context of victim–offender mediation programs, but it could be generalized to other forms of criminal or civil mediation. In this research victims were asked if they wanted to recover a loss or help the offender, to tell the offender of the impact of negative behavior, and to get answers about the crime. Offenders were asked if they wanted to make things right, to apologize, and be done with the episode. Finally, Carnevale et al. (1989: 224–228) asked mediators if they viewed participants as having "no interest in settling."

Dispute characteristics

The next construct among the antecedent factors is dispute characteristics. Three variables contribute to the construct: legal characteristics, conflict characteristics, and interpersonal dynamics. Operational definitions of *legal characteristics* are found in archival, client, and mediator data. Looking at case records, Bridenback et al. (1980: 14), Vidmar (1984: 527), McGillicuddy et al. (1987: 106 n. 1); Umbreit and Greenwood (1999: 239) and Wyrick and Costanzo (1999) list the type of cases referred to mediation. This variable can be defined several ways: whether the case is a misdemeanor or minor felony, whether it is a violation of property or an interpersonal dispute, the extent of legal liability, and the severity of violence involved in the crime. Vidmar (1985: 134) surveyed mediation participants to assess admitted liability. Wissler (2002: 652–653) asked mediators to note the type (e.g. business, personal injury, etc.) and legal complexity of the case. Kakalik et al. (1996: 331) also asked mediators and attorneys to assess the complexity of the legal issues and the difficulty of discovery (see also Wissler 2002: 652). Wissler (1999: 57–58; 2002: 650) relies on attorneys to report the legal status of the case with regard to discovery, motions to dismiss, and pending summary judgment.

We note that the next two variables – *conflict characteristics* and *interpersonal dynamics* – are probably highly related,[32] but for research purposes we attempt to distinguish the two. In the proposed model, conflict characteristics refers to descriptors of a set of events. The variable interpersonal dynamics describes the relations between the mediation participants.

Kressel (2000: 524–525) discusses several *characteristics of conflicts* he feels are relevant to any negotiation, including the intensity of the conflict, whether a conflict is over fundamental principles, and whether resources are scarce (see also Whiting 1994). Measures of conflict intensity exist in several data forms.[33] McGillicuddy et al. (1987: 108–109) created observational codes that described a continuum from hostile, contentious behavior to conciliatory behavior (see also Zubek et al. 1992:

554). Van Slyck et al. (1992: 80–82) measure intensity using client reports. Wissler (1999: 52) asks about a history of violence or abuse in marital disputes. She (2002: 653) also asked mediators about the contentiousness of both the client and the attorney relationships. Carnevale et al. (1989: 224–228) ask mediators to assess participant hostility (partially defined as interactional hostility; see also Irving & Benjamin 1992: 37). The Georgia Office of Dispute Resolution (GAODR 2000: 7–8; also Wissler 1999: 55) rely on mediators to gauge levels of acrimony. Different dimensions of the variable conflict characteristics exist in research by Van Slyck et al. (1992: 80–82) who asked clients about the duration of the dispute as well as whether the dispute involves tangible or intangible issues.[34] Kakalik et al. (1996) ask both mediators and attorneys to rate conflicts according to their overall complexity.

The final variable to operationalize conflict characteristics is *interpersonal dynamics*.[35] Many researchers use archival data to describe the relationship: whether people are family, quasi-family, acquaintances, or strangers, and if the relationship will continue after the mediation (cf. Bridenback et al. 1980: 10–14; McGillicuddy et al. 1987: 106 n. 1; Zubek et al. 1992; Whiting 1994: 249–250; Donnelly & Ebron 2000: 15). Studies based on client data operationalize interpersonal dynamics as characteristics of interactions. For example, for marital disputes, Thoennes and Pearson (1985: 120) describe the relationship with the spouse, their ability to achieve goals during the marriage, and their desire for or acceptance of a divorce. Irving and Benjamin (1992: 37) measure depression during a marriage. Van Slyck et al. (1992: 79) measured family functioning (e.g. family social climate, cohesion, etc.) prior to the mediation. Kakalik et al. (1996: 331) ask participants to assess how difficult the relations were between people prior to the mediation. Carnevale et al. (1989: 224–228) rely on mediator reports to assess the degree of trust between parties and whether people were intransigent.

Institutional context

Institutional context constitutes the final construct of the antecedent variables. The construct includes measures of: *program context, process access, process efficiency*, and *process information.* When framing future research agendas, McEwen and Wissler (2002) and McEwen (1999) call for scholars to link characteristics of programs to what happens during and after mediations.[36] But, it is unusual for studies to encompass characteristics like program sponsorship, governance structures, policies, and goals in analyses of mediation or outcomes.[37] In addition, most studies encompass only one program, making multi-program comparisons impossible. But Umbreit and Greenwood (1999: 238) use archival data (from program descriptions) to categorize the type of agency sponsoring mediation. In this study types included: private programs, community-based programs, church-based programs, probation programs, correctional facilities, prosecuting attorney's offices, victim services, the police, and a residential facility.[38] Wissler (2002) also relies on archival, mediator, and client data to compare five ongoing, pilot mediation programs in Ohio to characteristics of mediations conducted during settlement weeks in four Ohio courts. Drawing from Wissler (2002: 660 nn. 70, 71), data pertaining to program context would include policies that specify whether referral is voluntary or mandatory, the timing of referrals, the type of cases referred, and where the mediation program fits into the overall case management process of the court. Policies dictating mediator qualifications and the structure of mediation sessions are also relevant.[39]

According to Harrington (1985: 22), access to informal dispute resolution forums is important for two reasons: (1) lack of easy access – especially for minorities and the powerless – denies justice, and (2) direct involvement in informal proceedings enhances the effectiveness of law. Measures of *process access* reflect the concerns. For example, several studies rely on archival data to operationalize access as rates of involvement across cultural and ethnic groups (cf. Bridenback et al. 1980; Crosson & Christian 1990; Umbreit & Coates 1993; Kakalik et al. 1996; Donnelly & Ebron 2000). Donnelly and Ebron (2000) measure an additional dimension in the percentage of cases eligible for but exempted from mediation (e.g. people residing too far from the court, not suitable, case settled, etc.). Wissler (2002: 651) simply calculated the percentage of mediations held after being scheduled and the percentage of cases settled before the mediation date.

Measures of *process efficiency* are found primarily in archival data. Examples of measures include: the time lapse between filing and mediation (cf. Roehl & Cook 1989; Kelly & Duryee 1992; Wissler 2002; or, in Wyrick & Costanzo 1999, the length of time between the offense and referral to mediation); the length of time between the mediation and a scheduled trial date (Wissler 2002: 650); and the time between filing and final disposition (cf. Kakalik et al. 1996; Donnelly & Ebron 2000). In addition to gathering data from secondary sources, Kakalik et al. (1996: 332) asked mediators about referral times. One research team (Coates & Gehm 1989) operationally defines the variable *process information* using reports by participants on whether the program was clearly explained to them before the mediation (see also Umbreit et al. 2001: 129 for a description of a number of studies).

The Process Used

Figure 2.3 lists the constructs and variables we ascribe to a mediation process (figures 2.1 and 2.3 label the process T_m). The model presents a mediation process as two dominant dynamics. First, mediators must create environments where dialogs, problem analysis, and problem-solving take place (cf. Folberg & Taylor 1984; Moore 1986; Welton 1991: 112), and where the disputant has an active voice in the process (Gale, Mowery, Herrman & Hollett 2002). Various authors characterize effective mediations as encompassing trust, empathy, and rapport between participants (Menzel 1991: 14–15) as well as unabridged communication and boundaries, a commitment to problem-solve, awareness of both explicit and implicit issues, and affirmative listening (Thoennes & Pearson 1985: 117; Pearson et al. 1982: 18–19).[40]

We label this dynamic, considered an unmeasured construct, factors that prime personal readiness. Several variables operationally define the construct, including: *mediator empathy, feeling heard and understood, able to talk about perceptions and feelings, clarity, perceived self-efficacy,* and *hostile environment.* The construct and

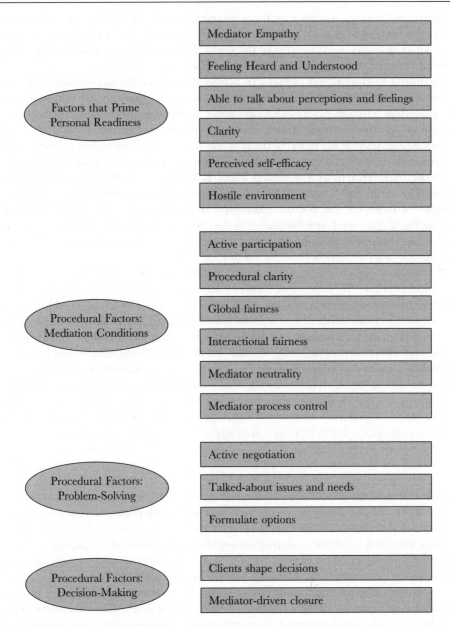

FIGURE 2.3 T_m = The mediation

related variables reflect the writings of Carl Rogers (1975, 1980), especially his philosophies about people, their ability to solve problems, and the role a third party
plays in supporting or drawing out those abilities.[41] The first construct also follows
directly from assumptions 2, 7, and 10.

We label the remaining latent constructs procedural factors, but think that the construct encompasses at least three components: the mediation conditions (including the variables – *active participation, procedural clarity, global fairness, interactional fairness, mediator neutrality,* and *mediator process control*); problem-solving (including *active negotiation, talked-about issues and needs,* and *formulate options*); and decision-making (including the variables *clients shape decisions* and *mediator-driven closure*). Thus, procedural factors begin when mediators and participants structure their mediation; continue while a mediator paces the mediation, and manages power, anger, and crises; then expands as mediators and participants use emerging insights to identify options and resources; and concludes with mutual commitments to change (cf. Thoennes & Pearson 1985: 117; Menzel 1991: 14–15).[42] The construct follows our assumptions 3, 4, 5, and 10, and expresses many of Deutsch's (1973, 1991, 2000) distinctions between competitive and cooperative problem-solving. In fact, several variables cited in the proposed model operationally define conditions described by Deutsch and others.[43]

Factors that prime readiness[44]

Table 2.2 lists constructs, variables, and references relating to the mediation process.[45] We begin our review with variables that operationally define factors that prime personal readiness.[46] Measures of *mediator empathy* can be found in all three data forms. Zubek et al. (1992: 555) use observational codes to categorize mediators according to whether they created rapport, expressed concerns for the welfare of each person, and reassured people. Several researchers ask clients if their mediator expressed concern for their needs or the needs of their children (cf. Emery & Wyer 1987a: 182;[47] Kelly & Duryee 1992: 42). McGillicuddy, et al. (1987: 110) asked clients if the mediation atmosphere was friendly and warm (see also Kelly & Duryee 1992: 42), and if the mediator established trust. Wissler (1999) asked clients if they were treated with respect. Finally, Lim and Carnevale (1990: 264) asked mediators about the tactics they use such as developing rapport, speaking the client's language, using humor, and developing trust between the parties. So, regardless of the data source, common components of mediator empathy include rapport, warmth, emotional safety, and respect.

Measures of the second variable, *feeling heard and understood*, attempt to elicit information reflective of internal states (i.e. people feel free to talk and feel that what they say is acceptable). We would argue that this construct carries considerable weight in any mediation context, but even more weight in programs that emphasize what Umbreit et al. (2001: 124–125) call a non-directive, humanistic mediation model, the distinction being between programs that emphasize settlements versus those that emphasize dialog *per se*. Measures of this variable exist in archival and client data. For example, Zubek et al. (1992: 555–556) rely on observational codes to assess whether a mediator exhibited genuine understanding, accurately interpreted their clients' thoughts and emotions, expressed a client's perspective, and whether they praised clients for past actions, for actions taken during the mediation, and for current positions. Thoennes and Pearson (1985:

TABLE 2.2   Variables describing the mediation process (T_m)

Factors That Prime Personal Readiness	Procedural Factors: Mediation Conditions	Procedural Factors: Problem-Solving	Procedural Factors: Decision-Making
Mediator empathy *Archival data* Zubek et al. 1992 *Client data* Emery & Wyer 1987a; McGillicuddy et al. 1987; Kelly & Duryee 1992; Wissler 1999 *Mediator data* Lim & Carnevale 1990 **Feeling heard and understood** Umbreit et al. 2001 *Archival data* Zubek et al. 1992 *Client data* Thoennes & Pearson 1985; Emery & Wyer 1987a; 1987; Pruitt et al. 1990; Meierding 1993; Jones & Bodtker 1998, 1999; Wissler 2002 **Able to talk about perceptions and feelings** *Client data* Wall & Dewhurst 1991; Irving & Benjamin 1992; Kelly & Duryee 1992; Pearson & Thoennes 1989; Umbreit 1991; Shapiro & Brett 1993; Wissler 1999; Donnelly & Ebron 2000; GAODR 2000; Wissler 2002 *Mediator data* Wissler 1999; Lim & Carnevale 1990	**Active participation** **a. Client attended the mediation** *Archival data* Shaw 1989; Van Slyck et al. 1992; Wissler 2002 *Client data* Kelly & Gigy 1989; Irving & Benjamin 1992; Kelly & Duryee 1992 *Mediator data* Wissler 1999, 2002; Jones & Bodtker 1998 **b. Client helped shape the process** Keashly & Newberry 1995 **Procedural clarity** Thoennes & Pearson 1985; Kressel 2000 *Archival data* Zubek et al. 1992 *Client data* Thoennes & Pearson 1985; Jones & Bodtker 1998; Donnelly & Ebron 2000 *Mediator data* Lim & Carnevale 1990 **Global fairness** *Client data* Thibaut & Walker 1975; Leventhal 1976; McEwen & Maiman 1981; Tyler 1987; Vidmar 1985; Bies & Moag 1986; Lind & Tyler 1988; Pruitt et al. 1990; Shapiro & Brett 1993; Stienstra et al. 1997; Wissler 1999, 2002; Donnelly & Ebron 2000	**Active negotiation** *Archival data* Zubek et al. 1992 *Client/Attorney data* Umbreit & Coates 1993; Wissler 2002 *Mediator data* Carnevale et al. 1991; McGillicuddy et al. 1991 **Talked-about issues and needs** Lind et al. 1990; Cobb 1994 *Archival data* Zubek et al. 1992 *Client data* Thoennes & Pearson 1985; GAODR 2000; Umbreit 1991 **Formulate options** *Archival data* Zubek et al. 1992 *Client data* Emery & Wyer 1987a; Irving & Benjamin 1992; Meierding 1993; Wissler 1999, 2002	**Clients shape decisions** Thibaut & Walker 1975; Tyler 1987 *Client data* Brett 1986; McGillicuddy et al. 1987; Folger 1977, 1986; Emery & Wyer 1987a; McGillicuddy et al. 1987; Kelly & Duryee 1992; Kelly & Gigy 1988; GAODR 2000; Wissler 2002 **Mediator-driven closure** *Archival data* McGillicuddy et al. 1987; Zubek et al. 1992 *Client data* Kelly & Gigy 1988; Kelly & Duryee 1992; Irving & Benjamin 1992; Meierding 1993; Jones & Bodtker 1999; Wissler 1999; Stienstra et al. 1997; Donnelly & Ebron 2000 *Mediator data* McGillicuddy et al. 1987; Lim & Carnevale 1990; Wissler 1999

TABLE 2.2 (Cont'd)

Factors That Prime Personal Readiness	Procedural Factors: Mediation Conditions	Procedural Factors: Problem-Solving	Procedural Factors: Decision-Making
Clarity	**Interactional fairness**		
a. Understand self, personal issues, and needs	*Client data* Kelly & Gigy 1988; Irving & Benjamin 1992; Wissler 1999, 2002; Donnelly & Ebron 2000		
Wall & Dewhurst 1991			
Client data Thoennes & Pearson 1985; Kelly & Gigy 1988; Pearson & Thoennes 1989; Meierding 1993; Jones & Bodtker 1998; Wissler 2002	*Mediator data* Lim & Carnevale 1990; Wissler 1999		
	Mediator neutrality		
b. Understand other's needs, issues, and point of view	Kressel 2000; Rifkin et al. 1991; Cobb 1994; Greatbatch & Dingwall 1989; Welton 1991		
Pruitt & Rubin 1986; Bush & Folger 1994	*Client data* Bridenback et al. 1980; Cook et al. 1980; Welton & Pruitt 1987; Kelly & Gigy 1988; Wall & Dewhurst 1991; Irving & Benjamin 1992; Kelly & Duryee 1992; Meierding 1993		
Client data Thoennes & Pearson 1985; Kelly & Gigy 1988; Umbreit 1991; Welton 1991; Kelly & Duryee 1992; Umbreit & Coates 1993; Jones & Bodtker 1998; Wissler 1997, 1999	*Mediator data* Lim & Carnevale 1990		
	Mediator process control		
Mediator data Lim & Carnevale 1990	Thoennes & Pearson 1985; Antes et al. 1999; Kressel 2000		
Perceived self-efficacy:	*Archival data* Wall & Dewhurst 1991; Zubek et al. 1992; Cobb 1994		
Deutsch 1973; Weiss-Wik 1983; Kelly & Gigy 1988; Kelly & Duryee 1992; Riskin 2003	*Client data* Thoennes & Pearson 1985; Kelly & Gigy 1988; Umbreit 1991; Kelly & Duryee 1992; Irving & Benjamin 1992; Meierding 1993; Stienstra et al. 1997; Wissler 1999; Donnelly & Ebron 2000		
Hostile environment			
Archival data Zubek et al. 1992; Kelly & Duryee 1992	*Mediator data* Lim & Carnevale 1990; Kakalik et al. 1996		

120) asked people if the mediator gave them a chance to express their point of view (see also Pruitt, Peirce, Zubek, Welton & Nochajski 1990, who asked if people were allowed to talk about basic issues). Emery and Wyer (1987a: 182; also Pruitt et al. 1990; Wissler 2002: 661) flipped the question by asking people if their feelings and views were understood. Meierding (1993: 161) created another variation by asking clients if they felt the mediator was aware of their needs as well as their spouse's needs. Jones and Bodtker (1998: 191; 1999) asked clients if the mediator listened to their concerns.[48]

The third variable, *able to talk about perceptions and feelings*, is similar to the second, but pertains to actions rather than an implied internal state. Measures are found in studies of clients and mediators. Affirmative questions have been written several ways. Wall and Dewhurst (1991: 74) ask people if they were allowed enough time to say what they needed to say. Another approach is to ask people if they were allowed to express their feelings fully or were silenced (cf. Irving & Benjamin 1992: 44; Kelly & Duryee 1992: 43; Shapiro & Brett 1993; Wissler 1999; Donnelly & Ebron 2000: 81; GAODR 2000: 11; Wissler 2002: 661). Pearson and Thoennes (1989) create a variation that asks if the mediator encouraged talk about the problem/supported talk about point of view. Umbreit (1991: 195) focuses on whether a mediator allows victims to describe the negative impact of the crime, and whether offenders liked the opportunity to face their victim and talk (see also Umbreit et al. 2001: 124). Finally, Lim and Carnevale (1990: 264) asked mediators if they let participants blow off steam (also see Wissler 1999).

Following the reasoning of Rogers (1975) that uncensored expression of concerns and issues relates to greater introspection and clarity, we include variables that measure *clarity*. To begin, Wall and Dewhurst (1991: 72–73) coded mediator utterances for how far they: clarified meaning, tried to hear the other side of the story, and forced people to look at statements made. Client and mediator data articulate two subsets of the variable, the first being *understand self, personal issues and needs*. Researchers commonly ask participants and sometimes their attorneys if the mediation and mediator actions facilitated insight (cf. Thoennes & Pearson 1985; Pearson & Thoennes 1989; Jones & Bodtker 1998: 191; Wissler 2002: 664). Additionally, several researchers define clarity in relation to factual content. Examples include, Kelly and Gigy (1988: 47), who ask if the mediation helped identify important issues and problems, if people needed more financial information or help in understanding details of property and financial issues, or if they received enough information to protect their self-interest. Meierding (1993: 162) asks if people understood details of financial settlements, custody, support, and other issues. Wissler (2002: 664) asked clients if they were better able to assess the strengths and weaknesses of their own case.

Understanding your own point of view more clearly is just one aspect of effective problem-solving. Pruitt and Rubin (1986: 148–151) talk about techniques of understanding each other's needs as well. This includes: listening below the surface; being attentive to points that are emphasized; drawing from your knowledge of the other's values and standards; and being aware that the same issue may have different meanings to different people. We label this second subset of the variable *clarity: understanding other's needs, issues, and point of view.*[49] Most measures exist as client data. A common approach is to ask about improved understanding of the other's point of view or needs (cf. Thoennes & Pearson 1985: 120; Pruitt & Rubin 1986; Kelly & Gigy 1988: 47; Umbreit 1991; Jones & Bodtker 1998: 191; Wissler 1999, 2002: 664). Wissler (1997: 5) relies on attorneys for data on whether people understand each other's positions as well as the strengths and weaknesses of each other's cases. Welton (1991: 106) asked people if they gained understanding of the impact of the dispute on the victim and society. This is similar to Umbreit and Coates (1993), who looked at increased awareness of the impact of negative behavior. Kelly and Duryee (1992: 43) include a question in their research that taps a logical extension of clarity, namely if people could put anger aside and focus on the children.[50] Finally, Lim and Carnevale (1990: 264) asked mediators if they discussed the interests of others and tried to clarify needs of the other party.

Perceived self-efficacy. An expression of power, labeled *perceived self-efficacy* in the model, represents a potentially important variable. Two studies relevant to this chapter measure self-efficacy. Kelly and Gigy (1988: 45, 47) asked mediation participants if they could now stand up for themselves and take more responsibility for managing their personal affairs (similar to Kelly & Duryee 1992: 42). These studies approximate a definition of power offered by Weiss-Wik (1983) in his discussion of classic negotiation texts (i.e. feeling you can get something done).

Even lacking widespread use as a variable, various theorists assume this form of power is highly relevant to problem-solving situations. For example, Deutsch (1973: 85, 395) describes power as a situational phenomenon, being shaped by characteristics of the situation as well as a person's characteristics. Power shifts across situations even for the same person.[51] Without using the word power, Riskin (2003: 30) describes how mediator actions invoke at least two forms of power: "*almost any conduct* by a mediator *directs* the mediation process, or the participants, toward a particular procedure or perspective or outcome, on the one hand or, on the other, *elicits* the parties perspectives and preferences-and then tries to honor or accommodate them." Borrowing from Riskin's thinking, all types of mediator actions relate to party self-determination directly, by directing or forcing, or indirectly by eliciting or framing reactions. The distinction is close to Steiner's (1981) delineation of external power (force) and internal power (compassion, empathy). Yet: "nearly any move by a mediator can have both directive or elicitive aspects or intents or effects" (Riskin 2003: 32).

Hostile environment. Two studies define a final variable under factors that prime readiness, namely a situation that may negate the positive effects of all of the previous variables – a hostile environment. Zubek et al. (1992: 556) code and track hostile communication (hostile questions, sarcasm, angry displays, putdowns, character assassination, etc.). Kelly and Duryee (1992: 43) ask people if they quit because they could not stay in the same room with a spouse or if their spouse was too angry or unreasonable.[52]

Procedural factors: mediation conditions

The model continues with constructs and variables that assess the context of the mediation proper. The first construct in this trio is procedural factors: mediation conditions. *Active participation, procedural clarity, global fairness, interactional fairness, mediator neutrality,* and *mediator process control* operationally define this construct. *Active participation* reflects two types of measures: *client attendance* and *client helped shape the process* of mediation. Measures of attendance are found in all three types of data. Archival data indicate whether people and their representatives attended their scheduled mediation sessions (Shaw 1989: 136; Van Slyck et al. 1992: 82; Wissler 2002: 657). Client reports capture information on who attended, how many sessions occurred, and the length of the mediation (cf. Kelly & Gigy 1989: 275; Irving & Benjamin 1992: 41). Irving & Benjamin (1992: 41) also note whether mediation participants attended jointly or individually (i.e. in dialog or caucus sessions). Where people ceased to participate, Kelly & Duryee (1992: 43) asked if they quit because they lacked sufficient information or felt confused. Some studies ask mediators: whether people and their representatives participated more or less actively (e.g. did people talk: Wissler 2002: 658); whether the mediation was terminated due to reports of domestic violence (Wissler 1999: 71, 115); whether their client made a sincere effort; whether they were ready to mediate; and whether they stopped participating because they were unable to come up with ways for solving the problem (Jones & Bodtker 1998: 197).

Active participation could also be defined as *clients helped shape the process.* Keashly & Newberry (1995: 279) note that much of the literature on pre-decision control confounds process and content control. The distinction calls for closer empirical scrutiny, and the variables need more development.[53]

Procedural clarity, the next variable used to define mediation conditions surfaces when mediators clearly describe the purpose and boundaries of a mediation (cf. Thoennes & Pearson 1985: 117).[54] An example can be found in Zubek et al. (1992) as codes that record mediator assurances such as: "I won't write anything incriminating in the agreement." or "Caucuses are confidential." Client assessments of procedural clarity include questions like: "Mediator explained the process clearly, explained confidentiality" (Jones & Bodtker 1998: 191); and "I understood the rules and procedures" (Donnelly & Ebron 2000: 81). There are also negative measures such as: the rules were confusing; the mediation was confusing; I did not know what was going to happen (Thoennes & Pearson 1985: 120; Donnelly & Ebron 2000: 81). Finally, Lim and Carnevale (1990: 264) asked mediators if the goals of the mediation had been made clear.

Measures of *global fairness* are found in many studies in data from participants and their attorneys. Typically, measures rely on generally worded questions: Was the process fair? (cf. Thibaut & Walker 1975; Leventhal 1976; McEwen & Maiman 1981; Vidmar 1985: 138–139; Tyler 1987: 371; Lind & Tyler 1988; Pruitt et al. 1990; Shapiro & Brett 1993: 1171–1172; Stienstra, Johnson & Lombard 1997; Wissler 1999: 74, 77; 2002: 661–663). Donnelly and Ebron (2000: 81) specified if the rules and procedures were fair. Bies and Moag (1986) asked if the mediator was fair in implementing the process.

Measures of *interactional fairness* tend to be more specific than those of global fairness. From past research, this variable is multi-dimensional and includes: mediator respect of clients, attention to client rights, and balance of power. Measures created from client responses define interactional fairness in several ways. Donnelly and Ebron (2000: 81; also Wissler 2002: 661) define the variable as: treated with dignity and respect. Wissler (1999: 116) defined it as: the mediator tried to even out bargaining imbalances. Irving and Benjamin (1992: 44) defined the variable in both positive and negative terms. Their positive definition is: mediator attended to client rights. Negative expressions include: my partner had an advantage, and mediator favored spouse's point of view. Their questions are similar to the Kelly and Gigy (1988: 47–48) questions: my spouse had an advantage over me during the mediation, and I was on the defensive. Two sets of measures were created from data supplied by mediators. The Lim and Carnevale, (1990: 264) factor scales include two questions: the mediator helped people save face and suggested face-saving proposals. Wissler's (1999: 113) records of mediator actions includes: tried to even out bargaining imbalances.

Mediator neutrality. The mediation literature is replete with descriptions of mediators as neutral third parties. The construct constitutes a core value for mediators, but is poorly defined (Kressel 2000).[55] Several theorists and researchers have questioned what neutrality means and how it is expressed in practice. Welton (1991: 113) discusses common assumptions, while Rifkin, Millen, and Cobb (1991; see also Carnevale 1992; Cobb 1993) question the feasibility of those assumptions. Both Cobb (1994) and Greatbatch and Dingwall (1989) review tapes of mediation sessions to illustrate gaps between what mediators aspire to and what they actually do. A number of studies measure the variable in ways that reflect its complexity. One approach defines neutrality as impartial versus partial behavior (cf. Wall & Dewhurst 1991: 74; Kelly & Gigy 1988: 47; Irving & Benjamin 1992: 44; Kelly & Duryee 1992: 42; Meierding 1993: 162). Several other studies measure neutrality as: the mediator is concerned about and values outcome for both sides (cf. Bridenback et al. 1980; Cook, Roehl & Sheppard 1980; Welton & Pruitt 1987). Lim and Carnevale (1990: 264) asked mediators if they avoid taking sides.

Mediator process control comprises a final variable defining procedural factors: mediation conditions. Kressel (2000: 533–534) suggests that good mediators maintain control of the process. He also notes the value of a mediator's substantive competence in discussing substantive issues. Substantive expertise potentially heightens a mediator's sensitivity to each person's interests and constraints, allowing mediators to shape the direction of negotiations strategically. But Antes, Hudson, Jorgensen, and Moen (1999) raise an interesting, as yet untested, question about how to define process control: is control indicative of mediations that flow in predictable sequential stages (reminiscent of Dewey's logic model of 1938) or can a mediator control a mediation that evolves as dialog and problem-solving needs shift? Might the sensitivities that Kressel (2000) notes improve a mediator's "intuition" about process shifts, thus improving both control and effectiveness?

Thoennes and Pearson (1985: 117) lay out the type of activities that comprise the variable. For these researchers, successful mediators maintain the pace of a mediation so that clients do not feel rushed or held back. They focus conversation on the most relevant issues. They promote open, honest communication. They balance power, reduce tension, and ensure that people feel responsible for their settlement.

Cobb (1994: 60), in an analysis of taped mediations, follows a similar reasoning. She has found that simply controlling the process is not enough: "mediators need to regulate the construction of stories with respect to narrative coherence; this mandate defies the traditional distinction between the process of mediation and the content of the dispute: To regulate the process, mediators must manage the construction of the content."[56] As yet, we lack studies that dissect and operationalize measures to this degree.

Measures of mediator process control exist in all three types of data. Archival measures produced by Wall and Dewhurst (1991: 72–73) operationalize the variable several ways: mediators softened language, changed the topic, reframed prior utterances into a proposal, emphasized points of agreement, and maintained control of the mediation. Similarly, Zubek et al. (1992: 556) rely on coded tapes to show that some mediators make early pronouncements about their competence, credentials, or knowledge.[57] As mediations progress, they also shape the dialog by critiquing participant behaviors during the mediation, as well as past behaviors. They may critique current positions (e.g. you are being unreasonable). Codes of transcripts also include: mediators used filters to channel communication (e.g. selective hearing) and structured negotiations (e.g. by posing joint problems to be solved, structuring an agenda, challenging people to develop new ideas, suggesting new ideas, asking for reactions to new ideas, asking embarrassing questions that create doubt, and interjecting to maintain order in the negotiation).

Measures derived from client surveys (sometimes of participants and sometimes of their attorneys) vary from less to more specific indicators of control. Less specific measures include: mediator facilitated communication (Thoennes & Pearson 1985: 117; Stienstra et al. 1997); mediator helped people negotiate more reasonably (Meierding 1993: 162); mediator facilitated confrontation (Umbreit 1991: 195). More detailed measures include: mediator maintained focus on issues, encouraged effective negotiation, allowed destructive communication, wasted time by not talking about important issues, we kept going over old ground, mediator did not stop spouse from acting destructively (Kelly & Gigy 1988: 47–48; Irving & Benjamin 1992: 44; Kelly & Duryee 1992: 42). Wissler (1999: 113) adds: mediator summarized frequently. Donnelly and Ebron (2000: 81) add: the process brought out all the issues.

Measures derived from mediator data also note ways mediators establish and maintain control over a negotiation. Additional actions include: devise a framework for negotiations, help prioritize issues, cover general issues first, settle simple issues first, simplify the agenda, take responsibility/make concessions, focus negotiations on the issues, press parties hard, move them off positions, say they are unrealistic, focus caucuses on the issues, call for frequent caucuses, keep people at the table, and express pleasure at progress (Lim & Carnevale 1990: 264). Finally, Kakalik et al. (1996) note that some mediators ask for written information prior to meeting, require lead counsel to attend, work with people with settlement authority, caucus (with and without attorneys present), and evaluate the case for each side.[58]

Procedural factors: problem-solving

The next construct in the model under the process of mediation is *procedural factors: problem-solving.* Putnam and Holmer (1992: 137–141) focus our attention in a general way on "issue development" as one approach to framing. This approach looks at how issues develop during a negotiation, assuming that they shift as they are conceptualized and reconceptualized during the ongoing dialog.[59] Within this construct the model encompasses variables like: *active negotiation, talked about issues and needs,* and *formulate options.* Our discussion of previous measures starts with *active negotiation.* Archival data analyzed by Zubek et al. (1992: 555–556) produced descriptors of active negotiation including: joint problem-solving (e.g. open communication, collaboration to clarify issues, generating and critiquing ideas, exchange of information), mutual concern for each other's interests, protecting personal needs, and contentious behavior (e.g. hard bargaining, threats, and heavy positional statements).

Umbreit and Coates (1993: 576) rely on client responses to describe active negotiation in terms of people having an opportunity to directly participate in problem-solving and being able to talk to the other person (e.g. to ask questions, hear answers, apologies). Wissler (2002: 665) asked attorneys if mediation helped them: talk to opposing counsel and expedite discovery. Some studies rely on mediators to provide data to operationalize active negotiation. Examples include: how participants interact (e.g. effective negotiation, good problem-solving, people held back, people not interested in coming up with solutions), and whether people developed new proposals (Carnevale, Putnam, Conlon & O'Connor 1991: 128–129; McGillicuddy et al. 1991).

The next variable under procedural factors: problem-solving is *talked about issues and needs.* We see this variable as an instrumental variation of the earlier variable, feeling heard and understood. It refers to dialog that specifically advances facts and interests that are important to a negotiation and a solution.[60] The archival data collected by Zubek et al. (1992) rated the importance of issues. Measures derived from client data allow participants to discriminate between the relevance of issues. Examples of questions include: mediation facilitated talk about the problems and issues (Thoennes & Pearson 1985: 120); all of the important issues were discussed (GAODR 2000: 11); and the conversation created assurance the offender would obtain help (Umbreit 1991: 195).

The last variable in the model to measure procedural factors: problem-solving is *formulate options.* Zubek et al. (1992) created a seven-point scale of joint problem-solving from their archival data. The code references: generating and critiquing ideas, creative invention of alternatives. Several studies rely on data from clients and include questions like: knew about available options (Emery & Wyer 1987a: 182); mediator made helpful suggestions (Irving & Benjamin 1992: 44); mediator helped people create options (Meierding 1993: 162); and mediator suggested options (Wissler

1999: 113). Wissler (2002: 656) asked mediators about their actions including: helping people evaluate their case, evaluating a case for clients, or staying silent.

Procedural factors: decision-making

Two variables: *clients shape decisions* and *mediator-driven closer* operationally define the final construct of procedural factors: decision-making. The variable *clients shape decisions* further articulates the distinction between process and outcome control.[61] Examples of questions that measure client control, as articulated by clients and sometimes attorneys, include: clients actively involved in working out an agreement (McGillicuddy et al. 1987; Wissler 2002: 661, 665); people had control over decisions (Emery & Wyer 1987a: 182); and both parties had equal influence over the terms of the agreement or over the outcome (Kelly & Gigy 1988: 48; Kelly & Duryee 1992: 42); and people helped determine the outcome (GAODR 2000: 11).

Mediator-driven closure constitutes the last variable among the procedural factors relating to decision-making. Sometimes researchers confound process control and settlement pressure. For example in a discussion that compares a mediator's style to effectiveness, Brett, Drieghe, and Shapiro (1986: 280) define "dealmakers" as those mediators who keep parties together, encourage compromise, propose settlements, and informally evaluate possible outcomes should the mediation fail. For these same authors, a mediator who relies on "shuttle diplomacy" typically separates parties while developing concrete solutions as they move from one caucus to another. Kolb (1983: 150) just looks at style, without comparing actions to effectiveness, and posits two types: "orchestrators" and "dealmakers." Orchestrators control interactions between the mediation participants while allowing them freedom to develop agendas and settlement options. Dealmakers propose and push settlement options. Future research could analyze this variable in conjunction with other variables, such as formulate options and clients shape decisions, to clarify if mediation participants relate mediator assertiveness to their effectiveness.[62]

Archival data provide measures of mediator forcefulness, ranging from light to heavy pressure tactics (McGillicuddy et al. 1987: 108–109) as well as descriptions of tactics such as urging agreement, noting the cost of an impasse, and making threats (Greatbatch & Dingwall 1989; Zubek et al. 1992: 557). Measures based on client data add detail to descriptions of the variable. For example, Kelly and Gigy (1988: 47; Kelly & Duryee 1992: 42) asked participants whether: the mediator did/did not impose his/her values on me; the participant needed more practical advice about what to do – how to decide; and the mediator proposed ways to settle. Irving and Benjamin (1992) asked if the mediator pushed compromises or influenced outcomes (see also Donnelly & Ebron 2000: 75–76). Meierding (1993: 162) asked if people were pressured to sign an agreement and distinguished by whom (i.e. by a spouse, the mediator or both; see also Wissler 2002: 661). Jones and Bodtker (1999: 26) were more specific in asking if the mediator pressured people to go along with something they really did not want. Questions developed by Wissler (1999: 69) cover a range of possibilities such as: mediator recommended a particular settlement, kept silent about an appropriate settlement, evaluated merits of the case, and suggested possible settlement options. Finally, Stienstra et al. (1997) asked attorneys if their mediator pressured too much or too little.

A few studies ask mediators about their efforts to influence closure, such as suggesting settlement, trade-offs among issues, or compromises; and evaluating the merits of the case or disclosing their opinion of the merits (cf. McGillicuddy et al. 1987: 109; Lim & Carnevale 1990: 264; Wissler 1999: 106; 2002: 656). Even though each study relies on similar questions, each also offers variations that, if combined into a single index, could produce a potentially powerful measure.

Short-Term Outcomes (T₁)

Mediation outcomes have traditionally served to define whether a mediator or mediation program is doing a "good job" (Duffy 1991). Thus, outcome and effect-iveness have been equated in practice, and sometimes in theory (Kochan & Jick 1978). But defining what constitutes a "good job" is difficult.[63] During the several decades that mediation has burgeoned beyond its labor roots in the United States, it has been asked to serve many roles (Herrman 1993), such as: (1) enhanc-ing institutions (e.g. improving the public's access to justice while also improving court efficiency; Hofrichter 1982: 194–196);[64] (2) improving the match between various types of disputes and forums for resolving disputes (Sander & Goldberg 1994); (3) enhancing disputant capacities for self-awareness and changed behaviors as well as a greater understanding of the needs of others involved in the dispute (Bush & Folger 1994); and (4) enhancing community capacities to resolve disputes without violence or institutional intervention (Danzig 1982; Merry 1982). Because mediation serves multiple masters, it is no surprise that various studies operationalize an assortment of outcome measures.[65]

The discussion in this section pertains to short-term outcomes.[66] The following section pertains to long-term outcomes. Figure 2.4 outlines several variables we define as short-term outcomes, including the constructs of: *disputant beliefs and attitudes*, measured by several forms of satisfaction, attitudes about the settlement, measures relating to anxiety, and one measure that taps changes in functioning; *conflict resolved*, measured by characteristics of the agreement and the relationship at the end of the mediation; and *institutional context*, measured by indicators of efficiency, effect-iveness, and cost. Table 2.3 lists variables and references used to operationally define each construct.

Disputant beliefs and attitudes

The first four variables to define attitudes and beliefs relate to satisfaction. The variable *satisfaction with the court/judicial system* relies on data provided by clients. Operational definitions focus on satisfaction with the court's role and whether the court had a bad or good effect on the participant (Emery & Wyer 1987a: 182; Emery & Jackson 1989: 12–15). Umbreit and Coates (1993: 575) asked if the case was handled fairly by the system, and if people were satisfied with how the case was pro-cessed by the judicial system. Coates and Gehm (1989) asked people whether their

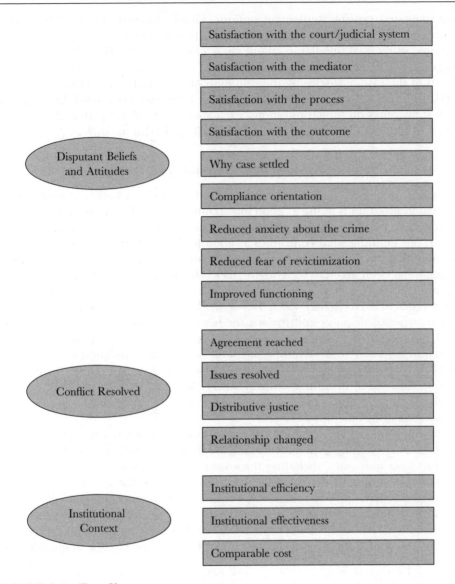

FIGURE 2.4   T$_1$ = Short-term outcomes

understanding of the justice system had improved as a result of their experience. Umbreit et al. (2001: 130) note seven studies that rely on survey data to measure whether victims were satisfied with the referral of their case to mediation.

Satisfaction with the mediator, the second satisfaction measure, relies on data from clients, their attorneys, and mediators.[67] Global ratings by clients range from excellent to terrible (Zubek et al. 1992; Stienstra et al. 1997). More detailed descriptors include: the mediator was skilled, competent, and trustworthy; the

TABLE 2.3 Variables describing short-term outcomes (T₁)

Disputant beliefs and attitudes	Conflict resolved	Institutional context
Satisfaction with the court/judicial system *Client data* Emery & Wyer 1987a; Emery & Jackson 1989; Umbreit & Coates 1993; Coates & Gehm 1989; Umbreit et al. 2001 **Satisfaction with the mediator** *Client data* Bridenback et al. 1980; Cook et al. 1980; Lehmann 1986; Wall & Dewhurst 1991; Kelly & Duryee 1992; Irving & Benjamin 1992; Zubek et al. 1992; Stienstra et al. 1997; Wissler 1999 *Mediator data* Carnevale et al. 1991; Irving & Benjamin 1992; Lehmann 1986 **Satisfaction with the process** *Client data* Davis et al. 1980; Cook et al. 1980; Harrington 1985; McGillicuddy et al. 1987; Thoennes & Pearson 1985; Coates & Gehm 1989; Kressel et al. 1989: 58; Kelly & Gigy 1988; 1989; Pearson & Thoennes 1989; Irving & Benjamin 1992; Shapiro & Brett 1993; Wall & Dewhurst 1991; Zubek et al. 1992; Donnelly & Ebron 2000; Kelly & Duryee 1992; Jones & Bodtker 1999; Umbreit et al. 2001; Wissler 2002 *Attorney data* Wissler 1997; Stienstra et al. 1997; Donnelly & Ebron 2000 *Mediator data* Carnevale et al. 1991; Kakalik et al. 1996; Jones & Bodtker 1998; Irving & Benjamin 1992	**Agreement reached** *Archival data* Bridenback et al. 1980; Cook et al. 1980; Slaikeu et al. 1985; McGillicuddy et al. 1987; Donohue 1989; Emery & Jackson 1989; Kressel et al. 1989; Wall & Dewhurst 1991; Umbreit 1991; Van Slyck et al. 1992; Zubeck et al. 1992; Burrell et al. 1994; Donohue et al. 1994; Whiting 1994; Jones & Bodtker 1998; Donnelly & Ebron 2000 *Client data* Bridenback et al. 1980; Coates & Gehm 1989; Pearson & Thoennes 1989; Welton 1991; Irving & Benjamin 1992; Umbreit & Coates 1993; Wissler 1997 *Mediator data* Hiltrop 1989; McGillicuddy et al. 1991; Irving & Benjamin 1992; Kakalik et al. 1996; GAODR 2000 *a. Agreement rate* Benjamin & Irving 1995; Kelly 1996 *Archival data* McGillis 1986; Gehm 1990; Emery & Wyer 1987b *Mediator data* GAODR 2000	**Institutional efficiency** *Archival data* Bridenback et al. 1980; Emery & Jackson 1989; Benjamin & Irving 1995; Kelly 1996; Donnelly & Ebron 2000; Wissler 2002 *Client data* Coates & Gehm 1989 *Mediator data* Kakalik et al. 1996 **Institutional effectiveness** *Client data* Emery & Wyer 1987a; Emery & Jackson 1989; Coates & Gehm 1989 *Mediator data* Kakalik et al. 1996 **Comparable cost** Benjamin & Irving 1995 *Client data* Pearson & Thoennes 1988; Menzel 1991; Wissler 1997; 1999; Donnelly & Ebron 2000 *Archival data* Kakalik et al. 1996; Kelly 1996

Satisfaction with the outcome

Client data Kelly & Gigy 1988; Wall & Dewhurst 1991; Kelly & Duryee 1992; Zubek et al. 1992; Emery & Wyer 1987a; McGillicuddy et al. 1991; Irving & Benjamin 1992; Stienstra et al. 1997; Wissler 1999; Jones & Bodtker 1999; Donnelly & Ebron 2000;

Mediator data Jones & Bodtker 1998; Wissler, 1999; Kakalik et al. 1996

a. reactive devaluation

Stillinger et al. 1988; Welton, 1991

Why case settled

Mediators, attorney, and client data

GAODR 2000

Mediator data Wissler 1999

Compliance orientation

Mayer 1989

Client data Coates & Gehm 1989

Mediator data Carnevale et al. 1989; Carnevale et al. 1991

Attorney data Donnelly & Ebron 2000

Reduced anxiety about the crime

Umbreit & Coates 1993

Reduced fear of revictimization

Client data Umbreit 1991; Umbreit & Coates 1993; Umbreit et al. 2001

Improved functioning

Duffy & Thomson 1992

Issues resolved

Nader & Todd 1978; Benjamin & Irving 1995

Archival data Bridenback et al. 1980; Koopman et al. 1984; Zubeck et al. 1992

Client data Bridenback et al. 1980; Thoennes & Pearson 1985; Kelly & Gigy 1988; Emery & Wyer 1987a; Shaw 1989; Irving & Benjamin 1992; Umbreit & Coates 1993; Wissler 2002

Mediator data Mathis & Yingling 1990; Wissler 1999; Kakalik et al. 1996

Distributive justice

Peachey 1989

Archival data Bridenback et al. 1980; McGillicuddy et al. 1987; Zubeck et al. 1992

Client reports Pearson & Thoennes 1989; Wall & Dewhurst 1991; McEwen & Maiman 1984, 1989; Umbreit 1991; Meierding 1993; Whiting 1994; Donnelly & Ebron 2000

Mediator data Leventhal, 1976; Pearson & Thoennes 1989; Carnevale et al. 1991

Relationship changed

Bush & Folger 1994; Benjamin & Irving 1995; Kelly 1996

Client data Emery & Wyer 1987a; Kelly & Gigy 1988; Pruitt et al. 1990; McGillicuddy et al. 1991; Keashly & Newberry 1995; Wissler 1997, 2002; Donnelly & Ebron 2000

Mediator data Zarski et al. 1985; Irving & Benjamin 1992; Kakalik et al. 1996; Wissler 1999

mediator was fair; the mediator did a good job making each disputant's position clear (Lehmann 1986; Wall & Dewhurst 1991: 74–75; Umbreit et al. 2001: 134); the mediator handled the case seriously and served the client's needs (Bridenback et al. 1980; Cook et al. 1980; Kelly & Duryee 1992; Wissler 1999: 74, 77); and the mediator cared (Flaten 1996). Irving and Benjamin (1992: 44) add a negative indicator: would have preferred another mediator.

Mediator data operationalize this variable as: feelings of goodwill and trust were created toward the mediator, people were satisfied with mediation efforts (Carnevale et al. 1991: 128; Irving & Benjamin 1992: 43). Perceptions of a good relationship between mediators and their clients represents yet another measure of the variable (Lehmann 1986).

Satisfaction with the process, both positive and negative descriptors, is perhaps the most common measure of short-term disputant attitudes. Several studies rely on client data to pose global questions that measure procedural satisfaction (cf. Cook et al. 1980; Davis, Tichane & Grayson 1980; Harrington 1985; McGillicuddy et al. 1987: 110; Kelly & Gigy 1989: 277–280; Kelly & Duryee 1992; Irving & Benjamin 1992: 44; Zubek et al. 1992; Jones & Bodtker 1999: 26; Donnelly & Ebron 2000: 76; Umbreit et al. 2001: 131–133; Wissler 2002: 661–662 n. 79). More specific questions probe whether: the process was fair (Wall & Dewhurst 1991: 74); we could look at the real issues (Pearson & Thoennes 1989); meeting the offender was satisfying (Umbreit et al. 2001: 131); I would recommend mediation (cf. Kelly & Gigy 1988: 47–49; Coates & Gehm 1989; Kressel, Butler-DeFreitas, Forlenza & Wilcox 1989: 58; Kelly & Duryee 1992; Wissler 2002: 661–663); and mediation is not as rushed as court (Pearson & Thoennes 1989: 19).

Negative expressions of the variable tap specific indicators: would not recommend mediation, people were angry during the session, people needed/wanted more legal advice (Thoennes & Pearson 1985: 120–123); the process made communication worse, went over old conflict, the process was confusing (cf. Kelly & Gigy 1988: 47–49; Coates & Gehm 1989; Kressel et al. 1989: 58); sessions were tense and unpleasant, expectations and the actual process were not well matched (there was neither counseling nor arbitration), too rushed, issues not fully aired (Pearson & Thoennes 1989: 19–20); needed/wanted more time and sessions, more involvement of others in the sessions (Irving & Benjamin 1992: 44); the process was frustrating, we feel bad about the process (Shapiro & Brett 1993: 1171–1172); and the case disrupted my daily affairs, was inconvenient (Donnelly & Ebron 2000: 76).

Wissler (1997: 4–5) and others gather information from attorneys. These studies define the variable as: mediation provided an opportunity to settle, it was a good process that brought people to the table, and we could define and resolve the key issues (Wissler 1997: 4–5); fair procedure, case settled because of mediation, would choose mediation again (Stienstra et al. 1997); and mediation is not worthwhile if it results in an impasse (Donnelly & Ebron 2000: 84).

A few studies rely on data from mediators, with the predominant approach being to ask a general question on satisfaction (cf. Carnevale et al. 1991: 128; Kakalik et al. 1996; Jones & Bodtker 1998: 197), although Irving and Benjamin (1992: 43) asked if the process had a positive impact on husbands and wives.

Satisfaction with the outcome is the final measure in this series. Clients and mediators provide data for these measures. Client measures include global questions: Were you happy/satisfied with the outcome/the agreement? (Wall & Dewhurst 1991: 74; McGillicuddy et al. 1991; Irving & Benjamin 1992: 43; Zubek et al. 1992); or Were you dissatisfied with the outcome? (Kelly & Duryee 1992). Emery and Wyer (1987a: 182) ask if people won/lost what they wanted (see also McGillicuddy et al. 1991), and were satisfied with the decisions and the fairness of decisions. Kelly and Gigy (1988: 48) ask if people were dissatisfied with their settlement, if they would have done better in court. Measures based on attorney data are found in Stienstra et al. (1997), Wissler (1999: 108), Jones and Bodtker (1999: 26), and Donnelly and Ebron (2000: 82). Each study uses a global measure such as: satisfied with the outcome or the result of the mediation. The same is true of studies that rely on mediator data (cf. Kakalik et al. 1996; Jones & Bodtker 1998: 197; Wissler 1999: 109).[68]

As a subset of this satisfaction measure, we include a construct that exists in the literature but has not yet been operationalized. The construct is *reactive devaluation*. Stillinger, Epelbaum, Keltner, and Ross (1988) suggest that people undervalue concessions made by others in a mediation while feeling that their concessions are greater. At the same time, Welton (1991: 110–115) discusses the difficulty of changing negative perceptions of others when people are problem-solving. While we did not find measures of reactive devaluation in the literature, the construct is potentially important.

Finally, several rarely used but distinct measures exist in the literature. As with reactive devaluation, we include them in this chapter to suggest their potential utility. Attitudes about *why the case did or did not settle* is the first example. The Georgia Office of Dispute Resolution (GAODR 2000: 8–14) asked participants, attorneys, and mediators why their case settled or not. Options included: people were ready to settle, people understood common interests, they were not that far apart to start with, people found creative solutions, people did not want to go to trial, people wanted to put the matter behind them, they needed to settle for financial reasons, people were too upset, the positions were too far apart, important information was missing, mediation occurred too early or too late, more discovery was needed, a key person was missing, no one had the authority to settle, and an attorney was absent or obstructive. Wissler (1999: 73) asked a similar question of mediators and offered these options: people were unreasonable, disparate evaluations, unresolved factual issues, missing information, domestic violence, and mental disability.

Compliance orientation is yet another example. Mayer (1989) offers suggestions based on the writings of Etzioni (1975, 1980). Mayer predicts that the probability of compliance with any agreement relates to factors influencing or supporting an agreement. For example, the probability of compliance is greatest when people agree to act in ways that support their previously held values or norms (defined as a normative influence). Compliance is slightly less likely if people simply think it will produce rewards (defined as a utilitarian-calculative influence). The probability of compliance diminishes when the agreement to act is based on fear of negative consequences, coercion, or threats (defined as a coercive-alienative influence). Actual research relies on client, attorney, and mediator data. Coates and Gehm (1989) ask participants about their perceptions of a lack of leverage to insure compliance. Attorneys were asked if people who reach agreement through mediation are more likely to comply (Donnelly & Ebron 2000: 84). Carnevale et al. (1989: 227) created a general settlement scale for mediator responses. The scale includes questions on lasting agreement reached and no future problems expected (see also Carnevale et al. 1991: 128 for a similar question on "a lasting agreement reached, people will comply with it over time").

The literature on victim–offender mediation offers two additional variables of interest. Umbreit and Coates (1993) construct a simple question to measure *reduced anxiety about the crime*. Measures of *reduced fear of revictimization* assess residual client fear of the offender (Umbreit 1991: 195; Umbreit & Coates 1993; Umbreit et al. 2001: 135–136).

The final variable in this set of variables to measure short-term disputant attitudes and beliefs is *improved functioning*. The variable is unique to a study by Duffy and Thomson (1992), who administered before-after surveys to mediation clients. Surveys assessed psychological functioning as defined by Maslow's hierarchy. The method and measure enabled researchers to compare perceptions of functioning at two points in time.

Conflict resolved

Conflict resolved is the second construct in the model pertaining to short-term outcomes. The construct encompasses measures pertaining to *agreement reached, issues resolved, distributive justice,* and *relationship changed. Agreement reached,* especially measures developed from court or mediation programs files, is perhaps the most common measure of short-term conflict resolution. Examples of this measure emerged in 1980 and exist in current research (cf. Bridenback et al. 1980; Cook et al. 1980; Slaikeu, Culler, Pearson & Thoennes 1985; McGillicuddy et al. 1987; Donohue 1989: 326; Emery & Jackson 1989: 10; Kressel et al. 1989: 58; Wall & Dewhurst 1991: 73; Umbreit 1991: 194; Van Slyck et al. 1992: 82; Zubek et al. 1992; Burrell, Narus, Bogdanoff & Allen 1994; Donohue et al. 1994: 266; Whiting 1994: 251; Jones & Bodtker 1998: 190; Donnelly & Ebron 2000: 72).[69] Fewer studies gather information from clients and mediators by asking people to report if an agreement was reached (cf. Bridenback et al. 1980; Coates & Gehm 1989; Pearson & Thoennes 1989; Welton 1991; Irving & Benjamin 1992: 43; Umbreit & Coates 1993; Wissler 1997: 4; 2002: 665–666). Similarly, mediators and attorneys have been asked to report if an agreement was reached (cf. Hiltrop 1989; McGillicuddy et al. 1991; Irving & Benjamin 1992: 42; Kakalik et al. 1996; GAODR 2000: 7).[70]

We classify the variable *agreement rate* as a subset of agreement reached. Both Benjamin and Irving (1995: 57) and Kelly (1996: 375–376) review the mediation literature with regard to reported rates of agreement. Most measures are simple computations that compare the actual number of agreements to the number of mediations held. Research conducted by McGillis (1986: 58–61), Gehm (1990: 179), and Emery and Wyer (1987b: 474) provide examples of rates computed from archival data.[71] The Georgia Office of Dispute Resolution (GAODR 2000: 7) computed a rate from mediator reports.

The variable *issues resolved* helps researchers interpret agreements. As Nader & Todd (1978) as well as Benjamin and Irving (1995: 57–58) suggest, it is important to know if agreements cover a range of issues and if they are comprehensive.[72] Zubek et al. (1992) use their archival data to operationalize these ideas. This research team matched items in an agreement with observations of issues raised during a mediation. Other studies that rely on archival data define the content of agreements (i.e. money paid, apologies, agreement to change behavior, etc.; cf. Bridenback et al. 1980: 12; Koopman, Hunt & Stafford 1984).

A number of studies elicit perceptions about the resolution from clients. Bridenback et al. (1980: 20–28; also Thoennes & Pearson 1985; Kelly & Gigy 1988: 48; Wissler 2002: 666–667) ask participants if monetary provisions were included and how much, if apologies were given, how much was settled, if custody and visitation arrangements are complete, temporary or partial in nature, or if no issues were resolved. Additional measures include: reached a lasting agreement (Emery & Wyer 1987a: 182), presenting problem resolved (Shaw 1989: 136–137), the agreement meets the child's needs (Irving & Benjamin 1992: 43), and the agreement includes help for the offender (Umbreit & Coates 1993). Studies that rely on mediator data operationalize similar ideas, including: no agreement, partial or full agreement (Mathis & Yingling 1990; Wissler 1999: 71) or resolved or narrowed monetary, liability, or other types of issues (Kakalik et al. 1996).

The variable *distributive justice* provides another means of interpreting a resolution. Peachey (1989: 302) defines distributive justice in two ways, as *equality* (where each person receives an equal share) and as *equity* (where each person shares in the outcome per some principle, need, or proportion).[73] Some measures based on archival data simply note whether both the complainant and respondent agreed to act or whether various points in the agreement favor the complainant or respondent (Bridenback et al. 1980; McGillicuddy et al. 1987). Zubek et al. (1992) compared agreements to issues raised by both the complainant and respondent. They then computed an issue gratification score as well as an importance score to determine if the agreement achieved an integrative solution.

A number of studies rely on client data to operationalize distributive justice by asking people if "the outcome was fair" (Pearson & Thoennes 1989; McEwen & Maiman 1989; Wall & Dewhurst 1991: 74; Umbreit 1991: 195; Meierding 1993: 162; Whiting 1994: 252; Donnelly & Ebron 2000: 75). McEwen and Maiman (1984, 1989) provide a slightly different definition of fair: both the defendant and plaintiff were obliged to act (similar to the archival measure). A common definition drawn from mediators is: no adverse affects on anyone (Leventhal 1976; Pearson & Thoennes 1989; Carnevale et al. 1991: 128).

The final measure under the construct conflict resolved is *relationship changed*. Bush and Folger (1994) posit that a conflict is not resolved unless the presenting relationship or interaction changes. Benjamin and Irving (1995: 61–62) reviewed a number of studies that operationalize the variable as changed perceptions of ex-spouse, reduction in conflict, increase in communication, trust, and understanding. Kelly (1996: 379) also reviews studies that capture data on change and reports relatively short-lived increases in cooperation and improved communication.

Measures based on client and attorney reports dissect this variable even more. Emery and Wyer (1987a: 181–182) compared a mediation and a control group on three scales: acrimony, acceptance of marital termination, and depression. Related definitions focus on reports of improved interactions during the mediation, anticipation that the relationship will improve, and anticipation that people will be able to solve conflicts in the future (cf. Kelly & Gigy 1988: 45–48; Pruitt et al. 1990: 36; McGillicuddy et al. 1991; Keashly & Newberry 1995; Wissler 1997: 5; Donnelly & Ebron 2000: 75; Wissler 2002: 665). Mediators also contribute to measures of this variable. Details of these measures include: better communication-reconciliation (Zarski, Knight & Zarski 1985); mutual talk, mutual help, cooperation, closeness, decreased perceptions of people having serious problems (Irving & Benjamin 1992: 42–43); and improved relations (Kakalik et al. 1996; Wissler 1999: 109).

Institutional context

The final set of variables included in the model under short-term outcomes follow up on the antecedent variables within institutional context. Operationalization of construct at this stage of the model focuses on *efficiency, effectiveness,* and *comparable cost.* Measures of *institutional efficiency* exist in archival, client, and mediator data. A typical archival measure tracks how long it takes to dispose of the case (cf. Bridenback et al. 1980; Emery & Jackson 1989: 11; Benjamin & Irving 1995: 61; Kelly 1996: 376; Donnelly & Ebron 2000: 25–26). Wissler (2002: 651–652) compiled information on the number and length of mediation sessions. Benjamin and Irving (1995: 61) compared mediated and litigated cases on whether mediation involves fewer sessions. Coates and Gehm (1989) ask clients about the time lag between the commission of a crime and a mediated resolution. Kakalik et al. (1996) asked mediators how long the mediation lasted, whether it reduced discovery time, and speed of disposition.

Measures of *institutional effectiveness* are found in studies of client data. Questions include: whether rights were protected (Emery & Wyer 1987a: 182; Emery & Jackson 1989: 13) and whether understanding of the justice system improved (Coates & Gehm 1989). Kakalik et al. (1996) relied on mediator feedback to measure timing in relation to the overall case and appropriateness for mediation.

Comparable cost is the last variable in this set. Benjamin and Irving (1995: 62) briefly review other studies that look at cost issues. Kelly (1996: 376) used archival data to compare mediated and litigated cases with regard to expenses, including whether mediation saved the government money. Kakalik et al. (1996) also rely on archival data to track the cost of court personnel as well as the cost of attorney's fees to clients. Clients and sometimes attorneys have been asked if they thought mediation reduced costs (cf. Pearson & Thoennes 1988; Menzel 1991; Wissler 1997: 8, 1999: 79–80; Donnelly & Ebron 2000).

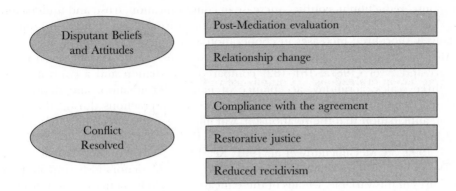

FIGURE 2.5 T_2 = Long-term outcomes

Long-Term Outcomes (T_2)

The proposed model organizes measures of long-term outcomes according to two constructs: *disputant beliefs and attitudes* (operationalized as post-mediation evaluation and relationship change) and *conflict resolved* (operationalized as compliance with the agreement, restorative justice, and reduced recidivism).[74] Figure 2.5 presents the schematic we are defining under long-term outcomes and table 2.4 details studies noted in the text.

Disputant beliefs and attitudes

Client perceptions of the experiences serve as the basis of measures of the variable *post-mediation evaluations*. Bridenback et al. (1980) collected data on satisfaction from clients six to 12 months after the mediation occurred. Van Slyck et al. (1992: 83) assess perceptions of the agreement (e.g. fair), the utility of the mediation, and the mediator (e.g. understanding, fair, neutral, and listened) three months after the mediation. Similarly, Meierding (1993: 162) focused on perceptions of the mediator (e.g. aware of parties' needs, bias, assistance with negotiation and creating options). A study by Donnelly and Ebron (2000: 40) investigates perceptions approximately three years after the mediation. Their questions pertain to: fair procedure, satisfaction with the result, trusting the mediator, competence of the mediator, able to tell your story.

The second variable, *relationship change*, is also based in client perceptions.[75] A study by Shaw (1989: 136) focused on parent–child mediations. The follow-up measure tapped whether the child was more manageable. This is similar to a Van Slyck et al. (1992: 83) study that used questions pertaining to improved interactions and ease of talking to a parent or child (see also Donnelly & Ebron 2000: 44–45). Other studies focus on adult conflicts and ask people if and how their relationships have changed (cf. Carnevale et al. 1991: 128; Welton 1991: 112; Irving & Benjamin 1992: 43). Typical issues are: relationship improved, new problems are unlikely to arise; perceptions of the other changed for the better; and continuing anger and guilt.

TABLE 2.4   Variables describing long-term outcomes (T₂)

Disputant beliefs and attitudes	*Conflict resolved*
Post-mediation evaluations	**Compliance with the agreement**
Client data Bridenback et al.	Kelly 1996
1980; Van Slyck et al. 1992;	*Archival data* Umbreit 1991; Umbreit & Coates 1993
Meierding 1993; Donnelly	*Client data* Vidmar 1985; McEwen & Maiman 1984,
& Ebron 2000	1989; McGillicuddy et al. 1987; Pearson &
Relationship change	Thoennes 1989; Van Slyck et al. 1992; Meierding
Client data Shaw 1989;	1993; Whiting 1994
Pruitt 1995; Carnevale	*Mediator data* McEwen & Maiman 1984, 1989;
et al. 1991; Welton 1991;	Roehl & Cook 1989; Pearson & Thoennes 1989;
Van Slyck et al. 1992;	McGillicuddy et al. 1991; Welton 1991; Pruitt 1995
Irving & Benjamin 1992;	***a. Percentage of claim paid***
Donnelly & Ebron 2000	*Archival data* McEwen & Maiman 1981; Vidmar 1985
	Restorative justice
	Peachey 1989
	Archival data Gehm 1990; Umbreit & Coates 1993
	Client data McEwen & Maiman 1981, 1984
	Mediator data Carnevale et al. 1991
	Recidivism
	Archival data Umbreit & Coates 1993; Meierding
	1993; Kressel et al. 1994; Donnelly & Ebron 2000
	Client data Shaw 1989; Pearson & Thoennes1989;
	Donnelly & Ebron 2000

Conflict resolved

Three variables operationalize the long-term latent construct conflict resolved. The first is *compliance with the agreement*. Kelly (1996: 377) provides a short review on compliance and relitigation rates. Research relies on all three forms of data to construct measures of compliance. Archival measures tend to reflect evidence of successful completion of the agreement, including where restitution was provided (cf. Umbreit 1991: 194; Umbreit & Coates 1993: 578). Client reports are similar; some researchers ask participants if compliance was complete or partial (cf. Vidmar 1985: 137–138; McEwen & Maiman 1984, 1989; McGillicuddy et al. 1987; Pearson & Thoennes 1989: 21; Van Slyck et al. 1992: 83; Meierding 1993: 162; Whiting 1994: 251). Measures based on perceptions of mediators tend to assess intent to follow through (cf. McEwen & Maiman 1984, 1989; Roehl & Cook 1989; Pearson & Thoennes 1989; McGillicuddy et al. 1991; Welton 1991; Pruitt, 1995). McEwen and Maiman (1981) as well as Vidmar (1985: 137) offer an archival measure *percentage of claim paid* that we are treating as a subset of the variable compliance with the agreement.

The next variable, *restorative justice,* is consistent with Peachey's (1989: 302–308) concept of making a wrong right, and more specifically with Zehr's (1990) emphasis on shifting problem-solving away from concerns about violations of law and toward concern for individuals. Mediations that restore justice involve the victim, offender, and community in dialogs that create solutions that "promote repair, reconciliation, and reassurance" (Zehr 1990: 181).[76] Gehm (1990: 179), as well as Umbreit and Coates (1993: 573–574), use archival data to measure the variable as compensation to victim, service to the community or victim, and an apology. McEwen and Maiman (1981, 1984) rely on client reports and questions about time payments versus immediate payment. Carnevale et al. (1991: 128) asked mediators if their clients gained or recouped valuable resources.

Recidivism is the final variable in the model. Umbreit and Coates (1993: 578–579), as well as Meierding (1993: 159), use court records to see if there were requests for court action after a mediated agreement had been filed, including: a request to set an agreement aside, a record of changes in a family's circumstance that might invoke a modification of the agreement, or requests for enforcement of an order. Kressel, Frontera, Forlenza, Butler and Fish (1994: 71) and Donnelly and Ebron (2000: 72) record dismissals, trials, and modifications. Shaw (1989: 136) relies on participant reports of whether the child had returned to court. Similarly, Pearson and Thoennes (1989: 21–22), as well as Donnelly and Ebron (2000: 43–44), rely on client reports of any additional legal action.

DISCUSSION

Mediation research conducted in natural settings provides a panoply of opportunities to explore, test, and refine our understanding of effective problem-solving, and especially how the introduction of third parties enhances or detracts from the process of resolving conflicts. The model suggested in this chapter, with accompanying constructs, variables, measures, and references, supports both deductive and inductive reasoning as well as both qualitative and quantitative data collection. It supports intense analysis of the dynamics of a mediation proper. By detailing a very broad contextual frame, we hope practitioners as well as scholars will achieve new insights into practice dynamics and their relationships to outcomes. In fact, we hope the model and supporting resources will encourage tests of numerous theories, challenges to the model, and development of new ways of thinking about mediation.

Selected Implications for Research

Intrepid researchers with the time and support for the creation and analysis of very complex data sets could test and examine various subsets of relationships. To do so would require access to clients before, during, and after their mediations. In addition, the ideal would be to have access to information describing the systems that support a mediation program, as well as data from mediators and attorneys in order to create interlocking quantitative and qualitative data sets.

Short of a full analysis, the model lends itself to testing select theories and has the potential to refine our understanding of problem-solving. Two theories, noted earlier in this chapter, serve as examples of possible approaches. Hypotheses from psychology suggest possible ways interveners support people as they struggle to solve problems individually and in groups (cf. Rogers 1975, 1980). Hypotheses suggested by the social psychology of problem-solving explore the problem-solving process *per se* (cf. Deutsch 1991, 2000).[77]

A Possible Application from Psychology

Figure 2.6 displays some of the relationships that might be hypothesized if a researcher turned to psychology to understand mediated problem-solving.[78] Working from

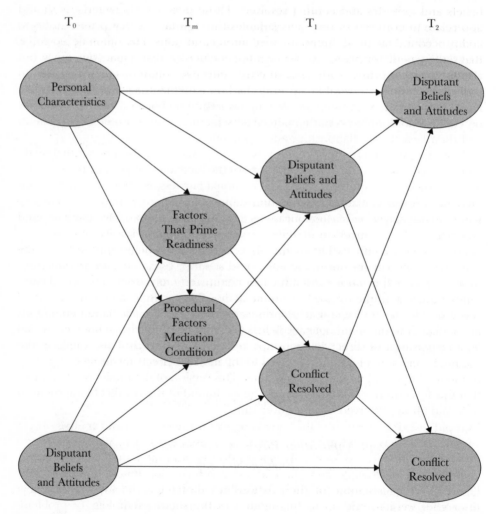

FIGURE 2.6   A model rooted in psychology

assumptions 2 and 7 (i.e. people prefer harmony and verbalization encourages reflection and a higher level of reasoning), coupled with some basic tenets from psychology (e.g. given a non-judgmental environment, people are enabled to solve their own problems: cf. Rogers 1980), we might predict that both short-term (T_1) and long-term (T_2) outcomes, primarily disputant beliefs and attitudes and conflict resolved, relate to the antecedent conditions (T_0) of personal characteristics and disputant beliefs and attitudes. Exploring all the possible relationships suggested by this segment of the model would require significant development, but it is possible to highlight a few, exemplar relationships.

We could hypothesize, for example, that certain personal characteristics of the mediator (e.g. skills as defined by Herrman et al. 2001; philosophies described by Herrman et al. 2002; the demographics researched by Kruk 1998; and experience as noted by Zubek et al. 1992) directly effect the T_1 and T_2 outcomes of disputant beliefs and attitudes and conflict resolved. Those personal characteristics should also relate to both sets of outcome variables through factors that prime readiness and procedural factors defining the mediation conditions. The rationale would be that skilled mediators with experience intervene in ways that impact outcomes, but also in ways that prime readiness and create effective conditions that then lead to positive outcomes. We would want to probe how a mediator's characteristics relate to the variables mediator empathy, feeling heard and understood, able to talk about perceptions and feelings, clarity, perceived self-efficacy, and hostile environment, and then how these relationships affect outcomes.

By staying within a framework from psychology we would also predict that mediator characteristics would affect conditions of the mediation, especially the variables active participation, global fairness, interactional fairness, mediator neutrality, and mediator process control. These relationships would then, in turn, relate to higher scores on the various satisfaction measures in T_1 as well as the variables issues resolved and relationship changed in the latent construct of conflict resolved in T_1.

Psychology takes the existence of crisis as a given. If we included sets of variables within the construct of disputant beliefs and attitudes at T_0 (including willingness to participate, expectations about the mediation, and motivation to resolve the dispute) in this simplified model, it would be possible to explore how these factors relate directly to both factors that prime readiness and the mediation conditions and indirectly to disputant outcome beliefs and attitudes. A further refinement would be a comparison of direct relationships between T_0 beliefs and attitudes and the T_1 and T_2 outcome of conflict resolved to the indirect effects involving factors that prime readiness and mediation conditions. This version of the model would predict that the T_m conditions would enhance the likelihood of the conflict being resolved over and above observed changes over time.

A Second Application Based on the Social Psychology of Problem-Solving

Figure 2.7 suggests some of the relationships that might be hypothesized if a researcher were to rely on writings found in the social psychology of problem-solving to understand mediation processes. Working from our assumptions 3, 4, 5,

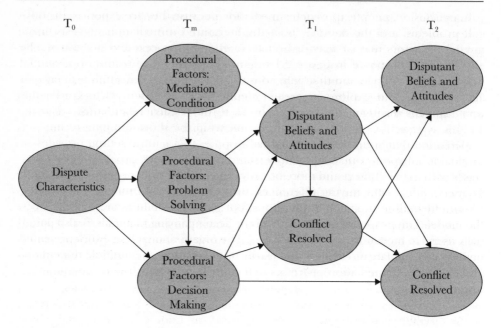

FIGURE 2.7   A model based on theories of problem-solving

6, 8, 9, and 10 (mediations begin with a competitive conflict, challenge resistance to change, expose people to new information through dialog, and help them create new options that support a consensual outcome that varies from original positions), one could test the indirect relationships between the dispute characteristics at T_0 to disputant beliefs and attitudes as well as conflict resolved at both T_1 and T_2. The test would involve controlling for early dispute characteristics while examining how process effectiveness, as defined by the procedural factors at T_m, contributes to change at both T_1 and T_2.

Deutsch (2000) and others define an effective problem-solving process as one that turns competition into collaboration. The model presented in figure 2.7 emphasizes that definition by focusing attention on the relationships internal to T_m, primarily on the relationships between the variables encompassed by the three procedural constructs. This model posits that mediation conditions directly contribute to problem-solving and that problem-solving factors contribute directly to decision-making. In this summary, we do not distinguish between the several variables used to define mediation conditions, problem-solving, and decision-making, although suggestions from other theories could easily guide the further development of hypotheses. Thus, this model hypothesizes a linear pattern of relationships between the constructs labeled procedural factors. It also suggests that mediation conditions, problem-solving, and decision-making relate directly to disputant beliefs and attitudes at T_1. But based on what appears to be a logic of cumulative effects (cf. Dewey 1938; Moore 1986), we would hypothesize that the greatest effect on short-term and long-term outcomes would emerge after a complete problem-solving process evolves during a mediation.

In conclusion, people approach a mediation because they are experiencing diffi-cult problems, and the complexity of the literature on mediation suggests that a myriad of factors may or may not relate to effective process and outcomes. The global model proposed in figure 2.1 organizes similar measures into operational definitions of variables and then into constructs. This model, hopefully, will encour-age researchers to explore in greater depth how antecedent factors influence what happens during a mediation to break through barriers, enhance creativity, and motivate actions that would solve problems in the short and long term.

Mediation that addresses interpersonal disputes in a natural setting provides an invaluable mirror to our deeper understanding of effective problem-solving pro-cesses both in this context and more broadly. The global model presented here could be used, with accompanying references, to pursue tests of a number of theories. We briefly outline two such applications, but many possibilities are embedded in the model. The proposed model, with all the accompanying materials, is also poten-tially useful to mediators and their trainers. The organizational framework presented here could stimulate discussions that clarify thinking about the multiple dimensions and outcomes of mediation processes that contribute to constructive resolution of disputes.

NOTES

Authors' note. The Mediator Skills Project (MSP) received funding from the William and Flora Hewlett Foundation, the State Justice Institute, and the Consortium on Negotiation and Conflict Resolution. The views expressed in this chapter reflect a growing understand-ing of the authors, and not the policies or priorities of any of our sources of support. As a part of the MSP team, Dawn Goettler Eaker and Kate Fogarty contributed immeasurably to the development of this chapter.

1   While various cultures embrace mediation in different ways, for purposes of this chapter we distinguish formal mediation from informal mediation that occurs with the aid of family, friends, or acquaintances. Formal mediation interjects non-aligned strangers into a conflicted dialog. We also note that this chapter pertains to the less directive end of a continuum of processes subsumed by the label of mediation. More directive types of mediation include hybrid forms such as med-arb (Brett & Goldberg 1983b; Ross & Conlon 2000) and advisory/evaluative mediation (Brett & Goldberg 1983a). Wall and Rude (1989: 194–195) studied judges who mediate. Their list of strategies that judges use would, for some mediators, define the directive end of the continuum. Mediation as described here elevates a mediator's process expertise over his or her subject matter expertise, and certainly over any formal authority to settle a dispute. Indeed for the type of mediation referenced here, mediators possess no explicit authority to settle a conflict. Even so, knowledge of collaborative problem-solving creates con-siderable power to influence – even mold – what is said, perceptions, negotiations, and any product of the negotiation (Warren 1954; Stevens 1963: 125; Walton & McKersie 1965: 119, 159; Folberg & Taylor 1984, chapter 3; Moore 1986: 24–43; Riskin 1996: 2). Formal mediation today, hopefully, supports many of the goals of third party con-sultation as defined by Fisher (1983: 304).

Readers might note that McEwen and Wissler (2002) as well as Hensler (2002) call for more research on the basic assumptions that have been used over the past several decades to propel mediation into various institutional settings. These authors open up questions about the interface between mediation and courts. Macfarlane (2001: 665 n. 4) notes that asking the question of whether settlement is "good" or "better" than adjudication is linked to a better understanding of why people settle. This chapter does not pose or answer the question, but it does more explicitly define the components of "good settlement."

2 Ross and Conlon (2000: 416) suggest that short of comparisons between mediation and arbitration, contextual variations (e.g. labor, small claims, and consumer complaints, etc.) impact the problem-solving role very little. Shapiro and Brett (1993) is an exception. Their field test involved coal miners with formal grievances who were assigned to either mediation or arbitration conditions.

3 Wall and Dewhurst (1991: 64) point out that many mediators operate by trial and error. To encourage more reflective practice, Lang and Taylor (2000: 134) posit a need for mediators to relate their personal beliefs, values, and assumptions consciously to their work. Otherwise: "A mediator . . . is merely tinkering with a situation, trying out strategies and techniques without knowledge of why those skills might or might not be appropriate." Mediator awareness supports effectiveness since, as Menkel-Meadow (1984: 759 n. 11) observes, how negotiators conceptualize the purpose of their work and how they define what constitutes effective action shapes what they do.

4 This chapter originated as a review presented by the Mediator Skills Project (MSP) at the University of Georgia to the annual meeting of the Society of Professionals in Dispute Resolution (Herrman, Gale, Hollett, Goettler & Fogarty 1998a, 1998b). Gadlin (2002) articulates one way the proposed model is useful to mediators, and, we would add, to trainers. By laying bare a time-sequence framework that both deconstructs and defines components of a mediation, the proposed model demystifies mediation in the context relevant to this chapter. Demystification carries risks (e.g. people could challenge the model, and that would be good) and rewards (e.g. mediators and trainers could think about how each and every construct in the model affects mediation practices).

Immersion in the review process uncovered a number of measures that combine several dimensions into a single measure (cf. Thoennes & Pearson 1985; Kelly & Gigy 1988), but in ways that obscure important relationships. Druckman (2001) makes a good argument for disaggregation when he distinguishes between how negotiators reach closure from the outcome of a negotiation. Likewise, Hollett, Herrman, Eaker, and Gale (2002) validate a measure of mediation effectiveness that distinguishes mediation processes from end products.

So, measures described in this chapter sometimes reference specific questions within more complex measures. This means we interpreted and assessed how variables suggested by other researchers might relate to effective mediation, and, when needed, lifted variables out of existing measures and sometimes moved variables from one time to another (e.g. a measure created from exit surveys might be cited in the proposed model as an antecedent variable). For example, the Bridenback, Bales, and Planchard (1980) questions about previous contact with the judicial system are cited in the model as an antecedent variable. We hope our "moving the furniture around" clarifies and does not offend.

5 Others as far back as 1963 noted the same gap (cf. Stevens 1963: 122–123; Kochan & Jick 1978: 209; Wall 1981: 157).

6 Wall and Dewhurst (1991: 64–65) note the prescriptive nature of mediation training materials.

7 Menkel-Meadow (1984) is similar to Zartman and Berman (1982: 12–13), who rely on game theory to define effective negotiation. For Zartman and Berman, effective negotiators eschew a zero-sum philosophy and adopt one that supports mutual benefit (i.e. the goal being to "do better," not destroy; see also Weiss-Wik 1983: 715–716; Weitzman & Weitzman 2000: 188; Deutsch 2002). By comparison, Thibaut and Walker (1975: 109) suggest that some people prefer adversarial sparring, especially when legal representatives bolster a case at the expense of an opponent.

8 Like Silbey and Merry's (1986) description of mediator behavior, our review was initially not theory-driven. We simply tried to locate operational definitions of mediation effectiveness for use in our research.

9 In order to focus on "real world" problem-solving, this review excludes research on "small group" conflicts occurring under experimental conditions (Weiss-Wik 1983: 717). Rolph and Moller (1995: 7) define experimental designs as the "gold standard" of evaluation research. But as McEwen (1999: 330) points out, research based on experimental designs limits our ability to understand how mediation is affected by and affects broader social contexts. Deutsch (2002: 312–313) notes the value and the pitfalls of experimental studies based on game theory. Findings from these two types of research could be compared at some point in the future, but such a comparison falls beyond the scope of this chapter.

10 Compare Strauss (1978) and Menkel-Meadow (1984) to Ross and Conlon (2000: 416).

11 We also exclude research on multiparty, large-group mediations because of the probability of considerable differences in antecedent and procedural factors.

12 Considerable tension exists among mediation professionals over whether mediators should evaluate the legal/factual merits of a case, only facilitate negotiation, or combine models in actual practice. Each form of mediation may or may not be distinct and effective for different types of cases (cf. Kakalik, Dunworth, Hill, McCaffrey, Oshiro, Pace & Vaiana 1996: 2 n. 3; Kruk 1998; Riskin 1996, 2003). This is an example of a researchable question begging for empirical analysis.

13 While the review focuses on mediation conducted in the shadow of courts, the utility of the proposed model is not limited. It might also apply to mediations conducted at the behest of an institution (e.g. employment mediations mandated by an internal grievance mechanism of a government or private sector organization or a complaint that reaches a federal agency like the Justice Department or EEOC).

14 Young (1991) reminds us that any negotiation involves more than rational choices; choices are shaped by arational and other "noise" as well.

15 Janis and Mann (1977: 45–80) point out that conflicted decisions are typically experienced as unpleasant and distressing, with the degree of distress being a function of how much a person wants to hold on to their current position.

16 Folger et al. (1997: 114–115) note an inability to define "truth." In any interaction, people continually redefine their relationships with each other. So: "Perception mediates objective reality, although of course reality imposes certain limits on the implications of perception . . . Of course, perception is not immutable either" (Zartman & Rubin 2000: 13).

17 Discussions of phase structures are more commonly found in the negotiation literature (cf. Holmes 1992), but Weitzman and Weitzman (2000: 187, also Johnson & Johnson 1989) suggest a time sequence that is relevant to effective mediation. Their model begins with an unresolved conflict, a claim, and a rejection (consistent with Felstiner, Abel &

Sarat 1980–81). It continues with people moving from ineffective problem-solving to effective problem-solving when talk stimulates diagnosis and thoughts about alternative ways of solving the problem. Once people surface and evaluate alternatives, they possess sufficient information to choose solutions and commit to actions that change the offending situation. A contingency approach, proposed by Carnevale, Lim, and McLaughlin (1989), makes similar assumptions about a time sequence. The model that follows conforms in many ways to suggestions made by Sacks, Reichart, and Profitt (1999) about a need for longitudinal research designs capable of capturing information on relationships before and after an intervention as well as information about context and culture.

18   This review includes studies based on two types of data. *Secondary data* – drawn primarily from court records – indicate organizational priorities. Between the late 1970s through the 1980s, courts adopted a number of reforms, including creating several nationally visible mediation programs (cf. Bridenback et al. 1980; McGillis 1980, 1986; Clarke, Valente & Mace 1992). To demonstrate accountability, program administrations used secondary data to describe program functioning (cf. Bridenback, Palmer & Planchard 1979; Bridenback et al. 1980; Cook, Roehl & Sheppard 1980). Many current studies continue to rely on secondary data because access is easy and such data produce important information (see Clarke et al. 1992; Kakalik, Dunworth, Hill, McCaffrey, Oshiro, Pace & Vaiana 1996; Wissler 1997).

   Client-based data (encompassing both clients/client attorneys and mediators) – primarily as survey data from actual participants – provide slightly more insight into mediated problem-solving than secondary data. Because mediators and clients may experience interventions in different ways, our review distinguishes between the two sources of information. Electronically tapped data support even greater scrutiny of interactions, but legal boundaries pertaining to confidentiality make recording difficult. Surveys are also easier and quicker to analyze than taped data, a consideration for mediation program administrators and funders who require timely evaluations of mediation effectiveness.

19   Mnookin and Ross (1999: 6–24) discuss three barriers to effective conflict resolution. While their discussion focuses on the act of negotiation, these factors – among a number of sources of influence – may influence participant thinking before the mediation. Barriers include: (1) mindsets that foreshadow logical, tactical strategies to maximize gains; (2) cognitive filters that shape how people interpret information, evaluate risks, set priorities, and experience loss or gains; and (3) structural contexts that constrain negotiation.

20   We clearly include the mediator as one of the negotiators. Figures 2.2–2.5 use circles and, where needed, sextagons to denote unmeasured, theoretical constructs. Squares denote variables that appear in the literature in operational form. Throughout the proposed model, lists of variables are presented as suggestions, not as exhaustive presentations.

21   Macfarlane (2001: 667–678) calls for attention to both structural/institutional contexts and intrapsychic contexts (i.e. attitudes and beliefs) in studies that look at settlement negotiation processes.

22   The point that antecedent characteristics cannot, in reality, be distinguished from the dynamics of a mediation and the outcomes is made by several chapters in this handbook. The reality of communication, its impact on thinking, a person's sense of self, and how people define a conflict are in constant flux, a constant state of reformulation (see Macfarlane 2001: 673–674).

23 The Weiss-Wik (1983: 718–722) review of experimental studies suggests several other measures such as a need to maintain face, a need for social approval, and a need for achievement. These are potentially important sources of variation regardless of whether the negotiator is the mediator or the client.

24 Kressel (2000: 529–533) notes that professionals in dispute resolution frequently invoke neutrality as a core value, but the construct lacks grounding in research. He suggests substituting acceptability, which we think is a form of rapport-building.

25 Leonard Riskin (2003: 9) updated an often referenced schematic for categorizing mediators' work styles or orientations. His observation on how mediators work speaks to the values and goals mediators bring to a mediation: "the conventional wisdom of mediator trainers and authorities held that the mediator did not predict court outcomes or tell parties how to resolve their dispute; in fact, however, many did so." In addition, Riskin (2003: 9–11) notes that many mediators at the time of his article focused on legal claims, tried to reach legally relevant settlements, and were not predisposed to work with other needs and interests or to support self-determination by parties.

26 Umbreit and Greenwood (1999: 241) surveyed victim–offender mediation programs and developed a range of mediator training hours.

27 This is an example of where MSP interpretation comes into play. Carnevale et al. (1989: 224) constructed two factors from a list of dispute characteristics. One, labeled "hostility," included a question on receptivity to mediation. But the second factor was labeled "resistance to mediation," implying a degree of involuntary participation. However, on their face, questions comprising the factor (i.e. no trust in the mediator, wanted to control the process, too many issues) relate to something other than willingness to participate.

28 McGillis (1986: 43–46) categorizes programs according to the level of coercion during intake. Some introductory letters simply say that a service is available. Others explicitly state negative consequences arising from a lack of participation. Still other programs refer cases outright from the bench to mediation at the time of an initial hearing. In a national survey of victim–offender mediation programs, Umbreit and Greenwood (1999) defined voluntariness as: reports that victims used the services voluntarily, victims could leave the mediation at any time, and whether the offender was required to meet with the victim (and admit their guilt before mediation).

29 The construct of voluntariness is a complex construct. One might assume that mediation participants forced into the forum resist the process. In Deutsch's (1973, 2000) terms, perceptions of force would contribute to a continuation of competitive behavior (cf. Umbreit & Coates 1993: 571). At the same time, attribution theory (Kelley 1971) suggests that perceptions of voluntary participation enhance the potential for trust and by extension cooperative problem-solving.

30 In a study of the perceived legitimacy of courts, Tyler (1984: 55) looks at how expectations shape subsequent satisfaction with courts. Of note are expectations about the objective/actual outcomes and about equal versus unequal treatment. These two variables are not included in the proposed model because we lack examples of operational definitions. Even so, we consider them to be potentially important variables. In a later essay on concerns about mediation, Tyler (1987: 371–372) relates expectations to several psychological variables, one being consistency. Consistency is defined as a comparison. People form opinions about possible outcomes well before they actually negotiate. Disputants then judge third parties by whether the actual outcome measures up to expectations and whether the treatment was evenhanded. Two additional expectations are also defined: ethical appropriateness and dishonesty. Again, these sources of

variation are not included in the model for lack of inclusion in past studies. Future studies should take them into consideration both as expectations and as *post hoc* reports.

31   They also coded perceptions of whether disputants were attempting to influence the mediator.

32   Advances in communication and problem-solving research clearly explore the complexity of the relationship between how people frame or articulate a conflict, what is at stake, attribution of motives, expectations of how others will act, definitions of fair treatment, and the framing of preferred outcomes (Macfarlane 2001: 678–708). As noted in other endnotes, there is a constant interplay between sources of variation noted in T_0 to T_{1-2}.

33   Umbreit et al. (2001: 125) introduce another source of variation, namely whether people are disputants or victims and offenders. There is a presumption that a pair of disputants present different issue dynamics in comparison to victims and offenders. This may be true, but it is also an empirical question (e.g. is a victim of a divorce substantially different from a victim of a property crime?).

34   The measure is similar to the Weiss-Wik (1983: 719–720) distinction between intangible and tangible needs and goals.

35   Kressel (2000: 525) suggests that unequal power is an important variable. We not only concur, but think it is a critical piece of any model. Unfortunately our review failed to uncover operational definitions of the variable in this context.

36   An even more exciting and profound possibility is to link research on mediation sanctioned by courts with scholarship on the mobilization of law, or, according to Black (1973: 126), "the process by which a legal system acquires its cases." According to Black, in the United States the majority of cases entering the legal system – through courts and police – are the result of a citizen complaint. A theoretical and practical link between these two areas of scholarship would begin to expose changing dynamics in the interchange between the public and the law. On a theoretical level such a blending would encourage more profound explorations into the changing roles of the law, into innovations that supposedly improve how the law functions, and perceptions of the law by the public. On a more practical level, it would invite thoughtful explorations into what the public knows about the law and alternative services like mediation offered by institutions that are surrogates of the law. Variables in the proposed model, such as participant perceptions of whether their participation in mediation is voluntary as well as their attitudes about how mediation program personnel function during case intake and after, beg for deeper analysis. Research that simply compares mediation programs across jurisdictions looking at the values of program personnel and attitudes of mediation participants against even short-term outcome measures would be of value. We need to explore simple questions like: who complains, who hires attorneys, how do they complain, what are the expressed attitudes of mediation program staff in regard to the public, in regard to attorneys, then what affect might these attitudes and patterns have on mediations and outcomes? On an even more applied level, the concept of mobilization of law opens the door to scrutiny of the public's knowledge of mediation. Practitioners have said for years that "we" need to educate the public, but where have "we" done so, and what effect does education have on mobilization, on intake, on institutional context, on mediations, and on outcomes?

37   Rolph and Moller (1995; see also Ostermeyer & Keilitz 1997) created a roadmap for programs to follow, but actual comparisons between programs of different structures are rare.

38   Since victim–offender mediation programs exist in several institutional contexts that also interface with the disputes at different points in a resolution process, an important

study would compare mediation processes and outcomes across these different settings (cf. Umbreit et al. 2001: 124). Such a comparison would produce new insights since each setting potentially supports different ways of framing the dispute, the disputants, and successful outcomes. For example, mediation programs housed in diversion settings might be very different from programs housed in pre-sentencing settings.

39 Plapinger and Stienstra (1996) compiled information on programmatic guidelines for the ADR programs in the federal district courts.

40 While we do not formally focus on narrative theories and narrative research methods, we assume that research drawn from narrative frames complements the proposed model, especially in this phase of the model. Unlike authors such as Kirkman (2002), we invite scholars to mix methods. Allow analysis of particular narrative dynamics to inform statistical analysis. Use contextual richness to enhance understanding of prediction.

41 Tyler (1984: 53), in a study of user satisfaction and perceived legitimacy of government services (e.g. courts, law enforcement, and even elected leaders), notes a failure to study the psychological aspects of encounters with legal institutions and political authority. In his study, satisfaction (and the perceived worth of the services) relates to much more than objective outcomes. He further notes that the failure extends to government services that provide alternative means of resolving disputes.

42 According to Homans (1961: 62), negotiations improve when issues are defined in detail, thus increasing the probability of differences in values (i.e. that each participant will place a value on different issues). In order to create the necessary level of detail, negotiators dissect any single issue into its composites. Pruitt (1981: 158) labels the process unlinking or *fractionating*. Unlinking reduces win-lose perceptions by encouraging people to weigh issues, concessions, and resolutions that are more easily traded. Unlinking also reduces the perceptual overload of an insurmountable barrier.

43 While figure 2.3 presents the constructs as distinct entities, we suspect they are related. We simply lack an empirically grounded understanding of how; therein lies the promise of future research. One potentially fruitful analysis might be to see if people who appear "ready" to problem-solve shift more easily from competitive to cooperative negotiation processes. They might also move easily within the mediation process (cf. Lang & Taylor 2000; Della Noce 2001). Outcome measures as defined in the proposed model might also show that expressions of participant and mediator satisfaction with the process would be high, relationships would change, and the conflict would be resolved.

44 This entire set of variables evolves in an atmosphere that supports understanding and change. How do you help people who are stuck? Macfarlane (2001: 674–675) describes the thinking behind this construct beautifully. We paraphrase: to resolve a dispute short of capitulation we must understand that the "reality" of a conflict is intertwined with how people understand the conflict. All sides must "see" (understand and comprehend) what led to the problem, what is at stake, and why certain outcomes are important personally for them and for others. Change hinges first on recognition and comprehension of self and other; second on a recognition that personal reality is socially constructed; and third on realities being continually made and remade during a mediation.

This is a tremendously complex topic and a different, very rich mode of study. It aligns with researchers in narrative analysis (cf. Mattingly 1998 in a study of occupational therapists). Narrative analysis adds specificity to the idea that stories, talk, description, and interaction promote clarity. For example according to Mattingly (1998: 5–6): "Stories have many purposes . . . They tell of experiences . . . their own and others, to entertain, to gossip, to confess, to argue, to reveal who they are. Often they tell . . . about

... experiences which are puzzling, powerful or disturbing, in order to render those experiences more sensible. Storytelling offers one way to make sense of what has happened and this makes stories essential to practice."

45   See Wissler (2002: 659 n. 67) for a similar, but less comprehensive list of constructs.

46   As we begin to explore a number of variables, we reiterate the probable interconnectedness between constructs and variables throughout the T_m phase of the model. In 1993 Cobb published an article based on interviews with mediators. The article underscores how much one aspect of a mediation influences other aspects. Factors contributing to mediation conditions (e.g. participation, perceptions of fairness, neutrality, and mediator process control) are probably influenced by and influence certain variables noted above in the readiness factors (e.g. feeling heard, able to talk, clarity, and perceived self-efficacy). Testing these interactions presents an interesting challenge for scholars and raises the need among practitioners and trainers to consider probable interactions.

47   This citation represents another example of where we use discretion in moving measures out of context. Data were collected well after the mediation, the timing suggests a long-term outcome not a process variable, but the measure is a retrospective report on the mediator's demeanor.

48   Tyler (1984: 68) asked a similar question in his study of user satisfaction with courts. The question posed was: "Did the judge listen to your side of the story?"

49   Bush and Folger (1994) emphasize the importance of this level of understanding to effective problem-solving. The idea is inherent in the writings of Homans (1961) and Menkel-Meadow (1984). Putnam and Holmer's (1992: 135–137) discussion of "frame categories" is also relevant to this area of analysis. These authors ascribe value to mediators who either do not get in the way of a free flow of information or who probe gently. There is also a flip side. Effective mediators may also, if they are trusted by all sides, induce reluctant or unaware participants to surface and reveal vital information (Mnookin & Ross 1999: 22).

50   We realize the question covers two topics. But it demonstrates how other researchers, consciously or not, connect self-expression and clarity.

51   A review of the extensive literature on power is beyond the scope of this chapter, but future research should not overlook both Rotter (1966) and Bandura (1986). Deutsch (1973: 395) notes an interplay between perceptions and efficacy, where people exercise more power in "facilitative" situations and less in "resistant" situations, or when personal aspirations are low or self-control high (see our tenth assumption as well as Zartman & Rubin 2000: 13–14 on the role of perceptions). Deutsch (1973: 395) also distinguishes between three forms of power: environmental power – an ability to influence your environment; relational power – an ability of one person to influence another; and personal power – an ability to satisfy one's own needs. Recent discussions of negotiation tactics define select power tactics as: force – direct application, making someone do something they would not otherwise do; non-direct power – threats of direct power that impel someone to comply or promises that compel; indirect power – manipulative interactions; and hidden power – tactics used to hide or suppress potential issues (Folger et al. 1997: 100–126).

52   This variable might relate to the earlier variable "interpersonal dynamics," but that is a question for future research.

53   The model includes a variable – mediator process control – to allow for comparison. Variables like mediator process control have been included in research, but applications continue the ambiguity and would benefit from more research.

54   Kressel (2000: 529) says this is one way a mediator creates rapport.

55 Wissler (2002: 661–663) simply asked clients and their attorneys if the mediator was fair.

56 These concerns echo a study of negotiation in complex organizations by Sheppard (1984), who distinguishes control over the process leading to a decision from control over what is discussed. Finally, we don't know the extent to which the balance of control between the parties and a "third" is important (i.e. the relative amount of the third party versus participant control over when, how, and who presents information).

57 We interpret this action as an act of control. Others might interpret it differently.

58 The job analysis referenced earlier (Herrman et al. 2002) produced a list of over 400 actions that mediators take throughout a mediation. Many represent ways mediators exert control.

59 The negotiation and communication literatures explore problem-solving dynamics in great depth. Covering those literatures would expand this chapter to a book, and several of the contributing authors delve into these bodies of knowledge. So given space limitations and a desire to give these authors an unimpeded voice, we simply offer two examples. As we discuss earlier stages of the proposed model, the writings of Putnam and Holmer (1992) help us consider that people think about or frame a conflict well before the mediation begins. Their discussion of reframing – the continuous redefinition of frames resulting from social interaction and communication – implies that reframing intensifies during the problem-solving phase of a mediation. Mnookin and Ross (1999: 22) suggest that negotiations falter when people fail to reframe effectively. They go on to note that effective mediators: "foster a problem-solving atmosphere, one that encourages the parties to move beyond political posturing and recriminations . . . to recognize fully the gains from an efficient and fair resolution."

60 Lind, Kanfer, and Earley (1990: 952) refer to this as having a voice. But simply telling your story – saying what you need or want – does not guarantee you will be heard and your needs addressed. Even though you must talk, your talk must also be elaborated by others. A lack of elaboration effectively silences a mediation participant (Cobb 1994: 58; see also Shapiro & Brett 1993).

61 Experimental studies indicate that people prefer to control decisions directly. If that is not possible, people try to indirectly control decisions by controlling opportunities to present information to each other and any third party (Thibaut & Walker 1975; Tyler 1987: 370). Brett (1986) talks about indirect outcome control (see also Folger 1977, 1986).

62 Mnookin and Ross (1999: 23) note that reactive devaluation – discounting settlement options when they are proposed by an adversary – can sometimes be avoided or reduced when a mediator suggests the options. A debate over the ethics of such acts continues within the field of mediation. For some mediators such suggestions operationally equate to mediator-driven outcomes. So for mediators holding these beliefs, dealmakers, orchestrators, and evaluators are not mediating. If we could include measures of several of these variables in the same study, we might be able to clarify the picture in a dispassionate way.

63 Marshall and Merry (1990) suggest that longitudinal analyses would yield more powerful evidence of effectiveness. They are right. But to date, appropriate data have not been readily available. This is a drawback of working in natural settings.

64 The issue is not whether a case will settle. Menkel-Meadow (1995a: 2664–2665) notes that settlement – as compared to an adjudicated decision – is now the norm. But it is important to understand if a particular settlement meets the emotional, procedural, economic, legal, political, or other needs of the disputants, the dispute, the public, and the institutions involved. While not formally proposing a hypothesis, there may be a

relationship between settlement characteristics that encompass more needs and the long-term stability of the solution.

65   To understand mediation we need to know more than just what people do; we also need to know what they think and feel about what they do, and how this relates to both the process and the outcome (cf. Kolb & Coolidge 1993).

66   Measures are typically based on exit surveys or face-to-face interviews that occur anywhere from one week to 16 weeks after the mediation – most are completed within five weeks of the mediation (cf. Emery & Wyer 1987a: 181).

67   When someone examines all of the measures subsumed by the construct of satisfaction with the mediator, the entire body of research underscores the complexity of the role. This is not surprising if the role is equated to that of a group leader (see Hare 1976: 278–303) responsible for moving conflicted people from a high state of tension, competition, and an inability to resolve a conflict to a lowered state of tension, collaboration, and effective problem-solving. An interesting research question might be whether satisfaction and perceived effectiveness change when mediators narrow or expand the diversity of roles they perform during the course of a mediation (i.e. is a mediator more effective when he or she performs multiple roles?).

68   Menkel-Meadow (1995a: 2693–2694) defines a good settlement by the existence of consent. She also notes the absence of consent when coercion (by a mediator, an attorney, the primary disputants, a court, or a mediation program) exists or where choices are mirages – either because litigants were extremely frustrated or because they could not wait to litigate or pay for litigation. Departures from consent call the legitimacy of any settlement into question, regardless of how settlement is achieved. Measures of satisfaction may be proxies for consent.

69   As noted earlier, a few of these studies rely on tapes of mediations.

70   Wissler (2002: 666) notes the following reasons for the lack of an agreement: serious disputes over the evaluation of a case, missing information, incomplete discovery, unresolved factual issues, unresolved legal issues, or unreasonable attorneys or clients. Lack of attorney preparation and lack of financial resources were also cited.

71   Although some rates fail to reflect negotiated agreements that occur before the actual mediation.

72   See also Menkel-Meadow (1995b: 126–127).

73   Mnookin and Ross (1999) employ both definitions and suggest that the probability of short-term outcomes improves when justice needs are addressed. They go on to say that the stability of agreements increases when those needs are addressed to everyone's satisfaction (implying a connection to long-term outcomes).

74   Our distinction between short- and long-term outcomes is somewhat arbitrary. In making the distinction, we tried to confine measures of long-term outcomes to those that were collected at least three months after the mediation. Some were collected as long as three years after the mediation. However, following this rule of thumb was not precise. Sometimes the content of a measure suggested that it was consistent with measures that occur earlier in the model.

75   Pruitt (1995: 372–373) initially thought that short-term success leads to long-term success. His results showed that long-term success is related more to relationship change than other forms of short-term success.

76   McCold (2001) notes that mediation programs relied on restorative justice approaches as early as 1971, but that theoretical explorations of the construct soon followed. People familiar with victim–offender mediation or victim–offender reconciliation programs realize that these applications began in and often continue in faith communities. Because

of the origins, words used to describe mediation dynamics are different from words and constructs referenced in the proposed model (e.g. atonement, accountability, forgiveness: McCold 2001: 43–44). An interesting research adaptation would involve operationally defining and measuring these constructs during the T_m phase of the model in order to compare short- and long-term outcomes where the dynamics were present or absent.

77 The reader will note in this discussion that certain constructs become the focus of analysis and others drop out. There are many more possibilities embedded in this model, most notably a focus on procedural justice (cf. Shapiro & Brett 1993) and its variant, procedural fairness (cf. Bies & Moag 1986). Our focus also drops the important potential of examining how the institution of courts affects the mediation of cases emerging in the court's shadow. The potential springs from the constructs of institutional context included in T_0 and T_1. Existing measures of these constructs could be used and new measures developed to explore how subsuming mediation programs within court structures affects how mediation proceeds. The ideas that Blumberg (1967) espouses open the potential for observable procedural variation between mediations from court-annexed mediation programs and private mediations even though procedures conducted in both contexts attempt to settle potential court cases. Another example involves Wall's (1981) exploration of the intersection of mediation and exchange theory. Exchange theory could be an important explanatory paradigm, but Janis and Mann (1977: 22–25) may be right. People may experience a difficult time collecting, interpreting, and assessing data on all possible positive and negative outcomes. Participants typically enter their mediation lacking a great deal of information. In addition, the form of mediation studied in this chapter increases the difficulty by relying on a cloak of confidentiality that isolates people from sources of information external to the mediation. Compressed negotiation time frames (e.g. from 30 minutes or longer) also inhibit information-gathering.

78 For the sake of visual clarity, even this depiction omits a few of the arrows suggested in the text.

References

Antes, J. R., Hudson, D. T., Jorgensen, E. O. & Moen, J. K. (1999) Is a stage model of mediation necessary? *Mediation Quarterly* 16(3, Spring), 287–301.

Bandura, A. (1986) *Social Foundations of Thought and Action.* Prentice-Hall, Upper Saddle River.

Benjamin, M. & Irving, H. H. (1995) Research in family mediation: review and implications. *Mediation Quarterly* 13(1, Fall), 53–82.

Bies, R. J. & Moag, J. S. (1986) Interactional justice: communications criteria of fairness. In R. Lewicki, B. H. Sheppard & M. H. Bazerman (eds.), *Research on Negotiation in Organizations*, vol. 1. JAI, Greenwich, pp. 43–56.

Black, D. J. (1973) The mobilization of law. *Journal of Legal Studies* 2, 125–149.

Blumberg, A. S. (1967) The practice of law as confidence game: organizational cooptation of a profession. *Law and Society Review* 1, 15–39.

Brett, J. M. (1986) Commentary on procedural justice papers. In R. Lewicki, B. H. Sheppard & M. H. Bazerman (eds.), *Research on Negotiation in Organizations*, vol. 1. JAI, Greenwich, pp. 81–92.

Brett, J. M. & Goldberg, S. B. (1983a) Mediator-advisers: a new third-party role. In M. H. Bazerman & R. J. Lewicki (eds.), *Negotiating in Organizations*. Sage, Beverly Hills, pp. 165–176.

Brett, J. M. & Goldberg, S. B. (1983b) Grievance mediation in the coal industry: a field experiment. *Industrial and Labor Relations Review* 37, 49–69.

Brett, J. M., Drieghe, R. & Shapiro, D. L. (1986) Mediator style and mediation effectiveness. *Negotiation Journal* 2(3, July), 277–285.

Brett, J. M., Barsness, Z. I. & Goldberg, S. B. (1996) The effectiveness of mediation: an independent analysis of cases handled by four major service providers. *Negotiation Journal* 12(3, July), 259–269.

Bridenback, M. L., Bales, W. D. & Planchard, J. B. (1980) *The Citizen Dispute Settlement Process in Florida: A Comprehensive Assessment*. Office of the State Courts Administrator, Tallahassee.

Bridenback, M. L., Palmer, K. P. & Planchard, J. B. (1979) Citizen dispute settlement: the Florida experience. *American Bar Association Journal* 65, 570–573.

Burrell, N. A., Narus, L., Bogdanoff, K. & Allen, M. (1994) Evaluating parental stressors of divorcing couples referred to mediation and effects on mediation outcomes. *Mediation Quarterly* 11(4, Summer), 339–352.

Bush, R. A. B. & Folger, J. P. (1994) *The Promise of Mediation*. Jossey-Bass, San Francisco.

Carnevale, P. J. D. (1992) The usefulness of mediation theory. *Negotiation Journal* 7(4, October), 387–390.

Carnevale, P. J. D., Lim, R. G. & McLaughlin, M. (1989) Contingent mediator behavior and its effectiveness. In K. Kressel, D. G. Pruitt & Associates (eds.), *Mediation Research: The Process and Effectiveness of Third-Party Intervention*. Jossey-Bass, San Francisco, pp. 213–240.

Carnevale, P. J. D., Putnam, L. L., Conlon, D. E. & O'Connor, K. M. (1991) Mediator behavior and effectiveness in community mediation. In K. G. Duffy, J. W. Grosch & P. V. Olczak (eds.), *Community Mediation: A Handbook for Practitioners and Researchers*. Guilford, New York, pp. 119–136.

Clarke, S. H., Valente, E., Jr. & Mace, R. R. (1992) *Mediation of Interpersonal Disputes in North Carolina: An Evaluation*. Institute of Government, University of North Carolina at Chapel Hill.

Coates, R. B. & Gehm, J. (1989) An empirical assessment. In M. Wright & B. Galaway (eds.), *Mediation and Criminal Justice*. Sage, London, pp. 251–263.

Cobb, S. (1993) Empowerment and mediation: a narrative perspective. *Negotiation Journal* 8(3, July), 245–259.

Cobb, S. (1994) A narrative perspective on mediation: toward the materialization of the "storytelling" metaphor. In J. P. Folger & T. S. Jones (eds.), *New Directions in Mediation: Communication Research and Perspectives*. Sage, Thousand Oaks, pp. 48–63.

Cook, R. F., Roehl, J. A. & Sheppard, D. I. (1980) *Neighborhood Justice Centers Field Test: Final Evaluation Report*. US Government Printing Office, Washington.

Crosson, M. T. & Christian, T. E. (1990) *The Community Dispute Resolution Centers Annual Report*. Office of the Court Administration, Albany.

Danzig, R. (1982) Towards the creation of a complementary, decentralized system of criminal justice. In R. Tomasic & M. M. Feeley (eds.), *Neighborhood Justice: Assessment of an Emerging Idea*. Longman, New York, pp. 2–24.

Davis, R., Tichane, M. & Grayson, D. (1980) *Mediation and Arbitration as Alternatives to Criminal Prosecution in Felony Arrests: An Evaluation of the Brooklyn Dispute Resolution Center*. Vera Institute of Justice, New York.

Della Noce, D. J. (2001) Mediation as a transformative process: insights on structure and movement. In J. P. Folger & R. A. B. Bush (eds.), *Designing Mediation: Approaches to Training and Practice within a Transformative Framework*. Institute for the Study of Conflict Transformation, New York, pp. 71–84.

Deutsch, M. (1973) *The Resolution of Conflict.* Yale University Press, New Haven.

Deutsch, M. (1991) Subjective features of conflict resolution: psychological, social, and cultural influences. In R. Vayrynen (ed.), *New Directions in Conflict Theory: Conflict Resolution and Conflict Transformation.* Sage, London, pp. 26–56.

Deutsch, M. (2000) Cooperation and competition. In M. Deutsch & P. T. Coleman (eds.), *The Handbook of Conflict Resolution: Theory and Practice.* Jossey-Bass, San Francisco, pp. 21–40.

Deutsch, M. (2002) Social psychology's contributions to the study of conflict resolution. *Negotiation Journal* 18(4, October), 307–320.

Dewey, J. (1938) *Logic: The Theory of Inquiry.* Holt, New York.

Dingwall, R. & Miller, G. (2002) Lessons from brief therapy? Some interactional suggestions for family mediators. *Conflict Resolution Quarterly* 19(3, Spring), 269–287.

Donnelly, L. F. & Ebron, R. G. (2000) *The Child Custody and Visitation Mediation Program in North Carolina.* North Carolina Administrative Office of the Courts, Raleigh.

Donohue, W. A. (1989) Communicative competence in mediators. In K. Kressel, D. G. Pruitt & Associates (eds.), *Mediation Research: The Process and Effectiveness of Third-Party Intervention.* Jossey-Bass, San Francisco, pp. 322–343.

Donohue, W. A., Lyles, J. & Rogan, R. (1989) Issue development in divorce mediation. In J. B. Kelly (ed.), *Empirical Research in Divorce and Family Mediation.* Jossey Bass, San Francisco, pp. 19–28.

Donohue, W. A., Drake, L. & Roberto, A. J. (1994) Mediator issue intervention strategies: a replication and some conclusions. *Mediation Quarterly* 11(3, Spring), 261–274.

Druckman, D. (2001) Turning points in international negotiation. *Journal of Conflict Resolution* 45(4, August), 519–544.

Duffy, K. G. (1991) Introduction to community mediation programs: past, present, and future. In K. G. Duffy, J. W. Grosch & P. V. Olczak (eds.), *Community Mediation: A Handbook for Practitioners and Researchers.* Guilford, New York, pp. 21–34.

Duffy, K. G. & Thomson, J. (1992) Community mediation centers: humanistic alternatives to the court system, a pilot study. *Journal of Humanistic Psychology* 32(2, Spring), 101–114.

Gale, J., Mowery, R., Herrman, M. & Hollett, N. (2002) Considering effective divorce mediation: three potential factors. *Conflict Resolution Quarterly* 19(4), 389–420.

Emery, R. E. & Jackson, J. A. (1989) The Charlottesville mediation project: mediated and litigated child custody disputes. *Mediation Quarterly* (24), 3–18.

Emery, R. E. & Wyer, M. M. (1987a) Child custody mediation: an experimental evaluation of the experience of parents. *Journal of Consulting and Clinical Psychology* 5(5), 179–186.

Emery, R. E. & Wyer, M. M. (1987b) Divorce mediation. *American Psychologist* 42, 472–480.

Etzioni, A. (1975) *A Comparative Analysis of Complex Organizations.* Free Press, New York.

Etzioni, A. (1980) Compliance structure. In A. Etzioni & E. W. Lehman (eds.), *A Sociological Reader on Complex Organizations.* Holt, Rinehart & Winston, New York, pp. 87–100.

Felstiner, W. L. F., Abel, R. L. & Sarat, A. (1980–81) The emergence and transformation of disputes: naming, blaming, claiming. . . . *Law and Society Review* 15(3–4), 631–654.

Fisher, R. J. (1983) Third party consultation as a method of intergroup conflict resolution. *Journal of Conflict Resolution* 27(2, June), 301–334.

Fisher, R. & Ury, W. (1981) *Getting To Yes: Negotiating Agreement Without Giving In.* Houghton Mifflin, Boston.

Flaten, C. (1996) Victim offender mediation: application with serious offenses committed by juveniles. In B. Galaway & J. Hudson (eds.), *Restorative Justice: International Perspectives.* Criminal Justice Press, Monsey, pp. 387–401.

Folberg, J. & Taylor, A. (1984) *Mediation: A Comprehensive Guide to Resolving Conflicts Without Litigation.* Jossey-Bass, San Francisco.

Folger, J. P., Poole, S. & Stutman, R. K. (1997) *Working Through Conflict: Strategies for Relationships, Groups, and Organizations.* Longman, New York.

Folger, R. (1977) Distributive and procedural justice: combined impact of "voice" and improvement on experienced inequality. *Journal of Personality and Social Psychology* 35, 108–119.

Folger, R. (1986) Mediation, arbitration, and the psychology of procedural justice. In R. Lewicki, B. H. Sheppard & M. H. Bazerman (eds.), *Research on Negotiation in Organizations,* vol. 1. JAI, Greenwich, pp. 57–79.

Gadlin, H. (2002) Framing new directions for theory from the experience of practitioners. *Negotiation Journal* 18(4, October), 327–330.

Galanter, M. (1974) Why the "haves" come out ahead: speculation on the limits of legal change. *Law and Society Review* 9(1, Fall), 94–160.

GAODR (Georgia Office of Dispute Resolution) (2000) *Participant Satisfaction Survey of Georgia's Court-Connected ADR Programs.* GAODR, Atlanta.

Gehm, J. (1990) Mediated victim–offender restitution agreements: an exploratory analysis of factors related to victim participation. In B. Galaway & J. Hudson (eds.), *Criminal Justice, Restitution, and Reconciliation.* Criminal Justice Press, Monsey, pp. 177–182.

Gergen, K. (1985) The social constructionist movement in modern psychology. *American Psychologist* 40, 266–275.

Greatbatch, D. & Dingwall, R. (1989) Selective facilitation: some preliminary observations on a strategy used by divorce mediators. *Law and Society Review* 23(4), 613–641.

Hare, A. P. (1976) *A Handbook of Small Group Research.* Free Press, New York.

Harrington, C. (1985) *Shadow Justice: The Ideology and Institutionalization of Alternatives to Court.* Greenwood Press, Westport.

Hensler, D. R. (2001) In search of "good" mediation. In J. Sanders & V. L. Hamilton (eds.), *Handbook of Justice Research in Law.* Kluwer Academic/Plenum., New York, pp. 231–268.

Hensler, D. R. (2002) Suppose it's not true: challenging mediation ideology. *Journal of Dispute Resolution* 2002(1), 81–99.

Herrman, M. S. (1993) On balance: promoting integrity under conflicted mandates. *Mediation Quarterly* 11(2, Winter), 123–138.

Herrman, M. S. (under review) Do select characteristics shape what mediators say they do? *Conflict Resolution Quarterly.*

Herrman, M. S., Gale, J., Hollett, N. L., Goettler, D. & Fogarty, K. (1998a) *Assessing the Relative Contributions of Personal and Professional Backgrounds, Programmatic Setting and Mediator Training to the Skills of Mediators – A Year End Report.* Report for the William and Flora Hewlett Foundation, Palo Alto.

Herrman, M. S., Gale, J., Hollett, N. L., Goettler, D. & Fogarty, K. (1998b) *Exploring What We Mean By a Good Mediation Outcome.* The Annual Meeting of the Society of Professionals in Dispute Resolution, September, Portland, Oregon.

Herrman, M. S., Hollett, N. L., Gale, J. & Foster, M. (2001) Defining mediator knowledge and skills. *Negotiation Journal* 17(2, April), 139–153.

Herrman, M. S., Hollett, N. L., Eaker, D. G., Gale, J. & Foster, M. (2002) Supporting accountability in the field of mediation. *Negotiation Journal* 18(1, January), 29–49.

Herrman, M. S., Hollett N. L., Goettler Eaker, D. & Gale, J. (2003) Mediator reflections on practice: connecting select demographics and preferred orientations. *Conflict Resolution Quarterly* 20(4), 403–427.

Hiltrop, J. M. (1989) Factors associated with successful labor mediation. In K. Kressel, D. G. Pruitt & Associates (eds.), *Mediation Research: The Process and Effectiveness of Third-Party Intervention.* Jossey-Bass, San Francisco, pp. 241–262.

Hofrichter, R. (1982) Justice centers raise basic questions. In R. Tomasic & M. M. Feeley (eds.), *Neighborhood Justice: Assessment of an Emerging Idea.* Longman, New York, pp. 193–202.

Hollett, N. L., Herrman, M. S., Eaker, D. G. & Gale, J. (2002) The assessment of mediation outcomes: the development and validation of an evaluative technique. *Justice System Journal* 23(3), 345–362.

Holmes, M. E. (1992) Phase structures in negotiation. In L. A. Putnam & M. E. Roloff (eds.), *Communication and Negotiation.* Sage, Newbury Park, pp. 83–105.

Homans, G. (1961) *Social Behavior.* Harcourt, Brace, Jovanovich, New York.

Irving, H. H. & Benjamin, M. (1992) An evaluation of process and outcome in a private family mediation practice. *Mediation Quarterly* 10(1, Fall), 35–55.

Janis, I. L. & Mann, L. (1977) *Decision Making: A Psychological Analysis of Conflict, Choice and Commitment.* Free Press, New York.

Johnson, D. W. & Johnson, R. T. (1989) *Cooperation and Competition: Theory and Research.* Interaction, Edina.

Johnson, D. W., Johnson, R. T. & Tjosvold, D. (2000) Constructive controversy: the value of intellectual opposition. In M. Deutsch & P. T. Coleman (eds.), *The Handbook of Conflict Resolution: Theory and Practice.* Jossey-Bass, San Francisco, pp. 65–85.

Jones, T. S. & Bodtker, A. (1998) Satisfaction with custody mediation: results from the York County custody mediation program. *Mediation Quarterly* 16(2, Winter), 185–200.

Jones, T. S. & Bodtker, A. (1999) Agreement, maintenance, satisfaction and relitigation in mediated and non-mediated custody cases: a research note. *Journal of Divorce and Remarriage* 32(1–2), 17–30.

Kakalik, J. S., Dunworth, T., Hill, L. A., McCaffrey, D., Oshiro, M., Pace, N. M. & Vaiana, M. E. (1996) *An Evaluation of Mediation and Early Neutral Evaluation Under the Civil Justice Reform Act.* Institute for Civil Justice, RAND, Santa Monica.

Keashly, L. & Newberry, J. (1995) Preference for and fairness of intervention: influence of third-party control, third-party status and conflict setting. *Journal of Social and Personal Relationships* 12(2), 277–293.

Kelley, H. H. (1971) *Attribution in Social Interaction.* General Learning Press, Morristown.

Kelly, J. B. (1996) A decade of divorce mediation research. *Family and Conciliation Courts Review* 34(3, July), 373–385.

Kelly, J. B. & Duryee, M. A. (1992) Women's and men's views of mediation in voluntary and mandatory settings. *Family and Conciliation Courts Review* 30(1), 34–49.

Kelly, J. B. & Gigy, L. L. (1988) Client assessment of mediation services (CAMS): a scale measuring client perceptions and satisfaction. *Mediation Quarterly* 19, 43–52.

Kelly, J. B. & Gigy, L. L. (1989) Divorce mediation: characteristics of clients and outcomes. In K. Kressel, D. G. Pruitt & Associates (eds.), *Mediation Research: The Process and Effectiveness of Third-Party Intervention.* Jossey Bass, San Francisco, pp. 241–283.

Kirkman, M. (2002) What's the plot? Applying narrative theory to research in psychology. *Australian Psychologist* 2002(March), 30–38.

Kochan, T. A. & Jick, T. (1978) The public sector mediation process: a theory and empirical examination. *Journal of Conflict Resolution* 2, 209–240.

Kolb, D. M. (1983) *The Mediators.* MIT Press, Cambridge.

Kolb, D. M. & Coolidge, G. G. (1993) Her place at the table: a consideration of gender issues is negotiation. In J. W. Breslin & J. Z. Rubin (eds.), *Negotiation Theory and Practice.* Program on Negotiation Books, Harvard Law School, Cambridge, pp. 261–277.

Koopman, E. J., Hunt, E. J. & Stafford, V. (1984) Child related agreements in mediated and non-mediated divorce settlements: a preliminary examination and discussion of implications. *Conciliation Courts Review* 22(1), 19–25.

Kressel, K. (2000) Mediation. In M. Deutsch & P. T. Coleman (eds.), *The Handbook of Conflict Resolution: Theory and Practice.* Jossey-Bass, San Francisco, pp. 522–545.

Kressel, K., Butler-DeFreitas, F., Forlenza, S. G. & Wilcox, C. (1989) Research in contested custody mediations: an illustration of the case study method. *Mediation Quarterly* 1989(24), 55–69.

Kressel, K. K., Frontera, E. A., Forlenza, S. G., Butler, F. & Fish, L. (1994) The settlement-orientation vs. the problem-solving style in custody mediation. *Journal of Social Issues* 50(1), 67–84.

Kruk, E. (1998) Practice issues, strategies, and models. *Family and Conciliation Courts Review* 36(2, April), 195–215.

Lang, M. D. & Taylor, A. (2000) *The Making of a Mediator: Developing Artistry in Practice.* Jossey-Bass, San Francisco.

Lehmann, H. J. (1986) Mediation and domestic violence. In J. E. Palenski & H. M. Launer (eds.), *Mediation: Contexts and Challenges.* Charles C. Thomas, Springfield, pp. 77–84.

Leventhal, G. S. (1976) Fairness in social relationships. In J. W. Thibaut, J. T. Spence & R. C. Carson (eds.), *Contemporary Topics in Social Psychology.* General Learning Press, Morristown, pp. 211–240.

Lim, R. G. & Carnevale, P. J. D. (1990) Contingencies in the mediation of disputes. *Journal of Personality and Social Psychology* 58(2), 259–272.

Lind, E. A., Kanfer, R. & Earley, P. C. (1990) Voice, control, and procedural justice: instrumental and noninstrumental concerns in fairness judgments. *Journal of Personality and Social Psychology* 59, 952–959.

Lind, E. A. & Tyler, T. R. (1988) *The Social Psychology of Procedural Justice.* Plenum Press, New York.

Macfarlane, J. (2001) Why do people settle? *McGill Law Journal* 46, 663–711.

Marshall, T. & Merry, S. (1990) *Crime and Accountability: Victim/Offender Mediation in Practice.* HMSO, London.

Mathis, R. D. & Yingling, L. C. (1990) Family functioning level and divorce mediation outcome. *Mediation Quarterly* 8(1, Fall), 3–13.

Mattingly, C. (1998) *Healing Dramas and Clinical Plots.* Cambridge University Press, Cambridge.

Mayer, B. (1989) Mediation in child protection cases: the impact of third party intervention on parental compliance attitudes. *Mediation Quarterly* 24, 89–106.

McCold, P. (2001) Primary restorative justice practices. In A. Morris & G. Maxwell (eds.), *Restorative Justice for Juveniles: Conferencing, Mediation, and Circles.* Hart Publishing, Oxford and Portland, pp. 41–58.

McEwen, C. A. (1999) Toward a program-based ADR research agenda. *Negotiation Journal* 15(4, October), 325–338.

McEwen, C. A. & Maiman, R. J. (1981) Small claims mediation in Main: an empirical assessment. *Main Law Review* 3, 237–268.

McEwen, C. A. & Maiman, R. J. (1984) Mediation in small claims court: achieving compliance through consent. *Law and Society Review* 18, 11–50.

McEwen, C. A. & Maiman, R. J. (1989) Mediation in small claims court: consensual processes and outcomes. In K. Kressel, D. G. Pruitt & Associates (eds.), *Mediation Research: The Process and Effectiveness of Third-Party Intervention.* Jossey-Bass, San Francisco, pp. 53–67.

McEwen, C. A. & Wissler, R. L. (2002) Finding out if it is true: comparing mediation and negotiation through research. *Journal of Dispute Resolution* 2002(1), 131–142.

McGillicuddy, N. B., Welton, G. L. & Pruitt, D. G. (1987) Third-party intervention: a field experiment comparing three different models. *Journal of Personality and Social Psychology* 53(1), 104–112.

McGillicuddy, N. B., Pruitt, D. G., Welton, G. L., Zubek, J. M. & Peirce, R. S. (1991) Factors affecting the outcome of mediation: third-party and disputant behavior. In K. G. Duffy, J. W. Gorsch & P. V. Olczak (eds.), *Community Mediation: A Handbook for Practitioners and Researchers*. Guilford, New York, pp. 137–149.

McGillis, D. (1980) *Policy Briefs: Action Guides for Legislatures and Government Executives*. National Institute of Justice, US Department of Justice, Washington.

McGillis, D. (1986) *Community Dispute Resolution Programs and Public Policy*. National Institute of Justice, Washington.

Meierding, N. R. (1993) Does mediation work? A survey of long-term satisfaction and durability rates for privately mediated agreements. *Mediation Quarterly* 11(2), 157–170.

Menkel-Meadow, C. (1984) Toward another view of legal negotiation: the structure of problem solving. *UCLA Law Review* 31, 754–842.

Menkel-Meadow, C. (1993) Lawyer negotiations: theories and realities – what we learn from mediation. *The Modern Law Review Limited* (May), 361–379.

Menkel-Meadow, C. (1995a) Whose dispute is it anyway? A philosophical and democratic defense of settlement (in some cases). *Georgetown Law Journal* 83, 2663–2696; repr. in C. Menkel-Meadow (ed.), *Mediation: Theory, Policy and Practice*. Ashgate, Dartmouth, pp. 39–72.

Menkel-Meadow, C. (1995b) The many ways of mediation. *Negotiation Journal* 11 (3, July), 111–136; repr. in C. Menkel-Meadow (ed.), *Mediation: Theory, Policy and Practice*. Ashgate, Dartmouth, pp. 217–242.

Menkel-Meadow, C. (2001) Introduction. In C. Menkel-Meadow (ed.), *Mediation: Theory, Policy and Practice*. Ashgate, Dartmouth, pp. xiii–xxxviii.

Menzel, K. E. (1991) Judging the fairness of mediation: a critical framework. *Mediation Quarterly* 9(1), 3–20.

Merry, S. E. (1982) Defining "success" in the neighborhood justice movement. In R. Tomasic & M. M. Feeley (eds.), *Neighborhood Justice: Assessment of an Emerging Idea*. Longman, New York, pp. 172–192.

Mnookin, R. H. & Kornhauser, L. (1979) Bargaining in the shadow of the law: the case of divorce. *Yale Law Journal* 88, 950–997.

Mnookin, R. H. & Ross, L. (1999) Introduction. In K. J. Arrow, R. H. Mnookin, L. Ross, A. Tversky & R. B. Wilson (eds.), *Barriers to Conflict Resolution*. PON Books, Cambridge, pp. 3–24.

Moore, C. (1986) *The Mediation Process: Practical Strategies for Resolving Conflict*. Jossey-Bass, San Francisco.

Nader, L. & Todd, H. F. (1978) *The Disputing Process: Law in Ten Societies*. Columbia, New York.

Ostermeyer, M. & Keilitz, S. L. (1997) *Monitoring and Evaluating Court-Based Dispute Resolution Programs: A Guide for Judges and Court Managers*. National Center for State Courts, Williamsburg.

Peachey, D. E. (1989) What people want from mediation. In K. Kressel, D. G. Pruitt & Associates (eds.), *Mediation Research: The Process and Effectiveness of Third-Party Intervention*. Jossey-Bass, San Francisco, pp. 300–321.

Pearson, J. & Thoennes, N. (1988) Divorce mediation research results. In J. Folberg & A. Milne (eds.), *Divorce Mediation: Theory and Practice*. Guilford, New York, pp. 429–452.

Pearson, J. & Thoennes, N. (1989) Divorce mediation: reflections on a decade of research. In K. Kressel, D. G. Pruitt & Associates (eds.), *Mediation Research: The Process and Effectiveness of Third-Party Intervention*. Jossey-Bass, San Francisco, pp. 9–30.

Pearson, J., Thoennes, N. & Vanderkooi, L. (1982) The decision to mediate: profiles of individuals who accept and reject the opportunity to mediate contested child custody and visitation issues. *Journal of Divorce* 6(1), 17–35.

Pines, A. M., Gat, H. & Tal, Y. (2002) Gender differences in content and style of argument between couples during divorce. *Conflict Resolution Quarterly* 20(1, Fall), 23–50.

Plapinger, E. & Stienstra, D. (1996) *ADR and Settlement in the Federal District Courts: A Sourcebook for Judges and Lawyers.* Center for Public Resources, Federal Judicial Center, Washington and New York.

Pruitt, D. G. (1981) *Negotiation Behavior.* Academic, New York.

Pruitt, D. G. (1995) Process and outcome in community mediation. *Negotiation Journal* 11(4, October), 365–377.

Pruitt, D. G. & Rubin, J. Z. (1986) *Social Conflict: Escalation, Stalemate and Settlement.* Random House, New York.

Pruitt, D. G., Peirce, R. S., Zubek, J. M., Welton, G. L. & Nochajski, T. H. (1990) Goal achievement, procedural justice and the success of mediation. *International Journal of Conflict Management* 1, 33–45.

Putnam, L. L. & Holmer, M. (1992) Framing, reframing, and issue development. In L. L. Putnam & M. E. Roloff (eds.), *Communication and Negotiation.* Sage, Newbury Park, pp. 128–155.

Raider, E., Coleman, S. & Gerson, J. (2000) Teaching conflict resolution skills in a workshop. In M. Deutsch & P. T. Coleman (eds.), *The Handbook of Conflict Resolution: Theory and Practice.* Jossey-Bass, San Francisco, pp. 499–521.

Rifkin, J., Millen, J. & Cobb, S. (1991) Toward a new discourse for mediation: a critique of neutrality. *Mediation Quarterly* 9(2), 151–164.

Riskin, L. L. (1996) Understanding mediators' orientations, strategies, and techniques: a grid for the perplexed. *Harvard Negotiation Law Review* 7(Spring), 1–34.

Riskin, L. L. (2003) Decision making in mediation: the new old grid and the new grid system. *Notre Dame Law Review* 79, 1–53.

Roehl, J. A. & Cook, R. F. (1989) Mediation in interpersonal disputes: effectiveness and limitations. In K. Kressel. D. G. Pruitt & Associates (eds.), *Mediation Research: The Process and Effectiveness of Third-Party Intervention.* Jossey-Bass, San Francisco, pp. 31–52.

Rogers, C. R. (1975) *Dealing with Social Tensions.* Hinds, Hayden & Eldredge, New York.

Rogers, C. R. (1980) *A Way of Being.* Houghton Mifflin, Boston.

Rolph, E. & Moller, E. (1995) *Evaluating Agency Alternative Dispute Resolution Programs: A User's Guide to Data Collection and Use.* Rand Corporation, Santa Monica.

Ross, W. H. & Conlon, D. E. (2000) Hybrid forms of third-party dispute resolution: theoretical implications of combining mediation and arbitration. *Academy of Management Review* 25(2), 416–427.

Rotter, J. B. (1966) Generalized expectancies for internal versus external control of reinforcement. *Psychological Monographs* 80(1), 1–28.

Rubin, J. Z. & Brown, B. R. (1975) *The Social Psychology of Bargaining and Negotiation.* Academic, New York.

Rubin, J. Z., Pruitt, D. G. & Kim, S. H. (1994) *Social Conflict: Escalation, Stalemate and Settlement.* McGraw-Hill, New York.

Sacks, M. A., Reichart, K. S. & Profitt, Jr., W. T. (1999) Broadening the evaluation of dispute resolution: context and relationships over time. *Negotiation Journal* 15(4, October), 339–345.

Sander, F. E. A. & Goldberg, S. B. (1994) Fitting the forum to the fuss: a user-friendly guide to selecting an ADR procedure. *Negotiation Journal* 10(1, January), 49–67.

Sandy, S. V., Boardman, S. K. & Deutsch, M. (2000) Personality and conflict. In M. Deutsch & P. T. Coleman (eds.), *The Handbook of Conflict Resolution: Theory and Practice.* Jossey-Bass, San Francisco, pp. 289–315.

Shapiro, D. L. & Brett, J. M. (1993) Comparing three processes underlying judgments of procedural justice: a field study of mediation and arbitration. *Journal of Personality and Social Psychology* 65(6), 1167–1177.

Shaw, M. (1989) Mediating adolescent/parent conflicts. In M. Wright & B. Galaway (eds.), *Mediation and Criminal Justice.* Sage, London, pp. 132–139.

Sheppard, B. H. (1984) Third party conflict intervention: a procedural framework. *Research in Organizational Behavior* 6, 141–190.

Silbey, S. & Merry, S. E. (1986) Mediator settlement strategies. *Law and Policy* 8(1, January), 7–32.

Slaikeu, K. A., Culler, R., Pearson, J. & Thoennes, N. (1985) Process and outcome in divorce mediation. *Mediation Quarterly* 10(December), 55–74.

Steiner, C. M. (1981) *The Other Side of Power.* Grove Press, New York.

Stevens, C. M. (1963) *Strategy and Collective Bargaining Negotiation.* McGraw-Hill, New York.

Stienstra, D., Johnson, M. & Lombard, P. (1997) *Report to the Judicial Conference on Court Administration and Case Management.* The Federal Judicial Center, Washington.

Stillinger, C. A., Epelbaum, M., Keltner, D. & Ross, L. (1988) *The "Reactive Devaluation" Barrier to Conflict Resolution.* Stanford Center on Conflict and Negotiation, Working Paper #3, Stanford.

Strauss, A. L. (1978) *Negotiations: Varieties, Contexts, Processes, and Social Order.* Jossey-Bass, San Francisco.

Thibaut, J. & Walker, L. (1975) *Procedural Justice: A Psychological Analysis.* Erlbaum, Hillsdale.

Thoennes, N. A. & Pearson, J. (1985) Predicting outcomes in divorce mediation: the influence of people and process. *Journal of Social Issues* 41(2), 115–126.

Tyler, T. R. (1984) The role of perceived injustice in defendants' evaluations of their courtroom experience. *Law and Society Review* 18(1), 51–74.

Tyler, T. R. (1987) The psychology of disputant concerns in mediation. *Negotiation Journal* 3(4, October), 367–374.

Umbreit, M. S. (1991) Minnesota mediation center produces positive results. *Corrections Today* (August), 192–197.

Umbreit, M. S. & Coates, R. B. (1993) Cross-site analysis of victim–offender mediation in four states. *Crime and Delinquency* 39(4, October), 565–585.

Umbreit, M. S. & Greenwood, J. (1999) National survey of victim–offender mediation programs in the United States. *Mediation Quarterly* 16(3, Spring), 235–251.

Umbreit, M. S., Coates, R. B. & Vos, B. (2001) Victim impact of meeting with young offenders: two decades of victim–offender mediation practice and research. In A. Morris & G. Maxwell (eds.), *Restorative Justice for Juveniles: Conferencing, Mediation, and Circles.* Hart Publishing, Oxford and Portland, pp. 121–143.

Van Slyck, M. R., Stern, M. & Newland, L. M. (1992) Parent–child mediation: an empirical assessment. *Mediation Quarterly* 10(1, Fall), 75–88.

Vidmar, N. (1984) The small claims court: a reconceptualization of disputes and an empirical investigation. *Law and Society Review* 18(4), 515–550.

Vidmar, N. (1985) An assessment of mediation in a small claims court. *Journal of Social Issues* 41(2), 127–144.

Wall, J. A. Jr. (1981) Mediation: an analysis, review, and proposed research. *Journal of Conflict Resolution* 25(1, March), 157–180.

Wall, J. A. Jr. & Lynn, A. (1993) Mediation: a current review. *Journal of Conflict Resolution* 37(1, March), 160–194.

Wall, J. A. Jr. & Rude, D. E. (1989) Judicial mediation of settlement negotiations. In K. Kressel, D. G. Pruitt & Associates (eds.), *Mediation Research: The Process and Effectiveness of Third-Party Intervention.* Jossey-Bass, San Francisco, pp. 190–212.

Wall, V. D. Jr. & Dewhurst, M. L. (1991) Mediator gender: communication differences in resolved and unresolved mediations. *Mediation Quarterly* 9(1, Fall), 63–85.

Walton, R. E. & McKersie, R. B. (1965) *A Behavioral Theory of Labor Negotiation: An Analysis of a Social Interaction System.* McGraw-Hill, New York.

Warren, E. L. (1954) Mediation and fact finding. In A. W. Kornhauser, R. Dubin & A. M. Ross (eds.), *Industrial Conflict.* McGraw-Hill, New York, pp. 292–300.

Weeks, D. (1992) *The Eight Essential Steps to Conflict Resolution.* Tarcher/Putnam, New York.

Weiss-Wik, S. (1983) Enhancing negotiators' successfulness. *Journal of Conflict Resolution* 27(4, December), 706–739.

Weitzman, E. A. & Weitzman, P. F. (2000) Problem solving and decision making in conflict resolution. In M. Deutsch & P. T. Coleman (eds.), *The Handbook of Conflict Resolution: Theory and Practice.* Jossey-Bass, San Francisco, pp. 185–209.

Welton, G. L. (1991) Parties in conflict: their characteristics and perceptions. In K. G. Duffy, J. W. Grosch & P. V. Olczak (eds.), *Community Mediation: A Handbook for Practitioners and Researchers.* Guilford, New York, pp. 105–118.

Welton, G. L. & Pruitt, D. G. (1987) The mediation process: the effects of mediator bias and disputant power. *Personality and Social Psychology Bulletin* 13, 123–133.

Whiting, R. A. (1994) Family disputes, nonfamily disputes, and mediation success. *Mediation Quarterly* 11(3, Spring), 247–260.

Winslade, J. & Monk, G. (2000) *Narrative Mediation.* Jossey-Bass, San Francisco.

Wissler, R. L. (1997) *Evaluation of the Pilot Mediation Program in Clinton and Stark Counties, August 1996 through March 1997.* Report prepared for the Supreme Court of Ohio, Columbus.

Wissler, R. L. (1999) *Trapping the Data: An Assessment of Domestic Relations Mediation in Main and Ohio Courts.* Grant report prepared for the State Justice Institute, Washington.

Wissler, R. L. (2002) Court-connected mediation in general civil cases: what we know from empirical research. *Ohio State Journal on Dispute Resolution* 17(3), 641–703.

Wyrick, P. A. & Costanzo, M. A. (1999) Predictors of client participation in victim–offender mediation. *Mediation Quarterly* 16(3, Spring), 253–267.

Young, H. P. (1991) *Negotiation Analysis.* University of Michigan Press, Ann Arbor.

Zarski, L. P., Knight, R., & Zarski, J. J. (1985) Child custody disputes: a review of legal and clinical resolution methods. *International Journal of Family Therapy* 7(2, Summer), 96–106.

Zartman, I. W. & Berman, M. R. (1982) *The Practical Negotiator.* University Press, Yale University Press, New Haven.

Zartman, I. W. & Rubin, J. Z. (2000) The study of power and the practice of negotiation. In I. W. Zartman & J. Z. Rubin (eds.), *Power and Negotiation.* University of Michigan Press, Ann Arbor, pp. 3–28.

Zehr, H. (1990) *A New Focus for Crime and Justice.* Herald Press, Scottdale.

Zubek, J. M., Pruitt, D. G., Peirce, R. S., McGillicuddy, N. B. & Syna, H. (1992) Disputant and mediator behaviors affecting short-term success in mediation. *Journal of Conflict Resolution* 36(3, September), 546–572.

Part II

MEDIATION AND NEGOTIATION
SET IN THEIR CONTEXTUAL
FRAMES

Chapter 3

Examining Mediation in Context: Toward Understanding Variations in Mediation Programs

CRAIG MCEWEN

INTRODUCTION: MEDIATION PROGRAM VARIABILITY AND THE RESEARCH CHALLENGES IT POSES

Much mediation in the United States is delivered through organized public and private programs that range widely along many dimensions. These programs frequently operate in the context of other institutions such as courts, agencies, or business organizations, in the shadow of varying legal rules, and with the engagement of professionals such as lawyers. The wide variations in program organization and context raise two important questions. First, how do the dramatic differences among programs and institutional contexts matter for the ways that mediation unfolds and that parties approach the process, use it, and respond to it? Second, how, if at all, does the introduction of mediation programs affect those organizations, institutions, and practices in which they are enmeshed? This chapter focuses on these questions in general relationship to the Herrman, Hollett, and Gale (HHG) conceptual model of mediation that incorporates aspects of institutional context.

The importance of the first of these questions is highlighted by the picture of "effective mediation" emerging from research and showing significant variation across programs. For example, Wissler (2004: 67) reports that, of ten studies of case-processing time in civil case mediation: five found mediation cases terminated more quickly than adjudicated cases; four found no difference in rates; and one found mediation cases took longer. One way in which Wissler accounts for these variations across studies is by differences in program structure and legal context. Such variations may have direct effects on patterns of party engagement in and response to mediation, but they can also influence other T_0 variables in the HHG model, such as the personal characteristics of disputants, their beliefs and attitudes, and the characteristics of disputes.

The second question focuses attention on a broadened view of institutional context at time periods beyond those envisioned in the HHG model – and the existing research which it brings together – as well as on the possible cumulative effects of mediation programs on courts, legal practices, organizations, and communities. The claim-making literature of mediation is full of aspirations for reduced court dockets, transformed communities, and more effective and efficient organizations. Virtually all mediation research, however, has focused on the parties engaged in mediation and their disputes. A more comprehensive agenda for mediation research would examine systematically the longer-term impacts, if any, that mediation programs have on their institutional environments.

Exploring Program Variability and Program Boundaries

The significance of program structures and contexts comes into sharper focus when one recognizes the enormous variety of mediation programs. They vary considerably in their philosophies, practices, and institutional contexts in ways that may matter to the experience of parties and to the outcomes of disputes. The early Community Boards Program in San Francisco, for example, sent out a powerful message about its goals of community empowerment. Case developers from the community contacted people in a dispute, and then program staff organized mediations (conciliations) using panels of community volunteers (DuBow & McEwen 1993). Each mediation unfolded according to a set of stages that volunteer mediators learned to follow carefully. Through this process, a wide range of disputes that never reached or were never touched by the legal system found their way into Community Boards mediations.

This community-based program stands in sharp contrast to one like the day-of-trial small claims mediation that the Maine courts put in place during the same period of time (McEwen & Maiman 1981). Parties in contested small claims cases were encouraged or directed by a judge to attempt mediation while the parties waited to have their cases tried. Solo mediators from the community were paid a small stipend to mediate those cases. If the mediation did not lead to a resolution, it would be followed closely by a trial. If the case reached a resolution, the agreement would be entered as the judgment of the court. By comparison to Community Boards, small claims mediation was much more heavily embedded in the legal system, less connected to community institutions, and thrust on parties with far less preparation. Despite their differences, these two programs may be much more similar to one another in the kinds of cases heard and in party involvement than they are to the many civil court mediation programs that rely heavily on participation by legal counsel in the midst of formal litigation. These sorts of variations in program structure and context would appear to be consequential for the nature of the mediation process, the experience of parties, the likelihood and kinds of settlements reached, and later compliance.

An examination of program structure and context calls attention to the importance of identifying the boundaries of "programs" in mediation research, whether it is the Community Boards program with five neighborhood offices or complex, state court-connected mediation program such as Florida's. That state program includes county, circuit, family, and dependency mediation and is administered under a state-wide set of formal rules and statutes. In 2002, the Florida program supported 5,000 mediators on court rosters in 20 judicial circuits. The program also mediated 76,000 cases (Press 2003: 58). But variation across jurisdictions is likely in the ways that such a sprawling program is administered as well as in local legal cultures. It might be more appropriate, therefore, for mediation researchers to think of the Florida "program" as 20 or more separate programs with some shared and some differing characteristics rather than as a single entity. Similar questions arise in other multi-site programs. Community Boards, for example, could be viewed as a single program or as five distinctive neighborhood programs. Because multi-site programs have a potential to vary internally in institutional context across sites, clarity and consistency in the definition of program boundaries will be important in advancing systematic mediation research.

Having reviewed in general terms the significance of program variability in relation to clearly defined boundaries, I now turn to the first of the central questions of the chapter: how do differences in program organization and context affect mediation processes, party responses, and dispute outcomes? The next section adds program structure and legal context to the three variables identified in the HHG model as constituting institutional context.

POTENTIAL EFFECTS ON MEDIATION OF ELEMENTS OF PROGRAM STRUCTURE AND LEGAL CONTEXT

In examining the potential of program and contextual variations that shape the processes and outcomes of mediation, the HHG model describes three general clusters of institutional context variables in the existing research literature – process access, process efficiency, and process information. This section of the chapter reviews each of these in turn and adds to the model by focusing on two additional categories of contextual variables that have received little attention in previous research – program structure and legal context. Each of these is comprised of a series of more particular variables that are likely to have important effects on mediation character and quality.

Process Access

There is a long and rich tradition of research and commentary on "access to justice," usually taken to mean access to formal legal procedures (Cappelletti & Garth 1978). Some of the early and continuing critiques of alternative dispute resolution have come from those who see the introduction of court-related mediation programs as diminishing access to courts and judicial decision-making (e.g. Hofrichter 1982; Hensler 2003). As mediation has grown in application, there is now more concern about access to mediation itself. Mediation programs vary with regard to their openness and availability to parties (McEwen & Williams 1998). Cost is one among many possible barriers to access that may shape the characteristics of parties and disputes entering mediation programs, each producing possible consequences for mediation processes and outcomes. Frequently, public mediation programs charge fees for mediation services or increase filing fees for the courts to pay for mediation. These costs, along with the time that is required to undertake mediation – and the potential loss of income that goes with it – could provide modest or significant disincentives for participation. These features of programs are part of their structure and need to be examined for their impact on the selection and types of cases as well as on the expectations of parties entering mediation.

Screening criteria also are debated for their appropriateness in limiting access to mediation of parties deemed vulnerable to harm during a mediation session. In particular, screening for domestic violence in divorce cases has received considerable attention as a matter of policy (Cole, McEwen & Rogers 2004: 12–14). Protocols for screening that are more or less restrictive will affect the mix of cases entering mediation. As noted below, commentators such as Hedeen (2003) have argued that program pressures to increase case volume may undermine the use of important screening protocols and subject some parties inappropriately to mediation. Program screening may, thus, be related to perceptions of fairness in mediation.

Process Efficiency – Timing of Mediation

Mediation may occur early or late in a disputing process and may be preceded by other dispute interventions or not, depending on that timing. Timing relates not only to efficiency of the process in terms of time, effort, and dollars expended, as the HHG model suggests, but also to the readiness of parties to negotiate meaningfully and to their orientation toward mediation. Lawyers often speak of "ripeness" of cases for settlement, believing that disputes may need to percolate for a while and that information may need to be gathered before parties will be willing or able to consider resolution seriously. Over time, parties may become more realistic about their options, understand more about the positions and situation of the other party as well as their own interests and goals, and be more emotionally disposed to settle. In civil litigation (including divorce) the relationship between discovery activity and settlement is fiercely debated. Lawyers often prefer to delay serious negotiation and settlement activity until completion of some or all discovery.

The timing of mediation in the disputing process is a function of program characteristics and rules and, when connected to courts, of legal rules, judicial management, and local legal cultures (see discussion below). Some mediation programs have been designed to occur earlier in the litigation process in the hope that they will have a more substantial effect in reducing costs by diminishing discovery and other litigation activity (e.g. Maiman, Karriker & Leighton 1998). On the other hand, other mediation programs, such as some settlement week programs, may focus on cases that have lingered longer on court dockets. The timing of mediation in relation to the beginning of a dispute thus varies widely from program to program. Because that timing may be related to various dimensions of mediation effectiveness, researchers should examine the program factors that influence it.

Process Information

In the HHG model, process information relates to the extent and character of provision of information to parties about mediation in advance of the process. The degree to which parties receive information about mediation will ultimately be a function of some aspects of program structure and legal advising – both treated below. Program structures may include an explicit educational component, as did the Community Boards program, through the advance work of outreach workers who informed community members about dispute resolution and of case developers who met individually with parties in advance of any mediation. Because mediation was entirely voluntary and operated independent of other institutions such as courts, Community Boards took on substantial responsibility for preparing parties. To some degree, private mediators have the same responsibility – essentially to market what they do to parties and to prepare them to enter the process. By contrast, mediation taking place under the sponsorship of courts may leave explanations to attorneys representing parties (and not all parties are represented) and particularly to mediators at the introduction of each session. Indeed, in some contexts a portion of mediator training is dedicated to learning how to explain mediation to parties. Once again, a vitally important contextual variable of process information must be examined both independently and in relation to the organization and structure of mediation programs as well as their legal contexts.

Program Organization and Structure

As the discussions of process access, efficiency, and information make clear, other factors relating to program organization and structure can influence these as well as other T_0, T_m, and T_1 variables in the model. This section describes some of the crucial aspects of program organization and structure: program sponsorship, funding, staffing, scale, and duration; program format; and program ideology and training.

Program sponsorship, funding, staffing, scale, and duration

Mediation programs vary significantly in their fundamental structures: sponsorship ranging across government, private for-profit, and private non-profit; funding by external sources or by the fees parties pay; staffing by lay or professional volunteers or by paid part- or full-time mediators; small volume to very large volume; and newer versus older. These general structural variables in turn affect access, the profiles of cases, and the characteristics of parties entering mediation and may influence the culture and practice of the program and its mediators.

Timothy Hedeen (2003: 273), quoting Albie Davis, argues that "form follows funding" in community mediation programs. In particular, he suggests that public – especially court – sponsorship in whole or in part creates special incentives for the operation of community mediation programs. For example, court-sponsored and publicly funded mediation programs face pressures to take in larger caseloads to justify their budgets. Since the pressure occurs in the context of a well-documented party reluctance to enter mediation voluntarily (e.g. Merry & Silbey 1984; Matz 1987; McEwen & Milburn 1993), programs may try to bring in clients by adopting coercive techniques such as "Requests to Appear that are nearly indistinguishable from criminal court summons" (Hedeen 2003: 273). These same pressures, Hedeen argues (2003: 274), lead to "relaxing the screen used to select appropriate cases." The effects of such techniques are not understood and are related to – but not the same as – program variation due to whether mediation is voluntary or mandatory. More broadly, Hedeen and others hypothesize that much about mediation, the mediation experience, and its outcomes is influenced by funding and consequent aspects of program structure and operation.

Similarly, it is plausible to wonder about the effects of providing mediation on a fee-for-service basis. Large-scale private mediation organizations have developed with nationwide practices, and their clientèles – by virtue of self-selection – are certain to be different from those served by public mediation programs, both demographically and probably in terms of motivation and preparation for mediation. But little research evidence about private mediation has been published. The implications of these poorly understood differences between private and public and between free and fee-based services remain to be examined by research. Similarly, we do not know much about differences among the styles, expectations, and effectiveness of mediators who are full-time professionals and those who give or sell time on occasion for court-connected or community programs.

In addition to sponsorship and funding, the duration of a program may be consequential. A recent law review symposium asks about mediation programs: what happens when a profession, practice or program "starts to capitulate to the routine" (Honeyman 2003: 9)? The general question raised is whether some of the spontaneity, imagination, and freshness that may characterize new programs is lost over time with growth and routinization. At the same time, worries about loss of freshness may be balanced with the apparent benefits of experience, the number of cases mediated being one of the few characteristics of mediators that predicts greater success in reaching settlements in civil cases (Wissler 2002: 678–679).

Arguably, variations in program sponsorship, funding, staffing, scale, and duration may relate to other institutional context variables, such as mode of entry into mediation, and to the characteristics of entering parties, as well as to such variables as process access, process information, and party perceptions of process and outcome.

Program format

In a society where face-to-face mediations are already substantially outnumbered by electronic forms of mediation, the format of the mediation process clearly needs to be examined by researchers. The rise of new forms of disputes in electronic commerce has prompted the development of high-volume programs for mediation (Katsh & Rifkin 2001). These mediation processes come out of entirely different institutional and relational contexts than traditional mediation. They rely on the written word rather than oral communication, are asynchronous, and may be highly abbreviated (Katsh & Rifkin 2001; Gibbons, Kennedy & Gibbs 2002). They represent a natural extension of other variations in mediation structure that may arise from the nature of sponsorship and the institutional context of disputes – for example, reliance on telephonic mediation in some cases in the Equal Employment Opportunity Commission mediation pilot program (McEwen 1994), appellate mediation programs (Wissler 2004), or use of mail in mediation programs carried out by consumer divisions of attorneys general (e.g. State of Maine Attorney General 2004). These variations in mediation format need comparative study as they relate to process access, information, and efficiency as well as party participation, expectations, and experience and as they influence the nature of the mediation process itself.

Program ideology and training

To what degree do program design and structure reflect the continuing debates within the mediation community about varying forms or styles of mediation, and how if at all do those differences matter in the nature and experience of the mediation process? Mediators themselves debate the virtues of various mediation styles and objectives (e.g. Bush & Folger 1994; Riskin 1996; Love 1997; Stulberg 1997). It is not at all clear how these debates are transformed into practice at the program level. But it is plausible to suppose that program ideology and training influence the kinds of activities that mediators engage in. At the same time, program ideology and practice may not be entirely consistent. In their study of employment mediation, for example, McDermott and Obar (2004: 75) observe that "it is a challenge for a facilitative program to prevent some mediators from using evaluative techniques."

Approaches to mediation appear to matter for several aspects of mediation effectiveness. In her research review chapter for this handbook (chapter 5), Wissler reports that active mediators who disclose views about case strengths and weaknesses, settlement value, and likely court outcome are more likely to settle cases and to have the parties view the mediation process as fair. McDermott and Obar (2004: 75) find, however, that both the charging party and the respondent in Equal Employment Opportunity Commission mediation "rate facilitative mediation more favorably than evaluative mediation." At the same time their research indicates that "evaluative mediation results in a higher monetary settlement" (McDermott & Obar 2004: 75). Much more research needs to be done to tease out the effects in varying contexts of differing mediation styles and the linkages between those styles and the organizational structures and ideologies of mediation programs.

Legal Context

Not only do program organization and structure matter in providing context for mediation processes and outcomes, but so also do legal institutions, rules, and processes. Legal context thus becomes a fifth institutional context variable in the

HHG model. Although some mediation programs operate quite removed from legal proceedings – for example in-school mediation, some community mediation, and online mediation – much mediation has close interconnections with the law. Lawsuits have been or might be filed in many consumer, small claims, and civil matters. Criminal cases may lurk in interpersonal disputes and are prominent in victim–offender mediation. Family law influences the ways that disputes between married partners and between parents and children play out (Mnookin & Kornhauser 1979). The reality or potential of intervention by legal actors creates a "force field" around mediation that has the potential to change virtually everything about it. This section sets out several dimensions of that "force field" that researchers should attend to in studying related mediation processes: local legal culture, participation by attorneys, court management, and legal rules governing mediation.

Local legal culture

The concept of local legal cultures was coined by Thomas Church and colleagues (Church, Chantry & Sipes 1978) to help interpret the widely variant paces of litigation from court to court, variations not explicable by caseloads. Clearly, lawyers practicing with one another and with judges and other court officials in particular locales come to develop their own expectations about what is normal, appropriate, and expected with regard to such fundamental matters as the timing of case settlement, the appropriateness of discovery, and the expectations about case outcomes. This makes the practice of law quite variable, even across locales that share the same laws and legal rules. Such local variations in legal cultures need to be understood as both causes and consequences of the operation of mediation programs because they can both affect the ways in which mediation is employed and, as argued in the last section of this chapter, be influenced by the widespread practice of mediation.

The existence of local legal cultures leads to significant variations in the ways that lawyers and judges act with regard to mediation. In research about divorce law practice in Maine, my colleagues and I discovered that attorneys in different parts of the state initiated mediation at rather different points in the life of the case and attended mediation with their clients at very different rates (Mather, McEwen & Maiman 2002: 59–61). The North Carolina courts studied by Clarke and Gordon (1997) varied significantly in the rates at which cases actually went into mediation, ranging from 31 percent to 74 percent of eligible cases in four courts and reflecting very different local practices by judges. The researchers explain this variation as follows:

> Judges varied in their attitudes about when mediation should be ordered. They also
> varied in their approaches to case management, with some instructing their assistants
> to pursue attorneys to ensure that deadlines were met for appointing the mediator
> and conducting the MSC [Mediated Settlement Conference] and others taking a more
> relaxed approach. (Clarke & Gordon 1997: 330)

These examples of variations in both court and lawyer practices suggest the importance of examining local legal cultures if one is to understand the efficiency and quality of mediation programs that are connected to courts and the formal legal process.

Participation by attorneys

Attorney participation in mediation is fundamentally important because lawyers have the potential to shape party expectations about mediation, their preparation for and engagement in the mediation process, and the fairness and outcomes of a mediation. When representing clients who could enter mediation, attorneys may serve as key informants for them about the process and its place in the dispute. Because they are "repeat players" (Galanter 1974), lawyers learn the system, know the local legal culture, and use that knowledge to assist and influence their clients. An understanding of how lawyers view mediation, strategize about it, interpret it to clients, and make use of the process in their practices is only beginning to emerge through research (e.g. McEwen, Mather & Maiman 1994; Macfarlane 2001).

Mediation programs connected to courts depend heavily on the perspectives and practices of the attorneys who practice regularly in those courts and who guide clients through mediation processes. As guides, lawyers have the inside track in shaping client expectations about the mediation process. For example, in the context of a mandatory mediation program an attorney could provide encouragement that disguises the mandate ("Now we have the opportunity to go to mediation which often helps parties reach a reasonable settlement"), or discouragement that underlines the mandatory and burdensome character of mediation ("Now we are required to go to mediation, just one more step before you can get your day in court"). Lawyers can guide clients toward more or less constructive behavior within mediation sessions through careful or desultory preparation (McEwen et al. 1994: 158–159) and by the behavioral model they themselves set (e.g. McEwen, Rogers & Maiman 1995: 1368–1371). Thus, understanding how lawyers view mediation and advise clients in its context is crucial if researchers are to comprehend the expectations of represented parties for mediation and their behavior in the process.

It is just as important to know how lawyers act when they attend and participate in mediation sessions. Research about divorce lawyers in Maine suggests that they have generally learned to play a supportive role and to encourage their clients to be active participants in the process (McEwen et al. 1994). In contrast, Sharon Press writes about the unexpectedly central role of civil lawyers in Florida's court-connected mediation programs:

In the 1988 oral arguments on the initial set of procedural mediation rules, Justice Barkett gave voice to the sentiment that the attorney, while allowed to be present at a mediation, was intended to play a very limited role. In today's practice, when parties are represented, the attorney will often play a major role in the mediation. (Press 2003: 60–61)

To the degree that the level of party participation in the process is important to mediation, attorney practices matter for its effectiveness.

Lawyer participation also matters in assessing the fairness of mediation processes. The extensive critical literature on divorce mediation, for example, argues that it systematically disempowers women (e.g. Grillo 1991; Bryan 1992). The empirical literature about party perceptions of the process does not resolve this question (e.g. Cole et al. 2004: 4–30). Since in the US legal system procedural fairness is thought to be provided through legal representation, I and colleagues have argued that lawyer participation in mediation helps resolve the fairness question for disputes that occur in the context of legal rules (McEwen et al. 1995). The practical and empirical question, then, is whether or not lawyer participation diminishes the effectiveness of mediation in other ways. The importance of lawyer participation for fairness and for outcomes is underlined in another context by McDermott and Obar (2004: 75), who conclude that it produces more economically favorable outcomes for complainants in employment cases going through EEOC mediation.

As important as lawyer participation may be, it is clearly not universal in mediation programs. Many parties whose disputes might come to mediation do not have lawyers. When attorneys are involved in the original dispute, they may be discouraged from or decline to participate in mediation. In much community and small claims mediation, for example, few parties have legal representation to begin with. In divorce too, many parties are also unrepresented, although they are much more likely to have attorneys in contested cases. In civil court, lawyers are frequently present. But the fact that lawyers represent disputing parties does not mean that attorneys are encouraged or choose to participate in the mediation process. By rule, statute, or practice, some divorce mediation programs, for example, discourage lawyer participation (McEwen et al. 1995: 1351), and in many such programs where participation is possible, attorneys choose not to accompany clients to mediation (McEwen et al. 1994: 153). Those studying the institutional context of mediation must thus pay close attention to the availability of lawyers in mediation cases and to the character of their participation in advising clients in and around the process, even if they are not present during mediation sessions.

Court management

Mediation programs that are connected to the judicial process find themselves dependent in a variety of ways on the rules and procedures for managing courts. Judicial management focuses on shaping the docket and moving cases through it expeditiously. Active judicial management includes close supervision over settlement processes and involvement of judicial personnel in meetings with parties, setting firm and early trial dates, encouraging voluntary exchanges of information to reduce discovery costs and time, and setting and enforcing deadlines for discovery and for motions (Kakalik et al. 1996a: 3–4). In any court, judicial management is a product of formal court rules, and local variants in practice and in the application of the rules. Mediation programs associated with courts find their interventions interwoven with these other activities for managing the flow and settlement of cases.

In examining the effectiveness of mediation, one must take account of court management procedures that independently affect such variables as case duration while also affecting the operation of mediation programs. The independent import- ance of judicial management strategies for at least one "effectiveness variable" was underlined by Rand's evaluation of judicial management in federal courts. Rand researchers found that:

> Four case management procedures showed consistent statistically significant effects on time to disposition: (1) early judicial management, (2) setting the trial schedule early, (3) reducing time to discovery cutoff, and (4) having litigants at or available on the telephone for settlement conferences. (Kakalik et al. 1996a: 89)

The linkages between judicial management and mediation programs were noted by Clarke and Gordon (1997: 220) in their study of North Carolina state court mediation programs as they observed variations in the ways that courts enforced common rules, making it quite easy (in some courts especially) to avoid media- tion. Thus, any research about the nature and effectiveness of mediation programs administered by courts must understand the judicial management practices of those courts as well. Judicial management practices may undermine, reinforce, or con- found the effects of mediation programs on important "effectiveness" variables.

Legal rules governing mediation

In the last 20 years, a growing number of legal rules and court rulings have emerged to define and shape the use of mediation. Writing over a decade ago, Carrie Menkel-Meadow (1991: 6) commented on the irony of the legalization of mediation: "A field that was developed, in part, to release us from some – if not all – of the limitations and rigidities of law and formal legal institutions has now developed a law of its own." Those legal rules have both intended and unintended effects and must be understood for their influence on both the mediation process and its effectiveness.

The statewide, court-connected mediation program in Florida provides examples of the influence of legal rules on mediation. One of the Florida rules permits the parties to stipulate exceptions to the statutory requirement about who should be present at mediation sessions. According to Sharon Press, this means that:

> Because an attorney speaks on behalf of the client, this [rule] can be read, appro- priately, as "unless stipulated by the attorneys." While I do not have hard data to support this trend, I have been told by mediators that there is a trend for the attorneys to agree that one or more party need not be present at the mediation. (Press 2003: 62)

Another rule, Press reports, provides flexibility to the parties (again largely their attorneys) in the selection of the mediator – either certified by the courts or not

– although the rule requires judicial review of uncertified mediators and court appointment of mediators when parties cannot agree. Once engaged in a system of procedural rules, lawyers can turn the process of mediation in unexpected directions, as the following report by Press indicates:

> Based on information shared informally by mediators and court administrators, the mediator is selected most often by agreement of the parties. Given that most parties are not as comfortable with judicial procedures as their attorneys, one would expect that the selection of the mediator is routinely made by the attorney rather than the party. Again, anecdotally, non-attorney certified mediators increasingly report that they are not selected in the initial ten-day period. Thus, the unintended consequence of providing flexibility is the decrease in the use of non-attorney mediators. (2003: 63)

These observations by the director of the Florida program make clear that legal rules and the ways in which they are interpreted and implemented by judges and lawyers in the context of varying local legal cultures can have substantial effects on such important variables as whether or not cases enter mediation, who is present in the mediation session, and the qualifications, training, and approach of the mediator.

Perhaps the most prominent and hotly debated legal rules regarding mediation are mandates to enter the process (Cole et al. 2004). These mandates are also among the more complex rules to understand in practice. Mandates clearly should relate in the HHG model to disputant beliefs and attitudes, particularly perceptions of voluntariness. They also are thought by some to relate to mediation effectiveness, with critics of mandates arguing that parties who do not choose mediation will take the process less seriously, resist it and settlement, and feel coerced. But legal mandates and party perceptions and behavior are distinctive variables and must be examined independently.

The empirical evidence is mixed, for example, about settlement rates in mandatory compared to voluntary civil mediation (Wissler 2004: 69), but the evidence about party perceptions of process suggests no differences in the experience resulting from different kinds of referral. The apparent lack of dramatic differences between voluntary and mandatory mediation in terms of several crucial effectiveness variables thus needs to be examined more fully to be understood. That examination and understanding might focus on how parties are introduced to the process (process information) by attorneys or other advisors, who may interpret mandatory entry in very different ways, as noted earlier, by underlining mediation as a requirement or softening it as an important opportunity. The issues of choice in mediation are also clouded by the context of court procedures and rules that already impose on parties a series of steps and activities, and could give "protective coloration" to a mandatory mediation requirement. As a result of this complexity, researchers examining mediation programs need to understand not only the formal structures of choice and requirement, but also the experiences and perceptions of parties in the context of local practices of providing advice by lawyers and others.

Potential effects of mediation programs on institutional context

In responding to the first organizing question for this chapter, the previous section has added to the HHG model of T_0 variables two additional variables – program structure and legal context – that are likely to influence the ways that mediation takes place and its effects on parties. The second organizing question for this chapter focuses on the effects that mediation programs themselves have on aspects of institutional context. Indeed, the rapid expansion of mediation in all sorts of institutional settings might be expected to have some social consequences. This section of the chapter in some sense goes beyond the HHG model, which focuses on individual mediation processes and their outcomes. Here I suggest that mediation research should also look at the cumulative effects over time of mediation practice and programs on four broad dimensions of institutional context: courts, legal profession, communities, and organizations.

Courts

Many courts have introduced mediation programs both because of the view that the mediation process can add significantly to the quality of justice and because it is hoped that mediation can divert cases from court and relieve heavy dockets. To date there is no empirical evidence to support these aspirations, but recent attention to the significant declines in the number of civil trials in the state and federal courts over the last decade has turned attention to these questions. A recent symposium on "The Vanishing Trial" (*Journal of Empirical Legal Research* 2004) includes examination of one possible cause – the rise in alternative dispute resolution programs that has corresponded historically with the declining trial rate (Stipanowich 2004). However, the direct linkage between the two phenomena remains unclear. Studies of community dispute resolution programs (McGillis 1997) and of particular state or federal civil mediation programs generally find no clear impact on court dockets (Kakalik et al. 1996b; Clarke & Gordon 1997), presumably because the numbers of cases mediated is relatively small and because other cases fill the time available. Perhaps future studies could focus on more subtle issues such as use of judicial time and how that changes, if at all, with the advent of mediation programs.

Lawyers

Lawyers who practice in such areas as civil, family, or employment law are likely in many areas of the United States to find themselves advising clients who must or may go to mediation. Many of these lawyers sometimes or commonly participate in mediation sessions. Significant numbers of attorneys also see the opportunity to serve as mediators as an asset to their practice, or perhaps as part of their responsibility to contribute to the justice system. Do these growing and sustained contacts with mediation make any differences to the ways that lawyers conceive of their own roles, work with clients, or strategize about cases? A few researchers have asked these questions in different contexts and have found suggestions that sustained experience with mediation does affect patterns and expectations of legal practice. For example, in her study of commercial litigators in Toronto and Ottawa, Julie Macfarlane (2001: 55–69) finds changes in one city in the ways that lawyers who have experienced mediation strategize about settlement outcomes and in the extent of preparation for cases. In our comparison of divorce lawyers in two states, my colleagues and I concluded that years of experience with mandatory mediation in Maine appear to have shifted the ways that divorce attorneys viewed the settlement process. The pattern was quite different from that seen by their peers in New Hampshire who, at the time, had virtually no experience with mediation (McEwen et al. 1994: 176–179). These studies only touch the edges of what could be fruitful work on law practice and the ways in which it both shapes and is shaped by significant engagement with mediation programs.

Communities

As noted earlier, some community mediation programs grew out of efforts to increase the number and power of institutions for resolving disputes in communities where traditional mechanisms for doing so by religious bodies, extended families, and elders had broken down. Goals of civic engagement, reduced violent conflict, and increased access to dispute resolution have been voiced by some advocates of community dispute resolution. Ray Shonholtz, for example, identified a wide range of goals for the Community Boards program in San Francisco, including two that focused primarily on the capacity and workings of local institutions: "strengthen[ing] the capacity of neighborhood, church, organization, school, and social service organizations to address conflict effectively" and "strengthen[ing] the role of citizens in the exercise of their democratic responsibilities" (quoted in Hedeen 2003: 271).

An assessment of the impact of the early Community Boards program on the San Francisco neighborhoods in which it operated found little large-scale impact, although it documented significant effects on the lives and perspectives of volunteers who participated in the program (DuBow & McEwen 1993). Commenting on the limited research evidence about the achievement of the broad social goals of community dispute resolution, Deborah Hensler concludes:

> There is little evidence that neighborhood justice centers have substantially reduced urban social conflict or contributed to a significant redistribution of power within communities, although they may well be helping neighbors work out minor disputes. (Hensler 2003: 195)

In turn, Professor Hensler worries about unintended effects of broadened access to mediation in the United States on institutional and individual expectations about the nature of justice. She worries, for example, about "a profound change in our view of the justice system. With increasing barriers to litigating, fewer citizens will find their own way into court" (Hensler 2003: 197). Examination of the broad consequences for individuals and communities of the significant increase in mediation programs remains a challenge for future researchers.

Organizations

Although organizations are not within the initial province of the proposed model, it is important to consider organizational contexts as possible sites of change resulting from the introduction of mediation programs. Interpersonal disputes within the context of the workplace or the school are common and increasingly subject to internal conflict resolution programs (e.g. Davis 1986). School-based mediation has been around for several decades, and some evidence suggests that changes in school climate might result from the most effective programs (Cole et al. 2004: 12–33). Mediation programs sponsored by employers might also be expected to have the potential to affect workplace norms and climate. Thus, mediation research needs to address not only the effects that differing managerial contexts have for the mediation of workplace or school disputes but also the impacts that such mediation programs may have on the organizations themselves.

SUMMARY AND CONCLUSION

This chapter began with two large questions about the impact of variables relating to institutional context and program structure on the mediation process and its outcomes for individual parties and about the consequences of mediation programs themselves for the institutional contexts in which they operate. Neither question has been systematically addressed by research, although summaries of research by Wissler (2002, 2004; chapter 5 this volume) in particular make a beginning at analysis and suggest both the importance of variation and the commonality of some patterns of results across disparate conditions. Clearly, institutional context matters in mediation and plays a significant part in the HHG model. The challenge for future research is to take systematic account of contextual variables both as causes and as effects. In this chapter, I have suggested adding two institutional context variables to the HHG model – program structure and legal context – and have examined the need for research on the impact of mediation programs on courts, lawyers, communities, and organizations.

An intriguing possibility for future mediation research would be to gather data on large numbers of mediation programs, treating them as units of analysis. Such research would require data not only on variables relating to program structure and context, as suggested in this chapter, but also on aggregate "effectiveness" variables such as average time to resolution, and rates of participation, settlement, and perceived fairness. The challenges of such research are enormous, particularly in developing comparable measures for variables measuring "effectiveness" and in gathering the data on sufficient numbers of programs. The benefits of such work could be substantial, however, and would come from highlighting the importance of *program* variables for analysis, something that does not frequently happen in most program-based research where they must be treated as constants – part of the background – rather than as variables.

The HHG model provides a comprehensive framework for micro-level analysis of mediation participants, processes, and outcomes, analyses that could be driven largely by theory or by practice and policy questions. Some of the variables in the HHG model are more subject to policy intervention than are others. For example, party characteristics and expectations may be affected by program policy and practice, but are largely "givens" by the time a mediation process is underway. Understanding which program variables are subject in some sense to "control" or "change" could help give priority to research that would inform policy and practice decisions. Many of the variables that matter to policy and practice are captured by this analysis of "institutional context." Serious incorporation of these variables into future mediation research may thus serve not only to build mediation theory but also to contribute to mediation practice and policy.

References

Bryan, P. E. (1992) Killing us softly: divorce mediation and the politics of power. *Buffalo Law Review* 40, 441–523.

Bush, R. A. B. & Folger, J. (1994) *The Promise of Mediation: Responding to Conflict Through Empowerment and Recognition.* Jossey-Bass, San Francisco.

Cappelletti, M. & Garth, B. (1978) *Access to Justice: A World Survey,* vol. 1. Sijthoff & Noordhoff, Alphenaandenrijn.

Church, T., Chantry, K. N. & Sipes, L. L. (1978) *Justice Delayed: The Pace of Litigation in Urban Trial Courts.* National Center for State Courts, Williamsburg.

Clarke, S. H. & Gordon, E. E. (1997) Public sponsorship of private settling: court-ordered civil case mediation. *The Justice System Journal* 19, 311–339.

Cole, S. R., McEwen, C. A. & Rogers, N. H. (2004) *Mediation: Law, Policy, Practice,* 2nd edn. West Group, Minneapolis.

Davis, A. (1986) Dispute resolution at an early age. *Negotiation Journal* 2, 287–297.

DuBow, F. & McEwen, C. (1993) Community boards: an analytic profile. In S. E. Merry & N. Milner (eds.), *The Possibility of Popular Justice: A Case Study of Community Mediation in the United States.* University of Michigan Press, Ann Arbor, pp. 125–168.

Galanter, M. (1974) Why the "haves" come out ahead: speculations on the limits of legal change. *Law & Society Review* 9, 95–160.

Gibbons, L. J., Kennedy, R. M. & Gibbs, J. M. (2002) Cyber-mediation: computer-mediated communications medium massaging the message. *New Mexico Law Review* 32, 27–73.

Grillo, T. (1991) The mediation alternative: process dangers for women. *Yale Law Journal* 100, 1545–1611.

Hedeen, T. (2003) Institutionalizing community mediation: can dispute resolution "of, by, and for the people" long endure? *Penn State Law Review* 108, 265–277.

Hensler, D. (2003) Our courts, ourselves: how the alternative dispute resolution movement is re-shaping our legal system. *Penn State Law Review* 108, 165–198.

Hofrichter, R. (1982) Neighborhood justice and the social control problems of American capitalism: a perspective. In R. L. Abel (ed.), *The Politics of Informal Justice: The American Experience.* Academic Press, New York.

Honeyman, C. (2003) Prologue: observations of capitulation to the routine. *Penn State Law Review* 108, 9–18.

Journal of Empirical Legal Studies (2004) Symposium on the Vanishing Trial, 1.

Kakalik, J. S., Dunworth, T., Hill, L. A., McCaffrey, D., Oshiro, M., Pace, N. M. & Vaiana, M. E. (1996a) *An Evaluation of Judicial Case Management Under the Civil Justice Reform Act.* Rand Corporation, Santa Monica.

Kakalik, J. S., Dunworth, T., Hill, L. A., McCaffrey, D., Oshiro, M., Pace, N. M. & Vaiana, M. E. (1996b) *An Evaluation of Mediation and Early Neutral Evaluation Under the Civil Justice Reform Act.* Rand Corporation, Santa Monica.

Katsh, E. & Rifkin, J. (2001) *Online Dispute Resolution: Resolving Conflicts in Cyberspace.* Jossey-Bass, San Francisco.

Love, L. P. (1997) Symposium: the top ten reasons why mediators should not evaluate. *Florida State University Law Review* 24, 937–949.

Macfarlane, J. (2001) *Culture Change? Commercial Litigators and the Ontario Mandatory Mediation Program.* Faculty of Law, University of Windsor, Windsor.

Maiman, R. J., Karriker, D. & Leighton, A. (1998) *The Maine Superior Court Alternative Dispute Resolution Pilot Project: Program Evaluation Final Report.* Edmund S. Muskie School of Public Service, Portland.

Mather, L., McEwen, C. A. & Maiman, R. J. (2002) *Divorce Lawyers at Work: Varieties of Professionalism in Practice.* Oxford University Press, New York.

Matz, D. (1987) Why disputes don't go to mediation. *Mediation Quarterly* 17, 3–9.

McDermott, E. P. & Obar, R. (2004) "What's going on" in mediation: an empirical analysis of the influence of a mediator's style on party satisfaction and monetary benefit. *Harvard Negotiation Law Review* 9, 75–113.

McEwen, C. A. (1994) *An Evaluation of the Equal Employment Opportunity Commission's Pilot Mediation Program.* Center for Dispute Settlement, Washington, DC.

McEwen, C. A. & Maiman, R. J. (1981) Small claims mediation in Maine: an empirical assessment. *Maine Law Review* 33, 237–268.

McEwen, C. A. & Milburn, T. (1993) Explaining a paradox of mediation. *Negotiation Journal* 9, 23–36.

McEwen, C. A. & Williams, L. (1998) Legal policy and access to justice through courts and mediation. *Ohio State Journal on Dispute Resolution* 13, 865–883.

McEwen, C. A., Mather, L. & Maiman, R. J. (1994) Lawyers, mediation, and the management of divorce practice. *Law & Society Review* 28, 149–186.

McEwen, C. A., Rogers, N. H. & Maiman, R. J. (1995) Bring in the lawyers: challenging the dominant approaches to ensuring fairness in divorce mediation. *Minnesota Law Review* 79, 1317–1411.

McGillis, D. (1997) *Community Mediation Programs: Developments and Challenges.* National Institute of Justice, Washington, also available at <www.ncjrs.org/txtfiles/165698.txt>.

Menkel-Meadow, C. (1991) Pursuing settlement in an adversary culture: a tale of innovation co-opted or "the law of ADR." *Florida State University Law Review* 19, 1–47.

Merry, S. E. & Silbey, S. (1984) What do plaintiffs want? Reexamining the concept of dispute. *Justice System Journal* 9, 151–179.

Mnookin, R. H. & Kornhauser, L. (1979) Bargaining in the shadow of the law: the case of divorce. *Yale Law Journal* 88, 950–997.

Press, S. (2003) Institutionalization of mediation in Florida: at the crossroads. *Penn State Law Review* 108, 43–67.

Riskin, L. (1996) Understanding mediators' orientations, strategies, and techniques: a grid for the perplexed. *Harvard Negotiation Law Review* 1, 7–51.

State of Maine Attorney General (2004) Consumer protection – consumer mediation. <www.maine.gov/ag/index.php?r=protection&s=mediation&t=>.

Stipanowich, T. (2004) ADR and the "vanishing trial": the growth and impact of "alternative dispute resolution." *Journal of Empirical Legal Studies* 1, 843–912.

Stulberg, J. (1997) Facilitative versus evaluative mediator orientations: piercing the "grid" lock. *Florida State University Law Review* 24, 985–1006.

Wissler, R. (2002) Court-connected mediation in general civil cases: what we know from empirical research. *Ohio State Journal on Dispute Resolution* 17, 641–703.

Wissler, R. (2004) The effectiveness of court-connected dispute resolution in civil cases. *Conflict Resolution Quarterly* 22, 55–88.

Chapter 4

Policy, Practice, and Politics: Bargaining in the Shadow of Whitehall

JANET WALKER AND SHERRILL HAYES

One cannot help but be fascinated . . . by something that can encourage men and women to sit down and try to just talk.

(Durrell 1990: 13)

INTRODUCTION

Fascination with the potential benefits of family mediation began in the UK in the mid-1970s. Thirty years on this fascination continues, despite the fact that relatively few divorcing couples use mediation. Constructive problem-solving is viewed as infinitely superior to litigation, although there are few studies which robustly test this assumption. Policymakers and practitioners continue to look for ways of promoting family mediation and encouraging couples to settle their differences through mediation rather than in court. There is no doubt that constructive conflict resolution is extremely sensible – it avoids destructive adversarial positioning, in which the needs and interests of the disputants are masked by what William Simon (1978) once referred to as "ritualist advocacy" in which the personal facts of the case are reconstructed to fit within legal rules and a rights-based culture.

Yet family mediation struggled for many years to find an appropriate niche in the family law business, being regarded as marginal, as a kind of Cinderella, until it was firmly embraced within reforming legislation in England and Wales in the mid-1990s. Although mediation has come out of the shadows, recent research conducted in the UK (Davis et al. 2000a; Walker 2001; Walker, McCarthy, Stark & Laing 2004) suggests that it is still a little-used option, in danger of being overshadowed by new approaches that family lawyers are developing as part of their legal services, including collaborative law and holistic legal practices.

In this chapter we reflect on the opportunities available to, and the challenges and dilemmas faced by, family mediators in the UK. We also consider the extent to which the model proposed in chapter 2 and the assumptions underlying it can provide a contextual framework for understanding mediation processes, the factors which influence mediation, and the outcomes mediation achieves. We draw heavily on our recent research relating to family mediation to illustrate the complexities inherent in what may initially have seemed, to the early pioneers of mediation, to be a straightforward concept and a deceptively simple process. It is a story of conceptual confusion and policy expediency.

Although most of the contributions in this handbook are written from a North American perspective, much of what is discussed is directly applicable to the UK, where practitioners have long been searching for balance (Jones, chapter 13, and Shapiro, chapter 14), seeking to understand the complexity of power (Saposnek, chapter 12), attempting to situate mediation within a broader spectrum of civil justice (Conlon, chapter 11), and trying to describe and refine those strategies which are most effective (Gray, chapter 8, Deutsch, chapter 17, Katz, chapter 18, and Avruch, chapter 19). Nevertheless, there are particular historical, social, and legal factors which render some of the confusions and dilemmas specific to family mediation practice in the UK. As we are examining the Herrman, Hollett, and Gale model presented in chapter 2 from a different cultural context it is essential to describe some of the circumstances which have shaped current mediation policy and practice in the UK since they inevitably impact on how the model can be applied and developed. This context is an important component of the "big picture" referred to in chapter 2, which so often remains elusive and which may be unwittingly ignored by researchers endeavoring to understand the mediation process and determine its effectiveness.

THE ORIGINS OF FAMILY MEDIATION IN ENGLAND AND WALES[1]

Social Changes

Family mediation in the UK is a product of social change and concerns about its consequences. The pace of change in contemporary, postmodern society has had an unparalleled impact on family life. In the 1970s, the number of divorces in England and Wales began to soar while the number of marriages began to fall. Expectations about the marriage relationship have shifted. Marriage is no longer based primarily on the wife's economic dependence on her husband and the pro-creation of children. Rather, individual fulfillment and mutual companionship have become the essential ingredients. This shift has significantly shaped the pattern of adult couple relationships since World War II (Giddens 1992). The private, companionate aspects of marriage are now rated more highly than the functional aspects of adequate income and good housing (Clulow 1995), and if personal fulfillment is not achieved there are few legal, economic, and social constraints to keep couples locked into unhappy unions (Walker 1995). Women's participation in the workforce is greater than ever before, families are smaller, and there are greater freedoms in terms of how personal relationships are conducted. Cohabitation is rapidly becoming a relationship of choice for heterosexual partners and over

40 percent of babies are born outside marriage (Kiernan 2004). Moreover, a new Civil Partnership Bill (2004) paves the way for the registration of same-sex partnerships as being akin to marriage.

Given these changes, it is not surprising that concerns have been expressed that "the social fabric of our [British] society is unraveling" (Lord Moran 1995), reflecting traditional, conservative values which continue to permeate debates about divorce in the USA as well as in the UK. The massive increase in divorce that has taken place over the past 30 years is frequently regarded as rocking the very foundations of society (Walker 1991, 1997). Therefore, buttressing marriage and supporting parenting have remained key policy priorities, which, as we will demonstrate, have made heavy demands on mediation practice. Indeed, the main thrust of our argument here is that policy agendas and political positioning are critical antecedent conditions (T_0) which have a heavy influence on what happens in mediation (T_m) and the outcomes it achieves $(T_1$ and $T_2)$. We believe that the institutional context, defined by a fairly narrow focus in the proposed model, is shaped by these broader conditions, and that the nature of this context in turn defines many of the personal characteristics of mediators, the beliefs and attitudes of mediators and disputants, and the range of dispute types which are considered suitable for family mediation. In our view, the model could be strengthened by an elaboration of the broader political and policy domains relevant to mediation, thus rendering it applicable to a variety of cultural, political, social, and legal contexts.

Political Context

The conservative, pessimistic view of divorce, which continues to influence family policy in England, also portrays children as the innocent victims of parental selfishness in which adult fulfillment is put before children's well-being and best interests (Popenoe 1993). The focus is on the damage caused to children and the desirability of protecting marriage as the surest foundation of family life (Lord Bishop of Worcester 1995). It was mounting concern about the plight of children living in lone-parent households that led to the development of family mediation in the UK. In 1974, the Finer Committee on One Parent Families recommended that mediation (or conciliation, as it was then termed) should be available to assist families deal with the consequences of divorce in a more civilized manner than is possible via an adversarial legal process (Finer 1974).

Unfortunately, successive governments failed to act on this recommendation, despite a rising divorce rate, and so a small group of divorce-associated professionals (including counselors, court welfare officers, and family lawyers) spearheaded the development of mediation. They did this in two ways: first, court welfare officers extended their services within divorce courts to offer court-based mediation; secondly, a deeply embedded child-saving philosophy held by a number of voluntary, charitable, community-based organizations has enabled them to embrace family mediation as part of their welfare provision. Although all those involved meant well in endeavoring to develop a more conciliatory approach to the resolution of matrimonial disputes, family mediation, having no coherent strategy, organizational framework, or mainstream funding, developed in a piecemeal, fragmented fashion. This disjointed institutional context has persisted and has been characterized by a recurring struggle within the community-based services for the financial resources to survive, and by confusion within the court-based services between statutory duties such as preparing welfare (custody[2]) reports, during which the practitioner has authority to intervene and recommend outcomes, and offering mediation, which is normally characterized by its voluntariness and the mediator's lack of authority, in the shadow of the court.

From Child Focus to All Issues

Although the Finer Committee expected mediation to be appropriate for resolving all kinds of matrimonial disputes, mediators in the UK originally restricted their remit to disputes involving the custody of and access (visitation) to children, leaving lawyers to deal with finance and property matters in the normal way. This is not surprising since the pioneer mediators traditionally worked in their parent professions with a focus on children, hence their enthusiasm for an alternative dispute resolution process which sought to minimize the detrimental impact of divorce on children. While this division of labor was comfortable for the professionals concerned and did not challenge the long-established role of the legal profession with its well-honed monopoly on managing the divorce process, it became apparent that it was not necessarily in the best interests of couples using mediation. The absurdity of encouraging parties to talk to each other in mediation about their children one day and leaving them to fight over money and property in court through their respective partisan lawyers the next was starkly revealed in research which found that couples who were in dispute about their children were highly likely to be in dispute about other matters also (Ogus, Walker & Jones-Lee 1989). Furthermore, the durability of agreements reached in mediation in isolation from other disputes was found to be problematic. In consequence, recommendations were made that mediation should tackle all the issues consequent upon divorce, enabling it to be regarded as a true alternative to litigation.

This recommendation provided the impetus for lawyers to become more closely involved in mediation and to develop a new, third kind of mediation practice located within the private sector. Their approach was based on a partnership between themselves and social work professionals, training and co-mediating together on all the issues a couple might bring. At the same time, mediators in the voluntary sector quickly adapted their approach to cover all issues, experimenting with a range of approaches, often involving lawyers as co-mediators or consultants. Slowly but surely, therefore, mediation practice in both the community-based and the private sectors embraced all issues, although concerns about children and parenting have continued to dominate the political agenda.

Research tracked the benefits and outcomes of all-issues mediation from the perspectives of clients, their lawyers, and mediators, using a range of research methods including direct observation of mediation practice and follow-up interviews with all those involved (Walker, McCarthy & Timms 1994). The research compared

102 couples who had experienced mediation on all issues with 298 couples who had experienced child-focused mediation. According to mediators, just over half of those who attempted to resolve all the issues completed the process, but most of those who began mediation managed to reach agreement on some of the issues. Moreover, disputants who attempted to resolve all issues regarded mediation as particularly helpful in terms of improving communication between them, helping them to negotiate together, and clarifying areas of disagreement. Indeed, all-issues mediation was more likely than child-focused mediation to achieve these broader outcomes. This study also showed that mediation is usually attempted at a time of high emotional stress, and that mediation helped some 40 percent of disputants to cope with the stresses and strains associated with their marital separation. The researchers concluded, therefore, that mediation can assist in the reconstruction of friendship and the remaking of cooperative relationships – two particularly important outcomes for parents who have to cooperate in the upbringing of their children well beyond the dissolution of the marriage. Such findings were encouraging for policymakers, and they provided positive messages for mediators with which to strengthen their demands that the UK government should place mediation at the heart of divorce reform.

Acknowledging Complexities

The research also challenged the previously unchallenged assumptions that the concept of mediation is straightforward and requires little elaboration (Walker et al. 1994). The researchers noted that mediation had derived increasing legitimacy in public discourse as a seemingly wholesome device for the resolution of conflicts at a range of levels, including in families. Yet it had become evident that mediation was not singular in form, nor was it concerned with the delivery of unambiguous goods. Rather, mediation appeared to be "a permeable form of intervention, subject to the 'pushes and pulls' of interests: those of users, of providers and the state. Moreover, these interests interact in a dynamic manner" (Walker et al. 1994: 160).

The researchers noticed tensions relating to the distinction between legal advice (the province of lawyers) and legal information (which is given in mediation, often by non-lawyers). Not surprisingly, disputants did not understand the distinction and expressed disappointment at the absence of guidance and the lack of information available during the mediation process concerning legal norms. The researchers concluded:

> Confusion, ambivalence and conflict cannot be adequately addressed by providing a catholic but confused service: distinct objectives require specification in an overall description and the ability to move between the procedures necessary for their particular achievement. (Walker et al. 1994: 160)

The pushes and pulls identified can be viewed as *antecedent conditions* (T_0), in which personal characteristics, beliefs, and attitudes and the institutional context were all influencing *the mediation* (T_m), and *short-term outcomes* (T_1). Whereas Herrman et al. take account of the personal characteristics, and the beliefs and attitudes, of the mediators and the disputants in their model, they also note that research investigating the effects individual differences have on the mediation process has been piecemeal (Sandy, Boardman & Deutsch 2000). Increasingly, the focus of our understanding of mediation has shifted from the disputants, and what they bring to mediation, to the mediators and what kinds of intervention they offer. Mediation users frequently arrive in mediation feeling confused, not only about their situation but also about the service they are about to receive. In order to address this problem, mediators need to be very clear about procedural factors and about the outcomes they are promoting.

Walker et al. (1994) argued that two related issues needed to be explored further: the organization and the profession of family mediation. These, it seems to us, remain central to current debates in the UK about the future of mediation practice and they are of critical importance to the Herrman et al. model. Although the ad hoc development of family mediation is not unique to the UK, the process of consolidation has never been completed and complex organizational tensions have tended to dominate the policy agenda. Mediation has been heavily influenced by setting (where should mediation be located – in court, in the community, or within legal practice?) and by the professional orientation of mediators (should they be social welfare professionals or lawyers or both?). Consequently, much time and effort have been spent in describing what mediation is *not*, in order to distinguish it from legal advice and representation, adjudication, negotiation, arbitration, therapy, and counseling. Very few attempts have been made to develop a coherent theoretical framework. Indeed, "theorizing" has tended to result in dialog about techniques (T_m), and training in mediation in the UK has primarily been about learning skills (Parkinson 1986), giving the impression that family mediation is a practice in search of a theory (Hayes 2004). Although mediation is seen by its users as a distinctive service, separate from counseling and reconciliation, disputants want mediators to recognize and pay attention to issues of healing and loss and to provide adequate information on which they can base decisions so that a new future can begin (Walker et al. 1994).

Research indicates that people facing separation and divorce want someone to help them "sort out the mess" and to restore some kind of order. They seem to expect dependency – at certain points in their personal journey they appreciate it – but see that the point of this is an emergence into self-determination and a need to resolve disputes both for their own sake and for their children's (Walker et al. 1994, 2004). It would appear from the research that readiness to mediate on all issues is a critical facilitating factor and that this readiness is an important antecedent condition (T_0) and not merely a feature of the mediation process itself (T_m). Moreover, the evaluation of all-issues mediation (Walker et al. 1994) revealed for the first time just how difficult and demanding the mediation process can be. It was often long (on average, couples attended between five and six mediation sessions over a period of four months) and arduous. Mediators have insisted that both parties attend together, and negotiate face to face. Within a fault-based adversarial divorce culture, this can be particularly stressful when the legal process focuses on allegations of fault and past misdemeanors at the same time as mediators attempt to focus on the future without exploring past hurts and wrongs. When the past has involved violence, negotiating with an abusive spouse may be unacceptable. Although screening for domestic violence is now required in practice, mediation is by no means an easy option for couples who are in the midst of personal distress and whose emotions are often running high.

Moreover, research in the UK suggests that one party is usually wanting separation and divorce while the other may be ambivalent or wanting to save the relationship (Walker et al. 1994, 2004). When disputants have wholly different agendas the mediator has a hard task maintaining a future focus and holding to settlement-seeking, problem-solving behaviors. That many couples do not stay the course in these circumstances is hardly surprising. The most important participants in mediation, therefore, are almost certainly the disputants themselves. Nevertheless, in order to facilitate constructive negotiation between them the institutional arrangements have to facilitate trust, fairness, safety, and civility (factors which prime readiness).

Accommodating Difference and the Search for Trust

All those who developed family mediation believed in an intervention which emphasizes negotiation rather than winning and losing, attends to the practicalities of ordinary living, and recognizes personal responsibility (couple power). Lawyers were aware of the personal, social, and economic costs of action from adversarial positions, counselors recognized that "mending" relationships is not restricted to reconciliation, and social welfare and court welfare professionals had moved beyond unreconstructed philanthropic autocracy. Nevertheless, it has been difficult for members of different professional groups to come together in a spirit of mutual trust. They have struggled to define themselves as mediators within a professional framework which recognizes and clings to parent disciplines and mores. Both users and providers of mediation have wanted a highly flexible organizational form which can respond to complex personal (disputants') and professional (mediators') agendas (T_0). The organization has also to facilitate the work of mediators and to affirm their professional competence, to address, symbolically at least, public concerns about the ending of marital relationships, and to ensure access to justice in its traditional sense. Only in the voluntary sector have discrete mediation services been established, while in the court-based and private sectors practitioners have embraced mediation as part of their everyday practice.

As a consequence of this somewhat ad hoc, opportunistic development across a wide variety of agencies and practice settings, family mediation in England has continued to steer a somewhat hazardous course, characterized by ambiguous and confused terminology,[3] differing ideologies on the part of the various professions involved, a multiplicity of practices, and a distinct tension between the legal principles applied by lawyers and the theoretical perspectives which guide social welfare professionals. Separate bodies were established to provide a professional reference point for mediators in the voluntary and private sectors respectively, and mediators working as court welfare officers practiced originally under the auspices of the Probation Service, now known as the Children and Family Court Advisory and Support Service. It is only since 1990 that some of these groups have come together to promote greater consistency in training, policy, and practice (e.g. through the founding of the UK College of Family Mediators in 1997). But tensions remain. Family lawyers have continued to voice concerns about the use of mediation to resolve financial matters if the mediator is not legally qualified. Lawyers and social work professionals have engaged in a rhetoric of partnership, but cooperation has had to cope with the fact that while legal practice has a clear identity, mediation has been more vaguely described.

Moving from the Shadows to Center Stage

Family mediation had not established itself as a discrete profession, and questions remained about the most appropriate organizational structure. But, by the 1990s, widespread agreement had emerged between all those involved that: (1) the current divorce legislation in England and Wales did nothing to facilitate constructive negotiation and (2) the personal, social, and economic cost of increasing numbers of divorces was too high. In November 1995, for the first time in 138 years, the UK government put forward proposals for divorce reform, within the Family Law Bill 1995. The government had been heavily influenced by the Law Commission view that divorce should be viewed as a process occurring over time (not merely a legal event), that divorce is almost always painful, and that the courts should be kept to a remit of adjudicating disputes, assuring due process, and enforcing orders, while counseling and mediation services should become important elements in a more constructive approach to marital dissolution (Law Commission 1988). At last, the government had fully embraced the notion of family mediation. Originally, it had recommended that there should be a mandatory personal interview for everyone wishing to initiate divorce in which, *inter alia*, information about mediation would be given, along with encouragement to try it (Lord Chancellor's Department 1993). This later shifted to provision for a mandatory one-to-one meeting in which a range of information would be provided in order to underpin four key objectives of family law which were spelt out on the face of the Bill.[4] These were:

- To support marriage.
- To promote a conciliatory approach to divorce.
- To reinforce the continuity of parenting.
- To provide protection from domestic violence and child abuse.

Family mediation had been placed at the heart of a reformed divorce process, yet members of both Houses of Parliament were more circumspect about its role. For example, one MP commented: "Mediation is a welcome principle and it will help in due course to take away a great deal of the acrimony from divorce" (Llwyd 1996: col. 249). But he was less convinced about the robustness of mediation when he referred to it as "the 'central plank' of the Government's proposals. As yet, we do not know whether that central plank will be made of teak or balsa wood" (Llwyd 1996: col. 252).

Another MP, Teresa Gorman (Billericay), was even less convinced about mediation, describing it as "nouvelle cuisine" when most people prefer "a good meal" and suggesting that the "presumption in favour of mediation is misplaced. At best it is idealistic. At worst, it is naïve" (Gorman 1996: col. 255). She may have been right in suggesting that the faith placed in mediation was idealistic and naive. The Conservative government had set an agenda for mediation which involved identifying marriages capable of being saved, helping couples to accept responsibility for the ending of their marriage by acknowledging conflict and hostility, dealing with feelings of hurt and anger, addressing issues which might impede the parties' ability to negotiate settlements amicably, and focusing on the needs of children (Lord Chancellor's Department 1995). This was a demanding agenda, which appears not only to encompass all the objectives of family law, but also to go beyond the agenda implied in the Herrman et al. model. Mediators, however, were hardly likely to challenge the efficacy of such a wide agenda, for fear of losing the support which policymakers were giving them. Faced with the prospect of a significant boost to their business, they did little to remedy or modify the government's inflated ambitions concerning their new role in the divorce process. Moreover, the government expected mediation to be the option of choice for the majority of divorcing couples. Eekelaar has described this as a clear example of government by persuasion:

> Mediation was not simply a method of bringing parties to an agreement; it was a further way of informing people about how they should have behaved, and should behave, and, through informing them about these matters, bringing pressure to bear on them to act in a "responsible" manner. (Eekelaar 1999: 387)

Critics of mediation often accused mediators of applying moral pressure to parents in a quest to make agreements which comply with a traditional model of parenting even after divorce (Dingwall & Greatbatch 1993). The belief, held by mediators and policymakers, that with the right legislation and the right processes in place divorcing couples can be helped to function in the right way (i.e. amicably and cooperatively) is almost certainly flawed.

During the stormy passage of the Family Law Bill through Parliament its central focus on mediation was somewhat weakened in favor of an increased focus on "saving savable marriages" through a period for reflection and an offer of counseling. Nevertheless, the emergent Act provided for mediation to be publicly funded and available to all, and policymakers retained their unrealistic hopes and ambitions that mediation would live up to all their expectations. The legislation fell short of directing people into mediation, and there was to be no presumption in its favor. The Family Law Act 1996 attempts to nudge people into mediation by requiring all disputants wishing to apply for legal aid for representation by a lawyer to attend a meeting with a mediator prior to being able to make such an application. The purpose of this meeting, known as a section 29 appointment, is to explain the benefits and process of mediation and to assess the suitability of the particular case. In other words, parties are required to consider mediation before negotiating their disputes through partisan lawyers. This raises serious dilemmas in respect of access to justice (Woolf 1996), and moreover makes the erroneous assumption that mediators offer the only route to conciliatory divorce. Our research, and that of others in the UK (Davis 1988; Davis, Cretney & Collins 1994; Davis et al. 2000a; Maclean, Eekelaar & Beinhart 2001), demonstrates that this is an unhelpful assumption which has further escalated professional rivalries.

FROM INNOVATION TO EVALUATION TO IMPLEMENTATION

The Family Law Act 1996 was considered to be one of the most radical and far-reaching reforms in family justice of the twentieth century. It was conceptually unusual because of its emphasis on counseling and mediation within legal proceedings, and the mandatory provision of information designed to promote personal responsibility and civility when marriages break down. In order to determine the best ways of implementing the new provisions for information meetings and publicly funded mediation, the government decided to set up a number of large-scale pilots which were to be evaluated prior to the new no-fault divorce process being introduced. A key message of the Family Law Act 1996 was that no longer should divorce legislation be merely concerned with the dissolution of a legal contract; rather, it must take account of the need to protect and preserve, as far as is possible, primary relationships. The Act represented a radical shift away from adversarial positioning toward a more informal, individualized system of justice. In this respect, the rigidity of mandatory information provision and the referral for a meeting with a mediator were strangely at odds with the new philosophy. However, despite an emphasis on mediation, neither section 29 appointments nor information meetings resulted in a significant diversion into mediation. While the government had hoped that, in a worst-case scenario, 40 percent of information recipients would use mediation, the research showed that only some 10 percent did so (Walker et al. 2004).

Davis and his colleagues who evaluated the provision of publicly funded mediation commented that the provision of public funding for mediation inevitably brought with it an expectation that people will behave in particular ways, in line with government policy, and that government support for mediation "reflects professional enthusiasm, with little regard to the low client base because the 'story' of mediation – its association with reasonableness and compromise – is appealing" (Davis et al. 2000a: xvii). Davis et al. (2000a) concluded that the mandatory referral to a meeting with a mediator is not an effective means of getting those who might benefit from mediation to consider it at what for them is the right time. Their research found that section 29 clients tended to lack understanding of mediation and have little motivation to attempt it. Mediators were faced with a somewhat unwilling or confused clientele, and had to "blend their account of the mediation process with claims for its advantages – frequently by reference to an unfavourable portrayal of the presumed alternative" (Davis, Pearce & Goldie 2000b: 214). Moreover, they found that mediators paid little attention to the parties' emotional state or to their intellectual capacity or articulacy, or to any attempt to identify outstanding legal issues. Nevertheless, the majority (77 percent) of section 29 referrals were deemed suitable for mediation, although this may not indicate a willingness to mediate, or sufficient understanding of mediation to give informed consent to do so. Davis et al. (2000b) argued that parties were being required to consider mediation when they had neither the capacity nor the desire to make procedural choices.

The evaluation of information meetings supports these findings (Stark & Birmingham 2001). When the benefits of mediation are explained they appear to be totally laudable. Most people indicated that it seemed a good idea, but that they probably would not use it, either because it was not appropriate or because their partner was unlikely to cooperate. The study of information provision, which collected data on almost 10,000 people, found that many factors have to be in place before mediation can work effectively, just as many factors have to be in place for a couple to get into mediation in the first place. Telling people about the advantages of mediation does not automatically result in their acting upon it in ways which are considered desirable in policy terms (Stark 2001). The antecedent conditions discussed in the model proposed in chapter 2 were found to pertain to each participant in the mediation process individually: each party (disputant) and each mediator. Personal characteristics, beliefs and attitudes, and dispute characteristics, vary between each of the participants, to the extent that readiness to mediate may be only partial. The evaluation of information provision found that the choice of which route to take through the divorce maze is influenced by each party's:

- knowledge of the services available
- understanding of processes
- sense of time and timing
- desired outcomes
- perceptions of cost
- perceptions of fairness

Stark (2001) concluded from the evaluation of information meetings that mediation is likely to be used only when all or most of the following conditions are satisfied:

- It is acknowledged that lawyers are not the only or the inevitable route through divorce.
- At least one of the spouses has more knowledge about mediation than just an awareness of the service, and understands the process – when and how to access mediation, how it works, and how it fits with other services.
- There are outstanding issues to be settled between the parties, whether financial, child-related, or both.
- Both parties are willing to go to mediation.

- Both spouses believe that negotiation between themselves is a better way of making arrangements, but have problems with or are uncertain about communicating directly with each other and view the presence of a third party as beneficial in this process.
- The parties have enough trust in each other to feel that negotiation is possible and that settlements reached will be adhered to.
- At least one of the parties has concerns about being fair.
- One or both parties wishes to minimize use of partisan lawyers.
- A mediation service is available which is accessible to the couple in terms of location, appointments, and affordability.

By contrast, mediation is unlikely to be used if *any one* of the following applies:

- Mediation is not well understood and/or is confused with counseling or reconciliation (people may be attracted to mediation for the wrong reasons).
- There is nothing to mediate about, because the parties are not in disagreement over finances or arrangements for the children.
- The parties feel able to communicate and negotiate directly with each other.
- The parties are unable or unwilling to communicate or negotiate directly with each other in any way, even if a third party is present.
- The parties do not trust each other at all, or do not trust each other in relation to matters which are still unresolved.
- One of the parties is unwilling to consider mediation as an option.
- At least one of the parties is so concerned with protecting their own interests and rights that they feel an overwhelming need for legal representation.
- The divorce is complicated by issues such as property, pensions, other assets, or arrangements for the children which require a high level of expert knowledge in order for resolution to be reached.

These antecedent conditions indicate that mediation is unlikely to be an option chosen by large numbers of people, particularly since it has often been regarded as an either/or option rather than as a process which can be engaged in, in conjunction with the use of other legal services. A study by Genn (1999) of the paths taken by people involved in civil and family disputes indicates that 99 percent of those experiencing divorce or separation problems took action of one sort or another in an attempt to solve their problem(s). The first point of formal contact was usually a family lawyer, and few of these recommended the use of mediation.

The non-use of mediation does not imply a non-conciliatory approach, however. The majority of those who participated in the information meeting pilots were aware of the importance of keeping conflict to a minimum and had attempted to follow the principles of a conciliatory approach, irrespective of whether they used lawyers, mediators, or the courts to resolve disputes (Walker & McCarthy 2001). This did not satisfy the New Labour government, however, which was disappointed by the results of the evaluations. It chose to abandon the most substantive part of the Family Law Act (which contained a reformed process of divorce) in favor of retaining an outdated and unpopular adversarial system. Mandatory information meetings were never implemented, although public funding for mediation was retained alongside section 29 appointments.

In retrospect, it can be argued that the Act attempted to do too much. There was an unrealistic expectation that information provision and mediation could save marriages, promote a constructive problem-solving culture, and introduce a new era of cooperative post-divorce parenting. While the Act would have removed punitive concepts of fault and blame, it sought to mold behavior in politically acceptable ways using mediation as a key intervention. Yet again, the same institutional context as that in which family mediation currently functions was proving to be enormously influential at all stages of the model proposed in chapter 2.

Reece (2003) argued that the divorce reform encompassed within the Family Law Act was a post-liberal reform in which the concept of autonomy (the ability to make choices) is embedded in and constituted by context, which is always an aspect of social relations. Not only were people expected to reflect on the steps they were taking, but they were expected to make the right choices as a result. In Reece's view, the object of the divorce process had "shifted from preventing, controlling or limiting divorce to educating the couple so as to make sure that they left the divorce process better citizens" (Reece 2003: 155). Thus there had emerged "an idealized image of divorce, constructed in discourses of welfare and harmony and representing only a variation on the theme of the 'happy-ever after' of fairy tales" (Reece 2003: 158).

The "good" divorce, constructed within discourses of harmony and welfare, "has become the ideal to strive for" (Sclater 1999: 177), and has inevitably been associated with mediation (Clulow 2000: 22) and the construction of the bi-nuclear family (Sclater & Piper 2000). Although the primary purpose of providing information to people wishing to embark on the process of divorce was to ensure that they had sufficient knowledge to make informed decisions about the steps they wished to take and to understand the consequences for themselves and their children, the new Labour government clearly recast the primary purpose as being to direct decision-making. There is no doubt that people valued the information they were given – over 90 percent of over 7,000 information recipients stated that they had found the information meeting useful (Walker & McCarthy 2001) – and that information meetings had achieved their original objective as envisaged within the Family Law Act. The government, however, chose to measure their success against what people did as a result of the information (Walker 2000). Because most people did not decide to save their marriage or opt for mediation, the Lord Chancellor[5] concluded that information meetings were not effective. Reece (2003) regards this interpretation, in which information provision is treated as a means of directing rather than improving people's decisions, as the most coercive aspect of post-liberalism's approach to divorce. Mediation has been at the heart of a subtle shift from enabling and empowering couples to make their own decisions – i.e. private-ordering – to seeking to influence the decisions themselves (Dewar 1998) and requiring and prescribing a particular result. This has proved to be a difficult role for mediators and one that may well explain subsequent client dissatisfaction with family mediation, which is contrary to the findings from research conducted prior to the Family Law Act and the availability of public funding for mediation. As a consequence, although in 1996 mediators in England and Wales had achieved the policy recognition they had long been seeking, the future for family mediation in the twenty-first century is by no means secure, largely because mediation has not been able to deliver on all the levels expected and public funding has served to constrain creative practice.

PICKING UP THE PIECES: MEDIATION BEYOND THE FAMILY LAW ACT

The government's decision not to implement divorce reform came as a particular blow for family mediators. They were faced with the prospect of promoting mediation within a continuing adversarial legal context and with no provision for all divorcing couples to be given information on which they could base choices and learn about the options available to them. At the same time, increasing numbers of family lawyers were embracing mediation as part of their legal practice (Roberts 2001). Since the government has expressed its continued commitment to providing appropriate support for families facing separation and divorce, and to finding novel ways of providing information and promoting conciliatory divorce within existing legislative processes, lawyers were well placed to extend their practice.

In order to develop practice, the government commissioned a two-year follow-up study of information recipients to provide an understanding of life-course trajectories: how people had lived their lives and reconstructed their family relationships (Walker et al. 2004). A postal questionnaire was sent to 3,909 of the original 9,330 information recipients (7,862 had attended an information meeting and 1,468 had received the information by post), and 1,491 completed questionnaires were returned. In-depth personal interviews were conducted with 131 people to explore the decisions they had taken. Great care was taken to ensure the reliability and generalizability of the data. Although response bias was minimal, data were weighted by variables for which some evidence of bias existed. The majority of the research respondents were divorced or in the process of divorce. The vast majority of these (over 80%) had consulted a lawyer, 10 percent had attended mediation and a further 2 percent had attended a section 29 appointment with a mediator but had not progressed into mediation. The follow-up study is important because it highlights a number of current dilemmas for mediation in relation to its post-liberal institutional context, the mediation process, and both short- and long-term outcomes.

Although 40 percent of respondents gave mediation some consideration, 56 percent of them rejected the idea because their partner was unwilling to attend. Mediation practice has so far failed to solve the problem of ensuring that both parties are willing to participate. The majority of those who did not use mediation had either reached their own agreements or had negotiated settlements through their respective lawyers.

For mediation users, the experience was not an unqualified success, however. The median number of sessions was three, but only 30 percent of 152 mediation users said that mediation had achieved all their objectives. The most common reason for ending mediation was that there seemed little prospect of making further progress (39%), and one in ten people opted out because it was not achieving anything. Some 62 percent of people left mediation with unresolved issues, and only 25 percent of disputants managed to resolve all the issues raised in mediation. The short-term outcomes (T_1) were particularly disappointing. Not only were settlement rates extremely modest (46%), but also, 38 percent of disputants were either dissatisfied or very dissatisfied (19%) with the process, with those not reaching agreements being the most dissatisfied. This dissatisfaction stemmed from a number of factors relating to issues remaining unresolved, partners being perceived as uncooperative, a lack of advice from mediators, and agreements being unenforceable. Of particular significance, however, is the claim that agreements were reached under pressure, with some people feeling that they had been forced into agreeing to future arrangements which conformed with the mediators' views about acceptable post-divorce relationships, particularly in relation to contact (visitation) and residence (custody). At the beginning of this handbook, Herrman et al. maintain that "mediation may be superior to giving in, adversarial sparring, or compromise" (p. 19). It would seem, however, that significant numbers of those who participated in the follow-up research gave in or made considerable compromises during mediation, and that problem-solving as such was itself highly compromised.

If we look at the longer-term outcomes envisaged in the Herrman, Hollett, and Gale model at T_2, these could be said to relate to the wider benefits of mediation, which go beyond helping couples to reach agreements, such as reducing conflict between disputants, improving communication between them, and helping them to be more cooperative and amicable. Mediation users in the follow-up study (Walker et al. 2004) did not feel that mediation had helped them to make divorce less distressing, or that it had helped them to improve communication, share decision-making, reduce conflict, or avoid litigation. Even those who managed to reach agreements were not all convinced that they had benefited in other ways. Although mediation had been promoted in terms of its wider benefits, few people in this study experienced these outcomes.

CURRENT DEBATES IN MEDIATION PRACTICE

So what has changed, and why is family mediation in England and Wales having to face some uncomfortable realities? It is our view that the institutional arrangements for mediation provision, together with a post-liberal political agenda, have had an unfortunate influence on mediation practice (T_m) and that some rebalancing is necessary if mediation is to retain its distinctive characteristics as an alternative dispute resolution process. We turn now to examine the extent to which the research in the UK supports this explanation, relating this specifically to the model proposed in chapter 2. First, we explore the characteristics of the mediators currently practicing in the UK; then we consider mediators' self-reports of practice; and finally we examine how certain mediator characteristics, especially practice setting, influence how mediators practice during the mediation process.

Mediator Characteristics

Although, historically, mediators in the voluntary or community-based sector have dominated mediation practice in the UK, the introduction of public funding created an increase in the numbers of mediators in the private (for-profit) sector, since, as Davis et al. (2000a) suggested, it had the potential to make mediation a profitable venture. Research conducted by Hayes (2002a, 2004) examined the characteristics of mediators throughout the UK and how differences between them may influence practice. Using a questionnaire mailed to all members of the UK College of Family Mediators (N = 761; n = 283[6]), Hayes found that UK mediators were most likely to be female (75%), hold a degree or professional qualification (80%), and be aged over 50 (55%). Most (64%) were working in the community-based sector, and nearly half (45%) had a background in the helping professions. Nevertheless, over a third of those practitioners who responded to the questionnaire were legally trained and practiced in the private sector. The training all mediators had received was similar, owing to the standardization of training programs.

Non-legally trained mediators in the community-based sector had higher levels of experience and devoted more of their professional practice to mediation than their legally trained counterparts in the private sector (Hayes 2002a). Despite this, mediation was usually a second job for practitioners, except for those who managed to combine mediation with mediation-related activities such as managing a mediation service, training, or supervising. Most mediators worked as sole-mediators (59%), although some used the co-mediation model primarily (31%). The types of case handled, and reported settlement rates, were similar across groups, but private-practice mediators spent fewer sessions and hours completing cases than those in the community-based sector (Hayes 2002a, 2004). The variations in professional background, levels of experience, and practice settings enabled Hayes to identify three sub-groups of mediators: community-based mediators with a background in social welfare and considerable mediation experience; private mediators with a background in law and less practice experience; and community-based mediators with neither a legal nor a welfare background and with considerable mediation experience. Although identification of these sub-groups of practitioners provided a context for understanding differences in respect of strategies, techniques, and interventions used with clients, the sub-groups were also interesting in themselves in that they show an increase in the number of lawyers practicing as mediators in the private sector compared with the numbers identified in previous research (Davis et al. 2000a), revealing an important contextual change regarding mediation in the UK. Although the majority of mediators are still mental health professionals, the "legalization" of mediation has attracted more lawyers, and this in turn has pushed practice toward a more "legal" model of settlement-seeking. This changing profile of mediators in the UK provides essential information about personal and dispute characteristics in T_0 to aid our understanding of procedural factors in the mediation process (T_m).

The Mediation Process

The focus on process and on mediator–disputant interaction has dominated most writing on mediation for many years, both in the USA (Slaikeu, Culler, Pearson & Thoennes 1985a; Slaikeu, Pearson, Luckett & Myers 1985b; Pearson & Thoennes 1988a, 1988b) and in the UK (Davis 1988; Dingwall & Greatbatch 1993, 2001; Davis et al. 1994; Walker et al. 1994; Hayes 2004). Research has attempted to uncover when, how, and why mediators use certain techniques and skills and how they influence process and outcomes. A wide range of methodologies have been used, but three have been prominent: self-report studies using questionnaires and interviews with mediators; simulated client studies in which mediators are required to work with "set" cases; and naturalistic observation of mediators in action, using either client observation or audio/videotapes of sessions. All these provide important insights into the mediation process and the beliefs and values of mediators. We look at each of these in turn.

Hayes' research (2002a, 2002b, 2004) adopted the same approach as Kruk's (1998) self-report study of mediators in Canada. Hayes examined the strategies, techniques, and interventions used by mediators throughout the UK during different stages in the mediation process and in different client and dispute situations. Mediators were offered a list of 43 of the most common strategies, techniques, and interventions chosen from the mediation literature and in consultation with family mediation professionals. Mediators were asked to choose the three most important strategies, techniques, and interventions for each situation presented, whether it was a stage in the mediation process or a particular client or dispute characteristic. Tables 4.1 and 4.2 show the choices they made.

These findings show that the focus of the mediation process itself is future-oriented and highly pragmatic, the mediators finding out about clients' issues, interests, and needs and then facilitating settlement-seeking. Managing conflict and facilitating communication appear to be integral to the process. These strategies are also central irrespective of the client and dispute characteristics, although the emphasis placed on some strategies varies according to the nature of the problem being explored. These findings fit well with the problem-solving construct in the model proposed in chapter 2, which encompasses variables such as *active negotiation*, *talked-about issues and needs*, and *formulating options*. Within each of these activities mediators use a range of skills and strategies. The results demonstrate that mediators see their role in the process as active, but also appreciate the importance of clients maintaining control over the content.

Further analyses of Hayes' (2004) questionnaire data demonstrate that particular background characteristics create systematic variations in the self-reported practices of mediators. During the general mediation process, practice setting was found to be the most influential characteristic, affecting 24 percent of the techniques mediators

TABLE 4.1   Strategies, techniques, and interventions most commonly used
during the mediation process (adapted from Hayes 2004)

Stage in mediation	Most commonly selected strategies, techniques, and interventions
Initial meeting (assessment/intake) N = 283	1. Assessment/history-taking (60%) 2. Educating/providing information (47%) 3. Defining/clarifying issues in dispute (39%) 4. Establishing ground rules (35%) 5. Using questions (17%)
Before working on disputes N = 283	1. Establishing ground rules (52%) 2. Defining/clarifying issues in dispute (48%) 3. Facilitating communication (30%) 4. Identifying interests and needs (23%) 5. Identifying positions (19%) 6. Contracting (18%)
During negotiation N = 283	1. Maintaining a future focus (29%) 2. Evaluating options for settlement (25%) 3. Facilitating communication (23%) 4. Reframing/positive connotation (23%) 5. Identifying interests/needs (18%) 6. Managing conflict (18%)
Ending stage N = 283	1. Summarizing (67%) 2. Drafting settlement (46%) 3. Reality testing (34%) 4. Maintaining a future focus (30%) 5. Evaluating options (19%)
Follow-up stage N = 106	1. Maintaining a future focus (34%) 2. Summarizing (25%) 3. Drafting settlement (20%) 4. Facilitating communication (19%) 5. Reality testing (19%)

chose when reporting what they do during the mediation process. Mediators in the community-based sector were more likely than those in private practice to use techniques such as "maintaining a future focus," "reframing," and "evaluating options for settlement," perhaps reflecting the government's expectations regarding their role in the divorce process, and their increasingly legalistic stance.

In the case of particular client and dispute situations the important variables were professional background (explaining 15% of the strategies used), practice setting (12%), mediation experience (12%), and gender (12%). The results demonstrate

TABLE 4.2 Strategies, techniques, and interventions most commonly used with specific client and dispute characteristics (adapted from Hayes 2004)

Client and dispute characteristics	Most commonly selected strategies, techniques, and interventions
Inability to come to terms with the end of marriage N = 283	1. Reflecting feelings (42%) 2. Exploring marital breakdown (29%) 3. Normalizing (23%) 4. Exploring spousal relationships (21%) 5. Reality testing (21%)
Impasse between parties N = 283	1. Reframing/positive connotation (28%) 2. Exploring resistance (27%) 3. Brainstorming (18%) 4. Identifying interests/needs (17%)
High-conflict couples N = 283	1. Managing conflict (52%) 2. Reframing/positive connotation (23%) 3. Reflecting feelings (20%) 4. Establishing ground rules (19%)
Power imbalances N = 283	1. Facilitating communication (27%) 2. Establishing ground rules (26%) 3. Identifying interests/needs (20%) 4. Directing communication (19%)
Spousal abuse N = 243	1. Establishing ground rules (54%) 2. Confrontation (26%) 3. Managing conflict (22%) 4. Holding to task (21%)
Child abuse or marked neglect N = 164	1. Exploring parent–child relationships (60%) 2. Referral (58%) 3. Educating/providing information (21%) 4. Establishing ground rules (20%)
Direct involvement of children in mediation session N = 136	1. Exploring parent–child relationships (39%) 2. Facilitating communication (32%) 3. Reflecting feelings (26%) 4. Normalizing (23%)
Culturally diverse clients N = 181	1. Facilitating communication (36%) 2. Defining/clarifying issues in dispute (33%) 3. Identifying interests/needs (31%) 4. Using questions (30%)

that particular background characteristics differ systematically in certain mediation situations. This provides some supporting evidence for the relationship described in the Herrman et al. model between *personal, dispute,* and *institutional* characteristics in T_0 and *procedural factors* in T_m.

Simulated client studies usually provide practitioners with a generalized case, based on actual case experiences. The researchers then collect data on their reactions to it. In the UK, a Scottish study conducted by Myers and Wasoff (2000) provided practitioners with written case "vignettes" and the researchers then interviewed practitioners about the strategies they would use. They explicitly compared mediators with different background characteristics, such as lawyers and social welfare professionals, and they found several major areas of difference between them. Lawyer mediators were more likely than non-lawyer mediators to offer overt direction during mediation, direct advice, and direction in respect of settlements. By contrast, non-lawyer mediators encouraged greater levels of client participation and required more input from disputants during mediation. Non-lawyer mediators were also more focused on client ownership of outcomes. Lawyer and non-lawyer mediators used different types of language with clients, with non-lawyers more likely to use the language of needs, responsibilities, and preferences, while lawyer mediators used the language of rights.

Nevertheless, despite their differences all practitioners reported an orientation toward conserving assets, minimizing process costs, facilitating compromise, reaching mutual agreement, and encouraging disputants to behave reasonably and sensibly. They attempted to minimize the apportionment of blame and saw themselves as being advocates for the children. Myers and Wasoff (2000) consider that this alignment with children, which is in tune with the political agenda, nevertheless compromises mediators' neutrality and impartiality, thus undermining mediation rhetoric. Myers and Wasoff also suggest that mediation can be a disempowering experience for some individuals, despite the empowering design of the process. These findings appear to support Reece's (2003) concerns that the post-liberalist approach to family law promotes particular kinds of behavior to achieve politically desirable outcomes.

Only a handful of mediation studies have utilized a naturalistic observational method, often pairing it with some type of electronic recording. Both audio- and videotaping have been used to record actual mediation sessions with clients. Although they suffer from certain limitations in terms of self-selectivity, inaudible recording, and observer effects, these taped and observed studies represent the most robust data available on mediator–client interactions. Observation has taken place in a diverse range of contexts, practice settings, and legal systems, and, in the USA, certain themes have emerged about the nature of work with clients: generally, the mediator is active in option generation, although remaining neutral regarding specific outcomes (Slaikeu et al. 1985a; Pearson & Thoennes 1988a, 1988b; Donohue 1991).

Although several researchers in the UK have observed or recorded the mediation process over the last 25 years (Davis 1988; Dingwall 1988; Ogus et al. 1989; Dingwall & Greatbatch 1991, 2000; Walker et al. 1994; Hayes 2004), much of this activity has been undertaken to help researchers understand the process under evaluation.

Dingwall and Greatbatch (2001), however, have undertaken in-depth conversation analysis at various times in the development of mediation, with a focus on mapping sequences of interaction, and have noted distinct changes in practice. They argue that mediation is now a more coherent client experience and that mediators have become much brisker and more focused in their work and distinctly more formal in style. Nevertheless, mediators work within structured parameters in respect of neutrality and impartiality. Dingwall and Greatbatch (2001) have consistently found that mediators hold strong values about what kinds of arrangements are in the best interests of children and that they seek to influence decision-making accordingly. In their view, client empowerment has given way to managed settlement-seeking, particularly as section 29 has tended to draw low-conflict cases into a formal pro-cess of mediation. Although the government had hoped that mediators would be able to detect marriages that could be saved, there is little evidence from Dingwall and Greatbatch's (2001) study that mediators look systematically for opportunities to promote reconciliation. Mediators have been as reluctant to assume a marriage-saving role as they have been willing to assume a child-saving agenda. Picking up the policy imperative to protect children from the detrimental impacts of divorce and to promote cooperative parenting has been unproblematic for mediators. Dingwall and Greatbatch (2000) have questioned whether mediators have the appropriate skills for dealing with the issue of reconciliation and have suggested that they avoid it wherever possible. Nevertheless, their research (2000, 2001) provides evidence of continuing wide variation in practice among mediators – what the researchers refer to as "a secret garden." They conclude that "there is clearly a problem in mediation in the variety of expertises that are brought to bear and the implications of this for the delivery of a consistent service" (Dingwall & Greatbatch 2000: 251). In their view, financial and client-focused mediations require skills of a completely different order from each other, perhaps supporting lawyers' concerns that mediators without legal training are not qualified to deal with the more technically complex issues surrounding money and property.

Hayes' (2004) observation of practice illustrated that, although there were strik-ing similarities in patterns of practice between lawyer mediators and social welfare mediators, practice setting and professional background did appear to be import-ant factors. Reflecting Dingwall and Greatbatch's (2001) observations, Hayes (2004) found that mediators with a social welfare background were much more comfortable dealing with children and parenting issues and seemingly less at ease addressing finance and property disputes. Even legally trained mediators within community-based settings were hesitant about financial issues. Legally trained mediators in private practice, by contrast, were confident in financial disputes but were less likely to explore parent–child relationships. These differences are clearly not a function of training, since mediators in the UK now have to achieve universal practice standards, but of the dominance of mediators' particular professional approaches. Certain skills become embedded in practice and their influence on the mediation process should not be ignored.

Hayes also found that community-based mediators took longer to complete medi-ation; were more likely to be involved in child-only cases and to use a co-mediation model when finances were involved; and worked more closely with other mediators and supervisors. Mediators from a social welfare background used active listening and counseling techniques with clients, including the "miracle question" from brief therapy and "reframing." Solicitor-mediators did not use these specific techniques during observations of their practice, but were more likely to use "questioning" and "reality testing." The observations were supported by interviews with the practitioners, who felt that their background and their other professional roles influenced the way in which they practice family mediation.

Hayes' (2004) explorations of practice setting found that practice diversity did not simply take place at the level of the individual practitioner, but also at the level of mediation setting. For example, most community-based mediators had little to do with the business side of practice unless they took on additional roles suchas manager, administrator, or supervisor. Mediators in private practice, by contrast, are used to running a business, accounting for the expenditure of public funding, and attracting new clients. Their businesslike approach has enabled them to embrace the new opportunities inherent in the government's agenda and to retain a gate-keeping role in the divorce process.

Relating Antecedent Conditions to the Mediation

Recent research in the UK into family mediation supports the relationship illustrated by the Herrman et al. model between the *antecedent conditions* and mediation process, and highlights the impact of institutional context (practice setting) on procedural factors (use of specific techniques). Although no one-to-one relationships have yet been developed, most studies have provided some evidence that private practitioners and community-based mediators practice in systematically different ways (Ogus et al. 1989; Dingwall & Greatbatch 1991, 2000; Myers & Wasoff 2000; Hayes 2002b, 2004).

The purpose of recent policies defining practice standards has been to create a more uniform process for disputants and to avoid what has been termed a "postcode lottery" in respect of the mediation experience. What researchers observe is a more standardized mediation procedure, but it remains the case that, although mediators have to demonstrate competence through a portfolio of cases, they "are examined on their knowledge of what they ought to be doing, rather than on their demonstration that they actually do it" (Dingwall & Greatbatch 2001: 381).

Dingwall & Greatbatch (2001) call for more attention to be paid to extending competence requirements to involve the submission of audio/videotapes of practice and greater periodic peer review. Whatling (2002) has argued for direct observation of practice by professional practice consultants since, in his view, this is the only way to uncover poor practice and bring about change. It remains unclear, however, what kinds of change might be made and whether these are likely to be a mere reflection of government policy agendas which fit with mediators' beliefs and values, or whether they will also encompass efforts to develop a more coherent theoretical and conceptual evidence base which is not politically motivated. The funding of mediation and the continuing development of standards are the most important practice issues currently facing mediators in the UK. Unless mediators revisit their own assumptions and beliefs about the purpose of mediation, however, we are likely to see an increasing fusion of mediation and legal services.

ASSUMPTIONS, VALUES, AND EXPEDIENCY

The model proposed in chapter 2 is grounded in several assumptions, the majority of which are implicit in current family mediation practice. Some of these assumptions, however, we would wish to challenge from the UK context. First, Deutsch's "ideal" (1991) – that we must understand the interplay of dispute resolution interactions and the broader socio-cultural context in order to understand conflict resolution – is in our view no longer merely an ideal. It is an essential requirement. Without this understanding, it is impossible to know whether, for example, the assumption that everyone prefers harmony to discord is valid.

Second, in the UK, referral to formal mediation does not necessarily signal that people are experiencing conflict characterized by a lack of cooperation. Some mediators, particularly those with a social welfare background, have argued that mediation is more akin to assisted decision-making than to dispute resolution, and that mediation can thereby assist most couples to resolve arrangements, irrespective of whether there is conflict. As it became possible to mediate all issues, so couples approaching mediation were not always "in dispute," but were seeking to resolve matters amicably and cooperatively – to receive skilled help in making decisions about how to manage and separate overlapping futures (Walker et al. 1994). Mediation became more like an alternative way of negotiating the ending of a marriage, using an impartial third party to assist negotiations rather than relying solely on partisan lawyers to negotiate at arm's length. Certainly, the Conservative government was persuaded of this position and hoped that many people would benefit from mediation. Section 29 appointments have almost certainly widened the intake net to include very low-conflict cases which would otherwise be dealt with by lawyers in a conciliatory manner. The verbalizing of "stories" and individual positions, another assumption underpinning the Herrman et al. model, is consistent with assisted decision-making, as there are always at least two versions of a marriage breakdown, however cooperative the parties remain.

Finally, it is axiomatic that people continuously attribute and redefine the meaning of actions, purposes, agreements, and identities. While there is no objective truth to be discovered with regard to past events, it does not follow that mediation cannot explore how past events are affecting the present and the future. The research indicates that a focus on the future and on achieving constructed, consensual agreements must take account of past realities since they influence present positions and determine acceptable futures. It is a fallacy to believe that people who are going through the dissolution of an intensely private, personal, and intimate relationship can be expected to ignore the reasons why the relationship is not sustainable. In research conducted in the 1980s (Ogus et al. 1989), the 1990s (Walker et al. 1994), and the new millennium (Walker 2001; Walker et al. 2004), people have consistently told researchers that they want: information about marriage, divorce, children, finances, and the divorce process; advice (legal and personal); access to counseling support; and help in resolving difficulties and disputes. Originally, settlement-seeking was only one of the goals of family mediation, but it is rapidly becoming the only goal as mediation is absorbed into the legal process. Research has shown that the people who were the most satisfied with mediation were those who had the opportunity to be heard and to tell their stories, and working through bitterness, hurt, and anger emerged as critical factors in enabling parties to cooperate as parents (Walker et al. 2004). If mediators are to uphold the government's policy agenda by focusing more and more on supporting parents, restructuring family relationships must be inextricably connected with this issue. This has long been recognized in other countries, such as Japan, which emphasizes the importance of the restoration of harmony, mutual apology, and pardon as necessary factors in mediation (Schimazu 1984; Wagatsuma & Rossett 1986).

Family mediators, as well as researchers in England and Wales, have noted a distinct shift in mediation practice and approach. The introduction of public funding has promoted national standard and competency assessments based on the more legal aims and objectives of dispute resolution, notably settlement-seeking. Since family lawyers now work to a defined protocol (Law Society 2002) which is highly conciliatory, and are experimenting with collaborative law, the fascination with encouraging men and women "to sit down and try to just talk" is no longer the exclusive province of mediators. Unless mediators do more than promoting settlements it is increasingly difficult to detect any "value-added." As Menkel-Meadow (1984) suggested, the negotiator's mindset is a critical variable. If it is driven by political expediency rather than acknowledged beliefs and values, the fundamental tenet of neutrality will be lost.

THE SEARCH FOR CLARITY

Following the demise of divorce reform in England and Wales, it became clear that we were not going to see the arrival of mediation "as the tidy insertion of a new 'third way,' fitted in comfortably alongside long-established roles." Rather, "Everything is in question: the identity of the mediator as autonomous professional, the lawyer as partisan, and the court as an instrument of third-party decision" (Roberts 2001: 273). Davis (2001: 374) argued that mediation has become a kind of hybrid – a settlement device within legal proceedings – in which mediators are required to devote themselves "to achieving success according to standards invented by lawyers." Paradoxically, mediators are awarded professional status as a result of certain skills which characterize the trade of mediation and adherence to a professional Code of Practice, yet, unlike lawyers and judges, they claim to exercise no statutory or legal authority. In this regard, Davis (2001) views mediation as an unfamiliar concept to most prospective users, who usually expect professionalism and authority to go together. Moreover, given the high level of enthusiasm among judges and lawyers for a more conciliatory approach, all that distinguishes them from mediators is that disputants perceive them as holding authority, a factor which some find comforting. By contrast, mediators appear not to hold any particular authority, a characteristic which some find frustrating (Walker et al. 2004). The distinct characteristic of authority may go some way toward explaining why the majority of divorcing couples seek help from lawyers and only a very few choose mediation.

Of course, mediators would argue that mediation does not merely replicate more traditional settlement-seeking approaches but offers much more to disputants: namely, a process which can improve the relationship between them by helping them to reduce conflict and to improve communication. Users of mediation in the Genn (1999) study understood mediation to be a process which helped to "sort out troubles." But if this role is being diminished in the quest for greater uniformity of practice and enhanced professionalism, it can be argued that the bureaucratization of mediation and its incorporation into the legal system have compromised its founding ethos of disputant empowerment and control, particularly as the political imperative has encouraged mediators to guide disputants toward preferred outcomes (Dingwall & Greatbatch 2000). Rather than offering an alternative dispute resolution process, mediators appear to offer a service which merely complements the legal process. Davis (2000: 271) argued that it is important to recognize and maintain the distinction between "mediation as a means of settling contested legal issues and mediation as an aid to negotiation which is independent of the legal process."

If mediation is expected to offer a replacement for lawyers and courts, it will fail. The focus on settlement-seeking, which is so powerful in legal culture, requires mediators to conform to a particular kind of legal-centric outcome measure in order to justify public funding. Furthermore, to be considered effective these mediated outcomes have to reflect government expectations that couples will behave in a civilized and reasonable manner. Research has indicated, however, that what people do in the immediate aftermath of separation is not always viewed as "reasonable" and that the relationship between the parties has often deteriorated to a point where constructive face-to-face negotiation is no longer a feasible option (Davis 2001; Walker 2001; Walker et al. 2004). This would appear to explain why most people think that mediation is a good idea, but decide that it is not for them. So they use lawyers to deal with the issues because mediation demands too much of them at a particularly stressful time.

Some interesting conundrums, therefore, emerge: as mediators are increasingly required to conform with a legal model of settlement-seeking, so lawyers "appear to think and behave disconcertingly like mediators for at least some of the time" (Davis 2001: 378). As mediation becomes increasingly integrated with legal provision it is increasingly regulated and narrows its remit. As lawyers adopt a conciliatory approach, so the non-lawyer mediators may lose their share of the mediation market. We can see this trend in both the USA and the UK. In 1983, 75 percent of US family mediators were mental health practitioners, who now account just 17 percent of mediators (Grebe 1999). In the UK, the private sector of lawyer mediators has similarly increased its mediation workload. Douglas and Murch (2002), in a study of family lawyers' responses to new policy and practice initiatives, suggest that the dilemma facing family lawyers lies in striking the correct balance between working as a lawyer and working as a family adviser. We might extend this to mediators, who have to strike a balance between offering a quasi-legal service and assisting couples to sort out problems, a role most mediators see as central. As one mediator claimed recently (Leigh 2004), clients often need to build trust and confidence, and often want to talk about wider issues such as the introduction of new partners or contact with grandparents, and talking can remove the blocks to reaching agreements. In Leigh's view, mediators "can offer time and space to look at these issues" (2004: 458). They can, providing the government is prepared to acknowledge this activity and allow public funding to cover more than focused settlement-seeking activities. Another mediator (Wilson 2002) has argued that linear thinking in terms of what mediation is and does is unhelpful. She believes that mediation "is not a tidy, logical process any more than the issues it deals with are simple, straightforward matters . . . Mediation is about uncertainty – indeed uncertainty is a fundamental component of the process" (Wilson 2002: 64). She goes on to assert: "Mediation is not a mechanical, replicable process, but a dynamic interaction with many intangibles and unknowns arising from unique sets of circumstances" (Wilson 2002: 67).

This uncertainty is very difficult for those who fund and quality-control mediation – they look for certainty in knowing precisely what mediation is. The model proposed in the handbook may assist here, since it recognizes mediation as a dynamic, interactive process to which various participants contribute. The ambiguity and uncertainty that practitioners such as Leigh and Wilson value can be accommodated within the model, as can many different mediator styles.

The next step is to use the model to help mediators deal with political agendas which expect them to promote particular kinds of post-divorce family living. In our view, the model would be more helpful if the institutional context which we have been describing and debating in this chapter were to be absorbed into the model. Herrman et al. have pointed out that it is unusual for research to encompass characteristics such as governance structures, policies, and sponsorship in analyses of mediation and outcomes. The changing face of family mediation in England and Wales has forced us to do so. Although we have described family mediation in the political context of England and Wales, we know that similar debates and pressures are prevalent in the USA. Mosten (2004) has pointed out that the trade-offs between regulations, creativity, accountability, regulation, and quality control have generated a vigorous dialog within the mediation community, and he poses the question: "What price has mediation (and the public) paid for the institutional acceptance that certification has provided?" (Mosten 2004: 295). He goes on to note the coercive pressure on mediators in the USA to settle cases and the concerns about whether lawyer culture will dominate mediation practice and subject it to compromise. We hope that the experience in England and Wales may sound a warning bell at this stage in the global development of mediation, which does indeed seem to have many masters. Having watched the political positioning in England and Wales, mediators in Scotland have rejected the offer of public funding for their services, preferring to remain independent of political masters.

Cretney (2003: 400) has argued persuasively that "family law reflects its historical development." We have attempted to demonstrate that family mediation also reflects its historical development, and is heavily influenced by political and moral positioning – what Smart (1997) referred to as modern-day social engineering and Cretney as paternalism. Dingwall and James (1988) argued over 15 years ago that family law exists in a constant tension between recognizing the family as a self-contained disputing arena and intervening to regulate the impact of disputes on non-participants.

Mediators have become caught up in this tension, which is essentially about the acceptable parameters of private-ordering, the legitimate role of the state in our everyday lives (Cretney 2003), and the extent to which mediation and support should be integrated with the family justice system or be valued as a social service with no direct link to the legal system. Any model which seeks to provide a contextual framework for mediation must be able to deal with these tensions.

NOTES

1   When discussing family mediation in England it is usual to refer to the United Kingdom as a whole. Nevertheless, legal jurisdictions vary. England and Wales share a family law jurisdiction while Scotland and Northern Ireland each has its own family law jurisdiction. Mediation practice across the UK is similar but there are important procedural, institutional, legal, and funding differences. The research conducted by the authors of this chapter refers primarily to England and Wales, and they have chosen to focus their discussion of family mediation on England and Wales.

2   The terms "custody" and "access" were replaced in England and Wales by the terms "residence" and "contact" following the implementation of the Children Act 1989. As a result, the terms "custody" and "access" are no longer used and neither legal nor physical custody is awarded to either or to both parents. There is a presumption that both parents should assume parental responsibility for their children. Residence describes the home in which a child lives most of the time. "Resident parent" is the term given to the parent with whom the child usually lives. Co-residence, the splitting of residence between two homes (as in joint physical custody in the USA), is unusual in England and Wales. The parent with whom the child lives is required to facilitate contact with the other (non-resident) parent. Contact is the right of the child, not the right of the non-resident parent. A parent can seek either a "residence order" or a "contact order" if arrangements cannot be agreed between the parents.

3   Mediation was originally known in the UK as "conciliation" – a term often confused with "reconciliation" by professionals, courts, and consumers.

4   See *Looking to the Future: Mediation and the Ground for Divorce: The Government Proposals*, Cm 2799 (1995) and the Family Law Bill (England & Wales) 1995.

5   The position of Lord Chancellor in England is akin to that of Minister of Justice in other jurisdictions. It is a hugely influential political position, and the Lord Chancellor, who sits in the Cabinet, is also Head of the Judiciary. The present government under Prime Minister Tony Blair is seeking to abolish the position as it is currently fashioned, but this requires primary legislation.

6   In this chapter, "N" denotes the total sample and "n" the sample included in the analysis.

REFERENCES

Civil Partnership Bill (HL) (2004). The Stationery Office, London.

Clulow, C. (1995) Marriage: a new millennium? In C. Clulow (ed.), *Women, Men and Marriage: Talks from the Tavistock Marital Studies Institute*. Sheldon Press, London, pp. 145–159.

Clulow, C. (2000) Supporting marriage in the theatre of divorce. In M. Thorpe & E. Clarke (eds.), *No Fault or Flaw: The Future of the Family Law Act 1996*. Jordan, Bristol, pp. 20–25.

Cretney, S. (2003) Private ordering and divorce: how far can we go? *Family Law* 33, 399–405.

Davis, G. (1988) *Partisans and Mediators*. Clarendon Press, Oxford.

Davis, G. (2000) Conclusion. In G. Davis et al. (2000a), *Monitoring Publicly Funded Mediation*. Report to Legal Services Commission. Legal Services Commission, London, pp. 269–274.

Davis, G. (2001) Reflections in the aftermath of the family mediation pilot. *Child and Family Law Quarterly* 13(4), 371–383.

Davis, G., Cretney, S. & Collins, J. (1994) *Simple Quarrels*. Clarendon Press, Oxford.

Davis, G., Bevan, G., Clisby, S., Cumming, Z., Dingwall, R., Fenn, P., Finch, S., Fitzgerald, R., Goldie, S., Greatbatch, D., James, A. & Pearce, J. (2000a) *Monitoring Publicly Funded Mediation*. Report to Legal Services Commission. Legal Services Commission, London.

Davis, G., Pearce, J. & Goldie, S. (2000b) An analysis of intake. In G. Davis et al. (2000a), *Monitoring Publicly Funded Mediation*. Report to Legal Services Commission. Legal Services Commission, London, pp. 201–228.

Deutsch, M. (1991) Subjective features of conflict resolution: psychological, social and cultural influences. In R. Vayrynen (ed.), *New Directions in Conflict Theory: Conflict Resolution and Conflict Transformation*. Sage, London, pp. 26–56.

Dewar, J. (1998) The normal chaos of family law. *Modern Law Review* 61(4), 467–485.

Dingwall, R. (1988) Empowerment or enforcement? Some questions about power and control in divorce mediation. In R. D. J. M. Eekelaar (ed.), *Divorce, Mediation, and the Legal Process*. Clarendon Press, Oxford, pp. 150–167.

Dingwall, R. & Greatbatch, D. (1991) Behind closed doors: a preliminary report on mediator/client interaction in England. *Family and Conciliation Courts Review* 29, 291–303.

Dingwall, R. & Greatbatch, D. (1993) Who is in charge? Rhetoric and evidence in the study of family mediation. *Journal of Social Welfare and Family Law*, 367–385.

Dingwall, R. & Greatbatch, D. (2000) The mediation process. In G. Davis et al. (2000a), *Monitoring Publicly Funded Mediation*. Report to Legal Services Commission. Legal Services Commission, London, pp. 229–255.

Dingwall, R. & Greatbatch, D. (2001) Family mediators: what are they doing? *Family Law* 31, 378–382.

Dingwall, R. & James, A. (1988) Family law and the psycho-social professions: welfare officers in the English county court. *Law in Context* 6(1), 61–73.

Donohue, W. (1991) *Communication, Marital Dispute and Divorce Mediation*. Erlbaum, Hillsdale.

Douglas, G. & Murch, M. (2002) Taking account of children's needs in divorce: a study of family solicitors' responses to new policy and practice initiatives. *Child and Family Law Quarterly* 14(1), 57–77.

Durrell, J. (1990) The proclamation "Justice is . . . just us." In J. M. Tannis (ed.), *A Tribute to Conflict Resolution Day of Ottowa-Carleton*, Captus Press, North York, Ont.

Eekelaar, J. (1999) Family law: keeping us "on message." *Child and Family Law Quarterly* 11(4), 387–396.

Finer, Sir M. (1974) *Report to the Committee on One-Parent Families*. Cmnd 5629. HMSO, London.

Genn, H. (1999) *Paths to Justice: What People Do and Think about Going to Law*. Hart, Oxford.

Giddens, A. (1992) *The Transformation of Intimacy: Sexuality, Love and Eroticism in Modern Societies*. Polity, Cambridge.

Gorman, T. (MP, Billericay) (1996) *Official Report (Standing Committee E)*. 14 May. London.

Grebe, S. (1999) Factors predictive of mediator style. Unpublished doctoral dissertation, Catholic University of America, Washington.

Hayes, S. (2002a) Family mediators in the UK: a survey of practice. *Family Law* 32, 760–764.

Hayes, S. (2002b) What do family mediators do? A look at practices and models. *Context: The Magazine of Family Therapy and Systemic Practice* 63, 39–41.

Hayes, S. (2005) Family mediation in the twenty-first century: policy and practice in England and Wales. Unpublished doctoral thesis, University of Newcastle upon Tyne.

Kiernan, K. (2004) Family futures. International Conference on the Family, celebrating the International Year of the Family, London.

Kruk, E. (1998) Practice issues, strategies, and models: the current state of the art of family mediation. *Family and Conciliation Courts Review* 34(2), 195–215.

Law Commission (1988) *Facing the Future: Discussion Paper on the Ground for Divorce* 170. Law Commission, London.

Law Commission (1990) *The Ground for Divorce*. 192. Law Commission, London.

Law Society (2002) *Family Law Protocol*. The Law Society, London.

Leigh, R. (2004) Mediation for all. *Family Law* 34, 458.

Llwyd, E. (MP, Meirionnydd Nant Conwy) (1996) *Official Report (Standing Committee E)*. 14 May. London.

Lord Bishop of Worcester (1995) *Official Report (H.L.)*. 30 November 1995 at col. 715. London.

Lord Chancellor's Department (1993) *Looking Forward to the Future: Mediation and the Ground for Divorce*. Cm 2424. London.

Lord Chancellor's Department (1995) *Mediation and the Ground for Divorce: The Government's Proposals*. Cm 2799. London.

Lord Moran (1995) *Official Report (H.L.)*. 30 November 1995 at col. 763. London.

Maclean, M., Eekelaar, J. & Beinhart, S. (2001) *Family Lawyers: The Divorce Work of Solicitors*. Hart, Oxford.

Menkel-Meadow, C. (1984) Toward another view of legal negotiation: the structure of problem-solving. *UCLA Law Review* 21, 754–842.

Mosten, F. S. (2004) Institutionalization of mediation. *Family Court Review* 42(2), 292–303.

Myers, F. & Wasoff, F. (2000) *Meeting in the Middle: A Study of Solicitors' and Mediators' Divorce Practice*. Scottish Executive Central Research Unit, Edinburgh.

Ogus, A. I., Walker, J. & Jones-Lee, M. (1989) *Report on the Costs and Effectiveness of Conciliation in England and Wales*. Lord Chancellor's Department, London.

Parkinson, L. (1986) *Conciliation in Separation and Divorce: Finding Common Ground*. Croom Helm, London.

Pearson, J. & Thoennes, N. (1988a) Divorce mediation: an American picture. In R. Dingwall & J. Eekelaar (eds.), *Divorce Mediation and the Legal Process*. Clarendon, Oxford, pp. 71–91.

Pearson, J. & Thoennes, N. (1988b) Divorce mediation research results. In J. Folberg & A. Milne (eds.), *Divorce Mediation: Theory and Practice*. Guilford Press, New York, pp. 429–452.

Popenoe, D. (1993) American family decline 1960–1990: a review and appraisal. *Journal of Marriage and the Family* 55, 527–555.

Reece, H. (2003) *Divorcing Responsibly*. Hart, Oxford.

Roberts, S. (2001) Family mediation after the Act. *Child and Family Law Quarterly* 3(3), 265–273.

Sandy, S. V., Boardman, S. K. & Deutsch, M. (2000) Personality and conflict. In M. Deutsch & P. T. Coleman (eds.), *The Handbook of Conflict Research: Theory and Practice.* Jossey-Bass/Wiley, San Francisco, pp. 289–315.

Schimazu, I. (1984) Procedural aspects of marriage dissolution in Japan. In J. Eekelaar & S. N. Katz (eds.), *The Resolution of Family Conflict: Comparative Legal Perspectives.* Butterworth, Toronto, pp. 116–123.

Sclater, S. D. (1999) *Divorce: A Psychosocial Study.* Ashgate, Aldershot.

Sclater, S. D. & Piper, C. (2000) Remoralizing the family? Family policy, family law and youth justice. *Child and Family Law Quarterly* 135(12), 135–151.

Simon, W. (1978) The ideology of advocacy: procedural justice and professional ethics. *Wisconsin Law Review* 29, 34–39.

Slaikeu, K. A., Culler, R., Pearson, J. & Thoennes, N. (1985a) Process and outcome in divorce mediation. *Mediation Quarterly* 10, 55–74.

Slaikeu, K., Pearson, J., Luckett, J. & Myers, F. (1985b) Mediation process analysis: a descriptive coding system. *Mediation Quarterly* 10, 25–53.

Smart, C. (1997) Wishful thinking and harmful tinkering? *Sociological Reflections on Family Policy* 26, 301–321.

Stark, C. (2001) Choosing a route through the divorce process. In J. Walker (ed.) *Information Meetings and Associated Provisions within the Family Law Act 1996: Final Evaluation Report.* Lord Chancellor's Department, London, pp. 475–491.

Stark, C. & Birmingham, C. (2001) The role of lawyers in divorce. In J. Walker (ed.), *Information Meetings and Associated Provisions within the Family Law Act 1996: Final Evaluation Report.* Lord Chancellor's Department, London, pp. 447–475.

Wagatsuma, H. & Rossett, A. (1986) The implications of apology: law and culture in Japan and the United States. *Law and Society Review* 20, 461–498.

Walker, J. (1991) Family mediation in England: strategies for gaining acceptance. *Mediation Quarterly* 8(4), 253–265.

Walker, J. (1995) *The Cost of Communication Breakdown.* BT Forum, London.

Walker, J. (1997) Family mediation. In J. Macfarlane (ed.), *Rethinking Disputes: The Mediation Alternative.* Cavendish, London, pp. 53–87.

Walker, J. (2000) Whither the Family Law Act. Part II. In M. Thorpe & E. Clarke (eds.), *No Fault or Flaw: The Future of the Family Law Act 1996.* Jordan, Bristol, pp. 3–10.

Walker, J. (ed.) (2001) *Information Meetings and Associated Provisions within the Family Law Act 1996: Final Evaluation Report.* Lord Chancellor's Department, London.

Walker, J. & McCarthy, P. (2001) Looking to the future. In J. Walker (ed.), *Information Meetings and Associated Provisions within the Family Law Act 1996: Final Evaluation Report.* Lord Chancellor's Department, London, pp. 835–862.

Walker, J., McCarthy, P. & Timms, N. (1994) *Mediation: The Making and Remaking of Co-operative Relationships.* Relate Centre for Family Studies, Newcastle upon Tyne.

Walker, J., McCarthy, P., Stark, C. & Laing, K. (2004) *Picking Up the Pieces: Marriage and Divorce Two Years After Information Provision.* Lord Chancellor's Department, London.

Whatling, T. (2002) The direct observation of mediation. *Family Law* 32, 623–627.

Wilson, B. (2002) The triumph of uncertainty, or "measuring mediation." *Family Law* 32, 64–67.

Woolf, Lord Justice (1996) *Access to Justice.* Lord Chancellor's Department, London.

Chapter 5

The Role of Antecedent and Procedural Characteristics in Mediation: A Review of the Research

Roselle L. Wissler

Introduction

Mediation program designers are faced with a number of decisions in their efforts to structure effective mediation programs. What types of disputes and disputants should be eligible for or referred to mediation?[1] What characteristics should the mediators possess? What approach should the mediators use during mediation? What type of mediation process should the program provide for disputants? What dispute and disputant characteristics should be matched with what mediator characteristics or approach? In brief, phrased in terms of the model presented in chapter 2: what dispute, disputant, and mediator antecedent characteristics[2] (T_0) and mediation process characteristics (T_m) contribute to favorable short-term (T_1) and long-term (T_2) mediation outcomes?

This chapter reviews the available empirical research addressing these key questions in the context of mediation programs that operate within the courts or in their shadow. To explore whether the same or different factors contribute to effective mediation in different mediation settings, I present research findings for several settings: domestic relations, community, small claims, general jurisdiction civil, and appellate civil mediation. By identifying which research findings have been fairly consistent, which present a mixed picture, and which questions remain unanswered, I hope to provide some answers for program designers as well as to identify issues for future research.

FOR WHICH DISPUTES IS MEDIATION MORE EFFECTIVE?

Interpersonal Dynamics and Conflict Characteristics

The disputants' relationship – both its nature and its contentiousness – had a different impact on mediation outcomes in different mediation settings. The nature of the disputants' relationship had no effect on settlement in small claims mediation, but did in community mediation. In small claims mediation, the likelihood of settlement was not related to whether the disputants had a past or continuing relationship or to the type of the relationship (e.g. personal or business) (McEwen & Maiman 1981; Vidmar 1984; Roehl, Hersch & Llaneras 1992; Wissler 1995). Small claims disputants involved in a continuing relationship, however, were somewhat more satisfied with their overall mediation experience than were disputants with no continuing relationship (McEwen & Maiman 1981). In community mediation, disputes involving a continuing relationship were more likely to settle in one study (Whiting 1994). In another study, disputes involving family members, neighbors, or friends were somewhat more likely to settle than those involving a business relationship (Cook, Roehl & Sheppard 1980). The nature of the disputants' relationship did not affect disputants' compliance with the mediated agreement (Cook et al. 1980; Whiting 1994) or their satisfaction with the mediator, the overall experience, or the agreement (Cook et al. 1980).

Whether the contentiousness of the disputants' relationship affected the mediation process and its outcomes also varied across mediation settings. Contentiousness played a larger role in those settings in which a greater proportion of disputes involved intimate and ongoing relationships.[3] In general civil mediation (Macfarlane 1995; Brett, Barsness & Goldberg 1996; Wissler 2002) and small claims mediation (Vidmar 1984; Wissler 1995), settlement was not related to the contentiousness of the disputants' relationship. In community mediation, the findings were mixed. In one study, settlement was less likely when the dispute involved escalation and severe prior incidents (Pruitt 1995). Disputes involving escalation and severe incidents *prior* to mediation also involved a higher degree of hostility, more competitive bargaining tactics, and less joint problem-solving *during* mediation (Pruitt 1995). These actions in turn were related to a lower rate of settlement and less disputant satisfaction with the agreement (Pruitt 1995). In another community mediation study, however, settlement was more likely when disputants had a history of repeated disputes, especially those associated with serious underlying problems. However, compliance was lower in those disputes (Felstiner & Williams 1980).

In domestic relations disputes, the contentiousness of the disputants' relationship had a large impact on the mediation process and its outcomes. Disputes were less likely to settle if there was a greater degree of spousal conflict, tension, acrimony, or anger (Kressel, Jaffee, Tuchman, Watson & Deutsch 1980; Thoennes, Pearson & Bell 1991; Irving & Benjamin 1992; Wissler 1999;[4] Bickerdike & Littlefield 2000; but see Kelly, Gigy & Hausman 1988). Higher levels of anger *prior* to mediation were associated with lower overall levels of problem-solving, greater disparity between spouses in problem-solving behavior, and more contentious behavior *during* mediation, which in turn were related to a lower rate of settlement (Bickerdike & Littlefield 2000). In addition, settlement was less likely if the disputants reported more problems cooperating, communicating, or co-parenting prior to mediation (Irving & Benjamin 1992; Thoennes & Pearson 1985; but see Kelly et al. 1988). The relationship between disputant reports of domestic violence and settlement or disputants' assessments of mediation were mixed (Thoennes & Pearson 1985; Chandler 1990; Ellis & Stuckless 1992; Wissler 1999). Compliance with the mediated agreement was less likely when the dispute involved pre-separation abuse and more serious disagreements (Ellis & Stuckless 1996).

Across mediation settings, settlement was also related to indicators of conflict intensity in addition to interpersonal dynamics. Settlement was less likely if the disputants previously had been to court or mediation in this dispute (Irving & Benjamin 1992); if the disagreement or disparity in the parties' positions was greater (Thoennes & Pearson 1985; Brett et al. 1996; Wissler 2002; but see Kelly et al. 1988); if liability was strongly contested or denied (Vidmar 1984; Roehl et al. 1992; Hermann, LaFree, Rack & West 1993; Wissler 2002; but see Wissler 1995); or if this dispute was linked to others (Brett et al. 1996). The size of the monetary claim by itself, however, was not related to settlement in small claims or general civil mediation (Woodward 1990; Roehl et al. 1992; Macfarlane 1995).

Research findings portray a mixed picture of the relationship between conflict complexity and mediation outcomes. The number of disputed issues was not related to settlement in some domestic relations studies (Kelly et al. 1988; Wissler 1999), but others found that disputes involving fewer issues or problems were more likely to settle (Thoennes et al. 1991; Irving & Benjamin 1992; Wissler 1999). In contrast, a community mediation study found that disputes involving multiple issues were more likely to settle and to report compliance than those involving a single issue (Whiting 1994). The number of named parties was not related to settlement in one civil appellate mediation study (Note 1979), but another study found that settlement was more likely in cases with fewer named parties (Hann & Baar 2001). The complexity of the issues in dispute was not related to settlement in two general civil mediation studies (Woodward 1990; Schildt, Alfini & Johnson 1994), but another study found that less complex cases were more likely to settle (Wissler 2002). The involvement of extended family or new partners in domestic relations disputes had a mixed impact on settlement (Irving & Benjamin 1992; Wissler 1999) and was not related to compliance (Meierding 1993). Years of marriage, a potential indicator of complexity in domestic relations disputes (Beck & Sales 2001),[5] was not related to settlement in some studies (Kelly et al. 1988; Wissler 1999), but others found that settlement was more likely in disputes involving shorter marriages (Irving & Benjamin 1992; Wissler 1999). Settlement was not related to the number of minor children (Wissler 1999).

Legal Characteristics

Across the different mediation settings, for the most part there was no relationship between general case types and mediation outcomes. In two studies of small claims mediation, the likelihood of settlement did not vary by case type (Roehl et al. 1992; Wissler 1995). Another small claims study found differences, however, with settlement most likely in cases involving unpaid bills and private sales and least likely in traffic accident cases (McEwen & Maiman 1981). In general civil mediation, most studies found no differences in settlement rates among case types (e.g. personal injury automobile, other torts, contracts) (Schultz 1990; McEwen 1992a; Macfarlane 1995; Kakalik et al. 1996; Wissler 2002). Two studies, however, found differences in settlement rates by case type: personal injury cases appeared to have a higher rate of settlement than contract cases in one study (Schildt et al. 1994), but a lower rate in another study (Macfarlane 2003). Other civil mediation studies suggested that differences in the rate of settlement might be found by looking at sub-types of cases within these broader case types (Schultz 1990; Hann & Baar 2001). The nature of the settlement varied by case type: non-monetary terms were included in a majority of settlements in contract cases, but seldom in personal injury (primarily car accident) cases (Wissler 2002). Participants' assessments of the process (Schildt et al. 1994) and the outcome (Schultz 1990) in general civil mediation did not vary by case type.

In civil appellate mediation, most studies found no substantial differences in the likelihood of settlement based on the subject matter of the case (Note 1979; Eaglin 1990; FitzGibbon 1993; Hanson & Becker 2002). But one study found that family law and probate cases were more likely to settle than contract and personal injury cases, which in turn were more likely to settle than employment and insurance cases (Task Force 2001). In domestic relations mediation, findings were mixed as to whether settlement rates varied depending on whether the case involved the final divorce or a motion to amend a prior divorce decree (Burrell, Narus, Bogdanoff & Allen 1994; Wissler 1999). In one study, disputes involving custody issues were more likely to settle than were disputes involving child support or visitation issues (Camplair & Stolberg 1990). The likelihood of settlement, however, depended not only on the type of issue but also on whether both parties agreed that issue was the most important one (Camplair & Stolberg 1990).

What Is the Impact of Disputant Characteristics and Attitudes?

Because disputant demographic characteristics are unlikely to be used as criteria for case selection in court-connected mediation programs, the impact of disputants' demographic and other personal characteristics on mediation outcomes will be only briefly summarized here. For the most part, research in different mediation settings found no consistent relationships between disputant characteristics (including gender, education, income, role as complainant or respondent, and status as an individual disputant or business representative) and settlement or disputants' assessments of mediation (Vidmar 1984; Kelly et al. 1988; Pearson & Thoennes 1988; Thoennes et al. 1991; Kelly & Duryee 1992; Hermann et al. 1993; Meierding 1993; Emery 1994; Whiting 1994; Pruitt 1995; LaFree & Rack 1996; Clarke & Gordon

1997; Maiman 1997; Wissler 1995, 1999, 2002).[6] The one exception, however, was that indicators of the defendant's ability to pay were related to compliance (McEwen & Maiman 1984; Roehl et al. 1992; Wissler 1995; Beck & Sales 2001). Disputant demographic characteristics might be useful in matching disputants to mediators, and the limited research findings regarding the interaction of disputant and mediator characteristics are discussed in subsequent sections.

Disputants' expectations about and preparation for mediation played an unclear role in mediation outcomes. Disputants who misunderstood the goal of domestic relations mediation and whose own goals differed from those of mediation were upset and annoyed (Pearson & Thoennes 1988). Small claims disputants were less likely to settle if they had competitive goals (e.g. to show the other person they couldn't be pushed around or to teach the other person a lesson) that were at odds with the goals of mediation (Wissler 1995). In several mediation settings, prior mediation experience was not related to settlement (Roehl et al. 1992; Maiman 1997; Wissler 2002), and its relationship with disputants' assessments of mediation was mixed (Maiman 1997; Wissler 2002). Disputants in general civil mediation who received more preparation for mediation by their attorneys were more likely to settle and to feel the process was fair than were disputants who had less preparation (Wissler 2002). In contrast, some efforts disputants made to prepare for domestic relations mediation decreased the likelihood of settlement (talking with court personnel or gathering more information about mediation), while others were not related to settlement (talking with one's attorney about mediation or reading the court's brochure) (Wissler 1999).

Not surprisingly, disputants' motivations concerning settlement affected the mediation process and the likelihood of settlement. In domestic relations mediation, settlement was less likely if the couple had not separated, had not filed for divorce, or was interested in reconciliation (Kelly et al. 1988). In some studies, settlement was less likely if one side was ambivalent about divorce (Kressel et al. 1980; Bickerdike & Littlefield 2000), but the non-mutual acceptance of divorce was not related to settlement in other studies (Thoennes & Pearson 1985; Kelly et al. 1988). Greater disparity in attachment between the disputants was related to greater disparity in problem-solving behavior during mediation, which in turn was related to a lower rate of settlement (Bickerdike & Littlefield 2000). In general civil mediation, cases were less likely to settle if a disputant was looking for a "jackpot" or if settlement was not in a disputant's financial interest (Brett et al. 1996).

WHAT MEDIATOR CHARACTERISTICS CONTRIBUTE TO EFFECTIVENESS?

Across mediation settings, most studies found that mediators who had mediated more cases or who had served as a mediator for more years had a higher rate of settlement than did mediators with less experience (Pearson & Thoennes 1985, 1988; Hann & Baar 2001; Wissler 2002; but see Wissler 1999). Mediation experience, however, was not related to disputants' assessments of the fairness of the mediation process (Wissler 1999, 2002). The amount of mediation training was not related to settlement (Wissler 1999, 2002), and its relationship to disputants' assessments of the fairness of the mediation process was mixed (Wissler 1999, 2002). No particular profession or educational degree was consistently associated with a higher settlement rate or greater disputant satisfaction (Roehl et al. 1992; Wissler 1999). In general civil mediation, the mediator's familiarity with the substantive issues in the case was not related to the likelihood of settlement or to disputants' assessments of the fairness of the mediation process (Wissler 2002).

More direct assessments of mediators' skills, specifically attorneys' ratings of mediator skillfulness based on their experience in civil appellate mediation sessions, were strongly related to whether the case settled and to whether attorneys felt the issues were clarified (Wissler & Rack 2004).[7] The seven dimensions on which mediators' skillfulness[8] was rated were: reducing tensions or animosities; helping participants objectively evaluate their arguments and case settlement value; identifying disputants' underlying interests and concerns; uncovering flexibility or willingness to compromise; generating new ideas and options for settlement; overcoming obstacles and impasses; and guiding the negotiation process. Although these ratings, taken together as a group, were related to both settlement and issue clarification to a similar degree, different individual skills made different relative contributions to these two outcomes. For instance, the mediators' skillfulness at uncovering flexibility or willingness to compromise and at overcoming obstacles were the two skills most strongly related to settlement, whereas the mediators' skillfulness at generating new ideas and options and at helping the participants evaluate the case were the two skills most strongly related to issue clarification (Wissler & Rack 2004).

The mediator's gender was not related to settlement and had no consistent effect on disputants' assessments of the process or the outcome in domestic relations mediation (Wissler 1999). In a small claims mediation program that used a co-mediator model, two female co-mediators had the highest rate of settlement and two male co-mediators had the lowest (Hermann et al. 1993). Disputants' satisfaction ratings, however, were highest with mixed-gender co-mediators (Hermann, 1993). The mediators' and the disputants' gender and ethnicity interacted to affect disputant satisfaction as well as the nature and dollar amount of the agreement (Hermann et al. 1993; LaFree & Rack 1996). For example, female claimants were less satisfied with the process when there were two female co-mediators, but minority claimants were more satisfied when there were two minority co-mediators (Hermann et al. 1993). It is not clear whether these gender and ethnicity effects would generalize to programs using a single-mediator model.

What Is the Impact of What Happens During Mediation?

Mediator Actions

Mediator actions during mediation cut across all the constructs under the mediation process component (T_m) of the model presented in chapter 2. Different studies have examined the question of mediator approach[9] at different levels, ranging from specific actions to more general styles. One finding that emerged in most mediation settings, discussed in detail below, was that settlement was more likely when the mediator was active rather than passive. The types of actions mediators took and their effectiveness, however, varied across mediation settings. A second finding observed in most mediation settings was that disputants who felt pressured to settle by the mediator were less likely to view the process as fair (Wissler 2004a).

In general civil mediation, settlement was more likely when mediators disclosed their views about the strengths and weaknesses of the case, possible solutions, the case settlement value, or the likely court outcome (Woodward 1990; McEwen 1992b; Cohn 1996; Wissler 2002; but see Brett et al. 1996). Although general civil disputants were more likely to feel the process was fair when mediators evaluated the case merits, they were less likely to think it was fair when mediators recommended a particular settlement (Wissler 2002). In one study of small claims mediation, settlement was more likely when mediators asked more questions and developed terms for payment, but was not related to other actions, such as suggesting specific solutions or discussing likely court judgments (Roehl et al. 1992). Another small claims study found, however, that settlement was not more likely when disputants rated the mediator as more active than passive (Wissler 1995). In community mediation, settlement was more likely, and disputants were more satisfied with the outcome, when mediators proposed agendas, raised new issues and solutions, and asked disputants to develop new ideas and react to them (Pruitt, McGillicuddy, Welton & Fry 1989; Pruitt 1995).

In domestic relations mediation, settlement was more likely when mediators discussed many options and possible solutions, structured the mediation process, focused on interests without ignoring relationship issues, and intervened during periods of greater conflict (Slaikeu, Culler, Pearson & Thoennes 1985; Donohue 1989; Pearson & Thoennes 1989; Donohue, Drake & Roberto 1994). An active and structured problem-solving style that tried to address the sources of impasse was associated with a higher rate of settlement, greater disputant satisfaction, more positive effects on the disputants' relationship, and a smaller percentage of cases engaging in subsequent court action (Kressel et al. 1994). Disputants were more likely to feel the mediation process was fair and that they had a better understanding of the other side's views when mediators encouraged them to express their feelings or summarized what they said (Wissler 1999). These same actions, however, were not related to settlement (Wissler 1999). When disputants reported domestic violence, settlement was less likely if mediators separated the disputants than if they did not separate the disputants (Wissler 1999). Some limited evidence suggests that certain mediator actions or styles were more effective with some types of cases than others (Kressel et al. 1980, 1994; Bickerdike & Littlefield 2000). For instance, a more narrow settlement-oriented approach was effective in settling disputes that involved low levels of conflict, little ambivalence, and good communication (Kressel et al. 1980, 1994). But the same approach was not effective in cases involving more intense conflicts (Kressel et al. 1980, 1994).

Disputant and Attorney Actions

Disputant actions during mediation also appear at various places under the mediation process component (T_m) of the model proposed in chapter 2. Several consistent findings emerged across mediation settings. First, settlement was more likely when disputants participated more actively during mediation (Pearson & Thoennes 1989; McEwen 1992b; Wissler 1999, 2002). Second, settlement was more likely when disputants engaged in more cooperative or joint problem-solving behavior and less contentious or competitive behavior, made more empathetic statements and fewer attributions of behavior, and showed less hostility (Slaikeu et al. 1985; Pearson & Thoennes 1989; Pruitt et al. 1989; Donohue et al. 1994; Pruitt 1995; Bickerdike & Littlefield 2000; but see Thoennes & Pearson 1985; Wissler 1995). Many of these same factors, as well as less use of verbal aggression and antisocial strategies during mediation, were associated with greater disputant satisfaction with and perceived fairness of the process and outcome (Pruitt et al. 1989; Pruitt 1995; Rudd 1996; Wissler 2004a). Greater joint problem-solving during mediation also was associated with improved long-term relations between the disputants (Pruitt 1995).

Only a few studies examined the impact of attorneys' presence and actions during mediation.[10] In small claims mediation, attorneys' presence was not related to settlement (Vidmar 1984; Roehl et al. 1992) or to disputants' long-term satisfaction (Hermann et al. 1993). In domestic relations mediation, disputes were more likely to reach a full settlement if only one or neither of the disputants had a lawyer present during mediation (Wissler 1999). When both disputants' attorneys were present, a partial settlement was more likely (Wissler 1999). When opposing counsel were more cooperative during general civil mediation, disputes were more likely to settle, and disputants were more likely to feel the mediation process was fair (Wissler 2002).

The Mediation Procedure and Environment

The relationship between settlement and aspects of the mediation procedure and environment, as assessed by disputants, varied across the different mediation settings. In small claims mediation, disputants who settled did not differ from those who did not settle in their perceptions that the mediator was neutral, trustworthy, warm, or competent; treated the disputants with respect and dignity; understood the issues; and was interested in their dispute (Roehl et al. 1992; Wissler 1995). Similarly, small claims disputants who settled did not differ from those who did not settle in their perceptions that the mediation session was thorough and not hurried, gave them an opportunity to tell their story, explored issues other than the money owed, was understandable, and permitted them to have control over the process and the outcome (Roehl et al. 1992; Wissler 1995).

In general civil mediation, in contrast, disputants who settled were more likely than those who did not settle to feel that they had a chance to tell their side of the dispute and had input into the outcome and that the mediator was neutral and understood their views (Wissler 2002). They did not differ, however, in whether they felt the mediator treated them with respect (Wissler 2002). In domestic relations mediation, disputants who settled were more likely than those who did not settle to feel that they had a chance to express their views, they were treated with respect, their dispute was handled seriously, and the mediator was neutral (Wissler 1999) and facilitated communication (Thoennes & Pearson 1985). In addition, domestic relations disputants who settled were more likely than those who did not settle to feel that mediation had helped them to better understand their own, their spouse's, and their children's needs, concerns, and feelings (Thoennes & Pearson 1985; Wissler 1999).[11]

In contrast to settlement, disputants' perception of the fairness of the mediation process[12] showed a consistent pattern of relationships with aspects of the mediation procedure across mediation settings. In small claims, domestic relations, and general civil mediation, disputants were more likely to say the mediation process was fair if they felt they had a chance to tell their side of the dispute; they had input into the outcome; and the mediator understood their views, was neutral, and treated them with respect (Wissler 2004a).

WHAT ARE THE RELATIONSHIPS AMONG OUTCOMES?

With regard to the relationship between settlement and other short-term (T_1) outcomes, a consistent finding that emerged across mediation settings was that disputants who settled in mediation were more satisfied with the process, outcome, and overall mediation experience than were disputants who did not settle (Pearson & Thoennes 1982; Kelly et al. 1988; Kelly & Gigy 1989; Kelly & Duryee 1992; Macfarlane 1995; Wissler 1995, 1999, 2002; but see Schildt et al. 1994). Settlement was not related to perceptions of process fairness in small claims mediation (Roehl et al. 1992; Wissler 1995; Maiman 1997), but was in domestic relations (Wissler 1999) and general civil mediation (Kobbervig 1991; Wissler 2002; but see Maiman 1997). Domestic relations disputants who settled, compared to those who did not settle, were more likely to report cooperation and improved relationships and were less likely to return to court after mediation (Pearson & Thoennes 1988).

With regard to relationships between short-term (T_1) and long-term (T_2) outcomes, one study found no relationship between disputants' satisfaction right after mediation and several months later (Pruitt 1995). Compliance generally was not related to disputants' perceptions of the outcome (McEwen & Maiman 1981; Vidmar 1985; Hermann et al. 1993; Pruitt 1995; Wissler 1995; but see McEwen & Maiman 1984). In some studies, however, compliance was related to disputants' perceptions of the process (Pruitt 1995; Ellis & Stuckless 1996; but see Wissler 1995). Across several mediation settings, compliance was related to several aspects of the nature of the agreement: whether it involved monetary payment or behavior change, the amount of money owed, the degree of specificity of the behavior change, and whether it involved a single immediate action or continuing actions (Felstiner & Williams 1980; McEwen & Maiman 1984; Roehl et al. 1992; Wissler 1995; Ellis & Stuckless 1996).[13] Finally, compliance was greater when the long-term relationship between disputants was better (Pruitt 1995).

CONCLUSION: ISSUES FOR FUTURE RESEARCH

Ideally, empirical research should be able to provide program designers with answers to questions concerning which dispute, disputant, and mediator antecedent characteristics (T_0) and mediation process characteristics (T_m) contribute to favorable short-term (T_1) and long-term (T_2) mediation outcomes. To date, however, researchers have devoted much less attention to these "second-order" questions than to the examination of mediation's overall effectiveness (Clement & Schwebel 1993; Benjamin & Irving 1995; Shack 2003; Lande 2004). Thus, few studies have examined the relationships among these components, and they have concentrated on a subset of the constructs in the model presented in chapter 2.

Notwithstanding the limited amount of research, several patterns were observed relatively consistently across multiple studies and mediation settings. Settlement in mediation was more likely if the dispute was less intense, if the disputants were motivated to settle, if the mediator had more mediation experience and was active during mediation, and if the disputants actively participated in a cooperative manner during mediation. Settlement generally was not related to legal case categories or to the mediator's amount of training or educational background. Disputants were more likely to view the mediation process as fair if the disputants were more cooperative and less hostile during mediation. Disputants were more satisfied with mediation if they settled, and compliance was related to disputants' ability to pay and to the nature of the agreement.

Some constructs were related to mediation outcomes in one mediation setting but not in other settings. Most notably, interpersonal dynamics played a large role in mediation outcomes in domestic relations disputes but virtually no role in general civil and small claims disputes. And features of the mediation process were related to settlement in domestic relations and general civil mediation but not in small claims mediation. Thus, researchers and program designers should not assume that the same construct will have the same effect, or can be measured in the same way, in different mediation settings. Accordingly, rather than a single model of effective mediation, there are likely to be different models of effective mediation for different mediation settings, each containing a somewhat different set of constructs and variables.

For some constructs, such as dispute complexity and disputants' expectations about and preparation for mediation, some studies did not find statistically significant relationships with outcomes while other studies in the same mediation setting did. There are several potential reasons for these mixed findings.

First, many studies, especially those of domestic relations mediation, involved a small number of disputes, making it more difficult to detect small relationships than in studies that included more disputes (Keppel 1973). To have confidence that a statistically non-significant relationship indicates no real underlying relationship, and not simply insufficient statistical power to detect a relationship, future studies should use adequate sample sizes. A meta-analysis, which takes into consideration the magnitude of relationships as well as their statistical significance, should be conducted using the findings of existing studies to provide a better overall picture of the impact of particular characteristics on particular outcomes (Rosenthal 1984).

Second, different studies measured the same constructs in different ways. Some statistically non-significant relationships might reflect that particular measures were overly broad and included a heterogenous set of disputes, making statistically significant findings less likely (Keppel 1973). For instance, disputes involving domestic violence differ on a number of dimensions, such as the frequency, recency, and severity of the abuse (Ellis & Stuckless 1992; Kelly 1996; Wissler 1999; Beck & Sales 2001); the disputants' current ability to cooperate (Pearson 1993); and whether disputants currently fear violence or feel unable to communicate on an equal basis (Chandler 1990). To the extent that these different patterns of domestic violence have different effects on the mediation process or outcomes, this variability would reduce the likelihood that "domestic violence" measured only as whether or not there had been abuse would have a consistent relationship with mediation outcomes. The mixed findings regarding disputant experience with and preparation for mediation similarly suggest that better and more nuanced measures are needed to permit a more accurate understanding of the impact of these factors. Researchers and mediators will need to weigh the potential benefits and costs, including the possible effect on the mediation process, of collecting more and more detailed information about disputes prior to mediation than typically is available. To assess whether it is a particular measure or the underlying construct that is (or is not) related to mediation outcomes, future studies should employ multiple measures of the same construct and examine whether the different measures produce similar or different findings.

Third, differences in the structure of different mediation programs in the same setting also could contribute to different findings across different studies (see also Irving & Benjamin 1992; Benjamin & Irving 1995; Lande 2004; Wissler 2004c; McEwen 2005). For example, programs that used more stringent criteria to screen out disputes involving domestic violence or other characteristics would have mediated disputes that fell into a narrower range on those characteristics. This would make it more difficult to detect a relationship between those characteristics and outcomes than in programs that used less stringent criteria (see also Thoennes & Pearson 1985). Similarly, programs that assigned mediators to particular types of disputes based on their skills would also be less likely to find statistically significant relationships between mediator characteristics and outcomes than programs that essentially assigned cases to mediators at random. If mediators with more training were routinely assigned to "hard" cases while those with less training were assigned to "easy" cases, the overall settlement rate for the two sets of mediators might be comparable and, as a result, mediator training would appear not to be related to settlement. Or a given mediator approach might appear to have a different impact on outcomes in different studies because the programs had a different mix of cases. Other differences in program structure, such as the timing and mode of referral, as well as differences in the broader community or legal context in which the programs operate, also could contribute to differences in findings (Wissler 2004c; McEwen 2005). At a minimum, future studies need to provide more detailed documentation of program structure and context so that these possible explanations for findings can be explored. More useful information, however, would be obtained by research that systematically varied elements of program structure and assessed their effects.

A final possible explanation of differences in findings regarding disputant characteristics is that some studies measured each disputant's level on the characteristic, other studies measured the average level of that characteristic for the pair of disputants combined, and still other studies measured the difference between the disputants on that characteristic. These different measurement approaches might produce different findings. For instance, one domestic relations study found that the amount of disparity in attachment between the two disputants was related to settlement and to the disputants' problem-solving behavior during mediation (Bickerdike & Littlefield 2000). The average level of attachment for the two disputants combined, however, was not related to settlement or to behavior during mediation (Bickerdike & Littlefield 2000). Future research needs to examine the pattern of relationships between disputant characteristics and the mediation process and outcomes using these different approaches to determine which is most useful in explaining mediation's effectiveness.

In addition to the above issues of sample size, measurement, and program structure, there are more substantive issues that future research needs to address. First, for the most part, studies have tended to examine the impact of individual antecedent characteristics on outcomes without adequately taking into consideration that various dispute, disputant, and mediator characteristics often are interrelated. The interrelationships among factors make it difficult to discern which particular characteristic plays a critical role in the mediation process or outcome. For example, apparent gender and ethnic differences in monetary outcomes in small claims mediation were largely explained by the legal claim type and the disputant's role as an individual or business representative (LaFree & Rack 1996). To tease apart the unique and combined influence of a set of characteristics, future studies need to use multivariate rather than only univariate analyses (Irving & Benjamin 1992; Lande 2004). In addition, the effect of a particular characteristic may vary depending on the presence of other characteristics. For instance, whether mediation was more likely to be effective in disputes involving low rather than high overt conflict depended on the degree of ambivalence about the divorce as well as other aspects of the dispute and the disputants' relationship (Kressel et al. 1980). Future research on dispute and disputant antecedent characteristics needs to examine how various characteristics interact to affect outcomes.

Second, mediation research has tended to follow a "black box" approach, examining the impact of dispute or disputant characteristics on mediation outcomes, and largely skipping over the mediation process (T_m), a prominent component of the model proposed in chapter 2 (see also Slaikeu et al. 1985; Irving & Benjamin 1992; Wall & Lynn 1993; Benjamin & Irving 1995; Kelly 1996, 2004; Beck & Sales 2000; Lande 2004; for exceptions, see Pruitt 1995; Bickerdike & Littlefield 2000). Studies that have examined mediator actions have tended to focus on what mediators do during the session rather than on the timing, frequency, and skillfulness of what they do (see also Kressel & Pruitt 1985). Research seldom has examined what types of mediator actions or approach are more effective with what types of disputes.

And few studies have examined the impact on outcomes of the nature of disputant interactions during mediation (for an exception, see Bickerdike & Littlefield 2000). A recent study suggests that disputants' interactions during the session had almost as large an impact as the mediator on disputants' perceptions of the fairness of the mediation process and outcome (Wissler 2004a). Future research needs to examine how antecedent characteristics affect the mediation process, how what happens in early phases of mediation affects what happens in later phases, how what takes place during mediation affects outcomes, and how differences in the mediator's approach and the mediation process alter the relationship between dispute and disputant characteristics and mediation outcomes (e.g. as illustrated in the applications in chapter 2). To the greatest extent possible, studies need to use one mediator approach with different types of disputes, and different mediator approaches with similar disputes, to examine for which disputes and disputants which mediator approach is most effective.

Third, the impact of antecedent characteristics and the mediation process on outcomes other than settlement, and especially on long-term outcomes, has seldom been examined (see also Sander 1995; Lande 2004). The available findings show that a given construct often had a different effect on different types of outcomes. For example, some characteristics that were associated with an increased likelihood of settlement either were not related, or were negatively related, to disputants' perceptions that the process was fair and to their compliance with the agreement. Future research needs to place more emphasis on examining the effects of antecedent and process characteristics on a broader array of outcomes, such as those listed in the model in chapter 2, that are relevant to a particular mediation setting.

Finally, although attorneys often are involved in the disputes mediated in some of the settings connected to or in the shadow of the courts (Wissler 1999, 2004c), their impact on the mediation process has seldom been examined (see also Beck & Sales 2000). Constructs relating to attorneys should be added or made more explicit at several places in the model presented in chapter 2: as antecedent characteristics (T_0) (e.g. their fee structure [see Kritzer 1986], their prior mediation experience [see Wissler 2002], and their attitudes and beliefs about mediation); during the mediation process (T_m) (e.g. how actively they participate in mediation [see Wissler 2002], how they interact with their client, and their views of the mediator's neutrality); and as short-term outcomes (T_1) (e.g. their beliefs and attitudes about the process, mediator, and outcome). One study, for instance, found that attorneys were more likely to discuss the use of mediation and other alternative dispute resolution (ADR) processes with clients if they thought the benefits of using ADR outweighed the costs and if more of their cases that went to ADR had settled (Wissler 2004b). Presumably, attorneys who had positive experiences in mediation not only would be more likely to discuss mediation with clients but also would discuss it in more favorable terms. Thus, attorneys' views of mediation are likely to affect not only the disputants' decision to use mediation (Pearson, Thoennes & Vanderkooi 1982; Wissler, Bezanson, Cranberg, Soloski & Murchison 1992), but also their attitudes and expectations about mediation, their experience during the process, and their satisfaction with the process and its outcomes.

In sum, researchers have much more work to do to develop a better understanding of the role the factors in chapter 2's proposed model play in order to provide program designers with information they can use to structure more effective mediation programs.

NOTES

The author thanks Bob Dauber and Craig McEwen for their comments.

1 Effectiveness is, of course, only one among a number of criteria on which this decision could be based (see Niemic, Stienstra & Ravitz 2001; Mack 2003).
2 This is only a subset of the constructs in the model proposed in chapter 2 that are relevant for program designers. For a discussion of other program design and context considerations, see Wissler (2004c) and McEwen (2006).
3 The percentage of disputes in which the disputants had a personal, "affective" (Silbey & Merry 1986), or continuing relationship varied across mediation settings. It was lowest in general civil (Clarke & Gordon 1997) and small claims mediation (McEwen & Maiman 1981; Roehl et al. 1992), was intermediate in community mediation (Felstiner & Williams 1980), and, of course, was highest in domestic relations mediation.
4 This study reported data from mediation programs in two states. This report is cited for each proposition it supports and, thus, when the findings in the two states are not the same, it is cited twice for a single issue.
5 Longer marriages tend to be associated with more children and assets (Beck & Sales 2001).
6 When a relationship between disputant characteristics and mediation outcomes was found, because of a high degree of intercorrelation among disputant characteristics, it was difficult to know to which particular characteristic to attribute that relationship (see Vidmar 1984; Hermann et al. 1993; LaFree & Rack 1996; Clarke & Gordon 1997; Wissler 2002).
7 Programs that used performance-based assessments reported that mediators' role-play performance during the selection process was related to subsequent on-the-job performance (Honeyman 1990; Honoroff, Matz & O'Connor 1990).
8 The data suggested that the skillfulness ratings did not simply reflect the frequency with which the mediators performed each of these seven actions (Wissler & Rack 2004).
9 I treat mediator actions as a mediation process (T_m) variable in this chapter. Several studies found that some mediators used a combination of approaches and varied their actions across cases, whereas other mediators tended to use a single approach in all cases (Vidmar 1984; Silbey & Merry 1986; Kressel et al. 1994; Bickerdike & Littlefield 2000; Wissler 2002). In programs where mediators use a consistent approach in most cases, mediator "style" might instead be considered an antecedent characteristic (T_0).
10 In some mediation settings (e.g. general civil and civil appeals), virtually all disputants had attorneys present during mediation; in other settings (e.g. small claims and community mediation), few disputants had attorneys present (Wissler 2004c). In yet other settings (e.g. domestic relations), the proportion of disputants with attorneys present in mediation varied greatly in different programs and studies (Wissler 1999; Beck & Sales 2000).

11   One might be tempted to conclude that the mediation process features that distinguished disputants who settled from those who did not settle are indicators of a more effective mediation process. However, because the typical methodology involved having participants rate these aspects of the mediation process after the close of mediation, it is instead possible that the fact of reaching (or not reaching) a settlement led disputants to have more favorable (or less favorable) views of mediation.

12   *Process fairness* appears in the model proposed in chapter 2 as both a short-term outcome (T_1) and as an aspect of the mediation process (T_m). In this chapter, I treat disputants' perceptions of the fairness of the process as a short-term outcome, consistent with the treatment of this concept in the procedural justice literature (Lind & Tyler 1988; Tyler & Lind 2000).

13   The findings of some of these studies should be interpreted with caution, however, because the compliance analyses were conducted for mediated and tried cases combined (McEwen & Maiman 1984; Vidmar 1985; Roehl et al. 1992; Wissler 1995). Accordingly, the patterns of relationships might be different for mediation cases alone.

REFERENCES

Beck, C. J. A. & Sales, B. D. (2000) A critical reappraisal of divorce mediation research and policy. *Psychology, Public Policy, and Law* 6, 989–1046.

Beck, C. J. A. & Sales, B. D. (2001) *Family Mediation: Facts, Myths, and Future Prospects.* American Psychological Association, Washington.

Benjamin, M. & Irving, H. H. (1995) Research in family mediation: review and implications. *Mediation Quarterly* 13, 53–82.

Bickerdike, A. J. & Littlefield, L. (2000) Divorce adjustment and mediation: theoretically grounded process research. *Mediation Quarterly* 18, 181–201.

Brett, J. M., Barsness, Z. I. & Goldberg, S. B. (1996) The effectiveness of mediation: an independent analysis of cases handled by four major service providers. *Negotiation Journal* 12, 259–269.

Burrell, N. A., Narus, L., Bogdanoff, K. & Allen, M. (1994) Evaluating parental stressors of divorcing couples referred to mediation and effects on mediation outcomes. *Mediation Quarterly* 11, 339–352.

Camplair, C. W. & Stolberg, A. L. (1990) Benefits of court-sponsored divorce mediation: a study of outcomes and influences on success. *Mediation Quarterly* 7, 199–213.

Chandler, D. B. (1990) Violence, fear, and communication: the variable impact of domestic violence on mediation. *Mediation Quarterly* 7, 331–346.

Clarke, S. H. & Gordon, E. E. (1997) Public sponsorship of private settling: court-ordered civil case mediation. *Justice System Journal* 19, 311–339.

Clement, J. A. & Schwebel, A. I. (1993) A research agenda for divorce mediation: the creation of second order knowledge to inform legal policy. *Ohio State Journal on Dispute Resolution* 9, 95–113.

Cohn, L. P. (1996) *Mediation: A Fair and Efficient Alternative to Trial.* Available online at <www.caadrs.org/studies>.

Cook, R. F., Roehl, J. A. & Sheppard, D. I. (1980) *Neighborhood Justice Centers Field Test: Final Evaluation Report.* National Institute of Justice, Washington.

Donohue, W. A. (1989) Communicative competence in mediation. In K. Kressel, D. G. Pruitt & Associates (eds.), *Mediation Research: The Process and Effectiveness of Third-Party Intervention.* Jossey-Bass, San Francisco, pp. 322–343.

Donohue, W. A., Drake, L. & Roberto, A. J. (1994) Mediator issue intervention strategies: a replication and some conclusions. *Mediation Quarterly* 11, 261–274.

Eaglin, J. B. (1990) *The Pre-Argument Conference Program in the Sixth Circuit Court of Appeals: An Evaluation.* Federal Judicial Center, Washington.

Ellis, D. & Stuckless, N. (1992) Preseparation abuse, marital conflict mediation, and post-separation abuse. *Mediation Quarterly* 9, 205–225.

Ellis, D. & Stuckless, N. (1996) *Mediating and Negotiating Marital Conflicts.* Sage, Thousand Oaks.

Emery, R. E. (1994) *Renegotiating Family Relationships: Divorce, Child Custody, and Mediation.* Guilford Press, New York.

Felstiner, W. L. F. & Williams, L. A. (1980) *Community Mediation in Dorchester, Massachusetts.* National Institute of Justice, Washington.

FitzGibbon, S. F. (1993) Appellate settlement conference programs: a case study. *Journal of Dispute Resolution* 1993, 53–107.

Hann, R. G. & Baar, C. (2001) *Evaluation of the Ontario Mandatory Mediation Program (Rule 24.1): Final Report: The First 23 Months.* Ontario Ministry of the Attorney General, Queens Printer, Toronto. Available online at <www.attorneygeneral.jus.gov.on.ca/html/MANMED>.

Hanson, R. A. & Becker, R. (2002) Appellate mediation in New Mexico: an evaluation. *Journal of Appellate Practice and Process* 4, 167–188.

Hermann, M., LaFree, G., Rack, C. & West, M. B. (1993) *The MetroCourt Project Final Report.* Institute of Public Law, University of New Mexico, Albuquerque.

Honeyman, C. (1990) The common core of mediation. *Mediation Quarterly* 8, 73–82.

Honoroff, B., Matz, D. & O'Connor, D. (1990) Putting mediation skills to the test. *Negotiation Journal* 6, 37–46.

Irving, H. H. & Benjamin, M. (1992) An evaluation of process and outcome in a private family mediation service. *Mediation Quarterly* 10, 35–55.

Kakalik, J. S., Dunworth, T., Hill, L. A., McCaffrey, D., Oshiro, M., Pace, N. M. & Vaiana, M. E. (1996). *An Evaluation of Mediation and Early Neutral Evaluation Under the Civil Justice Reform Act.* RAND, Santa Monica.

Kelly, J. B. (1996) A decade of divorce mediation research: some answers and questions. *Family and Conciliation Courts Review* 34, 373–385.

Kelly, J. B. (2004) Family mediation research: is there empirical support for the field? *Conflict Resolution Quarterly* 22, 3–35.

Kelly, J. B. & Duryee, M. A. (1992) Women's and men's views of mediation in voluntary and mandatory mediation settings. *Family and Conciliation Courts Review* 30, 34–49.

Kelly, J. B. & Gigy, L. L. (1989) Divorce mediation: characteristics of clients and outcomes. In K. Kressel, D. G. Pruitt & Associates (eds.), *Mediation Research: The Process and Effectiveness of Third-Party Intervention.* Jossey-Bass, San Francisco, pp. 263–283.

Kelly, J. B., Gigy, L. L. & Hausman, S. (1988) Mediated and adversarial divorce: initial findings from a longitudinal study. In J. Folberg & A. Milne (eds.), *Divorce Mediation: Theory and Practice.* Guilford Press, New York, pp. 453–473.

Keppel, G. (1973) *Design and Analysis: A Researcher's Handbook.* Prentice-Hall, Englewood Cliffs.

Kobbervig, W. (1991) *Mediation of Civil Cases in Hennepin County: An Evaluation.* Office of the State Court Administrator, St. Paul.

Kressel, K. & Pruitt, D. G. (1985) Themes in the mediation of social conflict. *Journal of Social Issues* 41, 179–198.

Kressel, K., Jaffee, N., Tuchman, B., Watson, C. & Deutsch, M. (1980) A typology of divorcing couples: implications for mediation and the divorce process. *Family Process* 19, 101–116.

Kressel, K., Frontera, E. A., Forlenza, S., Butler, F. & Fish, L. (1994) The settlement-orientation vs. the problem-solving style in custody mediation. *Journal of Social Issues* 50, 67–84.

Kritzer, H. M. (1986) *The Lawyer as Negotiator: Working in the Shadows.* Disputes Processing Research Program, Working Paper No. 4, Series 7, Institute for Legal Studies, University of Wisconsin-Madison Law School, Madison.

LaFree, G. & Rack, C. (1996) The effects of participants' ethnicity and gender on monetary outcomes in mediated and adjudicated civil cases. *Law and Society Review* 30, 767–797.

Lande, J. (2004) Focusing on program design issues in future research on court-connected mediation. *Conflict Resolution Quarterly* 22, 89–100.

Lind, E. A. & Tyler, T. R. (1988) *The Social Psychology of Procedural Justice.* Plenum, New York.

McEwen, C. A. (1992a) An evaluation of the ADR pilot project. *Maine Bar Journal* 7, 310–311.

McEwen, C. A. (1992b) *An Evaluation of the ADR Pilot Project: Final Report.* Bowdoin College, Brunswick.

McEwen, C. A. (2006) Examining mediation in context: toward understanding variations in mediation programs. In M. S. Herrman (ed.), *Blackwell Handbook of Mediation: Foundations of Effectiveness.* Blackwell, Oxford, pp. 81–98.

McEwen, C. A. & Maiman, R. J. (1981) Small claims mediation in Maine: an empirical assessment. *Maine Law Review* 33, 237–268.

McEwen, C. A. & Maiman, R. J. (1984) Mediation in small claims court: achieving compliance through consent. *Law and Society Review* 21, 155–164.

Macfarlane, J. (1995) *Court-Based Mediation for Civil Cases: An Evaluation of the Ontario Court (General Division) ADR Centre.* University of Windsor, Windsor.

Macfarlane, J. (2003) *Learning from Experience: An Evaluation of the Saskatchewan Queen's Bench Mandatory Mediation Program.* University of Windsor, Windsor.

Mack, K. (2003). *Court Referral to ADR: Criteria and Research.* Australian Institute of Judicial Administration, Melbourne.

Maiman, R. J. (1997) *An Evaluation of Selected Mediation Programs in the Massachusetts Trial Court.* Massachusetts Supreme Judicial Court, Boston.

Meierding, N. R. (1993) Does mediation work? A survey of long-term satisfaction and durability rates for privately mediated agreements. *Mediation Quarterly* 11, 157–170.

Niemic, R. J., Stienstra, D. & Ravitz, R. E. (2001) *Guide to Judicial Management of Cases in ADR.* Federal Judicial Center, Washington.

Note (1979) The Minnesota Supreme Court prehearing conference: an empirical evaluation. *Minnesota Law Review* 63, 1221–1257.

Pearson, J. (1993) Ten myths about family law. *Family Law Quarterly* 27, 279–299.

Pearson, J. & Thoennes, N. (1982) The benefits outweigh the costs. *Family Advocate* 4, 16–32.

Pearson, J. & Thoennes, N. (1985) Divorce mediation: an overview of research results. *Columbia Journal of Law and Social Problems* 19, 451–484.

Pearson, J. & Thoennes, N. (1988) Divorce mediation research results. In J. Folberg & A. Milne (eds.), *Divorce Mediation: Theory and Practice.* Guilford Press, New York, pp. 429–452.

Pearson, J. & Thoennes, N. (1989) Divorce mediation: reflections on a decade of research. In K. Kressel, D. G. Pruitt & Associates (eds.), *Mediation Research: The Process and Effectiveness of Third-Party Intervention.* Jossey-Bass, San Francisco, pp. 9–30.

Pearson, J., Thoennes, N. & Vanderkooi, L. (1982) The decision to mediate: profiles of individuals who accept and reject the opportunity to mediate contested child custody and visitation issues. *Journal of Divorce* 6, 17–34.

Pruitt, D. G. (1995) Process and outcome in community mediation. *Negotiation Journal* 11, 365–377.

Pruitt, D. G., McGillicuddy, N. B., Welton, G. L. & Fry, W. R. (1989) Process of mediation in dispute settlement centers. In K. Kressel, D. G. Pruitt & Associates (eds.), *Mediation Research: The Process and Effectiveness of Third-Party Intervention.* Jossey-Bass, San Francisco, pp. 368–393.

Roehl, J. A. & Cook, R. F. (1989) Mediation in interpersonal disputes: effectiveness and limitations. In K. Kressel, D. G. Pruitt & Associates (eds.), *Mediation Research: The Process and Effectiveness of Third-Party Intervention.* Jossey-Bass, San Francisco, pp. 31–53.

Roehl, J. A., Hersch, R. & Llaneras, E. (1992) *Civil Case Mediation and Comprehensive Justice Centers: Process, Quality of Justice, and Value to State Courts, Final Report.* Institute for Social Analysis, Washington.

Rosenthal, R. (1984) *Meta-analytic Procedures for Social Research.* Sage, Newbury Park.

Rudd, J. (1996) Communication effects on divorce mediation: how participants' argumentativeness, verbal aggression, and compliance-gaining strategy choice mediate outcome satisfaction. *Mediation Quarterly* 14, 65–78.

Sander, F. E. A. (1995) The obsession with settlement rates. *Negotiation Journal* 11, 329–337.

Schildt, K., Alfini, J. J. & Johnson, P. (1994) *Major Civil Case Mediation Pilot Program: 17th Judicial Circuit of Illinois.* Northern Illinois University, DeKalb. Available online at <www.caadrs.org/studies>.

Schultz, K. D. (1990) *Florida's Alternative Dispute Resolution Demonstration Project: An Empirical Assessment.* Florida Dispute Resolution Center, Tallahassee.

Shack, J. (2003) Mediation in courts can bring gains, but under what conditions? *Dispute Resolution Magazine* 9, 11–14.

Silbey, S. A. & Merry, S. E. (1986). Mediator settlement strategies. *Law and Policy* 8, 7–32.

Slaikeu, K. A., Culler, R., Pearson, J. & Thoennes, N. (1985) Process and outcome in divorce mediation. *Mediation Quarterly* 10, 55–74.

Task Force on Appellate Mediation (2001) *Mandatory Mediation in the First Appellate District of the Court of Appeal: Report and Recommendations.* California Court of Appeal, San Francisco. Available online at <www.courtinfo.ca.gov/reference/4_reports.htm#ADR>.

Thoennes, N. A. & Pearson, J. (1985) Predicting outcomes in divorce mediation: the influence of people and process. *Journal of Social Issues* 41, 127–144.

Thoennes, N. A., Pearson, J. & Bell, J. (1991) *Executive Summary of the Evaluation of the Use of Mandatory Divorce Mediation.* State Justice Institute, Washington.

Tyler, T. R. & Lind, E. A. (2000) Procedural justice. In J. Sanders & V. L. Hamilton (eds.), *Handbook of Justice Research in Law.* Kluwer Academic/Plenum, New York, pp. 65–92.

Vidmar, N. (1984) The small claims court: a reconceptualization of disputes and an empirical investigation. *Law and Society Review* 18, 515–550.

Vidmar, N. (1985) An assessment of mediation in a small claims court. *Journal of Social Issues* 41, 127–144.

Wall, J. A., Jr. & Lynn, A. (1993) Mediation: a current review. *Journal of Conflict Resolution* 37, 160–194.

Whiting, R. A. (1994) Family disputes, nonfamily disputes, and mediation success. *Mediation Quarterly* 11, 247–260.

Wissler, R. L. (1995) Mediation and adjudication in the small claims court: the effects of process and case characteristics. *Law and Society Review* 29, 323–358.

Wissler, R. L. (1999) *Trapping the Data: An Assessment of Domestic Relations Mediation in Maine and Ohio Courts.* State Justice Institute, Washington.

Wissler, R. L. (2002) Court-connected mediation in general civil cases: what we know from empirical research. *Ohio State Journal of Dispute Resolution* 17, 641–703.

Wissler, R. L. (2004a) *Correlates of Procedural Justice in Mediation.* Paper presented at the American Psychology-Law Society Annual Meeting. Scottsdale, Arizona, March 6, 2004.

Wissler, R. L. (2004b) Barriers to attorneys' discussion and use of ADR. *Ohio State Journal on Dispute Resolution* 19, 459–508.

Wissler, R. L. (2004c) The effectiveness of court-connected dispute resolution in civil cases. *Conflict Resolution Quarterly* 22, 55–88.

Wissler, R. L. & Rack, R. W., Jr. (2004) Assessing mediator performance: the usefulness of participant questionnaires. *Journal of Dispute Resolution* 2004, 227–255.

Wissler, R. L., Bezanson, R. P., Cranberg, G., Soloski, J. & Murchison, B. (1992) Resolving libel disputes out of court: the libel dispute resolution program. In J. Soloski & R. P. Bezanson (eds.), *Reforming Libel Law.* Guilford Press, New York, pp. 286–322.

Woodward, J. G. (1990) Settlement week: measuring the promise. *Northern Illinois University Law Review* 11, 1–54.

Chapter 6

Applying the Comprehensive Model to Workplace Mediation Research

BRIAN POLKINGHORN AND
E. PATRICK McDERMOTT

INTRODUCTION

Chapter 2 of this book presents a comprehensive model of mediation based on a descriptive review spanning more than four decades of research on interpersonal conflict. The model clearly synthesizes mediation research, as well as different theoretical lenses and various contexts where mediation is practiced at the interpersonal level. In this chapter we will apply, compare, and examine how the comprehensive model provides a frame that examines workplace conflict and our research on the United States Equal Employment Opportunity Commission's (EEOC) mediation program.[1] Our primary focus will be on research results from the first two of three studies conducted by the research team at the Center for Conflict Resolution at Salisbury University on the EEOC mediation program. The first study examines participant perceptions of the EEOC mediation process (McDermott, Obar, Jose & Bowers 2000). The second, companion, study focuses on the mediators' perspectives on the process (McDermott, Obar, Polkinghorn & Jose 2001), while a third study focuses on why employers decline an offer to mediate (McDermott, Obar & Jose 2003). It is worth noting that these three research projects were conducted long before the comprehensive model was developed, and yet there is a good deal of congruence. This chapter also demonstrates a variety of ways to examine the model and, as a result, add new information, constructs, and theoretical ideas.

We first provide an overview of the EEOC studies including the subjects and sampling technique, research protocol, survey instruments, coding of the mediator data, and finally the analysis. The second part then compares our research and results to the conceptual frames and variable measurements of the comprehensive model. Finally, the chapter concludes with a summary discussion on application of the comprehensive model to the research.

Background of the Research

The mediation of employment disputes has proliferated in recent years with state and federal offices launching mediation programs and private sector consultants providing a variety of mediation training, dispute systems design services and evaluation. The nationwide EEOC mediation program represents a major milestone in the growth of workplace mediation. Previous research on the EEOC mediation program points to major empirical findings on the success of this program (McDermott et al. 2000, 2001, 2003; McDermott, Polkinghorn, Jose & Obar 2002).

The Subjects and Sampling Technique

The two EEOC studies that we focus on in this chapter cover analyses of participant satisfaction with mediation from a procedural and substantive due process perspective and of the mediators' perspectives on the mediation process. Data were simultaneously gathered for both of these studies. Subjects in these studies include all participants (charging parties and respondents) and all mediators who took part in or otherwise conducted a private sector mediation session for the EEOC under the supervision of the one of the 50 EEOC field offices, from March 1 to July 31, 2000. The sampling technique captured every mediation session conducted during this time period so that the profile of the sample is exactly the same as the profile of the overall population of EEOC mediated cases for this period. A comparative analysis of this sample and the EEOC mediation case population verified that the sample in this study is completely consistent with the overall profile and characteristics of EEOC mediations (McDermott et al. 2000: 40–43).

Research Protocol

The research protocol requires mediators to complete a survey at the end of each mediation session and then place the completed survey in an envelope, seal it, and forward it to their local ADR coordinator. Participants complete a survey at the end of the session and place it in the accompanying sealed envelope. The ADR coordinator for each EEOC district office then forwards the packages to the research team.

The Survey Instruments

The survey instruments used in the studies were developed in consultation with EEOC headquarters personnel, piloted, and modified based on feedback. The first instrument, titled the "charging party" or "respondent" survey, is composed of a 22-item inventory that includes 14 questions that employ a five-point Likert-type response scale ranging from strongly disagree (1) to strongly agree (5). These questions focus on, among other things, "charging party" and "respondent" (i.e. employer) feedback concerning the mediator and various procedural and distributive justice measures. Of the remaining eight questions, five require a yes or no response, two allow for open-ended responses, and one incorporates a multiple-choice set of responses. So, the participant survey is primarily a quantitative instrument that focuses on program measures and theoretical constructs pertaining to various forms of justice (McDermott et al. 2000: Exhibit 3).

The response rate for "charging parties" was at least 46.25 percent. The phrase "at least" is used because the surveys were introduced in a rolling start by the various EEOC offices. Thus, an exact response rate is not determinable. The authors received a total of 2,209 surveys completed by the charging parties. Of these, 526 surveys were deemed unusable because some were blank or only partially completed. Most rejected surveys either did not indicate the case charge number or did not have a matching case number in the EEOC database. Without that information we were unable to match the mediator to the participants and have a complete "set" for the particular mediation session. This resulted in a total of 1,683 usable surveys. Thus, the effective participation rate for the charging parties was roughly 35 percent.

The response rate for "respondents" was at least 50 percent. Respondents returned 2,402 surveys and, after completing the same examination for completeness and missing information, there were 1,572 usable surveys. This is an effective respondent participation rate of 33 percent. The combined effective participation rate for the charging parties and respondents in the total sample is 34 percent.

The second survey instrument, entitled "mediator-results survey," is designed to measure mediators' perceptions of the parties, dynamics of the process, and the variety of outcomes that may result. With the exception of the questions pertaining to the characteristics and background of the mediation session (prior mediations, length of sessions, and outcome) and the skills of the parties' representatives (rated on a Likert scale) the questions are open-ended (McDermott et al. 2001: appendix A). While the participant survey in the first study is largely quantitative, the mediator survey in the second study is largely qualitative. Indeed for some open-ended questions, there are sub-parts that seek further and deeper elaboration.

The first set of questions addresses characteristics of the mediation. The remaining questions seek information from the mediator regarding the conduct of the parties at mediation, the resolution status of the mediation, participant actions that contribute to or interfere with the resolution of the dispute, barriers to the resolution of the dispute, turning points in the mediation, mediator tactics used to resolve a dispute, what the mediator would have done differently in those mediations where the dispute was not resolved, the skills of the parties' legal and non-legal representatives, and process improvement suggestions. There were a total of 4,776 cases mediated. The mediators returned a total of 2,062 completed usable surveys and the resulting response rate is 43.2 percent.

Data were also collected on each mediator prior to mediation using a separate survey instrument we developed entitled "Mediator Background and Style Survey." Every person who mediated a case filled out the survey. The purpose of this background and style survey was to obtain data concerning the mediator as well as identifying his or her style along a facilitative–evaluative continuum.

Coding Mediator Data and Analysis

Each mediator was asked to complete the questionnaire for every one of his/ her mediations. The data from the open-ended questions were team-coded by Drs. McDermott and Polkinghorn. In order to ensure greater inter-rater or inter-coder reliability, the coders worked side by side throughout the seven months of the coding process. Discussions of the raw data led not only to the development of new codes, but to the evolution of old codes. This part of the process involved hundreds of hours of coding and discussion. Each survey had to be read in its entirety and in many cases by both coders. The subjectivity of attributing cause and effect for each survey required the coders to discuss many of the surveys individually. In some cases it required both coders to read a survey, write down a set of ideas or working codes, then discuss/debate the interpretation until a consensus was reached on the most probable intent of the mediator. In the majority of cases the mediator was extremely articulate and clear in providing answers, thus making the interpretation of the data simpler and less subjective.

For two questions, the coders also entered their opinions regarding whether the mediator was attributing the failure to resolve the mediation to the charging party or the respondent, their representative(s), to any combination of parties or to some other discernible reason. Originally we assumed that mediators would be hesitant to provide many responses to this question, thus making our coding task more difficult. However, the mediators were quite willing to provide an ample amount of opinions on who or what caused the process to fail. It is interesting to note that few mediators claim they were the reason for the failure. After a thorough read of the survey, the coders determined which party or parties "caused" the mediation to stall or fail. Thus, the coders attempted to provide some additional perspective on which party interfered with resolution.[2]

Finally, we would like to note the robust nature of the analysis and the subsequent validity of the findings. Some may argue that qualitative data codes, constructs, and properties lists may be arbitrary, even with a high degree of measured inter-coder reliability. We agree to some extent that this is a hazard of qualitative analysis, but we have gone one step further and used these data coding patterns to test and develop a comprehensive "second generation" *quantitative* survey instrument that we subsequently used to evaluate the California Department of Fair Employment and Housing's mediation program.[3] The findings from that research project verify the validity of the codes found in the EEOC research.[4]

FRAMING THE EEOC WORKPLACE MEDIATION RESEARCH THROUGH THE COMPREHENSIVE MODEL

The comprehensive model provides a time sequence of pre-mediation (before, T_0), in situ mediation (during, T_m) and post-mediation (after, T_{1-2}) measures. The following section makes a comparison of the concepts and variables examined in our research to the comprehensive model. Even though the proposed model was not available when we were conducting our research, readers will note a great deal of similarity. The research relationship to the model suggests that researchers in various locales and times have used similar research foci, research protocols, research designs which in turn have produced complimentary findings.

Data Collected "Before" Mediation

T_0 represents "important characteristics antedating mediation." Proposed constructs include personal characteristics of disputants and mediators, disputant beliefs and attitudes, dispute characteristics, and the institutional context.

Personal characteristics: disputants

Overall, the EEOC research examines a large number of pre-mediation variables that fall within "personal characteristics" in the T_0 section of the proposed model. In the first EEOC study, considerable amounts of data were collected on disputant characteristics, including charging party and employer demographics (e.g. age, race, gender, size of company; McDermott et al. 2000: 41–42). This allowed us to examine mediation settlement rates, participant satisfaction on procedural versus distributive issues, and other measures vis-à-vis the demographic characteristics of the participants.

Personal characteristics: mediators

Our study also looked at mediator characteristics. Mediator background characteristics in our study include:

- number of mediations over the last five years
- extent of EEOC mediation training received by the mediator
- how well that EEOC training prepared the mediator for the mediation process
- mediator's professional occupation(s)
- whether the mediator was an advocate in an employment discrimination case, and if so, for what side
- type of mediator (contractor, pro bono, EEOC staff, etc.)
- number of EEOC cases mediated
- extent of mediator training
- number of mediations conducted

In addition to the above, we used the mediator style survey to identify the mediators' self-reported style. This Krivis and McAdoo (1997) survey consists of 25 statements describing various mediator tactics during the mediation. The mediators express their agreement or disagreement on a 10-point scale. We added two questions to the survey. The first asked if the mediators believed that their style changed from one day to the next and the other asked whether or not the mediators adjusted their style based on whether the parties were represented

TABLE 6.1   Mediator type

Responses	Frequencies	Percentages
Information provided		
EEOC staff mediator	1,329	80.0
Pro bono mediator	188	11.3
Contract mediator	143	8.6
Total responses	**1,660**	**100.0**
No information provided	402	19.5
Grand total	**2,062**	**100.0**
Total responses as % of grand total	N/A	80.5

by counsel. From these data, we were able to identify the mediators' style on an evaluative-facilitative continuum (see Riskin 1996, 2003).

Another mediator characteristic that we found important was the type of mediator – EEOC staff, pro bono, or contract (see table 6.1). These data can be matched to a variety of cases in order to examine the relationship between the mediator characteristics and other variables such as the disposition of the cases (settled, not settled) or the nature of the dispute (statute(s) at issue, basis of the charge and issue(s)).

Disputant beliefs and attitudes

When it comes to "disputant beliefs and attitudes" our study diverges from the comprehensive model. We did not examine this area in detail for one reason. The EEOC convening process is assumed to have identified parties who were willing to mediate in this voluntary program. Thus, there was an assumption that the parties were predisposed to mediation as a means of resolving the dispute. That being said, it is clear that our rich data would have been enhanced by a better understanding of the beliefs and attitudes of the parties, particularly to better understand why mediation may fail or succeed. Questions concerning the parties' motives for mediating would have been very valuable to understand the mediation process and outcome better.

The closest we got to beliefs and attitudes was to ask the parties whether they knew what they wanted coming into the mediation. We can see this as a factor that primes readiness and thus a T_m line of inquiry in the comprehensive model.

The third EEOC study, involving a separate questionnaire and protocol about two years after the first two studies, explored why employers decline mediation. This study found that the reason that employers declined to mediate an EEOC charge include that the merits of the case did not warrant mediation, that the employer was not concerned that the EEOC would issue a "reasonable cause" finding, and the employers' perception that if they agreed to mediate they were expected to agree to a settlement including a monetary payment (McDermott et al. 2003: 66). To better understand why employers declined to mediate we delved into employer beliefs and attitudes to a great degree, including the employers' past experiences with the EEOC, past experiences in employment litigation, past experiences with the EEOC mediation program, their representatives' prior experiences in these areas, their familiarity with the mediation process, and the extent of their investigation into the underlying facts of the dispute (McDermott et al. 2003: appendix A). The value of these data underscores the importance of understanding attitudes and beliefs prior to the mediation.

Dispute characteristics

The factors in the "dispute characteristics" section of T_0 in the comprehensive model (legal characteristics, conflict characteristics, and interpersonal dynamics) are all found in the EEOC research. The comprehensive model points out that archival data can be gathered in T_0 and table 6.2 provides a comparison of archival data on a few of the contextual and process characteristics of all EEOC cases in the present mediation research. One might argue that data presented here can also fit into the "institutional context" section of the model presented next, but it is placed here as comparative data for the types of disputes EEOC mediates. Data on company size, the specific statute, the nature or basis of the dispute, mediator type and representation allow for a direct comparison between our sample and the entire EEOC database.

The study gathered extensive data on the dispute characteristics, including whether or not the parties were represented by counsel, the statute at issue, the basis of the EEOC charge, and the disputed issue (see table 6.2). These particular classifications are used by the EEOC to categorize their charges, so they are the ones we used as well. This allowed us to analyze the data across many dispute characteristics to determine if our results were uniform across these categories, in addition to performing an in-depth analysis of how the program works across various personal and dispute characteristics.[5] We found that this was important for the EEOC to evaluate whether the program was performing at a certain level across various dispute characteristics and disputant characteristics.

Institutional context

Our first study provided a historical analysis of the EEOC charge-processing programs leading up to the present mediation program. This included a discussion of the types of cases referred/screened out of the process and how these cases fit into the overall case management of the EEOC program (McDermott et al. 2000: 24–34). These data on "process access" are part of our study. One access measure was how promptly the mediation was scheduled (McDermott et al. 2000: 60).

"Process efficiency" data are also collected using archival data for the starting point regarding the time between filing and time to mediation, as well as time to final disposition. This allows for a direct comparison of time to mediate a case versus other avenues.

TABLE 6.2 Comparison of the characteristics between our sample and the EEOC database (% of cases in the study)*

	EEOC mediation cases (March 1–July 31) (%)	Charging parties (%)	Respondents (%)
Company size			
15 to 100 employees	40.2	40.7	41.7
101 to 200 employees	13.7	14.9	14.1
201 to 500 employees	11.3	12	11.3
More than 500 employees	32	30.2	30.3
Statute			
Title VII	73.8	71.2	71.7
Age	19.2	21.4	21.1
Disability	22.3	23.5	24.1
Basis			
Religion	2.4	2.5	2.5
Gender	33.3	30.4	30.7
National origin	8.5	8.9	9.6
Race	35.2	37.9	37.7
Disability	23.1	23.3	23.8
Age	19.3	21.2	20.8
Issue			
Discharge	46.0	48.6	49.6
Terms and conditions	20.9	19.0	18.4
Harassment	19.1	17.1	16.8
Sexual harassment	12.1	10.4	10.6
Promotion	10.4	10.1	10.0
Wages	9.1	9.2	8.7
Discipline	8.9	9.2	9.0
Reasonable accommodation	8.8	8.6	8.7
Mediator type			
External	74	78.4	78.4
Internal	25	20.5	20.6
Representation			
Yes	N/A	41.3	58.5
No	N/A	57.7	39.8
Mediation status			
Mediation is completed	N/A	73.8	81.0
Mediation is ongoing	N/A	13.8	13.3

* The percentages do not all add up to 100 because some participants did not furnish the required information.

Data Collected "During" Mediation

T_m represents data on variables that focus on the dynamics of the mediation process. Our data support the validity of the categories of "factors that prime readiness," "procedural factors: mediation conditions," "procedural factors: problem-solving," and "procedural factors: decision-making." It will be seen that our survey questions and responses often cut across these various subcategories. The comprehensive model would have been helpful in survey design and interpretation of our results.

Table 6.3 presents data that can be found not only throughout T_m but also T_1. The reason data are presented here is to show one means of making a cross-comparison between various constructs in the comprehensive model. Table 6.3 highlights indicators relating to procedural justice, distributive justice, and specific mediator measurements. These concepts are found within the comprehensive model framework, in particular in the subparts labeled "procedural factors: problem-solving" and "procedural factors: decision-making," but also in T_1 "disputant beliefs and attitudes." It shows participants' familiarity with the process and mediator skills that impact participants' ability to solve problems and make decisions. It also provides data on distributive justice or outcome satisfaction measures.

Factors that prime readiness

A good deal of the data collected in the EEOC mediator study fall under the T_m part of the comprehensive model. In particular, the EEOC research with mediators produced a number of findings that might be labeled "human factor" elements that focus less on process and outcome patterns but more on feelings, listening, clearly communicating, and environmental factors. This "human factor" is similar to the comprehensive model's "factors that prime readiness." For example, table 6.4 presents a rich compilation of factors found in the readiness category. In addition to these data our first study measured the concept of empathy with a question concerning whether the participant felt that the mediator understood their needs (McDermott et al. 2000: 60, table VI).

Table 6.5 presents mediator conduct that facilitates the resolution of the dispute. Data in this table can be found in T_m under the "factors that prime readiness," "procedural factors: mediation conditions," and "procedural factors: problem-solving."

Table 6.6 highlights mediator perceptions regarding constructive conditions and conduct that produced turning points in the mediation. The concepts in table 6.6 are found throughout all four sub-parts of T_m: "factors that prime readiness," "procedural factors: mediation conditions," and "procedural factors: problem-solving."

Our mediation research also examined whether "hygiene factors" such as the quality of the physical location, office supplies, restrooms, photocopying, and other things impact the mediation process (McDermott et al. 2001: 40). We would classify "hygiene factors" as a subtle T_m "factor that primes readiness" and arguably it can also be seen as a "mediation condition." These variables have not been studied before, and are therefore not referenced in the proposed model. At the same time, we think they might contribute to effective mediation by creating an immediate context.

TABLE 6.3   Participant satisfaction based on mediator type*

Statements	Charging parties (n, %)		Respondents (n, %)	
	Internal*	External*	Internal	External
Procedural elements **(explanation, scheduling, and voice)**				
Adequate explanation	4.26 (1,277, 88.4%)	4.20 (343, 88.6%)	4.23 (1,189, 86.7%)	4.14 (311, 81.4%)
Prompt scheduling	**4.32** **(1,311, 88.6%)**	**4.16** **(346, 85.0%)**	**4.43** **(1,226, 91.8%)**	**4.27** **(317, 85.8%)**
Understood the process	4.37 (1,314, 91.9%)	4.31 (345, 91.3%)	4.54 (1,228, 96.0%)	4.50 (317, 95.0%)
Opportunity to present views	4.39 (1,314, 89.6%)	4.37 (346, 90.8%)	4.57 (1,227, 94.9%)	4.57 (320, 95.9%)
Mediator				
Mediator understood needs	4.32 (1,309, 86.6%)	4.23 (344, 85.5%)	4.31 (1,221, 87.1%)	4.30 (315, 86.3%)
Mediator helped clarify needs	4.28 (1,309, 85.1%)	4.18 (339, 82.0%)	4.17 (1,182, 79.8%)	4.16 (307, 77.5%)
Mediator neutral in the beginning	4.45 (1,313, 92.2%)	4.41 (344, 92.2%)	4.47 (1,229, 91.5%)	4.56 (321, 94.4%)
Mediator remained neutral	4.44 (1,305, 90.9%)	4.36 (342, 90.6%)	4.43 (1,227, 89.0%)	4.45 (321, 90.3%)
Mediator helped develop options	4.29 (1,303, 85.0%)	4.21 (341, 86.5%)	4.24 (1,215, 83.9%)	4.19 (314, 83.8%)
Mediator used fair procedures	4.34 (1,309, 88.5%)	4.33 (342, 88.9%)	4.44 (1,229, 91.9%)	4.45 (319, 92.2%)
Distributive elements				
Development of realistic options	**3.99** **(1,295, 76.5%)**	**3.83** **(336, 71.1%)**	3.99 (1,194, 75.5%)	4.02 (309, 75.7%)
Satisfaction with the fairness of the session	4.10 (1,294, 79.9%)	3.99 (337, 75.4%)	4.30 (1,227, 87.1%)	4.34 (316, 85.4%)
Satisfaction with the results	3.39 (1,213, 55.2%)	3.37 (318, 53.8%)	3.68 (1,156, 63.6%)	3.62 (307, 59.0%)

* Satisfaction is measured by the "mean responses" of the participants on a Likert scale (scale of 1 [strongly disagree] to 5 [strongly agree]) and by the percentage of participants who agreed or strongly agreed with the statements. The sample size (n) is also given for evaluation purposes. Figures in bold refer to statements where a statistically significant difference (evaluated at 95% confidence level) exists between the mean responses of the participants in cases mediated by "external" (non EEOC) mediators and those mediated by "internal" (EEOC) mediators.

TABLE 6.4 Charging party, respondent, and their representative conduct that facilitates the resolution of the dispute*

Responses	Frequencies	Percentages*
Charging party		
Flexibility and openness	687	56.2
Focus and preparation	143	11.7
Need for closure	82	6.7
Willingness to listen to lawyer	79	6.5
Total for charging party	**991**	**81.0**
Charging party's lawyer and representative		
Strategy and tactics		
"Reality check"	108	8.8
Flexible and compromising	79	6.5
Supportive	42	3.4
Expression or conduct that established commitment		
to resolution	29	2.4
Listened	23	1.9
Engaged in creative problem-solving	14	1.2
Preparation/advocacy skills	72	5.9
Demeanor	57	4.7
Other	5	0.4
Total for charging party's lawyer and representative	**429**	**35.2**
Respondent		
Flexibility and openness	327	26.7
Expression of a commitment to the resolution of		
the dispute	202	16.5
Good mediation skills	192	15.7
Apology/admission/remorse, empathy, or		
recognizing the charging party's concerns	157	12.8
Listening to mediator and charging party	125	10.2
Direct communication avoiding taking a position		
and/or the facts of the case	32	2.6
Total for respondents	**1,035**	**84.6**
Respondent's representative		
Demeanor	165	13.5
Expression of a commitment to resolution	121	9.9
Flexibility/willingness to compromise	87	7.1
Good mediation skills	80	6.5
Client convincing conduct	55	4.5
Focusing conduct	43	3.5
Expression of respect to CP	37	3.0
Other	16	1.3
Total for respondent's lawyer and representative	**604**	**49.4**
Total cases resolved	**1,223**	**100.0**

* Total number of resolved cases is 1,223. However, since some mediators have given multiple responses, the total number of responses (found at the bottom of each section) is much higher. Also note that the percentage given in the right column is only for the resolved cases.

TABLE 6.5   Mediator conduct that facilitates resolution of the dispute*

Responses	*Frequencies*	*Percentages**
Facilitative behavior		
Listening		
Listening, reflexive questioning, paraphrasing, restating, and facilitating catharsis	119	9.7
Reframing/use of probing questions	53	4.3
Helping parties see different vantage points	55	4.5
Clarifying facts/areas of agreement	38	3.1
Defusing negative emotions	33	2.7
Other		
Encouraging openness, honesty, and direct communication	129	10.5
Keeping parties focused	94	7.7
Encouraging resolution	62	5.1
Gaining trust/rapport	30	2.5%
Stepping back/letting parties fashion the remedy	30	2.5
Total for facilitative behavior	**643**	**52.6**
Evaluative behavior		
Reality-checking behavior	326	26.7
Evaluating the strengths and weaknesses of the dispute	83	6.8
Providing knowledge of the law/process	74	6.1
Exploring/proposing options	68	5.6
Active negotiation	7	0.6
Total for evaluative behavior	**558**	**45.8**
Personal style		
Demeanor	76	6.2
Empathy	54	4.4
Persistence	48	3.9
Neutrality	33	2.7
Optimism	12	1.0
Creativity	8	0.7
Total for personal style	**231**	**18.9**
Other strategies and tactics		
Caucuses	153	12.5
Process control	45	3.7
Transformative or "quasi-transformative" tactics	12	1.0
Control of the introduction of evidence	9	0.8
Effective use of pre-mediation calls	9	0.8
Other	37	3.0
Total for other	**265**	**21.7**
Grand total number of responses	**1,697**	**138.8**
Total cases resolved	**1,223**	**100.0**

* Total number of resolved cases is 1,223. However, since some mediators have given multiple responses, the total number of responses (found at the bottom of each section) is much higher. Also note that the percentage given in the right column is only for the resolved cases.

TABLE 6.6   Turning points of the mediation*

Responses	Frequencies	Percentages*
Communication		
Information obtained at mediation	537	43.7
Opening statement	9	0.7
Offer of evidence to support claim	8	0.7
Pre-mediation dialog	6	0.5
Total responses for this section	**560**	**45.8**
Attitudes		
Openness to compromise and resolution	317	25.9
Charging parties' willingness to compromise	66	5.4
Respondents' willingness to compromise	57	4.7
Parties' mutual trust	29	2.4
Shift from positional to interest-based discussion	10	0.8
Total responses for this section	**479**	**39.2**
The offer		
More money and other benefits	58	4.7
Respondent meeting all demands	42	3.4
Parties' reasonable initial exchange of offers	15	1.2
Parties' descriptions of the resolution offer	8	0.7
Communication of final offer	7	0.6
Total responses for this section	**130**	**10.6**
The mediator		
"Reality-checking"	56	4.6
Caucus	58	4.7
Encouragement	23	1.9
Other tactics	8	0.7
Keeping the parties focused	4	0.3
Total responses for this section	**149**	**12.2**
The representative		
Charging parties' lawyers	67	5.5
Respondents' lawyers	51	4.2
External parties	16	1.3
Participation of key players from the respondents' side	6	0.5
Removal of a participant	4	0.3
Total responses for this section	**144**	**11.8**

TABLE 6.6 (*Cont'd*)

Responses	Frequencies	Percentages*
Acknowledgment of feelings		
Recognition of charging parties' hurt	35	2.9
Recognition of each other's position	26	2.1
Admission of some liability/apology	24	2.0
Charging parties' venting/catharsis	19	1.6
Charging parties' admission of some liability	5	0.4
Charging parties' specific expression of need	4	0.3
Total responses for this section	**113**	**9.2**
Other variables		
Recognition of the costs of not settling	27	2.2
Parties' need to preserve future relationship	11	0.9
Charging parties "moving on with their life"	9	0.7
Strong desire to leave the mediation	7	0.6
Miscellaneous category	27	2.2
Total responses for this section	**81**	**6.6**
Grand total number of responses	**1,656**	**135.4**
Total cases resolved	**1,223**	**100.0**

* Total number of resolved cases is 1,223. However, since some mediators have given multiple responses, the total number of responses (found at the bottom of each section) is much higher. Also note that the percentage given in the right column is only for the resolved cases.

Procedural factors: mediation conditions

Mediator neutrality was an important procedural due process measure in our first study (McDermott et al. 2000: 54, table III). We also measured fairness and mediator process control, both described in the comprehensive model (McDermott et al. 2001: 16–17).

We considered the concept of "active participation" in ways that complement the comprehensive model. For example, in our research a procedural due process measure was whether or not participants felt as though they had a full opportunity to present their view during mediation. (See table 6.3 above.) Data were also collected on whether or not this was the initial mediation session (yes = 97.3%) and, if not (no = 2.7%), how many sessions occurred before this one (67.7% had one prior session), how many hours the previous session lasted (average of 4 hours), who attended, did they bring representation, how many sessions occurred and the length of the mediation (3.66 hours) (McDermott et al. 2000: 6–9, tables II–VI).

TABLE 6.7   Participant satisfaction with the mediator*

Statements	Charging parties Mean (n, %)	Respondents Mean (n, %)
The mediator understood my needs.	4.30 (1,669, 86.4%)	4.31 (1,552, 86.9%)
The mediator helped clarify my needs.	**4.25** **(1,665, 84.4%)**	**4.17** **(1,504, 79.3%)**
At the beginning of the mediation, I considered the mediator to be neutral.	4.44 (1,674, 92.1%)	4.49 (1,566, 92.0%)
The mediator remained neutral throughout the session.	4.42 (1,664, 90.7%)	4.43 (1,564, 89.1%)
The mediator helped the parties develop options for resolving the charge.	4.27 (1,661, 85.1%)	4.23 (1,545, 83.9%)
The procedures used by the mediator in the mediation were fair to me.	**4.33** **(1,668, 88.5%)**	**4.44** **(1,564, 91.8%)**

* Satisfaction is measured by the "mean responses" of the participants on a Likert scale (scale of 1 [strongly disagree] to 5 [strongly agree]) and by the percentage of participants who agreed or strongly agreed with the statements. The sample size (n) is also given for evaluation purposes. Figures in bold refer to statements where a statistically significant difference (evaluated at 95% confidence level) exists between the mean responses of the charging parties and respondents.

Table 6.7 provides direct measures of satisfaction with the mediator's performance that closely match the comprehensive model. In particular, the statements listed in table 6.7 fall directly in line with "procedural factors: mediation conditions" sub-parts: "procedural clarity," "global fairness," and "interactional fairness." These data directly address mediators' abilities to connect with the parties, assist in clarification of needs, act neutral, and promote fairness. Unlike the comprehensive model that shows other researchers using archival data and coded tapes to examine process control, the EEOC studies rely on participant and mediator surveys. Thus we discovered the importance of mediator process control in measuring the factors that relate to the outcome.

Table 6.8 focuses on the barriers to the resolution of the dispute. This barrier measure gets to the heart of the comprehensive model's decision-making and problem-solving issues.

Similarly, referring back to tables 6.4 and 6.5 we see the conduct of the parties and mediator that contributed to the resolution of the dispute, while table 6.8 points to the conduct that interfered with the resolution of the dispute. This conduct cuts across all four T_m factors.

Our study asks the mediators to describe what they would have done differently in those cases that were not resolved. We believe that this inquiry also fits into the

TABLE 6.8   The five most important barriers to the resolution of the charge

Responses	#1	#2	#3	#4	#5	Total*
Positional conduct of the parties						
Charging party's positional conduct	296 (36.50%)	85 (10.48%)	43 (5.30%)	19 (2.34%)	9 (1.11%)	452 (55.73%)
Respondent's positional conduct	158 (19.48%)	121 (14.92%)	60 (7.40%)	25 (3.08%)	11 (1.36%)	375 (46.24%)
Both parties' positional conduct	75 (9.25%)	17 (2.10%)	20 (2.47%)	7 (0.86%)	11 (1.36%)	130 (16.03%)
Sectional total	**529 (65.23%)**	**223 (27.50%)**	**123 (15.17%)**	**51 (6.29%)**	**31 (3.82%)**	**957 (118.00%)**
"Table conduct" of the parties						
Charging party table conduct	50 (6.17%)	75 (9.25%)	40 (4.93%)	19 (2.34%)	7 (0.86%)	191 (23.55%)
Respondent table conduct	47 (5.8%)	44 (5.43%)	23 (2.84%)	20 (2.47%)	7 (0.86%)	141 (17.39%)
Sectional total	**97 (11.96%)**	**119 (14.67%)**	**63 (7.77%)**	**39 (4.81%)**	**14 (1.73%)**	**332 (40.94%)**
Emotions/attitudes of the parties						
Charging party's emotions	34 (4.19%)	34 (4.19%)	27 (3.33%)	16 (1.97%)	5 (0.62%)	116 (14.3%)
Respondents' emotions	11 (1.36%)	21 (2.59%)	12 (1.48%)	7 (0.86%)	2 (0.25%)	53 (6.54%)
Sectional total	**45 (5.55%)**	**55 (6.78%)**	**39 (4.81%)**	**23 (2.84%)**	**7 (0.86%)**	**169 (20.84%)**
Conduct of the legal and non-legal representatives						
Charging parties' lawyer	36 (4.44%)	42 (5.18%)	20 (2.47%)	5 (0.62%)	5 (0.62%)	108 (13.32%)
Respondents' lawyer	25 (3.08%)	24 (2.96%)	18 (2.22%)	6 (0.74%)	3 (0.37%)	76 (9.37%)
Lawyers of both parties	0 (0.00%)	0 (0.00%)	0 (0.00%)	1 (0.12%)	0 (0.00%)	1 (0.12%)

TABLE 6.8 (*Cont'd*)

Responses	#1	#2	#3	#4	#5	Total*
The behavior of the non-legal representatives of the charging party	7 (0.86%)	6 (0.74%)	3 (0.37%)	1 (0.12%)	2 (0.25%)	19 (2.34%)
The behavior of the non-legal representatives of the respondent	4 (0.49%)	2 (0.25%)	3 (0.37%)	1 (0.12%)	1 (0.12%)	11 (1.36%)
Sectional total	**72 (8.88%)**	**74 (9.12%)**	**44 (5.43%)**	**14 (1.73%)**	**11 (1.36%)**	**215 (26.51%)**
Lack of respondent authority	**32 (3.95%)**	**23 (2.83%)**	**10 (1.23%)**	**4 (0.49%)**	**1 (0.12%)**	**70 (8.63%)**
External factors	**20 (2.47%)**	**11 (1.36%)**	**9 (1.11%)**	**4 (0.49%)**	**1 (0.12%)**	**45 (5.55%)**
Miscellaneous factors						
Lack of preparation	13 (1.60%)	14 (1.73%)	6 (0.74%)	2 (0.25%)	1 (0.12%)	36 (4.44%)
Intense personality clash	6 (0.74%)	4 (0.49%)	2 (0.25%)	3 (0.37%)	2 (0.25%)	17 (2.10%)
Lack of trust	3 (0.37%)	5 (0.62%)	5 (0.62%)	2 (0.25%)	1 (0.25%)	16 (1.97%)
Interference of legal issues/use of mediation for discovery	7 (0.86%)	11 (1.36%)	6 (0.74%)	5 (0.62%)	2 (0.25%)	31 (3.82%)
The lack of witnesses and legal representatives	10 (1.23%)	10 (1.23%)	11 (1.36%)	7 (0.86%)	3 (0.37%)	41 (5.06%)
The role of time	15 (1.85%)	4 (0.49%)	4 (0.49%)	3 (0.37%)	1 (0.12%)	27 (3.33%)
The respondent as a state entity	3 (0.37%)	5 (0.62%)	3 (0.37%)	3 (0.37%)	1 (0.12%)	15 (1.85%)
Mediator self-blame	2 (0.25%)	1 (0.12%)	2 (0.25%)	1 (0.12%)	1 (0.12%)	7 (0.86%)

TABLE 6.8   (*Cont'd*)

Responses	#1	#2	#3	#4	#5	Total*
Language/ communication difficulties	2 (0.25%)	2 (0.25%)	1 (0.12%)	2 (0.25%)	0 (0.00%)	7 (0.86%)
Party walkouts	2 (0.25%)	0 (0.00%)	2 (0.25%)	1 (0.12%)	0 (0.00%)	5 (0.62%)
Other	2 (0.25%)	6 (0.74%)	3 (0.37%)	5 (0.62%)	1 (0.12%)	17 (2.10%)
Total for other	**65** (8.01%)	**62** (7.64%)	**45** (5.55%)	**34** (4.20%)	**13** (1.73%)	**219** (27.00%)
Grand total responses	**860** (106.0%)	**567** (70.0%)	**333** (41.0%)	**169** (20.8%)	**78** (9.74%)	**2007** (247.6%)
Total unresolved cases						**811** (100.0%)

procedural problem-solving and decision-making areas. The data in table 6.9 present a dilemma when mediators are asked "What would you have done differently in a mediation that was not resolved?" While these data are collected immediately after the mediation (T_1) there is no place in this section of the model for such a construct. Rather, these data are best seen as a collection of immediate reflective thoughts and observations of the mediation at the T_m "problem-solving: decision-making" section of the model.

As discussed above, some measures may cross over these T_m categories. For example, we look at the mediators' perceptions of the skills and abilities of the parties' representatives. The skill of an attorney may be a factor that primes readiness, a mediation condition, and surely a problem-solving/decision-making factor.[6]

Collecting Data "After" the Mediation: Short-Term Outcomes

T_1 represents the short-term post-mediation products of the process. Short-term outcomes are divided into disputant beliefs and attitudes, conflict resolved, and the institutional context.

Disputant beliefs and attitudes

Our first study looked at disputants' beliefs and attitudes as of the end of the mediation day. This clearly is the type of short-term outcome contemplated by the comprehensive model.

TABLE 6.9   Mediators' perceptions of what they would have done differently to resolve the dispute

Responses	Frequencies	Percentages*
Pre-screening elements		
Thorough pre-mediation preparation	76	31.7
More comprehensive pre-screening of the cases	50	20.1
Pre-screening to ensure that appropriate decision-makers are present	18	8.0
Total for pre-screening elements	**144**	**60.0**
Changes in mediator strategies and tactics		
Stronger dose of reality-checking	24	10.0
Better use of caucuses	16	7.0
Timing	16	6.8
Better probing	10	4.2
Getting tougher	5	2.1
Speaking to parties alone	4	1.7
Other changes	13	5.4
Total for changes in mediator strategies and tactics	**88**	**36.7**
Other	**8**	**3.3**
Total number of responses	**240**	**100.0**
Total number of unresolved cases	**811**	
Responses as a function of the total cases		30.0

Throughout this chapter we have discussed some of these findings and provided accompanying tables on data pertaining to T_1 measures such as: "satisfaction with the mediator" (table 6.7), "satisfaction with the process" (table 6.3), "satisfaction with the outcome" (table 6.3), and "why the case settled" (tables 6.4, 6.5 and 6.6). As is mentioned in chapter 2, rarely do researchers ask the opposite question, namely, "Why did the case not settle?", but results for our research are shown in table 6.10.

In addition to the various measures of participant satisfaction cited above, in table 6.11 we combine constructs in T_1 by asking participants about their overall satisfaction with the process (procedural justice measures) in light of their satisfaction with the outcome (distributive justice measures) which, we believe begins to answer some pressing theoretical questions about the utility of the process, even in instances when the results are not optimal. It is worth noting that every single cell in table 6.11 shows a statistically significant difference (McDermott et al. 2000: 84, table XIX).

TABLE 6.10 Specific reasons cited for the non-resolution of the dispute*

Responses	Frequencies	Percentages*
Charging party's actions	427	52.7
Respondent's actions	373	46.0
Actions of both parties	249	30.7
Actions of the charging party's lawyer	104	12.8
Actions of the respondent's lawyer	54	6.7
Outside factors	67	8.3
Non-legal representatives	24	3.2
Lack of legal representation	6	0.7
Other	6	0.7
Total responses	**1,310**	**161.5**
Total number of unresolved cases	**811**	**100.0**

* Total number of unresolved cases is 811. Since some mediators have given multiple reasons, the total number of responses differs from actual number of unresolved cases. The percentage given is a function of the unresolved cases and not the responses of participants.

Our research explored process satisfaction responses a little further by asking about any progress that was made in failed mediation sessions. According to the literature review supporting the comprehensive model, researchers rarely examine cases that fail to reach settlement. In other words, the tough question to participants becomes, "Even though an outcome was not reached did you make any progress?" The responses to this question are shown in table 6.12. We believe that this is important because the eventual "conflict resolved" outcome may flow from what occurred in mediation but the mediation itself may be "unsuccessful" because the resolution has yet to fructify. For these mediations where there was not an immediate resolution, in both the charging party and respondent data we see that there is a skew toward disagreeing that progress was made. A little less than one-third of the participants did indicate that progress was made toward resolution of the dispute. One could arguably classify the mediation as a success even though it did not result in immediate resolution. This is an important T_1 measure as it portends a possible relationship change or other movement toward resolution.[7] Indeed, we think our research refines the T_1 "conflict resolved" classification by examining where progress was made in the resolution of the dispute even where the conflict was not resolved. We saw this as a "mini-win" and an important measure in understanding mediation as a longitudinal process.

A close examination of the constructs related to sub-parts of T_1 "disputant beliefs and attitudes" can be found throughout this chapter. However, the remaining five sub-parts of the T_1 model (satisfaction with the court/judicial system, reduced anxiety about the crime, reduced fear of revictimization, and improved functioning) were either not directly examined (quantitatively) or found in the open-ended (qualitative)

TABLE 6.11 Overall participant satisfaction based on their satisfaction with the mediation result*

Statements	Charging parties (n, %)		Respondents (n, %)	
	Satisfied	Not satisfied	Satisfied	Not satisfied
Procedural elements				
Explanation, scheduling, and voice				
Adequate explanation	**4.43** (826, 93.5%)	**3.94** (395, 79.2%)	**4.31** (886, 88.6%)	**3.94** (253, 77.9%)
Prompt scheduling	**4.47** (843, 92.2%)	**4.01** (398, 80.7%)	**4.49** (917, 92.6%)	**4.08** (259, 81.9%)
Understood the process	**4.53** (848, 96.5%)	**4.08** (397, 83.1%)	**4.63** (918, 98.1%)	**4.27** (260, 89.2%)
Opportunity to present views	**4.60** (845, 95.7%)	**4.05** (398, 80.7%)	**4.70** (923, 98.2%)	**4.20** (258, 84.9%)
Mediator				
Mediator understood needs	**4.58** (840, 95.4%)	**3.89** (397, 73.0%)	**4.50** (915, 94.3%)	**3.84** (257, 67.7%)
Mediator helped clarify needs	**4.57** (838, 95.0%)	**3.79** (396, 69.2%)	**4.38** (881, 87.2%)	**3.71** (252, 59.9%)
Mediator neutral in the beginning	**4.61** (845, 96.2%)	**4.16** (398, 84.7%)	**4.62** (922, 95.3%)	**4.15** (259, 82.2%)
Mediator remained neutral	**4.64** (839, 97.1%)	**4.09** (396, 81.6%)	**4.61** (922, 94.6%)	**4.01** (258, 76.7%)
Mediator helped develop options	**4.58** (841, 95.6%)	**3.75** (394, 65.2%)	**4.48** (911, 92.2%)	**3.59** (254, 60.6%)
Mediator used fair procedures	**4.57** (839, 95.8%)	**3.99** (398, 77.9%)	**4.62** (922, 97.4%)	**4.02** (260, 78.8%)
Distributive elements				
Development of realistic options	**4.44** (842, 93.5%)	**3.13** (389, 45.5%)	**4.38** (909, 90.8%)	**3.07** (246, 39.0%)
Satisfaction with the fairness of the session	**4.48** (838, 95.1%)	**3.45** (390, 55.6%)	**4.59** (920, 97.2%)	**3.65** (258, 62%)

* Satisfaction is measured by the "mean responses" of the participants on a Likert scale (scale of 1 [strongly disagree] to 5 [strongly agree]) and these scores are the top numbers in each cell. This is followed by the sample size and percentage of participants who agreed or strongly agreed with the statements. Figures in bold refer to statements where a statistically significant difference (evaluated at 95% confidence level) exists between the mean responses of the participants who were satisfied with the results and those who were not satisfied with the results of the mediation.

TABLE 6.12 Responses of participants whose claims were not resolved in mediation regarding whether "progress was made toward resolution"

Participant group	Total responses	Mean rating	Strongly agree/disagree (%)	Neither agree nor disagree (%)	Agree/strongly agree (%)
Charging parties	488	2.60	48.6	22.1	29.3
Respondents	486	2.72	41.6	30.9	27.6

responses. This may be due to researcher oversight, but we are inclined to think, based on our experience and research, that many of these measures may not necessarily pertain to the workplace mediation context.

Conflict resolved

The "conflict resolved" construct focuses on outcome measures ("agreement reached," "issues resolved," "distributive justice," "relationship changed") that reaffirm the link of "process to outcome." Our study examines a variety of outcomes including: complete (tables 6.3 and 6.9), partially complete (table 6.12) or no agreements (table 6.8).

Where our survey would have benefited from the comprehensive model is in the measure of "relationship change." We did not measure this on a short-term basis or for resolved versus unresolved cases.

Institutional context

Our research mandate did not include an analysis of the mediation program from an institutional context perspective. While not part of our study, the EEOC has found that cases that go to mediation are closed much quicker than cases that are investigated. We do know that the EEOC has relied on our data to highlight institutional efficiency. Our program studies actually end at the institutional context stage and become the evidence used by the agency to establish efficiency and effectiveness.

Collecting Data "After" the Mediation: Long-Term Outcomes

T_2 represents the long-term post-mediation products of the process. Our research is almost entirely focused on immediate post-mediation survey data and so the long-term T_2 focus is not a part of our study. However, excluding the time differential, many of the questions posed under the "post-mediation" construct focus on data presented throughout this chapter. We measure fairness of the procedure, satisfaction with the results, trust of the mediator, and competence of the mediator in a "post-mediation" survey, but not three, six, or 12 months out. Longitudinal research on mediation, as discussed in chapter 2, is an area that is, for practical reasons, in need of most attention by researchers and program directors.

In the participant study we did ask, at the end of the session and regardless of the "success" or "failure," if the participant would be willing to participate in the EEOC mediation program in the future. While this is an immediate post-mediation data-collection point we believe it does provide some indication or future projection of the likelihood of their willingness to possibly use the process again. The important point to note in table 6.13 is that, regardless of what a participant wanted going in or what they actually received as a result of participating, the vast majority (roughly 90%) would use the program/process again. This is an extremely telling result.

TABLE 6.13   Participants' willingness to participate in the EEOC mediation program in the future

	Total charging parties (%)	Total respondents (%)
For those who knew what they wanted going into the mediation: Did you obtain what you wanted going into the mediation?		
Yes	40.8	56.5
No	55.5	40.9
No response given	3.7	2.5
For those who responded YES to the question above: If you were a party to a charge before the EEOC in the future, would you be willing to participate in the EEOC's mediation program?		
Yes	95.2	97.5
No	2.2	0.7
No response given	2.6	1.8
For those who responded NO to the question above: If you were a party to a charge before the EEOC in the future, would you be willing to participate in the EEOC's mediation program?		
Yes	88.9	93.2
No	9.8	4.0
No response given	1.4	2.8

DISCUSSION ON THE APPLICATION OF THE
COMPREHENSIVE MODEL

Applying the comprehensive model to our EEOC mediation research provides new information on and insights into how various constructs influence the evolution of the model. As more researchers apply the model a utility-based dialog will undoubtedly emerge, and for our part the following discussion is our attempt to add to this worthy endeavor.

It is generally worth noting that the comprehensive model is methodologically an excellent example of a one-group, pre-test, post-test (with a second post-test) design as described in Cook and Campbell's seminal work *Quasi-Experimentation* (1979). If we take their basic equation:

$$O_1 - X - O_2 - O_3$$

where O_1 is the pre-test observation, X is the treatment (mediation), O_2 is the first post-test observation, and O_3 is the second post-test observation, by symbolically substituting the elements in the comprehensive model we get:

$$T_0 - T_m - T_1 - T_2$$

Although this is a simplistic analogy it does depict the temporal basis of the model and when and where certain types of data can be gathered. It is also similar to the linear decision science approach found in figures 2.1, 2.6, and 2.7 above.

Applying the comprehensive model to our EEOC research demonstrates some construct similarities and methodological benefits. One methodological strength of the model is the ability to gather data during the mediation (T_m) or treatment (X). Another notable distinction is that data collection occurs nearly continuously and incorporates primary and secondary data. As noted, the model also relies on multiple methods, and on inductive and deductive reasoning, as well as qualitative and quantitative analysis.

Theoretically, in our research we incorporate the logic of analytic induction, therefore recognizing and appreciating the strength of the mixed methods and mixed logic approach of the comprehensive model. There also appears to be some flexibility within the model to consider context, at least in terms of organizational and institutional systems measures. That is why our workplace research fits closely into the comprehensive model equation.

Based on our research in workplace mediation there are challenges in applying the model. First, the heavy reliance on psychological theory as the major framework, as well as a focus primarily on interpersonal dynamics and personal skills, may pose some challenges when translating the model to other social science disciplines and legal research. There obviously will be some degree of alteration in the unit of analysis for researchers from say sociology (groups) and anthropology (culture), and theoretical substitution for constructs, research design, and data collection may be difficult to achieve. Even so, the model provides a good starting point for researchers relying on other disciplinary constructs and paradigms.

Perhaps the biggest challenge in applying our research to the model is that, while many of the constructs match up, there are challenges in where they should be placed within the T_0, T_m, T_1, or T_2 sequence. For instance, some of the data gathered in T_0 on satisfaction with the mediator can be gathered in T_m and T_1. While some data can be collected at any time (mediator background or mediator style), others can only be gathered at specific points such as after the experience (treatment X or T_m). So as a framework and methodology within which to place data, we learned that, while there is similarity with constructs, there is less congruence on where these data fit into the model.

This tells us three things. The first is that the research design that drives the data collection, and the research tools that limit the types of data collected, directly impact the "goodness of fit" between data and where they line up in the model. In this chapter it is clear that our application of the comprehensive model informs us that there is a good deal of fit, and our research adds a few new constructs to the model.

Second, as noted at the beginning of the chapter, our research was conducted long before the model was developed. Yet what is most interesting to note from mediators' responses to our open-ended survey questions is that they are remarkably similar to the constructs presented throughout the comprehensive model, especially in T_0, T_m, and T_1. What this indicates is that mediators, those who practically apply their skills within the interpersonal mediation context, are indirectly supporting or even confirming many of the conceptual frames and operational measures within the comprehensive model. Taking this line of thinking to a personal level, we have been part of extremely unusual mediation process dynamics driven in part by cultural, economic, or political conditions that do not fit so neatly into any one model or framework. However, the developers of the comprehensive model have been clear in their encouragement of critical in-depth analysis that can lead to the addition of more constructs into the framework. This can also lead to the further development of another theoretical and analytical layer within which to place new constructs.

Finally, the application of our research to the comprehensive model leads us to believe that what may appear to some researchers and practitioners to be a linear (deterministic) or static (fixed) set of qualities is really a rather flexible framework and functionally dynamic model. It would be a mistake to interpret the comprehensive model too rigidly because, while far from perfect, it does possess a flexible characteristic between the various parts (T_0, T_m, T_1, and T_2). This is what puts the model into "motion" to create, expand, and evolve by incorporating more constructs, theoretical lenses, and methodological approaches. For instance, while we have conducted tests that examine the relationship between distributive and procedural justice we invariably used constructs and variables from all parts of the model that subsequently provided new knowledge. It is clear that there is great capacity to undertake more complex inferential inquiries such as multivariate analysis. This can be seen in figures 2.6 and 2.7 above. We also note from our experience that when using other statistical methods such as cluster analysis, which is an inductively driven process, we often create new constructs and avenues of inquiry that, while they may not fit perfectly into one specific part of the comprehensive model, certainly can be incorporated.

NOTES

1 Details of our research can be found by going to <www.conflict-resolution.org.sitebody/research/default.htm>.

2 While we may use words such as "interfere" when we discuss why a mediation did not result in a settlement, we do not make any value judgments as to whether the underlying conduct was correct or not.

3 The California Department of Fair Employment and Housing (CDFEH) asked the Center for Conflict Resolution research team to conduct a similar study of their mediation program based on the research design and protocols we used for the US EEOC. However, the CDFEH context of these two programs was different in regard to types of mediators used, provision of services, and other key characteristics so it is noteworthy to see similar results.

4 In the California study we used a closed-ended survey that was constructed out of the codes that were developed during the coding and analysis of the second EEOC study. Mediators in the California research were offered the opportunity to identify additional factors not set forth in our codes. We found very few additions, supporting the presumption that our codes were comprehensive. These codes are found in appendix A2 of *An Evaluation of the California Department of Fair Employment and Housing Pilot Mediation Program* located at <www.conflict-resolution.org.sitebody/research/default.htm>, or go to <www.dfehmp.ca.gov/News/PMP%20Eval%2004%20Evaluation.doc>.

5 Our study also asks each mediator to describe or list reasons why the conflict was settled or why it broke down and to identify the hostile and contentious behavior. While this could be placed in the antecedent dispute characteristics section, we believe that for timing purposes it is better placed in the in the T_m or T_1 sections.

6 We note that one could also place whether one is represented by counsel, and the skill of that counsel in the "dispute characteristics" category under T_0.

7 We note that researchers often cite such progress.

REFERENCES

Cook, T. & Campbell, D. T. (1979) *Quasi-Experimentation: Design and Analysis Issues for Field Settings*. Houghton Mifflin, Boston.

Krivis, J. & McAdoo, B. (1997) A style index for mediators. *Alternatives to the High Cost of Litigation*. 15, 157–167. <www.mediate.com/articles/krivis4.cfm> (November 9, 2004).

McDermott, E. P., Obar, R., Jose, A. & Bowers, M. (2000) *An Evaluation of the Equal Employment Opportunity Commission Mediation Program*. A report to the US EEOC can be found by going to <www.conflict-resolution.org.sitebody/research/default.htm> or to <www.eeoc.gov/mediate/report/index.html>.

McDermott, E. P., Obar, R., Polkinghorn, B. & Jose, A. (2001) *The EEOC Mediation Program: Mediators' Perspective on the Parties, Processes, and Outcomes.* A report to the US EEOC can be found by going to <www.conflict-resolution.org.sitebody/research/default.htm> or to <www.eeoc.gov/mediate/mcdfinal.html>.

McDermott, E. P., Jose, A, Obar, R., Polkinghorn, B. & Bowers, M. (2002) Has the EEOC hit a home run? An evaluation of the EEOC mediation program from the participants' perspective. In D. Lewin & B. E. Kaufman (eds.), *Advances in Industrial and Labor Relations*, vol. 11. Elsevier Press–JAI, Oxford, pp. 1–40.

McDermott, E. P., Polkinghorn, B., Jose, A. & Obar, R. (2002) *An Evaluation of the California Department of Fair Employment and Housing Pilot Mediation Program.* A report to the CDFEH can be found by going to <www.conflict-resolution.org.sitebody/research/default.htm> or to <www.eeoc.gov/mediate/mcdfinal.html>.

McDermott, E. P., Obar, R. & Jose, A. (2003) *An Investigation of the Reasons for the Lack of Employer Participation in the EEOC Mediation Program.* A report located at: <www.conflict-resolution.org.sitebody/research/default.htm> or <www.eeoc.gov/mediate/study3/index.html>.

Riskin, L. L. (1996) Understanding mediators' orientations, strategies, and techniques: a grid for the perplexed. *Harvard Negotiation Law Review* 7 (Spring), 1–34.

Riskin, L. L. (2003) Decision making in mediation: the new old grid and the new grid system. *Notre Dame Law Review* 79, 1–53.

Chapter 7

Restorative Justice Mediated Dialog

Mark S. Umbreit and Robert B. Coates

Introduction

Restorative justice mediated dialog is a conceptual frame that has utility for grouping and describing efforts at resolving conflict by engaging persons in face-to-face exchange. These approaches to conflict resolution have evolved out of the process of working with victims and criminal offenders. Today, these approaches are used at community levels to reduce or prevent the likelihood of offenses, for example, in acts of hate (Umbreit, Coates & Vos 2003), as attempts to divert offenders from the formal justice system, at the point of pre-sentence, after conviction, and even as institutionalized offenders attempt to reintegrate into the community (Maxwell & Morris 1993; Evje & Cushman 2000; Umbreit 2001; Coates, Umbreit & Vos 2003). These approaches are also used to resolve conflicts that never come to the attention of formal social control bodies, such as neighborhood conflicts that could lead to criminal charges. Some of these approaches, following extensive preparation over many months, have even been used to respond to requests of people who have survived an act of severe violence. These approaches allow victims, or a surviving family member of a loved one who was murdered, to seek answers and express their pain (Umbreit, Vos, Coates & Brown 2003).

Typically, the approaches which we group under this dialog rubric are victim–offender mediation/conferencing, family group conferencing, and peacemaking circles. We will describe each of these in more detail later. But as we considered the valuable contribution of the proposed mediation model developed and described in chapter 2 in this book, we felt we should note clearly that many practitioners of restorative justice dialog approaches do not consider what they do to be mediation. While many practitioners do describe themselves as mediators, many do not, preferring such descriptors as "facilitators."

The cornerstone restorative justice dialog approach initially developed in Kitchner, Ontario. It was refined and enlarged in Indiana in the late 1970s, and was called Victim Offender Reconciliation Program or VORP. While some programs still exist with that name, in the 1980s the bulk of those early VORP-type programs began calling themselves Victim Offender Mediation Program. The most recent evolution of the concept and name has yielded to Victim Offender Conferencing Program, in an attempt, in part, to distinguish conferencing from "traditional mediation." So, at the moment there are practitioners doing rather similar things under the various labels of reconciliation, mediation, and conferencing. Yet each emphasizes, to varying degrees, bringing persons harmed by conflict together to repair a harm.

While we make no suggestion here that all of what is described above is or should be called mediation, we do believe that the mediation model proposed in this book has considerable merit for how we think about, conduct research, and practice within a restorative justice dialog framework. So we will attempt here to provide a flavor of what we mean. The model described in chapter 2 is too vast and detailed to apply to restorative justice dialog in the space of a chapter. So we will highlight some of what we think it offers for further understanding dialog and mediation.

THE CONTEXT OF RESTORATIVE JUSTICE

Restorative justice dialog exists within the broad paradigm of restorative justice. That paradigm is drawn upon to foster actions other than dialog. For example, it is a framework that can guide system change such as that undertaken in Washington County, Minnesota (Coates, Umbreit & Vos 2002), Genesee County, New York (Wittman 2004), and Deschutes County, Oregon (Coates, Umbreit & Vos 2000).

Whether used to shape system change, dialog, or other interventions, restorative justice is value-driven. Howard Zehr, a pioneer in restorative justice practice and theory, offers several pithy comments that elucidate some of those values and principles. He writes in a recent work, *The Little Book of Restorative Justice* (2002: 25): "Restorative justice requires, at minimum, that we address victims' harms and needs, hold offenders accountable to put right those harms, and involve victims, offenders and communities in this process." Further, he offers that "restorative justice is an invitation for dialog and exploration" (2002: 10). Although a panoply of values may underpin any restorative justice effort, Zehr concludes one value is "supremely important: respect . . . respect for all, even those who are different from us, even those who seem to be our enemies" (2002: 36).

In practice, Zehr and Mika (1998) suggest that we are working toward restorative justice when we:

1 focus on the harms of wrongdoing more than the rules that have been broken;
2 show equal concern and commitment to victims and offenders, involving both in the process of justice;
3 work toward the restoration of victims, empowering them and responding to their needs as they see them;

4   support offenders while encouraging them to understand, accept, and carry
    out their obligations;
5   recognize that, while obligations may be difficult for offenders, they should
    not be intended as harms, and they must be achievable;
6   provide opportunities for dialog, direct or indirect, between victims and
    offenders as appropriate;
7   involve and empower the affected community through the justice process,
    and increase their capacity to recognize and respond to community bases of
    crime;
8   encourage collaboration and reintegration rather than coercion and isolation;
9   give attention to the unintended consequences of our actions and programs;
    and
10 show respect to all parties including victims, offenders, and justice colleagues.

After some 25 years, restorative justice programming is no longer on the peri-
phery of criminal justice. In 1994, the American Bar Association endorsed the
practice of victim–offender mediation and dialog. The association recommended
its use in courts throughout the country and also provided guidelines for its
use and development (American Bar Association 1994). In 1996, the New Zealand
Ministry of Justice issued a working paper on restorative justice for serious consideration as a federal policy (New Zealand Ministry of Justice 1996). The
Council of Europe, in 1999, specifically focused on the restorative use of mediation procedures in criminal matters, and adopted a set of recommendations to
guide member states in using mediation in criminal cases (Council of Europe
Committee of Ministers 1999). Meeting in 2000, the United Nations Congress
on Crime Prevention considered restorative justice in its plenary sessions and
developed a draft proposal entitled *UN Basic Principles on the Use of Restorative
Justice Programs in Criminal Matters* (United Nations 2000). These proposed principles encouraged the use of restorative justice programming by member states
at all stages of the criminal justice process. The proposed principles under-
scored the voluntary nature of participation in restorative justice procedures and
recommended the development of standards and safeguards for the practice
of restorative justice. A final proposal was adopted by the United Nations in
2002 (United Nations 2002). As the above deliberations and recommendations
suggest, restorative justice programs and policies are now being developed in
many parts of the world including Australia, Canada, European countries, Japan,
New Zealand, South Africa, several South American countries, Russia, South Korea
and the United States.

In the United States, a surprising expression of support for restorative justice is
emerging from victim advocacy groups. In the early years, most victim advocacy
groups adamantly opposed restorative justice measures; some still do. The National
Organization for Victim Assistance endorsement of "restorative community justice"
reflects this shift as well as the active participation of victim support organizations
in the ongoing restorative justice movement. This broad context of restorative
justice with its emphasis upon values and principles as well as its place in public

policy debate regarding criminal justice provides the backdrop for restorative justice dialog. In the model proposed by Herrman, Hollett, and Gale, these factors would be included under institutional context, antecedent variables, or T_0.

RESTORATIVE JUSTICE DIALOG: THREE APPROACHES

To provide a better understanding of what constitutes restorative justice dialog, three approaches that may be considered under this rubric will be briefly described: victim–offender mediation/conferencing (VOM), family group conferencing (FGC), and peacemaking circles (Circles). All three share the desire to bring together persons engaged in conflict to repair harm done and to enable individuals to move on.

Victim–Offender Mediation/Conferencing

Victim–offender mediation/conferencing is the oldest, most widely used, and most empirically grounded form of restorative justice dialog (Umbreit 2001). It is typically used with victims of property crimes or minor assaults, although increasingly it is being requested by victims of serious crimes. Depending upon the jurisdiction, participants may be referred by judges, probation officers, or attorneys. Occasionally individuals have heard of the programs on their own and seek assistance. It is expected that victims will voluntarily choose to participate in these programs. They may choose to participate for specific reasons. Many have questions about the crime that have never been satisfactorily answered. Some want the offender to know the impact of the crime for them. Some are looking for some kind of restitution. Some want to meet the offender in order to help him or her stay out of trouble in the future. While it is hoped that offenders, too, will volunteer to participate, it is certainly acknowledged that their decision to do so may be influenced by their perception of how meeting the victim might help or hinder their particular case.

Once an offender and victim have agreed to participate in mediation/ conferencing, typically a trained mediator/facilitator will meet with each separately one or more times before the actual session. This is done to listen to each individual's story, to share with them the process to be expected, to help participants shape realistic expectations, and to screen out those few individuals who are not appropriate for mediation. These trained mediators/facilitators are frequently volunteers and can represent a community presence in the process. The mediation session will include the victim, offender, and mediator. Often family members may be present as support, but these individuals usually play a secondary role.

The mediator's task is to facilitate a discussion between victim and offender so their questions and issues may be dealt with. If a restitution plan emerges, the mediator will often write up the details in a contract for the participants. In some jurisdictions, the mediator will report the results of the mediation to the courts and may have responsibilities for follow-up.

It should be clear that a mediator is not on a fact-finding mission. There is no question of guilt. In nearly all instances, the offender has already admitted guilt before being approached to participate. There is no dispute as in some other forms of mediation. Neither is victim–offender mediation/conferencing settlement-driven. Victim healing, offender accountability, and restoration of losses guide this work.

Family Group Conferencing

Family group conferencing originated in New Zealand and is used extensively in juvenile justice in that country (Maxwell & Morris 2001; McCold 2001). This approach emphasizes supporting offenders in taking responsibility for their actions and in changing their behaviors. Thus, the involvement of the offender's family is critical and expected. The victim's family is also invited. When deemed appropriate, key community members, such as a teacher or a police officer, may also be invited.

These conferences frequently take breaks for families to caucus to discuss what is happening in the larger conference and the next steps they may desire. In family group conferencing, guilt may not have been acknowledged, so even specific charges may be open for discussion. In New Zealand, at least, the family group conferencing coordinator is explicitly responsible for seeing that a specific plan develops. Plans address causes, reparation, and offender accountability. These facilitators are paid social service staff called Youth Justice Coordinators.

In North America, a somewhat different model of family group conferencing developed. This approach is frequently used with police officers as facilitators and typically relies upon a standardized, scripted template for facilitation. Family group conferencing is frequently formally embedded in part of the justice system (McCold 2001).

Peacemaking Circles

The peacemaking circles are rooted in North American indigenous cultures (Coates et al. 2003). For example, since the 1980s in the Yukon, First Nation people and local justice officials have developed partnerships between communities and formal justice agencies to build shared responsibility for handling crime problems through Community Peacemaking Circles (Stuart 1996; Pranis, Stuart & Wedge 2003). The circle is much more explicitly focused on harm done to community and community responsibility for supporting and holding accountable its members than the two approaches described above.

The circle process may be requested by offenders, victims, community members, or justice officials. Participation is voluntary. Sitting around the circle may be the offender and his or her family members and support persons, the victim and his or her family members and support persons, any number of community members, and perhaps a justice official. The circle process is facilitated by a circle keeper. Large circles may necessitate co-circle keepers.

In complex cases, smaller circles, perhaps one with the victim and their support persons and another with offender and their support persons, may meet before the larger circle meets to give people more opportunities to share their stories of what happened and to clarify what they would like to have happen now. In most instances, the circle keeper will meet with key participants before the circle takes place to become familiar with the individuals, the conflict that led to the referral, and participants' fears and hopes.

The actual circle process is guided by the circle keeper. The circle is often opened with a ritual designed to symbolize the work to be undertaken in the circle. For example, a fractured mirror may suggest the splintering of individuals, family, or community. A "talking piece" will be passed around the circle. Participants may only speak when holding the talking piece. Respectful listening with the heart as well as with the mind is central to the circle process; it is believed that using a talking piece encourages respectful listening and respectful dialog.

The first round of speaking may focus on the event that has brought people to the circle, i.e. what happened. The second round may focus on feelings at the time of the event and now. A third round may focus on reparation. Offenders are expected to make reparation to the community as well as to the victim. Decisions rendered by the circle are made by consensus. The circle is closed with ritual and frequently food is shared afterward.

A follow-up circle is typically held to determine if the participants have done what was expected and whether the circle needs to do more and meet yet again. In complex cases there may be a large number circles taking place over months or even years. The circle process can be very time-consuming and labor-intensive, but of the approaches described here, it typically involves the broadest cross-section of people touched by the conflict.

We should note that there is considerable variation within each of the approaches described above. That variation should be taken into account as researchers undertake to describe approaches and their impact. While victim–offender mediation/conferencing initially focused on the victim and offender, and sometimes included a support person for each, examples now abound where this approach is used with broader institutional/community conflicts. For example, it has been used as a means of resolving conflict among teen groups in high schools and as a means to responding to hate crime (Umbreit, Coates & Vos 2003).

The three approaches follow a broadly shared process, from preparation to meeting/conference to follow-up. The amount of time required, who is involved, and the emphasis devoted to each of these three stages varies considerably within and across the three approaches, reflecting differences in philosophy and even goals. These kinds of variations underscore the importance for researchers to adequately describe the program being studied. Too often, research focuses on what goes into a program (e.g. participant characteristics) and what comes out (outcomes) without paying adequate attention to describing what happens in the "black box." The Herrman, Hollett, and Gale model devotes considerable attention to this task as it addresses "variables describing the mediation process."

IMPLICATIONS OF THE PROPOSED MODEL FOR RESEARCH ON RESTORATIVE JUSTICE DIALOG AND VICE VERSA

The Importance of Time Order and Interaction of Variables

Two strengths of the proposed model are its emphasis on time order and the inter-action of the many variables identified in the resulting four stages. It is surprising how often these two areas are ignored in action research on restorative justice programs and therefore overlooked in training.

Careful attention to time order and interaction of variables has the potential for yielding a greater awareness of variation within and across restorative justice dialog approaches. In particular, it will enable researchers to begin to sort out the relative impact of a number of important domains or characteristics which currently tend to be measured in a dichotomous "present or absent" manner.

For example, each of the three approaches places some emphasis on the involvement of community members. Currently, at least in theory, peacekeeping circles are the most community oriented of the three. In the circle approach, com-munity participation may take place at numerous points in the process, including preparation, actual circle/conference, and follow-up. The variation of community participation is not an either-or issue. That participation varies across approach and within approach depending on the specifics of a particular case. The model suggests, as many do, a time order linearity that may be much less linear in practice than on paper. There is considerable interaction among variables within a given time phase.

Such careful attention can also begin to answer whether a given characteristic is an antecedent variable, an outcome variable, or some complex combination. For example, an important research question for all three approaches is why some people choose to participate in restorative justice dialog and others do not. In a recent study (Coates, Burns & Umbreit 2002), victims referred to a victim–offender conferencing program were interviewed about why they chose either to participate or not to participate in the program. Victims who had had personal crimes committed against them were more likely to participate than those who were victims of property crimes. In cases where the program intervention was designed to divert the offender from further court proceedings, fewer victims chose to participate than in cases where conferencing was offered as part of a pre-sentence investigation or after the court had handed down a sentence. Taken together, then, the "legal characteristics" and the "conflict characteristics" were related to victim willingness to participate. These findings were corroborated when victims were asked to identify the reasons why they chose to participate or not. The most often mentioned reason given for not participating was that it was not worth the time and trouble. The most frequently mentioned reason for choosing to participate was "hoped offender would be helped by meeting with me." That was closely followed by "wanted to hear why the offender did this to me" and "wanted offender to know how his/her actions affected me."

We suspect that there may be a more basic set of beliefs and attitudes that pre-dispose some individuals to be more willing to participate in this kind of program. Whether it is a basic philosophy of life, an orientation about citizen responsibility, or a sense of obligation, we do not know. But we expect that this is an area for further fruitful exploration. As we consider the proposed model as a framework for guiding research, we need to pay close attention to interaction of variables not only across time order phases but also within them.

Antecedents

The array of potential antecedents that may relate to dialog processes and outcomes is sometimes mind-boggling. Here, we will comment on only two that are mentioned in the proposed mediation model. The first is auspices, which we would identify as falling under program context. Early on in the restorative justice movement, and continuing to this day for many proponents, there has been a deep distrust of programs operated by the formal justice system. There was the belief, justified or not, that programs such as victim–offender mediation/conferencing and circles would lose their integrity and focus if administered by public institutions. This tension, while much less prevalent in situations where family group conferencing is the intervention of choice, remains a hot-button issue for many practitioners in the restorative justice field. At the same time, the public sector has long been involved in administering these sorts of programs (Umbreit & Greenwood 1999), and when dialog approaches are used to work with victims of severe violence, public institutions have proven pivotal (Flaten 1996; Umbreit 1998; Umbreit, Vos, Coates & Brown 2003).

In a recent study of victim–offender mediation programs operating in six Oregon counties (Coates et al. 2000), we had an opportunity to compare public versus private auspices because two of the six programs were operated by the county as part of its line item budgets. The other four were administered by private sector organizations. While there was considerable variation across programs regarding nature of referrals, number of cases, and mediation processes, there was no signific-ant difference in terms of outcomes such as participant satisfaction, assessment of helpfulness, willingness to recommend program to friends, and agreement com-pletion. Public or private non-profit auspices across the six programs, then, did not yield different outcomes.

Mediator characteristics are too often taken for granted in restorative justice research. This may in part be because many restorative justice advocates do not want the mediator/facilitator/circle keeper to play a dominant role in the process. As is so often said, their task is to assure a safe environment. Creating a safe place for dialog involves adequately preparing participants, coordinating with institu-tional officials if needed, and being ready to intervene if necessary. But there is a strongly held value that the work of mediation – asking and answering questions, the sharing of stories, any resulting agreements – should largely remain the responsibility of the participants. Nonetheless, these facilitators play pivotal roles. Sometimes they are underappreciated by the participants. Sometimes they are given too much credit. In either case, it behooves us to know who they are, for they do much to shape the process of dialog.

It seems to us that interest in mediator characteristics must go beyond demographics and skills to include philosophical orientation, length of experience with mediation/dialog, personal experience of life-changing conflict, and intent and expectations regarding the process and desired outcomes of restorative justice dialog. The person who chooses to be a circle keeper may be quite different from the individual who chooses to do victim–offender mediation within the context of prison. Or they might not be very different at all. The skilled negotiator may not be able to accept the silence of dialog, or to trust that the process of the circle will make things right. It may be that some individuals are better suited to one type of facilitator role over another, which does not mean that one role is better than another. The more we understand about who chooses to facilitate restorative dialog and why they choose to do so, the better we will be positioned to screen staff hires and volunteers and to do appropriate training.

Process Used

This is the traditional black box. As we indicated earlier, we believe it is important to describe as fully as possible what takes place in that box. Such ability to describe is not only necessary for assessment and evaluation, it is also necessary for those program developers who will want to replicate what has been studied. We do want to caution against mixing process variables with outcome variables. For example under "procedural factors: mediation conditions" described in the proposed model in chapter 2, we would suggest that, while "procedural clarity" focuses on the process of mediation, "global fairness" and "interactional fairness" are measures of immediate or short-run outcome which may influence other outcome variables such as satisfaction with the process or with the mediator.

The notion of control is anathema to many mediators/facilitators/circle keepers. Yet the proposed mediation model encourages practitioners to face squarely the question of control. Many who practice within restorative justice dialog approaches see themselves as different from those who work within the formal social control systems. These practitioners do not see themselves as authoritarian or directive. They prefer to use words such as sharing, partnering, and empowering to describe how they go about their work. Perhaps circle keepers are most resistant to the notion that they exercise control because they typically believe and repeatedly state within the circle that a "circle is a circle of equals," "each individual has an opportunity to participate and is equally responsible for process and outcome," and "decisions made by the circle should be by consensus."

Nonetheless, we submit that mediators/facilitators/circle keepers do exercise considerable control, explicitly and implicitly. Recognizing that exercise of control will vary within and across restorative justice dialog approaches, it does seem evident that the process, itself is controlled to a large extent by the mediator/facilitator/circle keeper. There is typically a flow to dialog that is rather similar across approaches, beginning with dialog about what happened that led to conflict, moving to feelings such as pain of loss as a result of the conflict, concluding with ways of making some form of repair to the victim/to the community. Participants know, to varying degrees, what to expect when encountering each other and are usually reminded about ground rules at the beginning of a meeting. If a disgruntled victim wanted to begin with reparation, most mediators/facilitators/circle keepers would step in to put things back in order. That this circumstance seldom happens is likely a testimony to the implicit control of the process that these coordinators exercise. In some dialog programs for victims of severe violence, mediators play the major role in determining when a victim is ready to meet with the offender. This has, at times, led to disagreements and conflict between mediators and victims who believe they are ready when the mediator does not. Even in peacemaking circles the opening ritual and explanation of ground rules shape the process and subtly serve, intentionally or not, to remind participants who is in charge. And even the use of a talking piece, while regarded as extremely valuable by participants – particularly those who are shy and less likely to speak up in a crowd – functions as a way of controlling dialog.

Likewise, facilitators in all three approaches are involved in controlling content. Particularly in the early stages of preparing participants to meet, they keep a sharp ear open for hot-button issues that may sidetrack the process or re-victimize the victim. For example, in many programs offenders are told not to ask for forgiveness. In other programs where the dialog process may take years to complete, forgiveness might be an issue upon which the victim works. Even in programs where coordinators see themselves as primarily empowering victims to meet the offender to get whatever questions they need answered in order move on with their lives, the victim will not be allowed to abuse the offender or encourage the offender to admit to crimes he or she has not already pled guilty to. Offenders and victims can and frequently do exercise considerable control over the questions and issues that will be discussed in a face-to-face meeting, and so do the coordinators/facilitators.

Perceived self-efficacy is a variable within the proposed mediation model that we wish to highlight because it so often comes up in interviews and conversations with persons who have experienced restorative justice dialog. We should point out that we would typically treat this variable as an outcome variable; it could be considered both as an immediate outcome and as a longer-term outcome. Statements from victims and offenders indicating that they feel "stronger," "more able to advocate for themselves," "more valued as community members," "wanting to contribute to future circle work," and "more able to speak up for themselves" are quite common. These kinds of sentiments are gleaned from listening to participants across the various dialog approaches. Such statements are likely more frequent from persons who have gone through severe violence dialog and those who have participated in circles. These feelings of newfound strength come from victims and offenders, young and old. A shy 8-year-old boy, who had been bullied on the school yard, credited the circle experience with giving him "a chance to stand up for himself." There are moments in interviews where participants speak with a sense of awe about the process and about themselves.

While these kinds of comments are extremely rewarding to those who work with these individuals, it would be very helpful to determine if these newfound strengths are reinforced over time or reflect a kind of "retreat-like euphoria" that rapidly diminishes under the pressures of day-to-day living. We would suggest, then, that this variable is one of those that should be measured over time. In our study of victims of severe violence in Texas and Ohio (Umbreit, Vos, Coates & Brown 2003) some interviews with victims and offenders occurred a year to three years after the encounter, clearly demonstrating a lasting positive self-efficacy impact.

Outcomes

Many of the short-term outcomes identified in the proposed mediation model have to do with satisfaction: satisfaction with the courts/judicial system, with the mediator, with the process, with the outcome/agreement. If there is an area that research on restorative justice has focused on over the years it is satisfaction: for VOM (Coates & Gehm 1989; Warner 1992; Umbreit & Coates 1993; Umbreit 1996; Bradshaw & Umbreit 1998; Evje & Cushman 2000; Umbreit, Coates & Vos 2001); for FGC (Maxwell & Morris 1993; McCold & Wachtel 1998; Fercello & Umbreit 1999; McGarrel, Olivares, Crawford & Kroovand 2000; Daly 2001); for Circles (Lajeunesse 1996; Matthews & Larkin 1999; Umbreit, Coates & Vos 2002; Coates et al. 2003). Across the approaches, victims and most offenders indicate high levels of satisfaction with the courts, mediator, process, and agreement. It seems to us that at this point more effort should be made to explain why participants are so satisfied with their dialog experiences. The proposed model has the potential for fostering the sort of research that will attempt to link antecedent variables and process variables with satisfaction. Some antecedent variables likely affect satisfaction directly. For example, it would be interesting to determine whether people who choose to participate in dialog are more predisposed toward innovation, the non-traditional, and change than those who are not willing to participate. And does such a predisposition, if it exists, make it likely that the participants will be satisfied with a non-traditional experience? This is a variation of the self-fulfilling prophecy that should not detract from the efficacy of dialog. But if such a link exists, it would have implications for screening and training.

Recidivism, in the justice community, remains a "bottom line" measure of success for any intervention. In the early years of development many restorative justice proponents resisted the notion that their interventions should live or die because of behavior for which society was responsible. How could a relatively brief encounter be expected to produce that much change in individual lives? There are still many practitioners who do not want their work closely tied to recidivism.

For many of us who have done research in this field for decades, it is actually rather surprising to see some of the findings from studies particularly on VOM and FGC. Regarding VOM, a host of studies have now been done across a number jurisdictions, including those in the United States, New Zealand, Canada, and England. Generally, the results show a positive reduction in reoffending behavior. Moreover, those who do reoffend, commit less serious offenses. Using a matched comparison group, Umbreit and Coates (1992) found such results across a four-state study. A randomly selected comparison study in Tennessee (Nugent & Paddock

1995) yielded similar results. Relying on the same cohort, as well as before and after measures, Wynne and Brown (1998), in a study in England, found that while 87 percent of offenders had previous convictions before mediation, 68 percent had no convictions during a two-year follow-up post-mediation. Similarly, juvenile offenders who went through VOM in two Oregon counties experienced a reduction in recidivism of 77 percent and 68 percent respectively when comparing the year before intervention with the year following intervention. And a rigorous reanalysis of 14 previous studies (Nugent, Williams & Umbreit 2003) involving a total sample of 9,037 juvenile offenders also found a significant reduction in recidivism for the VOM participants compared to the non-VOM participants.

Recidivism results for FGC follow a like pattern. A long-term study involving random assignment in Australia showed a 38 percent reduction in reoffending rates for FGC youth compared to a court-based group (Sherman, Strang & Woods 2000). A Bethlehem PA study showed reoffending declined for conference youth compared to a group that was referred, but did not participate, and to a control group. In Indianapolis, McGarrel et al. (2000) used a random assignment experimental design and determined that FGC diversion youth were statistically significantly less likely to have further justice system contact six months after the incident and six months after completion of the diversion program.

In a large meta-analysis conducted by the Canadian Department of Justice, Latimer, Dowden and Muise (2001) reviewed eight family group conferencing and 27 victim-offender mediation studies that used a control group or comparison group. They concluded that these restorative justice programs resulted in reductions in recidivism compared to non-restorative programs.

As we indicated earlier, consistent with the complexity of the proposed model, we are interested in seeing additional studies move toward attempting to explain more of the complexities that relate to the outcome variables. This is certainly needed for the variable recidivism, which is so often weighed down by political and philosophical debate. An ongoing effort to do just that is taking place in New Zealand (Maxwell & Morris 2001). These researchers are engaged in a longitudinal study of the effects of the family group conferencing experience for youth and parents. They have tracked over a hundred young people into their twenties and have obtained reconviction data on them. Several multivariate analyses were conducted to sort out predictors of reconviction and pathways to reoffending. These authors conclude that the chance of reoffending is lessened for young people who participate in family group conferencing even when other important factors are taken into account, such as adverse early experiences, other events which may be more related by chance, and subsequent life events.

MEDIATION DYNAMICS

The dynamics of mediation has actually been the focus of this entire chapter, just as it is the glue that binds the proposed mediation model. The more we can describe the interplay of the variables identified (and those unidentified) within and across the three time phases, the better we will understand how mediation/dialog works, what effects it has, and why. Even the model itself, along with the research available to us, makes it clear that we must expect variation upon variation as we study specific mediation/dialog programs. And yet there are patterns to be found within and across approaches.

For those of us in the restorative justice field, it is particularly helpful to consider how restorative dialog plays out in broader, overlapping social justice arenas. From 2001 through 2003, we had the opportunity to look at how dialog has been and is being used to respond to and prevent acts of hate (Umbreit, Coates & Vos 2003). Conflicts and potential conflicts were described across seven communities. The nature of the conflicts included a cross-burning at the home of a black family in an upscale neighborhood, racial conflict in a high school, racism across reservation boundaries, the murder of a transgendered youth in a small town rural community, a post 9/11 threat on a mosque and Muslim cleric, Arab–Jewish relations in an urban setting, and Somali and non-Somali exchange in an urban setting. Many of the key stakeholders and responders to these conflicts did not see themselves doing "restorative justice dialog," yet what they were doing in their natural settings paralleled and informed our understanding of such dialog. We discovered similarities and we saw possibilities that we hadn't been aware of before.

In hindsight – perhaps obvious, but certainly not known to us previously – was the notion that the focus and context of dialog could so readily flow back and forth from that of individuals most affected by conflict to the larger community which, too, is terrorized and at times shamed by crimes of hate occurring in its midst. We saw instances where a rather typical form of victim–offender dialog took place. That meeting was followed by a neighborhood gathering, or school-wide forum. In other places, a community-wide meeting was held to invite dialog. That was followed by smaller face-to-face encounters between a specific victim and offender. We concluded that "community dialogue may be the first or even the only dialogue response to a hate crime" (Umbreit, Coates & Vos 2003: 31).

In broad strokes, the process of dialog appears quite similar whether it is between a victim and an offender with some support persons present, or whether it is a community-wide forum with 200 people participating. The context, the initial conflict or threat of conflict, and the participant characteristics and motivation for participation varied considerably. And we cannot state strongly enough how open coordinators must be to cultural differences and sensitivities when attempting to address these emotionally charged conflicts engendered by hate. Adding these kinds of factors to an already dynamic approach to mediation/dialog only serves to heighten the elasticity, the richness, and the immediacy of such approaches.

Conclusion

The proposed mediation model constructed by Herrman, Hollett, and Gale has proven useful as we consider current restorative justice dialog studies and as we think about further efforts to explore the whats, hows, and whys of restorative justice dialog practice.

As we move forward with empirically based conceptual work, it behooves us to remain open to the discovery of yet additional variables not currently reflected in the model. That work will also benefit from appreciating the non-linear nature of dialog work even as we try to impose some conceptual order upon it. And we believe that further conceptual work will greatly benefit from longitudinal studies that can provide a better fix on time order and can provide data bases for sorting out interaction of variables over time.

REFERENCES

American Bar Association (1994) Criminal Justice Policy on Victim–Offender Mediation/ Dialogue. Approved August 1994. American Bar Association, Chicago.

Bradshaw, W. & Umbreit, M. S. (1998) Crime victims meet juvenile offenders: Contributing factors to victim satisfaction with mediated dialogue. *Juvenile and Family Court Journal* 49(3), 17–25.

Coates, R. B. & Gehm, J. (1989) An empirical assessment. In M. Wright & B. Galaway (eds.), *Mediation and Criminal Justice.* Sage, London, pp. 251–263.

Coates, R. B., Burns, H. & Umbreit, M. (2002) *Victim Participation in Victim Offender Conferencing: Washington County, Minnesota Community Justice Program.* Center for Restorative Justice and Peacemaking, University of Minnesota, St. Paul.

Coates, R. B., Umbreit, M. & Vos, B. (2000) *Obstacles and Opportunities for Developing Victim Offender Mediation for Juveniles: The Experience of Six Oregon Counties.* Center for Restorative Justice and Peacemaking, University of Minnesota, St. Paul.

Coates, R. B., Umbreit, M. & Vos, B. (2002) *Systemic Change Toward Restorative Justice: Washington County, Minnesota.* Center for Restorative Justice and Peacemaking, University of Minnesota, St. Paul.

Coates, R. B., Umbreit, M. & Vos, B. (2003) Restorative justice circles: an exploratory study. *Contemporary Justice Review* 6(3), 265–278.

Council of Europe Committee of Ministers (1999) *Mediation in Penal Matters. Recommendation No. R(99)19,* adopted September 15, 1999. Council of Europe Publications Office, Strasbourg.

Daly, K. (2001) Conferencing in Australia and New Zealand: variations, research findings, and prospects. In A. Morris & G. Maxwell (eds.), *Restorative Justice for Juveniles.* Hart Publishing, Oxford.

Evje, A. & Cushman, R. (2000) *A Summary of the Evaluations of Six California Victim Offender Reconciliation Programs.* Judicial Council of California, Administrative Office of the Courts, San Francisco.

Fercello, C. & Umbreit, M. (1999) *Client Satisfaction with Victim Offender Conferences in Dakota County, Minnesota.* Center for Restorative Justice and Peacemaking, University of Minnesota, St. Paul.

Flaten, C. (1996) Victim offender mediation: application with serious offenses committed by juveniles. In B. Galaway & J. Hudson (eds.), *Restorative Justice: International Perspectives.* Criminal Justice Press, Monsey, pp. 387–401.

Lajeunesse, T. (1996) *Evaluation of Community Holistic Circle Healing: Hollow Water First Nation,* vol. 1: *Final Report.* Thérèse Lajeunesse & Associates Ltd, Manitoba.

Latimer, J., Dowden, C. & Muise, D. (2001) *The Effectiveness of Restorative Practice: A Meta-Analysis.* Department of Justice Research and Statistics Division Methodological Series, Ottawa.

Matthews, S. & Larkin, G. (1999) *Guide to Community-Based Alternatives for Low Risk Juvenile Offenders.* Koch Crime Institute, Topeka.

Maxwell, G. & Morris, A. (1993) *Family, Victims and Culture: Youth Justice in New Zealand.* Social Policy Agency and Institute of Criminology, Victoria University of Wellington, Wellington.

Maxwell, G. & Morris, A. (2001) Family group conferencing and reoffending. In A. Morris & G. Maxwell (eds.), *Restorative Justice for Juveniles: Conferencing, Mediation and Circles.* Hart Publishing, Oxford.

McCold, P. (2001) Primary Restorative Justice Practices. In A. Morris & G. Maxwell (eds.), *Restorative Justice for Juveniles: Conferencing, Mediation and Circles.* Hart Publishing, Oxford.

McCold, P. & Wachtel, B. (1998) *Restorative Policing Experiment: The Bethlehem Pennsylvania Police Family Group Conferencing Project.* Community Service Foundation, Pipersville.

McGarrel, E., Olivares, K., Crawford, K. & Kroovand, N. (2000) *Returning Justice to the Community: The Indianapolis Juvenile Restorative Justice Experiment.* Hudson Institute, Indianapolis.

New Zealand Ministry of Justice (1996) *Restorative Justice: A Discussion Paper.* New Zealand Ministry of Justice, Wellington.

Nugent, W. & Paddock, J. (1995) The effect of victim–offender mediation on severity of reoffense. *Mediation Quarterly* 12, 353–367.

Nugent, W., Williams, R. & Umbreit, M. (2003) Participation in victim–offender mediation and the prevalence and severity of subsequent delinquent behavior: a meta-analysis. *Utah Law Review* 1, 137–165.

Pranis, K., Stuart, B. & Wedge, M. (2003) *Peacemaking Circles: From Crime to Community.* Living Justice Press, St. Paul.

Sherman, L., Strang, H. & Woods, D. (2000) *Recidivism Patterns in the Canberra Reintegrative Shaming Experiments (RISE).* Centre for Restorative Justice, Australian National University, Canberra.

Stuart, B. (1996) Circle sentencing in Canada: a partnership of the community and the criminal justice system. *International Journal of Comparative and Applied Criminal Justice* 20, 193–206.

Umbreit, M. S. (1996) Restorative justice through mediation: the impact of programs in four Canadian provinces. In B. Galaway & J. Hudson (eds.), *Restorative Justice: International Perspectives.* Criminal Justice Press, Monsey.

Umbreit, M. S. (1998) Restorative justice through victim–offender mediation: a multi-site assessment. *Western Criminology Review* 1(1), 1–29.

Umbreit, M. S. (2001) *The Handbook of Victim Offender Mediation: An Essential Guide to Practice and Research.* Jossey-Bass, San Francisco.

Umbreit, M. & Coates, R. B. (1992) *Victim Offender Mediation: An Analysis of Programs in Four States of the US.* Center for Restorative Justice and Peacemaking, St. Paul.

Umbreit, M. & Coates, R. B. (1993) Cross-site analysis of victim–offender mediation in four states. *Crime and Delinquency* 39, 565–585.

Umbreit, M. & Greenwood, J. (1999) National survey of victim offender mediation programs in the US. *Mediation Quarterly* 16, 235–251.

Umbreit, M., Coates, R. B. & Vos, B. (2001) *Juvenile Victim Offender Mediation in Six Oregon Counties.* Oregon Dispute Resolution Commission, Salem.

Umbreit, M., Coates, R. B. & Vos, B. (2002) The impact of restorative justice conferencing: a multi-national perspective. *British Journal of Community Justice* 1(2), 21–48.

Umbreit, M., Coates, R. B. & Vos, B. (2003) *Community Peacemaking Project: Responding to Hate Crimes, Hate Incidents, Intolerance and Violence through Restorative Justice Dialogue: Final Report.* Center for Restorative Justice and Peacemaking, University of Minnesota.

Umbreit, M., Vos, B., Coates, R. B. & Brown, K. (2003) *Facing Violence: The Path of Restorative Justice and Dialogue.* Criminal Justice Press, Monsey.

United Nations (2000) *Basic Principles on the Use of Restorative Justice Programmes in Criminal Matters.* ECOSOC Res. 2000/14. United Nations Economic and Social Council, Commission on Crime Prevention and Criminal Justice, Vienna.

United Nations (2002) *Restorative Justice: Report of the Secretary-General.* United Nations Economic and Social Council, Commission on Crime Prevention and Criminal Justice, Vienna.

Warner, S. (1992) *Making Amends: Justice for Victims and Offenders.* Avebury, Aldershot.

Wittman, D. (2004) *Genesee County Justice 2005.* Genesee County Justice Programs, Genesee County.

Wynne, J. & Brown, I. (1998) Can mediation cut reoffending? *Probation Journal* 45, 21–26.

Zehr, H. (2002) *The Little Book of Restorative Justice.* Good Books, Intercourse.

Zehr, H. & Mika, H. (1998) Fundamental principles of restorative justice. *The Contemporary Justice Review* 1(1), 47–55.

Part III

Exploring Powerful
Internal Dynamics

Chapter 8

Mediation as Framing and Framing within Mediation

Barbara Gray

Introduction

In this chapter I explore two important ways in which framing and mediation are linked. First, mediators use framing as an essential tool to perform their tasks as a third party – an activity that occurs during the T_m phase of the comprehensive model of mediation (see figure 2.1 above). My thesis is that framing as a mediation technique is essentially a social accounting process designed to establish interactional fairness (under the mediation condition at T_m) and to increase chances for resolution among the parties. I argue that different frames offer different social accounts of a conflict. The mediator's role is to help frame the conflict and its potential resolution in a way that all parties perceive to be fair. Mediator framing links to the procedural factors in the overall model proposed in chapter 2 and has the potential to affect the mediation conditions as well as the problem-solving process of the mediation (see figure 2.3 of the model).

In the first part of this chapter, I will describe several framing tasks that mediators undertake – all of which are intended to create a procedurally just context conducive to resolution. These include: framing the process and disputants' expectations, fairness and justice, the issues in contention, alternatives, and identity concerns. Thus, in the first part of the chapter, I pay particular attention to the mechanisms by which framing can transform disputes and disputants.

The second part of the chapter considers mediation itself as a frame. Here, frames and framing are construed much more broadly than within the context of a single mediation. A wide variety of frames that disputants might evoke in conflict situations are introduced, such as social control frames, power frames, and conflict-handling frames. Within this constellation of frames, mediation is positioned as one of several possible conflict-handling frames that disputants could, but often don't, adopt. I explore several reasons why disputants' framing of the conflict makes them leery of mediation (an issue salient to the pre-mediation phase of the proposed model in chapter 2, T_0).

Finally, the last section of the chapter explores third-party interventions that are designed to help maintain a civil dialog among disputants when mediation is not an accepted option. These interventions focus on narration, perspective-taking, and acknowledgment of critical identities, and are intended to honor disputants' existing frames while at the same time promoting possible frame enlargement so that disputants can begin to understand each other better. So, while they share many of the same underlying assumptions as mediation (e.g. assumptions 7, 8, and 10 outlined in chapter 2 of this volume, such as fostering cognitive disequilibrium to promote learning and stimulating higher levels of reasoning), these interventions are not intended to resolve the conflict, but rather to help disputants gain clarity on their own views and those of their counterparts and to foster construction of at least a small modicum of trust among them prior to any moves toward mediating an agreement.

THE ROLE OF FRAMING IN MEDIATION: FRAMES AND FRAMING

Framing, in general, refers to the process of constructing and representing interpretations of a situation (Tannen 1979; Gray 2003a). We engage in framing all the time, although it usually occurs without our awareness. Gregory Bateson (1975) introduced the notion of framing by illustrating how roughhousing between two brothers can quickly turn from one frame (play) to another (fight) if one of the brothers behaves too aggressively. If we say "the glass is half full" or "half empty," we are also using framing to describe how optimistically or pessimistically we view a situation. How we frame a situation also affects how we respond to it. For example, Tversky and Kahneman (1981) showed that people were more risk-averse if something was framed as a gain than if it was framed as a loss.

Gray (2003a: 11) notes that "framing involves shaping, focusing and organizing the world around us." We use frames to help us make sense of our own and others' actions. In doing so, we declare some aspects of our experience meaningful, while ignoring others. When we focus our attention on an event or an issue we are "imparting meaning and significance to elements within the frame and setting them apart from what is outside the frame" (Buechler 2000: 41). Through framing we also locate ourselves with respect to our experience. Our frame places us in relation to an issue or event and to other parties. For example, we can frame ourselves as "champions" of a cause or as "victims" of others' actions. We can frame others as "aliens" by emphasizing how they are different from us or as "compatriots" by focusing on our similarities.

While frames tend to impart a focus or interpretation that can last indefinitely, they are not immutable. People persist in relying on frames if they have proven to be useful and hold up under scrutiny. However, when people tenaciously cling to frames (and refuse to consider other points of view), conflicts can occur. If such relinquishment persists, conflicts can become intractable (Lewicki, Gray & Elliott 2003). However, in the face of new information, changing circumstances, persuasion, or reflection, people can and do change their frames. This change or "reframing" occurs when someone revises their interpretation of themselves, a situation, another person, or a group.

Framing in Mediation: Frames as Alternative Social Accounts

One way to conceptualize reframing in mediation is to think of frames as social accounts. When mediators frame issues for parties, in effect, they provide an alternative social account of the conflict. That is, they introduce (or at least attempt to introduce) a different way to make sense of the same circumstances because the current sensemaking employed by the parties leaves them stymied, if not frustrated and angry. By helping parties to reinterpret their circumstances, their counterpart's motivations, the range of possible solutions, and/or their own helplessness, opportunities for resolution may emerge. I will consider how social accounts are used to frame: (1) the process and disputants' expectations about mediation; (2) issues of justice and fairness; (3) the issues themselves; (4) alternatives; and (5) identity concerns. These activities fit under the mediation conditions and problem-solving steps that comprise "procedural factors" in figures 2.1 and 2.3.

Reframing the process of dispute resolving

One of the first tasks of a mediator is to help parties understand what they are undertaking. This occurs during the intake process during T_0. Despite its increased use over the last 25 years, many people know nothing about mediation and few can distinguish mediation from other dispute resolution techniques. Consequently, mediators need to help disputants make sense of or frame the mediation process as it is unfolding. This framing provides a social account of what the parties are trying to do and how they will interact during and (possibly) after the mediation. This social account rests on three fundamental premises. First, disputants will be the architects of any agreement that is reached. In this account, disputants, not the mediator, assume responsibility for the outcomes that are reached. Thus, they play an active rather than a passive role in the construction of solutions ("formulating options" in figure 2.3). Second, agreements emerge through non-adversarial dialog. Adopting this social account initially requires a leap of faith by disputants. Imagining they could behave non-adversarily (and that such behavior could produce a viable solution) may be outside their lived experience to date. Hence, this social account is, in effect, a fantasy or myth which, at the start of mediation, they may only be able to accept provisionally or skeptically. To fully embrace this social account, they will need to undergo a frame change, a schema-revision process (LaBianca, Gray & Brass 2000), which is only likely to occur if a satisfactory agreement can be found. In constructing this account of the process, the mediator essentially participates as a myth-maker, spinning a tale of possibility (Gray 1989). The mediator invites disputants into a world "that is made and imagined and that it can therefore be remade and re-imagined" (Unger 1987: 8). Finally, if disputants are going to embrace a mediated outcome, they must feel confident that mediation satisfies their sense of justice (Peachey 1989).

Reframing issues of justice and fairness

So, a second reframing task which mediators often undertake involves reframing what is considered just and fair by disputants. According to Peachey (1989: 316), "the mediator's recognition of and sensitivity to justice concerns is of paramount importance." Mediators must address both issues of procedural and distributive justice. Procedural justice occurs if the parties believe that the procedures adopted by the mediator are reasonable and even-handed and the mediator's actual behavior is consistent with their espoused behavior. In contrast to procedural justice, distributive justice involves ensuring that disputants concur that the outcomes reached are fair and equitable.

In the organizational justice literature, social accounts have been shown to reduce perceptions of unfairness among disputants by providing a mitigating explanation for a perceived distributive injustice (Sitkin & Bies 1993; Bies, Shapiro & Cummings 1998). The construction of such accounts may serve a similar purpose in mediated conflicts since concerns about what is considered fair or just are frequently at issue among disputants. In the overall model of mediation introduced in chapter 2, framing of fairness occurs in T_m during the process of establishing the mediation conditions (see figure 2.2).

Sitkin and Bies (1993) identified four ways that social accounts are used to manage people's perceptions of negative events. First, the account can introduce mitigating circumstances. This type of account acknowledges the injustice, but attempts to reduce or deny the culpability of the accused party. This could be done by attributing responsibility for the injustice to external events over which the accused has no control. Accounts based on mitigating circumstances help to reduce demands for retribution by "providing a plausible external attribution for the other's behavior" (Peachey 1989: 316).

A second type of social account is an ideological one. This account is designed to exonerate the perpetrator of the injustice by appealing to a higher value, such as: "It was for your own good." Considerable research has demonstrated the efficacy of ideological accounts (Folger & Cropanzano 1998: 146).

The third type of referential accounts, also called reframing accounts by Sitkin and Bies (1993), are intended to change the victim's frame of reference. Referential accounts can be either social or temporal (Folger & Cropanzano 1998). They are accomplished either by comparing the victim to someone less well off or by promising them a brighter future.

The fourth type of social account, penitential, involves the perpetrator of the injustice admitting responsibility and accepting culpability. Apologies, presuming they are sincere, are the best examples of penitential accounts (Folger & Cropanzano 1998).

Since a key task of mediation is to steer parties away from imputing blame, when parties attempt to incriminate each other mediators often reframe the blaming statement into a broader concern about fairness and redirect the parties' attention to how fairness for both (all) sides can be assured in future interactions. In doing so, they offer and encourage the parties to adopt an alternative social account of how the injustice can be understood and resolved. For example, mitigating or ideological accounts may be used in mediation to reframe one or both parties' culpability. By encouraging parties to explain the circumstances or the intentions behind an act, skillful mediators can then propose a reframing that redirects disputants' attention from blaming to prevention of future injustice. Referential accounts are also particularly useful for mediators (Wall 1981; Kolb 1985). In a study of labor mediators, "Kolb observed that mediators often provided disputants with referents that either lowered their expectations or made their current state of affairs seem less onerous by comparison" (Folger & Cropanzano 1998: 147).

Despite the potential that reframing of justice provides for crafting agreements, whether and how justice is achieved through mediation remains a contentious topic among mediation scholars. Not only does the practice of mediation differ from one context to the next (Kolb 1983), but critics of mediation question whether justice is seriously compromised when it is delivered through mediation. I take up these issues below in the second part of the chapter.

Reframing the substantive issues

Descriptions of mediators' tasks often include "reframing the issues" (Folberg & Taylor 1984; Moore 1986; Yarborough & Wilmot 1995). This is by far the most common use of framing in the mediation literature. Specifically, it refers to providing an interpretation of the issues in contention for the disputants. When mediators engage in this framing task, they are offering a reformulation of the issues in the conflict (Putnam & Holmer 1992) that hopefully creates or increases the prospect of cooperation among the parties. This task is often referred to as "reframing" because the mediator presents an alternative way of conceptualizing the conflict to the parties – transforming it from their own conceptions as a hopeless deadlock to a potentially resolvable problem. Used in this way, the ability to frame or reframe is considered an essential skill in the mediator's toolkit (Yarborough & Wilmot 1995).

Mediators frame the process for disputants by suggesting the potential for and steps to working toward a constructive solution. They also enlist disputants' participation by helping them appraise their alternatives to mediation and framing them as potentially less desirable options. (see "procedural factors: problem-solving" in figure 2.3 of the proposed model in chapter 2.) In the context of mediation, reframing most often refers to how the mediator talks about the issues in the dispute. For example, Moore (1986: 175) defines framing or reframing as "the preliminary definition of topic areas and issues that will be the focus of future negotiations." Putnam and Holmer (1992) refer to this as issue reframing. Reframing is a central technique in mediation practice "for freeing the disputing parties from old patterns so they can move forward to resolution" (Yarborough & Wilmot 1995: 135). The fundamental purpose of reframing is to shift the disputants from bipolar thinking to a more expansive view of the issues – one that introduces a greater number of, and hopefully more palatable, options that the disputants will embrace (see assumptions 7 and 8 in chapter 2). By encouraging disputants to talk differently to each other and to think differently about their choices, mediators hope to create constructive opportunities for resolution of the dispute.

The most typical approaches to reframing the issues involve: (1) reframing from positions to interests (Moore 1986; Fisher, Ury & Patton 1991; Yarborough & Wilmot 1995), and (2) finding superordinate goals (Sherif 1958). Reframing from positions to interests, involves restating the solutions that disputants express in terms of their underlying concerns (which may be satisfied through a variety of solutions). Since the differences between positions and interests and the value of searching for interest-based solutions have been explicated elsewhere (Lax & Sebenius 1985; Fisher et al. 1991), I will concentrate on the underlying social account that is being constructed through reframing of interests. Continuing the earlier notion of mythmaking, by reframing in terms of interests, the mediator is constructing two accounts for the parties. First, the mediator underscores that what each person cares about is important and needs to be addressed. Second, the mediator signals that there may be a way to satisfy at least some of each person's interests. So, once again, the implicit social account conveyed by the mediator is one of possibility and hope. As we will see below, however, when the issues at stake are rooted in identities, reframing in terms of interests is not sufficient.

Searching for superordinate goals refers to recasting small, discrete goals in terms of broader ones that are more likely to encompass both disputants (Sherif 1958). For example, if one disputant indicates that he or she is being underpaid while another complains his or her ideas are discredited, the mediator might suggest that both are interested in gaining recognition for their efforts. By moving to a more inclusive or slightly more abstract issue, disputants may each realize that the other's need (interest) is comparable to their own and may begin to appreciate other ways of satisfying their own or their counterpart's interests. Reframing in terms of superordinate goals is premised on the following social account – both parties share jointly held legitimate concerns.

Framing dispute resolution alternatives

Some framing activities occur repeatedly throughout the mediation process. When parties come to mediation, they often have the scepter of litigation or another form of authoritative decision-making looming in the background as a BATNA (best alternative to a negotiated agreement, Fisher et al. 1991). Initially, during T_0 of the proposed model, in order to get parties to the table, mediators may need to help them to reappraise the strength and attractiveness of their BATNAs compared to finding an agreement through mediation. Helping the parties create a social account of the comparative strength of these alternatives is what is meant by "framing dispute resolution alternatives." By exploring the real costs in time and money (e.g. the likelihood of a favorable court decision or the potential costs to the ongoing relationship of not finding an amicable agreement) mediators can often assist parties in (re)constructing their own social account in which mediation triumphs as the most appealing (or least unattractive) alternative. Reappraisal of these calculations may be necessary for some disputants periodically during the mediation and may surface again when the disputants are assessing whether or not to accept the mediated settlement.

Framing identity concerns

While substantive concerns can usually be reframed successfully as interests, when disputants remain intransigent because of identity-based concerns, mediators should use caution about reframing. As Rothman notes, "conventional approaches to handling interest-based disputes often serve only to exacerbate identity conflicts" (1997: 9). Identity concerns arise when disputants experience threats to the core of how they define themselves or their social group. In the face of identity threats, disputants often become defensive and volatile because there is nothing more fundamental to protect than one's (or one's group's) right to exist (Kelman 1999). Consequently, any attempt to reframe one's definition of self will likely be met with intense resistance.

Rather than attempting to negotiate away identities, mediators need to construct social accounts in which disputants' self-image, history, and/or group legitimacy is not only protected from threat but also acknowledged and honored (Rothman 1997; Elliott, Gray & Lewicki 2003). This is easier said than done since identities are maintained through social comparison processes (Tajfel & Turner 1985) in which groups elevate their own standing in society by demeaning that of others (Tajfel & Turner 1985; Gamson 1990). Stereotyping, belittling, and blaming other groups (as well as much more violent tactics) comprise the common currency of identity conflict. Moreover, blaming processes are fraught with projection – a process in which "the others from whom we most seek to dissociate ourselves are frequently repositories of the projected elements of ourselves that we least want to accept or acknowledge" (Rothman 1997: 27).

Consequently, the ultimate reframing that is needed to resolve identity-based conflicts among disputants involves withdrawal of their projections and re-embracing of the unclaimed, projected parts of themselves. This level of work goes well beyond traditional mediation and, in cases of bitter disputes like the Arab–Israeli conflict, painstaking trust-building steps are necessary to even initiate such delicate dialog (Kelman 1999). Montville (1995) likens these conversations to mourning processes because reclaiming one's projections involves acknowledgment of and contrition for past injustices experienced and committed by both sides. For conflicts rooted in identity issues, however, this level of reframing may be essential to achieving any lasting resolution of the conflict.

When identity-based conflicts (e.g. value-based environmental conflicts, conflicts over tribal land or artifacts, ethnic, race, or gender conflicts) arise but are less violent, attempts to reframe identity-based values into interests may still prove futile (Rothman 1997). Instead, in these processes, the social account must be constructed to recognize and acknowledge the underlying identity issues and to legitimize the identity-based concerns of aggrieved parties. Below I will consider some examples of how this can be accomplished. As our societies become more culturally diverse, identity issues can arise in two-party neighborhood or co-worker disputes (Ethier & Deaux 1990; Cox 1993) in addition to larger intergroup or international conflicts where identity issues flourish (Rothman 1997).

SUMMARY

So far I have described the role of mediators as reframers – agents who attempt to help disputants construct new social accounts of their interactions. These accounts are designed to enable disputants to conceive of their relationships in new ways and to transform the issues that have eluded resolution into viable agreements. An important point to keep in mind for any reframing attempt is that successful reframing involves timing and depends on the psychological readiness of the parties (Moore 1986). If parties do not buy into the process or are unconvinced that the outcome will be just, attempts to reframe the issues may be rejected out of hand. Mediators must sense when a particular reframing will be acceptable and when it may be premature. Interestingly, with careful attention to timing, mediators may be able to reintroduce a particular "framing" that had earlier been suggested and rejected, particularly if it is the mediator rather than an opponent who reintroduces it (Rubin & Brown 1975). Successful mediation rests in large measure on the parties' readiness to abandon their previous social account and at least provisionally accept the reframing offered by the mediator or by the other party.

MEDIATION AS A FRAME

The second major thesis I present in this chapter concerns mediation itself as a frame – one that conveys a particular social perspective on how disputes should be resolved (Abel 1982; Sheppard, Blumenfeld-Jones & Roth 1989; Gray 1994; Lewicki et al. 2003). In this section, I take a broader look at mediation as one among many frames that disputants may hold about conflicts and their evolution. The material for constructing the argument that mediation itself is a frame is drawn from two strands of research: critiques of mediation and research on intractable conflicts.

Critiques of Mediation

While the benefits of mediation over more adversarial approaches to dispute resolution have been extolled (Folberg & Taylor 1984; Kressel, Pruit & Associates 1989; Bush & Folger 1994), others view mediation with a more skeptical or jaundiced eye. Ongoing debate among legal and ADR scholars has provoked consideration of the limits of mediation and questioned whether mediation is appropriate or fair in certain circumstances (Galanter 1980; Abel 1982; Bush 1984; Menkel-Meadow 1995; Hyman & Love 2002). In contrast to the hopeful, optimistic view of conflict that mediation proponents espouse, critics of mediation adopt a more institutional or societal-level stance that considers whether societal-level interests are met and preserved by mediation (Galanter 1980; Abel 1982). Among the specific criticisms raised are questions concerning whether constitutional safeguards are preserved or lost when informal systems of justice are invoked. Those concerned about constitutional issues argue that contradictions arise to the degree that informal justice extends or reduces state control over disputants (Abel 1982). The loss of these safeguards undermines "the vitality of public systems of justice that are essential to the continuing consolidation of constitutional democracies" (Reuben 2000: 949). When mediation and other forms of ADR are bifurcated into public and private arenas of justice, the former presumably maintains the safeguards while the latter does not (Reuben 2000).[1]

Another issue raised by mediation critics lies in the inability of mediation to establish legal precedents. They charge that, by engaging in informal justice, mediation (and other forms of ADR) strip the judicial system of its mandate to establish just legal precedent for decision-making (Abel 1982; Hyman & Love 2002). The lack of public scrutiny of the proceedings and the lack of referential value of mediated decisions effectively undermines the development of law and thus impedes the dispensation of justice writ large.

Justice Frames

The debate over the extent to which mediation protects or inhibits justice, however, hinges on what frame for justice one adopts. Justice narrowly defined as legal justice (e.g. conforming to established legal rights and entitlements) differs widely from other models of justice rooted in communities, cultures, religions, or private norms for determining what is fair (Hyman & Love 2002). Conceptions of justice also differ because they are premised on different philosophies, ranging from the Kantian contractual view, to retributional approaches, to rights and duty-based or utilitarian orientations (see a detailed list of ethics frames identified in Wiethoff et al. 1999). As noted above, within mediation, differing frames for computing justice must be negotiated along with the substantive issues in dispute. Mediators can offer new framings but ultimately the disputants must decide the point at which the scales of justice are balanced. "The mediator must attend to the process, help the parties recognize the legitimacy of different perspectives on justice, and work towards a resolution that comports with the parties' considered views of a fair and acceptable outcome" (Hyman & Love 2002: 170).

An example can help to illustrate these different perspectives on justice. An eighteen-month mediation during 1996–98 over the management of land within Voyageurs National Park (VNP) ended in stalemate, in large measure because the parties couldn't agree on what was considered a just allocation of benefits to various user groups. Because Voyageurs is primarily comprised of large lakes, use of motorized equipment (e.g. motorboats, snowmobiles, and houseboats) was written into its enabling legislation in 1975 (a rare occurrence among US national parks). Over the years, however, opponents of the federal government's ownership of the VNP's parkland claimed that their rights and freedoms to use motorized equipment in the park were continually being chipped away by management decisions taken by the National Park Service. A key issue in dispute during the mediation pertained to the use of snowmobiles on the one large landmass (a peninsula) within the park. Efforts by environmentalists to limit the scope and timing of snowmobile use on the peninsula (in order to promote a wilderness-like area) were resisted by the park opponents who viewed the limitations as one too many diminutions of their rights to the land. Consider the frames of each group:

> *Park Opponent.* This is all part of the process of "incrementalism" used by the park service which will . . . slowly erode personal freedoms . . . Then local people will be forced to move on due to . . . an economy that can't survive.
> *Environmentalist.* We consider ourselves . . . a supporter of the park service, encouraging them to manage the park based on the way the park was established originally. We see ourselves as being responsible for the creation of the park . . . We have a responsibility to continue that work. (McHarg 2000)

In this example, the park opponents' rights-based justice frames clashed with the duty-oriented frames of the environmentalists who believed they had an obligation to preserve the land as wilderness for future generations (Gray 2003b). These conflicting ethics frames contributed substantially to the intractability of this conflict and the inability of mediation to provide an avenue for resolution. The fact that mediation is a forum in which justice norms are negotiated has been stressed by Hyman and Love (2002: 161):

> A sense of justice is in part a social phenomenon built on family and community beliefs and norms . . . When parties bring justice norms to a mediation and make them part of the discussion, they are educating each other, building justice norms in their family, workplace, business or community – in a manner parallel to (however different from) the public declaration of precedents and norms that litigation achieves.

Depending on how the parties conceptualize justice in the dispute, mediation may or may not be a vehicle for resolving it. In the attempted mediation over Voyageurs, not only did the parties disagree on the substantive outcomes, they also disagreed about whether their version of fairness could be achieved through mediation. Some accounts attribute the failure of the mediation to one local politician who, though not a member of the mediation panel, was powerful enough to sway key members to scuttle the final deal (see "Power Frames" below). An additional explanation for why the mediation failed lies in the conceptions some disputants held about how conflicts like the one over Voyageurs should be resolved. I take this issue up in the next section.

Conflict-Handling Frames

The fact that disputants differ in their conceptions of the available options for addressing a conflict is not new. For example, the dual concerns model of conflict handling (Thomas 1992) identified five different styles of responding to conflict: competing, compromising, accommodating, avoiding, and collaborating. These styles depict disputants' preferences for how to behave in a conflict but contain implicit assumptions about how the parties frame conflict (e.g. as about winning or relationships, in terms of assumptions about a fixed or expandable pie, etc.). Others have more explicitly emphasized how disputants experience or frame responses to conflicts (Sheppard et al. 1989; Pinkley & Northcraft 1994; Gray 2003a). Sheppard et al.

(1989) identified four frames that parties use to conceptualize the kind of dispute they faced: (1) right-wrong frames invoke ethical decision-making; (2) negotiation frames imply that the dispute can be worked out through give and take; (3) underlying conflict frames suggest that a conflict has deep-seated roots that may impede resolution; and (4) stop frames are predicated on the assumption that taking no action is the most advantageous approach to take. This typology of conflict-handling frames grew out of interviews with individual disputants involved in personal conflicts. Gray (2003a) offers a typology of conflict-handling frames that captures a broader array of alternatives available to participants in environmental and public policy conflicts. This typology represents an adaptation of one offered by Keltner (1994), identified as the struggle spectrum, a continuum of six aspects of struggle ranging from discussion to fighting. The expanded typology identifies ten conflict-handling frames including an "other" category for frames that did not align with any of those identified. See table 8.1 for a list of the ten frame categories. It is clear from the wide array of possible conflict-handling frames that the joint problem-solving frame (which includes mediation) does not necessarily hold a place of prominence in how disputants conceive of conflicts being handled. In fact, in some of the most intractable environmental conflicts reported by Lewicki et al. (2003), disputants had little conception of joint problem-solving as a viable option for addressing these conflicts. In the Voyageurs case, for example, many park opponents adopted struggle, sabotage and violence, or adjudication frames to achieve voice in the conflict. For example,

> *Speaker.* So then I was involved in land owner disputes. At one time we even had a statue – the one at the beginning of Rainier. You see that big Voyageur?
> *Interviewer.* Yes
> *Speaker.* . . . . He was sitting inside Voyageurs National Park on a four-acre island and it was our protest island. And we took this protest island and we divided it up into square feet . . . And we . . . took this island and divided it up into square foot sections, and we sold these square foot sections all over the country (*laugh*). And the idea was, is that we were gonna make this a permanent protest. And uh we were gonna have the island so dispersed that it would be very, very cumbersome for the government to take the island away. (From an interview with one stakeholder in the Voyageurs conflict, Gray, confidential research data)

Adjudication frame

An adjudication frame entails statements that imply that a third party, such as an arbitrator, the courts, judges, or judicial authority, should decide the dispute. Several examples of this frame were present in an interview with several motorized users from communities close to the park:

> The only chance we have, at least in this national park is the courts. I don't know about any other areas . . . And there's some of us that feel that the only way the issues are gonna be resolved is through litigation. Cause you get into the political arena and Washington and the congress, and uh, you know, if a bill ever does get through to do something positively there's members of congress that sell, and senate side that said they'd filibuster it in the senate to kill it. And if it does get passed, they've got assurances that Clinton will veto it. So, you know, where can you go? (Gray 2003b: 103)

TABLE 8.1   Conflict-handling frames

Frame type	Description
Avoidance, passivity	Preference for doing nothing, letting the matter rest, inertia, or taking no action.
Fact-finding	Preference for investigating, collecting more information, gathering scientific facts, and conducting research on the problem.
Joint problem-solving	Preference for community or joint action, finding common ground through negotiation, mediation, consensus-building, conciliation, etc.
Authority decides after consultation	Preference that local authorities, agencies, or institutions should gather input from a variety of stakeholders but retain the right to make the decision themselves.
Authority decides based on expertise	Preference that local authorities, agencies, institutions, or appointed boards make the decision because they have the technical knowledge and expertise to do so.
Adjudication	Preference that a third party (e.g. judge or arbitrator) makes the decision.
Appeal to political action	Preference for handling the problem through enacting or abolishing laws and regulations.
Appeal to market economy	Preference for negotiation of rights, searching for market solutions, and/or economic and system changes.
Struggle, sabotage, or violence	Preference for violent or non-violent confrontation, civil disobedience, sabotaging attempts at reconciliation and/or using force, among other techniques, to manage the conflict.
Other	Options that don't fit any of the above categories.

Environmentalists also tended to prefer adjudication and envisioned appeal to political action as another viable option for dealing with the conflict (Gray 2003b).

Appeals to political action frame

An appeal to political action frame recommends handling the problem through enacting or abolishing laws and regulations. This includes addressing the conflict through lobbying, referendums, electing people to offices, legislative actions, and/or making appeals to state or federal agencies to enact, change, or abolish laws.

Joint problem-solving frame

Most noteworthy is that few disputants in this conflict imagined or promoted joint problem-solving as their preferred approach (Gray 2003b), and few could hold the frames of the others in positive regard. Individuals using a joint problem-solving or consensus frame show preference for community or joint action, finding common ground among disputants often through mediation, collaboration, conciliation, and other collective processes. An example of this frame is seen in the following quote from one of the few disputants who did adopt this frame:

> I think there needs to be, if there's a way to have local input, but at the same time realizing that there's special managers that are here to manage the parks, Voyageurs in particular. That they take their input but that they don't cede their authority over to the locals. (Natural resource manager) (Gray 2003b)

Sadly, virtually none of the Voyageurs disputants entertained the possibility the conflict itself could be hurting the economic well-being of the gateway communities surrounding the park, and few could engage in the level of reframing necessary for enabling a successful collaborative solution to emerge. As Schön and Rein (1994: 171) cogently argued, "Codesign depends upon the ability of at least some of the actors to inquire into the intentions and meanings of other actors involved with them in controversy; and it is here, as we have seen, that situated frame reflection comes into play." Consequently, the Voyageurs conflict has remained intractable for over 40 years.

In another well-publicized natural resource case, joint problem-solving was eventually selected after the parties had engaged in more contentious tactics for several years. In this case, the reframing from contention to collaboration was championed by a member of each opposing camp who eventually came to appreciate that the need to save their town from economic peril (a superordinate goal) was more important than continuing the fight (Bryan & Wondolleck 2003).

Authority decides after consultation frame

An important distinction needs to be made between those who prefer the joint problem-solving frame and those who advocate the authority decides after consultation frame. This approach invites the stakeholders to present their information through activities like public hearings or informal meetings with decision-makers, but ultimately privileges those already in positions of authority (e.g. local authorities, agencies, or institutions) by assuming that they retain the right to make the decisions after gathering input from a variety of stakeholders. Confusion and ultimate loss of trust in agency officials often occurs when the officials and public stakeholders hold different frames about a joint activity they are undertaking. If the stakeholders believe they are participating in joint problem-solving while agency officials frame the interaction as an authority decides after consultation frame, the former typically feel resentful when their "recommendations" are not adopted and implemented as given.

The powerful role of framing in promoting social movement activism has been pointed out by scholars studying social movements: for example, in the nuclear disarmament movement (Benford 1993), the environmental justice movement in the US (Taylor 2000), and the growth of regional populism in Italy (Diani 1996). Taylor (2000) has convincingly argued that environmental justice framing was used to enlist people of color in the environmental movement during the 1980s and 1990s. "Framing environmental issues as social justice issues, comparing them to other labor and human rights issues, and connecting them to urban environments where they live and work enabled people of color to identify with the environmental movement, albeit via their own distinct brand of environmentalism" (Gray 2003a: 19).

Some scholars have also noted that, while movement organizers use frames to rally members to their cause, frame conflicts also erupt within social movements. For example, during the 1980s, proponents of the nuclear disarmament movement differed in their framing of how radical the movement should be (Benford 1993). Similarly, Canadian environmental organizations promoting green marketing campaigns clashed when their frames about the degree of advocacy they should adopt differed (Westley & Vredenberg 1991). In the early days of the environmental justice movement (EJM) in the US, mainstream environmentalists did not see eye to eye with the original proponents of the EJM. These groups did not overcome their frame differences until the Environmental Protection Agency intervened to legitimize the EJM's activities (Taylor 2000).

Proponents of mediation need to recognize that disputants can hold a myriad of frames about conflict and their stance toward it. At the extreme, people may even disagree on whether a conflict exists. For some, framing a set of circumstances as a conflict may not serve their needs, whereas it may advance the cause of others. The power of various disputants can be increased or decreased depending on how a relationship or dispute is labeled (Mather & Yngvesson 1980–81). The extent to which disputants frame the dispute in terms of power is the issue I address next.

Power Frames

Menkel-Meadow (2001) identified a host of contextual issues, including the negotiators themselves, that cause actual negotiation dynamics to deviate from that predicted by rational decision-making theories. One such issue is the relative power among the parties. Power is "measured by a variety of factors – perception, economics, need for resolution, legal or factual endowments, quality of agents or representatives, strength of constituencies, perceived sense of justice of one's cause" (Menkel-Meadow 2001: 260). Framing a situation as one that is "mediatable" may serve to obscure differences and restrict disputants' voice (particularly in asymmetric power situations). This could be done unwittingly or strategically to limit or quell dissent and preserve an existing power distribution (Gray 1994; Hardy & Phillips 1998). Low power parties who do come to the table may, in effect, perpetuate patterns of intimidation and consequently have less leverage and, therefore, negotiate away gains which they secure through advocacy and to which they might be legally entitled. Power differences (imputed to race and gender) are manifest in the differential success of women and minorities (relative to white men) who participate in mediation (Delgado, Dunn, Brown, Lee & Hubbert 1985; Grillo 1991) and in negotiated outcomes generally (Kolb & Williams 2000; Babcock & Laschever 2003). For example, power relations among the parties may also become salient in divorce mediations when issues of abuse are present. Mediation critics assert that formal legal proceedings afford greater protection to parties in these cases. Similar unjust prospects are suggested for parties who are shunted into court-annexed mediations without understanding their legal rights and entitlements (Nolan-Haley 1996). "Mediation becomes unjust if the issues it considers and the results it achieves stray too far from the issues and results that would obtain in the adjudicatory system" (Hyman & Love 2002: 158–9).

Struggles for power are often at the root of intractable conflicts, particularly those involving multiple parties (Gray 1989, 1994; Hardy & Phillips 1998). Attempts to overcome longstanding historical oppression lead groups to adopt a power lens to construct their interactions (Gray 2004a) and to mobilize recruits to champion their cause (Benford & Snow 2000). In an analysis of four intractable natural resource disputes, framing the dispute in terms of power (e.g. gaining authority, voice, resources, or sympathy, or building a coalition, using force or moral authority) was a dominant lens adopted by a wide array of disputants (Brummans et al. 2004), particularly environmental groups that rely on social mobilization tactics to keep their organizations alive. In the Voyageurs National Park conflict mentioned earlier, it is not surprising that disputants of all stripes used a wide array of power frames to make sense of their experiences in that conflict. With this framing as dominant, disputants on all sides of the conflict resorted to political strategies. Park opponents forced federal Congressional hearings in an attempt to decommission the park and relied on numerous forms of social protest to oppose park decisions. The Park Service, allied with environmental groups, countered with coalition-building strategies of their own. Some park opponents even charged that the federal mediation effort (described above) was a political ploy initiated by Senator Paul Wellstone to prevent him from having to take a public stand on the Voyageurs case and another hotly contested conflict over the Boundary Waters Canoe Area. These excerpts from interviews with motorized users who opposed the National Park Service's management efforts at Voyageurs exemplify frames rooted in power:

> *Speaker 1.* You have the environmentalist groups that have their . . .
> *Speaker 2.* . . . they have their wilderness agenda, they also have their tentacles right smack into the National Park Services . . . It's all politics . . . and they got the money
> . . .
> *Speaker 1.* . . . and they're in power . . .
> *Speaker 2.* . . . and they got the money and even when you complain to the politicians it still comes down to numbers. They know how to rally the numbers just like the National Rifle Association can put their people, whether its right or wrong, you know what I mean, they know how to rally their people. (Gray, confidential research data)

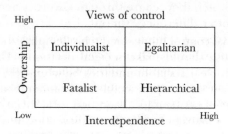

FIGURE 8.1   Social control frames

Social Control Frames

A final frame type that is particularly useful for making sense of intractable conflicts has been called social control frames (Gray 2003a). These frames are derived from an earlier conceptualization of worldviews depicted by Wildavsky and Dake (1990). Social control frames are useful for understanding disputants' expectations about decisions in society will be made. Figure 8.1 shows four types of social control frames that can be distinguished by their placement along two dimensions.

Individualist frames

When parties expect a high degree of ownership over decisions and believe they have little interdependence with others, they adopt individualist frames. Disputants with these frames expect that individuals should have a high degree of control over how societal issues are decided. They opt for little regulation and want the freedom to decide their own affairs with little interference from governments.

Fatalist frames

Parties with fatalist frames, on the other hand, have resigned themselves to having little control over their own affairs. They expert they have no choice but to accept tight controls over which they exert little influence. Hence, they opt out of any influence attempts themselves.

Egalitarian frames

At the opposite extreme are egalitarians who envision group or community control over the societal issues. Egalitarians envision widespread involvement in social decision-making that maximizes everyone's voice in decision-making and minimizes differences among individuals.

Hierarchist frames

The fourth type of social control frame, hierarchist, emphasizes that those individuals with technical expertise should make societal decisions. This framing envisions top-down control with clear social boundaries between decision-makers and non-decision-makers. In their study of intractable environmental disputes, Lewicki et al. (2003) also distinguished between local and non-local social control because some disputants preferred egalitarian frames, but believed local decision-makers should have responsibility for most decisions. Local refers to community, regional, and state-level control and national refers to federal, national, or global decision control. The two examples below illustrate the differences between local egalitarian and non-local hierarchist frames:

> [You] see one of this reasons that right now this is our last hope [is] if we can hold that water under state control. It isn't that the state isn't gonna manage the water with the . . . with whatever intent, with the intent of the national park, you know, in mind. They will manage it that way. It's just that we can be assured that at least we have a chance to be involved in the legislative process. On a state level we can play the politics. I mean if there's some rules and regulations that would come about on the water at least we have an opportunity to be involved in the process. (Local egalitarian; Gray, confidential research data)

> But point being we've gone on now for about 25 years and some issues have gone back and forth on the way they're either interpreted or they're regulated. And I guess I almost kind of feel at some point you need to kind of try to explain whether its through an informed consent process or whatever, and kind of draw a line in the sand this is the way this park is going to be managed, not vacillate back and forth. (Non-local hierarchist; Gray, confidential research data)

SUMMARY

We have seen that research on framing in intractable conflicts has identified several types of frames (including justice, conflict-handling, power, and social control) that create a wide array of lenses through which disputants experience and understand their interactions. Given these various frames, the likelihood that mediation is a dominant frame among these possibilities is relegated to a low probability, particularly in intractable conflicts. In the next section, we consider the implications of these alternative frames for conflict assessment processes and review some frame-based interventions that could be used as preliminary tools for intervening in disputes that are not yet (and may never be) ripe for mediation.

FRAME-BASED DISPUTE INTERVENTIONS

All four frames considered in the previous section, when considered together, form a complex array of lenses through which disputants approach conflicts. To conclude this chapter, two important implications of this plethora of frames for potential interveners need to be examined. First, the dispute resolution field needs an enriched model of conflict assessment – one designed to uncover the way disputants are framing the contested situation. Second, we need an array of frame-based interventions that can offer options, other than mediation, for increasing the prospects for civil dialog among the disputants in circumstances in which mediation or another dispute resolution process is not yet or maybe never will be possible.

Enriched Conflict Assessment

Traditional conflict assessment processes are generally designed to (1) understand the history and background of the conflict, (2) determine the relevant parties and their power relationships, (3) glean the positions, and, more importantly, the interests and BATNAs of the parties, and (4) diagnose whether or not the conflict lends itself to mediation. Incorporating framing into conflict assessment processes would expand the data collection process of assessment to include investigation of the way each disputant is framing the conflict. Interveners would want to pay attention to at least three of the four types of frames described earlier in this chapter (ethics, conflict management, and power) for interpersonal disputes and all four (including social control) for disputes dealing with public policy issues. Depending on the nature of the dispute, there may also be other types of frames (e.g. views of nature, loss versus gain frames, or health-oriented frames) that interveners should inquire about because they may also play a role in how a particular party understands the conflict. This enriched approach to conflict assessment will provide more data for determining whether or not a dispute is mediatable, and, it may motivate the intervener to adopt some of the techniques below if the conclusion is that the dispute is not yet ripe enough for mediation. Moore (1986) suggested that difficult, value-based conflicts can be reframed in terms of interests, but others have pointed to the intransigence of value-based or ideological conflicts (Rothman 1997; Littlejohn & Domenici 2000; Wade-Benzoni et al. 2002). Still others have alluded to an uneasy tension between the assertion that all disputes are potentially mediatable and the notion of intractable conflicts (Kriesberg, Northrup & Thorson 1989; Burgess & Burgess 1995; Lewicki et al. 2003).[2] Third parties who are considering intervening to establish a forum for joint problem-solving would do well to understand the patterns of all four of the frames disputants or groups of disputants hold in these controversies and to assess the tenacity with which disputants adhere to these frames. For disputes that involve multiple parties, it would seem that, because of their breadth and potency, social control frames and power frames, in particular, may be the most ingrained and therefore the least malleable of the frames I have considered.

Frame-Based Interventions

Although mediation has proven unsuccessful in intractable conflicts, other frame-based approaches that respect identity differences and promote voice have demonstrated some potential for opening a dialog among the disputants (Gray 2004b). These approaches, which I term "frame-based interventions," are predicated on different assumptions than mediation. Rather than trying to assist the parties in crafting a "solution" to the conflict (which they are unready or unwilling to do), these interventions are intended to make more modest gains in improving relations among the parties. Instead, they create opportunities for the disputants to investigate, "try on," and enlarge their own and others' frames about the conflict without having to give up (or abandon) any of their existing frames. The latter point is important because the approach tries to minimize any threats or challenges to the disputants' own framing while inviting them to try on more expansive frames. Frame enlargement draws on three overarching approaches:

1 Exploring one's own frame repertoire is accomplished by a series of exercises that enable participants to identify or classify their own frames in comparison to an array of other possible ways to frame the situation.
2 Perspective-taking exercises encourage disputants to begin to hear (without judgment) the ways other disputants experience the conflict. One way to accomplish this is through listening dyads, in which parties exchange their whole story frames with others in the dispute and try to weave a joint story that includes each of their relevant experiences.
3 Exploring stereotypes involves a counterintuitive appreciative process of finding value in that which a stereotype denigrates.

In general, frame-based interventions can be used to train parties who are in ritualistic, ideological, or historical conflict with each other (e.g. representatives of different federal agencies, pro-life versus pro-choice groups, racially divided groups, environmental proponents and opponents). Some of the interventions are designed for within-group and some for across-group work (see Gray 2004b for a more extended discussion of these approaches).

CONCLUSION

By adopting a framing approach to mediation and dispute resolution, I have highlighted several key components of the larger model of mediation introduced in chapter 2. In particular, frames represent important antecedent characteristics that parties import into the conflict arena. Because of their wider cultural exposure and their unique personal experiences, disputants view the conflict through a variety of different lenses. Interveners who want to introduce mediation or other dispute resolution options must recognize, first and foremost, that disputants may be constructing the conflict in many ways that may counter or impede third party efforts. Not only is it important for interveners to understand and anticipate these frames, but they must determine when mediation is an appropriate vehicle for resolution and when it is not and what alternative options could be introduced instead.

While the costs of conflict can be high for any group of disputants and mediation has enjoyed considerable success in ameliorating such costs, adopting a framing approach to mediation offers several fresh opportunities to reappraise mediation efforts. First, by focusing on framing within mediation, I have tried to highlight critical aspects of the original model of mediation that are likely to have a direct impact on the success of the mediation. How a mediator engages in framing will either enhance or impede reaching a mediated outcome. I argue that, without successful framing of the process and reframing of the issues, mediation is much less likely to conclude constructively. Thus, mediators must be cognizant and deliberate and reflexive about of all of their reframing initiatives. Second, by unpacking how disputants themselves are framing the conflict, we can get clearer insight into why conflicts persist and the fundamental disjunctures that make resolution elusive at times. Third, by articulating the role of framing in disputants' constructions of conflict, we can also begin to envision other mechanisms that may prove fruitful for maintaining civil dialog when mediation is neither possible nor desirable as a vehicle for dispute resolution.

Additionally, woven through my treatment of mediation in this chapter is the more subtle, yet fundamentally critical, question of who is framing what for whom? When parties submit to mediation (at least voluntary mediation), they are asked to assume responsibility for identifying and mutually agreeing to behaviors each will take to end the conflict. Yet many disputants do so without a well-developed knowledge of the nature of the process to which they are committing, or clear expectations about what it is intended (and not intended) to do (Peachey 1989). By considering the explicit role of the mediator as "framer," we are forced to ask questions about mediation ethics – just how influential are mediators or should they be in ushering parties to agreement? This is a topic of continuing debate within the profession – e.g. whether the mediator should function as a dealmaker or an orchestrator of agreements (Kolb 1983). The inherent tension here also turns on framing – regarding the extent to which mediators construe their role as finding an agreement at all costs versus relegating the responsibility for reaching agreement totally to the disputants themselves.

Adopting a framing perspective on mediation (and on conflict more generally) causes us to remember that disputants and third parties are actively engaged in the construction of conflict and its resolution – and that such discursive activity shapes the outcomes of their interactions. I hope to call mediators' attention to the power they wield in such constructions and to help them understand the implications of their actions and the stakes signified by disputants' frames. For example, critics of mediation might even assert that framing during mediation can be considered a subtle form of brainwashing that, in the interest of settlement, leaves the parties who submit to mediated settlements devoid of certain fundamental rights of jurisprudence. Similarly, without an awareness of and respect for disputants' frames, mediators may neglect or gloss over issues that are fundamental to disputants' identities.

In sum, third parties should not take the mediation task lightly. They should be mindful of the framing activities in which they are engaged and the decisions which ensue from them. These decisions, along with those of parties and organizations who adopt mediation, in the aggregate serve to frame choices about voice and justice in the larger society.

NOTES

1 Reuben (2000) proposes a way around this dilemma that he dubs "a unitary theory of alternative dispute resolution and public civil justice" by arguing that many ADR proceedings are conducted under state or federal auspices and consequently should be accorded these protections.

2 The philosophical differences at the root of this tension were highlighted during a discussion between researchers and a group of prominent public sector mediators at a dinner meeting of the Environmental Framing Consortium in Albuquerque, New Mexico during the 2000 meeting of the Society of Professionals in Dispute Resolution (SPIDR). The mediators indicated considerable unease with the notion of intractable conflicts.

REFERENCES

Abel, R. L. (1982) *The Politics of Informal Justice*, vol. 1. Academic Press, Orlando.

Babcock, L. & Laschever, S. (2003) *Women Don't Ask*. Princeton University Press, Princeton.

Bateson, G. (1975) *Steps to an Ecology of Mind*. Ballantine Books, New York.

Benford, R. D. (1993) You could be the hundredth monkey: collective action frames and vocabularies of motive within the nuclear disarmament movement. *The Sociological Quarterly* 34, 195–216.

Benford, R. D. & Snow, D. (2000) Framing processes and social movements: an overview and assessment. *Annual Review of Sociology* 26, 611–639.

Bies, R. J., Shapiro, D. L. & Cummings, L. L. (1998) Casual accounts and managing organization conflict: is it enough to say it's not my fault? *Communication Research* 15(4), 381–399.

Brummans, B., Putnam, L., Gray, B., Hanke, R., Lewicki, R. & Wiethoff, C. (2004) *Moving Beyond Stakeholder Groups: Profiles of Disputants Framing of Environmental Conflicts*. Working paper. Center for Research in Conflict and Negotiation, Pennsylvania State University, University Park.

Bryan, T. A. & Wondolleck, J. M. (2003) When irresolvable becomes resolvable: the Quincy library group conflict. In R. Lewicki, B. Gray & M. Elliott (eds.), *Making Sense of Intractable Environmental Conflict: Concepts and Cases*. Island Press, Washington, pp. 63–89.

Buechler, S. M. (2000) *Social Movements in Advanced Capitalism*. Oxford University Press, New York.

Burgess, G. & Burgess, H. (1995) Beyond the limits: dispute resolution of intractable environmental conflicts. In J. W. Blackburn & W. Bruce (eds.), *Mediating Environmental Conflicts: Theory and Practice*. Quorum Books, Westport, pp. 101–119.

Bush, R. A. B. (1984) Dispute resolution alternatives and the goals of civil justice: jurisdictional assumptions for process choice. *Wisconsin Law Review* 1984, 893–1034.

Bush, R. A. B. & Folger, J. P. (1994) *The Promise of Mediation*. Jossey Bass, San Francisco.

Cox, T. (1993) *Cultural Diversity in Organizations: Theory, Research and Practice*. Berrett-Koehler, San Francisco.

Delgado, R., Dunn, C., Brown, P., Lee, H. & Hubbert, D. (1985) Fairness and formality: minimizing the risk of prejudice in alternative dispute resolution. *Wisconsin Law Review* 1985, 1359–1404.

Diani, M. (1996) Linking mobilization frames and political opportunities: insights from regional populism in Italy. *American Sociological Review* 61, 1053–1069.

Elliott, M., Gray, B. & Lewicki, R. (2003) Lessons learned about the framing and reframing of intractable environmental conflicts. In R. Lewicki, B. Gray & M. Elliott (eds.), *Making Sense of Intractable Environmental Conflicts: Concepts and Cases*. Island Press, Washington, pp. 409–436.

Ethier, K. & Deaux, K. (1990) Hispanics in ivy: assessing identity and perceived threat. *Sex Roles* 22, 427–440.

Fisher, R., Ury, W. & Patton, B. (1991) *Getting To Yes*. Penguin Books, New York.

Folberg, J. & Taylor, A. (1984) *Mediation: A Comprehensive Guide to Resolving Conflicts Without Litigation*. Jossey-Bass, San Francisco.

Folger, R. & Cropanzano, R. (1998) *Organizational Justice and Human Resource Management*. Sage, Thousand Oaks.

Galanter, M. (1980) Legality and its discontents: a preliminary assessment of current theories of legalization and delegalization. In E. Blankenburg, E. Klausa & H. Rottleuther (eds.), *Alternative Rechtsformen und Alternative zum Recht*. Jahrbuch für Rechtssoziologicund Rechtstheorie, Westdeutscher Verlag, Opladen, vol. 6, pp. 11–26.

Gamson, W. A. (1990) The social psychology of collective action. In C. M. A. Morris (ed.), *Frontiers of Social Movement Theory*. Yale University Press, New Haven, pp. 53–76.

Gray, B. (1989) *Collaborating: Finding Common Ground for Multiparty Problems*. Jossey-Bass, San Francisco.

Gray, B. (1994) A feminist critique of collaborating. *Journal of Management Inquiry* 3(3), 285–293.

Gray, B. (1997) Framing and reframing of intractable environmental disputes. In R. J. Lewicki, R. Bies & B. Sheppard (eds.), *Research on Negotiation in Organizations*. JAI Press, Greenwich, vol. 6, pp. 163–188.

Gray, B. (2003a) Framing of environmental disputes. In R. Lewicki, R., B. Gray & M. Elliott (eds.), *Making Sense of Intractable Environmental Conflict: Concepts and Cases*. Island Press, Washington, pp. 11–34.

Gray, B. (2003b) The dialogue of intractability surrounding Voyageurs National Park. In R. Lewicki, R., B. Gray & M. Elliott (eds.), *Making Sense of Intractable Environmental Conflict: Concepts and Cases*. Island Press, Washington, pp. 91–125.

Gray, B. (2004a) Strong opposition: frame-based resistance to collaboration. *Journal of Community and Applied Social Psychology* 14(3), 166–176.

Gray, B. (2004b) *Interventions for Promoting Frame Reflection in Intractable Conflicts*. Paper presented at the conference on Multiorganizational Partnerships and Collaborative Alliances, Tilburg, The Netherlands, June 23–26, 2004.

Grillo, T. (1991) The mediation alternative: process dangers for women. *Yale Law Journal* 100, 1545–1610.

Hardy, C. & Phillips, N. (1998) Strategies of engagement: lessons from the critical examination of collaboration and conflict in interorganizational domains. *Organization Science* 9, 217–230.

Hyman, J. M. & Love, L. P. (2002) If Portia were a mediator: an inquiry into justice in mediation. *Clinical Law Review* 9, 157–193.

Kelman, H. C. (1999) *The Role of Social Identity in Conflict Resolution: Experiences from Israeli-Palestinian Problem-Solving Workshops*. Paper presented at the International Association of Conflict Management, June 22, San Sebastian, Spain.

Keltner, S. K. (1994) *The Management of Struggle: Elements of Dispute Resolution through Negotiation, Mediation, and Arbitration*. Hampton Press, Creeskill.

Kolb, D. M. (1983) *The Mediators*. MIT Press, Cambridge.

Kolb, D. M. (1985) To be a mediator: expressive tactics in mediation. *Journal of Social Issues* 41, 1–25.

Kolb, D. M. & Williams, J. (2000) *The Shadow Negotiation: How Women Can Master the Hidden Agendas That Determine Bargaining Success*. Simon & Schuster, New York.

Kressel, K., Pruitt, D. G. & Associates (eds.) (1989) *Mediation Research: The Process and Effectiveness of Third-Party Intervention*. Jossey-Bass, San Francisco.

Kriesberg, L., Northrup, T. A. & Thorson, S. J. (eds.) (1989) *Intractable Conflicts and their Transformation*. Syracuse University Press, Syracuse.

Labianca, G., Gray, B. & Brass, D. (2000) A grounded model of organizational schema change during empowerment. *Organization Science* 11(2), 235–257.

Lax, D. & Sebenius, J. (1986) *The Manager as Negotiator*. Free Press, New York.

Lewicki, R., Gray, B. & Elliott, M. (2003) *Making Sense of Intractable Environmental Conflict: Concepts and Cases*. Island Press, Washington.

Littlejohn, S. & Domenici, K. (2000) *Engaging Communication in Conflict: Systemic Practice*. Sage, London.

Mather, L. & Yngvesson, B. (1980–81) Language, audience, and the transformation of disputes. *Law and Society Review* 15(3–4), 775–821.

McHarg, N. (2000) Park Service chipping at [*sic*] away our rights. *Daily Journal* September 5, 1.

Menkel-Meadow, C. (1995) Whose dispute is it anyway? A philosophical and democratic defense of settlement (in some cases). *Georgetown Law Journal* 83, 2663–2696.

Menkel-Meadow, C. (2001) Negotiating with lawyers, men and things: the contextual approach still matters. *Negotiation Journal* 17(3, July), 257–293.

Montville, J. (1995) Complicated mourning and mobilization for nationalism. In J. Braun (ed.), *Social Pathology in Comparative Perspective: The Nature and Psychology of Civil Society*. Praeger, Westport, 159–174.

Moore, C. W. (1986) *The Mediation Process*. Jossey-Bass, San Francisco.

Nolan-Haley, J. M. (1996) Court mediation and the search for justice through law. *Washington University Law Quarterly* 74, 47–102.

Peachey, D. E. (1989) What people want from mediation. In K. Kressel, D. G. Pruitt & Associates (eds.), *Mediation Research: The Process and Effectiveness of Third-Party Intervention*. Jossey-Bass, San Francisco, pp. 300–321.

Pinkley, R. L. & Northcraft, G. B. (1994) Conflict frames of reference: implications for dispute processes and outcomes. *Academy of Management Journal* 37(1), 193–205.

Putnam, L. & Holmer, M. (1992) Framing, reframing and disuse development. In L. Putnam & M. E. Roloff (eds.), *Communication and Negotiation*. Sage, Newbury Park, pp. 128–155.

Reuben, R. C. (2000) Constitutional gravity: a unitary theory of alternative dispute resolution and public civil justice. *UCLA Law Review* 47, 949–1104.

Rothman, J. (1997) *Resolving Identity-Based Conflicts in Nations, Organizations and Communities*. Jossey-Bass, San Francisco.

Rubin, J. & Brown, B. (1975) *Social Psychology of Bargaining and Negotiation*. Academic Press, New York.

Schön, D. A. & Rein, M. (1994) *Frame Reflection: Toward the Resolution of Intractable Policy Controversies*. New York: Basic Books.

Sheppard, B., Blumenfeld-Jones, K. & Roth, J. (1989) Informal thirdpartyship: studies of everyday conflict intervention. In K. Kressel, D. G. Pruitt & Associates (eds.), *Mediation Research: The Process and Effectiveness of Third-Party Intervention*. Jossey-Bass, San Francisco, pp. 166–189.

Sherif, M. (1958) Superordinate goals in the reduction of intergroup conflicts. *American Journal of Sociology* 63, 349–358.

Sitkin, S. B. & Bies, R. J. (1993) Social accounts in conflict situations: using explanations to manage conflict. *Human Relations* 46, 349–370.

Tajfel, H. & Turner, J. C. (1985) The social identity theory of intergroup behavior. In S. Worchel & W. G. Austin (eds.), *Psychology of Intergroup Relations*. Nelson-Hall, Chicago, pp. 7–24.

Tannen, D. (1979) What's in a frame? Surface evidence of underlying expectations. In R. Freedle (ed.), *New Directions in Discourse Processes*. Ablex, Norwood, pp. 137–181.

Taylor, D. (2000) Advances in environmental justice: research, theory and methodology. *American Behavioral Scientist* 43(4), 504–80.

Thomas, K. W. (1992) Conflict and negotiation process in organizations. In M. D. Dunnette & L. M. Hough (eds.), *Handbook of Industrial and Organizational Psychology*, 2nd edn. Rand McNally, Chicago, pp. 889–935.

Tversky, A. & Kahneman, D. (1981) The framing of decision and the psychology of choice. *Science* 211, 453–458.

Unger, R. M. (1987) *Social Theory: Its Situation and its Task*. Cambridge University Press, Cambridge.

Wade-Benzoni, K., Hoffman, A., Thompson, L., Moore, D., Gillespie, J. J. & Bazerman, M. H. (2002) Barriers to resolution in ideologically based negotiations: the role of values and institutions. *Academy of Management Review* 27(1), 41–57.

Wall, J. (1981) Mediation: an analysis, review and proposed research. *Journal of Conflict Resolution* 25, 157–180.

Westley, F. & Vredenberg, H. (1991) Strategic bridging: the collaboration between environmentalists and business in the marketing of green products. *Journal of Applied Behavioral Science* 27(1), 65–90.

Wiethoff, C., Hanke, R., Wunch, J., Bryan, T., Jones-Corley, J. & Momen, M. (1999) *Master Codebook for the Environmental Framing Consortium*. Center for Research in Conflict and Negotiation, Pennsylvania State University, University Park.

Wildavsky, A. & Dake, K. (1990) Theories of risk perception: who fears what and why? *Daedalus* 119, 41–60.

Yarborough, E. & Wilmot, W. (1995) *Artful Mediation: Constructive Conflict at Work*. Cairns Publishing, Boulder.

Chapter 9

Does the Model Overarch the Narrative Stream?

JOHN M. WINSLADE AND GERALD D. MONK

INTRODUCTION

The impulse to construct an overarching model that accounts for everything within a given field is instinctively attractive. The search for such a theory has tantalized physicists for decades, or even centuries, and has spun off many fresh spurts of theoretical development. In the complexity of the study of human cultural and social endeavor, there have also been many efforts toward the creation of grand theories of history, culture, or of a universal psychology (Kuhn 1962; Cushman 1990; Newman & Holzman 1997; Fox & Prilleltensky 1999). While some of the models created by such efforts have exerted considerable influence for a time, they have usually come short of the dream of establishing lasting truth value (Burr 1995, 2003; Downing 2000; Seidman 1994). They have more usually been critiqued from a variety of perspectives, have created phalanxes of adherents and opponents, and have eventually settled into a position of partial influence within the competing forces that produce the history of an academic or professional discipline (Gergen & Gergen 1986).

So how do we respond to the model proposed in chapter 2 of this book, intended as it might be to establish an overarching model of mediation practice? How, indeed, might such a question even be addressed? The first question presupposes the second. We want to be careful here, that is, to treat with care the intentions of the authors of the model, the as yet unexplored territories that such a model might open up, and the possibilities for practice that might be enhanced by it.

We also want to be careful in another way, to remain faithful to some philosophical positions which we are ourselves committed to exploring, to some particular practices that we have found useful, and to some explorations of these practices in mediation that we have written about (Winslade, Monk & Cotter 1998; Winslade & Monk 2000). In other words, the model demands a response that represents an ethical engagement.

Our Frame

We start with the assumption that such an engagement can only be made from a position and in a way that attempts to be rigorous through making that position evident and open to scrutiny. We therefore need to declare that our starting point for response is a commitment to a philosophical position that draws from social constructionist writing (Gergen 1985, 1999; Burr 1995, 2003), narrative practice in mediation (Winslade & Monk 2000), family therapy (White & Epston 1990), poststructuralist discourse theory (Lacan 1977; Derrida 1978; Lyotard 1984) and selected aspects of the postmodern challenge to a modernist worldview (Gergen 1991, 1994). Immediately, as we make this declaration, we have stepped off the edge, have taken a step of interpretation, and established a position in a relation. For if we maintain a philosophical position from which to engage, then we are bound to inquire into the philosophical positions taken up within the model. We are drawn into relation with these assumptions in an explicit way and committed to exploring these assumptions.

Why Models?

One of the implications of this line of inquiry is that the very idea of constructing an overarching model of mediation comes into view. The impulse to construct a model that embraces everything itself deserves attention. Rather than jumping into the content of the model, we are compelled to address the philosophical status of its existence. Is an overarching model possible? Is it desirable? What might be the consequences for a field of knowledge or practice of such a development? Indeed, in what tradition of thinking does such a notion arise? These questions, and the latter question especially, might be described as a deconstructive, because they seek to locate the model in the presuppositions of a worldview (Downing 2000). These questions are epistemological, rather than simply ontological. They cannot be answered empirically.

Our response is a wary one. The impulse to construct overarching models in the social sciences has been critiqued by Jean-Francois Lyotard (1984) in terms of the construction of "grand narratives." It is not a neutral act in epistemological terms and itself locates the model, whether intentionally or otherwise, in a paradigmatic tradition. It is associated, we assume, with the modernist desire to create truth value through the deployment of the scientific ideal of objective observation, systematic categorization, atomization of details into linear causal explanations, and the gradual accrual of organized domains of knowledge. This is what Lyotard (and others) refer to as the modernist tradition (e.g. Gergen 1991; Burr 1995, 2003).

But knowledge, as Foucault (1972, 1980) argued, is inextricably linked with the discourses that dominate the social context out of which knowledge is produced. We refer to a discourse in Foucault's sense as a social practice dispersed through cultural interactions that exerts a dominating influence on what can be thought and spoken. Even though we respect the intentions of the authors to reorganize our understanding of accrued knowledge within the field of mediation, we are inclined towards a reading of the model as a product of the dominant discourses in the fields of mediation and research methods.

From this perspective, the emphasis on empirical studies in the construction of the model does not preclude it from being subject to philosophical inquiry. It must still be examined in the light of its ethical value, its implication in power relations, and its privileging of some perspectives over others. It must be expected to convey a sense of moral oughtness in the very words it chooses to use, as well as in the stories of mediation process that it pieces together. From a social constructionist perspective, it must necessarily be read as a model with a small "m," in preference to any pretension to overarch all other models.

Circumscribed Utility

On the other hand, such a reading does not preclude it from serving a useful purpose. It merely cautions against reading it in too grand a way. We would view the model as a perhaps useful way to organize a range of ideas about mediation into a relatively comprehensive account. As a "narrative," it attains a certain quality of being convincing, and therefore plausible, on the grounds of its relatively comprehensive coverage. But we would caution that any narrative, any model, must leave some things out, distort some things, privilege some things over others, and squeeze some things into categories where they fit uncomfortably, simply in order to maintain coherence. This model is no exception.

From the perspective of narrative mediation, there are many elements of mediation practice as we conceive of it that are not represented here, or can only be represented through performing some contortions of reinterpretation. In a way, we do not expect anything otherwise. And we are grateful for the opportunity to articulate some different assumptions in response to the model. In this way, it is indeed very useful to us. After exploring a little further some of the assumptions built into this model, this will be the main thrust of this chapter. We shall seek to make use of the model in order to articulate further a narrative perspective in mediation. We shall pose the question of how the model works from the point of view of narrative mediation, including asking about what aspects of a narrative approach might get emphasized, distorted or excluded in this model.

QUESTIONS ABOUT SPECIFIC ASSUMPTIONS BUILT INTO THE MODEL

1   One of the expressed aims of the model is to contribute to the development of greater consensus around the definitions of "key concepts and variables" in the mediation literature. Of concern to the model-builders here is the degree of "fragmentation" that results from the "panoply of conceptual and operational definitions" in mediation literature. While acknowledging the richness of possibility that the existence of different ways of defining concepts enables and acknowledging too the dangers of oversimplification, the model plumps for the

ideal goal of "synthesis." A social constructionist perspective would suggest to us a preference for the alternative option of celebrating and encouraging the development of greater variety in the definition of concepts. We would assume the social constructionist perspective that language is a form of social action (Burr 1995, 2003) and that concepts cannot be separated off from the practices they embody into neutral zones where consensus can be produced. Different concepts embody different practices and, as Foucault (1972, 1980) pointed out many times, a narrowing of definitions can lead to a totalizing tendency around a social norm within a field of knowledge that has quite substantial material effects in people's lives. In practice, consensus often leads to the establishment of dominance of one perspective over others. In the production of consensus, some practices are typically legitimated while others are necessarily consigned to the margins. Is it necessary? We do not think so. Why not proliferate the available concepts in order to continue to open up new possible practices rather than close them down through working toward consensus?

Our aim in writing about mediation in a narrative vein has been to practice deliberately from within a different set of discursive points of reference, that is, from a different set of concepts. It has been necessary for us at various points to eschew the existing language in the field of mediation in order to reach toward new forms of practice. There are many who respond to new ways of languaging mediation with confusion. They frequently cry "Foul!" and ask us to avoid the "jargon," which we often take to mean, "Please use the 'jargon' with which we are familiar, rather than your unfamiliar 'jargon.'"

There is no doubt something to gain from a consensus with regard to key concepts. It enables easier conversation between mediators, for example. And we would concede that some degree of consensus is necessary for a professional domain to flourish. But at the same time, we should not lose sight of the dangers of consensus and should be on the alert for what gets lost when norms established through consensus come to dominate other possible conceptions of practice.

2 The authors of the model are to be congratulated for explicitly stating their assumptions with regard to "socio-cultural context variables." They acknowledge that mediation interactions are always conducted in the context of an interplay with the socio-cultural contexts in which people live. However, they decide to pursue the pragmatic path of omitting specific analysis of these "variables" in the model because to do so would be too complex to handle in an already complex chapter. This decision is, from our point of view, critical. It shapes the model in a way that almost precludes a narrative perspective from being recognized within it.

The way that we think about mediation is to seek opportunity for the more explicit inclusion of the socio-cultural context in the process and the content of mediation conversations. We seek to do so through a focus on how people pursue their conflicts through the use of discourse, which will always require a consideration of dominant discourses or narratives. The socio-cultural context of mediation is not for us therefore a "variable" at all. This usage is itself an expression of a research paradigm that deserves questioning. We do not believe that the socio-cultural context can be "controlled" or "analyzed" separately from the process and content of the mediation itself. It is present in the words that we choose to use, and in the conventions of the expressions that use us (Fairclough 1992; Parker 1998). We are interested in it not from an idealistic or abstractly theoretical perspective but from the very pragmatic perspective of thinking about what to say in a mediation and how to respond to what other people say. Hence, we need to appeal this decision to treat the socio-cultural context as a set of "variables" that can be omitted from a model of the mediation process. One of our aims in working toward a narrative perspective in mediation practice has been to develop more explicit ways of including the socio-cultural world *more fully* in the practice of mediation. To omit it from this model might lead readers of the model to struggle to understand the intentions of narrative mediation practice.

3   Another feature of the model that we would want to raise questions about is the series of unproblematic references to terms such as disputant, mediator, interests, and needs as "characteristics" described in essentialist terms. As Vivien Burr (1995, 2003) has argued, a rejection of essentialism is a cornerstone of social constructionist thinking. Essentialism is the name given to the assumption that there is some kind of given, determined nature of persons or indeed of all objects in the world. From an essentialist perspective, words or concepts are secondary in importance to the underlying essence that pre-exists what they describe (Burr 1995, 2003). The constructionist perspective reverses this logic and argues that things like "personality" are the products of social interaction and discourse, rather than given in the nature of the person. Constructionist thinking therefore seeks to ask questions that constantly "de-naturalize" what is assumed to be natural. Essences are thus reconfigured as social constructions. Social constructions are by definition more susceptible to change through processes such as mediation and hence we consider many aspects of personhood as fluid and changing in response to social interaction, and discourse dynamics (Gergen 1991).

Hence, for example, concepts like "motivation" as an internalized characteristic of a person are not so readily accepted from a narrative perspective. They might be understood instead as the products of dialogical exchange or discursive positioning. The same might be said for mediator "empathy" as a personal characteristic. Why not think of it as a product of conversation? We would have serious questions about the assumption that disputants in conflict have some essential "interests" based on their psychological "needs" that underlie the positions they espouse in conflict situations. We would propose from a narrative perspective that a person's positions, interests, and needs are all constructed in discourse and that there is no underlying essence that can be referenced as more trustworthy than its "surface" manifestation. Hence, a model of mediation that takes for granted the value of negotiating change through the search for underlying interests is not necessarily warranted. We would not therefore accept as fundamental to a model of mediation the separation of positions and interests as accepted here.

4   The model is leavened with a number of constructionist insights in many places, but it also remains grounded in essentialized thinking in many places. One way in which this happens is in the discussion of concepts in a theoretical domain, followed by a process of "operationalizing" them into workable units of research or mediation practice. We are concerned that this leads to the creation of a degree of distance between "concepts" and domains of "practice" that is admittedly familiar in modernist social science, but nevertheless is open to question from a postmodern perspective (Lax 1989).

   Once we step out of the familiar patterns of essentialized thinking, then it starts to becomes problematic (which is different from saying wrong) to think of an attitude, a mindset, an expectation, a characteristic, a state of being, or even a demographic variable as inherent in a person, or in a relationship, or, for that matter, in a dispute. And there is an alternative. It is to approach persons, objects, and concepts from a discursive perspective. To look first for the work being done by discourse, rather than structural essences, to produce subjective experience and the social construction of life experience. To view people as positioned by dominant discourses and taken-for-granted assumptions that catch them up in patterns of thinking, feeling, speaking, and responding, indeed in the very conflicts that they bring to the mediator's attention.

5   The model appears to move from an analysis of individual characteristics to institutional characteristics that might affect the process and outcome of a mediation. It is this kind of progression that poststructuralist writers have set out to disrupt in recent decades and to claim that the role of language, or discourse, is not given enough emphasis in conventional social analysis. By this we mean the ways in which both individual utterances and institutional practices can be analyzed as formed out of discourse usage, rather than having a fundamental essence of their own (Foucault 1972). The work done by and through discourse appears to be downplayed from this analytical model. From a narrative perspective, we would rather see it given a much greater emphasis. There is moreover a growing literature about the practice of mediation that does indeed focus on discourse and language (see Garcia 1991, 1997, 2000; Cobb 1993, 1994; Greatbatch & Dingwall 1997, 1998) and this literature could be given an expanded place in the model. To do so would render the work of narrative mediators and researchers more visible.

How Does Narrative Mediation Fare in the Model?

We want now to concentrate on the things that are important for us to assert about narrative mediation and to consider what happens to these when they are examined in the light of the model. Is there a home for them in the model? Are they included or excluded? Does the model support or contradict what we want to explore in the development of narrative mediation? These are the kinds of questions that will guide our further interrogation of the model. We shall answer these questions by listing some cornerstones of narrative practice as we understand them and then asking how and where these principles fit with the model.

Goals of Narrative Mediation

From a narrative perspective, the goals of mediation are formulated differently from the ways that the model assumes. We would speak of aiming to help people separate themselves and their relationship from a conflict-saturated story and to reconnect with a story of cooperation, or understanding, or peace, or mutual respect (or whatever definition of the alternative story that the parties prefer). We deliberately focus on these goals rather than say "problem-solving" or "reaching agreement." Hence the elements of the model that assume that all mediation processes will include things like "option generating" are not always applicable. This is not to say that in a narrative mediation the process of "generating options" may not sometimes happen. But it is not necessarily central to the process we envisage.

Similarly, agreements may be reached in a narrative process, but we would understand these as plot events in the construction of a more satisfying narrative, rather than as the goals of the process of mediation itself. A formal written agreement may be only one moment in the development of such a narrative. We would expect it to have been preceded by many small moments of agreement, or mutual understanding, or unique outcomes (see White & Epston 1990; Winslade & Monk 2000) of cooperation, and also to be succeeded by further moments of plot evolution that arise in the working out of the agreement.

As a result, we do not assume that a satisfying relationship shift will be predicated on the formation of a formal basis for agreement. Rather, we would turn this assumption around and assume that the formal basis for agreement can be predicated on the recovery of a story of agreement that is frequently being masked by the attention given to the conflict story (White & Epston 1990). Therefore, as mediators, we focus on re-authoring the relationship story in order to address a problem issue, rather than addressing a problem issue in order to allow the relationship to go forward.

In the model as we read it, there is an interest in whether the relationship has changed. Change is, then, taken as a measure of mediation success. We would stress, however, a subtle difference. Since we believe that a narrative perspective starts from the assumption that people act on the basis of plausible stories rather than on the basis of hard facts, it becomes more important to focus on shifts in the *story* of the relationship, than on the relationship *itself*. From this perspective, so-called "self-report" becomes more reliable (in the sense of being a better predictor of future actions) than behavioral data.

Externalizing rather than Internalizing

In an effort to interrupt internalized ways of speaking frequently featured in conflict conversations, we try to develop externalized conversation. In this approach, we carefully use language in a way that presents to the parties the assumption that the conflict is not inherent in, or essential to, their nature as persons, or to the nature of their relationship. The practice of externalizing was developed in family therapy by Michael White and David Epston (1990). It takes its rhetorical force from its reversal of the common logic in psychology that focuses explanations for events on the inside of the person. An externalizing practice speaks about a conflict or a problem as if it were a third party in a relationship exerting influence over the persons, but not identified with either party. This way of speaking interrupts patterns of blame and guilt that frequently coalesce around a conflict story, and opens up space for the parties to have a different conversation than has been previously possible. It invites people to dis-identify with a conflict-saturated story in order to notice other possibilities for relationship. The spirit of an externalizing conversation is summarized in Michael White's (1989: 6) maxim, "It is not the person that is the problem; it is the problem that is the problem."

This is not the place to develop a full account of the practice of externalizing conversation either as a technique or as a theoretically consistent practice. We have done that elsewhere (Winslade & Monk 2000). What is relevant here is to ask questions about the fit between the model and this practice so central to narrative mediation. It would seem to fit most neatly under the heading of procedural factors, but does not coincide with any of the other procedural factors mentioned in the model. One can only assume that if model presented in chapter 2 were adopted by researchers, they would not be equipped to pick up on efforts made by narrative mediators to use language in this way.

Other Procedures in Narrative Mediation

Working from a foundation of externalizing conversation, mediators working in a narrative way would use a series of other procedures, described in more detail in Winslade and Monk (2000), for loosening the grip of a dominant story and developing an alternative story of relationship. These procedures would include:

- mapping the effects of the conflict story on the participants and on the relationship between them
- asking questions that attempt to deconstruct the dominant story by bringing into the foreground the taken-for-granted assumptions on which the conflict story relies
- mapping the discursive positions (after Davies & Harré's 1990 articulation of this concept) that have been crafted within the discourse of the conflict story
- asking the participants to evaluate the conflict story and its probable future trajectory
- inviting the participants to articulate their preferences for a future that is not limited by the conflict story
- asking about the existence of unique outcomes that would not be predicted by the conflict story
- listening for the implicit story of cooperation, or understanding, that is always present in the midst of a conflict story, and inquiring into its possibilities
- building the significance of these unique outcomes into a narrative that stands a chance of competing with the conflict story
- fashioning, in collaboration with the participants, an agreement that expresses the spirit of their preferred relationship story.

Evaluating the Fit

As already noted with regard to externalizing conversations, these important practices in narrative mediation are not to be found in the model. Again, they would not be out of place in the section on procedural factors in mediation (T_m). But the section on procedural factors concentrates on aspects of mediation that are based in the interest-based, problem-solving approach and assumed to be universal. Narrative mediation, along with perhaps some other approaches, serves as an awkward irritant with regard to such assumptions. It simply does not fit. We are advocating practices that cannot simply be grafted on to existing models.

It is worth stressing, though, that we are not complaining about the exclusion from the model of practices that are important for us with a view to claiming a space for these in the model. To include them might destroy the integrity of the model, which is not our intention. Nor would we expect that all mediators should be evaluated against criteria like ours that would only be relevant for someone practicing in a narrative way. Clearly the kind of practice we are advocating does not coincide with other mediation procedures, even though there are some points of overlap.

On the other hand, we would have grave misgivings about a research process that evaluated the work of a narrative mediator against the criteria specified in the section on procedural factors in mediation. To do so could produce an injustice and would fail to take account of paradigmatic differences or philosophical positions that cannot be integrated in any kind of facile way. The factors listed in the section on procedural factors simply do not fit the intentions and practices that we are interested in.

As a result, we would ask for some care with how the proposed model is read. It is not without value, but like all models, it is limited to a particular time and place, and the worldviews that feature there. Apart from anything else, it is largely American in the mediation and research practice that it articulates. This in itself means that it needs to be approached as a localized document rather than accorded global truth value. We would hope that the model can indeed be appreciated as a useful contribution to the mediation field, but in a more limited way than it appears to suggest itself. We see it as useful within the context of the mediation practices and worldviews that it represents. But, because it does not represent the whole domain of mediation practice, nor could be realistically expected to do so, it seems to us somewhat less than overarching the whole field.

Perhaps we can finish by exploring the "arch" metaphor a little further. We can imagine the field of mediation practice as a river flowing along a variety of streams in a common direction around some shingle banks built up by, and at the same time guiding, the flow of the river. This model arches nicely over some of the streams in this river and can serve as a useful vantage point for viewing the waters flowing beneath it. But it does not span all the streams in the river. Narrative mediation, as we conceive of it, flows down a different stream and around a different set of shingle banks. The arch of this model does not reach far enough to span this stream.

But, from the view accorded by those standing on the bridge created by this arch, it can be seen and distinguished from the other streams.

REFERENCES

Burr, V. (1995) *An Introduction to Social Constructionism*. Routledge, New York.

Burr, V. (2003) *Social Constructionism*. Psychology Press, London.

Cobb, S. (1993) Empowerment and mediation: a narrative perspective. *Negotiation Journal* 9(3), 245–259.

Cobb, S. (1994) A narrative perspective on mediation. In J. P. Folger & T. S. Jones (eds.), *New Directions in Mediation: Communication Research and Perspectives*. Sage, Thousand Oaks, pp. 48–66.

Cushman, P. (1990) Why the self is empty: toward a historically situated psychology. *American Psychologist* 45, 599–611.

Davies, B. & Harré, R. (1990) Positioning: the discursive production of selves. *Journal for the Theory of Social Behavior* 20(1), 43–63.

Derrida, J. (1978) *Writing and Difference*. University of Chicago Press, Chicago.

Downing, J. N. (2000) *Between Conviction and Uncertainty: Philosophical Guidelines for the Practicing Psychotherapist*. State University of New York Press, Albany.

Fairclough, N. (1992) *Discourse and Social Change*. Polity, Cambridge.

Foucault, M. (1972) *The Archaeology of Knowledge*, trans. A. M. Sheridan-Smith. Harper & Row, New York.

Foucault, M. (1980) *Power/Knowledge: Selected Interviews and Other Writings*. Pantheon Books, New York.

Fox, D. & Prilleltensky, I. (1999) *Critical Psychology: An Introduction*. Sage, Thousand Oaks.

Garcia, A. (1991) Dispute resolution without disputing: how the interactional organization of mediation hearings minimizes argument. *American Sociological Review* 56, 818–835.

Garcia, A. (1997) Interactional constraints on proposal generation in mediation hearings: a preliminary investigation. *Discourse and Society* 8(2), 219–247.

Garcia, A. (2000) Negotiating negotiation: the collaborative production of resolution in small claims mediation hearings. *Discourse and Society* 11(3), 315–343.

Gergen, K. (1985) The social constructionist movement in modern psychology. *American Psychologist* 40, 266–275.

Gergen, K. (1991) *The Saturated Self: Dilemmas of Identity in Contemporary Life*. Basic Books, New York.

Gergen, K. (1994) *Realities and Relationships: Soundings in Social Constructionism*. Harvard University Press, Cambridge.

Gergen, K. (1999) *An Invitation to Social Construction*. Sage, Newbury Park.

Gergen, K. & Gergen, M. (1986) Narrative form and the construction of psychological science. In T. R. Sarbin (ed.), *Narrative Psychology: The Storied Nature of Human Conduct*. Praeger, New York, pp. 22–44.

Greatbatch, D. & Dingwall, R. (1997) Argumentative talk in divorce mediation sessions. *American Sociological Review* 62(1), 151–171.

Greatbatch, D. & Dingwall, R. (1998) Talk and identity in divorce mediation. In C. Antaki & S. Widdicombe (eds.), *Identities in Talk*. Sage, London, pp. 121–132.

Kuhn, T. (1962) *The Structure of Scientific Revolutions*. University of Chicago Press, Chicago.

Lacan, J. (1977) *Ecrits: A Selection*, trans. A. Sheridan. Norton, New York.

Lax, W. D. (1989) Postmodern thinking in a clinical practice. In J. Shotter & K. Gergen (eds.), *Texts of Identity*. Sage, London, pp. 69–85.

Lyotard, J. F. (1984) *The Postmodern Condition*. University of Minnesota Press, Minneapolis.

Newman, F. & Holzman, L. (1997) *The End of Knowing*. Routledge, New York.

Parker, I. (1998) *Social Constructionism: Discourse and Realism*. Sage, Thousand Oaks.

Seidman, S. (1994) *The Postmodern Turn: New Perspectives on Social Theory*. Cambridge University Press, Cambridge.

White, M. (1989) *Selected Papers*. Dulwich Centre Publications, Adelaide, SA.

White, M. & Epston, D. (1990) *Narrative Means to Therapeutic Ends*. Norton, New York.

Winslade, J. & Monk, G. (2000) *Narrative Mediation*. Jossey-Bass, San Francisco.

Winslade, J., Monk, G. & Cotter, A. (1998) A narrative approach to the practice of mediation. *Negotiation Journal* 14, 21–42.

Chapter 10

A Facework Frame for Mediation

Stephen Littlejohn and Kathy Domenici

Introduction

People aim to present themselves honorably and wish to be treated with dignity – an ideal reflected in the metaphor of face. Originating in Chinese culture, the idea of facework was made popular in the US by sociologist Erving Goffman in his work on self-presentation (e.g. 1955, 1959). We define facework here as *a set of coordinated practices in which communicators build, maintain, protect, or threaten personal dignity, honor, and respect.*

In mediation, facework is the effort that participants and mediators put into managing face. Such work goes beyond managing the image of disputants, as it can also address others who may not be present at the mediation session, as well as relationships among participants and non-participants. Disputants who represent stakeholder groups may act in ways that are ultimately tied to the face of others and, in the end, for an entire community of stakeholders, including family members, neighbors, co-workers, or entire regional communities.

Our purpose in this chapter is to expand the concept of facework and to place it at the center of mediation communication. For us, facework is an overriding context for understanding disputant behavior and mediator interventions. We undertake several tasks in this chapter. First, we present a brief survey of literature on facework to provide a general background on the concept. Second, we expand the concept of facework and construct a meta-frame in which mediation practice can be understood. Third, we use this framework to support and enhance the model presented by Herrman, Hollet, and Gale in chapter 2. Finally, we discuss some implications of our work.

Research on Facework

Communication researchers with their colleagues in other fields have produced a copious knowledge base on facework (e.g. Cupach & Metts 1994; Ting-Toomey 1994;

Domenici & Littlejohn in press). Although we do not have space here for a complete review, a brief summary will help provide background on this fascinating topic. We rely largely on the recent review of Sandra Metts and Erica Grohskopf (2003) and, to add insights on facework in conflict, John Oetzel and his colleagues (2001). Cutting this literature in swaths, six generalizations are apparent.

First, communicators can achieve various types of face. The original idea of facework in China consisted of two types: *lien* (sometimes *lian*) and *mien-tzu* (or *mianzi*), corresponding respectively to *character* and *success in life*. We see these types of face commonly in mediation when, for example, disputants want to show that they have good motives (character) and that their positions are based on experience and knowledge (success). Since the Chinese version of face was first reported in the West (Hu 1944), many additional popular and useful models have been developed. Lim and Bowers (1991), for example, divide face into three types: autonomy, fellowship, and competence. *Autonomy face* is the feeling that we are unimpeded and free from intrusion or interference. A homeowner, for example, could feel threatened by a neighbor's objection to cutting down a tree on his property. *Fellowship face* is the desire for inclusion and acceptance, as would be the case when a divorcing spouse fights for more time with the kids. *Competence face* is a sense of ability and effectiveness, as can be seen, for example, in many workplace disputes based on the perceived threat to an employee's competence as a worker.

In their theory of politeness, Brown and Levinson (1987) write that face can be positive or negative. Positive face is the need to be respected and appreciated by others, while negative face involves the need to be free from intrusions and threats from others. Many mediated disputes arise precisely because parties feel that they are not appreciated or that the other person has intruded on their "space" in some way. Another model, from Ting-Toomey's face-negotiation theory (Ting-Toomey & Kurogi 1998; Ting-Toomey 2004), includes three types: self-face, other face, and mutual face. Mutual face is especially important in mediation, as it reflects the relationship among disputants and often is the key to resolution.

The second generalization is that facework addresses several important kinds of goals. Most research assumes that face is one of several possible communication goals. For example, a disputant may wish to gain a certain demand and in the process find it necessary to build or threaten face. In this way, facework may be an intermediate goal that supports a content objective, or it may be a goal in and of itself. Metts and Grohskopf (2003) organize facework into four meta-goals, which communicators may at different times attempt to achieve. The meta-goal of *constructing a positive or negative impression* would be evident, for example, when disputants in mediation build themselves up and attack the integrity of the other person. The second meta-goal is to *recover from a negative impression or restore a positive impression* that has been lost. The third is to *prevent attack or protect the integrity* of their impression. Finally, communicators frequently show *general social competence*, which is a kind of indirect facework. Simply by knowing and using normal conventions of speech and politeness, people can build their own face and that of others. Typical mediation groundrules, as one example, appeal to participants' sense of social competence and appropriateness.

The third generalization from the literature is that facework can be accomplished in a variety of ways. Individuals want to *present themselves positively*, and they will frequently *support the positive attributions of others*. When criticized or blamed, a person may *redress the situation* with an excuse, account, or apology, or support the redressive actions of others. Communicators may also use a variety of *preventative strategies* such as disclaimers or anticipatory accounts to protect the integrity of a positive impression. One can also protect another person's face by using a variety of politeness strategies. All of these kinds of messages are seen commonly in mediation.

Fourth, individual predispositions can influence facework strategies. Many dispositional variables have been studied. For example, facework has been associated with awareness, social anxiety, self-monitoring, self-esteem, and other variables (Leary & Kowalski 1990). Gender is also associated with facework, though the relationship is complex (e.g. Gardner, Van Eck Peluchette & Clinebell 1994). In mediation, we expect that disputants will do facework in different ways, in part because of their differing personalities and styles.

Fifth, facework effectiveness is determined by perceptiveness and social competence. Part of good facework involves reading social situations. It means being sensitive to indicators of status, power, tone, role, moods, dispositions, types of episodes, and communicator expectations. In other words, effective communicators are able to determine how and when impression management should be a concern (Berger & Bradac 1982; Leary 1995). In addition, effective facework also means knowing how to act with sufficient skill to accomplish face goals. This kind of social competence involves the ordinary conventions of conversation such as knowing when and how to be indirect and diplomatic (Grice 1975). Perceptiveness and social skill are two highly desirable qualities of mediators, and we always hope that disputants will also show a high level of skill in these areas, though this is not always the case.

Sixth, facework is cultural. In their landmark work on face negotiation, Ting-Toomey and her colleagues (e.g. Ting-Toomey & Oetzel 2002) show that face is a primary concern in all cultures, but that various cultures handle facework differently. Two dimensions of culture seem especially pertinent: individualism/collectivism (Triandis 1995) and power distance (Hofstede 1991). In *individualist* cultures, facework tends to be self-honoring and competitive, especially in conflict situations. In *collectivist* cultures, facework tends to be other-honoring with high mutual, or community, facework, in which cooperation is emphasized over competition or conflict. Indeed, mediation in Western societies acknowledges this difference and frequently works to transform the individualist orientation to a collectivist one. In cultures where *power distance* is high, rank and status are important indicators of face, and facework honors and attributes rank and status. In cultures where power distance is low, individual accomplishments are more important in building face. In intercultural encounters, face must be "negotiated" (Ting-Toomey 2004), and face negotiation requires abilities well beyond the skillful presentation of a single message. In the following section, we explore some of these complexities.

Expanding the Concept of Facework

For several years, we have advocated a set of five related characteristics of positive communication, in both conflict and non-conflict situations (Littlejohn & Domenici 2001). These are:

1 *collaboration,* or mutual decision-making
2 *empowerment,* or the ability to work effectively toward group benefits
3 *process management,* or attention to the "how" of communication
4 *safe environment,* or a feeling of freedom to explore, and
5 *facework.*

Recently we have come to believe that facework is more than a fifth dimension, that it is in fact the driving force of the other four characteristics. As such facework can be usefully employed as the general frame for constructive communication where the management of difference assumes importance. In other words, each of the other characteristics is built by and in turn contributes to positive facework, as figure 10.1 illustrates.

Mediators using a face-centric approach will look at how the actions of the participants constitute positive and negative facework. Interventions can be guided by answering the question, "What can I do now that would most help the participants achieve constructive facework?" The answer to this question is more difficult than traditional facework theory might predict.

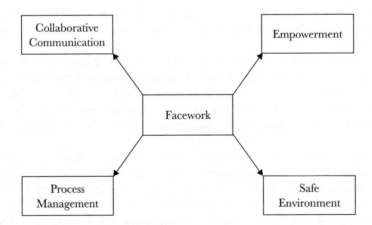

FIGURE 10.1   Facework at the center

Taking a Systemic View

Most of the research and theory on facework looks at individual acts addressed to self or other, but this individualist, act-oriented focus is challenged by a larger, systemic approach highlighting relationships and connections (Littlejohn & Domenici 2001). Taking a systemic view, the hard work of face over time honors individuals and communities and thereby builds effective relationships, establishes a basis for trust, and generates empowerment in systems of all kinds, from families to work-places, economic partnerships, and international relations.

Facework, then, is more than "making people feel good about themselves" or even maintaining cultural norms. It requires constant vigilance and demands simult-aneous and sometimes paradoxical mutual effort on a number of fronts. Facework is sometimes tough, and communicators do not always "feel good" about what is happening in the immediate moment, though they may have in mind honor and dignity for the larger community in the long run. Good facework, then, may mean working through hard places to achieve a better sense of purpose, worth, and dignity for everyone. Facework, conceived as a macro-frame, is an integral part of the process by which we construct meaning through communication. It is a process in the social construction of both identity and community, which has implications, not just for individuals in the immediate situation, but for entire systems and larger networks as well. How do we characterize facework within this larger system view? Two factors – focus of attention and scope of action – provide a useful approach to answering this question.

Focus of Attention

The focus of attention identifies the parts of the system the communicator is trying to affect. Three levels of attention seem especially important. The first of these is the person. Communicators do try to affect perceptions of self and other, trying quite directly to build or threaten a person's interaction. Compliments and apologies are simple examples. Attention to personal face in the moment is the most commonly understood application of facework, but it is not the only level of concern.

The second focus of attention is the relationship. Much of the time, facework aims to affect the relationship in some way, akin to what Ting-Toomey and her colleagues call mutual face (e.g. Ting-Toomey & Kurogi 1998). For example, we might compliment a colleague because we want to build a positive working relationship with this individual so that we can build honor and dignity for both of us.

A third focus of attention is the *system*. Here, facework is aimed at broader levels of concern, including, for example, the family, organization, community, nation, or world. A manager, for example, may criticize a supervisor in hopes that improvement will bring about a feeling of achievement among all employees in the department. Indeed, trying too hard to build the face of one employee isolated from the system can threaten the face of everyone else.

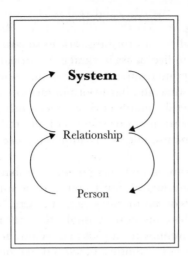

FIGURE 10.2 Focus of attention

Focus of attention becomes fascinating when we consider that communicators work on multiple levels simultaneously. Facework is rarely isolated to one of the above levels. Almost always, communicators address at least two of the above levels at the same time, so that each level provides a context for the other (figure 10.2). How might our hypothetical manager correct the behavior of one employee with minimal face damage, while maintaining a good working relationship and bringing about a feeling of strong productivity in the workgroup as whole?

Scope of Action

Although facework is usually thought of as a single act, it rarely is limited to one message or behavior. Facework is an interactional accomplishment, as communicators work together over time to manage face issues. For example, a workplace mediation between a manager and an employee may become a face negotiation in which the employee wants to rebuild personal face, while the manager wants to create an overall environment in which all employees, including managers, can feel honored and effective in their work. If done well, both personal and mutual face may be restored. The scope of action in face management is the broad context in which communicators in conflict situations address their differences. Facework is rarely limited to one message or a single act, but often includes a sequence of interaction that enables communicators to work through the hard places.

Borrowing from a model of contexts developed by Pearce, Cronen, and their colleagues (e.g. Pearce & Cronen 1980; Branham & Pearce 1985), we offer four broad categories that illustrate how facework becomes a mutual accomplishment over time. These are: (1) the act, (2) the conversation, (3) the episode, and (4) the life script. *Acts* are single messages that can threaten or build face. A teacher might tell students, for example, that they did well on an assignment. A *conversation* is an interaction consisting of a set of coordinated acts that together can build or threaten one's own face or that of others. For example, a couple may build parenting confidence as they discuss their child's report card. An *episode* is an event or series of connected events with a common theme or purpose. Facework is accomplished over time through a series of interactions, or episodes, of a certain type. For example, the performance review cycle within an organization may be carefully structured to set realistic goals, establish effectiveness among employees, and build a sense of achievement, while improving the quality of work for the entire organization.

Finally, we believe that something larger than episodes affects and is affected by acts of facework. At the highest level, this may be a kind of way of being, or *life script*. Sometimes called the moral order, this large context is comprised of a guiding set of principles that govern interaction (Pearce & Littlejohn 1997). Managers have a style, parents have a philosophy, and activists have a cause. Our identities as persons and communities affect and are shaped by communication patterns of facework enacted across the life span. Indeed, the way in which facework has played out in the life script can be a significant variable in readiness for mediation processes.

From a systems perspective, these four contexts for action – the act, the conversation, the episode, and the life script – are integrally connected, as depicted in figure 10.3. The accompanying tables 10.1 and 10.2 further define these connections and give examples. Human action is characterized by difference, and how we act into a situation will vary, depending upon life experience and the cultures that form our life scripts, the episodes that give structure to daily activity, the forms of conversation that comprise our social life, and the manners of speech and action we have learned in the many communities of which we have been a part.

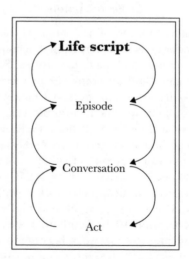

FIGURE 10.3   Scope of action

TABLE 10.1 The concept of facework*

Focus of attention	Scope of action			
	Act	*Conversation*	*Episode*	*Life script*
Person	An act that aims to affect self or other face.	A conversation aiming to affect face of self or other.	An episode of conversations aiming to affect self or other face.	A long-term series of episodes aiming to affect self or other face.
Relationship	An act of facework aiming to help define the relationship.	A conversation of facework aiming to help define the relationship.	An episode of conversations of facework aiming to define the relationship.	A long-term series of facework episodes aiming to define the relationship.
System	An act of facework aiming to help define the system.	A conversation of facework aiming to define the system.	An episode of conversations of facework aiming to define the system.	A long-term series of episodes of facework aiming to affect the system.

* Facework is a set of practices in which communicators build, maintain, protect, or threaten personal dignity, honor, and respect.

TABLE 10.2 Examples of facework*

Focus of attention	Scope of action			
	Act	*Conversation*	*Episode*	*Life script*
Person	Praising a child for doing well in a sports game so that he will feel good about himself.	Having a positive conversation with a child about her sports game in order to help build self-confidence.	Attending all of a child's sports games for an entire season to show that he is worthy and loved.	Showing a long-term attitude of interest and joy in children and their activities to help become happy adults.
Relationship	Giving a subordinate clear directions in order to establish a helping relationship.	Negotiating job goals with a subordinate in order to establish mutual respect.	Establishing a goal-oriented appraisal system in order to establish a climate of effectiveness in a work team.	Establishing a career commitment to employee participation and empowerment in order to build solid working relationships over time.
System	Establishing a no make-up policy in a class syllabus in order to help students become more responsible.	Having a class discussion in order to help students learn to think on their feet.	Using a discussion-based class method in order to help students learn good communication skills.	Adopting a teaching philosophy to achieve collaborative learning environments.

* Facework is a set of practices in which communicators build, maintain, protect, or threaten personal dignity, honor, and respect.

Differences can run deep, and the management of difference always involves an intricate coordination of meaning and action.

FACEWORK AND MEDIATION: ORIENTING TO THE MODEL

In chapter 2 of this volume, Herrman, Hollet, and Gale organize the research literature on mediation within a time-sequence, causal model consisting of three sets of variables – antecedents, processes, and outcomes. In narrative form, this model can be stated as follows:

under *conditions* in which (1) personal characteristics, (2) disputant beliefs and attitudes, (3) dispute characteristics, and (4) institutional context are conducive . . .

a *process* that (1) primes readiness, (2) establishes mediation conditions, (3) allows for problem-solving, and (4) permits appropriate decision-making can lead to . . .

short-term outcomes affecting (1) disputant beliefs and attitudes, (2) conflict resolution, and (3) institutional context and

long-term outcomes affecting (1) disputant beliefs and attitudes and (2) conflict resolution.

From a systemic point of view (Littlejohn & Domenici 2001), we would recast the model from a linear to a circular and reflexive one, noting that dispute processes constantly create a socially constructed set of conditions that in turn affect the process of mediation itself, as shown in figure 10.4. Here, facework reflects and shapes both conditions and mediation processes. In other words, facework is determined in part by the conditions in which communication takes place, facework in turn affects the mediation process, mediation process shapes facework, and facework adds to mediation conditions.

Sociologist Anthony Giddens (1976, 1977) refers to this circular process as structuration, in which conditions are built through interaction. In other words, as we act to accomplish mundane goals in life, our interactions create unintended consequences that create structures that affect future interaction. This process happens in all realms of social life, and conflict management is no exception. How we act in mediation will contribute to building larger structures that influence what we can do and say in the future. The conditions arising from interaction make some things possible and close off others. Emphasizing facework, we want to ask the question: How can we interact in conflict situations to create social arrangements that build honor and dignity and thereby open up new possibilities for action in the future?

In this section, we map our model of facework onto Herrman, Hollet, and Gale's model of mediation. Taking a systemic, structurational approach, we do this in two stages: first, by looking at mediation process and, second, by looking at mediation conditions.

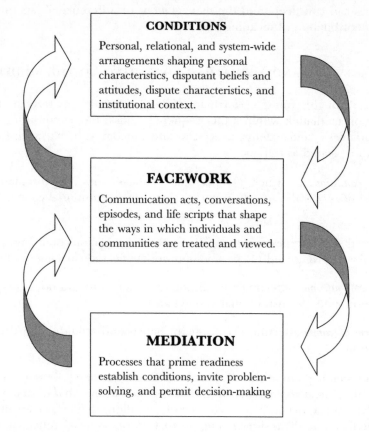

CONDITIONS

Personal, relational, and system-wide arrangements shaping personal characteristics, disputant beliefs and attitudes, dispute characteristics, and institutional context.

FACEWORK

Communication acts, conversations, episodes, and life scripts that shape the ways in which individuals and communities are treated and viewed.

MEDIATION

Processes that prime readiness establish conditions, invite problem-solving, and permit decision-making

FIGURE 10.4   Mediation

Mediation Process and Facework

Mediation processes, as depicted in Herrman, Hollet, and Gale's model, include two dominant dynamics that are conducive to the achievement of mediation goals. The first is the creation of environments where dialog, problem-solving, and decision-making can take place. Secondly, there exist factors that prime personal readiness for the mediation process, including mediator empathy, feeling heard and understood, being able to talk about perceptions and feelings, clarity, perceived self-efficacy, and hostile environment. Each of these clusters entail facework. The mediator can create an environment where facework shows a constant vigilance required to preserve people's honor. Certain mediation techniques could occur within an act, a conversation, an episode, or within the life script. Although disputants themselves do a great deal of facework, we emphasize here the work of the mediator. Let us begin with the life script.

Life script

Each of us possesses a dynamic life script, a road map for how we live our life. The life script answers questions like, "What kind of person am I?" "What is important to me?" "How do I act and communicate?" "How do I see myself as a mediator?" "Who are we as a community?" Even though our lives are full of paradox and contradiction, we try to negotiate the numerous challenges with some consistency and order, which becomes particularly clear when we crystallize a role such as that of mediator. Mediation, as a form of communication, embodies a variety of values and an orientation to conflict, exhibited as a style, a philosophy, a moral order. This "life script" is affected by and affects facework in mediation processes in a variety of ways.

As a cluster, the life script forms what might be called a moral stance that could include, for mediators, commitment to neutrality, orientation to the other, fascination with stories, and a spirit of open-minded exploration. People sometimes go into the mediation profession, in part, because of a set of life values that draws them to the field. Just as often, mediation training and practice can instill a way of thinking about difference that allows them to intervene constructively in disputes. To repeat a stereotype we have often heard from "recovering attorneys," the gap between the socialization encountered in law school and that required for mediation is wide, and attorney mediators will often say that they had to unlearn life script narratives when moving from one to the other.

As related to mediation process concerns, life script issues are clearly influential. For example, in showing mediator empathy, allowing participants to feel understood, and allowing them to talk about their perceptions and feelings – all factors that prime readiness – the ability and willingness to assume the perspective of others is critical. Notice how this life script commitment enables good facework. On the part of the mediator, it shows respect, and on the part of the disputant it honors the participant's own story.

A second example of the importance of the mediator's life script is the tendency to eschew polarized solutions and the inherent belief in multi-valued solutions. The shift from "resolving" a dispute to "solving a problem," is facilitated by this basic life script orientation, allowing at least the possibility of active negotiation, exploration of issues and needs, and the formulation of options – all variables of problem-solving within the Herrman, Hollet, and Gale model. Notice how the problem-solving orientation invites participants to show competence, intelligence, and open-mindedness.

As a final example, one's orientation to intervention – directive or non-directive – will in all likelihood be shaped by views of empowerment and expertise deeply embedded in one's worldview, which in turn will influence the extent to which a mediator defers to the judgment of disputants or pushes for certain solutions in the decision-making process. The face implications of this are serious. By assessing disputants' options and persuading them to follow a certain course of action in the interest of settling, a mediator may actually threaten the autonomy and competence of the parties themselves, while encouraging disputants to make their own clear, well-considered decisions, though creating stress in the short-term, may build face in the long term.

Episode

The life script provides resources and tools for structuring episodes of all kinds, just as episodes shape one's life script. When mediators advise us to "trust the process," they are essentially affirming this reflective relationship between the life script and the typical episode of mediation. Active participation and procedural clarity – both factors for establishing mediation conditions in the Herrman, Hollet, and Gale model – are issues related to the episode. Both of these factors provide opportunities for disputants to "do good work" and thereby honor themselves as persons and their relationship as disputants.

When approaching a mediation session, the mediator has a variety of preparatory decisions to make. Each decision has significance for a process that could help the individual feel honored and an integral player in determining their future. Mediators often discuss and decide about physical needs, such as room layout, lighting, chair and table arrangement, and room temperature and environmental factors. Other decisions include methods of greeting and seating participants, formal or informal tone of voice and dress, and what kind of materials and resources should be available. Further along, the mediator may invite participants to "set an agenda," which is an episode-structuring activity and a vital part of process management. This kind of work engenders a sense of active participation, which Herrman, Hollet, and Gale identify as important in establishing effective conditions within the mediation.

Mediations often occur over a series of meetings, especially in cases of prolonged or particularly complex situations. These "episodes" of conversations have a common overall theme (that which brought the mediation to the table) but may explore a variety of different topics throughout the meetings. The broader face accomplishments that are offered in an episode involve an intricate coordination of communication acts and conversations. Mediators can create personal readiness by framing the episode in ways that give honor to the participants.

A case that illustrates facework across an episode is a mediation one of us once conducted on an interesting and difficult custody case where the couple had never married. One of the parents had never seen the 4-year-old child until a recent point when that parent decided to get involved in the child's life. The couple had a variety of differences, from discipline philosophies, eating rules, requirements for bedtime and manners, and the everyday logistics of transporting the child and assuring his safety.

The mediator made some decisions about how to frame the episode that contributed to the comfort level of participating in such a potentially scary and tough conversation. The mediation was held in a home, a private, yet bright and cheery place to talk. The sessions were often referred to as "conversations about Johnny" rather than "custody mediation." Each session was begun with casual conversation about Johnny's antics, health, progress, and delightful personality. This deliberate framing as a session focused on the child rather than the parent's preferences established a common framing for the conversation. It led the parents to often wonder aloud, "Is this in Johnny's best interests?" When the parents would slip into personal and sometimes selfish requests or opinions, the mediator would acknowledge this interest, "You see bedtime as a time to wind down and relax, rather than wrestling and playing. Can you tell me some examples of Johnny's response to the quiet reading and music?" This acknowledgment allows that parent to feel that their perspective ("I do not want Johnny getting all riled up at bedtime") was heard, and redirected to the focus of the episode ("Let's focus on Johnny and the best decisions for him"). Facework in this mediation included a framing of the episode as in Johnny's best interests and repeated acknowledgment of each parent's interests with a redirection toward that frame.

Conversations

These are sequences of action with discernible structure that occur over time. You can often identify an episode because it will occur again and again. The structure of an episode both affects and is affected by the interaction, or conversations, that occur within episodes. Some episodes, like a street greeting, are characterized by a single simple conversation. Other episodes, like court hearings, are characterized by numerous conversations over time. A simple mediation can be a single conversation. A more complex mediation is probably more accurately divided into a series of conversations, sometimes spread over several sessions.

The first conversation that the mediator initiates as the session begins often offers a variety of face-managing messages. Each of these acts can signal that the mediators hope to honor each interaction and personal contribution. We often conclude our opening statements with some indication that "Mediation is a place where you get to say things that need to be heard and hear things that need to be said. Now which one of you would like to listen first?" By opening the mediation with a focus on listening, rather than privileging the speaker, we give a single message that "Listening is just as important as, if not more important than, speaking. Your perspective and stories need to be listened to." Within this single message, the implications for face set the scene for a session where good listening is a known assumption.

Throughout the ensuing conversations in a mediation, facework is accomplished across a series of interactions. In other words, positive or negative face is an interactional accomplishment. This facework context is the combination of messages that enables people to continue to feel safe and honored as communicators.

We once facilitated a meeting of educators and community leaders in Argentina who were discussing education models for their country. To provide structure to the meeting, we employed a method we call CVA, which stands for Concerns, Visions, and Actions. We present a triangular model, the points of which are designated as C, V, and A, and then lead the group through a series of discussions of each of these elements, noting how each is related to the other two.

The Argentines first discussed a vision for the development of new private and public models of education. This vision was forward-looking and described positively. The participants then broke into small groups to discuss their concerns. "When you consider this vision, what are you concerned about?" We, as facilitators, noted a distinct change in the tone of the conversation. The participants seemed to be grumbling and we overheard snatches of "This vision is impossible," and "We will never be able to change our education system." We were worried and began to discuss how we could change the agenda, in case the whole exercise fell apart due to critical talk and too idealistic visioning. When we brought the group back together to report on their concerns, they surprised us with their comments. They had considered the vision they created, and discussed their country's current state of affairs. They indicated to us "We know that we have a history of being overwhelmed with impossibilities. Now we believe that anything is possible." This group tapped into an emerging life script that indicated a commitment to building a new future that included a host of possibilities. Their life script enabled them to continue in the discussion, framed as one that connected visions to actions to concerns, and the session enabled them to explore their life script and use it to bring them together within a larger commitment for the future of their country.

We find it useful to think of the conversational structure of mediation as a series of stories (Littlejohn & Domenici 2001). Each party takes turns telling its respective version of what happened (stories of the past), what is going on now (stories of the present), and what they want to happen in the future (stories of the future). If the exercise is successful, disputants will actually craft a mutual story as well. This conversational approach accomplishes a number of face goals. First, by inviting stories, mediators begin to prime readiness by showing empathy, allowing participants to feel understood, and enabling them to share their perceptions and feelings. Instead of taking stories as depictions of fact and trying to decide who is distorting the truth, we grant legitimacy to each story, whether it is consistent with other stories or not. Successful mediators find in these stories the building blocks for solutions later in the mediation. Stories of the future are especially valuable because they invite negotiation, exploration of issues, and collaborative development of options.

Acts

Conversations are interactions comprised of messages that respond to other messages. From a communication perspective, every act responds to something that came before it and leads to something that will follow in a coordinated interactional pattern (Pearce & Cronen 1980). As one example, we prime readiness and build an effective set of conditions for mediation by many micro-interventions such as reflecting, summarizing, acknowledging, and framing. Although such acts can and do lead to mutually satisfactory outcomes, they also can build a sense of empowerment and recognition that can lead to salutary personal and communal outcomes (Bush & Folger 1994). Most basic mediation trainings tend to focus on individual acts in order to build skill, but experienced mediators know that their interventions are part of larger sequences of action.

Facework and Mediation Conditions

Consistent with the systemic model presented above in figure 10.3, we prefer to think of the outcomes of mediation as conditions that are built through acts, conversations, episodes, and life scripts. Consistent with our model, we address these conditions in terms of personal, relational, and system conditions.

Personal conditions

Excellent facework in mediation can have profound personal outcomes. We can feel empowered, competent, and respected. These results can build immediate satisfaction with the system, the mediator, the process, and the outcome; but, more important than these, in the long term personal empowerment and recognition will change the conditions that affect how individuals will interact with others in the future, including in conflict situations.

Relational conditions

Although personal conditions are important, relational outcomes are essential if mediation is to assume an important institutional role in society. Many mediators will tell you that the most profound effects of the process are not achieving settlements, but changing relationships, as noted in Herrman, Hollet, and Gale's model. Even the achievement of an agreement instead of a court settlement reflects a changed relationship. Any experienced mediator will recall cases in which the actual relationship between the parties improved, but perhaps more common is that future relationships can be impacted by how disputants experience the mediation process. When we think of relational conditions, then, we are concentrating on ways in which future interactions create an environment more conducive to constructive management of difference. People may come to think differently about how to handle conflict, and institutions may change to provide more opportunity for parties in conflict to communicate differently about their disputes.

System conditions

We have seen a transformation in agency conflict resolution processes in the past 30 years, as institutions adopt mediation as a regular part of the system of conflict resolution (e.g. Neumeier 2002). In many cases, these "new" options for resolving conflict in the workplace and the community provide disputants with the opportunity to talk directly about their issues. If we put facework at the center of this effort, we hold out the hope that people will think about and manage difference and interdependence in new productive ways.

THE FACEWORK FRAME AND SITUATED PRACTICE

How do we begin to think differently about mediation when we take a face-centric approach? Our orientation can change in several ways:

We come to value situated data. Each case is unique. Face is negotiated in every case, it spans beyond individual acts, and it impacts systems larger than what might be represented at the table. Facework is always fresh, as the participants, the situation, the history, the anticipated futures, and forms of talk will vary. Facework research demands local data, but it also provides a framework that helps us compare and learn from many cases.

We realize that mediation is a process of construction. Participants create a social world in the pattern of interaction in which they engage. For the researcher, the question is *what* gets made and *how* this gets created. More profound than identifying generalized correlations among variables, researchers must look at specific cases to determine the rich differences in how participants come to understand their experience, how they change their ways of relating, how they view conflict and difference, and how they come to define conflict resolution. The facework frame provides a context for understanding such aspects of the social reality in action. It gives us a basis for answering the question of whether the pattern of talk in the mediation helped to make a "better" world.

We see new connections. Not only do we tune in to perceptions of behavior, but we are able, with a facework frame, to see how actions connect – how they relate to what happened before, how they are organized across time to make conversations and episodes, and how they both reflect and impact honor and dignity across the community. In other words, this frame allows us to bring isolated perceptions of what is happening into a sensible pattern of interpretation.

We develop an ethic of practice. The facework frame provides a way to make decisions about how to proceed in moments that might otherwise be confusing or disjointed. It provides an end-in-view that enables us to keep the conversation going with some idea about what kind of world we are trying to make and how we might do so. Further, this ethic is based on the idea that every act is significant, but that acts only matter by virtue of their relationships to other acts. With this larger picture, we are able to make choices in complex situations.

We understand that mediators are always acting in an ongoing situation. There is always a dynamic system at play, always a system that extends beyond the parties themselves, and always a system with a history and a future. As mediators, we always become part of that system, if only briefly, from the moment we shut the mediation door. The facework frame provides a context for making sense of a system we are never fully prepared to understand completely, and it provides a basis for acting intelligently into that system. It is a basis for asking questions, learning more, and making sense of what participants do and say.

We have a sophisticated form of explanation more powerful than listing specific actions and outcomes. Among the many potentially valuable theoretical approaches, the facework frame provides a particularly humane set of categories that we can use to describe and evaluate what happened. Like the researcher, the practitioner can also ask, "What got made, and how was this made?"

We find a basis for moving forward. The facework frame enables us to learn systematically from experience in a way that can build toward virtuosity, as we experience an increasing number of ways in which aspects of facework connect. If you take strictly a settlement approach to mediation, facework becomes a mere tool for the achievement of a negotiated agreement. For us, however, facework is more than a tool. It is a form of communication with profound personal, relational, and systemic implications. We make our social worlds in the ways we communicate with one another, and mediation can embody forms of interaction that enable human beings to manage their differences with dignity and respect. We feel that the facework project takes a small step toward building a rationale and practice toward this end.

REFERENCES

Berger, C. R. & Bradac, J. J. (1982) *Language and Social Knowledge.* Edward Arnold, London.

Branham, R. J. & Pearce, W. B. (1985) Between text and context: toward a rhetoric of contextual reconstruction. *Quarterly Journal of Speech* 71, 19–36.

Brown, P. & Levinson, S. (1987) *Politeness: Some Universals in Language Usage.* Cambridge University Press, Cambridge.

Bush, R. A. B. & Folger, J. P. (1994) *The Promise of Mediation: Responding to Conflict through Empowerment and Recognition.* Jossey-Bass, San Francisco.

Cupach, W. R. & Metts, S. (1994) *Facework.* Sage, Thousand Oaks.

Domenici, K. & Littlejohn, S. W. (in press) *Communication and the Management of Face.* Sage, Thousand Oaks.

Gardner, W. L., Van Eck Peluchette, J. & Clinebell, S. K. (1994) Valuing women in management. *Management Communication Quarterly* 8, 115–141.

Giddens, A. (1976) *New Rules of Sociological Method.* Basic Books, New York.

Giddens, A. (1977) *Studies in Social and Political Theory.* Basic Books, New York.

Goffman, E. (1955). On face-work: An analysis of ritual elements in social interaction. *Psychiatry* 18, 213–231.

Goffman, E. (1959) *The Presentation of Self in Everyday Life.* Doubleday, Garden City.

Grice, H. P. (1975) Logic and conversation. In P. Cole & J. L. Morgan (eds.), *Syntax and Semantics*, vol. 3: *Speech Acts.* Academic Press, New York, pp. 41–58.

Hofstede, G. (1991) *Cultures and Organizations: Software of the Mind.* McGraw-Hill, London.

Hu, H. C. (1944) The Chinese concept of "face." *American Anthropologist* 46, 45–64.

Leary, M. R. (1995) *Self-Presentation: Impression Management and Interpersonal Behavior.* Brown & Benchmark, Madison.

Leary, M. R. & Kowalski, R. M. (1990) Impression management: a literature review and two-component model. *Psychology Bulletin* 107, 34–47.

Lim, T. S. & Bowers, J. W. (1991) Facework: solidarity, approbation, and tact. *Human Communication Research* 17, 415–450.

Littlejohn, S. W. & Domenici, K. (2001) *Engaging Communication in Conflict: Systemic Practice.* Sage, Thousand Oaks.

Metts, S. & Grohskopf, E. (2003) Impression management: goals, strategies, and skills. In J. O. Greene & B. R. Burleson (eds.), *Handbook of Communication and Social Interaction Skills.* Lawrence Erlbaum, Mahway, pp. 357–402.

Neumeier, E. (2002) The long and winding road: a look at the evolution of CR in the workplace. *ACResolution* 1(3), 20–23.

Oetzel, J., Ting-Toomey, S., Masumoto, T., Yokochi, Y., Pan, X., Takai, J. & Wilcox, R. (2001) Face and facework in conflict: a cross-cultural comparison of China, Germany, Japan, and the United States. *Communication Monographs* 68, 235–258.

Pearce, W. B. & Cronen, V. (1980) *Communication, Action, and Meaning.* Praeger, New York.

Pearce, W. B. & Littlejohn, S. W. (1997) *Moral Conflict: When Social Worlds Collide.* Sage, Thousand Oaks.

Ting-Toomey, S. (ed.) (1994) *The Challenge of Facework: Cross-Cultural and Interpersonal Issues.* State University of New York Press, Albany.

Ting-Toomey, S. (2004) Translating conflict face-negotiation theory into practice. In D. Landis, J. Bennett & M. Bennett (eds.), *Handbook of Intercultural Training.* Sage, Thousand Oaks, pp. 217–248.

Ting-Toomey, S. & Kurogi, A. (1998) Facework competence in intercultural conflict: an updated face-negotiation theory. *International Journal of Intercultural Relations* 22, 187–225.

Ting-Toomey, S. & Oetzel, J. G. (2002) *Managing Intercultural Conflict Effectively.* Sage, Thousand Oaks.

Triandis, H. C. (1995) *Individualism and Collectivism.* Westview, Boulder.

Chapter 11

Mediation and the Fourfold Model of Justice

Donald E. Conlon

Introduction

The goal of this chapter is to bridge between two literatures by applying a justice lens to the time-sequence model of mediation presented in chapter 2. To achieve this goal, I first sketch the development of the justice field. I will then apply a recently derived model of justice to the mediation model advanced by Herrman, Hollett, and Gale that forms the centerpiece of this book. My hope is that readers of this chapter will come away with a more thorough understanding of how justice is conceived, and a more thorough understanding of how justice informs the proposed time-sequence mediation model.

The Development of the Construct of Justice

Notions of justice and dispute resolution have been intertwined for centuries, though the systematic study of justice applied to dispute resolution procedures did not emerge until the 1970s. However, the dispute resolution context was a fruitful environment in which to develop two constructs related to dispute resolution process and outcome. These two constructs became known as procedural and distributive justice.

Distributive justice was the first fairness construct studied by social psychologists. Building on the work of Adams (1965), I define distributive justice as the perceived fairness of the outcomes one receives from a social exchange or interaction. This form of justice was originally construed by Adams (1965) in terms of equity. According to Adams, people determine fairness by first evaluating their perceived contributions or inputs relative to the outcomes they have received. They then compare this ratio to some comparison or referent standard to determine whether outcomes they have received for their efforts are fair.

Of course, equity rules are not the only standard that can be used to make decisions and promote fairness. Later work on distributive justice highlighted that other standards or decision rules can be applied and, depending on the context, be seen as distributively fair. For instance, equality rules argue that people should be rewarded equally – each should receive the same, or have the same opportunity to benefit. In the case of non-divisible "lumpy" resources (e.g. the biblical story of King Solomon cutting a baby in half), equality might be achieved by providing parties with an equal chance of receiving the outcome, such as by using a random draw (Young 1995). While equity and equality rules have received the most research attention (e.g. Adams 1965; Deutsch 1975; Leventhal 1976; Walster, Walster & Berscheid 1978; Pruitt 1981; Törnblom, Jonsson & Foa 1985), other rules can also be implemented (cf. Rescher 1966; Deutsch 1975, 1985). For instance, need rules argue that people should be rewarded based on their level of need or deprivation.

Researchers studying law and psychology noted that participants in dispute resolution procedures did not merely react to the outcomes that they received, but also to the process by which they received those outcomes. This led to the development of the construct of procedural justice, which I define as the fairness of the process used to arrive at decisions. Central figures in the development of this construct were Thibaut and Walker (1975), who published a book describing disputant reactions to different types of legal procedures in terms of their reactions to both the process used and the outcome received.

In their research, Thibaut and Walker characterized third party procedures in terms of the amount of process control and decision control each procedure afforded disputants. Mediation, for instance, was viewed as a procedure that afforded disputants high control over the process (as they typically had considerable opportunity to express their views in the procedure) and high control over the decision (as disputants were free to reject any decision suggested by a mediator). An adjudication procedure, by comparison, offers disputants similar levels of process control but low decision control, as in this procedure the third party (a judge) issues a ruling that is binding on the parties.

Thibaut and Walker's (1975) work suggested that disputants were willing to cede control over the outcome to a third party if they could continue to exert control or influence over the process. Thus, disputant process control or "voice" was seen as central to creating high levels of procedural justice. Other researchers elaborated our understanding of what characteristics of procedures enhanced procedural justice judgments. A multidimensional approach to procedural justice was advanced by Leventhal and colleagues (Leventhal 1980; Leventhal, Karuza & Fry 1980), who argued that procedures were fair to the extent that they met six criteria. Procedures needed to be:

1 *Accurate,* meaning that the information presented by parties (e.g. disputants, witnesses, experts) be truthful and correct. This means allowing decisions to be based on accurate information.
2 *Consistent temporally and interpersonally.* In other words, the procedure should guarantee similar treatment of all people who use the procedure, and follow the same rules and protocol each time it is used (i.e. with different people over time).

3 *Ethical,* meaning that the procedure conforms to the prevailing standards of ethics and morality.
4 *Correctable,* in that the process includes some mechanism to correct bad decisions.
5 *Able to insure bias suppression,* in the sense that the third party must not have a vested interest in a particular outcome or make decisions based on his or her own personal beliefs.
6 *Able to insure representation,* meaning that the procedure must insure that all affected parties have an opportunity to state their concerns and opinions. The representation element coincides with Thibaut and Walker's idea of the import-ance of giving disputant voice or process control.

By the 1990s a great deal of research on justice was moving away from a focus on legal procedures and towards a focus on organizational procedures. This likely occurred for two reasons. First, organizations provide a wide variety of con-texts where procedures are used. In addition to dispute resolution (often called disciplinary procedures in organizations), organizations use procedures for hiring, for performance appraisal, for determining salaries, for instituting layoffs, etc. Second, a number of scholars who were originally trained in social psychology moved to business schools. For example, Byrne and Cropanzano (2001) interviewed five scholars whom they viewed as the "founders" of organizational justice research. While most (three of five) of the founders were originally trained in social psycho-logy, four of the five now work in business schools.

The application of justice theory to organizations made a number of things about procedures and outcomes salient. For example, even within the same com-pany, the same ostensibly fair procedure (say, a performance appraisal procedure) could lead to very different employee reactions depending on how different man-agers might enact or implement the procedure. Initially this line of inquiry was referred to as interactional justice (Bies & Moag 1986). However, some scholars (e.g. Greenberg 1993) further distinguished this construct into two separate forms of justice labeled *interpersonal justice* and *informational justice.* Interpersonal justice focuses on the sensitivity, politeness, and respect people are shown by authority figures during procedures. Informational justice focuses on the explanations or information provided by decision-makers as to why certain procedures were used or why outcomes were distributed in a particular way – is this information thorough, reasonable, truthful, candid, and timely? Clearly, the constructs of inter-personal and informational justice focus more on the behavior of the person in the role of decision-maker rather than on the systemic or structural characteristics of procedures.

The Importance of the Fourfold Model of Justice

The fourfold model of justice I have elaborated (distributive–procedural–interpersonal–informational) has been validated in two separate studies by Colquitt (2001). A key advantage of this representation of justice over prior models is that by distinguishing specific forms of justice, one can more easily identify elements of procedures that might be lacking in some area, and thus recommend changes to the procedures themselves or the behavior of those involved in order to enhance fairness perceptions.

In addition, while some might view justice or fairness as an end unto itself, the four forms of justice described above have been meta-analytically linked to a number of different outcomes. (e.g. Colquitt, Conlon, Wesson, Porter & Ng 2001). While many of the studies in this meta-analysis looked at organizational outcomes, some of the studies focused on dispute resolution and included outcomes directly relevant to dispute resolution contexts such as decision satisfaction, compliance with decisions, and satisfaction with and trust of authority figures (e.g. Lind, Lissak & Conlon 1983; Lind, Kulik, Ambrose & De Vera Park 1993).

APPLYING THE FOURFOLD MODEL OF JUSTICE TO THE MEDIATION MODEL

Next, how do each of these four forms of justice inform the mediation model presented in chapter 2 of this book? A cursory glance at the model and its central constructs demonstrates that three of the four justice constructs (procedural, interpersonal, and informational justice) play a central role during the T_m phase – in other words, during the mediation proper. Distributive justice, with its focus on outcomes, is likely to have more relevance during the T_1 phase of the model. However, I expect that all four forms of justice will have some impact on short- and long-term outcomes (the T_1 and T_2 sections of the model). Moreover, some of the justice judgments may be influenced by actions that occur at the very beginning of the mediation process – in other words, the T_0 phase of the model. I approach this analysis temporally, beginning at this initial stage, move through the model, and, in the end, suggest relationships or hypotheses that might relate antecedent expressions of justice to short- and long-term outcomes as noted in the proposed model.

Justice and Antecedent Conditions

Three specific areas listed under antecedent conditions likely relate to justice judgments. Herrman et al. in chapter 2 of this book, discuss in the "Mediator characteristics" section that mediators ought to have certain skills or character- istics, including rapport-building and communicating substantive knowledge in ways that expand information and support evaluation of outcomes. Clearly, these concepts relate to interpersonal and informational justice. Establishing rapport would be accomplished in part by treating people sensitively and with respect. Communicating knowledge in substantive ways should enhance perceptions of informational justice, assuming the information communicated is viewed as credible, thorough, and tailored to disputants' specific needs.

However as the temporal model in chapter 2 makes clear, the antecedent characteristics that the mediator "brings to the table" is the *reputation* that third parties have cultivated over time for treating people fairly. Such reputations or expectations are part of the reason why some mediators are chosen more frequently to mediate disputes than others. At a system level, such reputations may also influence whether grievants are willing to use the procedure at all. If prior grievants have communicated to others that mediation was unpleasant or a waste of time, it is likely that the desire to use mediation will decline.

Positive or negative reputations that mediators or mediation procedures might accrue can also stem from characteristics described in the model as being part of the institutional context. Herrman et al. discuss the concept of *process efficiency* in terms of the temporal delays that occur before, during, or after mediation. Along with such objective measures of process efficiency, I would include participants' subjective reactions to these temporal elements of the procedure. A procedure that includes lengthy lead times for evidence-gathering might be looked at by one party as fair and appropriate, and by another party as a delay or stall tactic favoring the other party. Thus, structural variations in temporal aspects of procedures could influence multiple forms of justice.

For example, several studies in conflict and negotiation contexts have examined how time influences justice perceptions. In a study of the consumer complaint process, Conlon and Murray (1996) found that complainants who perceived that they had to wait a long time to get a reply from a company were less satisfied with the explanation the company ultimately provided. Beliefs that explanations are reasonable, and that such information was communicated in a timely manner, are central elements of informational justice (Colquitt 2001). Temporal delays may also influence perceptions of interpersonal justice. Slow responses to questions in mediation, or a procedure that appears to be moving at a tediously slow pace, could be interpreted symbolically by one or both disputants as meaning that a participant is not held in high respect or esteem. To the extent that delayed responses trigger feelings of disrespect, we can expect interpersonal justice judgments to be reduced. The key would appear to be striking a balance between expediency and giving participants the opportunity to state their case. As some research has shown, if third parties intervene and try to control the process or outcome too quickly, participants respond negatively even if the outcome received is favorable (Conlon & Fasolo 1993).

Finally, I note that the institutional context variable *process information* has an obvious connection to informational justice judgments, as defined by Herrman et al. (drawing on Coates & Gehm 1989), as to whether the program was clearly explained to people before the mediation. Thorough explanations are central to the experience of informational justice. However, what also cannot be overlooked is the importance of the phrase "before the mediation." Explanations received before events occur may be perceived more favorably than explanations received after (negative) events have occurred. Explanations prior to an event tend not to be viewed as having been constructed simply to excuse responsibility for negative outcomes (see Shaw, Wild & Colquitt 2003, for a meta-analytic review of the impact of explanations).

Justice and the mediation procedure

Clearly, the justice concepts we have described play their greatest role in the formal mediation section (T_m) of the model. Numerous activities occur at this stage that will influence procedural, interpersonal, and informational justice judgments. Herrman et al. describe 17 different actions that fall into four general categories describing the mediation process. Most of these 17 items relate to justice perceptions.

Beginning with procedural justice, Thibaut and Walker's original work noted that a key component of procedural justice is that disputants feel they have the opportunity to exercise voice or process control during the dispute resolution procedure. Similarly, Leventhal's justice model highlights that disputants should feel they have experienced representation in the procedure. These notions play out in many sections of the mediation model. Under "Factors that prime readiness," Herrman et al. discuss the importance disputants attach to *feeling heard and understood*, or being *able to talk about perceptions and feelings*. Under "Procedural factors: mediation conditions," Herrman et al. include disputant beliefs regarding *active participation* in the mediation, and under the heading "Procedural factors: problem-solving," I note the constructs of *active negotiation, talked about issues and needs*, and *formulate options*. I would argue that all six of these elements of mediation relate to the perceptions of control, influence, and representation that disputants feel during a mediation. I suspect that higher levels of these constructs work collectively to enhance procedural justice. A seventh concept from the model, *clarity*, is defined in terms of the mediator asking additional questions to increase understanding. This should also enhance disputant perceptions of voice/process control as it assures the disputant that the third party is actively considering and trying to understand what is being said.

An eighth and final element of the mediation process that should influence procedural justice judgments is *mediator neutrality*. This concept maps on nicely to the concept of bias suppression mentioned in Leventhal's model of procedural justice. Of course, as mentioned by Herrman et al., defining mediator neutrality can be problematic. Wittmer, Carnevale and Walker (1991) drew a useful distinction in their discussion of mediator bias or neutrality by distinguishing between the structural alignment of a mediator (which could include the mediator having a prior history with one party or having a network of relationships that people would view as favoring one party) and the overt support a mediator might show during the mediation. Their research, as well as subsequent research (e.g. Conlon & Ross 1993) suggests that disputants are less concerned about mediator prior relationships or alignment biases than they are about the level of bias that is shown during the mediation. Thus, it is the actions, not the prior history, that seems to matter to disputants in interpreting mediator neutrality, and which, in our context, would potentially influence procedural justice judgments.

Turning to interpersonal justice, I see several factors that are likely to influence these judgments. Recall that interpersonal justice focuses on the interpersonal treatment one receives from authority figures. Under the "Factors that prime readiness," I note two factors that are likely to relate to interpersonal justice. First,

I expect that *mediator empathy* would be quite relevant. Actions that reflect mediator empathy include expressing concern and sympathy for people, developing trust, and treating people with respect (e.g. Lim & Carnevale 1990; Wissler 1999). To the degree that a mediator accomplishes these goals, interpersonal justice judgments should be enhanced.

While interpersonal justice is usually construed in terms of the treatment one receives from authority figures, contexts such as mediation (and perhaps most interpersonal dispute resolution procedures) also have the opposing party present. Thus, depending on the parties involved and the intensity of the conflict, there may be numerous expressions of anger and hostility expressed by one disputant toward the other. This is nicely captured by Herrman et al. in their concept of *hostile environment.* The model makes explicit an important point – namely, that interpersonal justice in mediation contexts will be determined not only by the actions of the mediator, but by the actions of the other party in mediation. Clearly, mediators know that such statements can be problematic, and they may caucus privately with each disputant early in mediation in an effort to allow disputants to get their angry outbursts out of their system.

Turning to "Procedural factors: mediation conditions," I believe that *mediator process control* may influence interpersonal justice judgments. Herrman et al. describe this construct as reflecting the pace or control exerted by the mediator in moving the dispute resolution process towards conclusion – how long to spend on particular topics, when to clarify and probe for deeper issues versus when not to, etc. While this is a somewhat broader set of actions relative to many of the other specific factors in the mediation model, we can see where mediators have to strike a delicate balance between exerting too little control over the mediation (thereby letting the process get sidetracked, or be viewed negatively by one or both parties) and exerting too much control (which could lead one or both disputants feeling like they did not get to say what was on their mind). While this could be seen as impacting procedural justice, I suspect that such actions might be interpreted by disputants as indicative of a lack of sensitivity or respect for their interests, which could lead to a reduction in interpersonal justice. I see a very similar potential threat existing under "Procedural factors: decision-making," when Herrman et al. discuss *mediator-driven closure.* As this facet of mediation would include actions by the mediator such as being forceful and exerting pressure, there is the possibility for disputants to react negatively and believe that the mediator is not treating them properly.

I now consider informational justice. In viewing the mediation model, one concept under the heading "Procedural factors: mediation conditions" would influence these judgments. The concept of *procedural clarity* as described by Herrman et al. involves mediators clearly describing the goals, the events, and the constraints of the mediation procedure. Implicit in their description of this facet is the idea that this information is going to be conveyed prior to the onset of mediation. Again, as mentioned earlier, providing thorough information and explanations about procedures to be used or explaining why specific outcomes occur or may occur enhances informational justice, and such explanations are likely to be most effective when they are provided prior to, rather than after, the experience of a procedure or the receipt of an outcome (especially a negative outcome) from the process.

Two additional factors in the Herrman et al. model deserve comment before moving our discussion further. I note that two of the elements listed in the "Procedural factors: mediation conditions" section of the model refer explicitly to fairness judgments mentioned earlier (specifically, the *global fairness* and the *interactional fairness* constructs). I would argue that the fourfold model of justice provides a more precise nomenclature than does use of these two fairness constructs (along with distributive justice, to be discussed shortly). Thus, perhaps future versions of the mediation model might eliminate these two rather broad constructs and replace them with the more precise constructs developed and validated by scholars such as Greenberg (1993) and Colquitt (2001).

Finally, I consider distributive justice. While distributive justice is listed as a short-term outcome in the model, I believe that this justice judgment is typically developed late in the mediation procedure when attention is focused on determining the specific outcome from mediation. This is reflected in the model in the "Procedural factors: decision-making" stage under the heading "Clients shape decision." Examples of the types of questions that Herrman et al. provide that reflect this construct make clear that the focus is on disputant influence or control over what the outcome from mediation is going to be. As there is a strong connection between outcome satisfaction and outcome fairness, numerous studies have shown that the two effects relate to distributive justice. First, there is evidence that disputants prefer outcomes that they can claim ownership over to outcomes that are imposed on them by others. Given that outcomes from mediation are voluntarily (even if begrudgingly) agreed to by parties, there should be a belief that the outcomes are fair. Second, we know that perceptions of what outcomes are fair tend to be egocentrically biased – in other words, people prefer decision rules or allocation decisions that favor themselves over equally plausible rules that might favor others more (Babcock, Loewenstein, Issacharoff & Camerer 1995). Returning to the brief discussion of different kinds of allocation rules, a parent who has never been around his or her children might argue for an equality rule (joint custody), while the parent who has historically attended to the children almost exclusively might argue for an equity rule (past performance = sole custody). To the extent that clients are involved in shaping decisions, they may be able to exert influence that leads to outcomes that they cannot help but see as fair. These actions should also lead participants to feel that they have higher levels of both process and decision control, using the terminology of the original Thibaut and Walker (1975) model of procedural justice.

Justice and short-term outcomes

Turning to the short-term outcomes in stage T_1 of the model, I reiterate that distributive justice is the only form of justice to be listed in this section. At one level, this should not be surprising, as judgments of the other three forms of justice I have discussed can in fact be determined by participants prior to receipt of their outcome (i.e. they should already have a sense of whether they think the procedure was fair, whether they were treated with respect, and whether adequate explanations and communications were provided to them). However, it is also worth noting that outcomes themselves often lead to changes in these other justice judgments. Outcomes that are surprising (and in particular, more negative than expected) can lead disputants to more thoroughly consider why they received the particular outcome, which can lead to a re-evaluation of the procedure and how it was implemented (Wong & Weiner 1981). In fact, one recent model of justice (fairness theory) discusses in depth how unfavorable or surprising outcomes can lead participants to reassess their beliefs about the fairness of procedures (Folger & Cropanzano 2001). This suggests that a strong case can be made for placing all four justice perceptions into the "short-term outcomes" category.

The consequences of enhancing justice for short- and long-term outcomes

The Herrman et al. model outlines 21 specific short- and long-term outcomes that are classified into five general sets of outcome variables. Many of these specific outcomes have in fact been linked to one or more forms of justice. Of particular utility for this discussion are the results from several meta-analytic reviews of the justice literature (Colquitt et al. 2001; Cohen-Charash & Spector 2001), which have summarized many of the relationships found between justice variables and a variety of outcomes. For example, the Colquitt, et al. (2001) meta-analysis of over 180 studies reveals that all four forms of justice positively impact outcome satisfaction, evaluation of authority figures, and evaluations of authority systems. These three variables are analogous to the Herrman et al. concepts of *satisfaction with the outcome, satisfaction with the mediator,* and *satisfaction with the court/judicial system,* respectively. However, the Colquitt et al. (2001) study also presents information about the unique effects (variance explained) of each form of justice on these outcomes. For instance, distributive justice (not surprisingly) explains more unique variance in outcome satisfaction than do procedural, interpersonal, and informational justice. Distributive, interpersonal, and informational justice also explain more unique variance in evaluations of authority figures than does procedural justice. Informational and procedural justice explain the most unique variance in evaluations of authority systems.

Justice judgments have also been linked to disputant decisions to comply with decisions or outcomes reached, reflecting the two outcomes of *compliance orientation* and *compliance with the agreement* under short-term (T_1) and long-term (T_2) outcomes, respectively. Cohen-Charash and Spector (2001) report a modest weighted-mean correlation of .14 between procedural justice and compliance with decisions across three field samples in organizations. Studies in legal environments tend to show stronger support for a justice–compliance relationship. For instance, Lind et al. (1993: Study 1) examined disputants' willingness to accept (comply with) awards stemming from personal injury or breach of contract cases taken to arbitration (non-compliance would be a subsequent decision to take the case to trial). They report a correlation of .62 between procedural justice and award acceptance, as well as a correlation of .40 between a measure of "subjective outcome evaluation" (similar to distributive justice) and award acceptance. Using a median split on disputants' procedural justice judgments, they noted that, when the procedure was viewed as fair, arbitrated awards were accepted 79 percent of the time, whereas when the procedure was seen as unfair, such awards were accepted only 25 percent of the time. Clearly, justice perceptions matter when it comes to decisions to comply with outcomes, though we could find little work examining the relationships between interpersonal and informational justice and compliance.

Finally, I examine the potential connections between justice judgments and Herrman et al.'s variables of *reduced anxiety about the crime* and *reduced fear of revictimization*. While the justice literature has not historically been connected to these types of judgments, there has been some very recent work connecting justice judgments to stress perceptions. Judge and Colquitt (2004) examined the relationships between the four forms of justice discussed in this chapter and university faculty member perceptions of stress. These authors found that procedural and interpersonal justice had significant relationships with stress, while distributive and informational justice were not related to stress levels. However, we are not aware of any studies that have examined the connections between justice and stress-related outcomes within dispute resolution contexts.

CONCLUSIONS

As I hope this chapter has made abundantly clear, notions of fairness and justice can be influenced by a wide variety of activities that take place before, during, and after mediation. In addition, it is important to care about fairness judgments in part because these judgments often influence other outcomes from mediation. I would like to close by elaborating on three topics that strike me as in greater need of elaboration and distinction.

The first topic relates to the context of the mediation. This topic can manifest itself in at least three ways: the type of conflict, the importance of the issue in conflict, and the type of issue in conflict. I begin first by considering the type of conflict. For example, is the mediation concerning a workplace conflict (sexual harassment), a family conflict (divorce mediation), or some other conflict (e.g. consumer complaint, business-to-business dispute)? The context in which mediation is occurring can be a strong influence on which distributive justice rule might be salient or implemented. For instance, Schwinger (1986) argues that as relationships move from neutral to positive to very positive (e.g. from acquaintances to friends to family members), the salient justice norm will move from equity to equality to need, respectively. While this does not speak to the issue of when parties have a negative relationship, other work suggests that equity rules often are implemented when relationships are competitive or performance-focused (e.g. Reis & Gruzen 1976; Austin 1980).

Issues in dispute also differ in their level of importance to each party. While models of integrative bargaining and negotiation often make salient that disputants have different priorities across issues (thereby creating the integrative potential necessary for win-win settlements to emerge), parties still prefer to do well on their most important issues, and more important issues may also lead disputants to have more concern or emphasis on the other forms of justice (or the activities that enhance those forms of justice). For instance, the expression of voice or the sense of representation central to promoting procedural justice judgments may be more important when participants are involved in personal disputes than in organizational or business-to-business disputes if the former are more important to the disputant than are the latter. With important issues, perhaps part of the "outcome" one hopes to receive is simply having their opinions heard. One might expect that the more important the issue in dispute, the more important it is for a participant to "have their say" on the topic and express their process control through voice.

Finally, I note that properties of the issue in dispute may lead to variations in beliefs about how such an issue should be decided. Some recent work (Conlon, Porter & McLean Parks 2004) shows that what resource is being allocated leads to variations in both fairness judgments and beliefs that the allocation decision will lead to conflict among parties. Interestingly, these authors found that allocations of money (a most easily divisible resource) led to lower fairness judgments (regardless of what allocation rule was used) and higher beliefs that the decision would lead to conflict, than did allocating material "goods" (e.g. office furniture) or "status resources" (in this case, the authority to call a meeting). Having different types of resources increases the potential that people may imbue certain things with more value or status than others, which might explain differing preferences across parties for different allocation rules.

The second topic worth elaborating concerns how the process of mediation can lead to particular kinds of problems that may be more commonplace in mediation than in other third party procedures such as arbitration or adjudication. Because of its inherent informality, mediation might come to be seen by disputants in some cases as lacking in consistency (especially if a party has experienced prior mediations). In addition, the natural variance that exists in third party behaviors might be greater in mediation than in other procedures with more rigid sets of rules about propriety and behavior. As a result, concerns about bias suppression and ethicality may be greater threats in mediation than in other procedures. One way in which a mediator may ameliorate these concerns is by providing thorough up-front explanations about the procedure and what is likely to happen, followed by getting participant agreement on the process to be used. These last behaviors, which should enhance informational justice, will also then subsequently enhance procedural justice.

Finally, I realize that developing this chapter on justice intended for the dispute resolution literature has helped me realize an important shortcoming in the current work applying justice to the organizations literature. The organizational justice field needs to realize that in situations where multiple parties are involved (e.g. group decision-making), there are likely many instances where one's perception that they have been treated with politeness, dignity, and respect, and beliefs that parties refrained from improper remarks (in essence, interpersonal justice perceptions), ought to be measured in terms of how both the authority figure and the other parties behaved during the procedure. Currently, questions of inter-personal and informational justice are directed only toward the authority figure enacting a procedure. Yet, as is quite clear from mediation and other dispute resolution contexts, a disputant responds not only to the actions of the third party, but to those of the other disputant as well. In addition, current measures in the organizational justice field focus exclusively on equity – e.g. "To what extent does the outcome reflect the effort you have put into your work?" – whereas in many cases other justice rules are more appropriate. This suggests that future work should develop more items reflecting distributive justice (in particular other justice rules), and that the impact of other parties besides the authority figure should be examined.

References

Adams, J. S. (1965) Inequity in social exchange. In L. Berkowitz (ed.), *Advances in Social Psychology*, vol. 2. Academic Press, New York, pp. 267–299.

Austin, W. (1980) Friendship and fairness: effects of type of relationship and task perform-ance on choice of distribution rules. *Personality and Social Psychology Bulletin* 6, 402–408.

Babcock, L., Loewenstein, G., Issacharoff, S. & Camerer, C. (1995) Biased judgments of fairness in bargaining. *American Economic Review* 85, 1337–1343.

Bies, R. J. & Moag, J. F. (1986) Interactional justice: communication criteria of fairness. In R. J. Lewicki, B. H. Sheppard & M. H. Bazerman (eds.), *Research on Negotiations in Organizations*, vol. 1. JAI Press. Greenwich, pp. 43–55.

Byrne, Z. S. & Cropanzano, R. (2001) The history of organizational justice: the founders speak. In R. Cropanzano (ed.), *Justice in the Workplace: From Theory to Practice*. Lawrence Erlbaum, Mahwah, pp. 3–26.

Coates, R. B. & Gehm, J. (1989) An empirical assessment. In M. Wright & B. Galaway (eds.), *Mediation and Criminal Justice*. Sage, London, pp. 251–263.

Cohen-Charash, Y. & Spector, P. (2001) The role of justice in organizations: a meta-analysis. *Organizational Behavior and Human Decision Processes* 86, 278–321.

Colquitt, J. A. (2001) On the dimensionality of organizational justice: a construct validation of a measure. *Journal of Applied Psychology* 86, 386–400.

Colquitt, J. A., Conlon, D. E., Wesson, M., Porter, C. & Ng, K. (2001) Justice at the millennium: a meta-analytic review of 25 years of organizational justice research. *Journal of Applied Psychology* 86, 425–445.

Conlon, D. E. & Fasolo, P. M. (1990) Influence of speed of third-party intervention and outcome on negotiator and constituent fairness judgments. *Academy of Management Journal* 33, 833–846.

Conlon, D. E. & Ross, W. H. (1993) The effects of partisan third parties on negotiator behavior and outcome perceptions. *Journal of Applied Psychology* 78, 280–290.

Conlon, D. E. & Murray, N. M. (1996) Customer perceptions of corporate responses to prod-uct complaints: the role of explanations. *Academy of Management Journal* 39, 1040–1056.

Conlon, D. E., Porter, C. O. L. H. & McLean Parks, J. (2004) The fairness of decision rules. *Journal of Management* 30, 329–349.

Deutsch, M. (1975) Equity, equality and need: what determines which value will be used as the basis for distributive justice? *Journal of Social Issues* 31, 137–149.

Deutsch, M. (1985) *Distributive Justice: A Social Psychological Perspective*. Yale University Press, New Haven.

Folger, R. L. & Cropanzano, R. L. (2001) Fairness theory: justice as accountability. In J. Greenberg & R. Cropanzano (eds.), *Advances in Organizational Justice*. Stanford University Press, Palo Alto, pp. 1–55.

Greenberg, J. (1993) The social side of fairness: interpersonal and informational classes of organizational justice. In R. Cropanzano (ed.), *Justice in the Workplace: Approaching Fairness in Human Resource Management*. Erlbaum, Hillsdale, pp. 79–103.

Judge, T. A. & Colquitt, J. A. (2004) Organizational justice and stress: the mediating role of work–family conflict. *Journal of Applied Psychology* 89, 395–404.

Leventhal, G. S. (1976) *Fairness in Social Relationships*. General Learning Press, Morristown.

Leventhal, G. S. (1980) What should be done with equity theory? In K. Gergen, M. Greenberg & R. Willis (eds.), *Social Exchanges: Advances in Theory and Research*. Plenum, New York, pp. 27–55.

Leventhal, G. S., Karuza, J. & Fry, W. R. (1980) Beyond fairness: a theory of allocation preferences. In G. Mikula (ed.), *Justice and Social Interaction*. Springer, New York, pp. 167–218.

Lim, R. G. & Carnevale, P. J. (1990) Contingencies in the mediation of disputes. *Journal of Personality and Social Psychology* 58, 259–272.

Lind, E. A., Lissak, R. I. & Conlon, D. E. (1983) Decision control and process control effects on procedural fairness judgments. *Journal of Applied Social Psychology* 13, 338–350.

Lind, E. A., Kulik, C. T., Ambrose, M. A. & De Vera Park, M. V. (1993) Individual and corporate dispute resolution: using procedural fairness as a decision heuristic. *Administrative Science Quarterly* 38, 224–251.

Pruitt, D. G. (1981) *Negotiation Behavior*. Academic Press, New York.

Reis, H. & Gruzen, J. (1976) On mediating equity, equality, and self-interest: the role of self presentation in social exchange. *Journal of Experimental Social Psychology* 12, 487–503.

Rescher, N. (1966) *Distributive Justice*. Bobbs Merrill, New York.

Schwinger, T. (1986) The need principle of distributive justice. In H. Bierhoff, R. Cohen & J. Greenberg (eds.), *Justice in Social Relations*. Plenum, New York, pp. 211–225.

Shaw, J. C., Wild, E. & Colquitt, J. A. (2003) To justify or excuse? A meta-analytic review of the effects of explanations. *Journal of Applied Psychology* 88, 444–458.

Thibaut, J. & Walker, L. (1975) *Procedural Justice: A Psychological Analysis*. Erlbaum, Hillsdale.

Törnblom, K., Jonsson, D. & Foa, U. (1985) Nationality, resource class, and preferences among three allocation rules: Sweden vs. USA. *International Journal of Intercultural Relations* 9, 51–77.

Walster, E. Walster, G. W. & Berscheid, E. (1978) *Equity: Theory and Research*. Allyn & Bacon, Boston.

Wissler, R. L. (1999) *Evaluation of the Pilot Mediation Program in Clinton and Stark Counties, August 1996 through March 1997*. Report prepared for the Supreme Court of Ohio, 30 E. Broad Street, Columbus, OH 43266–0419.

Wittmer, J. M., Carnevale, P. J. & Walker, M. E. (1991) General alignment and overt support in biased mediation. *Journal of Conflict Resolution* 35, 594–610.

Wong, P. T. & Weiner, B. (1981) When people ask "why" questions, and the heuristics of attributional search. *Journal of Personality and Social Psychology* 40, 650–663.

Young, H. P. (1995) Dividing the indivisible. *American Behavioral Scientist* 38, 904–920.

Chapter 12

The Dynamics of Power in Child Custody Mediation

Donald T. Saposnek

INTRODUCTION

When two people enter into informal negotiations of any kind using personal power of persuasion and logic, each attempts to influence the other to his or her point of view. When this takes place in the more formal, restrained context of mediation, the stakes for exercising such persuasive personal power are higher. However, when the context is child custody mediation – which arguably may be considered one of the most intense contexts of negotiation – and each participant-parent feels that he or she is negotiating to maintain his or her relationship and connection with their child, the stakes escalate exponentially. Parents are vulnerable and filled with fear in many ways. The thought of negotiating their relationship with their child feels like a threat to their very survival. Saposnek (1983a: 23–24) notes:

> Each spouse's self-concept, lifestyle, moral values, competence as a parent, worth as a human being, and feelings of being lovable are threatened. Moreover, each spouse's capacity for flexible compromise, for empathy, and for dealing with often over-whelming feelings of anger, grief, jealousy, resentment, and revenge is also challenged. Both spouses have much to protect. They must each protect their own relationship with their children, their finances (often from threat by the other spouse), their integrity, and their sense of personal worth. They may feel subject to explicit and implicit criticism by their former spouse, by their children, by the judge, and even by the mediator. Each may put up a childlike resistance, for each will feel that his or her own inner child's emotional survival and autonomy are at stake. It is ironic that in this struggle, each spouse perceives himself or herself as powerless and the other spouse as powerful. The result is like a tug-of-war, with each spouse feeling over-powered by the other although in fact neither has moved an inch . . . a primary task of the mediator is to get the spouses apart when they feel stuck together.

The construct of power is of salient significance in the dynamics of custody mediation. Using the Herrman, Hollet, and Gale (HHG) model of mediation proposed in chapter 2, we can consider the numerous pertinent variables related to power dynamics within the model's chronologically sequential structure (T_0 = antecedent conditions; T_m = the mediation phase; T_1 = short-term outcomes; and T_2 = long-term outcomes).

DEFINITIONS

Dictionary definitions of the word "power" bring up the essence of the discussion in this chapter (*Webster's* 1959: 1145). The word is derived from the Latin root *potere* – "To be able; potent." Potency suggests two pertinent major categories of meaning: (1) power or control over oneself – a skill, competence or strength; the ability to do; capacity to act, capability of performing or producing; strength or vigor; and (2) power or control over others – influence or persuasion; the ability to control others; authority; sway; influence; having great influence, force, or authority. These definitions generally are inclusive of the types of power utilized by both the mediator and the clients in mediation, and they capture the realm of power discussed in this chapter.

THE NATURE OF POWER

While the first definition, "power over oneself," has neutral to positive connotations (and is related to a sense of self-efficacy and self-control), the latter usage, "power over others" tends to be viewed more negatively and is equated with coercion (Mayer 1987). It is this latter usage which characterizes much of the literature dealing with power between the parties in the context of mediation. Some view power as a basic aspect of every relationship (Haynes 1988a; Kelly 1995; Moore 1996), which becomes a concern in the midst of interpersonal conflict, and more insidiously within seriously conflictual relationships as in difficult divorces (Folberg & Taylor 1984). Folberg and Taylor (1984: 184) describe interpersonal power in terms of long-standing, familiar power patterns of "dominance and submission, deference and competition, dependence and competence." These emerge as ingrained patterns that function as "defense mechanisms . . . against the threat implied by the demand for equality inherent in the mediation process" (1984: 184–185). Saposnek (1998: 170) characterizes these patterns of power as "interactional reflexes" that are triggered by any of the countless reminders of the loss, mistrust, resentments, frustrations, and feelings of powerlessness and vulnerability that divorce so frequently elicits.

Regardless of their views, notions, and definitions of power, most theorists and practitioners in the field of mediation consider imbalances of power to be an important focus within the mediation process. Most mediators are trained to redress a power imbalance consciously in mediation wherever and whenever it shows itself, under the assumption that mediation requires a level playing field of power in order for equality and fairness to prevail in the couple's agreements. A mediator may assess the nature of a power imbalance initially, when determining whether or not to mediate, or later, when deciding whether or not to terminate while in process (e.g. in certain cases in which domestic violence has been revealed). Power balances certainly are an ongoing concern during mediation, as the mediator continually manages the clients' power.

Other mediators do not pursue the balancing of power as a particular goal to achieve. Rather, they work within the natural order of power balances established by a particular couple over the course of their relationship. This approach is based on the assumption that each participant in mediation has his or her own implicitly or explicitly designated domains of power that tend to dictate the dynamics of the negotiations within those particular topic areas. Some of these domains may be culturally and socially embedded and accepted as antecedent conditions to mediation (at T_0 in the proposed model in chapter 2).

For example, mothers have often been considered more knowledgeable about, and often serve as the "gatekeepers" of, their children, largely determining the father's involvement with them. This is shown to be the case both during marriage (Pleck 1997), as well as during separation and after divorce (Braver & Griffin 2000; Cohen, Cowan & Cowan 2002; Insabella, Williams & Pruett 2003; Kelly & Emery 2003). Fathers often are considered more knowledgeable about and influential regarding the family's financial matters. With their respective areas of knowledge being sources of power, each party retains a leading edge in the negotiations within those specific domains, as they pursue the primary goal of reaching an acceptable resolution to their presenting conflicts.

Expanding this issue further, Lang (2004) notes how a mediator's beliefs and thinking about power influences his or her assessment of power relationships and the development of appropriate interventions. As such, practice decisions follow beliefs (Lang & Taylor 2000) and influence both the process and outcome of mediation (i.e. directly influencing the mediator at T_0 and T_m, and indirectly influencing the clients at T_1 and perhaps T_2).

The question remains as to whether efforts to balance the power in mediation sessions or simply respect the couple's naturally established balance of power make any difference at all in outcomes (at T_1 or T_2). It is probably the case that, in the absence of empirical research on the issue, most mediators take an intermediate position on this matter.

Comments on the HHG Model Assumptions

In order to set in proper context further discussion about the power dynamics in custody disputes, it is important to add commentary to and clarification of how the assumptions made in the HHG model may or may not apply in these types of disputes.

HHG Assumption #1

"Any form of conflict resolution occurs in a social context."

Needs no commentary here.

HHG Assumption #2

"People prefer harmony to discord. Given a conducive problem-solving environment and in order to create harmony, people will act on their abilities for mature, independent, and responsible interactions."

Several characteristics of and situations within the power dynamics in custody mediations make this assumption questionable. The negative emotions experienced by many, if not most, divorcing spouses include hurt, rejection, loneliness, depression, anxiety, lowered self-esteem, and guilt. While many spouses are able to cope constructively with these difficult feelings, others cover up these vulnerable feelings with anger.

Anger generates power. It functions to intimidate and control others, to establish personal boundaries and to force the other to back off. It is often the case that one of the spouses (usually the one who is left) experiences such a significant degree of loss that it can only be managed by maintaining a high level of anger. To give up the anger too soon may leave that spouse feeling unbearably vulnerable and powerless. Often (particularly in stage T_0 and sometimes leaking into stage T_m) the angry spouse will persistently use anger as power (through blaming the other, blocking any attempt at resolution, and provoking discord) in unconscious efforts to prevent him or herself from feeling the deep loss. Most often, the other spouse will respond with equal levels of anger (as defense from the attack), with the couple appearing unable to stop their power struggles.

Mnookin and Ross (1999) list three barriers to effective conflict resolution: (1) mindsets that foreshadow logical, tactical strategies to maximize gains; (2) cognitive filters that shape how people interpret information, evaluate risks, set priorities, and experience loss or gains; and (3) structural contexts that constrain negotiation. To characterize the barriers to effective conflict resolution more accurately, I would add a fourth: powerful emotional states that distort, inhibit, sabotage, and shut down logical and rational thinking processes, and prevent effective negotiation. It is this fourth barrier that challenges the HHG assumption.

Two of the eight categories of spousal strategies identified by Saposnek (1983a, 1998) that are most relevant to our discussion of power are "power assertion strategies" and "revenge and retaliation strategies." Such strategies are a spouse's attempts to "gain some sense of security, personal power, and dignity . . . These interactional maneuvers with hidden personal agenda are similar to the functional strategies of children" (Saposnek 1983a: 136–137) discussed below. Power assertion strategies include such tactics as pushing to win sole custody, forcing a 50–50 percent split, demanding 51 percent, and changing the child's last name without consulting with the other parent. The central theme of power assertion strategies is to prove oneself as strong as or stronger than the other spouse, either to try to redress the experience of feeling dominated by the other spouse throughout the marriage, or by preserving a dominant status following a separation by staking out an aggressive claim regarding the custody issues. Mediation is often the first opportunity to assert such maneuvers.

Revenge and retaliation strategies have as their sole intent to hurt the other spouse. They include maneuvers such as demanding sole custody from a primary parent (to essentially deprive the primary parent of the child), demanding joint custody (to create a regular opportunity to interact with and emotionally torture the other spouse), and consciously frustrating visitations. Note that both the power assertion strategies and the revenge and retaliation strategies are carried out mercilessly, with little or no regard for the children's best interests. They are exclusively designed to generate discord, prevent harmony, and satisfy a distorted adult need. While one spouse can be the primary person who initiates these power strategies to generate conflict (Friedman 2004), the other spouse often soon joins in, and conflict ensues. The tenacity in the use of such spousal strategies challenges the very best of mediators.

Another example of disputants preferring discord over harmony is exemplified by spouses who were never able to achieve positive intimacy during the marriage, but persist in maintaining an attachment with each other through conflict and power struggles. Ricci (1980) called this phenomenon "negative intimacy," while Larson (1993) termed it the "connection conflict." The working premise is that, for many couples, negative intimacy is better than no intimacy. Couples who manifest this pattern are best characterized by the dysfunctional post-divorce spousal relationship categories identified by Ahrons and Rodgers (1987) as "angry associates" and "fiery foes." They are couples who cannot live together, yet cannot let go of each other. They persist in fighting during the divorce, in mediation, and for years thereafter (virtually in all stages of the HHG model). By no means do they strive for harmony, but rather they use their power to seek what they perceive to be the least detrimental alternative to personal pain.

HHG Assumption #3

"If someone experiences competitive interactions, the experience typically evokes competitive responses. Likewise, experiences of cooperation evoke cooperative responses."

Because of the underlying dynamics that drive the parents' use of power, this assumption does not necessarily hold up in custody mediations. If a disputant at T_0 holds an emotionally driven position strongly enough, then the competitive assertions of the other party will not necessarily evoke more competition, but may simply be disregarded and dismissed. For example, if a mother believes to her core that she is the better parent and that the father is a destructive and abusive parent, she is not about to let go of her assumption that she will retain primary custody of her child, no matter how competitively threatening or cooperative the father may act. She may feel neither cooperative nor competitive about the negotiations, but rather assured and confident that her plan obviously will come to fruition by mediation's end. In fact, she may take his threats as further evidence of his unworthiness as a parent, which may even increase her confidence in her position.

Likewise, if a father believes that he should and will be an equal parent (i.e. get 50–50 custody), he is not about to waver from this position, no matter how cooperative or competitive the mother might be in every other way. These strongly held positional beliefs at T_0 are often significantly enhanced during T_m when there are one or more external participants to the dispute (e.g. a lawyer, a new girlfriend, a grandparent, a therapist) supporting the parent and his or her positional belief. For example, it is not uncommon for a parent to enter mediation at T_m, appear to negotiate cooperatively and in good faith, but end the session by calmly refusing to agree. Sometimes, when asked, the parent will admit: "My lawyer told me to go through mediation, but not agree to anything. She said we would win in court." This would be an example of using a passive form of power (i.e. a passive-aggressive tactic). In its extreme version, dubbed "tribal warfare" (Johnston & Campbell 1988; Johnston & Roseby 1997), a cadre of extended family and friends take up the cause and give exaggerated support to the parent for asserting these positional beliefs. With such support, the parent feels secure in appearing cooperative but not budging on his or her position, even when the other parent is being genuinely cooperative.

Lastly, some individuals have personality characteristics of being oppositional and antagonistic which exaggerate in circumstances that are beyond their control, for example when that individual does not want the divorce. Antagonistic and oppositional stances, even in the face of cooperation, could be an antecedent condition for failure, even within an ideal model of positive, cooperative conflict resolution methods.

HHG Assumption #4

"Referral to formal mediation signals that people are experiencing a conflict characterized by a lack of cooperation (or poor communication, misunderstanding, etc.)."

There are two circumstances in child custody mediations in which this assumption may not be accurate. One circumstance is when both parents are in fact cooperative, but simply cannot agree on what is in the best interests of their children as they divorce and are seeking formal mediation to gather expert information on how to best serve the needs of their children through their divorce. They may experience legitimate differences of opinion, understand each other very well, but simply need the input of an expert and the guided structure offered by mediation, before making their decisions about post-divorce parenting plans. This is not a dynamic power struggle, but more of what might be deemed a "reality-based impasse" (Saposnek 1998: 170).

The other circumstance has to do with the nature and meaning of "communication." While most power struggles in mediation are quite complex and often attributed to "poor communication," Haley (1963) offered a refreshing point of view when he noted that, when two people are in a relationship, they cannot not communicate. Even if they are silent with one another, they are communicating that neither wishes to talk with the other. So, the concept of "poor communication" does not give much information about the nature of their power struggles, especially when one considers the patterns of communication of couples who are engaged in "connection conflict" or "negative intimacy." To those parties, their communications are exquisitely predictable and symmetrical, with each party knowing in advance what the other is about to say. Paradoxically, these could be considered "good" communications, and, thus, challenging to this assumption.

HHG Assumption #5

"The goal of formal mediation is to change a competitive conflict to a cooperative interaction characterized by: (a) effective communication, (b) less obstruction, (c) orderly discussion, (d) confidence in one's ideas coupled with support for the ideas and concerns of other participants, (e) coordinated efforts to resolve the conflict, (f) high productivity, (g) power-sharing and mutual power enhancement, and (h) acceptance that the problem is a mutual problem that can be overcome."

And:

HHG Assumption #6

"When confronted with a conflict, people express a great deal of attachment to their initial position – often a position based on preliminary and incomplete information."

When one is considering the intensity of the power struggles that occur in custody mediations, these ideal assumptions of conflict resolution may need revision. Because of the presence of a third, unrepresented, party – the children – who also happen to be the subject and object of the dispute, the goal for conflict resolution may be too lofty. A model that might be more fitting is one of "conflict management" rather than conflict resolution. Folberg and Taylor (1984: 25) make this important distinction:

> Conflict resolution creates a state of uniformity or convergence of purpose or means; conflict management only realigns the divergence enough to render the opposing forces less diametrically opposite or damaging to each other. Conflict management does not demand an identical aim, method, or process, as does conflict resolution, but simply one that is sufficiently aligned to allow unobstructed progress for the separate entities.

Because children are constantly growing and changing, divorced parents regularly need to modify their parenting plan. When the parents have been, and continue to be, in difficult power struggles over the co-parenting of their children, a more reasonable goal for a mediator would be to help them manage their conflicts. While some may be able to cooperate if they simply gain new information about the changing needs of their children on a regular basis, many respond to these changing needs by re-engaging in their ongoing power struggles with one another. Resolution of their parenting conflict is simply not attainable. Davis (2002) came to a similar conclusion in studying individuals in estranged relationships. She found that, while degrees of reconciliation were possible for many family relationships, this was never achievable for others. These estranged family members could, at best, manage their conflict enough to function courteously at family gatherings, but they never were able to resolve their core conflict.

We tend to idealize negotiation in conflict resolution as a linear process of rational discourse leading to a rational, fair, and equitable outcome. However, the reality is that negotiation is often irrational, circuitous, and, in the case of the higher conflict power struggles in custody disputes, it is often rageful and downright messy. It is frequently driven by emotional factors beyond what the structure of mediation can offer (Young 1991; Benjamin 2004). Further research is needed on the variables that predict more positive parental relationships at T_2.

HHG Assumption #7

"Verbalizing individual positions and stories provides the speaker and listener with an opportunity to develop a greater understanding of underlying needs and to stimulate higher-level reasoning."

With the essential breach of marital trust that is typically engendered in a divorce, fueled by the dynamic of "tribal warfare" (Johnston & Campbell 1988), the couple at T_0 often enter mediation already having "negatively reconstructed the spousal identity" (Johnston & Campbell 1988). This phenomenon describes the situation in which a party has rewritten marital history to reflect only the negative aspects of the spouse's identity and actions, thereby vilifying the other to maintain face-saving for having married that person and/or having left or been left by him or her.

If, with these entrenched points of view, the parties in the early stage of T_m are allowed to verbalize their individual positions and stories, anything but helpful understanding comes of it. To the contrary, with the higher-conflict couples, the more they are allowed to verbalize the positions that come from their distorted rewriting of marital history, the more the power struggle gets entrenched and amplified. Indeed, they all too soon begin engaging in "lower-level," rather than higher-level, reasoning.

It appears that the basis of HHG assumption #7 is that disputants are fully capable of rational, analytic thinking and that, given the opportunity in mediation, the parties will strive to be reasonable and understanding. Quite the opposite assumption is true with regard to the deeply emotion-based power struggles of parents in difficult custody mediations. Unless the mediator takes firm control over the process and establishes ground rules and a safe structure for further discussion, an irreversible impasse is imminent.

A disputant's beliefs and attitudes about the other at T_1 often remain unchanged by T_2. Although an agreement may be developed, its longer-term durability may be in jeopardy by virtue of the unchangeable negative perspective that each party has on the other. Moreover, if the children initiate their own strategies, the power struggle between these couples can easily erupt over the most minor of co-parenting issues. There is often little "understanding" achieved in mediation with these couples, in spite of their capacities to reach agreements, nonetheless.

HHG Assumption #8

"Exposure to different opinions, information, and interpretations of life experiences can arouse a state of cognitive disequilibrium that helps to thaw positions."

And:

HHG Assumption #9

"Uncertainty motivates an active search for more information."

This assumption generally has much truth. The body of social psychology literature in cognitive dissonance (Festinger 1957; Aronson 1980) does suggest that cognitive disequilibrium has the potential, at least temporarily, to release disputants from their positions. However, it also has the power to create the opposite effect – of entrenching positions further. One element that determines the valence of this power is the degree to which one has protective emotional attachment to one's position. In custody disputes, the emotional element is major. As discussed above, the attachment to positions is based upon the primary emotions of fear and sadness, and the secondary emotions of anger and revenge, that are most often generated by loss. These emotional wounds that divorcing people often suffer are at the core of their power struggles, and, in the face of challenges to their defenses (even with rational information, interpretations, and professional opinions), they often resolve the dissonance by clinging ever more tightly to their beliefs, attitudes, and positions. The challenge to the mediator at T_m is to facilitate enough resolution of the underlying emotional needs so as to free up the participant to be available to and, perhaps, curious about taking in the rational information and making a change in attitude first, and position second.

HHG Assumption #10

"At the same time, people continuously attribute and redefine the meaning of actions, purposes, agreements, even personal and social identities. So, there is usually no objective or even representational 'truth' to be discovered with regard to past events or experiences. Therefore, in mediation, the goal is not to discover the truth but to achieve a socially constructed, consensual agreement of terms and future actions."

This assumption finds no greater validity than with parents in custody disputes. It is often said that two spouses will describe their 20-year marriage in such divergent ways that the marital therapist must check her notes to make sure that they are talking about the same marriage! In the case of divorce, this phenomenon is often amplified many fold. A central element of the power dynamics of divorcing parents is that each attempts to convince not only the mediator, but everyone they know, and don't know, of the "truth" of their respective views about the other spouse. The stories are compelling to whoever will listen (including family, friends, neighbors, therapists, lawyers, evaluators, judges, and even strangers in the park). The problem is that the "truth" of each spouse's stories is almost always opposite from that of the other: For example, she says: "He was never around to interact with the kids and rarely participated in parenting. In fact, he never even wanted children!" He says: "I was the primary caregiver of the children since their birth. She was always out with her friends, leaving the children with me to care for. They regularly would ask me if their Mom even loves them. The children have always been closer to me."

Certainly, by T_0 and far into T_2, these "truths" show little change. Although the couple may be able to minimize their power struggles, their views of each other and of what happened in their failed marriage frequently remain polarized. This has serious developmental consequences for the children. If, over time, the children continue hearing these "different truths" presented by each parent, they remain very confused. Often, they come to believe that one of their parents must be lying, but, not being able to ascertain which one it is, they choose to disbelieve both of them. This tends to erode trust in those who should be their very base of honesty and truth.

Children's Strategies as Power

It is a given that the mediator has power, and that each of the parents has power, but the situation gets more complex when one factors in the power strategies utilized by children in custody disputes (Saposnek 1983a, 1983b, 1998). These strategies are common patterns of verbal and physical behavior that a child uses through the parents' divorce, with the intention (mostly subconscious, but some-times very conscious) to influence (and assert power over) their parents to resolve a strong need of the child. For example, a child may complain to her father that her mother has no food at her house, and then complains to her mother that her father has many girlfriends over at his apartment. The father may conclude that the mother is neglecting the child, which influences him to demand sole custody as he enters mediation. The mother may conclude that the father is not appro-priately protecting the child from his adult social life, which may influence her to demand reduced contact between the father and the child, as mediation begins. The irony of these responses is that, frequently, neither parent really understands that the child was utilizing a reuniting strategy, with the intent to have her father come back home to her mother's house and bring food, like he used to when they were married, and for her mother to invite her father back home and get rid of his new girlfriends. In this way, the child has attempted to arrange for her parents to talk with each other, solve her problem, and make the divorce go away.

Besides reuniting strategies, a very common strategy of children in divorce, Saposnek (1983a) identified eight others, which include strategies for reducing separation distress, detonating inter-parental tension, proving loyalty, and protecting self-esteem. The unfortunate irony of a child asserting these strategies is that the parents draw opposite and incorrect conclusions about the child's intentions and the meaning of the behavior. Rather than quell the parents' conflict, these strategies tend to fuel and escalate it and function as daunting forces that often influence mediation before it even begins (in the T_0 phase). Because children's strategies are not static, they may also influence the mediation process throughout the T_m phase, as the parents bring in "new data" on how the children have been acting or what opinions they have been voicing between sessions.

AN INTERACTIONAL SYSTEMS VIEW

As one begins to appreciate the complexity of the context of child custody mediation, linear notions of the use of power appear overly simplistic. We obtain more conceptual rigor when we expand the frame to a systems point of view, in which the various participants in the dispute (including the "direct" participants – i.e. the parents, the children and the mediator – and the "indirect" participants – the lawyers, therapists, extended family, friends, and others) are seen as using their respective powers to influence each of the participants (including the mediator) within the process and attempt to influence the outcome of the mediation. These influences operative within each of the phases of the HGG model will be discussed in more detail below.

POWER ISSUES IN THE VARIOUS STAGES OF THE HHG MODEL

Stage T_0

Many, perhaps most, of the power dynamics in custody disputes are present in their potential form, as antecedent conditions. The disputant characteristics, with the unique individual features of each spouse linked with the other to produce predictable interactional reflexes, express themselves, sooner rather than later, in power struggles and in efforts at resisting resolution of their disputes. The willingness of the parties to participate is shaped by intrapersonal factors (both cognitive frame and emotional state), interpersonal factors (by the nature of the couple's dynamic), and external factors of influence (by the nature and degree of influence by family, friends, lawyers, and therapists, as well as by whatever general information about divorce and mediation the participants have acquired).

Unique factors that complicate custody mediation include the following: when one party is willing to participate while the other is not; the degree of the clients' perception of "voluntariness" that is based on covert coercion by lawyers, judges, and even therapists; and the fact that motivation to resolve is not a static state, but a fluid, emotional process driven largely by fear, and it may change in midstream, for non-apparent reasons, at T_0 or T_m. Future research that maps the relationship between the eruption of power struggles and fear would be quite productive for our understanding of this process.

An important mediator characteristic at T_0 that likely predicts later success is the degree of a mediator's comfort with being in charge and setting up a clear and firm structure prior to commencing negotiations. This variable blends with the antecedent variable in the HHG model that is referred to as "institutional context" and deals with the mediator providing process information. When the mediator provides information about the process ahead and the rules of conduct, power struggles are minimized, since they tend to be fueled by lack of structure (Saposnek 1983a, 1998).

The HHG model refers to another antecedent variable of "process efficiency." In custody disputes, this variable is quite critical, but not in the way implied by the HHG model. A number of theorists have noted that power struggles can be reduced or avoided by managing inter-session time (Saposnek 1983a; Haynes 1988b; Benjamin 2004). This does not necessarily mean being efficient in the usual sense of the word of getting the job done more quickly and with minimum waste. Sometimes, there is much benefit in strategically slowing down the process and resisting client or attorney pressure to speed it up. Inter-session time allows much of the emotional charge to be processed and dissipated outside of the sessions, and allows the resumption of mediation in a calmer emotional climate.

Stage T_m

Mediator's power

The mediator's power (both as self-control and as control over others) is key to priming readiness and managing client power struggles. A mediator who conveys a sense of personal confidence and unflappable self-control in the face of client anger and conflict is more likely to gain the confidence of the clients, convey a sense of protection and safety over the process, and probably promote a better climate of client self-efficacy. The way that a mediator deals with power over others (i.e. over the process), however, is a function of the particular model that the mediator uses. Power utilization can range from ways that are very subtle and indirect, as in facilitative, transformative, and therapeutic models (Folberg, Milne & Salem 2004) and strategic models (Saposnek 1998), to ways that are quite overt, as in evaluative or hybrid models (Shienvold 2004). Regardless of the theoretical model that the mediator uses, the variables of mediator empathy and clarity of under-standing others' points of view seem central to minimizing power struggles.

There are, however, several caveats to this last point. For one, in cases of domestic violence, in which the abuser presents a rationale for how "she provoked me to beat her," a mediator who "empathizes and understands" that point of view can not only create a sense of betrayal and the loss of a sense of safety in the other party, but may also encourage more abuse. Yet Johnston and Campbell (1993) note that there is actually a variety of types of domestic violence, with each of fairly equit- able proportions, in which, in some types, there can be mutuality to the violence, as well as female-initiated violence. So one must be careful in making generaliza- tions about the directionality of the power imbalances in domestic violence. In the mediation context this is often unclear, and rarely does the mediator have access to information within the mediation context that could help determine the nature of a particular couple's power dynamics in this matter. Moreover, some mediators feel that screening for domestic violence and gaining such information is even beyond the scope of the duties of the mediator (Milne 2004).

Another caveat is that empathy often needs to be issued strategically (Benjamin 2004), rather than just simply in a straightforward manner. Strategic empathy allows the mediator the option to not respond empathically at times, if doing so is likely to irretrievably upset the balance of power between the parties. Just as early research on Carl Rogers' "client-centered therapy" demonstrated that subconsciously he was selectively empathizing with certain client feelings and not with others, mediators, too, selectively respond to feelings. A mediator cannot be naively empathic with- out risking escalation of power struggles and conflict.

Mediator neutrality has always been considered a core element of procedural maintenance of any good mediation process. However, in the realm of custody disputes, the fact that the subject of the negotiations is a third, unrepresented party, i.e. the child, creates complexity to this formula. In fact, there is a range of mediator beliefs about this issue. At the one end are those who believe that custody disputes are no different than any other disputes, and that a mediator must always maintain utmost neutrality (Haynes 1988a). At the other end are those who believe that the scope of the child custody mediator includes promoting and even protecting the best interests of the child (Saposnek 2004a).

When a mediator takes the former position, one of the parties may feel that the mediator is siding with the other parent, who is not looking after the child's best interests. When the mediator takes the latter position, one of the parties may feel that the mediator is siding with the other parent who is over-protective of the child and attempting to minimize the child's contact with the one parent. In either case, the nature of custody disputes necessitates the mediator taking a different perspective on power imbalances, and clarifying where he or she stands on the issue of advocacy for the child's best interests. While all would agree that the mediator should remain neutral on process, the crucial question is whether the child custody mediator should also remain neutral on outcome, and if not, whether that hampers global fairness and promotes excessive use of mediator power (Saposnek 1985).

Clients' power

As stated above, clients' sense of self-efficacy in mediation is a function of their perceived power. In custody mediation, with the exception of implicitly understood separate domains of real power in the form of control over the resources (i.e. the "gatekeeper" effect), power is manifested in a number of different ways. The obvious way is the exercise of overt power in the form of raised voices, persistence, intimidation, threats, and over-talking. The less obvious forms include exercising covert power, as in taking a one-down stance, assuming a victim stance, refusing (as in resisting closure of the agreement to symbolically forestall the final divorce event), and manifesting passivity and powerlessness (Watzlawick, Weakland & Fisch 1974). These forms of power are regularly seen in clients, but can also be strategically utilized by mediators (Saposnek 1986) throughout stage T_m. Again, in spite of these functional assertions of power, when asked, each parent almost always maintains the firm belief that the other parent has more power. This phenomenon elicits one of the most intriguing research questions: What is the relationship between the perception of power (locus of control) and actual power in negotiations in T_0 and T_m?

Stages T_1 and T_2

In looking at outcomes of child custody mediation, it would seem that compliance with a parenting plan would be a function of a parent's perceived power and control over the scheduled time with the child(ren) at mediation's end. After all, that is ostensibly why they were in mediation. However, that is not always the case. Sometimes, a parent appears satisfied with the outcome at T_1, but later, at T_2, reports dissatisfaction with the outcome, or reappears for a modification of the schedule. This can be due to countless reasons, each unique to custody mediation. For example: the parents, after leaving mediation, resume their long-standing, interactionally reflexive power struggle, and focus it on their child; the child, post-mediation, may initiate a strategy of his or her own by asking a parent to change the schedule again, tipping the balance established between the parents in mediation and re-creating the disequilibrium that was present prior to mediation; or, an intervening life event (e.g. job change, move away, new partner, school change) creates a new power struggle over the child's schedule.

At other times, compliance with a parenting plan at T_1 does not necessarily mean satisfaction with the plan. There are parents who will concede to the other parent an undesirable, more limited time-sharing schedule with their child and will comply, but will feel very dissatisfied with it all along. The concession is not from lack of a personal sense of power or self-efficacy, but because that parent believes that making the personal sacrifice of less time with their child is in the best interests of the child. That parent may know that fighting for more time may create more inter-parental conflict and may result in the child feeling more "caught in the middle," a status that has been consistently documented by research to be harmful to children (Garrity & Baris 1994).

Thus, compliance (in T_m) may mean giving up part of one's personal power experienced in T_0 and T_m, in order to achieve a more important overall outcome at T_2. This is often based upon the belief that *any* agreement outside of court/ litigation is better for both the parent and the child because of costs and emotional drain, and the mere fact that out-of-court dispute resolution most often reduces the longer-term acrimony and unilateral sabotages so characteristic of litigated custody decisions.

Because of the complexities presented by the very nature of custody disputes, the notion of compliance and satisfaction with an agreement, as well as with the mediator and the process, is qualitatively different than in other disputes. Children and the reorganized family are constantly changing in unpredictable ways, and a parenting plan serves only as a structure for the present. Life-events and a changing emotional climate between the co-parents have the power to necessitate modifications of the parenting plan and to compel the parents back into mediation. While the original issues may have been resolved, new issues are continually coming up as the child grows and changes.

After mediation, some couples are able to resolve future parenting disagreements between themselves (much the way most married parents regularly do), but only in cases in which the relationship between the parents has changed for the positive. This may be partly as a result of mediation, but it is mostly as a result of time passing and chance intervening life-events unfolding in a positive direction. As Irving and Benjamin (1995: 423) point out, an hour or two of mediation is unlikely to "transform intense marital conflict into affectionate cooperation, and intense distress into positive post-divorce family adjustment." This certainly says volumes about what can reasonably be expected from mediation at T_2.

In efforts to minimize dysfunctional power struggles and increase compliance and cooperation at T_2, future research in family mediation needs to explore methods for preventing family conflicts, preparing couples for mediation, screening of cases prior to mediation, and creatively exploring the mediation process, using micro methods such as time-sequence analysis (Becker-Haven 1990), in which the mediation process is broken down within each session into modes of intervention (Saposnek 2004b). Such efforts could lead to better predictability of the short-term (T_1) and long-term (T_2) outcomes. With such knowledge, we will be better able to manage the inherent power dynamics within and create more realistic and successful overall outcomes from the process of family mediation.

References

Ahrons, C. R. & Rodgers, R. H. (1987) *Divorced Families: A Multidisciplinary Developmental View.* Norton, New York.

Aronson, E. (1980) *The Social Animal,* 3rd edn. Freeman, San Francisco.

Becker-Haven, J. (1990) *Modes of Mediating Child Custody Disputes,* Working Paper No. 16. Stanford Center on Conflict and Negotiation, Palo Alto.

Benjamin, R. (2004) Strategies for managing impasses. In J. Folberg, A. L. Milne & P. Salem (eds.), *Divorce and Family Mediation: Models, Techniques, and Applications.* Guilford, New York, pp. 248–279.

Braver, S. L. & Griffin, W. A. (2000) Engaging fathers in the post-divorce family. *Marriage and Family Review* 29(4), 247–267.

Cohen, N., Cowan, P. A. & Cowan, C. P. (2002) *Understanding and Encouraging Fathers' Involvement with their Children: Integrating Research and Intervention*. Final report prepared for the Department of Social Services Office of Child Abuse Prevention, State of California, Sacramento.

Davis, L. (2002) *I Thought We'd Never Speak Again: The Road from Estrangement to Reconciliation*. HarperCollins, New York.

Festinger, L. (1957) *A Theory of Cognitive Dissonance*. Stanford University Press, Stanford.

Folberg, J. & Taylor, A. (1984) *Mediation: A Comprehensive Guide to Resolving Conflicts without Litigation*. Jossey-Bass, San Francisco.

Folberg, J., Milne, A. L. & Salem, P. (eds.) (2004) *Divorce and Family Mediation: Models, Techniques, and Applications*. Guilford, New York.

Friedman, M. (2004) The so-called high-conflict couple: a closer look. *The American Journal of Family Therapy* 32, 101–117. Also in *Family Mediation News* (Summer 2004), Association for Conflict Resolution, Washington, DC.

Garrity, C. B. & Baris, M. A. (1994) *Caught in the Middle: Protecting the Children of High-Conflict Divorce*. Lexington Books, New York.

Haley, J. (1963) *Strategies of Psychotherapy*. Grune & Stratton, New York.

Haynes, J. (1988a) Power balancing. In J. Folberg & A. Milne (eds.), *Divorce Mediation Theory and Practice*. Guilford, New York, pp. 277–296.

Haynes, J. (1988b) John Haynes' segment of *The Case of Willie: Three Mediation Approaches. Donald T. Saposnek, Florence Kaslow, John Haynes* [videotape]. Academy of Family Mediators, Lexington. Available through the Association for Conflict Resolution.

Insabella, G. M., Williams, T. & Pruett, M. K. (2003) Individual and coparenting differences between divorcing and unmarried fathers: implications for family court services. *Family Court Review* 41(3), 290–306.

Irving, H. H. & Benjamin, M. (1995) *Family Mediation: Contemporary Issues*. Sage, Thousand Oaks.

Johnston, J. R. & Campbell, L. E. G. (1988) *Impasses of Divorce: The Dynamics and Resolution of Family Conflict*. Free Press, New York.

Johnston, J. R. & Campbell, L. E. G. (1993). Parent–child relationships in domestic violence families disputing custody. *Family and Conciliation Courts Review* 31, 282–298.

Johnston, J. R. & Roseby, V. (1997) *In the Name of the Child: A Developmental Approach to Understanding and Helping Children of Conflicted and Violent Divorce*. Free Press, New York.

Kelly, J. B. (1995) Power imbalance in divorce and interpersonal mediation: assessment and intervention. *Mediation Quarterly* 13(2), 85–98.

Kelly, J. B. & Emery, R. E. (2003) Children's adjustment following divorce: risk and resilience perspectives. *Family Relations* 52, 352–362.

Lang, M. (2004). Understanding and responding to power in mediation. In J. Folberg, A. L. Milne & P. Salem (eds.), *Divorce and Family Mediation: Models, Techniques, and Applications*. Guilford, New York, pp. 209–224.

Lang, M. & Taylor, A. (2000) *The Making of a Mediator: Developing Artistry in Practice*. Jossey-Bass, San Francisco.

Larson, J. M. (1993) Exploring reconciliation. *Mediation Quarterly* 11(1), 95–106.

Mayer, B. (1987) The dynamics of power in mediation and negotiation. *Mediation Quarterly* 16, 75–86.

Milne, A. (2004) Mediation and domestic abuse. In J. Folberg, A. L. Milne & P. Salem (eds.), *Divorce and Family Mediation: Models, Techniques, and Applications*. Guilford, New York, pp. 304–335.

Mnookin, R. H. & Ross, L. (1999) Introduction. In K. J. Arrow, R. H. Mnookin, L. Ross, A. Tversky & R. B. Wilson (eds.), *Barriers to Conflict Resolution*. PON Books. Cambridge, pp. 3–24.

Moore, C. W. (1996) *The Mediation Process: Practical Strategies for Resolving Conflict*, 2nd edn. Jossey-Bass, San Francisco.

Pleck, J. H. (1997) Paternal involvement; level, sources, and consequences. In M. E. Lamb (ed.), *The Role of the Father in Child Development*, 3rd edn. Wiley, New York, pp. 66–103.

Ricci, I. (1980) *Mom's House, Dad's House*. Macmillan, New York.

Saposnek, D. T. (1983a) *Mediating Child Custody Disputes: A Systematic Guide for Family Therapists, Court Counselors, Attorneys, and Judges*. Jossey-Bass, San Francisco.

Saposnek, D. T. (1983b) Strategies in child custody mediation: a family systems approach. *Mediation Quarterly* 2, 29–54.

Saposnek, D. T. (1985) What is fair in child custody mediation. *Mediation Quarterly* 8, 9–18.

Saposnek, D. T. (1986) Aikido: a systems model for maneuvering in mediation. *Mediation Quarterly* 14–15, 119–136.

Saposnek, D. T. (1998) *Mediating Child Custody Disputes: A Strategic Approach*. Jossey-Bass. San Francisco.

Saposnek, D. T. (2004a) Working with children in mediation. In J. Folberg, A. L. Milne & P. Salem (eds.), *Divorce and Family Mediation: Models, Techniques, and Applications*. Guilford, New York, pp. 155–179.

Saposnek, D. T. (2004b) The future of the history of family mediation. *Conflict Resolution Quarterly* 22(1–2), 37–53.

Shienvold, A. (2004) Hybrid processes. In J. Folberg, A. L. Milne & P. Salem (eds.), *Divorce and Family Mediation: Models, Techniques, and Applications*. Guilford, New York, pp. 112–126.

Watzlawick, P., Weakland, J. H. & Fisch, R. (1974) *Change: Principles of Problem Formation and Problem Resolution*. Norton, New York.

Webster's New World Dictionary of the American Language (1959) The World Publishing Company, New York, p. 1145.

Young, H. P. (1991) *Negotiation Analysis*. University of Michigan Press, Ann Arbor.

Chapter 13

Emotion in Mediation: Implications, Applications, Opportunities, and Challenges

TRICIA S. JONES

INTRODUCTION

Dwayne, 14, was a young boy who had been brought in on charges of vandalizing a neighbor's car. The case was referred to a court-annexed mediation program. The neighbor, an elderly widower, was seeking damages for the vandalism. The intake information was very straightforward. Dwayne and several of his friends had decided one day to "trash" a classic Cadillac convertible that was the neighbor's pride and joy. They broke the windshield, ripped the seats, dented the hood, and scratched along the entire body of the car in several places. In full view of the neighborhood they meticulously ruined a car that the neighbor spent his evenings and weekends washing, waxing, and enjoying.

As the mediation began it was evident that the neighbor was confused about why the entire situation had happened and that Dwayne was having some intense emotions about the situation. During the opening statement it also became clear that the neighbor, an elderly gentleman in his eighties, was hard of hearing. As this became evident, Dwayne's sullen and angry face changed to one of bewilderment, recognition, and finally remorse. Dwayne had not known the neighbor could not hear. And there was something in that realization for Dwayne that fundamentally shifted his feeling about the situation and his role in it. In a moment, the landscape of the mediation had changed from a property conflict to an emotional conflict in a very specific relational context. The mediation conversation became an opportunity for Dwayne to explain that the vandalism of the car was his retaliation for the disrespect he and his friends had felt from the neighbor who had repeatedly "ignored" their attempts to say hello or engage in conversation as he waxed his car. They felt angry and humiliated (although Dwayne didn't use this language) and they felt justified in hurting what they knew the man valued most. But with the realization that the man had not been intentionally ignoring them, Dwayne saw his error. The rest of the mediation became a discussion between the neighbor and Dwayne about their neighborhood – how to make it better. They didn't negotiate about property values or restitution plans, but they did work out an arrangement for Dwayne to regularly help the neighbor with housework or car washing or whatever needed to be done. From a bargaining point of view the details of the agreement were sketchy to say the least. But when attempts to suggest the need for more clarity were not productive, it became clear that their work was done from their point of view.

Most mediators tell similar stories about mediations that seem more about feelings than facts; mediations that turn on an emotional fulcrum not well explained by mediation theory derived from rationalistic approaches to negotiation. Mediation theory has become more complex and focused on the role of emotion, especially in the past five years. But there is much more theory and research needed to develop a thorough understanding of emotion in the mediation process.

This chapter argues for a communication perspective on emotion in mediation to extend beyond heavily psychological orientations dominating recent emotion and negotiation theory and research. The implications of emotion for mediation are discussed in a brief overview of the nature of emotion and the centrality of emotion in conflict and mediation. Applications and opportunities are addressed by detailing ways in which mediators can improve their ability to identify disputants' critical identity-based emotions, use elicitive questioning to help disputants achieve a better understanding of their emotional experience underlying the conflict, and help disputants formulate reappraisals that change their emotional experience of the conflict. Opportunities come with challenges, and those challenges are introduced in the last section of the chapter, including consideration of strategic or manipulative emotional expression and cultural differences in emotional experience and expression.

CENTRALITY OF EMOTION IN CONFLICT AND MEDIATION

Scholarship on emotion wrestles with the definition of this complex phenomenon; but most scholars agree that emotion involves three components – cognitive, physiological, and behavioral (Kitayama & Marcus 1994). In this way, emotion is distinct from affect, mood, and feelings. Feelings are sensations that do not necessarily have cognitive components (Damasio 1994). Moods are distinguished from emotions in terms of duration and intensity, with moods being of longer duration and significantly less intensity (Morris 1992). Affect is the most general of the terms, encompassing the other three (Batson, Shaw & Oleson 1992). Although some negotiation theory and research concentrates on the impact of affect (and that literature will be noted later), this chapter focuses on emotion in mediation because of the more sophisticated information value and strategic potential in emotion than its less cognitive counterparts.

Emotion is an event rather than a thing, which contributes to the difficulty in studying it, measuring it, or manipulating it. Planalp (1999) explains the basic components of the emotion process. First there are objects, causes, or eliciting events – the something that emotion is about. The object is appraised or evaluated, producing the emotional experience in response to this situation, person, or event. The emotional experience also produces physiological changes, somatic reactions, which many scholars argue are the body's way of preparing for the next step of the process – action tendencies. Action tendencies are the motivation to express the emotion or behave in a certain way. Regulation is the ability to decide whether or not to engage in the action tendencies.

A debate still in progress is the extent of social and cultural influence on the nature of emotion. This chapter agrees with a "weak constructivist" position articulated by Oatley (1993) that acknowledges the biological/physiological dimensions of emotion (conceding the existence of a limited range of natural emotional responses), but emphasizes the extent to which emotions, even those that may be considered primary, are socially constructed or modified in action and interpretation (Shweder 1993).

Emotions can be seen as socially shared scripts that are culturally determined to some extent (Kitayama & Markus 1994). Functionally speaking, emotion scripts are used by social actors to define reality and negotiate it with others. Hochschild (1983) argues that emotions are the means through which people know the social world and their relation to it. As Duncombe and Marsden (1996) recently argued, people are able to participate in emotional lives because they have the ability to construct narratives of the self through discourse. The relationship between discourse and individual emotional behavior is the way they undertake "emotion work" to conform to or resist the ideologies that cultures have about emotion.

Jones (2000) argues that emotional communication is the essence of conflict interaction; that the triggering events that cause conflict are, by definition, events leading to appraisals resulting in perceptions of negative emotional experience. Conflict occurs when people perceive incompatible goals or interference from the other (Wilmot & Hocker 1998). Perceived interruption of plans and/or perceived discrepancies between our goals and reality are the things most identified as emotion-eliciting (Ortony, Clore & Collins 1988). Since the triggers of emotion and the triggers of perceived conflict are the same, to recognize that someone is in conflict is to acknowledge that he has been triggered emotionally. The implications of this principle for mediation are clear. Because the trigger for the dispute is inherently emotional, in uncovering the nature of the dispute the mediator is by necessity and without exception accessing emotional information. To gain a full understanding of a conflict (or the relational tensions, interests in the dispute, underlying concerns, opposing positions, etc.) mediators must attend to the emotional triggers that influenced how the disputants recognized and defined the conflict, and which emotion scripts they invoked (whether or not the disputants are even aware that they did so). Thus, mediators must undergo a profound shift in their thinking about emotion in mediation. Rather than seeing emotion as a side-effect of a conflict, mediators should appreciate emotion as a frame for the conflict, as a social construction through which the disputant defines the conflict reality.

A second key principle is that emotion morally frames conflict (Jones 2000). As others have argued, emotional experience is fundamentally moral. Values impact the experience of emotions, and emotions reveal underlying values (Manstead 1991).

People perceive a conflict because something has happened that seems "wrong," and they are not comfortable leaving or dispensing with the conflict until things have been made "right," or they have changed assumptions about the seriousness of the moral or normative violation occurring. Understanding emotional communication as a lens onto the ideology and morality of disputants enables a mediator to understand the emotional response of the disputant as a moral framing of issues and options. The mediator can better appreciate the possibilities of resolution and how those possibilities need to be presented to the parties to increase the potential for acceptance. Rhetorical presentation that does not resonate with the ideological frames in use by the disputants is likely to be disregarded out of hand. Other scholars have noted that understanding the moral dimensions of conflict is necessary for the creation of a "transcendent dialog" in which disputants not only learn to reflect on their own ideology, but become willing to entertain moral shifts in order to resolve conflict (Pearce & Littlejohn 1997).

The third principle of emotional communication in conflict states that emotional communication reflects core identity issues that impact conflict dynamics (Jones 2000; Jones & Bodtker 2001). Many scholars have explained the fundamental role of identity in conflict, and particularly in escalatory and intractable conflicts (Northrup 1989). Insults to identity can take precedence over economic value in conflict, leading disputants to reject economically superior outcomes if they come with too high an "identity" cost (Pillutla & Murnighan 1996).

Two theories of emotion emphasize the relationship of emotion and identity, Kemper's theory of emotion and power relations and Affect Control Theory. Kemper's (1978, 1993) theory of emotion gives primacy to the role of identity, in terms of perceived status and power. Kemper isolates two underlying relational themes: control of one member by another (power) and degree of positive social relations (status). In a dyadic relationship, four possibilities exist for each member: a person can feel that s/he: (1) has claimed or acquired an excess of power in the relationship; (2) has claimed or acquired an excess of status in the relationship; (3) has insufficient power in the relationship; or (4) receives insufficient status in the relationship. Kemper (1978: 37) explains:

> Since deficit of own power (or excess of other's power) is the social relational condition for fear or anxiety, and since loss of customary, expected, or deserved status (other as agent) is the basic relational condition for anger, it seems entirely compatible to suppose that specific social relational conditions are accompanied by specific physiological reactions, with the felt emotions as the psychological mediators between the two.

Affect Control Theory provides a formal model of emotions, behavior, and identity shifts during social interaction (Smith-Lovin & Heise 1988). According to this theory, emotions provide information about both the identity of an emoting actor and how well current social events are confirming that identity. When actors perform valued identities well they experience positive emotion (Stryker 1980). Actors can avoid or mitigate identity damage resulting from inappropriate behaviors by displaying certain emotions (e.g. remorse). Alternately, actors can expose their identities to social damage by displaying inappropriate affect while behaving otherwise normatively. Robinson and Smith-Lovin (1999) found that, in experimentally manipulated interactions, display of emotions that are affectively congruent with behaviors can reduce damage to identity from harmful behaviors and that the display of incongruent emotions can spoil identity.

In related research, Beersma, Harinck, and Gerts (2003) investigated the impact of insults on emotional response and conflict behavior in workplace conflict among people who are sensitive to threats to identity (discussed as honor sensitivity). They argued that reputation is a highly salient dimension of the self for those with high honor values.

According to Rodriguez Mosquera (1999: 13), honor "has to be socially claimed and recognized in order to have any value. When the self is humiliated or offended during a conflict, a person's claim to honor and to be treated with respect is denied" (Rodriguez Mosquera 1999: 13). Conflicts make defending or restoring one's honor salient. In honor cultures, honor can be defended or restored through actions such as aggression or expressions of anger. Therefore, individuals who attach much value to honor are likely to react to conflicts in a more aggressive manner than those who attach less value to honor (Rodriquez Mosquera, Manstead & Fisher 2000, 2002).

One way that a person may damage identity or "lose honor" in conflict is to be treated in a manner considered unfair or unjust. To the extent that a person is targeted for unjust treatment, and to the extent that s/he cannot retaliate or remediate the inequity, s/he suffers identity damage likely to result in negative emotional experiences that motivate the escalation of dysfunctional conflict behaviors. Homans (1974) argued that people treated fairly will experience positive emotions; but those who are under-rewarded will feel anger and those over-rewarded will feel guilty. His arguments have been confirmed in a variety of investigations of interpersonal relations (Gray-Little & Teddlie 1978; Hegtvedt 1990; Sprecher 1992). In conflict contexts, Hegtvedt and Killian (1999) examined how perceptions of procedural and distributive justice in negotiation influence emotional reactions to the process and the final outcome distribution. Using data from questionnaire responses provided by subjects in a computerized experiment, they found that perceived procedural justice enhances positive feelings about the negotiation and decreases depression over outcomes. The more a negotiation is viewed as fair, the more likely are expressions of pleasure and the less likely are expressions of negative feelings.

The application of these insights about emotion and identity in mediation should be obvious. The disputants' emotional responses in mediation reveal identity needs and face concerns to which mediators must be sensitive. Identity threats stimulate defensiveness that escalates conflicts (Rubin, Pruitt & Kim 1994). Threats to identity also invoke shame-based cycles that are difficult to circumvent, yet without circumvention often lead to spiraling unresolved shame and anger combinations (Retzinger 1991). Emotional communication, especially in mediation involving intimate partners, reveals much about the power and status expectations in the relationship that influence opportunities for resolution. Mediators who operate from a relational orientation assume that, in mediation, understanding emotion provides understanding of how parties have currently defined their relationship and how motivated they are to retain that definition or change it (Bush & Folger 2004).

RECENT ADVANCES IN NEGOTIATION LITERATURE

Conlon and Hunt (2002: 54–55) recently stated a conclusion concerning the need for negotiation theorists and researchers to embrace emotion more seriously:

> everyday negotiations are inherently much messier and more difficult to rationalize than the kinds of formal, economically-driven negotiations on which much of our current knowledge is based. Though it may be possible in some circumstances to formalize the outcomes of negotiations in quantitative terms, such as when negotiating a sales contract or collective bargaining agreement, more often than not it is infeasible to do so. Even in situations where some of the potential outcomes can be quantified, there are also likely to be other outcomes which are no less important, but are much more difficult to quantify . . . rather than simply trying to ignore or eliminate affect, it behooves us to try to find ways to help negotiators deal with it emotionally more effectively, both in themselves and in others.

In the past decade, other negotiation scholars have also noted the need for models of negotiation that include affect and emotion, and research that answers critical questions about emotion as an independent, intervening, and dependent variable in the process (Davidson & Greenhalgh 1999; Thompson, Nadler & Kim 1999). The motivation to attend to emotion has been enhanced by broader arguments of the role of emotion in social exchange processes and social formations. Lawler and Thye (1999), in an extensive review of the role of emotion in social exchange theories, identify six meta-theories of emotion, two for each facet of the exchange process – context, process, and outcome – that offer significant insight for exchange. Other scholars have argued that emotion in conflict has potential to impact on subsequent relations – both with the same partners and with others (Frank 1991).

Initial interest was in the general role of positive or negative affect in negotiation, with research supporting the assumption that positive affect generally made negotiators more cooperative and negative affect made negotiators more competitive (Isen, Daubman & Nowicki 1987; Baron 1990; Baron et al. 1990), although some research did not confirm this tendency (Weitzman 1996). This work was followed by a series of general reviews and proposed models of the role of affect in negotiation or organizational conflict.

Barry and Oliver (1996) presented a model of affect in negotiation detailing anticipatory affect (the affect experienced as one anticipates the nature of the upcoming negotiation), experienced affect (affect during the negotiation in response to tactics like offers and concessions) and post-negotiation affect (affect in response to outcomes and possible future or continuing interaction). Kumar (1997) emphasized a negotiator's regard for his or her opponent and perceived fairness of negotiation. He suggested that positive affect can promote persistence – a willingness of parties to keep working through things – and that negative affect may functionally signal a need for change. Lawler and Yoon (1995) describe how repeated negotiations between individuals can create positive feelings that increase their emotional commitment to the partner and motivate negotiators to a more relationship-driven approach. Thompson and her colleagues (1999) discussed the role of both experienced and expressed affect in negotiation processes.

Recently, more attention has been given to theory and research on the role of specific emotions, with the majority of attention given to anger. Baron and colleagues (Baron et al. 1990) demonstrated that anger could be reduced in negotiation by inducing an incompatible emotional state such as sympathy. Allred, Mallozzi, Matsui, and Raia (1997) found that negotiators who felt high anger and low compassion for their opponents achieved lower joint gains and had less of a desire to work together in the future. Allred (1999, 2000) has recently concentrated on developing his model of anger-driven retaliatory conflict based on attribution theory and cognitive appraisal theories of emotion, a model that is discussed in more detail in later sections of this chapter. These models extend earlier attribution models of the role of emotion in conflict (Betancourt & Blair 1992) and the tendency of negative emotion and negative attribution to create escalatory cycles in conflict (Pruitt, Parker & Mikolic 1997; O'Connor & Arnold 2001).

Van Kleef, De Dreu and Manstead (2004a, 2004b) investigated the interpersonal effects of anger and happiness in computer-mediated negotiations. In the course of a computer-mediated negotiation, participants received information about the emotional state (anger, happiness, or neither) of their opponent. Through a series of experiments participants conceded more to an angry opponent than to a happy one; and this effect was due to participants using the emotion information to infer the other's limit, and adjusting their demands accordingly. Angry communications (unlike happy ones) induced fear and thereby mitigated the effect of the opponent's experienced emotion. These results suggest that negotiators are especially influenced by their opponent's emotions when they are motivated to care about the other's emotional state and able to attend to the emotional cues. These authors do caution that the relationship between anger and negotiation response is mediated by a negotiator's need for cognitive closure, time pressure, and the opponent's perceived power. Sinaceur and Tiedens (2004) examined the effects of anger in face-to-face negotiations and reported that participants conceded more to an angry as opposed to a non-emotional counterpart. This body of research reports the same basic effect of anger on negotiation in face-to-face and computer-mediated interactions.

Similar effects have been found in studies involving negotiators from different cultures. Chiongbian's (2001) research examined whether US and Filipino negotiators who felt very angry and less compassionate would create fewer joint gains, claim a greater proportion of the joint gains, and have less of a desire to work with each other in the future. The results confirmed that European American and Filipino negotiators who judged the other party to be responsible for a negative act felt angry and less compassionate toward the other party, and that angry and less compassionate negotiators had less of a desire to work with each other in the future. Contrary to expectations, angry and less compassionate negotiators did not create less value, nor did they claim a greater proportion of the joint gains.

Less attention has been paid to applying some of these research findings to negotiation practice, though several scholars have begun that conversation. Adler, Rosen, and Silverstein (1998) provided specific recommendations for negotiators about how to manage emotions such as fear and anger during negotiation. Thompson et al. (1999), in contrast to the traditional view of emotion as a detriment to effective negotiation, encourage negotiators to engage in strategies including emotional tuning, neutralizing emotions, buffering emotions, and normalizing emotions. And Gray (2003) argues that effective negotiators know how to handle emotional outbursts, including how to respond when the other negotiator evokes their "nemesis." Shapiro (2004) has argued that negotiators should understand the relationship between emotion, autonomy, and affiliation, and learn to use emotion strategically to balance autonomy and affiliation needs as well as address more instrumental aspects of conflict.

RECENT ADVANCES IN MEDIATION

Much less theory and research has been produced concerning the role of emotions in mediation. To confirm this basic conclusion, revisit chapter 2 of this volume provided by Herrman, Hollett, and Gale. In their exhaustive review of research on interpersonal mediation they have few references to research that has examined emotion in mediation. Clearly, their model offers the opportunity for this important work to be included, but their review of the literature testifies to the absence of serious attention to emotion.

Only two studies have actually investigated how emotion may impact the mediation process or perceptions of mediation. Thompson and Kim (2000) demonstrated that negotiators' expressed emotions could impact the ability of third parties (e.g. mediators) to develop accurate perceptions of the negotiators' interests and intentions. Friedman, Anderson, Brett, Olekalns, Goates, and Lisco (2004) argued that anger expressed by participants in mediation may be counterproductive or productive. The authors tested these competing theories of emotion by using data from actual online mediations. Results showed that the expression of anger lowers the resolution rate in mediation and that this effect occurs in part because expressing anger generates an angry response by the other party.

Several popular books on conflict practice and mediation have argued for more attention to be given to emotion (Cloke 2001; LeBaron 2002; Bush & Folger 2004) yet none of them acknowledges the theoretical body of scholarship on emotion and seriously applies that knowledge to the mediation process or intervention. Their consideration of emotion depends on a predominantly "lay" understanding of emotion, which provides some insights, but is not sufficient to build theory or guide research on this phenomenon.

Jones and Bodtker (2001) discuss the potential application of a number of social science theories of emotion to mediation processes. They argue that mediators should be aware of important theory and research on emotional expression, the physiological component of emotion, and the cognitive processes of emotion. They articulate a variety of practice implications from these theories and argue for much more complex renderings of the role of emotion in mediation. Other mediation practitioners have called for more emphasis on emotion in mediation training (Lund 2000), family mediation practice (Parkinson 2000), and even public policy mediation applications (Podziba 2003).

The Need for a Communication Perspective

Communication scholars explore mediation as the social construction of meaning that is contextually impacted and creates a foundation for current and continuing relationships. As noted by Folger and Jones (1994: ix), "central to a communication perspective is the realization that conflict is a socially created and communicatively managed reality occurring within a socio-historical context." They describe three principles guiding a communication perspective. First, a communication perspective draws from a pragmatic and interpretive meta-theory, and attends to the microanalysis of verbal and non-verbal communication in order to examine the various patterns of process over time. Second, there is an appreciation of the social construction of meaning and interpretive structures as well as the continuous interplay between text and context. This does not mean that a communication perspective dismisses information that can be obtained from other perspectives, such as sociological or psychological approaches to mediation. It does mean that these insights are blended in an interaction frame to understand how psychological and sociological processes inform and influence the social construction of meaning through communication. Third, this perspective places discursive structures and features (the who, what, and how of conversational interactions) as primary skills for intervention and conflict management as well as analysis.

A communication perspective provides an effective way to study emotion in mediation and a powerful framework from which to consider practice interventions. There are four reasons why a communication perspective offers value for the consideration of emotion in mediation. First, as mentioned earlier, emotion is socially constructed and implemented through a variety of behavioral expressions impacted by culture and context. The perspective on the phenomenon should be congruent with the nature of the phenomenon; thus, a perspective that highlights the expressive component of emotion is critical.

Second, as conflict theorists know, and as negotiation theorists have recently advocated, the intrapersonal work on emotion in conflict is important but not sufficient. An interpersonal focus that examines the interplay of emotional experience and expression as an unfolding dynamic between disputants is required (Barry 1999).

Third, mediation is not well represented by perspectives or methodologies that isolate and reduce aspects of the process while trying to understand the underpinnings. For example, many mediation scholars agree with the argument that mediation is the production and management of narrative (Cobb 1994) even if they do not subscribe to a specific "narrative approach to mediation" (e.g. Winslade & Monk 2000). Cobb's early explanation of mediation as narrative "permanently *includes* the mediator as a co-participant in both the construction and the transformation of conflict narratives" (1994: 61–62), and "*requires* attention to narrative politics; as they unfold, some stories become dominant, others can be marginalized" (1994: 52). Emotional communication is essential to the telling of the story in mediation, and provides mediators with insights into the nature and felt experience behind the story.

Fourth, whether or not mediators want to attend to emotion, it is inevitable that the emotion is impacting not only a disputant's individual orientation and behavior, but the relationship in and beyond the mediation. Collins (1981, 1989, 1993) proposes that, in interaction rituals, at least two people who have a mutual focus infuse the interaction with emotional energy. This energy affects relational structure and stability, such that interactants will have enhanced social solidarity if they experience a common mood or emotion, and these feelings strengthen over time. Likewise, Kemper (1993) argues that the ritual nature of emotion in all interactions provides a particularly strong impact on the formation of group identity and social bonds. His theory of interaction situation chains attempts to link the micro-interaction at the group level with the macro social structures through the use of emotional energy.

EMOTION IN THE MEDIATION PROCESS

Chapter 2 of this volume provides a model of interpersonal mediation that should be reconsidered before discussing more specific foci on emotion in mediation process. In this chapter, Herrman, Hollett, and Gale distinguish between antecedent and process components of mediation. Daniel L. Shapiro (chapter 14) offers a valuable assessment of possible pre-mediation interventions to address emotional issues. The remainder of this chapter will be concerned with addressing emotional issues during the mediation process (T_m).

As Herrman et al. note, "mediators must create environments where dialogs, problem analysis, and problem-solving take place", which requires creating and supporting "trust, empathy, and rapport between participants" (p. 32). Among the key variables they define for "factors that prime personal readiness," the first dimension of the T_m stage, are several that are strongly related to effective emotional communication in mediation: *mediator empathy, feeling heard and understood, being able to talk about perceptions and feelings,* and *perceived self-efficacy.* Mediator empathy and being heard and understood require an appreciation of the disputants' emotions; without emotional communication there is no basis for either of these accomplishments. Obviously, to talk about perceptions and feelings, the mediator should know how to help the disputants talk about feelings, which will be discussed later as elicitive questioning to uncover emotion. And uncovering emotional experience as a basis for the conflict leads to perceived self-efficacy, especially in the facilitating reappraisal process as discussed later.

The second dimension of the T_m stage, procedural factors, also contains elements related to emotion: *global fairness, interactional fairness,* and *mediator neutrality* (in mediation conditions); and *talking about issues and needs* and *formulating* (in problem-solving). Earlier the link between perceived fairness, identity, and emotion was articulated. The more disputants perceive the mediation process and outcome as fair, the less likely they are to perceive harms to identity that create negative emotions which fuel dysfunctional behavior. As already mentioned, procedures that help disputants talk through issues and needs and formulate options for the conflict are the same processes that will be discussed as uncovering emotion and facilitating reappraisal. Although these processes can be done with attention to only the "facts" and "data" (indeed, the fact that mediators can do this is a criticism of all standard models of mediation training and practice), this chapter argues that these processes are inherently more effective when done with attention to emotional experience and emotional communication.

In the next section, three mediation skills are presented which provide ways to attend to and intervene with emotion in mediation. The first skill concerns a mediator's ability to "read" or decode the emotional experience of the other, and depends on an increased awareness of emotional communication cues. The second skill involves a mediator's ability to help the disputants articulate and understand their own emotional experiences through the process of elicitive questioning. And the third skill, facilitating reappraisal, is the mediator's ability to use non-directive questioning to help a disputant identify options that will move them past the emotional experience that is blocking them from managing the conflict.

Mediator Decoding: Three Critical Emotions

Mediators are traditionally not well prepared to identify a variety of emotion cues, such as those Planalp (1998, 1999) identifies: facial cues, vocal cues, physiological cues (the kinds of physical responses we see in high arousal states like sweating, nervous movement, twitching, etc.); gestures and body movements, and action cues (like physical activity – running, hiding, walking, singing); and verbal cues (emotion-laden terms, figurative language, word choice and language intensity). Without adequate sensitivity to verbal and nonverbal cues of emotion, mediators forgo essential information about the dispute.

Fussell's (2002) recent edited volume offers an overview of the current state of knowledge about the verbal communication of emotion. While emotional expression has traditionally been studied in terms of nonverbal cues, with heaviest emphasis on facial affect cues (Ekman & Friesen 1975), nonverbal channels alone are not sufficient for full understanding. Nonverbal cues do not signal the cognitive processes leading to the emotional experience, and cannot communicate about emotions

of the past and expected emotions of the future. Past events are particularly important in recounting experiences leading to a present understanding of a dispute.

Mediators are faced with a truly daunting task. They need to focus on emotional
communication markers offered by disputants in an attempt to identify the
emotional experience of the disputants and determine whether that emotional
experience requires or gives the opportunity for further intervention. Identity-
related emotions, or self-conscious emotions, as Lewis (1993) has labeled them,
are the most critical for discovery given the primacy of identity threats in conflict
escalation.

In this section we will share an introduction to verbal and nonverbal communication markers of three identity-related emotions: anger, contempt, and shame.
The exclusive focus on these emotions does not mean that other emotions are
unimportant in mediation. However, these three identity-based emotions have
been studied in more detail and have more elaborated marker systems than
many others. Put simply, they are not the only emotions that mediators should be
attending to, but they are emotions that have proven, generalized markers that
mediators can be trained to recognize, with understandable limits of efficacy.

Anger

As noted earlier, anger is the most researched emotion in the conflict literature.
Appraisal theories of emotion generally agree that anger is a response to perceived
injustice or intentional identity threat (Canary, Spitzberg & Semic 1998). Anger
happens when some rule or normative standard has been broken (Averill 1982),
and anger signals a needed change in current relational or instrumental circumstances (Daly 1991).

In the context of negotiation, Allred's (1999, 2000) model of anger-retaliatory
dynamics explains that people suffer from accuser bias and bias of the accused when
making attributions about the other which leads them to make assessments that
generate anger and retaliation cycles. Using one of Allred's (2000) examples:

- some harmful behavior occurs (Robin requests that Peg come in to work on a
  weekend)
- the accuser (Peg) perceives this in a biased way
- Peg assigns the responsibility for the harmful behavior to Robin
- Peg gets angry
- Peg retaliates (Peg tells Robin she needs to be more organized)
- the accused (Robin) perceives this from her bias
- Robin makes the judgment that she is not responsible for the harmful behavior
  so the retaliation is not fair
- Robin gets angry
- Robin counter-retaliates (Robin leaves Peg to finish the work by herself).

For Allred (2000), the key to understanding the cycle is to understand the
attributions being made by each disputant and the specific biases in attribution

processes that trigger anger, attributed responsibility, and justificatory retaliation. Not surprisingly, when Allred addresses how this anger-retaliation model may give insights into training interventions for negotiators or mediators, he suggests interventions that largely educate about attributional biases and how to overcome them. Among his suggested practice applications are:

1 Alternatives to venting anger: training people to reduce their attributional biases, and to be better able to take the perspective of the other (thus gaining a better understanding of their motivations and generating more unbiased assessments of the other).
2 Having mediators intervene when they detect an accuser bias at work; trying to help the accuser see this bias and entertain other possible explanations for the behavior.
3 Teaching someone alternative responses even in situations of justifiable anger.
4 Teaching reflective techniques that help people take more responsibility for their own behavior.
5 Encouraging the use of apology or explanation to mitigate anger of the other.

The applicability of Allred's model and practice prescriptions becomes stronger if mediators can identify specific verbal and nonverbal cues that signal anger. Communication scholars have attended to this more detailed level of analysis in several conflict practice contexts. In general, communication researchers have developed taxonomies of verbal markers of hostility in which anger displays figure prominently. Intense language usage has been found to mark the hostility or aggressiveness of a particular conflict and to indicate a person's emotional state during a disagreement (Donohue 1991; Gayle & Preiss 1998). Zwaal, Prkachin, Husted and Stones (2003) examined whether hostile people differ from non-hostile people on measures of emotional verbal behavior using the *Dictionary of Affect in Language*, which emphasizes use of activation and evaluation words as verbal markers of anger and hostility. Rogan (1995) investigated the intensity of conflict interactions using a measure of language intensity to examine transcripts of hostage negotiations. Among the markers of language intensity correlated with hostility and anger are:

1 Obscure words, including the use of uncommon words or phrases.
2 General metaphors, including words or phrases that took some effort to transfer their denotative meaning from the meaning conventionally associated with the terms.
3 Qualifying adjectives or adverbs, including words that modified other words by accenting the meaning of the first term.
4 Profanity or sex-based statements, including any language that approached the bounds of good taste.
5 Deathbed statements, including terms usually associated with death, decomposition, or afterlife, used metaphorically.
6 Written emphasis, including words that were underlined, enlarged, or emphasized by punctuation such as exclamation points or quotes.

Shaver, Schwartz, Kirkson, and O'Connor (1987) did a study to identify the ways in which we express anger. They found six clusters of angry behaviors ranging across verbal and nonverbal marker sets:

1 *Verbal attacks*, e.g. obscenities, cursing, verbally attacking the cause of the anger; yelling, loud voice, screaming, shouting, complaining.
2 *Physical attacks*, e.g. hands and fists clenched; aggressive, threatening gestures; attacking something other than the cause of anger; incoherent, out of control, emotional behavior.
3 *Nonverbal disapproval*, e.g. heavy walk, stomping; tightness in body; nonverbal demonstrations like slamming doors; frowning, mean or unpleasant facial expression; gritting and showing teeth; flushed face.
4 *Uneasiness*, e.g. crying; feelings of nervousness, anxiety, discomfort.
5 *Internal withdrawal*, e.g. brooding, withdrawing from situation; narrowing of attention to all but anger situation, obsessing, and
6 *Avoidance*, e.g. suppressing the anger, trying not to show or express anger.

Many of the nonverbal markers of anger noted by Shaver et al. (1987) have been studied as triggering events in escalatory conflict cycles (Worcel, Shields & Paterson 1999).

Given the range and detail of known anger markers, mediators can be trained to be more sensitive to disputants' experience and expression of anger. Understanding these markers can help mediators monitor levels of anger and identify issues that need to be discussed more thoroughly to understand the causes of anger. Finally, mediators' knowledge of anger markers is relevant for the identification of anger, but it is also helpful in the initial identification of other emotions. As Canary et al. (1998) state, anger is often a secondary emotion in the sense that it is the emotion we are more likely to experience and show in public even though it stems from other underlying emotional experiences like shame, guilt, and fear.

Contempt

Even with the renaissance of emotion scholarship in the social sciences, contempt remains the least studied emotion. That oversight is considerable given the conceptual and practical significance of contempt in conflict.

Izard (1977) describes contempt as a basic feeling of superiority over others and considers it the primary emotion fueling prejudice against groups thought to be inferior to one's own. Ortony et al. (1988) define contempt as a reproach emotion under the purview of attributions made about the other. Specifically, as figure 13.1 suggests, they argue that we make attributions about self and other that result in either positive (e.g. pride/admiration) or negative (e.g. shame/reproach) emotions.

The primary reproach emotions are contempt, disdain, and indignation. Although Ortony et al. (1988) define contempt as a response to the action of another, it can also be a response to an inherent characteristic of the other. Despite its appearance

Identity of agent	Praiseworthy appraisal of agent's action	Blameworthy appraisal of agent's action
Self	Approving of one's own praiseworthy action resulting in PRIDE emotions	Disapproving of one's own blameworthy actions resulting in SHAME emotions
Other	Approving of another's praiseworthy action resulting in ADMIRATION emotions	Disapproving of another's blameworthy action resulting in REPROACH emotions

FIGURE 13.1   Appraisals of agent-oriented emotions

on most "basic emotions" lists, there hasn't been nearly as much agreement on the expressive component of contempt as there has been for other basic emotions. Many researchers believe there is a universal facial expression for the emotion of contempt (Ekman & Friesen 1975). Like other emotions, the communication of contempt is not limited to facial displays. In some cultures there are unique emblems of contempt (Miller 1997). More generally, we can express contempt for others by engaging in acts that are intended to belittle and degrade them, to "put them in their place." There are two ways that contempt may be communicated: territorial intrusions, and threat displays.

- *Territorial intrusions.* Standing too close, touching, staring, shouting, and so on do not in themselves communicate contempt. But when the intruder disregards the negative signals of the other, the intruder's behavior becomes contemptuous.
- *Threat displays.* Some actions imply that the other disputant need not be taken seriously (or even needs help, as when overly supportive behaviors signal condescension), for example, rolling one's eyes, speaking very slowly as though the other can't understand, using insultingly simplistic language.

Less attention has been given to verbal forms of contempt. However, Gottman (1994) distinguishes characteristics of complaint, criticism, and contempt statements. While a complaint is a specific statement of anger, displeasure, distress, or other negativity, it is focused on a specific action or lack of action (e.g. "I am upset because you didn't take out the garbage tonight"). A criticism tends to be global and includes blaming the partner (e.g. "You never take out the garbage because you are lazy"). Contempt adds insult to the criticism: it is verbal character assassination (e.g. "You idiot, why can't you ever remember to take out the garbage?"). What separates contempt from criticism is the intention to insult and psychologically abuse the other, to "put them down." The most common verbal markers of contempt are insults and name-calling, hostile humor, and open mockery.

In conflict, displays of disrespect, or intentional demonstrations of perceived superiority can be linked with explosive, destructive escalatory cycles (Jones & Remland

1993; Remland, Jones & Brown 1994). Contempt fuels conflict by heightening identity damage (Haviland & Kalbaugh 1993). Predictably, contempt displays are often linked with shame cycles in conflict. As Lewis (1993) argues, the link between contempt and shame can be very important for group and interpersonal conflict. Does being treated with contempt cause shame? It may if we accept the evaluation of others and use it as a metric by which we see ourselves lacking in our general ability to meet expectations. If being treated contemptuously results in shame, it may result in shame reparation cycles discussed in detail by Retzinger (1991) and reported in the next section.

The exercise of contempt in mediation is even more dangerous than contempt in dyadic conflict. When a disputant behaves contemptuously in mediation the identity damage inflicted on the other is done in public, increasing the potential for embarrassment and discomfort. And if a mediator chooses to disregard the contemptuous display (for whatever reason), the target of contempt is likely to feel the display is being excused and possibly even endorsed by the mediator.

Shame

Retzinger and Scheff (2000) have contributed the most thorough understanding of the dynamics of shame in conflict. They have a taxonomy of shame markers for shame identification in mediation, and have explained how mediators can intervene in shame repair cycles, a dynamic they have discussed in detail over the past decade or so (Retzinger 1991; Scheff 1990, 1997). The basis of the shame-repair model is that: (1) the social bond is threatened, usually by some disrespectful behavior; (2) shame signals disrupt the bonding; (3) shame is denied (not acknowledged), leading to feelings of alienation and perceptions of the other as attacker; and (4) anger follows as a signal of degree of threat and as a means of saving face and perhaps repairing the bond (Lewis 1976). The cycle is exacerbated if the anger signals are not attended to by the other. This lack of attention is seen as further disrespect. However, if anger is attended to, the shame can be reduced and the bonds repaired (Retzinger 1991). The real key is that the shame component is often hidden from self and other. It is the hidden shame that does the damage, because, as long as it is hidden, there is no possibility for repairing the damaged bonds. It is the denial of emotion and the resulting alienation that lead to intractable conflict.

In mediation, Retzinger and Scheff (2000) argue that one way to impact entrenched narratives is to express hidden emotions underlying the narrative. "To begin to resolve a stuck conflict, mediators must help the clients acknowledge, or acknowledge for them, at least a small part of their alienation and hidden emotions in a way that leaves some of their dignity in tact" (Retzinger & Scheff 2000: 78). They argue that most disputants omit their emotions from their narratives. Disputants give facts in chronology but not the emotional experience behind them. The mediator's basic task is to help disputants formulate their stories, complete with emotional underpinnings, then be sure that these complete stories are heard and acknowledged. Even if the disputants cannot completely hear each other's stories, it is critical that the mediator hear and acknowledge them.

Mediators need special training to detect shame because it is so often hidden, disguised, or denied. Shame may occur in the overt form or the bypassed form. In the overt type there is obvious emotional pain, but it is misnamed as something else: "hurt, insulted, a failure." With the bypassed form there is little or no emotional pain evident. Instead, there is obsessive rumination, incessant talk, or hyperactivity. Bypassing seems to be the primary form used by men. In their mediation trainings, Retzinger and Scheff (2000: 82–84) use the following list of verbal and nonverbal markers of shame to help mediators see shame in action:

1   *Verbal markers*: alienation terms (rejected, dumped, deserted, rebuffed, abandoned); confusion terms (stunned, dazed, blank, empty, hollow); ridiculous terms (foolish, silly, idiotic, absurd); inadequacy terms (helpless, powerless, inferior, ineffective, unfit, impotent, trivial, meaningless); uncomfortable terms (restless, fidgety, anxious, nervous, uneasy); hurt terms (offended, upset, wounded, injured, intimidated); and mitigation terms – to make the situation seem less severe or painful (denying any impact, playing it "cool").
2   *Paralinguistic or nonverbal vocal markers*: vocal withdrawal, hiding behaviors, and disorganization of thought leading to disfluency; overly soft tone, hesitations, self-interruptions, filled pauses, long pauses, silences, stammering, stuttering, mumbling, laughed words.
3   *Visual markers*: hiding behavior (hand covering all or part of the face, gaze aversion, eyes lowered or averted), blushing, control behaviors (turning in, biting the tongue or lips, false smiling).

While Retzinger's approach assumes that shame is dysfunctional for conflict, Keltner, Young, and Buswell (1997) take a slightly different view, seeing shame as potentially functional appeasement behavior. Appeasement is the process by which we pacify or placate others in situations of potential or actual conflict. A person anticipates aggression and displays appeasement behaviors (apologetic, submissive or affiliative behavior) which prevents or reduces another's aggression. The use of appropriate appeasement displays leads to reconciliation because the appeasement displays generate positive emotions toward the appeaser. Interestingly, Keltner and colleagues (1997) believe that many dispute resolution processes, such as negotiation and court procedures (potentially including mediation), actually reduce the ability of people to strategically use appeasement displays and thus make it more difficult to repair and sustain reconciled relationships. Whether shame should be decoded because it is functional or not, mediators should be familiar with shame markers and use them to identify overt or hidden shame dynamics.

Uncovering Emotional Experience through Elicitive Questioning

At the core of uncovering the emotional experience of the disputants is appreciation for the cognitive appraisals that have led to the emotion. Weiner (1985, 1986) has an attribution theory of emotion in which he argues that an actor experiences a generalized or diffuse emotion first when the actor realizes his or her goal attempt is successful or has been blocked. These are "primitive" emotions; they motivate the actor to engage in more specific attribution processes which lead to specific emotions, much like the process that Lazarus (1991) describes.

Similarly, Kemper (1987) classifies primary and secondary emotions. Kemper (1987) argues that primary emotions, like fear and surprise, are physiologically grounded, and cross-culturally universal. Secondary emotions, like guilt, shame, and pride, are socially constructed.

Lazarus's (1991) theory of cognitive appraisal has received the most attention for its implications of practice in social support and conflict contexts, as will be discussed in the next section. Lazarus (1991) distinguished goal-congruent, or positive, emotions (i.e. compassion, happiness, hope, love, pride, and relief) and goal-incongruent, or negative, emotions (i.e. anger, anxiety, disgust, envy, fright, guilt, jealousy, sadness, and shame).

Whether an emotion is goal-congruent or goal-incongruent is the result of a two-stage appraisal process including primary and secondary appraisals. The identification of the emotional experience is a function of both appraisal processes acting in tandem.

Primary appraisals focus on the question: "Is the event or situation personally relevant?" There are three elements to be considered in making the primary appraisal:

- Does it impact on personal goals? (goal relevance)
- Does it make it easier or harder for me to achieve my goals? (goal congruence)
- Is it related to my identity in some important way? (ego-involvement)

All negative emotions arise from appraisals that the event or situation impacts on personal goals (is goal-relevant) in a way that makes it harder for one to achieve those goals (is goal-incongruent).

Secondary appraisals focus on additional issues that help determine the specific emotion felt. According to Lazarus (1991), there are three additional issues to consider:

- What or who is to blame for the event/situation? (judgments of accountability)
- How well can one solve the problem and manage one's feelings? (coping potential)
- How likely is it that things will get better or worse? (future expectancy)

One can be blamed for an incident and still be seen as not intentionally causing that incident. In conflict, the issue of blame is critical because other-blame is more likely to generate aggression toward the other while self-blame is more likely to cause aggression toward the self (Kottler 1994). Coping potential encompasses a sense of empowerment for the person. When coping potential is high, a person is less likely to feel trapped or desperate and more likely to realize they have options other than "fight or flight." If a disputant has a sense of future expectancy

– for example that the problem will definitely get worse – he or she may be more motivated to problem-solve and handle the problem. However, if the disputant feels the problem will get better without intervention he or she may be prone to avoid confronting the issue.

Some basic appraisal explanations for each of the goal-congruent and goal-incongruent emotions listed earlier are:

- *Anger*: someone has intentionally committed a demeaning offense against us or those close to us.
- *Anxiety*: we are facing an uncertain threat; we cannot make sense of the situation.
- *Disgust*: we want to get away from someone or something that we find offensive.
- *Envy*: we want something that someone else has.
- *Fear*: we face an immediate physical danger and feel powerless to prevent that danger.
- *Guilt*: we have done something or we want to do something that we know to be morally wrong.
- *Jealousy*: we hold a third party responsible for the threat of the loss of someone's affection.
- *Sadness*: we think we have experienced an irrevocable loss that is no one's fault, but that we cannot replace.
- *Shame*: we perceive that we have failed to live up to expectations in someone else's eyes; our identity is damaged and it is our fault.
- *Compassion*: we are moved by another's suffering and want to help them.
- *Happiness*: we are making progress toward our goals.
- *Hope*: we think something bad is going to happen but we want something better to happen and believe there is something we might do to make that happen.
- *Love*: we have affection for other people.
- *Pride*: we are able to take credit for something we did that we value.
- *Relief*: we have been experiencing a negative emotion and the situation changes for the better.

Most mediators are not trained to talk with disputants about their feelings, either as a means of uncovering them or as a means of altering them. Mediators are usually trained to have the person describe or talk about the event, but are advised not to allow the person to maintain too much of a focus on the past. While mediators are trained to "listen for feelings," they usually do not learn how to enable the disputant to talk through feelings. Thus mediators may acknowledge emotion, but not appreciate it as a conflict management tool.

Extrapolating from Lazarus's (1991) theory, we suggest that mediators learn to focus on feelings as critical to conflict management. This involves two steps: the use of elicitive questions to help identify the emotional experience of the disputant; and the use of elicitive questions to help the disputant reappraise the situation, thereby opening the possibilities for different resolution. The first step is addressed here.

To help a disputant identify his or her emotions, a mediator may ask elicitive questions such as:

- What are you feeling?
- Do you know why you are feeling this way?
- Did something specific happen to make you feel this way?
- How did that event help or hurt you?
- Do you think someone or something is to blame? If so, who or what?

There are a variety of ways that mediators can ask questions that uncover the emotional experience. Mediators should tailor the wording of these questions to their own style. They can also be encouraged to work with co-mediators to develop a host of possible questions that feel natural to them, but which are able to elicit the basic information.

As mentioned earlier, many people are unable to articulate their emotional experiences, either because they lack an adequate emotional vocabulary or because they have been taught to ignore their emotions (Rancer & Kosberg 1994). When a disputant cannot "name" their emotion, these questions can help the mediator identify the emotions that are operating. In this sense, the questions are doubly diagnostic. Identification of emotion can be done throughout the mediation. If the mediator can listen for implicit and explicit appraisals as the disputants discuss their situation, the mediator can identify their possible emotions without having to question them directly. Then, in caucus, the mediator can use more direct questioning to verify his or her assumptions.

Changing Emotional Experience through Facilitating Reappraisal

This third skill is the most important in terms of managing the conflict and moving disputants past blocks in their perception of the dispute. Decoding emotion is a critical mediator skill much like diagnosing a disease is a critical medical skill. It certainly accomplishes some of the T_m goals mentioned earlier – mediator empathy, feeling heard and understood, being able to talk about perceptions and feelings. However, to accomplish other T_m goals, particularly the goals of perceived self-efficacy and formulating options for resolution (in a problem-solving or relational mode), the mediator must hone the skill of facilitating reappraisal of the disputant's emotional experience.

Mediators cannot facilitate reappraisal by trying to "fix" the problem for the disputants or telling them how they should view their situation. The task for the mediator is to help them see things differently for themselves. This portion of the reappraisal process focuses primarily on the coping abilities of the disputants, which is similar in many respects to the process of empowering in mediation. According to Burleson and Goldsmith (1998), helpful questions in this effort could include:

- How important is this event to you – now and in the future?
- What might make it less important?

- How might this event have helped you in ways you haven't discussed?
- How important is it for you to blame the other in this situation?
- What does the blame do for you?
- What does it cost you?
- What might help you get past the blame? What would make it right?
- What have you done to deal with the situation?
- How well is that working for you?
- How do you feel as a result of trying that?
- What might you try that would help you feel better? Why might that make you feel better?

Of course, the mediator may not need or want to ask all of these questions (or to ask them in this way). If a disputant is not experiencing blame-based emotions, then questions about blame are not relevant. However, if a disputant is feeling sad, an emotion characterized by a feeling of powerlessness, the mediator may want to concentrate on questions about ways of coping that could improve the person's perception of their power resources in the situation, even if it does not change the "facts" of the situation.

As mediators become more adept at this process they will discover different question sets that are more germane for certain emotions. For example, if sadness is the primary emotion, questioning that facilitates reappraisal may be best focused on how the experience of sadness may help the person, what they gain from it, how they have dealt with sadness in the past, and what is similar in this situation to those previous situations. If fear is a primary emotion, questioning can concentrate on why the disputants value what they fear to lose, what other things might be substituted for the potential loss, what could be better if the loss occurred, why they assume the other wants to cause this loss, what they can do to replace the loss, or what they can do to honor the loss so that it has symbolic richness for them.

The process of facilitating reappraisal does more than simply identify courses of action to help alter the emotional experience. As Planalp (1999) argues, communicating emotion offers benefits simply by encoding an emotional experience into language. It helps disputants weave together thoughts and feelings, clarifying what is felt and why. It can help the disputant achieve an appropriate distance from the experience. And communicating the emotion can also provide a sense of control, giving disputants the notion of mastery over their emotions.

THE CHALLENGES OF MANAGING EMOTIONAL COMMUNICATION IN MEDIATION

The skills discussed in the preceding section are a good place to start for mediators who wish to treat emotion more seriously and use the power of emotional awareness in mediation. But there is no doubt that this chapter only introduces ideas that require more attention because the phenomenon of emotion is so much more complex than is acknowledged, both in contemporary mediation theory and certainly in contemporary mediation practice literature. Thus, this chapter ends with a brief acknowledgment of the major challenges in applying these skill suggestions.

The Complexity of Emotional Communication

Although strides have been made in the identification of emotional communication markers, there are no exhaustive taxonomies available to cover all possible forms of emotional expression. Planalp and Knie (2002: 55) lament: "Everyone knows that verbal and nonverbal cues fit together into integrated messages like interlocking pieces of a puzzle, but nobody really knows how . . . Nowhere is this more apparent than in the study of the messages of emotion." The complexity of emotional communication is increased by cultural differences in emotional expression, strategic versus spontaneous expression, and the experience of multiple emotions.

Cultural Differences in Emotion and Expression

Markus and Kitayama (1991) and Saarni (2001) argue that, as social constructivists agree, emotional experience and emotional expression are very culturally based. This is particularly true for identity-based emotions like the ones discussed in this chapter. Clearly, the nature and function of "ego-focused emotions" and "other-focused emotions" alter considerably if one has an independent or interdependent sense of self. Cultures that emphasize an independent sense of self focus more on ego-focused emotions. The reverse is true for cultures that emphasize an interdependent, or collective, sense of self. Cultural differences in emotional expression may be linked to culture as gender (Mongrain & Vettese 2003), race and ethnicity (Weathers, Frank & Spell 2002), nationality (Goddard 2002), and socio-cultural norms that influence the use of emotionality rules in discourse (Fiehler 2002).

Strategic versus Spontaneous Emotional Communication

In 1872 Charles Darwin published *The Expression of the Emotions in Man and Animals*. He wrote about the expression of emotion as a "coming out" from the body and argued that expression is a critical part of emotional experience. For him, emotional expression was spontaneous, natural, and non-strategic. A century later, Ross Buck wrote *The Communication of Emotion* (1984), and argued that, while emotional expression may be non-strategic, there are times when it is very strategic and inherently communicative: we communicate emotion symbolically and strategically.

Conflict scholars realize that strategic emotional expression is often used in negotiation and mediation. Barry (1999) argued that individuals can display emotion strategically to capitalize on their interdependence with negotiation opponents. In his exploratory research he found that people are more confident in their ability to use emotion-management tactics than other forms of premeditated deception. Kramer and Hess (2002) note that maintaining professional identities means appropriate emotional management in which positive and negative emotions are displayed in appropriate ways, which usually means masking. Andersen and Guerrero (1998) discuss five display rules that are used to strategically express emotion: simulation (displaying or feigning an emotion when no such emotion or feeling is present); inhibition (giving the impression of having no feelings when one actually has them); intensification (giving the appearance of having stronger feelings than one actually has); deintensification (giving the appearance of experiencing an emotion with less intensity than one is actually feeling it); and masking (communicating an emotion that is entirely different from the one that the person is feeling).

Mediators have two basic challenges with regard to the spontaneous expression of emotion by disputants. First, mediators may not be able to tell when an emotional expression is strategic, and the assumption is that more strategic expression has lower "information value" for the mediator in terms of decoding the emotional experience of the disputant. Second, the mediator may wish to encourage more spontaneous or more strategic expression of emotion so a disputant can "gain" something (e.g. sympathy, regard, credibility) in the mediation interaction. However, how and when to encourage either is exceptionally complex.

Risks of Emotional Interaction

Emotion is powerful and risky. When mediators encourage discussion of emotion they must realize that there are risks inherent to such discussion. As Honos-Webb et al. (2002) argue, people often assume, for good reason, that getting someone to "talk it out" is going to be helpful to that person. These authors indicate that this is not always true. Just as there are situations in which exploring negative emotions can be quite positive, there are other situations where exploring negative emotions is very negative.

Emotional conversation can trigger memory that heightens emotional experience and emotional flooding (LeDoux 1996). A critical aspect of emotional experience is memory. Highly emotional events are likely to be held fast in the memory for longer periods than less emotional events. Gayle and Preiss (1999) argue that the role of emotion in recalling relationship memories deserves serious attention. Salaman (1982) claimed that memories elicit the same intensity and variety of emotions that occurred when the original interaction happened. Research by Cloven and Roloff (1995) and Gayle and Preiss (1998) also suggested that unresolved confrontations trigger recurring emotional responses that frame future interactions. These findings suggest that emotional retrospective narratives are likely to affect current and future relational interactions.

Mediators shy away from any intimation that they are "doing therapy" in mediation; this reaction often results from a discomfort in leading a disputant into emotional and psychological realms that the mediator is not well trained to handle. This caution is professional, wise, and compassionate. There are emotional experiences and relational contexts that are beyond the expertise of a mediator without specific training in counseling and psychotherapy. Yet, even in much less risky interactions, mediators need to be sensitive to how much the recall and retelling of emotional experience in the past may impact the emotional experience of the present and the disputant's ability and willingness to move forward.

SUMMARY

Any discussion of interpersonal mediation is insufficient if it does not attend seriously to the role of emotion in the mediation process. Psychological theories of conflict and negotiation contribute insight into the how emotion may function by influencing negotiation strategy. Yet corresponding theory and research on emotion in mediation is in its infancy, as the literature review in chapter 2 of this volume attests. This chapter provides a rationale for why more work in this area is needed and advocates a communication perspective that underpins the application of emotional communication skills that mediators can use in mediation.

REFERENCES

Adler, R. S., Rosen, B. & Silverstein, E. M. (1998) Emotions in negotiation: how to manage fear and anger. *Negotiation Journal* 14(2), 161–179.

Allred, K. G. (1999) Anger and retaliation: toward an understanding of impassioned conflict in organizations. In R. J. Bies, R. J. Lewicki & B. H. Sheppard (eds.), *Research on Negotiation in Organizations*, vol. 7. JAI Press, Stanford, pp. 27–58.

Allred, K. G. (2000) Anger and retaliation in conflict: the role of attribution. In M. Deutsch & P. Coleman (eds.), *Handbook of Conflict Resolution: Theory and Practice*. Jossey-Bass, San Francisco, pp. 236–255.

Allred, K. G., Mallozzi, J. S., Matsui, F. & Raia, C. P. (1997) The influence of anger and compassion on negotiation performance. *Organizational Behavior and Human Decision Processes* 70, 175–187.

Andersen, P. A. & Guerrero, L. K. (eds.) (1998) *Handbook of Communication and Emotion: Research, Theory, Application and Contexts*. Academic Press, San Diego.

Averill, J. R. (1982) *Anger and Aggression*. Springer, New York.

Baron, R. A. (1990) Environmentally induced positive affect: its impact on self-efficacy, task performance, negotiation, and conflict. *Journal of Applied Social Psychology* 20, 368–384.

Baron, R. A., Fortin, S. P., Frei, R. L., Hauver, L. A. & Shack, M. L. (1990) Reducing organizational conflict: the role of socially-induced positive affect. *International Journal of Conflict Management* 1, 133–152.

Barry, B. (1999) The tactical use of emotion in negotiation. In R. J. Bies, R. J. Lewicki & B. H. Sheppard (eds.), *Research on Negotiation in Organizations*, vol. 7. JAI Press, Stanford, pp. 93–121.

Barry, B. & Oliver, R. L. (1996) Affect in dyadic negotiation: a model and propositions. *Organizational Behavior and Human Decision Processes* 67, 127–143.

Batson, C. D., Shaw, L. L. & Oleson, K. C. (1992) Differentiating affect, mood, and emotion: toward a functionally based conceptual distinction. In M. S. Clark (ed.), *Emotion*. Sage, Newbury Park, pp. 294–326.

Beersma, B., Harinck, F. & Gerts, M. (2003) Bound in honor: how honor values and insults affect the experience and management of conflicts. *International Journal of Conflict Management* 14(2), 75–94.

Betancourt, H. & Blair, I. (1992) A cognition (attribution)-emotion model of violence in conflict situations. *Personality and Social Psychology Bulletin* 18(3), 343–350.

Buck, R. (1984) *The Communication of Emotion*. Guilford Press, New York.

Burleson, B. & Goldsmith, D. (1998) How the comforting process works: alleviating emotional distress through conversationally induced reappraisals. In P. A. Anderson & L. K. Guerrero (eds.), *Handbook of Communication and Emotion: Research, Theory, Application and Contexts*. Academic Press, San Diego, pp. 246–281.

Bush, R. A. B. & Folger, J. (2004) *The Promise of Mediation*, 2nd edn. Jossey-Bass, San Francisco.

Canary, D. J., Spitzberg, B. H. & Semic, B. A. (1998) The experience and expression of anger. In P. A. Anderson & L. K. Guerrero (eds.), *Handbook of Communication and Emotion: Research, Theory, Application and Contexts*. Academic Press, San Diego, pp. 189–213.

Chiongbian, V. M. B. (2001) The effect of status and emotions on negotiation: evidence from the United States and the Philippines. *Dissertation Abstracts International: Section B: The Sciences & Engineering* 62(2-B), 1139.

Cloke, K. (2001) *Mediating Dangerously: The Frontiers of Conflict Resolution*. Jossey-Bass, San Francisco.

Cloven, D. H. & Roloff, M. E. (1995) Cognitive tuning effects of anticipating communication on thought on interpersonal conflict. *Communication Reports* 8, 1–9.

Cobb, S. (1994) Narrative in mediation. In J. Folger & T. Jones (eds.), *New Directions in Mediation: Communication Research and Perspectives*. Jossey-Bass, San Francisco, pp. 34–58.

Collins, R. (1981) On the microfoundations of macrosociology. *American Journal of Sociology* 86(5), 984–1014.

Collins, R. (1989) Toward a neo-median sociology of mind. *Symbolic Interactionism* 12(1), 1–32.

Collins, R. (1993) Emotional energy as the common denominator of rational action. *Rational Sociology* 5(2), 203–230.

Conlon, D. E. & Hunt, C. S. (2002) Dealing with feeling: the influence of outcome representations on negotiation. *International Journal of Conflict Management* 13(1), 38–59.

Daly, J. (1991) The effects of anger on negotiations over mergers and acquisitions. *Negotiation Journal* 7, 31–39.

Damasio, A. R. (1994) *Descartes' Error: Emotion, Reason and the Human Brain*. G. P. Putnam's Sons, New York.

Darwin, C. (1872) *The Expression of the Emotions in Man and Animals*. Philosophical Library, New York.

Davidson, M. & Greenhalgh, L. (1999) The role of emotion in negotiation: the impact of anger and race. In R. J. Bies, R. J. Lewicki & B. H. Sheppard (eds.), *Research on Negotiation in Organizations*, vol. 7. JAI Press, Stanford, pp. 3–26.

Donohue, W. A. (1991) *Communication, Marital Dispute, and Divorce Mediation*. Lawrence Erlbaum, Hillsdale.

Duncombe, J. & Marsden, D. (1996) Extending the social: a response to Craib. *Sociology* 30, 155–158.

Ekman, P. & Friesen, W. V. (1975) *Unmasking the Face: A Guide to Recognizing Emotions from Facial Cues*. Prentice Hall, Englewood Cliffs.

Fiehler, R. (2002) How to do emotions with words: emotionality in conversations. In S. R. Fussell (ed.), *The Verbal Communication of Emotions: Interdisciplinary Perspectives*. Lawrence Erlbaum, Mahwah, pp. 79–106.

Folger, J. & Jones, T. (eds.) (1994) *New Directions in Mediation: Communication Research and Perspectives*. Sage, Thousand Oaks.

Frank, R. (1991) Economics. In M. Maxwell (ed.), *The Sociobiological Imagination*. State University of New York Press, Syracuse, pp. 91–110.

Friedman, R., Anderson, C., Brett, J., Olekalns, M., Goates, N. & Lisco, C. (2004) The positive and negative effects of anger on dispute resolution: evidence from electronically mediated disputes. *Journal of Applied Psychology* 89(2), 369–376.

Fussell, S. R. (2002) The verbal communication of emotion: introduction and overview. In S. R. Fussell (ed.), *The Verbal Communication of Emotions: Interdisciplinary Perspectives.* Lawrence Erlbaum, Mahwah, pp. 1–16.

Gayle, B. M. & Preiss, R. W. (1998) Assessing emotionality in organizational conflicts. *Management Communication Quarterly* 12(2), 280–302.

Gayle, B. M. & Preiss, R. W. (1999) Language intensity plus: a methodological approach to validate emotions in conflicts. *Communication Reports* 12(1), 43–51.

Goddard, C. (2002) Explicating emotions across languages and cultures: a semantic approach. In S. R. Fussell (ed.), *The Verbal Communication of Emotions: Interdisciplinary Perspectives.* Lawrence Erlbaum, Mahwah, pp. 19–54.

Gottman, J. M. (1994) *What Predicts Divorce? The Relationship between Marital Processes and Marital Outcomes.* Lawrence Erlbaum, Hillsdale.

Gray, B. (2003) Negotiating with your nemesis. *Negotiation Journal* 19(4), 299–310.

Gray-Little, B. & Teddlie, C. B. (1978) Racial differences in children's responses to inequity. *Journal of Applied Social Psychology* 8, 107–16.

Haviland, J. & Kalbaugh, P. (1993) Emotion and identity. In M. Lewis & J. M. Haviland (eds.), *Handbook of Emotions.* Guilford Press, New York, pp. 327–340.

Hegtvedt, K. A. (1990) The effects of relationship structure on emotional responses to inequity. *Social Psychology Quarterly* 53, 214–228.

Hegtvedt, K. A. & Killian, C. (1999) Fairness and emotions: reactions to the process and outcomes of negotiations. *Social Forces* 78(1), 269–308.

Hochschild, A. R. (1983) *The Managed Heart: Commercialization of Human Feeling.* University of California Press, London.

Homans, G. C. (1974) *Social Behavior: Its Elementary Forms.* Harcourt Brace Jovanovich, New York.

Honos-Webb, L., Endres, L. M., Shaikh, A., Harrick, E. A., Lani, J. A., Knobloch-Fedders, L. M., Surko, M. & Stiles, W. B. (2002) Rewards and risks of exploring negative emotion: an assimilation model account. In S. R. Fussell (ed.), *The Verbal Communication of Emotions: Interdisciplinary Perspectives.* Lawrence Erlbaum, Mahwah, pp. 231–251.

Isen, A. M., Daubman, K. A. & Nowicki, G. P. (1987) Positive affect facilitates creative problem solving. *Journal of Personality and Social Psychology* 52, 1122–1131.

Izard, C. (1977) *Human Emotions.* Plenum, New York.

Jones, T. S. (2000) Emotional communication in conflict: essence and impact. In W. Eadie & P. Nelson (eds.), *The Language of Conflict and Resolution.* Sage, Thousand Oaks, pp. 81–104.

Jones, T. S. & Remland, M. S. (1993) Nonverbal communication and conflict escalation: an attribution-based model. *International Journal of Conflict Management* 4(2), 119–138.

Jones, T. S. & Bodtker, A. (2001) Mediating with heart in mind. *Negotiation Journal* 17(3), 217–244.

Keltner, D., Young, R. C. & Buswell, B. (1997) Appeasement in human emotion, social practice, and personality. *Aggressive Behavior* 23(5), 359–375.

Kemper, T. D. (1978) *A Social Interactional Theory of Emotions.* Wiley, New York.

Kemper, T. D. (1987) How many emotions are there? Wedding the social and autonomic components. *American Journal of Sociology* 93, 263–289.

Kemper, T. D. (1993) Sociological models in the explanation of emotion. In M. Lewis & J. M. Haviland (eds.), *Handbook of Emotions.* Guilford Press, New York, pp. 41–52.

Kitayama, S. & Markus, H. R. (eds.) (1994) *Emotion and Culture: Empirical Studies of Mutual Influence*. American Psychological Association, Washington.

Kottler, J. A. (1994) *Beyond Blame: A New Way of Resolving Conflicts in Relationships*. Jossey-Bass, San Francisco.

Kramer, M. W. & Hess, J. A. (2002) Communication rules for the display of emotions in organizational settings. *Management Communication Quarterly* 16, 66–81.

Kumar, R. (1997) The role of affect in negotiations: an integrative overview. *Journal of Applied Behavioral Science* 33, 84–100.

Lawler, E. J. & Yoon, J. (1995) Structural power and emotional processes in negotiation: a social exchange approach. In R. M. Kramer & D. M. Messick (eds.), *Negotiation as a Social Process: New Trends in Theory and Research*. Sage, Thousand Oaks, pp. 143–165.

Lawler, E. J. & Thye, S. R. (1999) Bringing emotions into social exchange theory. *Annual Review of Sociology* 25(1), 217–245.

Lazarus, R. S. (1991) *Emotion and Adaptation*. Oxford University Press, New York.

LeBaron, M. (2002) *Bridging Troubled Waters: Conflict Resolution from the Heart*. Jossey-Bass, San Francisco.

LeDoux, J. (1996) *The Emotional Brain: The Mysterious Underpinnings of Emotional Life*. Touchstone Books, New York.

Lewis, H. B. (1976) *Psychic War in Men and Women*. New York University Press, New York.

Lewis, M. (1993) Self-conscious emotions: embarrassment, pride, shame, and guilt. In M. Lewis & J. M. Haviland (eds.), *Handbook of Emotions*. Guilford Press, New York, pp. 563–573.

Lund, M. E. (2000) A focus on emotion in mediation training. *Family & Conciliation Courts Review* 38(1), 62–68.

Manstead, A. S. R. (1991) Emotion in social life. *Cognition and Emotion* 5(5/6), 353–362.

Markus, H. R. & Kitayama, S. (1991) Culture and the self: implications for cognition, emotion, and motivation. *Psychological Review* 98(2), 224–253.

Miller, W. I. (1997) *The Anatomy of Disgust*. Harvard University Press, Cambridge.

Mongrain, M. & Vettese, L. C. (2003) Conflict over emotional expression: implications for interpersonal communication. *Personality & Social Psychology Bulletin* 29(4), 545–555.

Morris, W. N. (1992) A functional analysis of the role of mood in affective systems. In M. S. Clark (ed.), *Emotion*. Sage, Newbury Park, pp. 256–293.

Northrup, T. A. (1989) The dynamic of identity in personal and social conflict. In L. Kriesberg, T. Northrup & S. J. Thorson (eds.), *Intractable Conflicts and their Transformation*. Syracuse University Press, Syracuse, pp. 55–82.

Oatley, K. (1993) Social construction in emotions. In M. Lewis & J. M. Haviland (eds.), *Handbook of Emotions*. Guilford Press, New York, pp. 341–352.

O'Connor, K. M. & Arnold, J. A. (2001) Distributive spirals: negotiation impasses and the moderating role of disputant self-efficacy. *Organizational Behavior and Human Decision Processes* 84(1), 148–176.

Ortony, A., Clore, G. L. & Collins, A. (1988) *The Cognitive Structure of Emotions*. Cambridge University Press, New York.

Parkinson, L. (2000) Mediating with high-conflict couples. *Family and Conciliation Courts Review* 38(1), 69–76.

Pearce, W. B. & Littlejohn, S. (1997) *Moral Conflict: When Social Worlds Collide*. Sage, Thousand Oaks.

Pillutla, M. M. & Murnighan, J. K. (1996) Unfairness, anger, and spite: emotional rejections of ultimatum offers. *Organizational Behavior and Human Decision Processes* 68, 208–224.

Planalp, S. (1998) Communicating emotion in everyday life: cues, channels and processes. In P. A. Anderson & L. K. Guerrero (eds.), *Handbook of Communication and Emotion: Research, Theory, Application and Contexts.* Academic Press, San Diego, pp. 30–45.

Planalp, S. (1999) *Communicating Emotion: Social, Moral and Cultural Processes.* Cambridge University Press, Paris.

Planalp, S. & Knie, K. (2002) Integrating verbal and nonverbal emotion(al) messages. In S. R. Fussell (ed.), *The Verbal Communication of Emotions: Interdisciplinary Perspectives.* Lawrence Erlbaum, Mahwah, pp. 55–78.

Podziba, S. L. (2003) The human side of complex public policy mediation. *Negotiation Journal* 19(4), 285–290.

Pruitt, D. G., Parker, J. C. & Mikolic, J. M. (1997) Escalation as a reaction to persistent annoyance. *International Journal of Conflict Management* 8(3), 252–270.

Rancer, A. S. & Kosberg, R. (1994) *Violence Prevention: A Communication-Based Curriculum.* Paper presented at the Speech Communication Association Convention, New Orleans, November.

Remland, M., Jones, T. & Brown, T. (1994) *Nonverbal Communication and Conflict Escalation: The Effects of Attribution and Predisposition.* Paper presented at the International Association of Conflict Management Convention, Eugene, OR, June.

Retzinger, S. M. (1991) *Violent Emotions: Shame and Rage in Marital Quarrels.* Sage, Newbury Park.

Retzinger, S. M. & Scheff, T. (2000) Emotion, alienation and narratives: resolving intractable conflict. *Mediation Quarterly* 18(1), 71–85.

Robinson, D. T. & Smith-Lovin, L. (1999) Emotion display as a strategy for identity negotiation. *Motivation & Emotion* 23(2), 73–105.

Rodriguez Mosquera, P. M. (1999) Honor and emotion: the cultural shaping of pride, shame and anger. Doctoral dissertation. University of Amsterdam, Amsterdam.

Rodriguez Mosquera, P. M., Manstead, A. S. R. & Fisher, A. H. (2000) The role of honor-related values in the elicitation, experience, and communication of pride, shame, and anger: Spain and the Netherlands compared. *Personality and Social Psychology Bulletin* 26, 833–844.

Rodriguez Mosquera, P. M., Manstead, A. S. R. & Fisher, A. H. (2002) The role of honor-concerns in emotional reactions to offenses. *Cognition and Emotion* 16, 143–163.

Rogan, R. G. (1995) Language intensity: testing a content-based metric. *Communication Reports* 8, 128–135.

Rubin, J. Z., Pruitt, D. & Kim, S. (1994) *Social Conflict: Escalation, Stalemate and Settlement,* 2nd edn. McGraw-Hill, New York.

Saarni, C. (2001) Epilogue: emotion communication and relationship context. *International Journal of Behavioral Development* 25(4), 354–356.

Salaman, E. (1982) A collection of memories. In U. Neisser (ed.), *Memory Observed: Remembering in Natural Contexts.* W. H. Freeman, San Francisco, pp. 49–63.

Scheff, T. (1990) *Microsociology: Discourse, Emotion, and Social Structure.* University of Chicago Press, Chicago.

Scheff, T. (1997) *Emotions, the Social Bond, and Human Reality: Part/Whole Analysis.* Cambridge University Press, Cambridge.

Shapiro, D. (2004) Emotions in negotiation: peril or promise? *Marquette Law Review* 87, 737–745.

Shaver, P., Schwartz, D., Kirkson, D. & O'Connor, C. (1987) Emotion knowledge: further exploration of a prototype approach. *Journal of Personality and Social Psychology* 52, 1061–1086.

Shweder, R. A. (1993) The cultural psychology of the emotions. In M. Lewis & J. M. Haviland (eds.), *Handbook of Emotions*. Guilford Press, New York, pp. 417–431.

Sinaceur, M. & Tiedens, L. Z. (2004) Get mad and get more than even: the benefits of anger expression in negotiation. Unpublished manuscript, Stanford University, Palo Alto.

Smith-Lovin, L. & Heise, D. R. (1988) (eds.) *Analyzing Social Interaction: Research Advances in Affect Control Theory*. Gordon & Breach, New York.

Sprecher, S. (1992) How men and women expect to feel and behave in response to inequity in close relations. *Social Psychology Quarterly* 55, 57–69.

Stryker, S. (1980) *Symbolic Interaction: A Social Structural Version*. Benjamin Cummings, Menlo Park.

Thompson, L. L., Nadler, J. & Kim, P. H. (1999) Some like it hot: the case for the emotional negotiator. In L. L. Thompson, J. M. Levine & D. M. Messick (eds.), *Shared Cognitions in Organizations: The Management of Knowledge*. Erlbaum, Mahwah, pp. 139–161.

Thompson, L. L. & Kim, P. H. (2000) How the quality of third parties' settlement solutions is affected by the relationship between negotiators. *Journal of Experimental Social Psychology* 6, 3–14.

Van Kleef, G. A., De Dreu, C. K. W. & Manstead, A. S. R. (2004a) The interpersonal effects of anger and happiness in negotiations. *Journal of Personality and Social Psychology* 86, 57–76.

Van Kleef, G. A., De Dreu, C. K. W. & Manstead, A. S. R. (2004b) The interpersonal effects of emotions in negotiations: a motivated information processing approach. *Journal of Personality and Social Psychology* 87(4), 510–528.

Weathers, M. D., Frank, E. M. & Spell, L. A. (2002) Differences in the communication of affect: members of the same race versus members of a different race. *Journal of Black Psychology* 28(1), 66–77.

Weiner, B. (1985) An attributional theory of achievement motivation and emotion. *Psychological Review* 92, 548–573.

Weiner, B. (1986) *An Attribution Theory of Motivation and Emotion*. Springer, New York.

Weitzman, M. (1996) An examination of the effect of affect on the outcomes and processes of negotiations. *Dissertation Abstracts International: Section B: The Sciences & Engineering* 56(9-B), 5210 [one-page abstract].

Wilmot, W. W. & Hocker, J. L. (1998) *Interpersonal Conflict*, 5th edn. McGraw-Hill, Boston.

Winslade, J. & Monk, G. (2000) *Narrative Mediation*. Jossey-Bass, San Francisco.

Worcel, S. D., Shields, S. A. & Paterson, C. A. (1999) She looked at me crazy: escalation of conflict through telegraphed emotion. *Adolescence* 34(136), 689–697.

Zwaal, C., Prkachin, K. M., Husted, J. & Stones, M. (2003) Components of hostility and verbal communication of emotion. *Psychology & Health* 18(2), 261–274.

Part IV

EXTENSIONS

Chapter 14

Preempting Disaster: Pre-Mediation Strategies to Deal with Strong Emotions

Daniel L. Shapiro

Introduction

A single poplar tree was the focus of a serious international crisis. The poplar tree sat in the Demilitarized Zone (DMZ) between North and South Korea. Each year, the tree would grow and obstruct the South Korean line of sight between a checkpoint and the "Bridge of No Return," a conduit between North and South Korea. And each summer, a South Korean team trimmed the tree.

On August 6, 1976, a group of US soldiers, UN officers, and South Koreans reportedly attempted to cut the tree, but they were chased away by North Korean soldiers (Korea Web Weekly 2003).

On August 18, a team of South Korean workers, eight UN guards, and two US officers approached the area to trim the poplar tree (globalsecurity.org 2003). The Korean People's Army from the North threatened to attack anyone attempting to trim it. Despite the threat, the team started to trim the tree. North Korean troops were ordered to attack US soldiers (Korea Web Weekly 2003). Two were killed, and several UN guards were injured.

As a result, both sides built up their military presence along the DMZ. Henry Kissinger, the US Secretary of State at the time, advised President Ford to respond by bombing North Korea. The president ultimately decided that a more appropriate strategy would be simply to cut down the tree.

On August 21, "Operation Paul Bunyan" was initiated. This was a joint mission of South Korean and UN-supported US troops with a single goal: to chop down the tree. Fifteen combat engineers returned to the site, along with an armed platoon, 27 helicopters, and a number of B-52 bombers. The tree was chopped down without fire drawn on either side, and in less than an hour the operation was complete.

This case illustrates how quickly the fuel of strong negative emotions can ignite a downward cycle of destructive conflict. A small dispute over tree-trimming mushroomed into a serious conflict resulting in armed conflict, multiple deaths, and a heightened risk of international war.

How could this tense conflict have been more effectively defused? Confrontation resolved the standoff, but also led to casualties and a nearly full-blown war. One alternative intervention could have been mediation. A third party could have interceded and helped the disputants deal with their differences more peacefully. Yet how can a mediator facilitate a problem-solving discussion when disputants' emotions are inflamed and constituents are hawking every action of every involved party?

In this chapter, I offer advice to mediators on how to deal with strong negative emotions before they hijack either party's ability to problem-solve their differences. First, I explain common ways in which strong emotions can jeopardize mediation success. Second, I propose three diagnoses about why mediators often fail to deal effectively with parties' strong emotions. Third, I suggest strategies to address each of these diagnoses. In the final section of the chapter, I return to the opening story about the conflict over the poplar tree and illustrate the use of this chapter's strategies in dealing more effectively with the conflict. This chapter argues that the T_0 phase of a mediation as described in chapter 2 of this book – before parties meet face to face – is an opportune time to reduce strong emotions and to strengthen the parties' relationship.

STRONG NEGATIVE EMOTIONS CAN HINDER DISPUTANTS FROM REACHING THEIR GOALS

The success of a mediation can be judged by the extent to which parties satisfy two important goals: affective satisfaction and instrumental satisfaction (Verba 1961; Shapiro 2000). Strong emotions can affect the ability of a mediator to reach each of these goals.

Affective Satisfaction

Affective satisfaction measures the quality of your emotional experience during the mediation (Verba 1961; Shapiro 2000). To what extent do you feel that your emotions were positive during the mediation? Do you feel that you were appreciated or put down? Affective satisfaction is a measure of your meta-emotions, your feelings about your feelings (Gottman, Katz & Hooven 1997). If South and North Korean officials meet and insult one another, each side might leave their meeting and admit feeling affective dissatisfaction. On the other hand, if each side treats the other with due deference, their resulting assessment of their affective satisfaction may be positive.

Instrumental Satisfaction

Instrumental satisfaction focuses on the degree to which your substantive work requirements are fulfilled (Shapiro 2004). A meeting between South and North Korean officials that ends with improved relations, but with no new ideas about how to deal with their issues, may be considered an affective success but an instrumental failure.

The Perils of Strong Negative Emotions

Emotions serve many valuable functions. They provide others and ourselves with information about our intentions and motivations (Scherer 1994). They prepare us for action (Frijda 1986). They recruit physiological changes that energize us to act in ways that meet our interests (Levenson 1994).

Yet intensely strong negative emotions – rage, frustration, humiliation, and the like – can threaten the ability of disputants to reach their instrumental and affective goals. In this section, I provide an overview of some of the risks posed by strong negative emotions.

Risks to Affective Satisfaction

Strong negative emotions can sidetrack, stall, or spoil the mediation process, leaving parties feeling little affective satisfaction. In the face of strong emotions such as anger, frustration, humiliation, or shame, it is hard for parties to listen to one another, to understand one another's interests, or to empathize with one another's situation (Shapiro 2004). Even if a mediator establishes procedures with great clarity, each party's strong emotions can fuel their own escalating emotions, as well as the emotions of the other party (Rubin & Pruitt 1994; Thompson 2001). Parties risk losing control of their own behavior and diverting the mediation process from important substantive issues.

Furthermore, strong emotions can hijack rational thinking (Goleman 1995), causing us to act in ways that we later regret. When experiencing rage or frustration, for example, disputants may damage their working relationship if they insult one another or storm out of the room. Without a good working relationship, neither side may trust the other. Joint problem-solving becomes more difficult, in part because neither side wants to share information if he or she thinks that the other side will use it to their advantage.

Risks to Instrumental Satisfaction

Anger, humiliation, and other strong negative emotions also tend to compromise the ability of disputants to maximize their instrumental satisfaction. Intense emotion can jeopardize a disputant's ability to: (1) create value by expanding the pie as much as possible (Mnookin, Peppet & Tulumello 2000; Bazerman, Baron & Shonk 2001), and (2) distribute value in ways that maximize the satisfaction of each party's interests (Lax & Sebenius 1986).

In terms of creating value, strong emotions tend to make people think that agreement with the other side is impossible. Whether the conflict is between North and South Koreans, the Hatfields and the McCoys, or a divorcing couple, parties come to believe that virtually no realistic options exist which can satisfy their mutual interests. They may resort to coercive tactics, including threats, demands, force, or violence (Rubin & Pruitt 1994). They also may buy into the "fixed pie" assumption

(Fisher, Ury & Patton 1991; Bazerman & Neale 1992), failing to believe that there may exist creative options for mutual gain.

Whether or not disputants "enlarge the pie," they face the challenge of distributing it. Satisfaction with the mediated outcome increases if parties base distribution upon objective standards or justice-based principles such as equity or equality (Folger & Greenberg 1985; Lax & Sebenius 1986; Fisher, Ury & Patton 1991; Thompson 2001). As a result, parties feel fairly treated in the short term. And in the long run, parties' perception that there is a fair method for distribution can positively affect relationship satisfaction and adherence to the mediated agreement (Thibaut & Walker 1975; Lind & Tyler 1988; Kumar, Scheer & Steenkamp 1995; Shapiro 2000).

When feeling strong emotion, however, disputants tend to distribute value in ways that fail to maximize the satisfaction of each party. Strong emotions can turn one's nuanced understanding of the world into a black-and-white, all-or-nothing view. As the boundaries between self and other rigidify, parties resolve the question of distribution by employing polarizing methods of distribution (Shapiro 2004). An extremely upset disputant is likely to give "all to my lover" and "nothing to my adversary." The disputant distributes value based on the valence of emotions he or she is experiencing – on whether the emotion is positive or negative – rather than on justice-oriented principles such as equity or equality.

DEALING WITH THE STRONG EMOTIONS OF DISPUTANTS

Most mediators work hard to help parties find agreement. They are well trained in the skills of mediation. They know how to facilitate discussion, reframe statements, and aid parties in creating options for mutual gain. Yet even with good intentions and skill in problem-solving, mediators are often challenged by the emotional complexities involved in the conflicts they mediate. This is not surprising, as the issues of mediation span topics as emotionally complicated as disputes over child custody, family inheritance, termination of business partnerships, and political sovereignty. Even trained psychologists would need significant time and expertise to come to an understanding about the underlying emotional dynamics of such disputes.

Despite the fact that emotions play a critical role in many conflicts (Greenhalgh & Chapman 1995; Shapiro 2000), mediators tend not to deal with strong negative emotions as well as they could. In this section, I describe three diagnoses to explain this gap, and in the next section I offer strategies to deal with each diagnosis respectively.

The Dangers of a "Wait-and-See" Strategy

How should mediators deal with the strong emotions of disputants? Some enlist what I term a "wait-and-see" strategy. The mediators bring the parties together, facilitate problem-solving, and wait to see if parties get angry or upset. The hope is that no strong negative emotions will emerge. If either party does express strong negative emotions, the mediator enacts crisis management tactics, such as calling for a break or separating parties into individual caucus rooms. The wait-and-see strategy has questionable appeal for two main reasons.

We cannot avoid the impact of emotions on us

The wait-and-see strategy allows disputants and the mediator to avoid open discussion of emotions. Unless emotions are clearly sidetracking the mediation, the mediator and parties assume that they can steer clear of them.

However, while it is plausible that mediators and parties can avoid *talking* about emotions, it is not possible to steer clear of their impact on the mediation. To be avoidable, emotions would have to be discrete, static phenomena – like poles on a ski slope around which a skilled skier can steer. But this conception of emotions is misguided. Emotions are a lived experience, arising before we are cognizant of them and inescapable in their subjective effect on us. Evidence clearly shows an impact of emotions – as well as their more diffuse cousin, moods – on human judgment, memory, and decision-making (Fiske & Taylor 1991). To emphasize this point, Robert Solomon (1993) suggests the term "surreality" to describe the notion that our emotions constitute our personal sense of reality. We cannot escape our emotional experience.

In fact, avoiding "emotion talk" can make matters worse. Disputants often feel a need to express their emotions. They want to feel "heard" by the other party and by the mediator. Without the time to share their emotional experience, parties may aggressively state their case early on, demeaning the other's perspective and initiating a volley of derogations and negative emotions.

Avoiding emotions can make efforts at problem-solving less effective

Many people believe that a focus on emotions will reduce their ability to problem-solve. Avoiding conversation about emotions is seen as a tactic to maintain a "rational" discussion.

This strategy is untenable. Emotions cannot be expunged from parties' problem-solving efforts. To the contrary, emotions (and affect more generally) have an automatic impact on our subjective experience, which influences how we deal with others, how we perceive ourselves, and how we view problems. Shapiro (2001) argues that we are in a state of "perpetual emotion," and empirical research supports that notion (e.g., Bargh and Chartrand 1999).

Furthermore, if it were possible to avoid emotions altogether, we would lose a great ally in problem-solving. Emotions amplify motivation (Tomkins 1970). They signal the importance of an issue to us and point us toward issues about which we care. Personally important goals – both instrumental and affective – are called to the forefront of our attention and given urgency. Hence, an awareness of emotions, one's own and those of others, provides valuable information about interests and motivations.

In conclusion, the wait-and-see strategy leaves the mediator and parties in a dangerously vulnerable position: at the whim of emotions.

The Illusion that We Can Get Rid of Emotions

If we cannot avoid emotions, then maybe we should get rid of them as they arise? Freud popularized the process of venting, proposing that the vigorous expression of strong emotions reduces their intensity. The theory suggests that, just like a boiling kettle, people experiencing strong emotions need to let off steam. Otherwise, the strong emotions will swell into a psychological malady or physical ailment.

The "venting hypothesis" provides an incomplete picture of how to deal with strong negative emotions. In fact, empirical evidence suggests that venting can escalate the intensity of emotions. Consider a classic study by Ebbesen, Duncan, and Konecni (1975). These investigators arranged interviews with engineers and technicians who recently had lost their jobs. The interviewer guided conversation in one of three directions: toward their supervisor ("What action might your supervisor have taken to prevent you from being laid off?"), toward the company ("In what ways has the company not been fair with you?"), or toward themselves ("Are there things about yourself that led your supervisor not to give you a higher performance review?"). The findings clearly show that the expression of anger in the interview did not reduce feelings of anger. Rather, discussing anger about their supervisor or toward the company increased feelings of anger toward that target, but not toward others. These results suggest that talking about anger can create and escalate feelings of anger.

So should disputants *never* talk about their emotions, even if they are upset? Should they simply suppress their strong negative emotions? No. But mediators who allow disputants to vent need to be conscious of their reason for doing so. Expressing negative emotions is helpful to the extent that it helps deal with distress (Kennedy-Moore & Watson 1999; Allred 2000). Talking privately with each disputant about their feelings about the conflict can relieve each disputant of an emotional burden. At the same time, the process of their understanding their emotions can, in itself, help soothe strong emotions. If parties are able to put into words their subjective experience, they are better able to understand, compartmentalize, and take control of their emotions. They can think about how to handle their internal world. Thinking and feeling go hand in hand, each aiding the other.

In contrast, having disputants rant and rave for hours about the "evil intentions of the other party" is likely to heighten relational tension. The act of unleashing anger becomes a rehearsal of the very attributions that initially triggered it (Allred 2000). Hence, people who vent unyieldingly can become angrier. And if they generate additional negative thoughts about the person who they think wronged them, the words and ideas they express will tend to construct a *more* negative situation. Thus, encouraging parties to vent, if done without a clear purpose in mind, imperils the mediation process.

The Failure to Deal with Emotional Resistance

Parties often come to mediation dressed in emotion-resistant armor. They are resistant to changing their own behavior and assume that "the other must change, but not me!" Two factors often underlie this resistance.

A loss of identity

Most parties have more at stake in a mediation than just the possibility of substantive losses. They fear the loss of a part of their identity. Once they have established a sense of identity for themselves and in the eyes of the other disputant, it can be emotionally taxing to change that identity. To play a new role in relation to the other party means a loss of certainty about how to act – and how they will feel – in the "new" relationship. Essentially, they lose a part of themselves.

The pain of this loss is depicted well in the Charlie Chaplin film *The Gold Rush*. Every time Chaplin enters his house, just as the door is about to shut, a big board drops on his head. One day, Chaplin walks in the house and, to his surprise, no board falls. Confused, he stops for a moment, opens the door, walks out of his house, walks in again, and slams the door shut. The board drops on his head. Chaplin relaxes, and life proceeds as usual (Kitron 2003).

If a person were to tell Chaplin, "Fix that board so it does not fall on your head," he might resist. He is accustomed to a world in which his welcome home is represented by a board falling on his head. While most disputants do not face problems as unusual as Chaplin's, one can recognize the underlying challenge that change is hard to do. And it is especially hard when disputants feel obligated to change their own sense of identity. Often, an important part of disputants' identity is wrapped up in the conflict. They might see the other as an adversary and them as doing no wrong. Or they might see themselves as out to prove their competence and the other's incompetence. Whatever the case, modifying one's sense of identity entails losing a part of who they currently are. This is true even if change will lead to a better life and a resolved conflict.

Prospect theory (Kahneman & Tversky 1979; Levy 1992) helps us to understand the emotional resistance to changing one's identity. This theory suggests in part that "losses loom larger than gains." People are more averse to loss than welcoming of comparable gain. Even if the future holds promise, the current state of affairs holds certainty. Losing a part of one's identity can be seen as a significant risk to one's sense that the world is predictable and stable (Northrup 1989).

History of a bad relationship

Prior relationships may affect resistance to change. A disputant may consciously or unconsciously associate the current conflict with previous ones. A party may have experienced grave mistreatment in the past and now becomes almost paranoid in an attempt to shield himself or herself from a repetition of the trauma. The party cognitively transfers characteristics from the previous situation into the current situation and makes negative attributions about his or her counterpart. Hence, it becomes difficult for the traumatized party to listen openly and without bias to the counterpart.

To summarize so far, mediators do not always deal with strong negative emotions of disputants as well as they could. I have discussed three diagnoses of this problem: that mediators try to avoid emotions, try to get rid of emotions, or fail to deal with emotional resistance to the extent possible.

STRATEGY

It is helpful, but not enough, to understand the diagnoses that produce a deficit in mediator effectiveness. As important, mediators need an action plan to help them deal with these diagnostic challenges. In this section I offer such advice for mediators.

Don't Wait and See: Conduct a Pre-Mediation Caucus with Each Party

The wait-and-see strategy is reactive. Perhaps parties can avoid talking about emotions, but the variety of affects people experience has an unavoidable impact on their subjective experience. Failing to deal with emotions early on simply means that emotions can run their own course – whether or not that course is congruent with the goals of the disputants. Given this, it is advisable for mediators to deal proactively with the emotions of disputants. Avoiding emotions makes it likely that problems will erupt (Moore 2003).

If mediators should not wait to deal with disputants' strong emotions until they arise, when should they start dealing with such emotions? The mediation model presented in chapter 2 offers the groundwork for a possible solution. This model describes the stages of mediation. But rather than assuming that the first stage begins as a joint meeting between parties and mediator, Herman, Hollett, and Gale outline a "T_0" stage of mediation. This stage occurs *before* the disputants meet jointly with the mediator. I will refer to a pre-mediation, individual meeting between a mediator and a single party as a "pre-mediation caucus."

A pre-mediation caucus is a particularly apt time for mediators to begin to appreciate the emotions of each party (Mathis, Tanner & Whinery 1999; Moore 2003; Poitras, Bowen & Byrne 2003). From the perspective of disputants, this stage provides an opportunity to share their conflict narrative with the mediator, who can listen to the party's narrative with undivided attention. Thus, the disputants can feel "heard" and recognized, at least by the mediator (Bush & Folger 1994; Billikopf-Encina 2002). They also can feel assured that, during the joint mediation session, the mediator has a clear understanding of their narrative, even if the other side appears not to understand. The mediator becomes their ally.

From the mediator's perspective, a pre-mediation caucus holds much promise. If each side sees the mediator as their ally, the mediator's ability to facilitate the mediation process is enhanced. Parties are more likely to trust the guidance of the mediator, allowing him or her to help parties communicate their interests and emotions.

While a pre-mediation caucus provides no guarantee that strong negative emotions will not be provoked later in the session, the mediator will be in a much better place to deal with any strong emotions that *are* expressed. Having learned about each party's emotions from the outset, the mediator can better help the parties understand one another and better lead the mediation process. The mediator will tend to have a good understanding of which issues are emotionally "safe" to discuss early on and which are flammable and worth suspending until rapport improves between the disputants.

During pre-mediation, the mediator wants to explore answers to such questions as:

- What is the current conflict about?
- How intense are the feelings of each side toward the other?
- How did the conflict arise?
- What is the history of the relationship between the disputants?
- How does each party currently feel toward the other? What might be possible "causes" of those feelings?
- Aside from the current mediation, has anything been done to try to deal with the conflict? What?

Rather Than Get Rid of Emotions, Focus on Relational Identity Concerns

Given that emotions are an integral part of any human interaction (Shapiro 2001), mediators can use them to help disputants reach their instrumental and affective goals. By understanding the emotions of parties, the mediator can gain insight into the intentions and motivations of each party (Tomkins 1970). With this insight, the mediator can guide discussion in ways that help each party to understand their own and the other's motivations, as well as approaches to satisfying those motivations.

Yet a mediator can easily get overwhelmed if he or she tries to decipher the complex motivations and intentions that underlie each emotion that arises in each party in the mediation. Emotions are dynamic. They come and go. To try to "catch" each emotion, to analyze the intentions it conveys, and to use that information constructively is much too time-consuming for most mediators (Fisher and Shapiro, 2005).

Turn your attention to relational identity concerns

One way to deal with this problem is to recognize that there is a small subset of motivations that, in conflict situations, tend to underlie a great many emotions. This subset of motivations is known as *relational identity concerns* (Shapiro 2002). They are "concerns" because we experience a felt desire for their satisfaction. They are "identity concerns" because the concerns motivate us to preserve a positive sense of self. And they are "relational identity concerns" because they focus our attention on our perceived identity in relation to the other party. Is the other party respecting us to the degree we expect or deserve?

In different relationships, individuals have a different threshold for the satisfaction of their relational identity concerns. In deciding upon a vacation location with one's spouse, a person may feel little desire for autonomy, thus welcoming collaborative decision-making. In negotiating a business deal with another firm, that same person may demand a great deal of autonomy and leave little room for collaboration.

Research in a variety of disciplines has converged upon two relational identity concerns – autonomy and affiliation – as basic dimensions of human existence (Angyal 1941; Bakan 1966; Bem 1974; Deci & Ryan 1985; Benjafield & Carson 1986; Wiggins 1991). These concerns are similar to conceptual dichotomies in the field of negotiation. See, for example, Kolb and Williams' description of advocacy and connection (2000) and Mnookin, Peppet, and Tulumello's "tension" between assertiveness and empathy (2000).

The first of these relational identity concerns, *autonomy*, describes the freedom to act, think, and feel as one would like – without the imposition of others. Mediation itself, for example, is typically predicated on the assumption that disputants can decide their outcome in accordance with internalized, personally accepted principles and not in response to coercion from the mediator or other parties.

Each party's desire for autonomy can become apparent early in the mediation. Who decides who talks first? For how long does each person get to talk? Is one party pressuring the other into believing that there is only one "right" conflict narrative? Or is one party telling the other that they have no reason to be as upset as they are? These actions are all potential impingements on a party's autonomy, and they can lead to strong negative emotions.

The second relational identity concern, *affiliation*, is the interpersonal closeness or distance that one party feels toward the other. To what degree does each party feel a sense of colleagueship with the others at the mediation table? Who feels excluded?

Stimulate positive emotions by improving each party's sense of affiliation and autonomy

Rather than trying in vain to get rid of emotions, the mediator can use relational identity concerns to improve the emotional climate. In this section, I offer illustrative ways for a mediator to help parties build affiliation and autonomy during a pre-mediation caucus.

"Wait a minute!" you might be thinking. How can the relationship between parties improve in the pre-mediation caucus – before parties have had the opportunity to interact with one another? To answer that question, consider the concept of affiliation. It is a psychological concept. The degree of interpersonal closeness between two parties is determined not only by the way people treat one another in an actual human interaction, but also by how each party *perceives* their relationship with the other (Cashdan 1988). Parties who reinterpret their understanding of their relationship with the other can positively impact their sense of affiliation with the other (Lazarus 1991).

Thus, during the pre-mediation caucus, the mediator can build affiliation between parties. After learning from a party about their perspective on the conflict, the mediator can shift conversation to positive elements of the disputants' relationship.

Each party might be encouraged to talk about a time when their relationship with the other was better than it currently is. What did the relationship feel like then? How did each party interact with the other? What were some of the strengths of that relationship? Such an exploration can help a party see their affiliation with the other party in more nuanced, less black-and-white terms.

There are many ways that the mediator can help satisfy each party's concern for autonomy during the pre-mediation caucus. For example, simply allowing the party to share their conflict narrative can give them a sense of liberation. It can be surprisingly satisfying for parties to have the space and time to express their personal experience of the conflict. Also, the mediator can talk with each party about ways their autonomy feels impinged. How has the disputant been constrained by the behavior of the other? Did one party make a big decision without consulting the other?

If a party admits being upset around issues of autonomy, the mediator may work with the party to understand the context in which the frustration arose. Next, the mediator may encourage the disputant to reflect on ways in which the *other's* autonomy may feel impinged on. The goal is not vindication of the other's behavior, but rather improved understanding. As parties understand the perceived constraints on their behavior and on that of the other party, they can develop a sensitivity to each party's concern for autonomy.

From the Outset, Help Parties Reflect Upon Whether to Let Go of their Emotional Resistance

Dealing with parties' resistance to change is an important activity of the mediator. As mentioned earlier, two factors often underlie emotional resistance. Parties may fear a loss of their identity, or they may fear a repetition of unsavory past circumstances and become protective of their current identity.

To deal with emotional resistance, a mediator first wants to understand what is motivating the resistance. Sometimes resistance is for good reason; sometimes it is not. But the people who hold the answer to that question are the parties themselves. And the only people who can reduce resistance are also the parties themselves. Thus, the mediator does not want to coerce a party to let go of their resistance. Rather, he or she wants to help the parties become aware of any resistance they might have and to give them the space and time to make a conscious choice about whether or not to maintain it. Parties can consider questions such as: "What might be making it tough to work with the other party? What are some of your fears if the conflict continues? What are some of your fears if you and the other reach an amicable agreement?"

Whether the cause of emotional resistance rests in a fear of change or in a fear of a recurring, troubling relationship, if a party wants to change, he or she needs to acknowledge that fact. Just as ex-smokers are more likely to stay away from cigarettes if they make a public pronouncement of their intentions (Prochaska & Di Clemente 1983), the same is true for disputants. Stating one's intentions to let go of resistance is a step in the right direction.

The next step is meant to transition the disputant through the often painful experience of modifying his or her identity. There is usually no avoiding the emotional pain of reconceptualizing one's relational identity. To help the process along, the mediator may help the disputant to grieve over the lost identity. Grieving entails mourning the lost elements of oneself. The mediator can ask questions such as, "What would you miss if you built a collegial relationship with the other party?"

A final step in overcoming resistance is for the disputants to work toward creating a revised relationship. In essence, disputants need to recraft their roles in relation to one another. For example, disputants may revise their roles from "adversaries" to "colleagues working side by side" (for details, see Fisher & Shapiro 2005).

A RETURN TO THE POPLAR TREE: PREEMPTING DISASTER

This section of the chapter returns to the conflict over the trimming of the poplar tree. I will turn the case into a hypothetical and explore what might have been done differently to avoid the loss of lives and to further reduce the risk of international war. The purpose of this section is not to identify the most effective process of problem-solving, but rather to consider how a mediator might induce parties into an emotional state conducive to cooperative work.

The Scenario

Today is August 4, 1976, the day after a group of US soldiers, UN officers, and South Koreans reportedly attempted to cut the tree but were chased away by North Korean soldiers. As a mediator with an international reputation for impartiality, you receive confidential calls from the United States government and from South Korean officials to see if you would be willing to conduct backchannel mediation to stop this brewing conflict at the DMZ. All involved parties, even the North Koreans, recognize the high risk associated with this small incident over a poplar tree and want to avert full-blown war.

The complications of the case become immediately apparent to you. First off, which parties should be included in the mediation? The UN? South Koreans? North Koreans? The United States? Other concerned states, such as China, Japan, and the USSR? Should you hold multiple sets of mediations between various parties? Because there is a crisis at hand, your goal is to keep the mediation as simple as possible. You arrange for the initial conversation to involve a senior US representative, a top South Korean representative, and a trusted confidante of Kim il-Sung. The risks of excluding the UN, China, Japan, or others from the talks are significant, but time limitations prevent you from going that route.

By good fortune, a representative from each country – even North Korea – agrees to attend this highly secret meeting, which begins tomorrow, August 6, 1976, on a military base in a neutral location outside of Asia.

Conducting a Pre-Mediation Caucus

As you arrive at the base, you are informed that the South Korean official will be arriving within the hour. With tempers boiling and fear tangible, the officials are probably in no mood to problem-solve.

Rather than wait and see if the representatives will explode in anger or get along during the mediation, you decide to hold a pre-mediation caucus with each official. Each will be able to share his perspective of this situation, which gives you the opportunity to gauge the quality and intensity of each person's emotions and perhaps to reduce the intensity of strong negative emotions through active listening and understanding.

The South Korean official indeed arrives first. You meet with him in private, diagnosing substantive areas of disagreement as well as relational identity concerns. Regarding the latter, you inquire about the cause of the tensions and listen carefully for themes related to autonomy and affiliation.

Focusing on autonomy

He is outraged at the audacity of North Koreans trying to prevent the tree trimming. He explains that trimming the tree is a routine procedure from year to year. Why stop the procedure this year? He indicates that many South Koreans feel that their autonomy is impinged on by the North Koreans' unilateral demand not to cut the tree.

He reflects on the larger issues that divide the two countries. There is a constant fear, he says, that North Korea is going to militarily overtake South Korea and limit political, cultural, and social autonomy. He worries that accepting any demands from North Korea will undercut the long-term interest of South Korea to maintain its autonomy. To concede would make South Korea, and perhaps even their close ally, the United States, appear weak.

As a mediator, you make a mental note of this fear of looking weak. You suspect that this fear may manifest during the face-to-face mediation. You foresee the possibility that a party may try to assert his autonomy much more strongly than is called for by the discussion – in order to look strong.

Focusing on affiliation

At first, the South Korean official speaks angrily about the North Korean political system. He calls it the "enemy." However, as conversation continues, the tone of his voice changes. He describes grave disappointment that the two countries cannot just get along. "Why are we killing our children like this? We speak the same language. We share the same history. Yet we live in two utterly different countries." This revelation is a gem for the mediator to remember. It can be a valuable way to frame the face-to-face meeting later on between the parties – helping them build affiliation as colleagues facing a joint problem rather than seeing each other as adversaries.

Dealing with Resistance to Change

You ask the South Korean what options he sees to improve the current situation. His response: "Either they win or we do." You inquire as to what he means, and he clarifies: "We refuse to change our behavior. They issued the threats. They are out to get us. We will not concede in the face of threat."

His resistance certainly has some basis in reality. North Korea has tried numerous times to invade the South. Yet now, at this time of crisis, neither party apparently desires magnification of this single issue to international proportions.

You explain to him that it may be possible to find a creative agreement that meets every party's interests – without anyone "giving in." He hears you say that, but he holds on to his resistance. You realize that if his resistance were to manifest in the mediation, it could offend the North Korean representative and spoil the entire mediation process. So you try to learn more about the basis of his resistance. You question him about what he sees as the risks and benefits of collaborative work with the North Koreans. He thinks hard, then lists some of the pros and cons. Still, he clings to his resistance. You do not want to force his cooperation; in fact, you cannot. Yet you do want to make sure that any resistance he sustains is based not on irrational fear, but rather on sound judgment. So you decide to take a different approach to help him get a more complete picture of the conflict. You ask him how the current crisis might look from the perspective of the North Koreans. At first, he refuses to talk about the other's perspective. But with some friendly coaxing, he tries. He suggests that Kim il-Sung may fear that the US, with support from South Korea, is preparing to attack North Korea. The official recalls that there were training exercises of US military forces along the DMZ starting in June 1976. The South Korean official admits that Kim il-Sung probably has good reason for his suspicions, however ill founded they actually are. The official concludes that these fears may have prompted Kim il-Sung's sensitivity to the poplar tree trimming in August. With this new understanding of the relational identity concerns and resistances, both you as a mediator and the South Korean are better equipped for the challenges of the upcoming face-to-face mediation.

Moments later, you learn that the North Korean has arrived. You conclude your conversation with the South Korean, meet the North Korean representative, and engage him in a two hour pre-mediation caucus. The questions you ask him are virtually identical to those you asked the other official. By holding a pre-mediation caucus focused on substantive and emotional issues, you learn about the important concerns to North Koreans. Then, after the US representative arrives, you repeat the entire process for a third time and then organize an initial face-to-face mediation between the parties late in the day.

Once it comes time for the face-to-face mediation, you have already developed a solid understanding of each party's interests and relational identity concerns. You have lessened their emotional resistance to change. They feel that you have heard their narrative, so they are less likely to "act out." And each has a greater understanding of their own partisan perceptions, as well as those of the other parties. Combined, these pre-mediation strategies leave the parties emotionally ready to cooperate and problem-solve.

SUMMARY

Mediators do not always deal with strong negative emotions of disputants as well as they could. I have discussed three diagnoses of this problem: that mediators try to avoid emotions, try to get rid of emotions, or fail to deal with emotional resistance.

To deal with these diagnoses, a mediator can hold a pre-mediation caucus, focus on relational identity concerns, and give each party time to decide whether or not to let go of emotional resistances to change. As the mediator holds a pre-mediation caucus with each of the parties, he or she reduces the risk that strong emotions will overwhelm the impending face-to-face mediation, and problem-solving becomes more effective.

REFERENCES

Allred, K. G. (2000) Anger and retaliation in conflict. In M. Deutsch & P. Coleman (eds.), *The Handbook of Conflict Resolution.* Jossey-Bass, San Francisco, pp. 236–255.

Angyal, A. (1941) *Foundations for a Science of Personality.* Commonwealth Fund, New York.

Bakan, D. (1966) *The Duality of Human Existence: Isolation and Communion in Western Man.* Beacon, Boston.

Bargh, J. A. & Chartrand, T. L. (1999) The unbearable automaticity of being. *American Psychologist* 54(7), 462–479.

Bazerman, M. H., Baron, J. & Shonk, K. (2001) *You Can't Enlarge the Pie: Six Barriers to Effective Government.* Basic Books, Cambridge.

Bazerman, M. H. & Neale, M. A. (1992) *Negotiating Rationally.* Free Press, New York.

Bem, S. L. (1974) The measurement of psychological androgyny. *Journal of Consulting and Clinical Psychology* 42, 155–162.

Benjafield, J. & Carson, E. (1986) A historicodevelopmental analysis of the circumplex model of trait descriptive terms. *Canadian Journal of Behavioural Science* 17(4), 339–345.

Billikopf-Encina, G. (2002) Contributions of caucusing and pre-caucusing to mediation. *Group Facilitation: A Research and Applications Journal* 4, 3–11.

Bush, R. A. B. & Folger, J. P. (1994) *The Promise of Mediation: Responding to Conflict through Empowerment and Recognition.* Jossey-Bass, San Francisco.

Cashdan, S. (1988) *Object Relations Therapy: Using the Relationship.* Norton, New York.

Deci, E. L. & Ryan, R. M. (1985) *Intrinsic Motivation and Self-Determination in Human Behavior.* Plenum Press, New York.

Ebbesen, E., Duncan, B. & Konecni, V. (1975) Effects of content of verbal aggression on future verbal aggression: a field experiment. *Journal of Experimental Social Psychology* 11, 192–204.

Fisher, R. & Shapiro, D. (2005) *Beyond Reason: Using Emotions as You Negotiate.* Viking, New York.

Fisher, R., Ury, W. & Patton, B. (1991) *Getting to YES: Negotiating Agreement without Giving In.* Penguin Books, New York.

Fiske, S. T. & Taylor, S. E. (1991) *Social Cognition.* McGraw-Hill, New York.

Folger, R. & Greenberg, J. (1985) Procedural justice: an interpretive analysis of personnel systems. *Research in Personnel and Human Resources Management* 3, 141–183.

Frijda, N. H. (1986) *The Emotions: Studies in Emotion and Social Interactions.* Cambridge University Press, Cambridge.

Frijda, N. H. (1993) The place of appraisal in emotion. *Cognition and Emotion* 7(3–4), 357–387.

Frijda, N. H. & Swagerman, J. (1987) Can computers feel? Theory and design of an emotional system. *Cognition and Emotion* 1(3), 235–257.

Gilligan, C. (1982) *In a Different Voice.* Harvard University Press, Cambridge. globalsecurity.org (2003) <www.globalsecurity.org/military/ops/paul_bunyan.htm>.

Goleman, D. (1995) *Emotional Intelligence.* Bantam Books, New York.

Gottman, J. M., Katz, L. F. & Hooven, C. (1997) *Meta-Emotion: How Families Communicate Emotionally.* Erlbaum, Hillsdale.

Greenhalgh, L. & Chapman, D. I. (1995) Joint decision making: the inseparability of relationships and negotiation. In R. M. Kramer & D. M. Messick (eds.), *Negotiation as a Social Process.* Sage, Thousand Oaks, pp. 166–185.

Kahneman, D. & Tversky, A. (1979) Prospect theory: an analysis of decision under risk. *Econometrica* 47, 263–291.

Kennedy-Moore, E. K. & Watson, J. C. (1999) *Expressing Emotion: Myths, Realities, and Therapeutic Strategies.* Guilford Press, New York.

Kitron, D. G. (2003) Repetition compulsion and self-psychology: towards a reconciliation. *International Journal of Psycho-analysis* 84(2), 427–441.

Kolb, D. M. & Williams, J. (2000) *The Shadow Negotiation.* Simon & Schuster, New York.

Korea Web Weekly (2003) <www.kimsoft.com/2000/bunyan.htm>.

Kumar, N., Scheer, L. K. & Steenkamp, J. E. M. (1995) The effects of supplier fairness on vulnerable resellers. *Journal of Marketing Research* 32, 54–65.

Lax, D. & Sebenius, J. K. (1986) *The Manager as Negotiator: Bargaining for Cooperation and Competitive Gain.* Free Press, New York.

Lazarus, R. S. (1991) *Emotions and Adaptation.* Oxford University Press, New York.

Levenson, R. W. (1994) Human emotion: a functional view. In P. Ekman & R. J. Davidson (eds.), *The Nature of Emotion: Fundamental Questions.* Oxford University Press, Oxford, pp. 123–126.

Levy, J. S. (1992) An introduction to prospect theory. *Political Psychology* 13(2), 171–186.

Lind, E. A. & Tyler, T. (1988) *The Social Psychology of Procedural Justice.* Plenum, New York.

Mathis, R. D., Tanner, Z. & Whinery, F. (1999) Evaluation of participant reactions to premediation group orientation. *Mediation Quarterly* 17(2), 153–159.

Mnookin, R. H., Peppet, S. R. & Tulumello, A. S. (2000) *Beyond Winning: Negotiating to Create Value in Deals and Disputes.* Harvard University Press, Cambridge.

Moore, C. W. (2003) *The Mediation Process: Practical Strategies for Resolving Conflict.* Jossey-Bass, San Francisco.

Northrup, T. A. (1989) The dynamic of identity in personal and social conflict. In L. Kriesberg, T. A. Northrup & S. J. Thorson (eds.), *Intractable Conflicts and their Transformation.* Syracuse University Press, Syracuse, New York, pp. 55–82.

Poitras, J., Bowen, R. E. & Byrne, S. (2003) Bringing horses to water? Overcoming bad relationships in the pre-negotiation stage of consensus building. *Negotiation Journal* 19(3), 251–263.

Prochaska, J. O. & Di Clemente, C. C. (1983) Stages and processes of self-change of smoking: toward an integrative model of change. *Journal of Consulting and Clinical Psychology* 51, 390–395.

Rubin, J. Z. & Pruitt, D. G. (1994) *Social Conflict: Escalation, Stalemate, and Settlement.* McGraw-Hill, New York.

Scherer, K. R. (1994) Emotion serves to decouple stimulus and response. In P. Ekman & R. J. Davidson (eds.), *The Nature of Emotion: Fundamental Questions*. Oxford University Press, Oxford, pp. 127–130.

Shapiro, D. L. (2000) *Negotiation Residuals: The Impact of Affective Satisfaction on Long-Term Relationship Quality*. Program on Negotiation at Harvard Law School Papers 2000, Cambridge.

Shapiro, D. L. (2001) A negotiator's guide to emotion: four "laws" to effective practice. *Dispute Resolution* 7(3), 3–8.

Shapiro, D. L. (2002) Negotiating emotions. *Conflict Resolution Quarterly* 20(1), 67–82.

Shapiro, D. L. (2004) Emotions in negotiation: peril or promise? *Marquette Law Review* 87(4), 737–745.

Shapiro, D. L. (2004) *Vertigo: Dealing with Strong Emotions in Negotiation*. Working Paper of the Harvard Negotiation Project. Cambridge, MA.

Solomon, R. (1993) *The Passions: Emotions and the Meaning of Life*. Hackett, Indianapolis.

Thibaut, J. & Walker, L. (1975) *Procedural Justice: A Psychological Analysis*. Erlbaum, Hillsdale.

Thompson, L. (2001) *The Mind and Heart of the Negotiator*. Prentice Hall, Upper Saddle River.

Tomkins, S. S. (1970) Affect as the primary motivational system. In M. B. Arnold (ed.), *Feelings and Emotions: The Loyola Symposium*. Academic Press, New York, pp. 101–110.

Verba, S. (1961) *Small Groups and Political Behavior: A Study of Leadership*. Princeton University Press, Princeton.

Wiggins, J. S. (1991) Agency and communion as conceptual coordinates for the understanding and measurement of interpersonal behavior. In W. M. Grove & D. Ciccetti (eds.), *Thinking Clearly about Psychology: Personality and Psychopathology*, vol. 2. University of Minnesota Press, Minneapolis, pp. 89–113.

Chapter 15

The Meaning of "Social" in Interpersonal Conflict and its Resolution

Sandra Schruijer and Leopold S. Vansina

Introduction

A handbook on interpersonal mediation has in our view to include a social psychological perspective. Mediating is a social process that takes place between minimally three individuals, two of whom being involved in a conflict, a third acting as a mediator. In chapter 2, Herrman, Hollett, and Gale informed us that complex mediation processes, i.e. those involving conflict between large groups or organizations, are not dealt with in the proposed model and literature review. Although it is understandable and justifiable to reduce complexity, we will argue in this chapter that such reduction should not imply that the social identities of the persons in question are ignored. Based on our work on multiparty collaboration, as researchers, consultants, and trainers, we "reframe" the domain of mediation by: (a) pointing to the role of social identities and social contexts in interpersonal and intergroup interactions; (b) exploring the complex interplay of conflict, collaboration, and collusion; and (c) enriching the concept of mediating by relating it to the way multiparty interactions can be facilitated successfully.

In order to understand interpersonal mediation processes one cannot exclude people's social identities, as it would mean that we look at individuals without them having, for example, a gender or a nationality. Furthermore, these social affiliations gain meaning by including the social context in which mediation takes place. Only then can we understand the behaviors enacted by the protagonists. A second argument we introduce is that the concept of mediation invokes a conflict frame. Indeed most of social psychology has studied the means to reduce conflict. We argue that it is imperative to study conflict and collaboration jointly if one is to gain a fuller understanding of the dynamics of social relationships. In the subsequent section we illustrate how we work with our understanding of the dynamics of social relationships, in our work as both researchers and consultants. We end with formulating implications for the study of and interventions in interpersonal mediation.

SOCIAL: INTERPERSONAL OR INTERGROUP, OR, INTERPERSONAL AND INTERGROUP?

What individual behavior enacted in a social relationship is purely individual, i.e. not influenced by that person's social embeddedness in groups, categories, and/or society? We cannot think of any. Although it seems possible to separate interpersonal behavior from intergroup behavior, it is not so easy. Individuals are embedded in groups and these groups in turn are embedded in society. Individuals cannot be reduced to individual identities, as that would imply that we study persons without considering their gender, age, nationality, organizational role, or parental status. Although individuals and their interpersonal relationships may be the focus of analysis, we cannot really understand their interactions if we ignore their social affiliations, identities, and interests. And understanding what gender means to anyone in a particular situation we have to understand what gender means in the larger society. So, contextual analysis is to be involved too.

Consider the following anecdote. While running through the corridor of the department one day, Sandra Schruijer found her path was blocked by an elderly man carrying a cello. He asked: "Are you a secretary or are you a student?" Suppressing her irritation, she pointed out that other alternatives existed. Ignoring her comment, he indicated that he needed a telephone – quickly. She made clear that she could not help him and suggested he go back to the place on campus he came from. She walked off without waiting for an answer. After an hour her anger subsided, and she reflected on the event. Statistically speaking his assumption made sense: the university is very male-dominated when it comes to academic staff. However, by applying this to a single case he made Sandra a "victim" of prejudice. But she may have confirmed his prejudice. He may have thought: "Women who run around here are either students or secretaries. And if she is not she must be a bitch in order to fight for her place in this male-dominated institution." And Sandra had behaved like a bitch! Later she related this story to a group of male military officers. One commented: "Why do women always think that men think that women are bitches?" And on and on it can go.

Were all these people acting as individuals, as group members, or both? How did their embeddedness in social categories and their experiences in society shape their behavior and comments? We cannot say what the man in question thought, but we can say that Sandra used his group membership as an explanation for his and her own behavior.

By omitting complex, multiparty interactions, Herrman et al. have also excluded such social analysis of individual and interindividual behavior. Although one may focus on the interaction between individuals, they may still act (partly) as group members. Tajfel and Turner (1979: 40) define intergroup behavior as: "any behaviour displayed by one or more actors toward one or more others that is based on the actors' identification of themselves and the others as belonging to different social categories." They make a clear distinction between two types of social behavior, namely interpersonal and intergroup behavior. Intergroup behavior takes place when one or more individuals behave toward (an)other(s) in terms of their membership of different social groups or categories. When individuals act toward (an)other(s) in terms of their personal relationships and their individual characteristics, it is called interpersonal behavior. Both types of behavior are two extremes of a continuum. In daily life social behavior will mostly be a combination of both types. Interpersonal and intergroup aspects of relationships coexist. Social identity theory (Tajfel & Turner 1979) stresses the potential importance of a person's identification with his or her group membership in determining behavior. Social identity refers to "that part of the individual's self-concept which derives from their knowledge of their membership of a social group (or groups) together with the value and emotional significance of that membership" (Tajfel 1981: 225). People strive for a positive self-concept. One's group membership may help build that self-concept.

All mediation relationships mentioned by Herrman et al. involve social identities. In chapter 2, Herrman et al. describe protagonists' demographic characteristics that have an impact on the mediation process and outcome. But aren't demographics group characteristics par excellence? How to interpret those differences if we do not know the social meaning of these characteristics in the interaction? Likewise, mediation that is taking place in parent–child relationships, boss–subordinate relationships, or neighbor relationships all potentially involves, in varying degrees of importance, group interests and social identities. That is even true for what some see as the most intimate relationship, namely marriage. A heterosexual relationship can actually be seen as both a purely intergroup (man and woman) and a purely interpersonal (intimacy between two individuals) relationship. Hence both personal and social identities are involved in the relationship.

Depending upon (changes in the) context and the issue under consideration, both personal and social identities may be triggered, in different and varying degrees. Therefore, it is important to understand the context of the mediation relationship. For example, a conflict that has arisen between a Dutch and a Turkish colleague cannot be worked with without understanding their different ethnic group memberships and especially what the meaning and nature of that inter-ethnic relationship is in society. Are we talking about a conflict in Turkey or in The Netherlands? It makes quite a difference when a Turkish employee has a conflict with his Dutch boss in The Netherlands as compared to a situation when a Turkish boss has a conflict with his Dutch employee in The Netherlands. Not only are social identities involved in both instances, but also they are probably quite different in meaning as the latter example is inconsistent with the existing status and power relationships between Dutch people and Turks in Dutch society.

The larger society is relevant too if it concerns cross-cultural differences in mediation between people coming from different countries or regions, as we encountered unexpectedly in our research on cross-cultural differences in the resolution of inter-group conflict. Together with our Indian colleagues we were devising comparable questionnaires to be distributed among supervisors and their employees in both The Netherlands and India (DeRidder 1992; DeRidder, Schruijer & Tripathi 1992; Singh & Sinha 1992). The idea was to think of situations in which a supervisor violated a norm toward his or her subordinate and vice versa. We then studied the reaction to those norm violations detailed in the questionnaires. To our surprise, our Indian colleagues in their final questionnaire had formulated all 36 hypothetical situations in the plural while those in The Netherlands had done so in the singular. Our colleagues explained that the singular would make no sense to the respondents. From our perspective the plural would be unintelligible. The same issues surfaced in our questionnaire concerning Dutch and Turkish people in The Netherlands, on the one hand, and Hindus and Muslims in India on the other (Ghosh, Kumar & Tripathi 1992; Schruijer 1992).

Rather than attributing differences to culture only, one should try to understand observed differences in a larger institutional context. For example, Lawrence's (1991) observation that Dutch managers are tolerant, as they are not likely to dismiss employees if they make mistakes, says more about the differences in labor law between England and The Netherlands than about value differences. Finally, one should be aware that not only does context influence social interactions in various ways, but also such context may be, rightly or wrongly, presented as relevant and so be used to serve one's interests. For example, the Dutch "poldermodel" pertains to a particular, consensus-oriented interaction style between the country's social partners. It is easily invoked to cut down on time spent in meetings, as in: "we in The Netherlands 'polder' too much."

In interpersonal conflict situations as dealt with in this book – between parents and their children, between husband and wife, between neighbors, between superiors and subordinates, between colleagues – the larger societal and organizational context is expressed in norms, values, institutional practices, and laws, for example around who is to get custody of children of divorced parents, when children can make what type of decision for themselves, the way neighbors are formally and informally expected to relate to one another, etc. In all this, social categorizations are involved as expressed in social identities, belief systems, social representations, norms, values and problem definitions. One's group membership and its social/societal meaning will have an impact on the way the problem is framed, is to be explained, and is to be dealt with (namely in interpersonal or in intergroup ways; Schruijer & Lemmers 1996).

And then there is the micro-context, which can influence the mediation process and outcomes in various ways. Stephenson has shown in his negotiation research that several factors can affect the salience of intergroup and interpersonal aspects of the relationship, for example: procedural requirements, formality of the communication system, eye contact, third party evaluation and number of negotiators present (Stephenson 1984).

The mediator should not be forgotten as a source of influence. Although expected to be neutral, she or he may not be perceived as such and/or may deliberately be framed as biased for various (self-serving) reasons. Shared social characteristics or group affiliations among the mediator and one of the parties in conflict may be put forward in order to position the mediator in a particular favorable or unfavorable light. The other party may resist allegations of partiality if the mediator seems to suit his or her interests. Since the mediator is the third party in a conflict between two other parties, he or she is likely to be fought for. Real or imagined shared social characteristics or relationships may lead to (imagined) support from the mediator for one's own point of view. This may add to the self-perceived strength and rightfulness of one party. Equally, around certain issues, both protagonists may experience a sense of interdependency or common social identity, that is, if they resemble one another more vis-à-vis a particular social characteristic than they each resemble the mediator. Such an event could be used as an opportunity to develop the protagonists' relationship for the better.

In practice, however, it is not at all easy to distinguish personal dispositions from social factors like group affiliation or representation. The reduction of conflicts to individual dispositions and/or interpersonal conflicts, excluding such social factors, reduces the effectiveness of mediation efforts. The individuals involved may come to some agreement, but it may, intentionally or not, isolate them from their social context. Upon returning to their real-life settings they often are unable to live up to the agreements because of pressures from their respective groups, pressures they can neither change nor ignore because they risk becoming excluded.

Conflict Resolving or Enhancing Collaboration?

Thus far we have spoken about conflict between interacting parties. It is amazing how much attention has been devoted by social psychology to the reduction to conflict and how little to the development of collaboration. Absence of conflict does not imply collaboration. Conflict, on the other hand, may be part and parcel of collaboration and may even be needed for collaboration to occur effectively. Successful negotiation outcomes are preceded by a conflict phase. Such a phase is less manifest in less successful negotiations (Stephenson 1981). But perhaps the terms conflict and collaboration need to be defined further. In *The American Heritage Dictionary of the English Language* (2000), the terms are described as follows:

Collaborate

1   to work together, especially in a joint intellectual effort;
2   to cooperate treasonably, as with an enemy occupation in one's country.

Conflict

1   a state of open, often prolonged fighting; a battle of war;
2   a state of disharmony between incompatible or antithetical persons, ideas, or interests; a clash;
3   a psychic struggle, often unconscious, resulting from the opposition of simultaneous functioning of mutually exclusive impulses, desires, or tendencies;
4   opposition between characters or forces in a work of drama or function, especially opposition that motivates or shapes the action of a plot.

The term collaboration has two quite different meanings. The double meaning of collaboration is also noticeable in day-to-day language where collaboration for many is associated with those Dutch and Belgians who actively sympathized with the Germans during World War II. The term is perceived negatively and therefore is mostly avoided. By collaboration, we mean all conscious efforts to work together on a given or set task, taking into account the diversity (e.g. of values, views, knowledge) of the parties involved.

Conflict has a more widespread negative connotation as reflected in all meanings ("war," "clash," "struggle," "opposition"). In our view such descriptions distract from the potential benefits of conflict. With conflict we refer to the tense or uneasy situation that can emerge when parties state their interests, come forward with their honest opinion or conviction, and do not shun expressing their own identity. The diversity of ideas, interests, and identities is not avoided or suppressed but faced or even capitalized on so as to address the common task successfully. We use the term *task conflict* to describe such a state of affairs, in contrast to *relational conflict*, in which the task is not served but the other party is defeated, or both parties end up in stalemate. In task conflict the realization of a positive distinctiveness vis-à-vis the other party remains present. But insofar as the need is recognized, it can be fulfilled by valuing each party's uniqueness without hampering task fulfillment (Tajfel & Turner 1979; Rijsman 1983).

Task conflict is the opposite of collusion. The definition of collusion in the *American Heritage Dictionary* is "a secret agreement between two or more parties for a fraudulent, illegal, or deceitful purpose." We would like to broaden the term to include implicit agreements and relationships that are not consciously secret, but unconsciously enacted. They are not necessarily for fraudulent, illegal, or deceitful purposes, but they serve one's own interests (and are often kept vague). In a collusive climate parties neglect to confront others with their diverse interests, while they unduly and prematurely agree with one another. They deny their diversity and suppress or avoid any disagreement to maintain an illusion of harmony (cf. groupthink, Janis 1972).

Herrman et al. assume that people prefer harmony to discord, and expect people to act responsibly and independently to achieve such harmony. We argue that the opposite may be true, especially under conditions of stress or insecurity. The need for harmony helps people avoid conflict. They avoid facing the issues and are seduced into collusion. A collusive climate is as destructive to successful collaboration as relational conflict. Diversity (e.g. of ideas, contributions, points of view) is essential and needs to be cherished rather than being reduced through conformity, power, or collusion. It follows that one cannot assess the effectiveness of solutions reached only by measuring satisfaction or whether an agreement has been reached or not. The reality base of the protagonists' satisfaction and their agreement need to be checked too.

Sometimes, it might be necessary to stimulate conflict when collusion prevails or task conflict is lacking (Brown 1983). When relational conflict looms, the adoption of conflict reduction techniques can be useful. Collaboration is a dynamic process with various phases and features.

MULTIPARTY COLLABORATION AND ITS FACILITATION

As researchers and consultants we are interested in the dynamics of multiparty collaboration. We conceive of multiparty collaboration as the emerging social system between two or more (legally independent) parties that is formed to address a concern, problem, or opportunity. A jointly defined goal is developed in the process of collaborating rather than being present from the very beginning. The parties, because of their unique contribution to this goal (that, since the goal is not socially shared from the start, may not be appreciated), are interdependent, while remaining autonomous vis-à-vis other goals or problem domains. Collaboration, therefore, does not imply the creation of a new entity at the expense of the existing entities. Instead, a new entity is added to the existing ones (Vansina, Taillieu & Schruijer 1998; Schruijer 2002). Examples of collaborations we study would be joint ventures, public–private partnerships, regional development initiatives, processes of interactive policymaking, but also multidisciplinary and multifunctional teams in hospitals and universities. We use the term "multiparty" to indicate that we do not restrict ourselves to the study of only two parties, which often is the maximum number in social psychological research.

During successful collaboration enough common ground is created to allow the unique value of each group, insofar as it is relevant for the task, to be recognized, accepted, and valued (Vansina et al. 1998). The diversity in perspectives, interests, identities, and potential contributions present, if handled properly, results in a broad problem definition, in creativity and a wide-ranging generation of solution alternatives, in the legitimacy of the chosen strategy, in energy and commitment to implementation, and, finally, in the capability to govern the emerging collaborative system. Apart from realizing the common goal, in which the participating parties can recognize their own interests, successful collaboration also helps in realizing a positive social identity through mutual validation (Rijsman 1997).

Gray (1989) has described the characteristics of a successful collaboration process. It unfolds from an underorganized situation in which parties act independently of each other toward a more strongly organized system in which decisions are made jointly. Solutions emerge because differences are constructively dealt with, in pursuit of the jointly defined goals. These goals are not given from the start, but are developed in the initial stages of the collaboration process. Parties feel jointly responsible for the solution of the problem or the realization of the opportunity and the execution of tasks that follow. Decisions are binding and constituencies too experience commitment to continue to work together and to carry out the decisions.

In multiparty collaboration in which parties are legally independent although they are interdependent in relation to the *problématique* or domain, the power of position is of little help (Theobald 1987). The interdependence in relation to a particular domain makes them stakeholders to that domain (Gray 1989, 1996). Within this context collaborative leadership is emerging as a response to the changing dynamics of these new social realities. The notion of collaborative leadership is, however, still ambiguous, not well defined, and described from different perspectives.

Svara (1994: 7) conceives of collaborative leadership as a form of leadership which stresses "empathic communication, think[ing] in win-win terms, rather than seeing ... interests in conflict with those of others, and us[ing] synergism to make the whole greater than the sum of the parts." Others, like Theobald (1987) see collaborative leadership as a necessity in the absence of positional authority. The notion of collaborative leadership runs counter to the dominant leadership concepts, principles, and practices, which for certain tasks, in certain contexts, are effective, but which fail in achieving voluntary commitment from different interest groups (Schruijer & Vansina 2004).

Bryson and Crosby (1992) have introduced in the title of their book the phrase "leadership for the common good" based on shared power. Chrislip and Larson (1994: 138) see "collaborative leaders" as people who "catalyze, convene, energize, and facilitate others to create visions and solve problems." The collaborative leadership role is a process-oriented one. A collaborative leader identifies and brings together relevant stakeholders, brings them to the table, and helps them to deal with one another in a constructive manner. Such leaders do not possess a formal authority or power position and do not try to obtain them. They attempt to minimize power and status differences between the parties, while helping them to recognize their interdependencies and valuing the diversity present. They furthermore foster conditions for creating and building trust between the parties and between the parties' representatives (Vansina 1999).

Huxham and Vangen (2000: 1171) define leadership in multiparty situations as a series of "mechanisms that are central to shaping and implementing collaborative agendas." Some of these mechanisms are outside of the direct sphere of influence of those participating, namely, the structure of the collaboration and the type of participants, the collaboration process (for example, the method of communicating with and informing the participants), and the leadership roles as enacted by individuals, groups, and organizations. Some leadership activities can be undertaken by all involved, for example influencing the agenda proactively, empowering people, and mobilizing the participating organizations. Huxham and Vangen attribute the success of collaborative partnerships largely to the energy and stamina of individual leaders.

Feyerherm (1997: 1) describes leaders in a multiparty context as people "who influence the course of events, the way issues get framed and resolved, and the people who influence the outcomes of the gathering." The emphasis is more on "framing the reality of others" than on facilitating the negotiation processes that result in a social construction of a particular domain, a "negotiated order" as Strauss (1978) calls it. Both "leaders" seek consensus but through distinguishable routes. In Feyerherm's frame, then, the convergence of different frameworks can be explained in terms of leadership behavior "that surfaces underlying assumptions and beliefs, helps create new alternatives, and initiates collective actions by providing structures and proposals" (Feyerherm 1997: 8). Activities are perceived by the members as leadership behavior when they foster the reaching of consensus. This implies that there is already a latent recognition that collaboration is the appropriate approach for dealing with that particular problem domain.

Not all multiparty issues start from that condition. In such instances, leadership is not perceptually linked to achieving a more or less agreed task, because there is neither an agreed definition of the task, nor a shared recognition of the inter-dependencies between the parties; nor is there an agreement on a strategy for task accomplishment. In situations like these, one starts from an earlier stage where people come together because they just have an interest or a concern related to a particular domain, and vague implicit expectations about desirable outcomes. Within this context, Gray (1989, 1996: 62) introduced the concept of "convener."

According to the *American Heritage Dictionary*, to convene means "to cause to come together formally, convoke." Gray (1996: 63) uses the notion of convener as the one who convenes in a broader sense to depict "one or more shareholders who create a forum for deliberations among the stakeholders and entice others to participate." He or she creates conditions for the different parties to collaborate. In her earlier work (Gray 1989), she lists the issues that need to be resolved successively in order to achieve effective completion of multiparty collaboration. The issues are grouped together under three phases that logically follow one another. These are the problem-setting phase: to arrive at an agreement among the stakeholders to talk about the issues; the direction-setting phase: to negotiate an agreement on actions to be taken; and the implementation phase: to manage the interorganizational relations toward effective implementation of the negoti-ated agreement. From the listed issues to be resolved, we learn that much more is required than just bringing the various parties together in a room, as has been proclaimed by Weisbord (1992). The convener does much more than just convene the interested parties.

Gray (1996: 63–65) describes four types of conveners/convening:

1 *Legitimation.* "Conveners using the legitimation mode possess formal authority and respond to an invitation from others stakeholders to organize the problem domain."
2 *Mandate.* "Stakeholders who convene by mandate elect to exercise the formal power they possess within the domain to assemble other stakeholders."
3 *Facilitation.* In this mode conveners "rely on their credibility, influence and/or knowledge as a source of informal authority."
4 *Persuasion.* Conveners rely on "informal authority and their own initiative."

But other participants may contribute to the creation of the necessary conditions for collaboration too. The legitimation base of the convener may subsequently change over time, or she or he may be pressured to intervene in the evolving processes. Intervening or not intervening poses an issue, a moral issue according to Schuman (1996), because "how" parties decide is subject to moral scrutiny just as much as "what" is being decided. Process interventions have an influence both on process and on content.

The three basic forms of conflict resolution – mediation, third party consultation, and arbitration – rely on the neutrality of a "third" party. Arbitration is a process by which a third person or group, either chosen by the disagreeing parties or appointed by statutory authority, solves the existing conflict. The neutrality of that third party is either established by the consent of the conflicting parties, or by appointment of a statutory authority. In arbitration it is this third party that decides on the solution for the disagreement that is binding on the parties involved.

Mediation refers to an emergent or contracted intervention to help solve conflicts and disputes between two or more parties. The impact of mediation is threefold: (1) a transformation of the conceptualized relations between the parties; (2) the restoration of a communication system between the parties to prevent distortions of perceptions and breakdowns in communication; and (3) clarification of the range or attractiveness of alternatives available in the situation. In mediation the parties eventually decide on the compromise or alternative solution, not the mediator. The mediator may be concerned about the outcome of the dispute, or may wish to make a good impression on one or more parties, but she or he should be neutral and impartial (Pruitt & Carnevale 1993). Bercovitch (1992) questions the neutrality of mediators as their presence changes the structure of the dispute: a dyad is transformed in a triad that cannot be neutral. Furthermore the mediator is a member of other organizations with their own interests that may interfere with the mediator's task. And even when the mediator is objectively neutral, he or she may not be perceived as such by the parties.

Third party consultation is another form of conflict resolution by a third party in which a consultant or facilitator assists the conflicting parties in gaining a better understanding of one another in relation to their conflict in order to help them to resolve it themselves. Impartiality and neutrality are again basic requirements. Third party consultation differs from the other two forms in the kind of professional expertise that is required to take on that role. In mediation and arbitration, expertise in the nature of the conflict or the domain is required, while in third party consultation the expertise resides primarily in understanding the dynamics of intergroup conflicts, their possible origins, and the processes leading to resolutions or aggravation (Fisher 1983, 1993). This does not mean that expertise in process and an understanding of context are not important in the work of mediators and arbitrators.

Search conferences (Emery 1997) are designed to create a learning and planning community of stakeholders in a particular domain. They have been organized over the years within a wide variety of domains, ranging from the stakeholders in an industrial organization to stakeholders in the development of an economically deteriorated community (Weisbord & Janoff 1995; Bunker & Alban 1997). Facilitators are neither passive nor non-directive. They design the sequence of tasks to be performed and they manage all plenary sessions in which the stakeholders come together. They observe conditions for effective communication, practice openness, and share their understanding of the dynamics at work. They, however, leave all "responsibilities for content and outcome to those who have to live with the consequences" (Emery 1997: 397).

"Professionals" like arbitrators, mediators, third party consultants, facilitators, or the staff of search conferences should be neutral toward the outcomes and impartial toward the parties. They work in more confined roles to realize more clearly defined tasks. "Non-professionals" or stakeholders seem to operate from a wider variety of roles (content- and process-orientation) in a basically non-hierarchical context. They may mediate, facilitate, or structure the agenda. By definition they are not impartial, nor are they neutral toward the eventual outcome of the deliberations. However, they allow, even encourage, the other members to question and review any improper insertion or imposition of their own interests. Over time, when understanding the dynamics of multiparty collaboration becomes more widespread, collaborative leadership may be exerted by the stakeholders themselves. It then becomes a function through which several stakeholders share the responsibility for creating conditions for collaboration. When the diversity of interests becomes conflictual they may decide to fall back on a "professional."

Our Work on Multiparty Collaboration and General Findings

After having reviewed our considerations concerning the social aspects of interpersonal mediation, the role of conflict in collaboration, and the implications for the facilitation of multiparty collaboration, we will present our observations based on our work in this domain. Rather than providing detailed observations for projects separately, we will briefly state in what type of projects our findings are based, refer to individual studies, and then focus on those phenomena that we often encounter.

We developed a simulation called "The Yacht Club," which enables participants to learn, by experience, about multiparty dynamics (Vansina, Taillieu & Schruijer 1999). The simulation is based on a regional development concern that emerged in Russia 12 years ago. Seven legally independent parties, each with a stake in regional development, have the possibility of addressing their concerns and opportunities and of interacting with other parties. Participants choose a party of their liking and are asked to identify with the interests of that party. It is made clear that it is not a role-play – they can be themselves. The main ground rule of the simulation pertains to interaction possibilities. We set up a schedule providing slots in which members of a maximum of three different parties can meet simultaneously and slots in which all parties can come together and communicate via representatives. Between 18 and 40 people can take part in the simulation. We have run simulations inside and outside of Europe with managers, consultants, and students, either in open programs or in company-specific programs. The total number of simulations we have conducted amounts to approximately 60. The simulation itself lasts for a full day, plus a part of the morning of the next day. During the simulation we observe without intervening.

The second day consists of an extensive reflection on the dynamics observed. We first ask each party to review their goals, strategies, and outcomes. Subsequently these, as well as intergroup perceptions, are exchanged in a plenary. We then explore and review the dynamics of the simulation over time, with the participants. We share our observations, yet do not claim to have seen more or better than the participants, just from a different perspective. We do not single out individuals; rather, we conduct the discussion in terms of roles, functions, and group behaviors and interests. The results of three questionnaires we distribute before, during, and at the end of the simulation are discussed. Then we ask participants to exchange their experiences concerning their back-home organizations and discuss which aspects of the dynamics they recognize and what can be done about this back home. At the end of the day we share relevant concepts concerning multiparty collaboration. Sometimes we organize a follow-up meeting during which we deepen the participants' conceptual understanding while also showing videotapes made of their collective meetings in the simulation. We ask them to observe and discuss what is happening and to think about possible interventions. In some workshops their learning is supported by writing a reflection paper.

Apart from the simulation that we have been running over the last eight years and that we continue to use, we are or have been involved in various action research and consulting projects. These concern, for example, the rethinking and formulation of the mental health policy in Malta. In the early 1990s, Leopold S. Vansina was asked to help with a fundamental change in this policy. The minister who initiated the change was well aware that the implementation of a new policy required wide endorsement beyond the acting government and its administration. The island community needed to recognize its relevance, its benefits, and its less pleasant consequences. Individual and small group interviews were organized with professionals (e.g. psychiatrists, psychologists, nurses) and parties (e.g. police, unions, employers, patients, ex-patients) which either had difficult working relations with or held opposing views on policy changes. Gradually more stakeholders (e.g. parents' groups and voluntary associations) were identified and included. Eventually, we ended up with about 15 parties in a two-day working conference. Expectations, concerns, and the anticipated negative consequences of a more liberal and modern mental health policy were listed and debated. At times, existing conflicting relations between professionals – which were perceived by many as interpersonal – had to be dealt with as intergroup issues originating from an outdated power and income structure in the mental health care system. For the well being of the total community, the staff tried to hold on to a neutral role, by seeing the conflicts and diversity of opinions in relation to the development of a more effective policy (the special characteristics of this had been listed by the parties). The working conference produced a lot of suggestions and concrete plans to curb most of the feared negative consequences of a more liberal, modern mental health policy (e.g. special training or educational programs for the parties facing direct interactions with patients and ex-patients). Most importantly, however, the stakeholders present had gained an understanding of one another's expectations and concerns, and had learned to make those difficult distinctions between interpersonal and interparty issues.

A current project of Sandra Schruijer involves facilitating a group consisting of representatives of 20 different organizations from the building industry in The Netherlands. Together they are exploring how they can be more effective in satisfying clients' needs while simultaneously reducing costs. It is an open network among competing and collaborating organizations, coming from various positions in the chain. Meetings are organized as a total system, as well as with heterogeneous systems that work on a common theme. Projects for concrete collaboration are being thought through. Another project concerns action research around the shellfisheries in The Netherlands, in which various interest groups, coming from nature preservation organizations, the fishing industry, government, and research institutes, come together to discuss the future of the shellfisheries and inform new policy (Schruijer, Neven & Boonstra 2004). We are observing interactions in certain workshops from a social science and policy science perspective, conducting interviews, and feeding back and discussing our observations.

We would like to present here some general observations, as we do at some point in almost all our projects. The first category of observations deals with the meaning people attach to the term *collaboration*. It appears that collaboration is to many a rather vague concept that they feel is mostly descriptive of people's behavior. Often when we feel that relational conflict or collusion is the name of the game, participants think that they work quite well together. Conflict avoidance is often confused with collaboration. It strikes us how easily the popular term "win-win" is used while the actual behavior of the involved parties is quite different. There is also confusion about whether collaboration in itself is something good or not. Rather then seeing collaboration as a way to realize one's own gain and joint gain, participants think that they cannot talk about their own needs and interests any more. The only alternative people envisage is solely pursuing their own interests while not taking into account those of others, often resulting in a positional power game. Still, the rhetoric of collaboration is often used, having multiple, different meanings as inferred from the way people actually behave.

Based on the simulation we have discovered at least six different meanings (Schruijer 2002):

1 collaboration as absence of competition; collaboration as a truce;
2 collaboration as a defense system with which parties can control each other's actions, or through which the weaker parties align to protect themselves against the powerful;
3 collaboration as a form of working autonomously yet at the same time and in the same place as others;
4 collaboration as the intention to bring parties together (and perhaps also doing that), combined with the hope that collaboration will occur spontaneously and automatically;
5 collaboration as a puzzle that needs solving with the assumption that the ideal solution can be "computed'; and
6 collaboration as a deal or an accumulation of bilateral deals; collective meetings are purely intended to sign off what has already been agreed. A deal, combined with handshake and signature, is seen as proof of collaboration.

Whether it is a matter of not knowing what collaboration is or of not being able to transform sincere intentions and good ideas into action remains to be explored further. We can only conclude that working with diversity in a constructive way (i.e. not engaging in either win-lose interactions or collusion, while being willing to embrace task conflict and being able to avoid or solve relational conflict) is not something that comes to people naturally (Vansina et al. 1998).

Earlier we noted that social psychology has occupied itself mostly with understanding the determinants, processes, and resolution of conflict rather than of collaboration. This preoccupation becomes more intelligible when we observe how quickly win-lose dynamics emerge between parties who have not found out about each other's interests, goals, or even positions. Group-serving biases as expressed in expectations, attitudes, and attributions become the basis for behavior, which in turn creates conditions for the realization of self-fulfilling prophecies. A lack of openness about one's ideas, interests, and concerns coincides with a growing gossip circuit, unchecked assumptions, and flourishing fantasies. Once such a climate is created, it tends to reinforce itself. It becomes more and more difficult, without adequate intervention, to change.

Collaboration is mostly understood in interpersonal terms. This may partly be due to insufficient insight into intergroup dynamics, an inclination to reduce complexity or downplay contextual influences. It strikes us frequently that, rather than thinking in terms of social systems consisting of relationships between individuals or groups and their interdependencies, people tend to think in terms of individuals or groups as autonomous entities that can exert unilateral control or can act and succeed independently of others. This explains how interpersonal conflict can erupt without concomitant insight into how such conflict may be related to underlying group interests and identities. Likewise, intergroup conflict sometimes is softened by informal and interpersonal relationships between members of the different groups.

Something that strikes us over and over gain is the need for clarity and simplicity. Apparently people cannot stay very long in a position of not knowing, uncertainty, or not understanding. One expects to be able to resolve such feelings soon. In complex situations this may take a while, however (and many never completely come about – nor would that be desirable), leading to increased frustration and impatience. As a consequence, diversity and complexity are reduced too drastically and prematurely. This is manifested in intolerance of further exploration, exclusion of parties, continual postponement of complex issues, externalization of frustration, psychologizing, lack of reflection, and calls for a strong leader – a strong leader who will relieve us from having to struggle with thinking and coping with complexities, from considered choices about justice and one's responsibilities as a member of a social system, or as a citizen of the world. The wish to be free to pursue without concern one's self-interest may well be the greatest obstacle to learning about collaboration or conflict-handling. These are not only phenomena that we encounter in our work on multiparty issues – we see them in society all the time, and it concerns us deeply. Learning and development are only possible if one allows oneself not to know and is willing to engage in a joint and inclusive exploration.

That brings us to the last category of observations we want to share here, namely, the difficulties of enacting the role of a "leader" who "helps the collaborative agenda to move forward" (Huxham & Vangen 2000: 1159). There is little notion among participants in multiparty interactions of what type of leadership function is suitable to their aims and how that could be translated into particular roles. Most expect leaders to behave in line with the currently fashionable caricature of a successful leader: powerful, charismatic, dominantly present, decisive, risk-taking. And indeed the tendency exists for those taking up a leadership role to live up to at least some of these expectations. Rather than facilitating, mediating, and "creating and maintaining conditions for getting the most out of the diversity of perspectives, competences, resources that parties bring to the table, while simultaneously enabling the different parties to realize their objectives" (Vansina et al. 1998), they easily become managers or judges of ideas and proposals formulated by the participating parties. Not only is their neutrality often questioned; by behaving in such a way they have become interest parties themselves and they take away the responsibilities of the stakeholders.

IMPLICATIONS AND INTERVENTIONS

We conclude this chapter by formulating some implications of our analyses for those working in the domain of interpersonal mediation. Our main message is that interpersonal relations need to be situated in a social, ideological, and structural context, meaning that protagonists' social identities have to be taken into account and that contextual analysis is needed to understand the ways in which social identities are involved. Any relationship encompasses different yet interdependent levels of analysis: impacting upon the interpersonal relationship is, as we have said, the protagonists' social identities and the underlying intergroup relationship, in turn embedded in a larger system (organization and/or society). And then there are the three individuals (protagonists and mediator) with their intra-individual dynamics and relationships with each other and other individuals. Such a complex system, including its history, needs to be critically examined and at least minimally understood so as to be able to explore and understand how the issue(s) at stake are constructed: in interpersonal terms and/or intergroup terms? Whose construction is it? And what interests lie behind such a construction? In other words, a mediator needs to sort out what the intergroup basis is for the interpersonal conflict.

Second, we introduced the term collaboration as a complement to the term conflict and added a third term, namely collusion. Here too it is important to explore the protagonists' framing of the issue at hand. Is a conflict frame or a collaboration frame employed? In whose interest? Do the people involved share the same frame? Is it realistic to reframe conflict into collaboration? To what extent is the collaboration achieved of a collusive nature?

Finally, based on our work on multiparty collaboration we have elaborated on the term mediation and related it to leading multiparty interactions. Elsewhere we have formulated what we think is important for collaborative leaders to be and do (Vansina et al. 1998; Schruijer 2002). She or he has to be able to deal with ambiguity and complexity, be comfortable enough with "not knowing," and with frustrations that are projected onto him or her, as the legitimacy of the leader (or facilitator) may be undermined by holding them responsible for the lack of success or questioning their neutrality. Moreover she or he can be seduced into formulating solutions too fast, thus reducing the diversity of ideas, interests, and points of view prematurely. A capacity to contain and to hold on to the "messiness" of the situation is called for (Vansina 1999; Schruijer 2002). It seems to us that such competences equally apply to the "traditional" interpersonal mediator.

Given the apparent need for clarity, speed, and predictability, and the difficulties people have in staying with complexity, it makes sense to mentally prepare protagonists with the knowledge that the process may take a while, can be painful and frustrating, and that solutions and agreements can only be found after having started with and worked through difficulties and ambiguities. In our work on multiparty issues, for example, we sometimes get the feeling that people are relieved to find out that is it quite natural that there is no trust to start with but that it needs to be worked on. Such mental preparation is comparable to the intervention of emotional inoculation Janis and Mann (1977) have described.

Helping protagonists to reflect on their interactions with their mediator seems no superfluous luxury. Reviewing regularly can become a rich source of learning (Vansina 2004). Our "Yacht Club" simulation not only contributes to experiencing the importance of reviewing, but also enriches one's understanding of the dynamics of conflict and collaboration in and of a complex social system. Such experiential learning, including of course reflecting on one's experiences, can add greatly to the effectiveness of attempts to resolve relational conflict and enhance true collaboration.

REFERENCES

American Heritage Dictionary of the English Language, 4th edn. (2000), <bartleby.com>.

Bercovitch, J. (1992) The structure and diversity of mediation in international relations. In J. Bercovitch & J. Rubin (eds.), *Mediation in International Relations: Multiple Approaches to Conflict Management*. St. Martin's Press, New York, pp. 1–29.

Brown, L. (1983) *Managing Conflict at Organizational Interfaces*. Addison-Wesley, Reading.

Bryson, J. & Crosby, B. (1992) *Leadership for the Common Good: Tackling Public Problems in a Shared-Power World*. Jossey-Bass, San Francisco.

Bunker, B. & Alban, B. (1997*) Large Group Interventions: Engaging the Whole System for Rapid Change*. Jossey-Bass, San Francisco.

Chrislip, D. & Larson, C. (1994) *Collaborative Leadership*. Jossey-Bass, San Francisco.

DeRidder, R. (1992) Dutch employee relations: supervisors' and subordinates' perspectives. In R. DeRidder & R. Tripathi (eds.), *Norm Violation and Intergroup Relations*. Oxford University Press, Oxford, pp. 116–136.

DeRidder, R., Schruijer, S. & Tripathi, R. (1992) Norm violation as a precipitating factor of negative intergroup relations. In R. DeRidder & R. Tripathi (eds.), *Norm Violation and Intergroup Relations*. Oxford University Press, Oxford, pp. 3–37.

Emery, M. (1997) The search conference: design and management of learning with a solution to the "pairing" puzzle. In E. Trist, F. Emery & H. Murray (eds.), *The Social Engagement of Social Science: A Tavistock Anthology*, vol. 3, *The Socio-Ecological Perspective*. University of Pennsylvania Press, Philadelphia, pp. 389–412.

Feyerherm, A. (1997) *Leading M.E.N.: Perspectives on Leadership in Multistakeholder Environmental Negotiations*. Paper presented at the Academy of Management, Boston.

Fisher, R. (1983) Third party consultation as a method of intergroup conflict resolution: a review of studies. *Journal of Conflict Resolution* 27, 301–334.

Fisher, R. (1993) Towards a social-psychological model of intergroup conflict. In K. Larsen (ed.), *Conflict and Social Psychology*. Sage, London, pp. 109–122.

Ghosh, E., Kumar, R. & Tripathi, R. (1992) The communal cauldron: relations between Hindus and Muslims in India and their reactions to norm violations. In R. DeRidder & R. Tripathi (eds.), *Norm Violation and Intergroup Relations*. Oxford University Press, Oxford, pp. 70–89.

Gray, B. (1989) *Collaborating: Finding Common Ground for Multiparty Problems*. Jossey-Bass, San Francisco.

Gray, B. (1996) Cross-sectoral parties: collaborative alliances among business, government and communities. In C. Huxham (ed.), *Creating Collaborative Advantage*. Sage, London, pp. 57–79.

Huxham, C. & Vangen, S. (2000) Leadership in the shaping and implementation of collaboration agendas: how things happen in a (not quite) joined-up world. *Academy of Management Journal* 43, 1159–1175.

Janis, I. (1972) *Victims of Groupthink*. Houghton Mifflin, Boston.

Janis, I. & Mann, L. (1977) *Decision Making*. Free Press, New York.

Lawrence, P. (1991) *Management in The Netherlands*. Clarendon Press, Oxford.

Pruitt, D. & Carnevale, P. (1993) *Negotiations in Social Conflict*. Open University Press, Buckingham.

Rijsman, J. (1983) The dynamics of social competition in personal and categorical comparison situations. In W. Doise & S. Moscovici (eds.), *Current Issues in European Social Psychology*, vol. 1. Cambridge University Press, London, pp. 279–312.

Rijsman, J. (1997) Social diversity: a social psychological analysis and some implications for groups and organizations. *European Journal of Work and Organizational Psychology* 6, 139–152.

Schruijer, S. (1992) On what happens when Dutchmen and Turks violate each other's norms: a perfect match of mutual expectations? In R. DeRidder & R. Tripathi (eds.), *Norm Violation and Intergroup Relations*. Oxford University Press, Oxford, pp. 51–69.

Schruijer, S. (2002) *Delen en helen: over conflict en samenwerking tussen groepen* [Parts and wholes: about conflict and collaboration between groups]. Published inaugural address, Tilburg University, Tilburg.

Schruijer, S. & Lemmers, L. (1996) Explanations and evaluations by Turks and Dutchmen of norm violating ingroup and outgroup behaviour. *Journal of Community and Applied Social Psychology* 6, 101–108.

Schruijer, S., Neven, I. & Boonstra, F. (2004) *Reflexive Analysis of the Dutch Policy on Shellfish Fisheries*. Paper presented at the 11th Conference on Multi-Organizational Partnerships, Alliances and Networks, Tilburg.

Schruijer, S. & Vansina, L. (2004) The dynamics of multiparty collaboration and leadership. In T. Camps, P. Diederen, G.-J. Hofstede & B. Vos (eds.), *The Emerging World of Chains and Networks: Bridging Theory and Practice*. Reed Business Information, The Hague, pp. 219–234.

Schuman, S. (1996) The role of facilitation in collaborative groups. In C. Huxham (ed.), *Creating Collaborative Advantage*. Sage, London, pp. 126–140.

Singh, R. & Sinha, J. (1992) The darker side of the worker–manager relationship in a coal area in India. In R. DeRidder & R. Tripathi (eds.), *Norm Violation and Intergroup Relations*. Oxford University Press, Oxford, pp. 90–115.

Stephenson, G. (1981) Intergroup bargaining and negotiation. In J. Turner & H. Giles (eds.), *Intergroup Behaviour*. Basil Blackwell, Oxford, pp. 168–198.

Stephenson, G. (1984) Intergroup and interpersonal dimensions of bargaining and negotiation. In H. Tajfel (ed.), *The Social Dimension: European Developments in Social Psychology*, vol. 2. Cambridge University Press, Cambridge, pp. 646–667.

Strauss, A. (1978) *Negotiations: Varieties, Contexts, Processes, and Social Order*. Jossey-Bass, San Francisco.

Svara, J. (1994) *Facilitative Leadership in Local Government: Lessons from Successful Mayors and Chairpersons*. Jossey-Bass, San Francisco.

Tajfel, H. (1981) *Human Groups and Social Categories: Studies in Social Psychology*. Cambridge University Press, Cambridge.

Tajfel, H. & Turner, J. (1979) An integrative theory of intergroup conflict. In W. Austin & S. Worchel (eds.), *The Social Psychology of Intergroup Relations*. Brooks/Cole, Monterey, pp. 7–24.

Theobald, R. (1987) *The Rapids of Change*. Knowledge Systems, Indianapolis.

Vansina, L. (1999) Towards a dynamic perspective on trust-building. In S. Schruijer (ed.), *Multi-Organizational Partnerships and Cooperative Strategy*. Dutch University Press, Tilburg, pp. 47–52.

Vansina, L. (2004) The art of reviewing. In G. Amado & L. Vansina (eds.), *The Transitional Approach in Action*. Karnac, London, pp. 227–254.

Vansina, L. & Taillieu, T. (1997) Diversity in collaborative task-systems. *European Journal of Work and Organizational Psychology* 6, 183–199.

Vansina, L., Taillieu, T. & Schruijer, S. (1998). "Managing" multiparty issues: learning from experience. In W. Pasmore & R. Woodman (eds.), *Research in Organizational Change and Development*, vol. 11. JAI Press, Greenwich, pp. 159–181.

Vansina, L., Taillieu, T. & Schruijer, S. (1999) *The Yacht Club: A Simulation of Multigroup Processes*. Professional Development Institute, Korbeek-Lo.

Weisbord, M. (1992) *Discovering Common Ground*. Berrett-Koehler, San Francisco.

Weisbord, M. & Janoff, S. (1995) *Future Search*. Berrett-Koehler, San Francisco.

Chapter 16

Manager as Mediator: Developing a Conflict-Positive Organization

DEAN TJOSVOLD AND FANG SU

When a minister lives among calumniators, flatterers, and sycophants, though he may wish the state to be well governed, is it possible for it to be so?

Mencius, influential Confucian scholar

When two [people] in business always agree, one of them is unnecessary.

(William Wrigley, American businessman)

INTRODUCTION

Organizations have developed formal structures, such as grievance committees and ombudsman's offices, to mediate conflicts between employees and have hired mediators to cope with escalated labor–management conflict and sharp divisions between units. Mediation research and practice as developed in the other chapters of this book are highly relevant and useful for guiding these efforts. Mediation, though, is much more prevalent in organizations than only in terms of these formal approaches. Employees continually disagree over issues, interpersonal treatment, and attitudes. Rather than hire third party specialists, managers are expected to handle conflicts as they make decisions and resolve differences among employees. However, most managers have little formal training in conflict and are unprepared to meet the demands of mediation.

Conflict is part of interdependence and occurs in dyads, or two-person relationships, as well as in groups, which can be defined as two or more persons who depend upon and interact with each other, normally face to face. Organizations are structured relationships designed to accomplish an established purpose and typically have a management structure, including an authority hierarchy, designed to promote coordination.

This chapter examines the role and methods of mediation as illuminated by the model presented in chapter 2 of this volume and as applied to organizations.

It proposes that, in addition to formal mediation, conflict is so prevalent and potentially so constructive, that mediation needs to be built into the everyday activities of organizations. The organization's culture and methods should be developed to support managers and employees so that they are able and willing to mediate and manage their conflicts successfully.

Applying mediation knowledge in organizations is important because many conflicts occur within work, social, and community organizations, and they are often complex and difficult to manage. It is also useful to consider mediation in organizations because they embed conflicts within a set of relationships. Conflicts involve members with an ongoing relationship within a wider context of other individuals and groups. A conflict between supervisors, for example, is likely to affect and to be affected by their employees and their superiors. In organizations and in many other settings, most conflicts develop out of a larger set of interpersonal relationships and are influenced by these relationships.

This chapter applies mediation knowledge relevant to portions of the model presented in chapter 2 to organizations. It emphasizes the antecedent variables (T_0) of disputant beliefs and attitudes that affect conflict dynamics. It uses Deutsch's (1973) theory of cooperation and competition to argue that disputants' perceptions that they are trying to resolve a conflict for cooperative goals (mutual benefit) or to further competitive interests (win at the other's expense) very much affect their interpersonal dynamics. The personal characteristics of the disputants and mediators, the legal and conflict characteristics of the disputes, and the institutional context are also vital, but their effects can be understood in terms of how they affect the cooperative or competitive perceptions of the disputants.

Interpersonal dynamics noted in the T_0 phase of the model presented in chapter 2 very directly and critically affect mediation, including any conflict processes presented in the T_m phase of the model, especially social problem-solving. Like chapter 2, this chapter highlights the value of social problem-solving and supplements it by reviewing the research literature that details the nature of social problem-solving when dealing with a wide variety of conflicts. The model presented in chapter 2 proposes that environment very much affects social problem-solving. Studies reviewed in this chapter document important social conditions and interpersonal dynamics under which open-minded social problem-solving is likely to occur, thus relating directly to constructs defined as disputant beliefs and attitudes, as well as institutional context, described in the T_0 phase of the model presented in chapter 2.

The model presented in chapter 2 identifies institutional context as an important antecedent to mediation and conflict dynamics in phase T_0. This chapter elaborates that the internal context of an organization, such as its leadership and culture, affects the dynamics and outcomes of conflict as well as the demands of customers, social values, and other elements of the external context.

The model presented in chapter 2 also specifies that conflicts can affect disputant beliefs and attitudes, resolutions, and the institutional context in the short term (T_1) and in the long term (T_2). This chapter proposes that these types of outcomes, in both the short term and the long term, are critical for organizations.

Organizations require managers and employees to work together over time; if possible, conflicts should strengthen the relationship of managers and employees with each other. Disputants must reach agreements that allow them to move forward. Ideally, conflicts are resolved so as to change organizational procedures and values in ways that help managers and employees work more effectively and manage their conflicts more successfully in the future.

Poorly managed conflicts cost organizations significantly and disrupt their goals (Tjosvold & Janz 1985). The theme of this chapter is that training managers and developing organizations that support mediation and the constructive management of conflict are wise investments. Training in the sensitivities and skills of mediation prepares managers to fulfill a significant part of their responsibilities. Organizations should develop the norms, structures, and patterns that provide a facilitative institutional context for conflict management. Unfortunately, the values and procedures of most organizations are conflict-negative and orient their members to avoid conflict and, when that fails, to escalate and try to win. Organizations prosper when they apply mediation knowledge to help managers become effective mediators and develop their values and methods to support constructive conflict management.

This chapter has five sections. The first part outlines the value of organizations becoming conflict-positive. The second section elaborates on the chapter's theme that managers need to be skilled mediators to fulfill their responsibilities and that developing conflict-positive values and methods can very much help managers and employees mediate and resolve their conflicts. The third part reviews research indicating that constructive controversy has provided a useful way to characterize the social problem-solving for managing conflict in organizations and that cooperative goals are an important antecedent to this problem-solving. The fourth section outlines the basic steps to using this research so that organizational members have a common understanding and framework for managing conflict. The final part concludes with the value of managers as skilled mediators and of a conflict-positive organization for meeting contemporary demands.

BECOMING CONFLICT-POSITIVE

Organizations have traditionally been built upon two related assumptions: conflict is harmful and can be avoided (Tjosvold 1991). These assumptions have fostered common values (e.g. be rational) and roles (e.g. superiors decide). However, neither assumption is true. Developing our organizations based on more realistic views of conflict will be a challenge for many years to come.

Conflict pervades organization life. Each person within a department is unique, and they all see the world from their own perspective. They inevitably develop different opinions and reactions. Even less realistic is the expectation that different groups, often separated by distance and diverse training, will be able to work harmoniously. Indeed, as organizations move toward teams, form alliances, and enter the global marketplace, the notion that they will be able to work without conflict becomes completely fanciful and dysfunctional. The first rule of management, according to Jack Welch, is to face reality (Tichy & Sherman 1993). To deny conflict is to deny reality.

As suggested by the model proposed in chapter 2, a number of research programs have shown that conflict can be a highly constructive force (Cosier 1978; Eisenhardt & Bourgeois 1988; Jehn 1995, 1997). Expressing diverse views has been found to stimulate exploration of issues, understanding of the advantages and disadvantages of various options, and the creation of high-quality solutions that people are committed to implement (Tjosvold 1982, 1998). Managing conflict can also strengthen relationships and resolve anger and other feelings that may divide people (Tjosvold 2002; Tjosvold & Su in press). Managing conflict is key to realizing the potential of teamwork within and between organizations.

But managing conflict in organizations cannot be left to a few managers specifically trained in mediation. Moving from a conflict-negative organization to a conflict-positive one helps group members, departments, alliance partners, and customers deal with their many conflicts.

MANAGER AS MEDIATOR

Traditional, conflict-negative organizations expect managers to deal with conflicts expeditiously in order to restore the harmony needed for people to work productively. The hierarchy assigns superiors the responsibilities and grants them the authority and power to resolve conflicts. Increasingly skeptical about this approach, managers and researchers are experimenting with different leadership styles.

Effective leaders work with and through other people to accomplish goals. To accomplish this, contemporary leaders want to involve employees more in developing goals and making decisions. In this way, more information is available to make decisions. Employees should then also appreciate the rationale for the decision and realize what they and others must do to implement the decision.

Today's leaders are to empower and develop their employees so that they are more skillful. Transformational leaders promote teamwork among employees and direct it to accomplish vital organizational goals. By developing close, in-group relationships with individual employees, leaders can help them perform their jobs and become organizational citizens who contribute to the welfare of the organization.

Many managers, though, fall far short of these ideals. Surveys of US employees consistently indicate that over 60 percent believe that their boss is the biggest source of stress on the job (Hogan, Curphy & Hogan 1994). Despite all the discussion about empowerment and teamwork, many employees feel alienated from their leaders.

What is not much appreciated is that contemporary leadership approaches demand constructive conflict to be effective. Employees must be able to express their opposing views and integrate them to take advantage of the opportunities to participate in decision-making. Both teamwork and maintaining a strong leader relationship require that employees and managers deal with relational and task conflicts.

Training managers in mediation can contribute significantly. But managers must work with and through employees if they are going be successful mediators. It is not enough that managers want conflicts to be managed. Managers and employees should together become more oriented and able to make their conflicts productive. The next section argues that they should together learn cooperative, problem-solving values and methods to manage their conflicts.

Research on Productive Conflict in Organizations

Managers and employees need clear, credible guidance on how they can develop their organizations to support their conflict management. The anchor model identifies social problem-solving as a central ingredient to successful conflict management. Our studies document the value of social problem-solving for a wide range of issues and conflicts, specify the interactions that contribute to it, and identify conditions under which it occurs.

Social Problem-Solving

Constructive controversy has proved a useful way to understand the social problem-solving that develops and implements quality solutions to organizational conflicts. Controversy occurs when decision-makers express their opposing ideas, opinions, conclusions, theories, and information that at least temporarily obstruct resolving the issue. Experiments in the West and in China have documented the dynamics in controversy and, specifically, how controversy can promote decision-making (Tjosvold 1982, 1998; Tjosvold & Sun 2000, 2003; Tjosvold, Hui & Sun 2004).

People in controversy, especially when they seek mutually acceptable solutions, have been found to be open to new and opposing information. Confronted with an opposing opinion, they have felt uncertain about the adequacy of their own position, indicated interest in the opponent's arguments, and asked questions to explore the opposing views. They have demonstrated that they knew the opposing arguments and understood the reasoning others used to examine the problem and develop the opposing perspective. They have taken information seriously and incorporated opposing positions into their own thinking and decisions.

Constructive controversy occurs when people work to integrate their diverse ideas. Studies show that constructive controversy results in high-quality, implemented solutions (Tjosvold 1982, 1998; Tjosvold & Sun 2000, 2003). When relying on constructive controversy, participants use opposing ideas to develop a more complete awareness and appreciation of the complexity of the problem and create a solution that responds to the complete information. These studies have shown that constructive controversy interaction – that is, expressing opposing views openly and respectfully, seeking mutually acceptable agreements, listening and understanding each other, and combining ideas – promotes quality solutions.

Cooperation Goals for Constructive Controversy

Organizational members, though, often do not discuss their opposing views openly and constructively. Indeed, researchers have been most impressed with how members avoid and suppress their conflicts, especially in collectivist cultures like China's (Kirkbride, Tang & Westwood 1991; Tse, Francis & Walls 1994). Our studies have used Deutsch's (1973) theory of cooperation and competition to identify when people are more or less able to use constructive controversy (Tjosvold 1998).

According to Deutsch (1973), the way goals are structured affects the outcomes of groups by shaping how individuals interact (Deutsch 1980; Johnson, Maruyama, Johnson, Nelson & Skon, 1981; Johnson & Johnson 1989; Stanne, Johnson & Johnson 1999). Goals may be structured so that individuals promote the success of others or obstruct the success of others, or goals may be unrelated. When a situation is structured cooperatively, individuals' goal achievements are positively correlated. Individuals perceive that they can reach their goals if and only if the others also reach their goals. When a situation is structured competitively, individuals' goal achievements are negatively correlated. Each individual perceives that when one person achieves his or her goal, all others with whom he or she is competitively linked fail to achieve their goals. With independent goals, individual achievements are unrelated.

Organizational members' beliefs about how their individual goals are related critically affect their expectations, interaction, and outcomes. With cooperative goals, people believe that as one person moves toward goal attainment others move toward reaching their goals. They understand that others' goal attainment helps them; they can be successful together. With cooperative goals, people want each other to perform effectively, for such competence helps each person be successful. They interact in ways that promote mutual goals. In particular, they are able to discuss their views on various issues for mutual benefit.

Whether people conclude that their goals are primarily cooperative or competitive, Deutsch (1973) proposed, profoundly affects their orientation and intentions toward each other. In particular, goal interdependence affects their attitudes and expectations about each other's abilities as well as how people are likely to use their abilities.

Organizational members with cooperative goals can realistically expect that people want each other to succeed. They conclude that others are motivated to express their views so that they can act effectively in pursuit of their goals. As individuals succeed, everyone moves toward goal attainment. Because it is in their own self-interest to promote others' goal attainment, people share information, express their opinions, and combine their ideas to resolve conflicts. They expect that others will use a conflict for mutual benefit. They believe they can rely upon each other and are sensitive and responsive to each other. With these positive expectations, organizational members want to identify and help each other apply their abilities for team success.

However, in competition, people develop a much different perspective on others' abilities. They expect each other to work for their own goals at the expense of others. They do not expect others to provide information and ideas to help them act effectively, for that would frustrate their own, personal goal attainment. This atmosphere restricts and distorts information.

Generally, competitive goals have been found to lead to conflict avoidance. People withhold information and ideas in the expectation that they can win the competition and outdo each other (Deutsch 1973; Tjosvold 1998). However, at times, avoidance is not possible or suitable, and people employ tough bargaining tactics to pressure and even to deceive the other as they try to "win" the contest by having their position dominate.

With independent goals, organizational members have few incentives to express and use their diverse perspectives to assist each other. Independence induces an indifference to the interests of others and a tendency to avoid conflict, but like competition it can also lead to escalating conflict (Deutsch 1973). Indeed, independence has often been found to be as alienating as competition (Johnson, et al. 1981; Johnson & Johnson 1989; Stanne et al. 1999). As an organization imposes interdependence upon its members, members' believing and acting as if their goals were independent may seem to be an active rejection of others.

AGREEING HOW TO DISAGREE

In a traditional organization, employees are unprepared to manage conflict. Conflict is an aberration and a sign of failure. People turn to their managers, expecting them to resolve conflicts expeditiously so that the work of the organization can proceed. It is much more realistic and consistent with research documenting the value of managing conflict openly to develop the values, procedures, and skills of employees and managers so that they are confident that they have a common framework for resolving and using their conflicts. They have agreed about how they will disagree. The constructive controversy and cooperative goals framework provides research-based guidance.

A first step is for organizational members to understand the cooperative problem-solving approach to conflict and appreciate how it is an alternative to viewing conflict as a competitive fight over opposing interests. They might review the model presented in chapter 2, mediation research, and research on cooperative conflict. They then clarify confusions between cooperation, conflict, and competition, gaining a clearer understanding of how constructive controversy can guide their social problem-solving to enhance relationships and productivity.

Then people can commit themselves publicly to managing their conflicts openly and cooperatively. They realize that they cannot transform their ways of working overnight, but credibly convey that they are motivated to learn cooperative ways of managing conflict. In this way, they see each other as direct, open-minded, and responsive people who want to manage their differences.

Commitment motivates action to put cooperative values, procedures, and skills in place. Team members develop the norms, allocation of rewards, and mediation and conflict training that will support their handling conflicts cooperatively and are practical, appropriate, and powerful for their situation. They find resources that describe procedures and processes they can use to develop their skills.

People should strive for ongoing development and continual improvement. Ideally they study cooperative conflict, rededicate themselves to learning, and help each other refine their abilities and skills. Learning to manage conflict is an ongoing journey, not a one-stop trip.

For example, fish farmers were discovering that they needed to manage their conflicts cooperatively as they were discovering they were in a tough business. The founder thought his company could get rich quick by growing fish in the beautiful waters off British Columbia, Canada. But the price for fish did not continue to rise, though the costs of paying for the excessive investments and feed did. Everyone would have to operate efficiently and effectively to reduce costs to make the company viable. Farm managers could not simply be allowed to hire more employees to supplement ineffective ones. Employees could not be allowed to waste expensive feed.

A new CEO described his vision of a conflict-positive, lean organization. He pledged to be direct and honest with the farm managers, distributed budgets and future projections, and told them that only if they were effective could the company succeed. The fish farmers read about and discussed cooperative conflict and teamwork and quickly saw how they were critical to improve organizational and individual effectiveness and job security.

After reading, the farm managers brainstormed ways that they could establish and use cooperative conflict. They developed a company-wide bonus plan to help them feel more cooperative. They improved how the farm managers could communicate with each other via radio. They assigned several managers to one team and scheduled times when they could discuss issues face to face.

Several months later, they reviewed cooperative conflict, practiced team problem-solving skills, and evaluated the success of their plans. They were confident that they were developing the spirited teamwork that would help them try to meet the challenges of an unforgiving market.

Becoming more conflict-positive is often easier before tough difficulties and challenges emerge. A medical testing company's task force on developing a new computer system had a workshop on cooperative conflict soon after it was formed. By studying and discussing cooperative conflict, task force members publicly recognized that they would disagree and that their differences could be quite useful for designing a system that worked for the various groups in the company.

They developed rules and norms for how their group would deal with their differences. They were also able to allay suspicions they had about each other. The nurses and lab technicians heard and saw first-hand that the supposedly arrogant computer specialists were quite willing to listen and wanted a system that served their "customers." Task force members very much enjoyed the camaraderie and stimulation of their group and the company got a system that was on time and which lived up to expectations.

POSITIVE CONFLICT FOR FUTURE CHALLENGES

Investing in cooperative, constructive conflict may seem to be a distraction, whereas training in technical skills and technology seem much more promising investments. Yet mediating conflict in organizations and developing cooperative conflict are becoming more relevant and useful. Today's organizations have too many conflicts and too many demands to change to brush aside strengthening their conflict abilities.

Ongoing improvement is a necessity for organizational survival and prosperity. In the fiercely competitive marketplace, companies must continually improve the quality and delivery of their products or be overtaken by aggressive rivals. Organizations must innovate under continual pressure. They must speed new products to the marketplace, and once they are copied, upgrade their products and services.

In addition to dealing with the conflict that is part of change and adaptation, organizations are facing increasing diversity in their make-up. Professionals and specialists trained in their own areas and disciplines are needed to operate complex technology and solve contemporary problems. Marketing, sales, production, and research and development are asked to work together on new product teams and task forces. Because of employee mobility and immigration, organizations are becoming more gender and ethnically diverse.

Many managers are taking up the challenges to innovate and change. They are instituting participative management to involve employees in helping the organization change. Cross-functional work groups have the responsibility to manage themselves and solve complex problems for the organization. Hierarchies are being squashed and management layers reduced to lower costs and improve quality. Managers are structuring their organizations around markets to focus on serving their customers.

Less appreciated is that, to become more empowered and make organizational innovations work, managers and employees must develop intensely cooperative goals and the abilities to manage their conflicts. Then they can combine their different specialties, orientations, and opinions to empower the organization to improve quality and serve customers.

The conflict-positive perspective suggests important research issues as well as these practical implications. Ongoing basic issues include identifying antecedents of when conflict participants take a cooperative rather than a competitive approach that in turn fosters constructive controversy, and the conditions when constructive controversy is more and less useful. Studies are also needed on the methods and conditions that help organizations become conflict-positive. In this global marketplace, research is needed to identify the conditions under which cooperative goals and constructive controversy contribute to the management of conflict between individuals, groups, and organizations with different cultures. Case studies of managers and employees together learning to manage their conflicts effectively would be useful. In addition to basic knowledge about conflict management, understanding how to help managers and employees learn to mediate their conflicts to make them constructive will continue to be a challenge for practitioners and researchers alike.

Contemporary forces are smashing traditional bases of security for people and organizations. People recognize that organizations cannot provide lifetime employment and that the organization does not have guaranteed customers and income. Managers and employees will increasingly find security for themselves and their organizations by developing the confidence and ability to use their conflicts to take advantage of change. The research noted here and in chapter 2 relating to cooperative conflict can be a basis upon which to develop adaptive, innovative organizations.

NOTE

The authors thank David W. Johnson for his very helpful advice. They also appreciate the Hong Kong University Grants Council for its support of this paper, grant project no. TDG01-04LU2.

REFERENCES

Cosier, R. A. (1978) The effects of three potential aids for making strategic decisions on prediction accuracy. *Organizational Behavior and Human Performance* 22, 295–306.

Deutsch, M. (1973) *The Resolution of Conflict.* Yale University Press, New Haven.

Deutsch, M. (1980) Fifty years of conflict. In L. Festinger (ed.), *In Retrospections on Social Psychology.* Oxford University Press, New York, pp. 46–77.

Eisenhardt, K. M. & Bourgeois, L. J. I. (1988) Politics of strategic decision making in high-velocity environments: toward a midrange theory. *Academy of Management Journal* 31, 737–770.

Hogan, R., Curphy, G. J. & Hogan, J. (1994) What we know about leadership: effectiveness and personality. *American Psychologist* 49, 493–504.

Jehn, K. A. (1995) A multimethod examination of the benefits and detriments of intragroup conflict. *Administrative Science Quarterly* 40, 256–282.

Jehn, K. A. (1997) A qualitative analysis of conflict types and dimensions in organizational groups. *Administrative Science Quarterly* 42, 530–557.

Johnson, D. W. & Johnson, R. T. (1989) *Cooperation and Competition: Theory and Research.* Interaction Book Company, Edina.

Johnson, D. W., Maruyama, G., Johnson, R. T., Nelson, D. & Skon, L. (1981) Effects of cooperative, competitive and individualistic goal structures on achievement: a meta-analysis. *Psychological Bulletin* 89, 47–62.

Kirkbride, P. S., Tang, S. F. Y. & Westwood, R. I. (1991) Chinese conflict preferences and negotiating behaviour: cultural and psychological influences. *Organizational Studies* 12, 365–386.

Stanne, M. B., Johnson, D. W. & Johnson, R. T. (1999) Does competition enhance or inhibit motor performance? A meta-analysis. *Psychological Bulletin* 125, 133–154.

Tichy, N. M. & Sherman, S. (1993) *Control Your Destiny or Someone Else Will.* Doubleday, New York.

Tjosvold, D. (1982) Effects of approach to controversy on superiors' incorporation of sub-ordinates' information in decision making. *Journal of Applied Psychology* 67(2), 189–193.

Tjosvold, D. (1991) *The Conflict-Positive Organization: Stimulate Diversity and Create Unity.* Addison-Wesley, Reading.

Tjosvold, D. (1998) The cooperative and competitive goal approach to conflict: accomplishments and challenges. *Applied Psychology: An International Review* 47, 285–313.

Tjosvold, D. (2002) Theory oriented reviews for applied psychology. *Applied Psychology: An International Review* 51, 387–393.

Tjosvold, D. & Janz, T. (1985) Costing effective vs. ineffective work relationships: a method and first look. *Canadian Journal of Administrative Sciences* 2, 43–51.

Tjosvold, D. & Su, F. S. (in press). Managing anger and annoyance in organizations in China: the role of constructive controversy. *Group & Organization Management.*

Tjosvold, D. & Sun, H. (2000) Social face in conflict among Chinese: effects of affronts to person and position. *Group Dynamics: Theory, Research, and Practice* 4, 259–271.

Tjosvold, D. & Sun, H. (2003) Openness among Chinese in conflict: effects of direct discussion and warmth on integrated decision making. *Journal of Applied Social Psychology* 33, 1878–1897.

Tjosvold, D., Hui, C. & Sun, H. (2004) Can Chinese discuss conflicts openly? Field and experimental studies of face dynamics in China. *Group Decision and Negotiation* 13, 351–373.

Tse, D. K., Francis, J. & Walls, J. (1994) Cultural differences in conducting intra- and inter-cultural negotiations: a Sino-Canadian comparison. *Journal of International Business Studies* 24, 537–555.

Chapter 17

Mediation and Difficult Conflicts

MORTON DEUTSCH

INTRODUCTION

By focusing on difficult conflicts, this chapter starts at the end, rather than at the beginning, of the excellent comprehensive model advanced by Herrman, Hollett, and Gale in their introductory chapter. In other words, I am concerned with conflicts that do not typically end up in T_1 or T_2 with a constructive resolution in which the parties involved all feel satisfied with their outcomes. I shall consider several types of difficult conflicts, ranging from those in which mediation would appear to be impossible to those in which mediation is possible but difficult and not usually successful. The purpose of my discussion will be to identify some of the major factors which obstruct or facilitate the successful mediation of conflict. My discussion is abstract and not focused on understanding the details of specific cases of difficult conflicts. As Kenneth Kressel (2000: 524) has wisely stated: "Mediation is not a magic bullet for resolving any and all conflicts."

Four types of conflict will be discussed:

1. *A conflict between a terrorist group and a state.* In the conflict that I examine, none of the factors considered in the first time period (T_0) of the model is conducive to the acceptance of mediation by the parties in conflict. As a consequence, one can expect the conflict to persist until one side or the other is defeated or until social, economic, and political changes make the conflict passé.

2. *A hostage situation where the hostage-taker is surrounded by the police.* Here, the factors listed under T_0 are often more ambiguous. It is often up to the hostage negotiator (who in reality is frequently a mediator between the hostage-taker and such public authorities as the chief of police or the mayor) to mold all of the factors listed under T_0 to make them more favorable to mediation. In addition, the intense time pressure and, often, the emotional instability of the hostage-taker require special sensitivity and skills of the negotiator-mediator if there is to be a successful resolution of the hostage situation (T_m and T_1 of the model).

3   *A conflict between deeply held moral values or worldviews* is often difficult to resolve
    because prior conflicts have often made the factors at T_0 not conducive to con-
    tact and mediation. In addition, untutored dialog between the parties often has
    negative rather than positive outcomes. In my consideration of such conflicts,
    I discuss a form of dialog ("transcendent eloquence") which a mediator can
    facilitate that may provide more favorable outcomes. This action has some
    relevance to T_m, T_1, and T_2 of the model.

4   *A competitive conflict, involving opposed interests, which is not already embittered.* Here,
    I consider two types of win-lose conflict: one in which there is little possibility
    or desire to transform this type of conflict into a win-win conflict and one in
    which such a possibility exists. In the former type, I discuss the importance
    of the institutional context in making the win-lose conflict a regulated com-
    petition, which in various ways limits and controls the destructiveness of the
    conflict. Here I consider the questions: What are the conditions necessary for
    the institutionalization and regulation of the conflict? What are the conditions
    that make it likely that the regulations will be adhered to by the conflicting
    parties? This part of my chapter elaborates in some detail some factors which
    might be considered under the heading "Institutional Context" in the T_0 phase
    of the model presented in chapter 2. In my discussion of the transformation
    of "win-lose" to "win-win" conflicts, I consider not only some of the character-
    istics of the parties in conflict and the institutional context which affect the
    possibility of conflict transformation (T_0 of the model), but also the skills required
    of the mediator in facilitating such a transformation (also T_0 as well as T_m phases
    of the model).

CONFLICT BETWEEN A TERRORIST GROUP AND A STATE

The term "terrorist group" has often been used by those who control an oppressive
state to refer to any group that employs armed force and violence to overthrow
those who control the government. Such groups rarely consider themselves to be
terrorists. They are more apt to view themselves as "freedom fighters," "rebels,"
or "revolutionaries." There are many instances – as, for example, in the American
Revolution – when colonial powers had to yield to such groups and negotiate a
withdrawal from control over the population which they had dominated. Similarly,
there are instances in which such groups – as, for example, in South Africa – have
forced an oppressive minority government to negotiate a transfer of power over the
government from the dominating minority to the representatives of an oppressed
majority of the population. There are more instances in which a change in power
relations has occurred only after extensive violence, I believe, than instances which
such changes have occurred after successful, peaceful negotiations with the assistance of third parties.[1] Why is this so?

   I know of no historical research which would shed light on this question, and
I believe it would be very useful to do such research. While I am not a historian,
I would like to examine, in the abstract, an extreme case to see what light it can shed

on why successful, peaceful negotiations rarely occur between states and terrorist groups. The terrorist group is Al Qaeda, led by Osama Bin Laden, and the state is the United States, the leading military and economic power in the world.

It seems somewhat absurd to ask the following question because the answer seems so obvious: Why has not anyone proposed that the US government and the Bin Laden group mediate their conflict? The obvious answer is that no one believes that a successful mediation is possible. Nor do they believe that either the US government or Al Qaeda would be willing to negotiate about their conflict. Nor can either side or any third party compel such negotiation. Moreover, it is not clear what the conflict is about apart from each side's intent to destroy the other's power to inflict harm and, also, to attain its objectives.

The United States certainly wants to destroy Al Qaeda's capability to engage in all of its forms of violence and especially its abhorrent terrorist violence against civilians and civil targets. It also seeks to undermine the support that Al Qaeda receives from many Muslims throughout the world who see the United States as a "Great Satan" that flouts and harms Muslim religious values and political-economic interests. As I see Al Qaeda's aims, they are to weaken the "Great Satan" so that they can pursue their objective of installing theocratic, Islamic states in areas populated mainly by Muslims. They may also aim to extend Islamic influence over non-Islamic populations.

Thus, the conflict between Al Qaeda and the United States is non-negotiable for the following reasons: (a) each side considers itself to be in a zero-sum or win-lose competitive conflict with the other: the more one side gains, the more the other loses; (b) each side believes that the other side's deeply held worldviews are fundamentally different, evil, and irreconcilable with its own; (c) they perceive that they have few or no common interests; (d) neither side believes that the conflict is negotiable and each believes that the other has no interest in negotiation; and (e) there is no third party which could persuade or compel both sides to such a negotiated settlement to their conflict.

Conflicts of this sort can be ended by: (a) defeat or destruction of one side by the other, as has occurred in various revolutions (e.g. the American, French, and Russian revolutions); (b) the development of hurting stalemates which erode one or both sides' motivation or ability to engage in the conflict (as in the conflicts in South Africa, East Timor, and Northern Ireland); or (c) social-political-economic-cultural-historical changes which reduce or eliminate the bases for the conflict in the parties, or changes in their milieu which make the conflict irrelevant or relatively unimportant. There are some unlikely possibilities under (c). For instance, a catastrophic event (for example a large meteor striking the earth, producing drastic changes in the climate and geological formations) might make the conflict relatively unimportant and irrelevant to other issues of personal, familial, tribal, and national survival. Or, over an extended period of time, there might be sufficient political, economic, cultural, social, and educational change in the United States and in Islamic nations and among Muslims so that the animus toward the United States would largely disappear, as would the support for the terrorist activities of Al Qaeda.

Professionals in the field of conflict resolution would, I believe, distinguish between a short-term and a long-term perspective in dealing with terrorism (Welsh & Coleman 2002). The short-term perspective places its emphasis on reducing terrorism primarily on military, economic, and political actions against the terrorists and their terrorist organizations. A long-term perspective places its emphasis on bringing about the social, political, economic, educational, and cultural changes which would reduce the conditions which breed terrorism and which enable terrorists to have easy access to weapons and political targets. As is true for most destructive conflict, there is a need for both a short- and a long-term perspective: a short-term perspective to reduce the destruction and a long-term perspective to alter the conditions which give rise to the destructive conflict.

HOSTAGE NEGOTIATION

Unlike the conflict between Al Qaeda and the United States, most hostage situations are short-term crisis situations in which the goal of the hostage-taker is not to kill the hostages but rather to satisfy some specific or nebulous demand. Similarly, the goal of the public authority (the police or military who surround the hostage-taker) is not to kill the hostage-taker but, rather, to free the hostages and to have the hostage-taker surrender. Negotiation in such situations is often possible because the authority doesn't want the hostages harmed and because the hostage-taker doesn't want to be killed (and he or she knows that the authority has the capability of doing this) or has some need which the authority can fulfill (for example making a public statement that is broadcast).

In a very interesting discussion among hostage negotiators (from present and former members of the New York City Police Department Hostage Negotiation Team as well as from a crisis negotiator for the FBI),[2] I learned that the basic concepts underlying the practice of hostage negotiations are similar to those generally underlying the successful practice of negotiation and mediation. The key differences relate to the degree of emotional tension involved for all of the participants, the intense time pressure, and the necessity of dealing with great sensitivity with the potential for emotional instability in the hostage-taker, the hostages, and other concerned parties. The hostage negotiator is often negotiating not only with the hostage-taker but also with the chief or authority who determines if and when to use force to overcome the hostage-taker, as well as what can be offered to the hostage-taker to encourage the good treatment and safe release of the hostages.

What are the basic concepts employed by the hostage negotiator?

1   *Lower tension.* Take the time to allow the situation to cool down, to allow the drunken hostage-taker to sober up, to permit the emotionally upset to calm down. Encourage them to talk and to continue to talk by active listening which shows understanding and by putting questions and eliciting responses which keep the conversation going. Explain why things take time, why responses to demands cannot be immediate. Speak in a voice that is calm and responsible, considerate, and respectful.

2   *Establish credibility.* As an experienced hostage negotiator stated:

> One of the things we do, or try to do, when we have a dialog, is to start off by
> asking a simple question. That is "Do you want me to lie to you?" That is what the
> negotiator *starts off with*, after giving his name. As crazy as hostage-takers can
> be (and they can be very, very crazy), I've never had any of them ever say "Yes,
> please lie to me." So one of the things we do early on is to make a contract with
> them – we are not going to lie to them; they understand that by our not lying to
> them, we might say some things to them that may upset them, but we are going
> to work our way through that. There is an agreement on both sides: "You are not
> going to lie to me, I may get upset by some of the things you are going to say,
> and you will be with me the whole time and we will work this out." (Cambria,
> De Filippo, Louden & McGowen 2002: 337)

3   *Establish a relationship* by treating the hostage-taker with dignity and respect and
     insisting on similar treatment in return. Help the hostage-taker retain self-esteem
     and "face" by employing terms like "coming out" rather than "surrender."
4   *Reframe the situation.* The hostage negotiator seeks to reframe the situation from
     a purely adversarial relation to a situation where "We are in this together,"
     and where together they have to work out a solution that will be acceptable
     to the hostage-taker as well as to the authority. The hostage-taker is given the
     opportunity or is empowered to participate in a cooperative solution to the diffi-
     cult situation that he, the hostages, and the authority are in. For this to occur,
     the hostage negotiator "must display an empathetic posture" (Cambria et al.
     2002: 339) and communicate a sincere desire for the hostage-taker to come out
     of this situation safely, for the situation to be resolved peacefully with no one
     getting hurt. This is a key aspect of the negotiation process and very difficult
     to do, not only because of the resistance from the hostage-taker which needs
     to be overcome, but also because of the attitudes among the "hardliners" in
     authority who are inclined to use force to resolve the situation. They view
     negotiation as "coddling" the hostage-taker, more appropriate to sympathetic
     social workers and sob sisters than the police.
5   *Getting to yes.* Through subtle suggestions, the negotiator will seek to get the
     hostage-taker to make a demand to which the authority will be able to say yes.
     This requires careful listening for the expressed and also implicit interests of
     the hostage-taker to find an acceptable demand that he or she can be subtly
     encouraged to make.

I do not know if there are any statistics indicating what percentage of hostage
negotiations turn out to be successful. Success appears to be most likely if the
negotiator has a good deal of experience (and employs the five concepts listed
above); if the negotiation has continued over an extended period of time without the use of violence on either side; if the hostage-taker prefers survival with
incarceration to a violent death, and is not a member of a fundamentalist terror
group. Apparently hostage-takers who are criminals (e.g. surrounded in the course
of robbing a bank) or who are emotionally unstable or mentally ill are more apt to
accept the encouragement of the negotiator to make a demand that is acceptable
than is a committed member of a terrorist group.

INTRACTABLE CONFLICT BETWEEN DEEPLY HELD MORAL VALUES OR WORLDVIEWS

In this section, I discuss intractable conflict. Sometimes such conflicts arise from differences in deeply held moral values or worldviews. Other times they develop about specific issues, such as who shall control a given piece of land. As a specific conflict endures and becomes intractable, it commonly becomes "moralized." That is, the conflicting parties enmesh their specific positions and claims in larger moral values which justify and provide what they believe to be, and emotionally feel as, the moral superiority of their position and claims. Thus, in this section, I first consider an approach to intractable moral conflicts. Such an approach is, I believe, implicit in other approaches to intractable conflicts: problem-solving workshops dealings with intractable conflicts between or within nations, divorce mediation, and family therapy. However, as I have pointed out elsewhere (Deutsch 1988), internal conflicts within a party involved in an external conflict often contribute to or promote "intractability" because the internal conflict generates a need to maintain the external conflict. I shall not here deal with the important issue of therapy or other methods of reducing the internal conflict.

As Pearce and Littlejohn (1997: 153) have pointed out:

> Intractable moral conflicts are not easily resolved and, in many cases, may not be resolvable. Indeed, many such conflicts should not be resolved, but they can be argued in more humane, enlightening, and respectful ways . . . Needed is a format or setting in which trust can be built between conflicting parties, a forum in which and an atmosphere in which beliefs are put at risk of change, not by influence from the other party but by self-reflection.

Pearce and Littlejohn (1997: 157–167) describe the characteristics of the discourse (termed "transcendent eloquence") which enable a change in the dynamics of the relationship between the two parties and a change in the sense of identity by one or both sides in the conflict. As Northrup's (1989) analysis of intractable conflict suggests, frozen conflict can begin to thaw when the foregoing two types of change occur. Pearce and Littlejohn identify five general characteristics of transcendent eloquence:

1 *Philosophical.* This attempts to uncover the knowledge, being, and values that lie behind the positions in conflict. It attempts to move discussion from intractable struggle over issues to a more fundamental level at which the parties must pause and reflect.
2 *Comparative.* This attempts to create categories and a language that enable compassion between two otherwise incommensurate systems. In essence, this involves a shift from experiencing the conflict within one's moral order to viewing it from an outside, more inclusive and objective point of view. The creation of such higher-level categories can provide new ideas and a common reference for reconsidering the statements and actions of both sides.

3 *Dialog.* This attempts to move the discussion from statements meant to convince to statements designed to explore. It seeks to create an open-minded, respectful conversation between moral people with moral differences, and to construct an overarching truth that is acceptable within the larger human community within which the moral conflict exists.

4 *Critical.* Transcendent eloquence aims to help each side recognize its own fallibility as well as the fallibility of the other so that moral choices are made, critically, by comparing the weaknesses and strengths of each side's views from the perceptions of a more inclusive, objective point of view.

5 *Transformative.* This seeks to change the context of the conflict so that it is not about "good" versus "evil," about "winning" or "losing." It aims to transform it to one of mutual understanding and mutual respect so that interactions are enabled that are mutually beneficial as well as beneficial to the larger moral community to which both sides belong.

Transcendental eloquence is a form of a constructive discourse and interaction among parties in conflict which is desirable but often difficult to achieve. It seems more achievable when the conflict is between individuals rather than between groups. It appears to be less achievable when the conflict is not exclusively a moral/ worldview conflict but also a conflict over the power to dominate, to control, or to eliminate those whose moral standpoint or worldview are in conflict with one's own views.

Without describing it as such, a number of social scientists and social practitioners have attempted to create a discourse and interaction between parties involved in an intractable conflict which could be characterized as similar to transcendental eloquence. Ronald Fisher (1997), in his excellent book *Interactive Conflict Resolution*, describes the work of such pioneers as Burton, Kelman, Doob, Azar, Wedge, Mitchell, Volkan, Saunders, Montville, Kriesberg, Bar-on, Bargal, and many others as well as his own work, all of whom have created workshops that seek to develop constructive dialog and interaction between parties in an intractable conflict. In my paper "Negotiating the Non-Negotiable" (Deutsch 1988), I have described a therapeutic approach to a married couple involved in an intractable conflict about the nature of their marriage.

Below, I characterize what, I posit, are the conditions necessary to establish a constructive interaction and problem-solving orientation to an intractable conflict. These conditions, I believe, are common to the various approaches indicated above.

1 A hurting stalemate (see Zartman 2000 for a full discussion of this condition).

2 Recognition that one cannot impose a solution which may be acceptable or satisfactory to oneself (or one's group) upon the other, and that a solution requires the agreement of the other.

3 Belief that the other has also recognized that a solution has to be mutually acceptable.

4 Hope that a mutually acceptable agreement can be found.

5 Confidence that if a mutually acceptable agreement is concluded both sides
   will abide by it. If the other is viewed as unstable, lacking internal control of
   oppositional forces, or untrustworthy, it will be difficult to have confidence in
   the viability of an agreement unless one has confidence that third parties are
   able to guarantee the integrity of the agreement.

The conditions listed above are essential to begin the process of constructive
dialog to search for or to create a mutually acceptable agreement and to build the
mutual confidence and trust that, if an agreement is reached, it will be adhered
to by both sides. To develop a process of constructive dialog other conditions also
appear to be necessary. They include:

1 The availability of skillful third party facilitators who are respected by and
   are acceptable to the parties in conflict. Burton (1987), Deutsch and Coleman
   (2000), Doob (1993), Fisher (1994), Galtung (1976), Kelman (1992), Lederach
   (1995), Mitchell (1981), Rouhana and Kelman (1984) and Volkan (1991), among
   others, have written about this.
2 The establishment of a safe, supportive, secure, and comfortable environment
   which encourages constructive dialog. This involves creating rules and procedures which provide to the conflicting parties mutual security from physical
   harm, humiliation, or damage both during their own interactions and in their
   relations with others who are not directly involved in the discussions.
3 The humanization of the other. During bitter conflict each side tends to dehumanize
   the other and develop images of the other as an evil enemy. Opportunities
   must be created for the participants – who have developed their views as a result
   of their experiences in their family, their school, and their neighborhood – to
   place their viewpoints in a personal context. They also should be provided with
   opportunities for learning how similar, as well as different, their experiences
   have been in their roles as parents, spouses, professionals, supervisors, sub-
   ordinates, neighbors, etc. Further, they should have occasions in which they
   can interact with one another informally in a friendly manner about common
   interests and around topics not directly related to the issues in conflict – for
   example pictures of children, health, food, sports, TV, movies, and education.

If the foregoing conditions of constructive dialog have been created, the possibility
of transcendental eloquence and creative cooperative problem-solving has emerged.
Their full development will depend on the skills of the third party facilitator,
the capabilities of the conflicting parties, and their abilities to plan for foreseeable
problems such as new, emerging conflicts between the conflicting parties and
oppositional tendencies to agreement within each of the parties.

It is important to recognize that even if a tentative reconciliation has begun between
the former bitter adversaries, new conflicts will inevitably occur. Beforehand, one
should plan for and develop the fair rules, procedures, experts, institutions, and
other resources for managing such conflicts constructively and justly. Otherwise, a
conflict managed poorly is apt to reignite mutual hostility and distrust.

Among the conflicts that often occur are those stimulated by the extremists on one or both sides. During a protracted and bitter conflict, each side tends to produce extremists committed to the processes of destructive conflict as well as to its continuation. Attaining some of their initial goals may be less satisfactory than continuing to inflict damage on the other. Both sides need to cooperate in curbing extremism and in restraining actions by extremists that stimulate and justify a vicious circle of mutually reinforcing extremism on both sides.

Finally, it is vital to understand the fragility of transcendental eloquence and cooperative problem-solving in their early stages. It takes repeated experiences of successful, varied, mutually beneficial cooperation to develop a solid basis for mutual trust between former enemies. In the early stages of reconciliation, when trust is required for cooperation, the former enemies may be willing to trust a third party (who agrees to serve as a monitor, inspector, or guarantor of any cooperative agreement) but not yet willing to trust one another. In the early stages, it is especially important that cooperative endeavors be successful. This requires careful selection of the opportunities and tasks for cooperation so that they are clearly achievable as well as meaningful and significant.

When the conflict is between individuals or between small groups all of whom are able to participate in the kind of constructive dialog described in the preceding pages, then a stable and acceptable agreement may be reached between the conflicting parties. Such an agreement will often involve a lowering of the initial levels of aspiration of both sides which is based on the recognition that the realities of each side and of the situations in which they are immersed do not permit the realization of their full hopes. However, as Coleman, Hacking, Steven, and Fisher-Yoshida (2003) have pointed out, most disputes involve more than the conflicting dyad (individual or group) that is directly involved in the dialog. In many conflicts, there are multiple individuals and groups who have interests in the conflict and its outcomes. This is often the case even for an interpersonal conflict as, for example, between a husband and wife in which children, in-laws, and the extended family may have considerable relevance to and involvement in the conflict.

The existence of multiple stakeholders in a conflict presents an important issue to the convener-facilitator or mediator or therapist who is seeking to aid the conflicting parties to resolve or manage their conflicts constructively. The issue is: who should be directly involved or represented in the conflict resolution process – whether it be a mediation, workshop, or a therapeutic intervention? Divorce mediators (e.g. Kressel) and family therapists (e.g. Minuchin) in the United States, who generally deal with a nuclear family structure, indicate that the children should be involved or represented (when they are not old enough to be able to represent their own interests) as well as the parents. In conflicts within extended families, one could assume that it would be appropriate to have the key decision-makers as well as the conflicting parties directly involved. To have an impact on the conflict as a result of participating in an interactive problem-solving workshop for a conflict between or within nations, it appears that participants should be "influential" (i.e. people who can influence the public and/or decision-makers) or informal policy advisors to the decision-makers (see Fisher 1997: 193).

Understandably, it is very difficult to do rigorous, systematic research to assess the effectiveness of the problem-solving workshops, divorce mediations, and family therapy dealing with intractable conflicts. There are often no "control groups;" the criteria for different degrees of success are not clear; there are few case studies and even fewer have had systematic data collection about the potential effects on whom and what over a period of time. Nevertheless, there is reason for some degree of optimism (see Kressel & Pruitt 1989). Kressel (2000), in his discussion of the effects of divorce mediation, indicates that divorce mediation produces greater satisfaction with the agreements and fewer future court challenges to the agreements reached than agreements reached through a legal process only. Similarly, Fisher (1997: 194–195) in his analysis of the reported outcomes of 76 problem-solving workshops involving conflicts within or between nations, reports the following findings:

1   In almost all of the interventions, there was increased understanding and im-
    proved attitudes. Only 13 percent of the workshops had no direct or indirect
    effect on the peace process.
2   In 41 percent of the cases, it was reported by either the workshop participants
    or the workshop facilitators that the improved understanding and improved
    attitudes had an indirect but positive influence on the peace process.
3   In 17 percent of the cases, there emerged from the workshop documents, plans,
    or initiatives that were contributions to the peace process.
4   In situations where negotiations were ongoing between the conflicting parties,
    26 percent of the workshops appear to have made direct contributions to the
    negotiations by analysis of resistances, formulations of issues, and the creation
    of frameworks for agreement.

Although some degree of optimism is warranted from these results, there is also the harsh reality that many of the workshops dealt with conflicts that are still festering (e.g. the Israeli–Palestinian conflict, the Catholic-Protestant conflict in Northern Ireland, and the Greek–Turkish Cypriot conflict).

It is a truism that the best way to manage destructive, intractable conflicts is to prevent them. In a paper published a decade ago (Deutsch 1994), I outlined a utopian and ambitious program for the prevention of destructive conflict. It suggested what the different institutions – political, economic, educational, reli-gious, and cultural – could do to prevent destructive conflict, and David Hamburg (2002) has summarized the extensive work done by the Carnegie Commission on Preventing Deadly Conflict under his leadership. This book contains the most comprehensive discussion of the many issues involved in preventing deadly con-flict. It draws upon the work of many distinguished scholars from varied disciplines to indicate how the conditions favoring prevention can be developed. Hamburg makes it clear that the human and economic costs of destructive conflicts are so high (as is also the case for such physical diseases as polio) that the major effort should be directed at their prevention rather than at their treatment once they have become virulent.

A COMPETITIVE CONFLICT INVOLVING OPPOSED INTERESTS

In the three prior sections I have discussed conflicts which, typically, are not only perceived to be competitive, win-lose conflicts by the parties involved, but also are ones in which deep distrust and hostility as well as strongly entrenched negative beliefs and attitudes between the parties often exist based upon a history of negative interactions between the parties in conflict. These competitive conflicts are difficult to resolve because of the negative feelings, attitudes, beliefs, and history in which such conflicts are embedded.

When win-lose conflicts are not embedded in embittered relations they are often much easier to manage. There are two types of such conflicts that I consider below: a regulated, win-lose conflict which ends with a winner and loser, the winner defeating the loser in a contest conducted under agreed-upon rules, and a win-lose conflict which is transformed into a win-win conflict through negotiation.

Regulated Competition

Regulated competition is a pervasive form of dealing with win-lose conflicts. It exists in sports, games, a true free-market economy, in judicial and arbitration systems, among academic departments competing for the opportunity to hire new faculty, in collective bargaining, among job-seekers, between adversaries in a duel of honor, among suitors for an exclusive relation with a potential mate, and so on.

It is evident that competitive conflicts can be limited and controlled by institutional forms (e.g. collective bargaining, the judicial system), social roles (mediators, conciliators, referees, judges, policemen), social norms (fairness, justice, equality, nonviolence, integrity of communication), rules for conducting negotiations (when to initiate and terminate negotiations, how to set an agenda, how to present demands), and specific procedures (hinting versus explicit communication, public versus private sessions). These societal forms may be aimed at regulating how force may be employed, as in the code of a duel of honor or in certain rules of warfare; or it may be an attempt to ascertain the basic power relations of the disputants without resort to a power struggle, as is often the case in the negotiations of collective bargaining and international relations; or it may be oriented toward removing power as the basis for determining the outcome of conflict, as is often the case in judicial processes.

With regard to regulated conflict, it is pertinent to ask two central questions: (1) What are the conditions necessary for the institutionalization and regulation of conflict? (2) What are the conditions that make it likely that the regulations will be adhered to by the parties in conflict? Why would adversaries engage in a duel of honor rather than attempt to kill one another without regard to any rules? In a duel, when would a duelist prefer to die rather than to cheat?

The development of conflict regulation

For conflict regulation to develop, several preconditions seem required. First of all, the conflicting parties must themselves be organized. As Dahrendorf (1959: 226) has pointed out, "So long as conflicting forces are diffuse, incoherent aggregates, regulation is virtually impossible." Unless each party is sufficiently internally coherent and stable to act as an organized unit so that the actions of its components are controlled and unified in relation to the conflict, it is evident that regulation cannot be effectively developed or maintained. Thus one is not likely to engage in a duel of honor with an opponent who is so unstable and impulsive that his actions are uncontrollable – and it cannot be predicted with confidence that he will follow the rules.

Second, each party to a conflict must be willing to recognize the legitimacy of the other party and be committed to accepting the outcome of the regulated conflict, even if it is considered to be unfavorable to his interests. For example, an employer who is confronted with demands from a number of his workers may feel that those demands do not represent the wants of the majority of his employees and may refuse to recognize them. Under such conditions, it is unlikely that the conflict between the employer and his workers will be limited and regulated by rules and procedures acceptable to both sides. Also, if either an employer or a union makes clear its intention to refuse to accept the outcome of a regulated conflict if it believes the outcome is undesirable, there is little incentive for the other side to submit to being regulated. Similarly, it is hard to have a duel of honor if your opponent is not willing to accept your right to challenge him. Nor are you likely to participate in such a duel if you know that your opponent will attempt to have you injured in some underhanded way of he is defeated fairly by you.

Third, it should be noted that the conflicts that are regulated are not likely to be the unprecedented ones. A conflict that is recurrent provides a base of experience for developing the procedures, institutions, facilities, and social roles for limiting its destructiveness. It would be reassuring to be able to report some evidence that demonstrates that repeated experience with a given type of conflict leads to its more productive management. Unfortunately, I could find no significant research bearing upon this issue.

Finally, and perhaps most importantly, the regulation of conflict is most likely to develop when both sides to a conflict are part of a common community. This is so for several reasons. The community may be adversely affected by an unrestrained conflict and may, hence, exert pressures on the conflicting parties to regulate and limit their conflict and to follow the rules once they have been agreed upon. In addition, as members of a common community having similar values, traditions, and language, it may be easier for the conflicting parties to agree on rules and procedures for regulating the conflict than if they do not have this correspondence of background. Also, a common community is likely to help provide the knowledge, resources, and facilities that can expedite the development of methods of regulating a conflict. Prior experience with similar conflicts may have led the community to develop institutions and procedures for dealing with the type of conflict in which the parties are engaged. A duel of honor presupposes that the duelists have a common code of honor, a code to which all members of a given community will adhere if they want to be esteemed within that community. It also presupposes a set of social roles and procedures that have been carefully articulated within the community and that help to limit and specify the actions that may be taken by the adversaries.

Adherence to the rules

A full examination of the conditions that influence whether rules (norms, agreements, contracts, laws, and the like) are adhered to or violated would lead to a discussion of the different forms of rule violation and social deviance, their genesis and control. Such an undertaking is beyond the scope of this work. However, it seems reasonable to assert that adherence to the rules is more likely when:

1 *The rules are known.* How accessible is the information about the rules? How much publicity have they been given and through what media of communication? How motivated and able is the individual to acquire and absorb knowledge of the rules?

2 *The rules are clear, unambiguous, and consistent.* How easy is it to understand the rules, and how clear are their implications? If one conforms to one rule, does this lead to a violation of other rules because the rules are not internally consistent?

3 *The rules are not perceived to be biased against one's own interests.* How fair are the rules? Do they give the adversary an advantage he or she would not otherwise have?

4 *The other adheres to the rules.* With how much confidence can one predict that the other side will also follow the rules if one abides by them? If the other violates the rules, will it be out of ignorance or mischief?

5 *Violations are quickly known by significant others.* If violations of the rules occur, how quickly will they be identified? How much advantage will the violator gain before the violation is detected? Who will know of the violations, and how influential are they?

6 *There is significant social approval for adherence and significant social disapproval for violations.* How strong are the internalized values of conscience in the conflicting parties? Do important people and groups in the community care about whether the rules are supported or violated? Are esteem and other social benefits granted for adherence to the rules, and are there significant negative sanctions for those who violate them?

7 *Adherence to the rules has been rewarding in the past.* Have prior experiences with the rules been rewarding or frustrating? Is there a legacy of trust or suspicion with regard to the rules and the way they have been administered in the past?

8 *One would like to be able to employ the rules in the future.* Do the adversaries envision a future that will be better because they have worked toward the preservation of the current system of rules, or is the outcome of the specific conflict more important to them than the preservation of the system? Is the system of conflict regulation held in such disrepute that the conflict participant is more concerned with destroying the system than with resolving the specific conflict?

The Transformation of Win-Lose to Win-Win Conflicts

Although win-lose conflicts can be regulated so that they are not barbaric struggles, one may ask under what conditions a regulated competitive or win-lose conflict will turn into a win-win conflict. Thus, it is relevant to ask, for example, under what conditions the institutions and procedures of collective bargaining between union and management result in industrial peace rather than in industrial warfare.

One of the most extensive studies that attempts to answer this question was carried out under the aegis of a committee, the National Planning Association, that included many of the leading scholars and practitioners of industrial relations in the United States. The results of this investigation were published in 14 monographs, which included case studies of harmonious union–management relations in many different industries and in many different contexts. In the conclusions to their final report (National Planning Association 1953), they list the following basic causes of industrial peace:

1   There is full acceptance by management of the collective bargaining process and of unionism as an institution. The company considers a strong union an asset to management.
2   The union fully accepts private ownership and operation of the industry; it recognizes that the welfare of its members depends upon the successful operation of the business.
3   The union is strong, responsible, and democratic.
4   The company stays out of the union's internal affairs; it does not seek to alienate the workers' allegiance to their union.
5   Mutual trust and confidence exist between the parties. There have been no serious ideological incompatibilities.
6   Neither party to bargaining has adopted a legalistic approach to the solution of problems in the relationship.
7   Negotiations are "problem-centered" – more time is spent on day-to-day problems than on defining abstract principles.
8   There is widespread union–management consultation and highly developed information-sharing.
9   Grievances are settled promptly, in the local plant whenever possible. There is flexibility and informality within the procedure.

In brief, negotiations involving conflicts of interest are more likely to have acceptable outcomes for the parties involved to the extent that they take place in a context of cooperative relations. Harmonious relations are less likely to occur if both sides: (a) feel that their existence or their rights are under threat from the other side; (b) think that their survival is endangered by external competition from other firms or from other rival unions; (c) are torn by internal factionalism that gets displaced onto the union–management relationship; (d) have little local autonomy so that agreements cannot be responsive to local conditions; (e) are constantly subjected to changing conditions as a result of such factors as changes in technology, alterations in the market, seasonal variations, and turnover in management or union personnel.

Third parties, such as mediators, can play a critical role in transforming a win-lose into a win-win conflict. As I mentioned in the section on intractable conflicts above, they may help to transform an embittered conflict by encouraging and enabling the conflicting parties to engage in a dialog of transcendent eloquence. When the conflicting parties are not embittered, a third party may find it is less difficult to facilitate the development of a cooperative orientation and problem-solving process to a conflict.

There are three types of skills that are useful for third parties (such as mediators, conciliators, counselors, or therapists), as well as the participants in a conflict, in developing and implementing successfully an effective, cooperative problem-solving process. For convenience, I label them "rapport-building skills," "conflict resolution skills," and "group process and decision-making skills."

First, there are the skills involved in establishing effective working relationships with each of the conflicting parties and between the conflicting parties if you are the mediator; or with the other, if you are a participant. Some of the components of this broad category include such skills as breaking the ice; reducing fears, tensions, and suspicion; overcoming resistance to negotiation; establishing a framework for civil discourse and interaction; and fostering realistic hope and optimism. Thus, before negotiations begin between two individuals or groups perceiving each other as adversaries, it is often useful to have informal social gatherings or meetings in which the adversaries can get to know one another as human beings who share some similar interests and values. Skill in breaking the ice and creating a safe, friendly atmosphere for interaction between the adversaries is helpful in developing the pre-negotiation experiences likely to lead to effective negotiations about the issues in dispute.

A second, related set of skills concerns developing and maintaining a cooperative conflict resolution process among the parties throughout their conflict. These are the skills that are usually emphasized in practicum courses or workshops on conflict resolution. They include identifying the type of conflict in which you are involved; reframing the issues so the conflict is perceived as a mutual problem to be resolved cooperatively; active listening and responsive communication; distinguishing between needs and positions; recognizing and acknowledging the other's needs as well as your own; encouraging, supporting, and enhancing the other; taking the perspective of the other; identifying shared interests and other similarities in values, experiences, and so on; being alert to cultural differences and the possibilities of misunderstanding arising from them; controlling anger; dealing with difficult conflicts and difficult people; being sensitive to the other's anxieties and hot buttons and how to avoid pressing them; and being aware of your own anxieties and hot buttons as well as your tendencies to be emotionally upset and misperceiving if they are pressed so that these can be controlled.

A third set of skills is involved in developing a creative and productive group problem-solving and decision-making process. These include skills pertinent to group process, leadership, and effective group discussion, such as goal- and standard-setting; monitoring progress toward group goals; eliciting, clarifying, coordinating, summarizing, and integrating the contributions of the various participants; and maintaining group cohesion. This third set also includes such problem-solving and decision-making skills as identifying and diagnosing the nature of the problem confronting the group; acquiring the relevant information necessary for developing possible solutions; choosing the criteria for evaluating the alternatives (such as the "effects" on economic costs and benefits, on relations between the conflicting parties, and on third parties); selecting the alternative that optimizes the results on the chosen criteria; and implementing the decision through appropriate action.

As Rubin, Pruitt, and Kim (1994: ch. 10) point out, there are a number of different types of outcomes that may result from a cooperative problem-solving approach to a conflict: a compromise; an agreement on a procedure for deciding who will win; an integrative win-win solution. Clearly, the most desirable outcomes involve the integrative win-win solution.

How are win-win solutions developed? Rubin, Pruitt, and Kim (1994) describe several different types of integrative solution: expanding the pie, nonspecific compensation, log-rolling, cost-cutting, and bridging. Fisher, Ury, and Patton (1991: ch. 4) have a very helpful discussion of inventing options for mutual gain, as do Lax and Sebenius (1986: ch. 5) in their consideration of the question: "Creating value, or where do joint gains really come from?" Deutsch and Coleman (2000: ch. 17) presents some guidelines for developing a creative approach to conflict. The important points are that win-win solutions to conflict often require a good deal of creative effort, and that creativity can be fostered through the acquisition of certain types of knowledge, attitude, and skills. A central function of a mediator is to help the parties in conflict to develop a creative approach to their conflict. As Betty Reardon, a noted peace educator, once said, "The failure to achieve peace is in essence a failure of imagination" (personal communication).

Summary and Conclusion

In this chapter I have discussed four types of difficult conflict in order to consider the conditions under which a constructive negotiation or mediation is apt to occur. From the discussion of the conflict between Al Qaeda and the United States, it is apparent that when the willingness to negotiate is lacking in both sides and there is no third party sufficiently influential or powerful to induce the conflicting parties to negotiate, neither negotiation nor mediation will occur.

In a hostage situation, where the hostage-taker is surrounded, a skillful, sensitive negotiator can sometimes create a successful negotiating situation by establishing his or her credibility, decreasing tension and time pressure, creating a mutually respectful relationship, reframing the conflict as a mutual problem to solve, and by suggesting mutually acceptable solutions. This is harder to do when the hostage-taker is a member of an ideologically or religiously inspired terrorist organization than if the hostage-taker is involved in a criminal act or is mentally disturbed.

Intervention in a protracted, moralized intractable conflict is most apt to be successful after a hurting stalemate has been reached. The objective of the intervention is to create safe conditions under which a mutually respectful, constructive dialog can develop a cooperative problem-solving orientation to this conflict which results in cooperative work to resolve the conflict. The embittered relations, distrustful attitudes, the barbarities committed, the investments in the perpetuation of the conflict, and the history which has been developed during the protracted conflict often make a more benevolent, constructive relation between the conflicting parties difficult to achieve. Success, if it occurs, is often the result of a long, sustained, and dedicated process from influential third parties as well as from peace-seeking elements within each of the conflicting groups.

The Geneva agreement for the Palestinian–Israeli conflict negotiated by unofficial but influential Palestinians and Israelis illustrates an interesting approach to moving a constructive process forward when the leadership of an influential third party (the Bush administration of the United States) and the leadership of the two conflicting parties (Sharon and Arafat) seem immobilized. The Geneva agreement provides a detailed, practicable, and realistic solution to the conflict which can be used to mobilize external third parties as well as large segments of the Palestinian and Israeli populations to overcome both the resistances to a constructive peace and the immobilization of the current leadership in the United States, Israel, and the Palestinian Authority.

When a conflict is not embedded in a history of embittered and destructive relations it is much easier to manage. In the final section of this chapter I discussed the conditions under which win-lose conflicts can be regulated so that the win-lose competitions between conflicting parties are conducted under fair rules which are adhered to by both the winners and the losers. Then I considered how conflicts which are perceived to be win-lose conflicts by the parties involved can be transformed into win-win conflicts. Basically, the transformation process is a process that one hopes can be employed in all types of conflict, appropriately modified for the different types. However, this chapter suggests that this hope is over-optimistic. As it has indicated, some conflicts are not accessible to the process of negotiation and mediation, and some that are accessible have great difficulty in achieving successful resolution through negotiation and mediation.

It is important to recognize that many of the most difficult conflicts to resolve constructively emerge from aspects of our national and international political, economic, educational, health, and cultural systems (see Deutsch 2002). Many groups and individuals experience systemic injustices (oppression) in all or some of the systems just mentioned. The conflict between those who feel oppressed and humiliated by the status quo and those who feel advantaged by it or threatened by its change are often among the most difficult to resolve. For their constructive resolution, the underlying injustices, as well as the feelings of humiliation of the oppressed and of threat by the advantaged, must be addressed.

One final note. I have not discussed the need for and the possibilities of doing research on the complex issues that I have considered in this chapter. Yet it should be apparent that we have little well-grounded theoretical and practiced knowledge in this area, and much research is necessary to develop such knowledge so as to have more frequent, successful interventions in difficult conflicts. While it is beyond the purpose of this chapter to detail the research that is required, it is evident that we need many more well-constructed case studies of successful and unsuccessful interventions. We also need carefully controlled laboratory studies of such limited and specific questions as how to establish a mutually respectful and constructive dialog between people who have an embittered relationship of long standing.

NOTES

1 As I have indicated elsewhere (Deutsch 2002), overthrow of an autocratic government has only rarely led to a new democratic government.
2 This took place at the 2002 Hewlett Theory Centers Conference at the John Jay College of Criminal Justice in New York City in the spring of 2002. See *Negotiation Journal* (2000) 18(4, October) for a report of this discussion as well as other presentations at the conference.

REFERENCES

Burton, J. (1987) *Resolving Deep-Rooted Conflict: A Handbook.* University Press of America, Lanham.

Cambria, J., De Filippo, R. J., Louden, R. J. & McGowen, H. (2002) Negotiation under supreme pressure. *Negotiation Journal* 18(4), 331–344.

Coleman, P. T., Hacking, A. G., Steven, M. A. & Fisher-Yoshida, B. (2003) Reconstructing ripeness: a study of constructive engagements in complex, intractable, systems of conflict. Unpublished. Box 53, Teachers College, Columbia University, New York.

Dahrendorf, R. (1959) *Class and Class Conflict in Industrial Society.* Stanford University Press, Stanford.

Deutsch, M. (1988) On negotiating the non-negotiable. In B. Kellerman & J. Z. Rubin (eds.), *Leadership and Negotiation in the Middle East.* Praeger, New York, pp. 248–263.

Deutsch, M. (1994) Constructive conflict resolution for the world today. *International Journal of Conflict Management* 5, 111–129.

Deutsch, M. (2002) *Oppression and Conflict.* Plenary address given at the annual meeting of the International Society of Justice Research in Skovde, Sweden, June 17, 2002.

Deutsch, M. & Coleman, P. T. (2000) *The Handbook of Conflict Resolution: Theory and Practice.* Jossey-Bass, San Francisco.

Doob, L. (1993) *Intervention: Guides and Perils.* Yale University Press, New Haven.

Fisher, R. J. (1994) Generic principles for resolving intergroup conflict. *Journal of Social Issues* 50(1), 47–66.

Fisher, R. J. (1997) *Interactive Conflict Resolution.* Syracuse University Press, Syracuse.

Fisher, R., Ury, W. & Patton, B. (1991) *Getting To Yes: Negotiating Agreement without Giving In,* 2nd edn. Houghton Mifflin, Boston.

Galtung, J. (1976) *Peace, War and Defense: Essays in Peace Research II.* Christian Ejlers, Copenhagen.

Hamburg, D. A. (2002) *No More Killing Fields: Preventing Deadly Conflict.* Rowan & Littlefield, Lanham.

Kelman, H. C. (1992) Informal mediation by the scholar-practitioner. In J. Bercovitch & J. Z. Rubin (eds.), *Mediation in International Relations: Multiple Approaches to Conflict Management.* St. Martin's Press, New York, pp. 64–96.

Kressel, K. (2000) Mediation. In M. Deutsch & P. T. Coleman (eds.), *The Handbook of Conflict Resolution: Theory and Practice.* Jossey-Bass, San Francisco, pp. 522–545.

Kressel, K., Pruitt, D. G. & Associates (eds.) (1989) *Mediation Research: The Process and Effectiveness of Third Party Intervention.* Jossey-Bass, San Francisco.

Lax, D. A. & Sebenius, J. K. (1986) *The Manager as Negotiator: Bargaining for Cooperation and Competitive Gain.* The Free Press, New York.

Lederach, J. P. (1995) *Building Peace: Sustainable Reconciliation in Divided Societies.* The United Nations University, Tokyo.

Mitchell, C. R. (1981) *Peacemaking and the Consultant's Role.* Gower, Westmead.

National Planning Association (1953) *Causes of Industrial Peace.* National Planning Association, Washington.

Northrup, T. A. (1989) The dynamic of identity in personal and social conflict. In L. Kriesberg, T. A. Northrup & S. J. Thorson (eds.), *Intractable Conflicts and their Transformation.* Syracuse University Press, Syracuse, pp. 55–82.

Pearce, W. B. & Littlejohn, S. W. (1997) *Moral Conflict: When Social Worlds Collide.* Sage, Thousand Oaks.

Rouhana, N. N. & Kelman, H. C. (1994) Promoting joint thinking in international conflict: an Israeli–Palestinian continuing workshop. *Journal of Social Issues* 50(1), 157–178.

Rubin, J. Z., Pruitt, D. G. & Kim, S. H. (1994) *Social Conflict: Escalation, Stalemate, and Settlement,* 2nd edn. McGraw-Hill, New York.

Volkan, V. D. (1991) Psychological processes in unofficial diplomacy meetings. In V. D. Volkan, J. V. Montiville & D. A. Julius (eds.), *The Psychodynamics of International Relationships.* Lexington Books, Lexington, pp. 207–222.

Welsh, N. A. & Coleman, P. T. (2002) Institutionalized conflict resolution: have we come to expect too little? *Negotiation Journal* 18(4), 345–350.

Zartman, I. W. (2000) Ripeness: the hurting stalemate and beyond. In P. C. Stern & D. Druchman (eds.), *International Conflict Resolution After the Cold War.* National Academy of Sciences, Washington, pp. 225–250.

Chapter 18

Enhancing Mediator Artistry: Multiple Frames, Spirit, and Reflection in Action

Neil H. Katz

Introduction

When I first accepted Margaret Herrman's invitation to write a chapter for this book, I did so out of flattery in being asked and personal admiration for what Margaret has accomplished and contributed in her professional life. It was only a few days later that I became anxious about honoring my agreement. My daunting task was to read other chapters from an impressive list of contributors and still *add value* to the volume by weaving an original and coherent theme that would comment on the opening chapter and somehow cover the landscape of the book. I wasn't at all sure what I would do and how it would contribute.

As fate would have it, once in a while I come across a body of knowledge that alters the way I look at the world, the meaning I assign to people and events, and the thinking that forms my strategy and actions. Fortunately, this occurred recently when I participated in a workshop on "Leadership, Power and Spirit," led by Robert Marx of the University of Massachusetts-Amherst. The workshop was based primarily on two books – a brilliant work by Lee Bolman and Terrance Deal called *Reframing Organizations: Artistry, Choice and Leadership* (3rd edition, 2003), and *The Wisdom of Solomon at Work: Ancient Virtues for Living and Leading Today* (2001) by Charles Manz, Robert Marx, and others. Each of these books is primarily situated in organizational life and focused on organizational leadership. Yet I believe they have significant relevance to our work as mediation practitioners and scholars. Indeed, all of my recent conflict intervention work, including my mediation efforts, has been heavily influenced by my awareness and integration of this material.

Bolman and Deal's work illuminates four "frames" which serve as "windows to look out on the world and lenses which bring the world into perspective and sharper focus." These frames function as a "cognitive map" which affects what to look for, what it means, and what to do. Therefore the frames serve both as a diagnostic tool and as a model for planning strategy and taking action. The frames allow for sophisticated judgment to help us to make sense of our experience and engage in multifaceted and effective action. Furthermore, knowledge and use of multiple frames facilitates a more holistic and penetrating perspective on people and events, helps avoid individual blindness, and expands choices and effectiveness.

THE BOLMAN AND DEAL FRAMES

Let us now examine the four frames explicated by Bolman and Deal before we speculate on how they might add value to the theory and practice of mediation, as well as serve as one possible framework to relate to the contributions to this bold and groundbreaking volume of work. Through their research on effective organizational leaders, Bolman and Deal identify four "frames" or perspectives that these leaders used to make sense of complex situations and guide their strategy and actions. The four frames or lenses are the structural frame, the human resource frame, the political frame, and the symbolic frame.

A Structural Frame

Structural leaders see their primary task as addressing confusion and chaos by clarifying goals, roles, and expectations. The main activities of a structural leader are to establish, maintain, and reaffirm procedures and policies, focus on tasks, facts, and logic (as opposed to personalities and emotion), and to design and implement a structure to fit circumstances and align with the environment. It is important for the leader to make sure the structure is clear to everyone and appropriate for what needs to be accomplished so that people can perform well and achieve goals. Meetings are formal occasions to transmit facts and information, conduct objective analysis, and make rational decisions. The metaphor for understanding the structural frame is the "well-oiled machine" or "factory," with the leader serving as the *architect* or *analyst*.

A Human Resource Frame

The human resource leader addresses anxiety and uncertainty by primarily focusing on human needs, desires, and building positive relationships. The leader's main task is to keep people involved and participative, and to keep communication open where participants share information and feelings. By being responsive to the needs of individuals and supportive of their goals, leaders can count on their dedication and loyalty. Leaders demonstrate their responsiveness by communicating warmth and concern, listening to and respecting the aspirations of others, and giving people the resources, autonomy, and opportunity to succeed and do their job. Decision-making is an open, empowering, consensus-based process to ensure understanding and commitment. The metaphor for understanding the human resource frame is the "extended family" with the leader serving as the *facilitator* or *servant*.

A Political Frame

The political leader addresses conflicts and feelings of disempowerment by creating forums where issues can be negotiated and alliances redrawn. A good leader is an advocate and astute negotiator who understands politics and is comfortable with conflict, realizing that conflict is often about scarce resources and the distribution of resources (who gets what). The main agenda of the political leader is to manage conflict as productively as possible by creating a power base and exercising influence carefully, particularly with key players. Recognizing that individuals and groups will not get everything they want and that there will always be enduring differences in values, beliefs, information, perceptions, and interests, the leader creates arenas where they can jockey for influence, negotiate their differences, and come up with reasonable compromises. The political leader understands that the meetings and decision-making forums are mainly an opportunity to air conflicts, exercise or gain power, and win concessions. The metaphor for this frame is the "jungle" with the leader posing as the *advocate* or *negotiator* who assists the parties with survival.

A Symbolic Frame

The symbolic leader deals with the formidable barriers of loss of direction and hope and clinging to the past by providing vision, meaning, and inspiration. Symbolic leaders believe their most important job is to give people something that they can believe in. They realize that events have multiple meanings, so what is import-ant about events is not what actually happened, but what it means to people. The focus of symbolic leaders is on creating meaning, belief, and faith, and they do this by the use of metaphors, ceremonies, rituals, myths, stories, and artifacts. The symbolic leader communicates passion, is visible and inspiring. Meetings and conflict resolution procedures are used to develop shared values and negotiate meaning, maintain an image of cooperativeness, responsibility, and accountability while participants act out various roles and share symbolic gestures in a dramatic ritual. Indeed, the metaphor for this frame is the "theater" or "temple" whereby the leader serves as *playwright, poet,* or *prophet.*

Using Frames

Let us examine how the intentional use of these multiple frames can enhance our mediation practice. I believe this knowledge can affect our practice on several levels – the ability to understand the dynamics of the dispute, the ability to build rapport with the disputants, the ability to understand our role in a holistic way, and our ability to formulate and deliver more effective interventions. For instance, familiarity with the *structural frame* facilitates mediator empathy and understand-ing for disputants who see much of their existence in terms of rules, policies, and believe strongly in rationality and logic. Mediators will create safety and comfort for disputants with a high structural valency (disposition) by emphasizing discernible stages to the mediation process, staying focused on the goals of mediation, and enforcing adherence to ground rules that are established. The mediation environment, including factors such as location of the meeting, placement of the chairs and the participants, and equipment in the room, would all be of importance in looking at the world through the structural frame.

The structural frame also has implications as to how mediators conceive of their role and how they determine the success and outcome of the mediation. Mediators who view themselves as *analysts* or *architects* are mainly concerned with building and establishing a conducive *environment* in which rational disputants can exchange facts and information (as well as feelings). The mediation itself is seen as a formal occasion for making decisions based on new information, with the outcome being the ability to feel OK about the rationality of the decision and to return to a life of increased predictability and order. Satisfaction will be primarily measured on the settlement of the conflict along rational lines: Were the issues at least partially resolved and an agreement reached? Was the decision the "best" that could have happened given the facts and logic of the situation including the personalities and idiosyncrasies of the disputants and the case, and the possible penalties of no settlement? Did the mediation allow the parties to claim *authorship* of the agreement by having developed it, shaped it, and agreed to it?

From the vantage point of the human resource frame, the role and work of the mediator will be quite different. The leadership role is as *servant* or *catalyst* of the "extended family" and the work of the mediator is to demonstrate *caring* for family members, serve human needs, and tend to the human interactions and the relationship among members. Fulfillment and satisfaction of the mediation session will be measured by the extent that feelings were expressed and understood, fundamental human needs were acknowledged and accepted, and communication was open and honest. The meeting itself will be viewed as a somewhat informal occasion for sharing feelings and for involvement in issue exploration and joint problem-solving to engender commitment. The mediator will view him or herself as an understanding, empathetic parent figure whose main job is to support and empower the disputants, communicate warmth and concern, listen to and respect their aspirations, and extend the opportunity to the disputants to discuss their different perceptions and problem-solve. Of course, in this frame, the ultimate goal will be the repair of the relationship emerging with increased understanding and empathy from the human dialog that takes place and the transformation of the human heart.

Mediators operating out of the political frame will view their role and the mediation process quite differently. Their role will be the *negotiator* or *overseer of the jungle* who will keep the inhabitants safe by being an advocate for the parties and the process and assist the parties in the hard, trade-off bargaining that will allow each of them to save face and survive. The job of the mediator will be to provide an *arena* for negotiation and compromise and, if possible, rally the disputants against an even more formidable outside enemy (perhaps the legal institutions and procedures, or people who would covertly or overtly benefit by the continuation of hostility). The mediator will look for common interests and use persuasive techniques to influence key stakeholders to bargain and settle. Most importantly, mediators will recognize that enduring differences in values, beliefs, information, interests, and perceptions of reality are laws of the jungle, and that the goal of mediation is to assist the parties to recognize both their power and the limitations of their power, and to bargain in a trade-off environment as they jockey for position and use the mediation session as a competitive occasion to win points. Satisfaction will emerge from the fact that power was acknowledged and exercised, that losses were minimized and some gains were realized, and that some form of *justice* was achieved and survival was assured.

Mediators who operate out of the symbolic frame exercise considerable influence through the definition of their role and their behavior. Given the mediator's assumption that much of life is ambiguous and uncertain, the mediator sees his or her chief job as to create meaning for the participants. The mediator as *prophet, poet,* or *playwright* doesn't concern him or herself with facts, logic, and rational analysis as much as developing hope and faith, meaning and direction through the creation of symbols supported by rituals, ceremonies, stories, and metaphors. The mediation session itself is viewed as a dramatic event for "actors" to acknowledge and share responsibility, produce symbols (such as an apology or some other form of "olive branch"), negotiate the meaning of certain actions and events, and to confirm values and provide opportunities for bonding even among those who were (or are) in conflict. Some of the main tools for the mediator are to interpret the conflict story in a way that teases out meaning and positive purpose, articulates a persuasive and inspiring vision of a less conflictual reality, demonstrates to the actors their key role in contributing to a more compelling and meaningful story, and to use dramatic and visible symbols (stories, rituals, and artifacts) to involve and inspire people. The success of the mediation will be measured not so much in terms of the settlement of outstanding issues, or repairing of the relationship, but in assigning new meaning to the whole experience of the conflict and the mediation session, the restoration of *faith* in the continuing mystery of life, and the feeling among the disputants and the mediators of living a life that has *significance.*

Applications to Mediation

Now that we have explored how the mediator might operate within each of the frames, which ones might be the most important for the mediator to pay more attention to in order to enhance their capability to effectively engage? Bolman and Deal's research supports the contention that most of us rely most heavily on one or two frames to support our analysis, diagnosis, and interventions. Traditionally, managers (and, I suspect, mediators) tend to rely on logic and structure, and good communication and rapport-building skills to control the mediation process and gain the trust and cooperation of disputants. This observation suggests that the political and symbolic frames are the most underutilized frames and, therefore, might give us the most benefit by their use. I believe this could apply to mediators and their practice. In regard to the political frame, the ethic of justice and the acknowledgment of the primary role and need for disputants to engage power and exert influence over decisions are central to the success of mediation and disputant satisfaction. The mediator's ability to create an effective arena, and engage and direct the parties in interest-based negotiations, even within a context of limited resources and jungle-like rivalries, is a vital part of the mediation challenge.

Ultimately, expanded and intentional use of the symbolic frame might have the most potential to expand our understanding of the "magic of mediation" and enhance our mediation practice. Mediators might more consciously use the tools of the symbolic frame, such as storytelling or myths, to shape meaning and create inspiration and hope for the parties and redirect their efforts. Let me share a personal experience when I consciously used the symbolic frame and it seemed to have a huge positive impact on the parties. I was working as a facilitator/mediator with a national labor-management partnership council with a large federal social service agency. The respective labor and management teams were not making progress on any agreements, and there was much bickering and contentious behavior between the teams and even among the teams. The negotiators seemed entrenched in their positions and were blaming each other for the lack of movement. I knew I needed to do something but was not sure of what to do. Fortunately, I remembered a story that former president Jimmy Carter told about the Camp David 1978 negotiations between the Egyptians and the Israelis. Carter spoke about a key moment in the negotiations that he thought was pivotal in reaching an agreement between President Anwar Sadat of Egypt and Prime Minister Menachem Begin of Israel. After several weeks and many attempts to forge an agreement, it looked like all was lost and the parties were packing their bags to go home. Carter visited the Israeli delegation to say farewell to Begin and his associates. It so happened that Begin had requested pictures of President Carter for his grandchildren. Following the suggestion of one of his young staff members, Carter had signed the pictures and placed the name of one of Begin's numerous grandchildren on each one. As Begin accepted the pictures from Carter, he gazed at each one and slowly spoke the name of each grandchild. As he did this, his eyes filled with tears. Moments later he ordered his entourage to unpack their bags and redouble their efforts to get an agreement. According to Carter, the overall interest of negotiating an agreement that might create a better life for children and grandchildren then became the overriding concern in the mind and heart of both men. No doubt this was always an interest that motivated the negotiators to come to Camp David. However, it might have gotten lost or placed backstage as powerful heads of state engaged in tough positional bargaining to win victories and satisfy egos. The picture incident, however, placed the interest of a more peaceful future for children and grandchildren solidly center stage and refocused the parties on their ultimate goals. Days later, an agreement was reached that has established peace between the Israelis and the Egyptians for over 25 years.

What does this have to do with the symbolic frame and the way in which I conduct my interventions? At the height of tension between my federal government labor-management teams, I told them the story I had heard about Camp David. After the story, I pulled a picture of one of my daughters out of my wallet, asked them to look at it, and then told them how this daughter had been in the throes of a serious illness and was now making progress, at least partially because of the emotional support and financial help from the agency they represented. I told them how this assistance had allowed our family to hire very good medical care for our daughter that seemed to make a difference in her recovery. And I told them how thankful I, and my family, were to the agency that made that high-quality care possible and available, and how we would have suffered more if they had not been there in a time of critical need. The humane and compassionate assistance from folk in their agency had made a significant impact.

The story had the intended effect. As in Camp David, the intervention seemed to refocus the parties on why they were negotiating (their ultimate interest of serving the public at a time of critical need), who would benefit by their possible cooperation, and who would lose by their in-fighting. Just as at Camp David, the parties did not discuss the story, but immediately vowed to redouble their efforts to "work together and get it done." And my parties labored well into the night to come up with more "yes-able proposals" that culminated in a more fruitful dialog and important agreements the next day.

"Spirit" and Negotiations

A second book, *The Wisdom of Solomon at Work: Ancient Virtues for Living and Leading Today*, has also had a significant impact on my consulting practice and might add to our understanding of the role and characteristics of exemplary mediators. In *The Wisdom of Solomon*, Charles Manz, Robert Marx, and their colleagues ruminate on the notion of "spirit" by writing about virtues that have endured and weathered the passage of time and are reflected in and reinforced by different religious traditions over the centuries. Though each of the virtues is introduced through a biblical character and demonstrated through stories from the Old Testament, the authors relate the enduring values to contemporary professional practice. The virtues explicated in the book are:

- the faith of Job
- the courage of David
- the compassion of Ruth
- the integrity and justice of Moses
- the wisdom of Solomon

Even though the authors primarily give examples of these virtues being exercised and modeled in business practice, the understanding of and modeling of these virtues might very well be important in uncovering the heart and soul of effective mediators. Let me suggest some ways in which these virtues might relate to the essence of both mediators and mediation practice.

The compassion, courage, and faith of any mediator will be tested early on, and throughout the mediation session. Compassion, characterized by having empathy for the struggle and suffering of others as well as "how deeply we choose to see beyond ourselves and how deeply we choose to respond to what we see," will be a major determinant of the mediator's ability to create and maintain rapport with the disputants, and of the willingness of the parties to transform their understanding of the dispute and broaden their options on ways to address their differences. The mediator's courage, defined as "staying present to life's most difficult challenges, to work with them, and to learn from them," will be tested when third parties enforce ground rules and introduce various interventions to assist the parties. Most of all, faith, to "consistently do the right thing" and strongly believe in the ethos and benefits of mediation as opposed to other dispute resolution processes is essential as the mediator faces many pitfalls within his or her mediation practice that challenge his or her assumptions, values, and beliefs.

It is the acting out of faith, courage, and compassion that enhances the potential for integrity and justice. The authors view integrity as the virtue that leaders display by acting responsibly and consistently, and "empowering others to be responsible for and address their own inner struggles." Mediators display integrity by allowing the parties to define the issues, explore options, and voluntarily commit to action plans if they so desire. And mediators pursue justice when they emphasize fairness, and model impartiality, equality, and respect for the disputants and their rights throughout the mediation process.

All of these other virtues are in support of the most fundamental virtue – the wisdom of Solomon, which is characterized by a "wise and discerning mind" that allows one to display "superior judgment" and choose "a sound course of action." And, at best, mediators are able to access transcendent wisdom, a deep form of "knowing that flows from reflection upon experience and is sensitive to human encounters with life."

INTEGRATING REFLECTION AND PRACTICE

A third book that I continually revisit, and that has had a considerable influence on my consulting work is *The Reflective Practitioner: How Professionals Think in Action* (1990) by Donald Schön. This work has allowed me to think about what I do, assume a more professional and confident persona, and talk about what I do and what I am in a professional context. Schön postulates that successful practitioners do much more than the common notion of others that we "fly by the seat of our pants" or engage in an impulsive "hit-or-miss" mentality and behavior. In his study of professional practitioners in various fields, Schön discovered that the successful practitioners were indeed "reflecting in action" and, in fact, "becoming a researcher and testing theory in the practice context." Like good jazz musicians, successful professionals get a "feel" for the material they are working with and make on-the-spot minor adjustments to phenomena they encounter. When they are "in the groove" (in the mediation context, "in the groove" might be when numerous mediator interventions yield the desired result), the actions become more repetitive and routine and the intuitive, spontaneous performance yields intended results. But when intuitive performance leads to surprises, pleasing or promising or unwanted, expert practitioners then need to respond by "reflection in action." As the professional surfaces and criticizes his or her initial understanding of a phenomenon, constructs a new description of it, and tests the new description by an on-the-spot experiment, a new "theory in action" emerges. Thus, the experiment serves to generate a new understanding of the phenomenon and a change in the situation brought about by the new action.

Why might this perspective offered by Schön be important to mediators and the field of mediation research? I suspect it might be useful in several ways. One way is how we think about ourselves and present ourselves to the public. At best, we are practitioners who perform in professional situations much like lawyers, doctors, accountants, teachers, or other professionals. By logging time in our profession, we also "practice" our craft so we are prepared and ready to encounter somewhat similar situations again and again. Therefore, our professional practice becomes more repetitive and routine, and our knowing-in-practice becomes tacit and spontaneous. Our reputation among our peers and the public as "successful professionals" is enhanced, and our confidence and competence grow.

However, Schön warns that this "upside" of professional practice also has a potential "downside." As we become more respected and comfortable in our "practice" and our analysis and actions become more predictable and repetitive, we might be susceptible to "over-learning," and prone to miss important opportunities to think about what we are doing. The way to overcome this vulnerability is to continue to operate as a "reflective practitioner" throughout our career so we can display "principled flexibility," continue to learn and respond to both familiar and unfamiliar phenomena, enhance our effectiveness with our clients, and strengthen the public's perception of what we do and our status as valued professionals.

ENHANCING THE MODEL IN CHAPTER 2

How does the knowledge in these three books add to our understanding of the magic of the mediation process and potentially refine the effectiveness of mediators? And where does this material intersect with or expand the comprehensive model offered by Herrman, Hollett, and Gale? I believe this discussion directly addresses some of the antecedent conditions (T_0), particularly the *disputant and mediator characteristics.* Researchers and practitioners could sharpen their understanding and practice by diagnosing which of the four frames is dominant in the mediator and the disputants, and which of the frames is foremost in the party's characterization of the dispute. This knowledge could result in more effective "frame matching" between the mediator and the disputants while the mediator keeps in mind the advantages of a multi-frame approach. Furthermore, the wisdom of these three works, particularly the Bolman and Deal text, speaks directly to the *structural, human, and political factors that prime readiness* (T_m) such as procedural clarity, mediator empathy, feeling heard and understood, ability to talk about perceptions and feelings, and global and interactional fairness. And in terms of short- and long-term outcomes (T_1 and T_2), the four-frame material certainly speaks to how one will measure success and whether factors such as *agreement reached* and *issues resolved* are more or less important than other factors such as *distributive justice* and *relationship change.*

Perhaps the discussion of these three books also suggests some omissions in the "comprehensive model." The *Reframing Organizations* material speaks to the advantage of having all four frames at your disposal when analyzing complex situations, and deciding upon and delivering interventions. The flexible cognitive disposition advocated by Bolman and Deal enhances our thinking about "concepts and tools" available to expert mediators. The ability and willingness to use all four frames might very well enhance our understanding of the nuances of the dispute, as well as expand our intervention options and our ability to gain and maintain rapport with the disputants. The *Wisdom of Solomon* material has the potential to remind mediators of the core values or virtues underlying the theory and practice of mediation. And Donald Schön's work on *The Reflective Practitioner* reinforces our belief in mediation as a professional practice and helps our understanding of what we are doing and how we explain what we do to our critics and admirers.

Does the existing model incorporate all of these possibilities? I'm not sure. Maybe the description of mediator characteristics would need to include flexible cognitive disposition (i.e. the ability and willingness to utilize the four frames) and the reflection-in-action mindset of the reflective practitioner. And maybe we would need to fit in some of the core virtues somewhere in the model to more effectively tap in to the "spirit" of mediation. Yet it is perhaps wise to remember that the subtitle of *Reframing Organizations* includes "artistry." Artists spin their craft and interpret experience for us in new ways so that we may envision, explore, and pursue unimagined possibilities. Expert mediators rely on a rich mixture and accumulation of lifetime lessons that afford them the knowledge, skills, and wisdom to bring to life the "magic" of mediation. Their artistry transforms how we view our disputes and how we interpret the intentions and actions of others and ourselves. As much as we try, we will never quite understand and explain art or magic with rational thought, technical language, and sophisticated diagrams by themselves. Models, even ones as expertly crafted and comprehensive as the one in this book, can only approximate what is done, and speculate on its impact. Our noble efforts in this volume illuminate more than was known before. Yet the animating force or "soul" of mediation remains somewhat mysterious and elusive, and, like art, has to be fully experienced to even begin to be understood and truly appreciated.

REFERENCES

Bolman, L. G. & Deal, T. E. (2003) *Reframing Organizations: Artistry, Choice and Leadership,* 3rd edn. Jossey-Bass, San Francisco.

Manz, C. C., Manz, K. P., Marx, R. D. & Neck, C. P. (2001) *The Wisdom of Solomon at Work: Ancient Virtues for Living and Leading Today.* Berrett-Koehler, San Francisco.

Schön, D. A. (1990) *The Reflective Practitioner: How Professionals Think in Action.* Basic Books, New York.

Chapter 19

Of Time and the River: Notes on the Herrman, Hollett, and Gale Model of Mediation

Kevin Avruch

Based upon more than four decades of research and practice in interpersonal mediation, the model proposed by Herrman, Hollett, and Gale (HHG) deserves the appellation bestowed on it by many of the contributors to this volume: "comprehensive." Adopting a linear, phase-structure, or time-sequential approach, the model depicts and structures mediation as it proceeds through four main stages: T_0, which describes conditions antecedent to the mediation; T_m, describing those conditions pertaining to the formal mediation "event" or "session"; and two post-event stages, T_1 specifying short-term outcomes or "end products" and T_2 for long-term results. Because the model assumes that conditions are never fixed but vary according to characteristics of personnel, situation (narrowly conceived), and context (more broadly conceived), they are in turn useful in constituting sets of variables which, when operationalized through reference to the empirically rich literature on mediation practice, can contribute to theory-generation and theory-building, and to the testing of hypotheses derived from these theories.

What makes the model "comprehensive" is the range and diversity of conditions (specifiable as variables or organized as possible measures) in each of the T-stages (see tables 2.1–2.4 above). Four decades of research and practice have been well mined to produce this catalog of conditions, and then some sophisticated conceptualization of the dynamics of interpersonal relations, disputing, and problem-solving have been put in the service of turning the catalog into a dynamic model of the mediation process. Importantly, the modelers are aware of what (other) sources of diversity or variation they leave relatively unspecified in this model: contexts related to or generated by radically different cultures, for example. Such careful circumscription in the face of comprehensiveness increases our confidence in the model. For all these reasons, Herrman, Hollett, and Gale are fully justified in claiming that their model presents us with a "new platform for formal theory testing."

As the chapters in this book amply demonstrate, the model is also useful for generating critical discussion around the nature of third party mediation per se. This forms the core of my brief remarks and "notes" on the HHG model in this chapter. But first I want to distinguish the HHG model as (precisely) a *model* of the mediation process from its role as a *theory* of mediation. Models may well (as Herrman, Hollett, and Gale claim) generate theories and testable hypotheses, and models are always, at least implicitly, based themselves upon some (at least partial) theories, but it is important not to mistake the model for the theory that undergirds it. As admirably explicit and comprehensive of the mediation process as the HHG model is, it is less so as a fully developed theory of mediation. What theory there is (there must be!) in the HHG model is largely implicit. To be sure, some of this theory is indirectly revealed in the section in chapter 2 where they describe the basic "assumptions of the model." These assumptions constitute the taken-for-granted axioms (the "primitives" of any theory) upon which the model is based. Some examples include: "People prefer harmony to discord." "Competition brings forth competition, cooperation calls forth cooperation." "Uncertainty motivates an active search for more information." Such axioms are to be understood as in part ontological: they comprise a "theory" of human nature and universal human psychological functioning. One potential challenge to such assumptions (to all ontological assumptions, in fact) comes from the domain of radical cultural variation – the ethnographic record, in other words (Avruch 1998). As already noted, however, this source of potential variation has been delimited "out" of the model. But we need not travel to other cultures to question some of these assumptions.

For example, Donald Saposnek, in his chapter analyzing the dynamics of power in child custody mediation (chapter 12), comments on how some of these assumptions do not hold in emotionally laden child custody disputes where, among other dynamics, "anger generates power." In such situations, among other things: (a) one party, autistically hostile, may emphatically prefer discord to harmony; (b) one party may react, consequently, agonistically or competitively even when approached cooperatively; while (c) the affectively charged combination of rage and power imbalance can "sabotage" or shut down rational problem-solving, short-circuiting the search for "more information" in the face of uncertainty (in fact, rage "resolves" any uncertainty.)

Other parts of the implicit HHG theory of mediation are buried more deeply than in stated assumptions. Perhaps the contribution by Winslade and Monk (chapter 9), following their work on "narrative mediation" (2000), makes this point more critically than any other in this volume. Reacting most strongly to the circumscription of "sociocultural context" already mentioned, they also question the epistemological status of such notions as "problem-solving," "motivation," "mediator empathy," "needs," or "interests" as objectively determinable (and determinative) internal states or engines of an "actor." Indeed, they question the very vocabulary of "variables" and "operationalized measures." Their metaphor is the "story" and they see mediation in the terms of a narrative flow or "stream" rather than a third party intervention in a phase-structured process. They subject the HHG model not to the empiricist and "modernist" criteria of hypothesis-generating positivism, but to the Foucauldian criterion of discursive plausibility. And they point briefly to the ethical implications of command-and-control that are consequential to the few dominant discourses of a society. In this way they do not so much question the power of HHG theory as the appropriateness of any (grand) theorizing project in general – Herrman, Hollett, and Gale's included. Theirs is a postmodernist approach to another largely critical literature on mediation, mainly from scholars working in the law and society tradition, including Nader (1998), Galanter (1974), Harrington (1985), and Grillo (1991). This critique argues that mediation, or alternative dispute resolution (ADR) in general, disempowers certain kinds of people, such as women, minorities, or the working poor. Though noted briefly by Herrman, Hollett, and Gale, this aspect of mediation is not elaborated or addressed in this volume. Nevertheless, in addition to that by Winslade and Monk, some of the chapters on mediation and "justice," such as those by Conlon (chapter 11) or Umbreit and Coates (chapter 7), can be read with this critique in mind.

Beyond a postmodernist interrogation of the positivist underpinnings of the model in general, or a political critique of (North American) mediation as a late-capitalist social form, what remains most deeply embedded and problematic in the theory of HHG mediation has to do, in my view, with the nature of mediation itself, particularly the role, function, or tasks of the mediator as a third party intervener. This is what comes out of my reading of most of the chapters in this volume, where authors who bring decades of experience in research or practice in their own areas of expertise react to the wealth of material and possibilities presented by the HHG model. The resulting "dialog" across chapters is for me the most valuable contribution of this book. But at times the dialog also seems strained, as though in trying to fit or make sense of their own areas of expertise in research or practice in terms of the HHG model some of the authors can't help but problematize two aspects of the model that Herrman, Hollett, and Gale themselves take unselfconsciously for granted: the linear and temporalized phase structure of the process and the nature of the third party they call "mediator." These are, I shall argue, two aspects of the same problem.

Take the nature of the mediator first. It is not the case, of course, that the HHG model denies any variability in the role. On the contrary, part of the conditions under stage T_0 in the model specifies, alongside disputants, a set of "mediator characteristics." But these are conceptualized as *personal* characteristics and, beyond demographic categories like sex or age, further as those skills and knowledge mediators need to possess to be effective – particularly communication and process-management skills. Certainly these are important dimensions of variation that a mediator would manifest, and ought not to be ignored, but they remain personal dimensions, and take for granted their variation around the third party intervener called "mediator." What does this sort of creature look like? How stable is it? Crucially, does it appear to look the same way in many of the chapters in the book?

In fact, although the personal characteristics, skills, knowledge, and social background of mediators are expected to vary, the overall sense of what a mediator is seems to be taken for granted, an unexamined amalgam of the classic descriptions of the role and its tasks, right out of, for example, Folberg and Taylor (1984), Moore (1986), or Wilmot and Hocker (2001). Prototypically: the mediator is neutral and impartial, an "outsider" to the dispute and unrelated to the parties, lacking the power and authority to stipulate decisions or settlements (or, indeed, enforce compliance with them). The paradigmatic mediation is conceived as a one-off "session" even if separated in two or more parts by some days. Functionally, the mediator mainly "facilitates" the process of negotiation between the parties, and any agreement arising from this negotiation must be one that the parties themselves "own." For their part, the parties come to mediation voluntarily. There are other prototypical characteristics, but these will suffice for now.

That we operate cognitively in terms of "prototypes" is not surprising, and in fact is unavoidable. But what we must remember is that prototypes are *constructed* cognitive entities, and that (a) they never describe a comprehensive picture of the phenomenal world they purport to depict (i.e. not all entities "covered by" the prototype resemble the prototype), and (b) prototypes can vary either with variations in the phenomenal world or in the "cognitive communities" inhabiting such worlds.

These points are based on the pioneering work on prototypical thinking by the cognitive psychologist Eleanor Rosch (1972, 1975, 1976). Within a given "cognitive community" (say, "a culture"), agreements on typicality will generally be high. For example, in the category of things called "birds," Rosch shows that high protoypicality for Americans resides in such birds as "robin" and "sparrow," with low agreement on prototypicality for "emu" and "penguin," with "crow" and "parrot" falling somewhere in the middle. In other words, when one calls up a mental image of "a" bird, it is likely to be a robin, and unlikely to be an emu – or a turkey, for that matter. This is not to say, of course, that complex cognition cannot recognize turkeys, owls, or flamingos as kinds of birds, but that – for reasons of cognitive economy – we think in terms of prototypes and such prototypes structure our thinking (and probably also our learning). Rosch herself worked cross-culturally, and following her work cultural anthropologists and psychologists have demonstrated how prototypes in fact may vary from culture to culture – for example, prototypes for "tree" among American and Tzeltal children differ significantly (see Keller 1978; D'Andrade 1995: 115–121).

Now let's return to our "prototypical" mediator and ask how such an implicit and embedded construct can structure our thinking so that we take the very category, as prototypicalized, for granted: "Mediators are neutrals as robins are birds." Importantly, just as complex (or "adult") cognition understands that "chickens" are birds too, so can complex cognition deal with the fact that not all mediators are "neutral." In fact, adverting to the "outsider/neutral" characteristic mentioned above, one of the first modifications urged on our prototypical thinking about mediators came from practitioners with extensive cross-cultural experience, who realized that in other cultures not outsider/neutrals but rather what they called "insider/partials" were the rule – and thus the prototype. Missing such prototypical variation is one of the costs of delimiting or keeping socio-cultural context "constant," as the HHG model does. John Paul Lederach argued this based upon his Central American experience (Wehr & Lederach 1991), and more recently work in some Middle Eastern societies has demonstrated the same phenomenon (Abu-Nimer 1996). Yet another critique of mediator neutrality has political sources, already mentioned (the work of Nader, for example); and today the entire notion of third party neutrality as a key or defining characteristic is subject to critical questioning, as in Bernard Mayer's recent *Beyond Neutrality* (2004). Among other things, all this demonstrates that in an emergent (and one hopes still vigorous) field of inquiry prototypes are subject to revision – on the whole an encouraging finding.

But one need not go to cross-cultural work or political critique to find a certain instability in the prototype of the mediator. In fact, my thinking in this direction was stimulated precisely by my readings of several of the chapters in this book. While Winslade and Monk, as mentioned, are the most far-reaching in this sense, portraying the "prototypical" mediator as storyteller or even, alongside the parties, a collaborative co-creator of stories (see also Cobb 2004), they are hardly alone in this volume in conceiving and portraying non-prototypical mediators. For instance: Morton Deutsch (chapter 17), regarding difficult conflicts when "regular" mediation fails, and mediation appears irrelevant, nevertheless borrows Pearce and Littlejohn's (1997) notion of "transcendental eloquence" as a key mediator skill in such intractable conflicts. But such a mediator is somehow different from our prototype. Donald Conlon sees mediators working through a mediation as jugglers of complex construals of four different sorts of "justice," while Mark Umbreit and Robert Coates focus on the mediator as a facilitator of dialog striving particularly for "restorative justice" in the context of victim–offender dialogs. Daniel Shapiro (chapter 14) tackles the thorny issue of strong emotion, arguing against the popular notion of third parties encouraging angry disputants to "vent" their affect "away." Here the mediator resembles more an object-relations therapist than a negotiation facilitator.

Still on emotions, Donald Saposnek adds consideration of power to the mix in child custody disputes and, inter alia, questions the idealization of "negotiation in conflict resolution as a linear process of rational discourse leading to a rational, fair, and equitable outcome" (p. 267), indicating that the mediator is often involved in a "circuitous" process (more on this below). Dean Tjosvold and Sofia Su Fang (chapter 16) analyze the manager as a mediator. Managers are hardly outsider/ neutral, or even mildly disinterested, third parties – again not quite our prototype. And Neil Katz (chapter 18), borrowing Bolman and Deal's (2003) four frames or metaphors for organizations and their leaders, finds them relevant to conceiving different sorts of mediators as well.

I found Katz's chapter particularly suggestive. The four frames Katz discusses are the *structural* frame (where metaphorically the organization is a well-oiled machine and the leader an architect or analyst); the *human resources* frame (the organization is a extended family and the leader is a facilitator or servant); the *political* frame (the organization is a jungle and the leader is an advocate or a negotiator for the parties); and the *symbolic* frame (the organization is a "theater" or "temple," and the leader is playwright, poet, or prophet). Building upon Katz's own interesting discussion of these frames and metaphors, I suggest they correspond neatly to four major understandings of mediation current today. The structural frame is perhaps closest to our prototype, the "standard model" mediator if you will, focusing on conflict analyst and dispute systems or process designer/architect (cf. Moore 1986). The human resource frame, with its relational and family metaphors, seems to me to echo the concerns of transformational mediation (Bush & Folger 1994). The political frame, concerned with power and justice, brings to mind the rather activist, politically engaged and "trouble-making" third party work of such Quakers as Adam Curle (1986) or C. H. Yarrow (1972), or even some of Larry Susskind's third party work in the public policy arena (Susskind & Cruikshank 1987). Finally, the symbolic frame, with its playwright/poet/prophet roles, brings us back to the mediator as master narrator or storyteller, to Winslade and Monk.

I have not mentioned here all the different contributors to the volume, and some do indeed deal with a mediator that seems "prototypical" and befits the standard model. But referring to the chapters cited above, I would argue that what emerges in this volume overall is a tremendous diversity – alternatively an uncertainty or instability – in what exactly a mediator is and does. Certainly the semantic distance separating facilitator, manager, therapist, advocate, poet, and prophet would seem to undermine our confidence in a secure and stable prototype. The question is: Should this also undermine our confidence in the HHG model of mediation?

I will argue that it shouldn't, though it should make us rethink some key aspects of the model, most particularly its linear (unidirectional) and temporal structure. Part of the problem has to do with our primary conceptualization of mediation as a third party intervention in a (prototypically!) two-party situation. Bercovitch echoed many definitions of mediation when he wrote that "Mediation is, at least structurally, the continuation of negotiation by other means" (1997: 127). But negotiation, relying upon the core heuristic of the market and "buyer-seller" is a particularly robust idea, even cross-culturally so, while any third party intervention seems far more conditional and contingent by comparison. This is demonstrated even in Bercovitch's own work on international mediation – perhaps accounting for his adding a sub-clausal qualification to his definition: "at least structurally." From the beginning the idea that mediation was simply "facilitated negotiation" seemed less than fully sustainable. In the same article in which Bercovitch begins with the simplest of definitions, he goes on to cite contemporary work by Carnevale (1986), Kressel (1972), Stuhlberg (1987), and Touval and Zartman (1985), all of which offer more or less expansive typologies of mediators (roles and tasks), and "complexify" the idea. The more we mediate, and the more we study and analyze its practice, the more uncomfortable does the basic definition (and its prototype) appear. Instead, we have come to recognize that the addition of a third party – any third party – to a dispute or negotiation seems to transform some of its key parameters and dynamics. A single robin in a cage has somehow become a full and many-specied aviary, and not one that is so well confined.

What does mediation, or the mediator, look like if we admit its multifarious manifestations and forms and the instability of its prototype? How does this affect the HHG model? To begin, let me go to the problem I characterized as the linear and temporalized, phase-structure, nature of the model – and to another metaphor: the river.

The language of positive science and systems theory is comfortable thinking of the mediation, as the HHG model does, in terms of a temporally sequential, phase-structured, and causal process in different states with different inputs (in T_0

and T_m) and outputs (T_1 and T_2). But reading the model and the papers that sought to "navigate" it put in my mind a different metaphor and language – hinted at in Winslade and Monk – the "mediation process" as a flow or stream, as a river, and the mediator as the intentional vessel traveling down the river toward its end. The various inputs can be thought of as conditions of the river (that in turn condition its flow), or, more graphically, as incoming streams or rivulets that "feed" and so transform it. Outputs are usually simple to tell: the sea or another, larger river. In humanly altered riverscapes, dams are possible, and in deserts rivers can simply flow in one brief season, evaporate, and lead nowhere discernible: dry wadis. But we tend to think (protoypically) of rivers flowing in one direction, irreversibly.

Now anyone who has traveled much on rivers, or lived off them, knows that they are, depending on conditions and location, complex and ever-changing things. (It's time to reread Twain's *Life on the Mississippi!*) And if we cast the HHG model in terms of our riparian metaphor, I think on the whole the metaphor does very well at capturing the model's sense of the mediation process. Nevertheless, some of the contributors to the volume, for example, Littlejohn and Domenici (chapter 10), who focus on "facework" in mediation, point to one of the limitations of such a conception of mediation flow, namely its linear and unidirectional nature. They suggest a "circular" flow. Umbreit and Coates, writing of mediated dialog in the context of restorative justice, also react to the strong linearity of the HHG model, stressing the non-linear nature of dialog work.

Let me suggest another limitation. No matter how complex our understanding of the river as an ever-changing (even, invoking Gaia, as a "living") entity might be, if we imagine a vessel traveling "down" it we instinctively presume that the vessel itself remains unchanged. It doesn't start as a canoe and end as a steamer. Even Twain, that master observer of the Mississippi, did not imagine *his* boat changing form as it traveled (though he certainly understood that *the river is not the same river* if it's traveled by oar, sail, or steam). Here we come back to the HHG model. For however complexly understood and represented the mediation "stream" is in this model, the underlying presumption is that the same sort of "vessel" – the mediator – travels intentionally – navigates – down it. Yet what many of the chapters in this book demonstrate (as so much other research on mediation practice demonstrates) is something different: how variegated is the mediator form, how "unstable" and resistant to easy prototyping the role of this third party intervener actually is. And just as the river is not the same river if traveled by different sorts of vessels under different modes of power, so too is the mediation process something different as different sorts of third parties enact the mediator's role. To push this analogy one last step: we can all understand how the river can destabilize a vessel. Can we understand how, in much more seismically sensitive ways, the vessel may also destabilize the river?

No doubt I've pushed this analogy, however Gaia-friendly, too far. My point is to have us look at the unidirectional linearity of the HHG model "flow" critically (as some of the authors in fact do), and also to regard more closely the one main and unquestioned "given" in the model, beyond noting variation in "personal characteristics" at T_0, and that is the nature of the mediator him or herself.

We have several typologies of mediator roles, functions, or tasks from which to choose, as noted above. I want to call attention to a typology presented by Christopher Mitchell in 1993 and then, influenced by notions of contingency, introduced by Fisher and Keashly (1991) – another stage or phase-structured temporalized model, of conflict and conflict resolution more generally – refined in a later publication (see Mitchell 1993, 2003). It will be noted that Mitchell's 14 mediator tasks and roles are divided into three different stages, corresponding to HHG's T-values (with T_1 and T_2 collapsed into a single "Post-Agreement" stage; see table 19.1).

TABLE 19.1   Core mediator roles and tasks in conflict resolution

Intermediary role	Tasks and functions
	Pre-negotiation
Explorer	Determines adversaries' readiness for contacts; sketches range of possible solutions
Reassurer	Reassures adversaries that other not wholly bent on "victory"
Decoupler	Assists external patrons to withdraw from core conflict; enlists patrons in other positive tasks
Unifier	Repairs intra-party cleavages and encourages consensus on interests, core values, concessions
Enskiller	Develops skills and competencies needed to enable adversaries to reach a durable solution
Convener	Initiates process of talks, provides venue, and legitimizes contacts and meetings
	During talks/negotiations
Facilitator	Fulfills functions within meetings to enable a fruitful exchange of versions, aims, and visions
Envisioner	Provides new data, ideas, theories, and options for adversaries to adapt; creates fresh thinking
Enhancer	Provides additional resources to assist in search for positive-sum solution
Guarantor	Provides insurance against talks breaking down and offers to guarantee any durable solution
Legitimizer	Adds prestige and legitimacy to any agreed solution
	Post-agreement
Verifier	Reassures adversaries that terms of agreement are being fulfilled
Implementer	Imposes sanctions for non-performance of agreement
Reconciler	Assists in long-term actions to build new relationships among and within adversaries

Source: Adapted from Mitchell (2003: 84).

There are at least three ways to interpret Mitchell's 14 roles in terms of the HHG model of mediation. Perhaps with the exception of the "implementer" role (able to impose sanctions on non-compliant parties), first, and fundamentally, they collectively argue against a single prototype for "the mediator," unless of course one methodologically restricts the definition of "mediator" to only one or two of the possible 14 roles, probably around "facilitator." This would indeed preserve the prototype but at the cost of losing a great deal of information about what "mediator-like" third parties actually do in the real and multifarious world – precisely the point made by several of the chapters in this book.

The second interpretation, perfectly amenable to the model, is to see "the" mediator changing roles/functions/form as the process unfolds. In other words, to see mediator characteristics as conditional and consequential not only at T_0 but also throughout T_m. Depending on how broadly we conceive the role, perhaps even changing consequentially, post-agreement, through T_1 and T_2. Alternatively, we can also think of this as the "mediation changing the mediator," or as a successful and effective mediator as one who is receptive to role/task change throughout the process. Certainly the HHG model can accommodate this thinking.

But the third interpretation, as noted by Mitchell himself, is most interesting for the model. Mitchell points out that given the contradictory nature of some of these roles, for example those of "unifier," which works within a party to reduce cleavages, or "enskiller," working on behalf of a single disputant, it is unlikely that they would be acceptable to the other side later on in the process – they would be seen as highly partial and not neutral, for example. In other words, the same person cannot play all the roles as the process unfolds. (Think of how the Quaker American Friends Service Committee, working for many years to build skills in the Palestinian community in order that the Palestinians may one day pro-ductively engage the Israelis as symmetrical partners in peace negotiations, have entirely and irrevocably lost the confidence of the Israelis to act as "neutrals" in any way – although the whole point of Friends' activism is, in their view, ultimately in the service of peace.) This notion that the same third party cannot mediate throughout the process, and that by implication no single and unique actor called mediator is possible for all conditions and contexts in a conflict or dispute, comes closest to representing some of the insights found in some of the chapters in this book. What remains most intriguing after considering the HHG model and the fine chapters which utilize it is the light it sheds on the complexity of the nature of the mediator as "the vessel" traveling intentionally down the mediation "stream."

What would the HHG model look like in order to accommodate this observa-tion? Can we preserve its unidirectional flow? These are questions we have hardly touched on here. (I understand the Chicago River has been made to flow "back-ward," at least at times; but then so too have the dead voted in local elections there.) One great value of the HHG model is that it stimulates this sort of thinking. It should, in fact, help us more clearly to conceptualize that mediators may shift shape or form as the process unfolds, and help us to see what this "form-shifting" of the mediator looks like, through "time and the river."

REFERENCES

Abu-Nimer, M. (1996) Conflict resolution approaches: Western and Middle Eastern lessons and possibilities. *American Journal of Economics and Sociology* 55, 35–52.

Avruch, K. (1998) *Culture and Conflict Resolution*. United States Institute of Peace Press, Washington.

Bercovitch, J. (1997) Mediation in international conflict. In W. Zartman & L. Rasmussen (eds.), *Peace Making in International Conflict: Methods and Techniques*. United States Institute of Peace Press, Washington, pp. 125–153.

Bolman, L. G. & Deal, T. E. (2003) *Reframing Organizations: Artistry, Choice, and Leadership*. Jossey-Bass, San Francisco.

Bush, R. B. & Folger, J. P. (1994) *The Promise of Mediation*. Jossey-Bass, San Francisco.

Carnevale, P. (1986) Strategic choice in mediation. *Negotiation Journal* 2, 41–56.

Cobb, S. (2004) *Witnessing in Mediation: Toward an Aesthetic of Practice*. Institute for Conflict Analysis and Resolution, George Mason University, Working Paper 22.

Curle, A. (1986) *In the Middle: Non-Official Mediation in Violent Situations*. Berg, Oxford.

D'Andrade, R. (1995) *The Development of Cognitive Anthropology*. Cambridge University Press, Cambridge.

Fisher, R. J. & Keashly, L. (1991) The potential complementarity of mediation and consultation within a contingency model of third party intervention. *Journal of Peace Research* 28, 29–42.

Folberg, J. & Taylor, A. (1984) *Mediation*. Jossey-Bass, San Francisco.

Galanter, M. (1974) Why the haves come out ahead: speculation on the limits of legal change. *Law and Society Review* 9, 95–160.

Grillo, T. (1991) The mediation alternative: process dangers for women. *Yale Law Review* 100, 1545–1610.

Harrington, C. (1985) *Shadow Justice: The Ideology and Institutionalization of Alternatives to Court*. Greenwood, Westport.

Keller (Dougherty), J. (1978) Salience and relativity in classification. *American Ethnologist* 5, 66–79.

Kressel, K. (1972) *Labor Mediation: An Exploratory Survey*. Association of Labor Mediation Agencies, New York.

Mayer, B. (2004) *Beyond Neutrality: Confronting the Crisis in Conflict Resolution*. Jossey-Bass, San Francisco.

Mitchell, C. R. (1993) The process and stages of mediation: two Sudanese cases. In D. Smock (ed.), *Making War and Waging Peace: Foreign Intervention in Africa*. United States Institute of Peace Press, Washington, pp. 139–159.

Mitchell, C. R. (2003) Mediation and the Ending of Conflicts. In J. Darby & R. MacGuinty (eds.), *Contemporary Peacemaking: Conflict Violence and Peace Processes*. Palgrave, London, pp. 77–86.

Moore, C. (1986) *The Mediation Process: Practical Strategies for Resolving Conflicts*. Jossey-Bass, San Francisco.

Nader, L. (1998) Harmony models and the construction of law. In K. Avruch, P. Black & J. Scimecca (eds.), *Conflict Resolution: Cross-Cultural Perspectives*. Greenwood, New York, pp. 41–59.

Pearce, W. B. & Littlejohn, S. W. (1997) *Moral Conflict: When Social Worlds Collide*. Sage, Thousand Oaks.

Rosch, E. (1972) The structure of color space in naming and memory for two languages. *Cognitive Psychology* 3, 337–354.

Rosch, E. (1975) Cognitive representations of semantic categories. *Journal of Experimental Psychology* 104, 192–233.

Rosch, E. (1976) Cognitive reference points. *Cognitive Psychology* 7, 532–547.

Stuhlberg, J. (1987) *Taking Charge/Managing Conflict.* D. C. Heath, Lexington, MA.

Susskind, L. & Cruikshank, J. (1987) *Breaking the Impasse: Consensual Approaches to Resolving Public Disputes.* Basic Books, New York.

Touval, S. & Zartman, I. W. (eds.) (1985) *International Mediation in Theory and Practice.* Westview, Boulder.

Twain, M. (1996) *Life on the Mississippi.* Oxford University Press, New York.

Wehr, P. & Lederach, J. P. (1991) Mediating conflicts in Central America. *Journal of Peace Research* 28, 85–98.

Wilmot, W. & Hocker J. (2001) *Interpersonal Conflict.* McGraw-Hill, New York.

Winslade, J. & Monk, G. (2000) *Narrative Mediation: A New Approach to Conflict Resolution.* Jossey-Bass, San Francisco.

Yarrow, C. H. (1972) *Quaker Experiences in International Mediation.* Yale University Press, New Haven.

Chapter 20

Mediation at the Millennium

DEAN G. PRUITT

INTRODUCTION

Mediation is a growth industry. Formal mediation has long been practiced in industrial and international relations; but in the past 25 years, it has spread into almost every conceivable realm of conflict, from the relations between children on the playground to the sentencing of murderers. Informal mediation – by friends, co-workers, family members, and the like – has always been with us. But many people (e.g. managers) are now being trained to do a better job in that capacity.

Mediation practice, theory, and research have been dominated by a tradition that stresses the goal of settling the present conflict and offers problem-solving as the preferred methodology. Some of the chapters in this handbook rely heavily on this tradition, especially Herrman, Hollett, and Gale's chapter 2 and chapter 5 by Wissler (though neither of these is exclusively based on this tradition). But many of the chapters present amendments and challenges to this tradition. That means that the field is growing conceptually and that this handbook is an excellent place to learn about this growth.

My first task in this overview chapter will be to summarize the problem-solving-to-settlement tradition, or model, of mediation, to which a number of authors including myself have contributed over the years (Pruitt 1981, 1995; Kressel & Pruitt 1989; Duffy, Grosch & Olczak 1991; Moore 1996; Kressel 2000; Wall, Stark & Standifer 2001; Bercovich 2002; Pruitt & Kim 2004). Then I will summarize what I see as the key amendments and challenges to this tradition, drawing on the chapters of this book and other sources. Part of the latter section will compare and contrast the traditional approach with these new developments and speculate about links among the latter. These first two sections will be mainly concerned with the process used, which occurs at point T_m in the Herrman et al. four-phase model, and its impact on short-term (T_1) and long-term (T_2) outcomes. Finally I will present a critique of the new developments, focusing primarily on those designed to rebuild troubled relationships. That section will mention some theoretical and research frontiers.

THE TRADITIONAL MODEL

The traditional, or problem-solving-to-settlement, model views mediation as third-party-assisted negotiation. It stresses the importance of building integrative or win-win agreements, which the disputants find acceptable because their interests or needs are more or less met. Such agreements are seen as having many advantages over simple compromises or grossly uneven settlements. In addition to need satisfaction, they are assumed to encourage compliance, contribute positively to the future relationship between the disputants, and provide benefit to the organization or society of which the disputants are members.

Traditional mediators ordinarily guide the process through a series of stages such as the following:

1   Venting – all parties present a history of the conflict and their opening positions
2   Shifting the focus from the past to the future
3   Clarifying the issues
4   Generating possible solutions to these issues
5   Choosing among these solutions
6   Developing an implementation plan

Problem-solving takes place at the second, third and fourth stages of this progression. The aim of problem-solving is to devise a mutually acceptable agreement. Problem-solving is accomplished by seeking out the interests (goals, values, needs) underlying the disputants' positions and their priorities among these interests. A search is then made for options that speak to the most important of interests on all sides, and the best of these options is chosen.

Joint problem-solving, in which the disputants work together in search of a win-win solution, has been shown to maximize the likelihood that agreement will be reached and will satisfy the parties' interests (Zubek et al. 1992; Wissler, chapter 5 in this handbook). Most mediators feel that they should make minimal interventions when joint problem-solving is going on.

Unfortunately, the ideal of joint problem-solving is often not fully feasible. Disputants are too rigid to analyze the interests and priorities underlying their own positions. Or if they understand these interests and priorities, they are too distrustful of each other to talk about them openly. Or they are too hostile to seek a solution that satisfies the other party's interests. In such cases, they may not make the transition to a future orientation required by stage 2 and are likely to circle through a set of demands and accusations rather than engaging in joint problem-solving. If this happens, the mediator must step in and facilitate joint problem-solving or engage in problem-solving himself or herself. Research shows that the less the disputants are doing for themselves, the more active the mediator must become (Donohue 1989; Hiltrop 1989).

The mediator can set an agenda, interview the parties about their underlying interests and priorities, provide discreet information about the other party's

interests, analyze the issues, encourage the disputants to think up mutually beneficial solutions, devise such solutions himself or herself, or try to precipitate an
agreement. A favorite mediator tactic is "caucusing," that is, meeting with each
side separately. In caucus sessions, disputants become less emotional, they are more
likely to provide information about their interests and priorities, and they are often
willing to engage in problem-solving with the mediator, which can yield some good
ideas (Welton et al. 1992).

When the disputants do not trust each other, as is often the case, trust in the
mediator is crucial to get problem-solving going (Deutsch, chapter 17 in this handbook). This puts special requirements on the mediator. He or she must be seen
as unbiased. In small communities (e.g. villages, the international community), it
is not always possible to find a mediator who is equally close to both sides. But, it
is essential that he or she be seen as neutral on the issues at hand (Conlon & Ross
1993). If that cannot be achieved, co-mediation may work, with one mediator closer
to the first side and the other to the second.[1] The mediator must also work hard
to build rapport with the disputants, giving them a chance to present their case,
engaging in empathic listening, showing a concern about their welfare, and building a reputation for being truthful (Deutsch, chapter 17). Mediators can also try
to build trust between the disputants, emphasizing values and goals they have in
common (Katz, chapter 18).

Amendments and Challenges to the Traditional Model

The Mediator as Expert Advisor

In some realms, the disputants are simply over their heads with regard to the
issues and the mediator must give them expert advice. Saposnek (chapter 12 in
this handbook) and Walker and Hayes (chapter 4) argue that this is often the
case in divorce and custody mediation, where legal issues and the stages of child
development loom large. Sometimes there is no real conflict and the parties are
mainly seeking knowledge from the third party. This challenges the traditional
assumption that mediation is always assisted negotiation; to quote Walker and
Hayes, it sometimes is "assisted decision-making." In such cases, disputants are
likely to be disappointed if the mediator takes the traditional route of keeping
quiet unless they begin to argue.

Another kind of expert advisor, the accountant, is seldom mentioned in the
mediation literature. Accountants who can put a monetary value on an estate or
business often work wonders in resolving conflicts between heirs or former business partners.

Conflict within Organizations

Tjosvold and Fang (chapter 16 in this handbook), while by no means rejecting the
traditional model, write about the special case of mediation within organizations.

They argue that conflict is inherent in the division of labor, which produces differing perspectives, goals, and values. These differences must be confronted in a problem-solving manner or organizational functioning will decline. Yet there is a strong tendency in most organizations to avoid confrontation in the mistaken belief that overt conflict is inherently disruptive.

This means that most organizations must be deeply reformed to make them "conflict positive." New norms must be developed to confront conflict in a cooperative manner, and managers must be trained to be mediators and rewarded for playing this role.

What this adds to traditional mediation theory is a focus on organizing for mediation. Mediation is a relatively uncommon method of dealing with conflict (Sheppard 1983; Kolb 1986; Keating et al. 1994) and yet has considerable potential. Hence organizations, and by extension other social systems, need to reform their procedures to make mediation more likely to occur and to succeed. Potential mediators must be identified and trained and new norms must be developed that motivate them to play this role and ensure that mediation is accepted by disputants and rewarded by the system. Other authors with a similar perspective include Johnson and Johnson (1991), who have developed mediation systems for public schools, and Ury, Brett, and Goldberg (1988), who have constructed such systems in communities with periodic conflict problems.

Frame Analysis and Reframing

A "frame" is a way of labeling a situation that determines how one perceives it and acts toward it. As a third party who is mainly working on intergroup disputes, Gray (chapter 8 in this handbook) has found it useful to identify the frames disputants use to understand their conflicts and help them rethink these frames if they are counterproductive.

The traditional model embodies some elements of reframing. Thus mediators typically try to discourage a "right-wrong" frame, in which the disputant's goal is to prove that I am right and you are wrong; a "sell my position" frame, in which the goal is to dominate; and a "hopeless dialog" frame, which views the mediation as a waste of time. Instead they try to sell a "both parties succeed" frame and a "potentially resolvable problem" frame. Furthermore, they often try to reframe the presenting issues so that they reflect the parties' underlying interests and their priorities among these interests. Thus the issue of whether the son gets a drum set or his father gets a quiet household is reframed into how the son can gain recognition in school without annoying his father. What Gray adds to this part of the tradition is to sharpen mediator attention to the parties' incoming frames and give names to the typical frames that are found.

Gray's chapter in this handbook (in company with Deutsch's chapter) is most innovative in its discussion of "framing dispute resolution alternatives" in the broader context where mediation is only one possible approach to conflict. Alternatives to a "consensus" frame, which may lead to negotiation or mediation, include a "power struggle" frame (in which the goal is "gaining authority, voice, resources, sympathy or building a coalition or using force or moral authority"), an "individualist" frame (in which the goal is to limit the other party's interference with one's decisions), a "hierarchist" frame (in which one accepts top-down decision-making as legitimate), or another version of the "hopeless dialog" frame (in which one sees no possibility of action).

Gray argues that mediators should not directly challenge frames but engage in "frame enlargement," expanding the parties' framing perspectives. She has developed exercises to help parties to: (a) identify their own frames, (b) compare them to other possibilities, and (c) gain insight into the other party's frames.

Promoting Perceived Justice

Traditional mediators often try to shift disputant attention away from a quest for justice or fairness (a type of "right-wrong" frame) to an effort to find a solution that serves both parties' interests. However, a long tradition of psychological research (starting with Adams 1965) has revealed that humans have a deep yearning for justice, which means that such a diversion can be partially successful at best. Concern about justice for one's group is often stronger than concern about justice for oneself, creating even larger problems for the mediation of many intergroup conflicts. Clearly mediators must be concerned about justice rather than trying to sweep it under the rug. They must adopt procedures and encourage outcomes that seem fair to the disputants or risk failing to reach agreement or reaching an agreement that will not stick.

Conlon (chapter 11 in this handbook) has provided readers with a very useful summary of the rich literature on justice. Four basic types of justice can be distinguished: distributive justice, which is "the perceived fairness of the outcomes one receives;" procedural justice, which is the perceived "fairness of the process used to arrive at decisions;" interpersonal justice, which is the perceived "sensitivity, politeness, and respect people are shown by authority figures during procedures;" and informational justice, which is the extent to which authority figures provide explanations "as to why certain procedures were used or why outcomes were distributed in a particular way." Research evidence suggests that all four types of justice are related to outcome satisfaction and to positive evaluation of authority figures in organizations, courts, and police work (Lind & Tyler 1988; Cohen-Charash & Spector 2001; Colquitt et al. 2001). Furthermore, perceived procedural fairness is predictive of readiness to abide by arbitration judgments (Lind et al. 1993) and readiness to comply with agreements reached in community mediation (Pruitt 1995).

Not mentioned by Conlon are two other forms of justice that have a bearing on mediation: retributive justice, which is a perception that the other party has been punished for his or her misdeeds, and restorative justice, in which an offender "puts right" the harms inflicted on his or her victim. The desire for retributive justice often keeps people out of mediation or makes them unwilling to reach a mediated agreement. What can mediators do about this? Gray (chapter 8) suggests ways of reframing the conflict that may reduce the desire for retribution. These include attributing the accused party's behavior "to external events over which the accused has no control," "comparing the victim to someone less well off," or redirecting attention to the prevention of future injustice. In addition, Peachey (1989) suggests that restorative justice may diminish the demand for retributive justice.

A restorative justice movement began some years ago and has produced a number of novel procedures, the best known of which is victim–offender mediation. These procedures have a number of goals that are outside the scope of conventional mediation, including empowering the victim and reintegrating the offender into the community. An overview of these procedures is provided by Umbreit and Coates in chapter 7 of this handbook.

Enhancing Disputant Capacity

Because traditional mediators place so much emphasis on building win-win agreements, they largely overlook disputant capacity to deal effectively with conflict. Yet this is short-sighted if their goal is joint problem-solving, as it should be and usually is. Several of the chapters in this handbook deal with capacity-building; and there is a related line of thinking (transformative mediation) that is not represented here. These contributions emphasize such interrelated goals as relationship-building, disputant empowerment, facework, management of negative emotions, and narrative restructuring. Some of these authors view capacity-building as a useful supplement to traditional mediation; others argue that it should altogether replace the goal of building an agreement.

Facework

By "face" is meant "personal dignity, honor, and respect" (Littlejohn and Domenici, chapter 10 of this handbook). Face is first and foremost the view that others have of us. But by extension it is also part of our self-image – our sense of being adequate and good – and hence our self-respect. Saposnek (chapter 12) suggests that conflict (he is referring to marital conflict) often produces a sense of loss of control and lowered self-esteem. This implies that disputants will often come into mediation with a feeling that their adequacy and honor – their face – is at stake. Shapiro (chapter 14) adds that disputants often fear changing their view of a conflict – their narrative – because it implies that they are not so competent and right as they previously believed. This suggests that joint problem-solving, with its openness to the other party's viewpoint, will often be viewed with suspicion because it is seen as a threat to face.

All of this implies that facework – in which mediators "build, maintain, [or] protect . . . personal dignity, honor, and respect" – is an essential part of mediation. Littlejohn and Domenici suggest three ways in which mediators can engage in facework. One is to convince the disputants that their perspectives have been heard, understood, and taken seriously. This grants those perspectives legitimacy and hence accords dignity and respect to the people possessing them. A second is to encourage active participation by the disputants – agenda-setting, idea development, and the like – which helps them "feel honored and an integral player in determining their future." A third is to frame the issues in terms of lofty common goals that bring out the best in the participants and hence contribute to their self-respect and respect for each other. Thus a custody mediation becomes a discussion of "What is in Johnny's best interests?" and an interdepartmental dispute is reframed as "What is our vision of the best future for our company?"

Littlejohn and Domenici argue that such facework encourages problem-solving and also has the potential to improve the parties' relationship and enhance their sense of effectiveness (disputant empowerment). Hence it contributes to both the success of mediation and the parties' capacity for future problem-solving.

There appears to be a close relationship between facework, as described by these authors, and two of the types of justice discussed above: procedural justice and interpersonal justice. As Conlon describes them, procedural justice is primarily a matter of allowing disputants to control the process they are in and to state their views in a way that is "heard and understood," and interpersonal justice entails showing respect to the disputants. Could these authors be talking about much the same thing but using different words? Perhaps procedural and interpersonal justice are effective because they maintain or enhance disputant face, an assertion that is not far from Tyler's (1990: 150) suggestion that procedural justice is important because it enhances people's "sense of personal worth."

Managing negative emotions

Two of the chapters in this handbook – those by Shapiro and Saposnek – focus attention on the management of negative emotions, such as anger, frustration, and humiliation. Both agree that these emotions stand in the way of problem-solving. Shapiro argues that negative emotions "tend to make people think that agreement with the other side is impossible," make it "hard for parties to listen to one another, to understand one another's interests, or to empathize with one another's situation," and "can hijack rational thinking." Furthermore, they reduce the attraction of win-win agreements. which help the other side as well as oneself. Saposnek asserts that negative emotions (his analysis mainly concerns anger) encourage rigidity, "power assertion strategies" designed to "redress the experience of feeling dominated by the other," and "revenge and retaliation strategies." These strategies, in turn, tend to generate vicious circles of dominance and counter-dominance, accusation and counteraccusation during the mediation session.

These authors also agree that when negative emotions abound, the mediator must be especially empathic, understanding and showing an understanding of the parties' perspectives. This reduces the sense of threat in the situation, relieves the disputants from having to tell and retell their aggrieved story, enhances flexibility, and allows the mediator to regulate the discussion to diminish the attention given to the most volatile issues. In advocating mediator empathy, these authors are in line with most mediation theorists.

However, it is important to note that, in being empathic, mediators must walk a very fine line. Research evidence (Johnson 1971) suggests that empathy that is too warm and sympathetic tends to *provoke* rigidity rather than reduce it. Furthermore, as Saposnek points out, overt empathy can endanger the appearance of mediator neutrality, creating a "sense of betrayal . . . in the other party." The latter suggests that heavily empathic displays are best made in caucus sessions rather than in joint sessions. Shapiro seems to agree with this position, arguing that pre-caucus sessions should be used in heavily emotional conflicts, allowing the parties to vent without provoking a battle with each other and allowing the mediator to exhibit sufficient empathy that both sides view the mediator as "their ally."

The main point of difference between these authors is in their optimism about overcoming negative emotions and the hostile relationships that accompany them. Shapiro seems to feel that by venting their negative emotions, disputants can gain an understanding of the sources of these emotions and move beyond them to a sounder relationship with each other. This process is aided by a mediator who helps them to cope with the loss of "identity" that comes from agreeing that the opponent may be right in some things. Walker and Hayes (chapter 4) agree with Shapiro, arguing that divorcing couples must "tell their stories" and work through their "bitterness, hurt, and anger" so that they can later cooperate in parenting.

However, Saposnek (who also works with divorcing couples) disagrees with this assessment. He feels that anger and the accompanying desire to dominate the other party are usually so heavily entrenched that they cannot be overcome in mediation. In such situations, the mediator can and should limit emotional displays during the mediation session, but seldom can reduce hostile feelings or induce an improved relationship. In most cases, the best one can hope for is an armed truce in which the parties remain estranged but agree to behave in ways that are "less diametrically opposite or damaging to each other." To achieve such an outcome, Saposnek advocates a great deal of mediator control over the session. "Unless the mediator takes firm control over the process and establishes ground rules [that minimize power struggles] and a safe structure for further discussion, an irreversible impasse is imminent." In this recommendation he agrees with traditional mediation theory, which advocates greater mediator control the more hostile the disputant interchange. But he disagrees sharply with most modern theorists, including the advocates of procedural justice and facework, described earlier, and the traditions of narrative restructuring and transformative mediation, still to be discussed.

Narrative restructuring

While facework and the management of negative emotions can be seen as adjuncts to traditional mediation that improve its effectiveness, the proponents of narrative mediation see themselves as engaged in a totally different enterprise (Winslade and Monk, chapter 9). They view the basic job of the mediator as a cognitive or linguistic one: flushing out and restructuring the parties' narratives – the stories they tell about the history of the conflict and their "patterns of thinking, feeling, speaking, and responding" with respect to the conflict. Such narratives are usually highly oversimplified, painting the self as victim and the other as aggressor and showing little understanding of the other's perspective (Cobb 2003). Hence, they tend to poison the relationship between the parties. In this tradition, the aim of the mediator is to restructure the parties' narratives so as to help them to become more capable of dealing productively with each other. This is a form of capacity-building.

In narrative mediation, there is little use for the traditional mediator's focus on positions and interests, because these are functions of the entering narratives and are likely to change as the narratives change. Win-win solutions may be discovered as a result of narrative restructuring, but that is not the fundamental goal of mediation. Another distinction from traditional mediation is that the latter sees good agreements as fostering good relationships whereas narrative mediation turns this assumption around and views improved relationships as necessary for the achievement of good agreements.

Winslade and Monk propose a number of techniques for "loosening the grip of the dominant story and developing an alternative story of relationship," including the following:

1   Externalization – fostering a view of the conflict as a third actor that "exerts influence over the [parties] but [is] not identified with either party." I assume that this includes recognition of the conflict spirals (Pruitt and Kim 2004) that so often drive escalated conflict forward.
2   Surfacing the "taken-for-granted assumptions" on which the narrative is based.
3   Asking the disputants to project ahead as to where the conflict story will take them.
4   Listening for the "implicit story of cooperation and understanding that is always there, and bring it to the fore."

In addition, Cobb (2003) recommends increasing the complexity of narratives by uploading new information into them through subtle questions.

Transformative mediation

There is one other mediation tradition that has gained importance in recent years but is not represented in this book: transformative mediation (Bush & Folger 2005). Transformative mediation seeks to develop two elements of disputant capacity: *recognition*, which is an improvement in the relationship that entails "some degree of understanding and concern for one another despite their disagreement" (2005: 14) and *empowerment*, which is an improvement in "self-respect, self-reliance, and self confidence" that allows disputants to "mobilize their own resources to address problems and achieve their goals" (2005: 13). As with narrative mediation, the goal of reaching a win-win agreement is not an integral element of success.

The technique of transformative mediation is very nondirective. The mediator imposes no order of business. He or she does not structure the conversation or attempt to control hostility. Instead, the parties are encouraged at every point to make their own decisions about process and substance. This fosters self-reliance, which these authors see as the key to relationship-building. The mediator's main job is to reflect – summarize and sharpen – what is being said. This helps the parties understand each other and encourages them to make ever more revealing comments. Positive statements about the other and statements that indicate a can-do attitude are reinforced.

Transformative mediation seems most closely related to the facework approach to mediation discussed above, which also stresses the goals of relationship-building and empowerment. In both approaches, the mediator encourages the parties to tell their stories, takes these stories very seriously, and rewards the parties for taking the high road. Furthermore, though transformative mediation does not have the goal of achieving perceived justice, its techniques have the potential to build a sense of procedural and interpersonal justice.

CRITIQUE

This book is a rich tapestry of insights about mediation. Traditional mediation, with its emphasis on problem-solving to agreement, is well represented. But many of the chapters show how theory and practice have moved beyond this base, with new developments in the construction of mediation systems, frame analysis, promoting perceived justice, and enhancing disputant capability through facework, managing negative emotions, and narrative restructuring. Most of the new developments can be seen as complementing and enhancing the traditional approach. But one of them – narrative restructuring – challenges this tradition as focused on the wrong goals and employing the wrong methods. So also does transformative mediation.

As with many rapidly developing applied fields, empirical research lags well behind the frontiers of theory and practice. The traditional approach is informed and supported by a host of studies cited by Herrman and by Wissler. But the new developments remain largely in the realm of practice-informed speculation.

Some of the new developments seem non-controversial and nearly universal in their applicability. Who can quarrel with the general importance of mediation training and the development of mediation systems, promoting perceived fairness, examining disputant frames, or acting in ways that maintain or enhance disputant face? However, the same cannot be said about those approaches that attempt to build disputant capacity for conflict resolution, especially the ones that try to repair damaged relationships by dispelling negative emotions, narrative restructuring, or transformative mediation. Most of my critique concerns these approaches. Three questions need to be answered about them: Should mediators try to repair relationships? If so, how should it be done? Can repairing relationships supplant the traditional practice of problem-solving to agreement? I will try to answer these questions in the next three sections.

The Importance of Relationship-Building

There is clearly a controversy between the advocates of managing negative emotions, narrative, and transformative mediation, on the one hand, and Saposnek, on the other. Pessimism about improving highly hostile relationships is not in the vocabulary of Shapiro, Winslade and Monk, or Bush and Folger.[2] Nor are they likely to be happy with Saposnek's highly controlling style of mediation, which is 180 degrees opposite to the permissive style of Bush and Folger and opposed to most of the advice of new-wave theorists.

I take a middle position in this matter and argue that relationship-building is much more important in some circumstances than others. For example, Phillips (2001) maintains that some disputants only want help in building an agreement and are *not interested in improving their relationship*. Such people are likely to resent and reject mediators who have an automatic policy of relationship-building (though mediators may have to persuade them to engage in this activity if it turns out that their hostility stands in the way of agreement). A subclass of these people may be simply *seeking expert advice*, a circumstance sometimes encountered in divorce mediation (Saposnek, chapter 12 this handbook; Walker and Hayes, chapter 4). Imagine these people's reactions if confronted with a determinedly nondirective mediator or one who insists on digging up the past.

Research suggests that there are also *certain kinds of issues* where building relationships is unimportant. Thus research findings indicate that strained relationships do not interfere with reaching agreement in civil and small claims mediation (Wissler, chapter 5).

There are three possible advantages to relationship-building: promoting joint problem-solving, which is the best way to achieve a win-win agreement; encouraging later compliance with the agreement; and facilitating problem-solving in post-mediation conflicts. This suggests that relationship-building is of diminished importance when it is possible to reach a *self-enforcing agreement* (e.g. a debt that can be paid on the spot) or when the parties are in a *non-continuing relationship*.

Sometimes disputants face a choice about whether or not to continue a relationship. Before embarking on relationship repair, mediators should acquaint them with the time and trouble it is likely to entail, so that they can make an informed decision about whether to try it. Mediators who have a policy of always trying to build "recognition" between the parties could be accused of having a hidden agenda.

The importance of trying to improve a relationship may also depend on the *degree of escalation* in that relationship. Fisher and Keashly (1990: 236–237) distinguish four levels of escalation in the relationships between parties:

1 *Discussion*, in which "perceptions are still accurate, commitment to the relationship strong, and belief in possible joint gain predominant."
2 *Polarization*, in which "trust and respect are threatened, and distorted perceptions and simplified stereotypes emerge."
3 *Segregation*, in which "competition and hostility are the basic themes and the conflict is . . . perceived as threatening basic needs."
4 *Destruction*, in which "the primary intent of the parties is to destroy or at least subjugate each other through the use of violence."

At the *discussion* level, relationship-building is unnecessary because the parties already have a good relationship. They may, nevertheless, be having enough trouble resolving a conflict that they seek (or someone imposes) mediation. Traditional mediation has a lot to offer such disputants, for example, sharpening the issues, developing an agenda, encouraging a discussion of the interests underlying their positions, explaining the other party's interests if that party is reluctant to talk about them, questioning high aspiration levels, dispelling an incorrect assumption that the other party is about to concede, etc.

Fisher and Keashly argue that relationship-building is most appropriate at the *polarization* level of escalation, as a preliminary to conventional mediation. These writers are mainly interested in intergroup and international conflicts, so they recommend such techniques as problem-solving workshops (see Fisher 1997), where people of good will from both sides come together with a trained leader to gain an understanding of the conflict and of each other. But the argument can be extended to the relationship-building methods discussed in this handbook.

In the Fisher–Keashly model, the usefulness of relationship-building has a curvilinear relationship to level of escalation. It is unnecessary at the discussion level and so difficult at the *segregation* and *destruction* levels, that these authors recommend that the third party instead try to contain the conflict by limiting the parties' destructive communications and actions. For containment, they have in mind mediator threats or bribes and peacekeeping, of the kind found in international relations. But their position sounds most like that of Saposnek in this handbook, who is also pessimistic about relationship-building in the highly emotional environment of custody mediation. It will be recalled that he recommends that the mediator take firm steps to limit hostile displays while urging the disputants to talk about the problems they have in common despite their basic estrangement.

The Fisher–Keashley model suggests that Shapiro, Winslade and Monk, and Bush and Folger may be right about the importance of relationship-building in many moderately escalated disputes, and Saposnek may be right about the importance of problem-oriented mediator guidance in many heavily escalated disputes.

Saposnek assumes that disputants can often settle common problems despite a continuing high level of hostility. I would argue that *this is true if their motivation to reach a settlement is strong enough.* An example can be seen in a study of the negotiations that produced a ceasefire in the Nagorno-Karabakh war (Mooradian & Druckman 1999). These negotiations and the agreement reached in them were precipitated by a dramatic upsurge in battlefield casualties, which produced a "ripe" moment in which both sides were motivated to escape the conflict. The relationship between the parties was nevertheless extremely bitter and remains so to this day, though the ceasefire still holds strong. This study implies, though by no means proves, that *the importance of relationship-building diminishes with increased motivation to settle.* Both of the italicized hypotheses in this paragraph can be tested empirically.

How to Build Relationships

Four of the methods mentioned earlier are said to help improve relationships: facework, negative emotion management, narrative restructuring, and transformative mediation. How do we choose among these methods? First, we should probably observe mediators working within these traditions to see if they actually differ in the way they behave and, if so, how. Then, if actual differences are found, we need an evaluation study or studies to determine the short-term and long-term success of these methods. A clever follow-up study would look at combinations of useful methods to see how they interact. There are two possible outcomes of such a study: (a) the methods are compensatory – combinations are no better than one of them used alone; (b) the methods are complementary – they work better in combination than if used alone.

The latter conclusion fits the results of a well-designed experiment on marital therapy (Jacobson & Follette 1985). There were three conditions: behavioral exchange therapy ("which focuses on increasing the frequency of positive exchanges" at home), communication/problem-solving training (which teaches the couple "communication skills aimed at more effective conflict resolution"), and a combination of the two. Six months later, relationships were better in couples who had the combined therapy than in those who had either of its components alone.

To sort out the issue of how best to improve escalated relationships, a theory about the components of such relationships would be useful. Pruitt and Olczak's (1995) MACBE model of escalated relationships provides such a theory on the level of the individual. This argues that five kinds of "structural" change can take place when relationships deteriorate:

1 *Motivation* – the parties become motivated to exact retribution by showing each other up or hurting each other.
2 *Affect* – the parties begin to harbor hostile feelings toward each other.
3 *Cognition* – the parties develop negative perceptions of each other and unfavorable narratives about their prior interaction.
4 *Behavior* – hostile and maladaptive behavior sequences characterize the relationship.
5 *Environment* – each party has a set of polarized supporters who encourage or reinforce hostility toward the other party.

In mildly escalated situations, only one or two of these changes is likely to have taken place. After a careful diagnosis, therapy can be directed to those particular structures. But heavily escalated relationships usually involve most or all of these changes, and these changed structures support each other, making escalation very imbedded. Hence, therapy directed at only one subsystem is likely to produce at best a temporary improvement.

Strained relations between groups are produced and maintained by similar structural changes, for example, the development of group goals of retribution (motivation) and group traditions about the origins of a conflict (cognition).[3] Other kinds of changes in groups include the development of militant leaders and conflict-committed subgroups such as the PLO and the IRA. Conformity pressures within groups add a further element of imbeddedness to heavily escalated relationships (Pruitt & Kim 2004).

Interventions aimed at reversing three of the MACBE components in interpersonal settings are discussed in this handbook: (1) negative affect (chapters 12 and 14); (2) cognition (chapters 8 and 9); and (3) the motive of retribution (chapter 8). There are also methods for dealing with polarized support groups, for example, bringing them into the mediation session.[4]

Consider the problems that narrative mediation is likely to encounter in a heavily escalated situation. Narratives and other cognitions may well be *initially* responsible for the development of hostile motives, emotions, and support groups and the emergence of militant leadership. However, the latter structures, once formed, gain an existence of their own and cannot always be reversed by cognitive changes. Hence, a revised narrative that emerges from mediation may subsequently be undermined by unresolved revenge motives or contact with polarized friends or co-workers. Furthermore, narratives that blame the other and exonerate the self often serve as rationalizations for hostile motivation, emotion, or behavior and can be originated or reinforced by militant leaders with vested interests in maintaining the conflict. All of this suggests that, in heavily escalated conflicts, narrative analysis should be supplemented by methods that attack other structures.

If narrative mediation has a problem with heavily escalated conflicts, the problem should be even larger for transformative mediation, with its lack of attention to any of the structural changes that occur when conflicts heat up. One waves a magic wand of reflective listening and somehow all these impediments disappear. While Saposnek may be too pessimistic about the possibility of overcoming heavily hostile relationships, Bush and Folger seem vastly over-optimistic about the universal value of their nondirective methodology.

The MACBE model and its extension to intergroup escalation poses a challenge for further development of mediation. Only a handful of writers and practitioners are developing methods for dealing with the various components of heavy escalation, and my impression is that most of them have only scratched the surface. For example, there is only minimal guidance about how to deal with vengeful motivation and none at all about how to rid a group of militant leadership (except for heavy-handed police practices that are far from the purview of mediation). Clearly more thinking is needed in these areas.

Is Relationship Repair Enough?

The advocates of narrative restructuring (Winslade and Monk) and transformative mediation (Bush and Folger) claim that their methods supplant, rather than supplement, the traditional problem-solving-to-agreement approach. This implies that the problems that bring people into mediation are often ephemeral, a result of improper narratives that can be corrected and hostile relations that can be reversed. Hence, problem-solving is not always needed in the end.

While this may be true in some cases that come to mediation, it is decidedly not the case in many others. At the end of the day, the parties will still have to decide about the details of custody and visitation, how much money if anything is owed for failure of a product, what to do about the young man who is stalking his former girlfriend, whether or not a merger will take place, and whether there will be a ceasefire or continuation of a war. In addition, many conflicts are ultimately due to social structures that will continue to exist despite an improvement in people's relationships (Dugan 2001). Thus there is a built-in divergence of interest between production and sales, labor and management, worker and homemaker, wealthy and poor, powerful and weak that cannot be dispelled by a better set of narratives or greater recognition of the other party. Narrative mediation may help identify such structures, but it cannot easily alter them or dispel the divergence of interest they generate.

All of this suggests the need for greater modesty by the advocates of these methods. While narrative restructuring and transformative mediation may enhance disputants' capacity to deal with each other, most disputants will still have to solve the problems that brought them to mediation. And old-fashioned problem-solving-to-settlement mediation will often be needed in the end.

Conclusions

This handbook began with an "anchor" chapter (chapter 2), which made a significant effort to state a research-based framework for understanding mediation. The four-phase model that is part of this framework is a useful contribution, as is the compendium of variables and methods of measurement used in prior research. Both should prove quite valuable to people who are trying to think more clearly about the field or are designing research on it. Subsequent chapters in the book suggest that there may be too many credible, new, practice-based initiatives and too many unresolved controversies to allow construction of a definitive theory of mediation at this time. Furthermore, the field is developing at such a commendable rate that any effort to impose a standard set of concepts on it would be counterproductive. We need to let a thousand flowers bloom, because the traditional model of mediation is clearly too limited.

At the same time we need empirical research to sort out the lilies from the dandelions and to add to the luster of the lilies. I mentioned earlier an experiment (Jacobson & Follette 1985) that examined the joint effect of two techniques of marital therapy, one traditional (behavioral contacting) and one relatively new at the time (communication/problem-solving training). This is only one of many well-designed experiments concerning marital therapy, a close cousin of mediation. Is there any reason why mediation researchers cannot follow a similar path?

Notes

1 Pruitt (in press) cites cases in which a co-mediation chain has produced agreement between governments or political factions: party A talks to intermediary 1, who talks to intermediary 2, who talks to party B.

2 However, Cobb (2003), another narrative mediator and theorist, seems keenly aware of the difficulties of improving relationships in highly escalated conflicts.
3 Volkan (2001) calls such traditions "chosen traumas."
4 Mediation in traditional societies often involves community meetings that involve family and friends of the parties on both sides (Gulliver 1979). Family group conferencing and peacemaking circles, as described by Umbreit and Coates (chapter 7 of this handbook), have a similar format. Bunker and Alban (1997) have carried this concept into organizational settings and run workshops attended by everybody who works in a factory, to discuss knotty policy problems and directions for the future.

REFERENCES

Adams, J. S. (1965) Inequity in social exchange. In L. Berkowitz (ed.), *Advances in Experimental Social Psychology*, vol. 2. Academic Press, New York, pp. 267–299.

Berkovich, J. (ed.) (2002) *Studies in International Mediation*. Palgrave Macmillan, New York.

Bunker, B. B. & Alban, B. T. (1997) *Large Group Interventions*. Jossey-Bass, San Francisco.

Bush, R. A. B. & Folger, J. P. (2005) *The Promise of Mediation*, revised edn. Jossey-Bass, San Francisco.

Cobb, S. (2003) Fostering coexistence in identity-based conflicts: towards a narrative approach. In A. Chayes & M. Minow (eds.), *Imagine Coexistence*. Jossey-Bass, San Francisco, pp. 294–310.

Cohen-Charash, Y. & Spector, P. (2001) The role of justice in organizations: a meta-analysis. *Organizational Behavior and Human Decision Processes* 86, 278–321.

Colquitt, J. A., Conlon, D. E., Wesson, M., Porter, C. & Ng, K. (2001) Justice at the millennium: a meta-analytic review of 25 years of organizational justice research. *Journal of Applied Psychology* 86, 425–445.

Conlon, D. E. & Ross, W. H. (1993) The effects of partisan third parties on negotiator behavior and outcome perceptions. *Journal of Applied Psychology* 78, 280–290.

Donohue, W. A. (1989) Communicative competence in mediators. In K. Kressel, D. G. Pruitt & Associates (eds.), *Mediation Research*. Jossey-Bass, San Francisco, pp. 322–343.

Duffy, K. G., Grosch, J. W. & Olczak, P. V. (eds.) (1991) *Community Mediation: A Handbook for Practitioners and Researchers*. Guilford, New York.

Dugan, M. A. (2001) Imaging the future: a tool for conflict resolution. In L. Reychler & T. Paffenholz (eds.), *Peacebuilding: A Field Guide*. Lynne Rienner, Boulder, pp. 365–372.

Fisher, R. J. (1997) *Interactive Conflict Resolution*. Syracuse University Press, Syracuse.

Fisher, R. J. & Keashly, L. (1990) A contingency approach to third party intervention. In R. J. Fisher (ed.), *The Social Psychology of Intergroup and International Conflict Resolution*. Springer-Verlag, New York, pp. 234–238.

Gulliver, P. H. (1979) *Disputes and Negotiations: A Cross-Cultural Perspective*. Academic Press, New York.

Hiltrop, J. M. (1989) Factors associated with successful labor mediation. In K. Kressel, D. G. Pruitt & Associates (eds.), *Mediation Research*. Jossey-Bass, San Francisco, pp. 241–262.

Jacobson, N. S. & Follette, W. C. (1985) Clinical significance of improvement resulting from two behavioral marital therapy components. *Behavior Therapy* 16, 249–262.

Johnson, D. W. (1971) Role reversal: a summary and review of the research. *International Journal of Group Tensions* 1, 318–334.

Johnson, D. W. & Johnson, R. T. (1991) *Teaching Children to be Peacemakers*. Interaction Book Company, Edina.

Keating, M. E., Pruitt, D. G., Eberle, R. A. & Mikolic, J. M. (1994) Strategic choice in every-day disputes. *International Journal of Conflict Management* 5, 143–157.

Kolb, D. M. (1986) Who are organizational third parties and what do they do? In R. J. Lewicki, B. H. Sheppard & M. H. Bazerman (eds.), *Research on Negotiation in Organizations*, vol. 1. JAI, Greenwich, pp. 207–227.

Kressel, K. (2000) Mediation. In M. Deutsch & P. T. Coleman (eds.), *The Handbook of Conflict Resolution*. Jossey-Bass, San Francisco.

Kressel, K. & Pruitt, D. G. (1989) Conclusions: a research perspective on the mediation of social conflict. In K. Kressel, D. G. Pruitt & Associates (eds.), *Mediation Behavior*. Jossey-Bass, San Francisco, pp. 394–435.

Lind, E. A., Kulik, C. T., Ambrose, M. A. & de Vera Park, M. V. (1993) Individual and corporate dispute resolution: using procedural fairness as a decision heuristic. *Administrative Science Quarterly* 38, 224–251.

Lind, E. A. & Tyler, T. R. (1988) *The Social Psychology of Procedural Justice*. Plenum, New York.

Mikolic, J. M., Parker, J. C. & Pruitt, D. G. (1997) Escalation in response to persistent annoyance: groups vs. individuals and gender effects. *Journal of Personality and Social Psychology* 72, 151–163.

Mooradian, M. & Druckman, D. (1999) Hurting stalemate or mediation? The conflict over Nagorno-Karabakh, 1990–95. *Journal of Peace Research* 36, 709–727.

Moore, C. W. (1996) *The Mediation Process*. Jossey-Bass, San Francisco.

Peachey, D. E. (1989) What people want from mediation? In K. Kressel, D. G. Pruitt & Associates (eds.), *Mediation Behavior*. Jossey-Bass, San Francisco, pp. 300–321.

Phillips, B. A. (2001) *The Mediation Field Guide*. Jossey-Bass, San Francisco.

Pruitt, D. G. (1981) *Negotiation Behavior*. Academic Press, New York.

Pruitt, D. G. (1995) Process and outcome in community mediation. *Negotiation Journal* 11, 365–377.

Pruitt, D. G. (in press) Escalation, readiness for negotiation, and third party functions. In I. W. Zartman & G. O. Faure (eds.), *Escalation and Negotiation*. Cambridge University Press, Cambridge.

Pruitt, D. G. & Kim, S. H. (2004) *Social Conflict: Escalation, Stalemate, and Settlement*, 3rd edn. McGraw-Hill, New York.

Pruitt, D. G. & Olczak, P. V. (1995) Beyond hope: approaches to resolving seemingly intractable conflict. In B. B. Bunker, J. Z. Rubin & Associates (eds.), *Conflict, Cooperation, and Justice: Essays Provoked by the Work of Morton Deutsch*. Jossey-Bass, San Francisco, pp. 59–92.

Sheppard, B. H. (1983) Managers as inquisitors: some lessons from the law. In M. H. Bazerman & R. J. Lewicki (eds.), *Negotiation in Organizations*. Sage, Beverly Hills.

Tyler, T. R. (1990) *Why People Obey the Law*. Yale University Press, New Haven.

Ury, W. J., Brett, J. M. & Goldberg, S. (1988) *Getting Disputes Resolved*. Jossey-Bass, San Francisco.

Volkan, V. D. (2001) Transgenerational transmissions and chosen traumas: an aspect of large-group identity. *Group Analysis* 34, 79–97.

Wall, J. A., Stark, J. B. & Standifer, R. L. (2001) Mediation: a current review and theory development. *Journal of Conflict Resolution* 45, 370–391.

Welton, G. L., Pruitt, D. G., McGillicuddy, N. B., Ippolito, C. A. & Zubek, J. M. (1992) Antecedents and characteristics of caucusing in community mediation. *International Journal of Conflict Management* 3, 303–318.

Zubek, J. M., Pruitt, D. G., McGillicuddy, N. B., Peirce, R. S. & Syna, H. (1992) Short-term success in mediation: its relationship to prior conditions and mediator and disputant behaviors. *Journal of Conflict Resolution* 36, 546–572.

Chapter 21

A Trainer Responds to the Model

Zena D. Zumeta

The model that Margaret S. Herrman, Nancy Hollett, and Jerry Gale pose in chapter 2 is a sophisticated, comprehensive model of the mediation process. For me, as a trainer, it is exceedingly helpful for several reasons. Mediation training has been a collection of techniques hung on a theory for most of the short time this field has existed. What the authors offer is a way to look at the context of both theories and techniques. Negotiation theory and technique has a longer history and a more sophisticated approach than mediation. The authors take the best of that theory and research, and apply it to a mediation model.

I consider myself a facilitative mediator in the nomenclature of Riskin's (1996) original grid. I teach a sequential model of mediation, knowing that this is only an approximation of the approach that I and other sophisticated facilitative mediators use. And yet a sequential model is helpful to beginning mediators, because it offers a skeleton on which to hang actions and a theory to approach a new way of problem-solving for most beginning mediators.

My assumption is that through practice mediators will veer away from the model, and begin to add their own touches to the process. In fact, many new mediators have come to my advanced workshops and approached me, with trepidation, saying that they have strayed in one way or another. I assure them that this is just fine. But my teaching does not give them any help in the post-model assessment. The addition of this new model will assist me in this immensely. Because the authors ground their model in research, training participants will be able to test out whether their variations on my model will help them to achieve better results.

The authors point out that results may be either substantive (agreement) or procedural (communication, understanding). In fact, this aspect of the model is especially helpful. For too long, trainers and practitioners have argued back and forth as to whether substantive or procedural outcomes are more important, appropriate, and mediative. Because this model allows for both approaches, it is much more useful to trainers, who can focus on either one, or even focus on both.

I use a seven- or eight-step model (an additional step is in the family mediation model) using the acronym MEDIATE(S).[1]

1   **M**easure appropriateness and design
2   **E**xplain the process
3   **D**raw out information
4   **I**dentify and frame issues
5   **A**sk for needs, interests, and options
6   **T**est options and negotiate
7   **E**nd the mediation
8   (**S**ee the whole family)

My model differs from many mediation models in that it starts with pre-mediation. In fact, I practice and teach a model where I would ideally meet with each participant prior to the mediation, and talk with the lawyers involved both together in a conference call and separately in separate calls. Thus, I was very pleased to see that the model proposed in chapter 2 also started with pre-mediation.

ANTECEDENT CONDITIONS (T_0)

The first thing I noticed about the model is the attention it pays to the pre-mediation state of the mediator, the parties, the type of dispute, and the context of the mediation (T_0). Current models of mediation pay woefully little attention to these factors, and yet in my practice and teaching of mediation I have, over the years, spent more and more time assessing these very factors. It is very helpful to have them set out in this orderly way for a trainer to refer to. Their T_0 will lead to a great expansion of my discussion of "M" in my model, and to a vocabulary for consideration of many factors in determining appropriateness, timing, and approach to particular mediations. Antecedent conditions proposed in chapter 2 are *personal characteristics* (of mediator and disputants), *disputant beliefs and attitudes, dispute characteristics,* and *institutional context.* As a trainer, these categories will allow me to focus the attention of training participants on these items. This will lead to more discussion and understanding of these antecedent conditions as factors in the mediation process. It will allow trainers to focus on each of these factors separately and explore how each makes a difference for the mediator. Moreover, research within these categories will allow me to discuss which characteristics, beliefs, attitudes, and contexts make a difference to the mediation process and outcomes, and in what way. That would be a very exciting addition to training.

Forty-hour training has become the norm for teaching mediation outside the academy. Academic programs are now able to focus more on sub-areas of theory and practice. Hopefully this model, and the research that supported it and will come out of it, will expand the teaching of mediation so that advanced training will become a norm. Perhaps even 40 hours will be seen as insufficient for training in an entire field of knowledge.

Mediation Characteristics (T_M)

Next, the authors of the proposed model take a look at factors within the mediation process itself. One of the helpful things that they do is to clump and label groups of considerations. This allows trainers to do more than just list requirements for effective mediation, which is what usually happens now. In the future, trainers can focus on how each of these requirements works in the mediation process. This is ground-breaking work. I assume that, as academics and practitioners work with these concepts, they will be expanded, rearranged, some discarded, and new concepts added. This is just the beginning, but what a beginning!

For the trainer, this is a goldmine. The first construct discussed in the model is *factors that prime personal readiness*. This construct includes: mediator empathy, feeling heard and understood, able to talk about perceptions and feelings, clarity, perceived self-efficacy, and hostile environment. What is most important here is that the authors are looking at research that is trying to measure these things. For example, for mediator empathy, they note that rapport, warmth, emotional safety, and respect are found to be components of empathy across many studies. For the trainer, this helps to define several items.

In the old paradigm of training, mediator empathy is simply one of many techniques suggested to create rapport and help parties move along toward resolution. What the authors have added to the trainer's arsenal is that mediator empathy is not simply a technique; it is a technique to be used at a particular point in the mediation – the beginning. One reason to use this technique at the beginning is that it helps to prime the readiness of the parties, while also allowing mediators to draw on empathy later in a mediation as needed to reinforce a participant's sense of safety to problem-solve. Additionally, the trainer now can say that there are other factors that help to prime personal readiness, and here is what they are.

The other areas included are aspects of the parties. Even the listing is helpful for trainers. We can point to this list and help train mediators to look for particular abilities and perceptions on the part of the parties in assessing the appropriateness and design of the mediation process.

Perceived self-efficacy is a very interesting variable to me. In both employment and divorce mediations, it is clear that actual efficacy is less important than a party's perceived self-efficacy. It is very helpful for the authors to note this factor. It would be extremely helpful to have researchers look at how this plays out during mediations. Some parties are very powerful, but because they perceive themselves to be low in power they come across as a Mack truck. A particularly helpful bit of research would be a comparison of perceived versus actual efficacy in negotiation. The next step would be to note how a mediator could help parties observe their actual efficacy.

One of the most exciting aspects of this book for a trainer is that it points to many areas that will be rich for advanced training. It would be wonderful if researchers and trainers in the future could put together exercises for teaching assessment of these areas such as perceived self-efficacy.

Procedural Factors

Of the many procedural factors that the authors discuss, one of the most important for trainers to track is mediator process control, since this is one of the most hotly discussed issues in the mediation community. If there were more research, and more controlled research, on the effect of different approaches to process control, it would greatly assist the trainer. In particular, it would be helpful to know if specific antecedent conditions suggest particular process controls; or whether certain controls work better in different parts of the mediation; or whether timing is more important than anything else. For now, all we have is our own experience and intuition about these things, and some studies that have looked at limited issues around these topics. Trainers and mediator trainees will benefit from more research.

For the trainer, research on issues of procedural clarity is very important. Although I train in a particular procedure, I don't emphasize the importance of relating that procedure to the parties. If the research clarifies that this makes a big difference in party empowerment, ability to negotiate, comfort, trust, etc., that would definitely change my approach to training on this issue. The research noted by the authors states whether the mediator made the procedure clear; what is missing still is the relationship between procedural clarity and outcomes.

Mediator Neutrality

The authors note that there is no consistency in the operational definition of mediator neutrality. Here is an area where more research would definitely change the teaching of mediation. Neutrality is such a central tenet of mediation. The construct infuses all areas and fields of mediation, and more research would have a sharp and deep impact. In conducting advanced training, I have noted that there are many different assessments by mediators of neutral behavior and neutral impact. It is also clear that clients have very different views of what makes for neutral behavior. Is neutrality a specific set of behaviors, or should it be defined from the parties' perceptions? If a mediator plays to the parties' perceptions, but acts in ways that objectively do not seem neutral, is that still neutrality?

One of the discussions about neutrality entails "cold" versus "warm" neutrality. That is, to what extent can a mediator empathize with the parties and still remain neutral? Is the concept of "balancing" between the parties sufficient to achieve neutrality, or is that really a rationalization of mediator behavior that trainers should warn against? Or, is that really what we should be teaching?

Just as there has been little focus up until now on antecedent conditions to mediation, there has been little focus on what exactly makes up neutrality. A fascinating study would be to ask the mediator and both parties about: (1) what they perceived as mediator actions that were both neutral and partial, and (2) which actions made a difference, either negatively or positively, to the mediation. My hunch is that trainers and mediators would be very surprised by the parties' answers. Connecting the parties' feelings about particular mediator actions to factors that prime readiness would allow trainers to be much more precise in teaching the analysis of the process to use and options for mediator interventions.

I believe that there is a great connection between factors that prime readiness (particularly mediator empathy, feeling heard and understood, able to talk about perceptions and feelings, and perceived self-efficacy) and perceptions of interactional fairness. If that is the case, precise mediator neutrality might be less important to the parties than help from the mediator to understand what is going on with the other party and reactions of each party to actions on the part of the other party.

Mediator Problem-Solving and Decision-Making

As with the variable above, it would help trainers immensely if mediator approaches to decision-making could be assessed in terms of their effectiveness with particular types of clients or disputes. What leads parties to decide if more or less intrusiveness by the mediator is helpful? When is suggesting options more or less effective? When is predicting judicial outcomes more or less welcome? Information regarding these issues that could be passed on to training participants would be most welcome.

It would be immensely helpful, for instance, to know if there are objective ways to assess whether the mediator is focusing on the most important issues. Or, is a focus on needs and interests important to do before or after looking at options?

One of the biggest discussions among mediators is how and when options should be put forward during a mediation. Should the mediator suggest options? Suggest an outcome? Or is it better for the parties to do all of that? Any research that could shed light on these differences would totally change the shape of mediation discussions within the field. Additionally, it is my observation that many mediators skip this stage of the process entirely, simply asking for proposals and commenting on them. For a trainer, it would be immensely helpful to know whether a formal brainstorming step results in better outcomes, or whether any creative response to proposals is sufficient.

As for mediator efforts to drive closure, there are many discussions of what is the most effective approach for a mediator to take. Right now the discussions are ideology-driven rather than research-driven. It is difficult for a trainer to state with any precision under what circumstances a hands-off stance is most helpful, and when mediator suggestions or even formal recommendations would be most helpful. Research connecting types of disputes, types of disputants, mediator forcefulness, and outcomes would be most welcome to help in the teaching of mediators.

SHORT-TERM OUTCOMES (T_1)

The proposed model suggests that outcomes in mediation are judged from many different viewpoints, ranging from self-awareness to improving institutional effectiveness. Further complicating the picture is that parties themselves have varying reasons for participating in mediation, and varying standards for judging outcomes. These varying uses for mediation complicate the task of the trainer in defining and training people to be effective mediators. For example, a court mediation program may focus on settlement of the issue that was brought to court. On the other hand, the mediator and/or parties may focus on whether the underlying issue was settled (e.g. a motion to modify parenting time may be brought to court but the underlying issue may actually be child support; or a lawsuit may be brought against a hospital for damages, but the plaintiffs really want to understand what happened during surgery, or want an apology from the doctor or hospital).

I agree with the authors that what might be most helpful is to look at data about why the case settled or did not settle. What helped and what hurt in the parties' efforts to reach resolution? Here might be concrete keys for trainers to point to as to what will indeed make a difference in ability to settle. For example, a key person missing from the negotiations: if it turns out that, statistically, missing people are very important in why a case did or did not settle, it would again make a case for more pre-mediation work on the part of the mediator, and trainers should emphasize the importance of who attends a mediation in their training. If, on the other hand, parties' readiness or the timing of a mediator turn out to be more statistically important, then trainers should focus more on those issues. As a trainer, it would be very exciting to be able to point to such data in emphasizing the importance of particular assessments or techniques.

The authors bring out one concept, reactive devaluation, that is very interesting. As a mediator, I have noted that participants devalue the concessions of the other party and overvalue their own. In fact, I sometimes resort to keeping a formal tally sheet to show what concessions each party has made. However, I rarely teach this as a technique. It would be great to see research on both the concept as it relates to outcomes, and on techniques to deal with it.

Long-Term Outcomes (T_2)

The proposed model offers only two concepts concerning long-term outcomes, *disputant beliefs and attitudes* and *conflict resolved*. My belief is that institutional measures could also be included under this part of the model. The authors note that the distinction between short-term and long-term is somewhat arbitrary. In that sense, for the trainer, the distinction may not be as important as one might initially think. However, it would be very helpful for trainers to find out what actually affects long-term outcomes of both disputant attitudes and actions, including compliance, long-term resolution, and recidivism.

Advanced versus Basic Training

Basic Training

Much of the model presented by the authors is material taught in basic mediation training, with the exception of antecedent conditions (T_0). I believe that it is important that more of T_0 be taught in basic mediation. Mediators and/or intake staff should be taught many of the issues brought up in T_0 for assessment purposes. In fact, the outline of the issues in T_0 could be put into an intake questionnaire for both training and assessment purposes.

Most of T_m is taught in basic mediation training. Mediator empathy, ability of clients to speak their mind, and other factors that prime readiness are regular parts of basic mediation training. Also included are issues of procedural fairness, interactional fairness, and other mediation conditions. Problem-solving issues and decision-making issues are likewise central components of basic mediation training. Like T_0, outcomes data (T_1, T_2) is not often taught in basic training. There is usually a nod to data on agreements reached and satisfaction with the process, but these are not considered important parts of mediation training.

One issue in discussing what is covered in basic versus advanced training, of course, is what is considered basic or advanced. Specialty training often includes outcome data (e.g. victim–offender mediation training often includes data on recidivism with juvenile offenders). Specialty training is sometimes considered basic mediation training and sometimes advanced mediation training, and can be taught either way. If it is a basic training, the role-play examples are taken from the specialty area, and the focus of the didactic portions of the training is in that area; but basic mediation skills are also taught. If it is an advanced training, most often only the specialty material is taught.

So one question is: How much of the research material should be taught in a basic training as opposed to an advanced training? One place to present research material would be to indicate toward the end of a training the areas that have been or are being researched, to give participants an idea of the issues in the field. Another would be to acknowledge that basic training workshops use a particular approach, and that participants may want to modify their approach to fit better with their personalities and their changing knowledge and understanding as they become more sophisticated.

As to particulars that could be taught in basic training, some examples include: the components of empathy (rapport, warmth, emotional safety, and respect), components of neutrality, and mediator decision-making. Expansion of these areas in basic training makes absolute sense, as they are foundation issues for new mediators, and will help mold their initial approach to practice. In addition, keys for settlement would be a good area for basic training.

Advanced Training

The model and components of the model are a goldmine for advanced training. So many issues can be explored in advanced training that could assist a mediator in assessing their approach to mediation and the efficacy of their practice. In advanced training, the trainer and the participants can go into many more nuances than is possible in a basic training. Discussions can be held on specific areas, and research findings can be brought in for thoughtful assessment of practice. Conferences put on by mediation organizations such as the Association for Conflict Resolution and the American Bar Association Section of Dispute Resolution would be greatly enhanced with short workshops on particular topics brought out by research in many of these areas.

Examples of areas ripe for advanced presentation and discussion:

- Neutrality and perceptions of neutrality
- Perceptions by the parties as to why a case settled or did not settle
- Perceptions of self-efficacy by parties and their effect on settlements
- Reactive devaluation and methods of counteracting its effect on settlement
- Mediator coaching of individual clients and its effect on perceptions of neutrality and settlement
- The relationship between attention to antecedent conditions (T_0) and outcomes (T_1 and T_2).

This list could go on and on. What is very clear is the helpfulness of translating research into practice. So, the more researchers and trainers can learn from each other, the more both can assist the practitioner.

One unsettling factor in advanced training is the number of mediators who don't take advanced training at all, or whose advanced training is all in substantive specialty areas rather than in mediation theory, research, or skills. It would no doubt be helpful for researchers to begin to do advanced training for trainers, to keep us up to date! Many states are now requiring advanced training, which should help reverse the first problem. However, almost none specify the content of that training. The more training that is available to help improve the quality of mediation, the better.

CONCLUSION

The work done by Herrman, Hollett, and Gale is astonishing in its depth and breadth. It will be exceedingly helpful to trainers as well as researchers and practitioners. I can't thank them enough for their hard work, perceptivity, and willingness to put forth a new model for the mediation world to work with. And I can't wait to see how it changes my practice and my teaching of mediation.

While the authors of the proposed model note that they are not advocating one application of the model over another, the research connections proposed and presented in figures 2.6 and 2.7 are enticing. These connections (and others) are, of course, what would be most helpful for trainers to find out about. It is here that research will be most helpful to trainers and students of mediation.

Once researchers take up the challenge embodied in both the proposed model and other chapters of this handbook and either test parts of the proposed model or present innovative spinoffs, all I need is for someone to summarize the outcomes of the research and tell me which research areas have sufficiently solid results that trainers should use them to base their training on!

Anyone willing?

NOTE

1   Created by and used with permission of Susan Hartman, Peace Talks, Ann Arbor, MI.

REFERENCE

Riskin, L. L. (1996) Understanding mediators' orientations, strategies, and techniques: a grid for the perplexed. *Harvard Negotiation Law Review* 7(Spring), 1–34.

Chapter 22

Conclusion

MARGARET S. HERRMAN

This handbook began with a goal of organizing existing information in a way that clarifies a complex and wide-ranging literature. A second, but equally important, goal was to prompt a lot of questions that might help mediators, negotiators, trainers, or scholars think about mediation in innovative ways. Authors contributing to this handbook represent some of the best minds currently working with negotiation and mediation as both practitioners and scholars, an incredible blend of talent and awareness. Their multi-faceted understanding reveals the nuances and complexities of mediation, especially for readers who read the entire handbook or a substantial number of chapters.

The collective emphasis may feel different, not just to new mediators. As Pruitt notes in chapter 20 of this handbook, the interest in mediation and negotiation traditionally focused on outcomes – whether settlements happened and whether participants followed through on their settlement. But this handbook opens up other aspects of mediation as being equal to or more important than outcomes. To begin, the model presented in chapter 2 details antecedent or contextual factors as well as the dynamics within an actual intervention as much or more than outcomes. All of part II carries this exploration into antecedent factors forward along with later voices like those of Gray, Schruijer and Vansina, and Avruch, who expand the idea of context. Thanks to Wissler's chapter 5, outcomes are not ignored, but Wissler clearly connects outcomes to antecedent factors using the findings from a number of studies. To take the theme further, when Deutsch (chapter 17), and Gray (chapter 8), describe a variety of contextual characteristics, they introduce a cautionary note to those who still think mediation offers an answer to life's persistent questions. They are asking practitioners to assess the context of a conflict thoroughly before deciding on any form of intervention. Shapiro (chapter 14), also emphasizes the importance of contextual awareness, especially when a conflict is emotionally charged. These authors are clearly cautioning against naive interventions. All of the chapters in part III delve deeply into different aspects of the internal dynamics of problem-solving: power, emotions, manifestations of justice, facework, and the actual talk of a mediation. All represent important focal points for advanced training as well as more research.

The natural tendency for readers is probably to read select chapters. But after reading the whole book, I know that the full impact of the handbook emerges when all of the chapters are allowed to perk in your mind. The wide range of ideas presented by all of the contributing authors suggests so many new avenues for thought, research, and teaching. Editing this handbook was delightful. I learned a lot, and each chapter gave me new reasons to appreciate where this field is going. So I close this conversation by sharing some of what I have learned by experiencing the action-reaction-action nature of this handbook.

THE PROGRESS OF OUR THINKING

The area of practice and scholarship relating to conflict resolution or conflict engagement (as Mayer 2004 suggests) has evolved significantly for over at least a 40-year period. As demonstrated by the array of chapters in this handbook, the scholarship of this field draws ideas and hypotheses from many intellectual and practical disciplines. New scholarship as well as evolving intervention techniques will benefit from conscious attention to the knowledge and skills offered within as many of these disciplines as possible.

The breadth of information communicated in this handbook affirms that our understanding of the dynamics of mediation and negotiation has evolved well beyond a formative period. But our full potential lies ahead. As Mayer (2004) notes, we are not there yet. This handbook presents new ideas and challenges old paradigms. Readers are being asked to stretch beyond current shibboleths (e.g. ideas that shape thinking, especially of people just coming into the field; invocations of neutrality represents but one example), and beyond self-imposed boundaries (e.g. untested proclamations about the nature of mediation) and assumptions (especially that models derived from Caucasian and Eurocentric comfort levels are "ideal ways to mediate"). This handbook considers the setting of a mediation seriously, while also detailing intimately the moves during a mediation, and furthermore how mediators and other participants are influenced in subtle and not so subtle ways by the interplay of context and the narrative of a problem-solving conversation.

EMBRACING COMPLEXITY

The sophisticated ideas and techniques presented in this handbook underscore the complexity of problem-solving, especially when problem-solving involves more than one person partnering with an intervener. Chapter 2 chronicles the roots of our thinking about mediation. Some people will read the chapter and stop there, but I hope not. Winslade and Monk say that the model presented in chapter 2 should be considered as a little "m" not an "M." We raised the same caution. But the message bears repeating, especially in a context of writers over the past decade pummeling scholars and practitioners with ideologies about the "right way to mediate" and about "valid subjects for study." The second goal of this handbook will be achieved when readers experience the wonder and complexity of different ways to solve problems, different texts to explore, and broad frames of reference.

I invited contributing authors to critique, add to, and test ideas presented in chapter 2 in ways that move thinking and understanding forward. People took me up on my request, and readers will find a myriad of suggestions about future research and practice innovations between the covers of this handbook. I offer two examples. First, Winslade and Monk (chapter 9), challenge the dominance of "agreements" as the end stage or even the *sine qua non* of mediation. They note that mediations may not stop with an agreement, since the talk – the narrative – may not stop with a formal agreement. This point presents a beautiful opportunity to test and possibly change the content of training. To test the idea, I would frame a series of hypotheses that begin with contextual characteristics, including – but not limited to – the forum in which the mediation occurs. All of part II describes various ways in which forums or institutional contexts impinge on the conduct of a mediation, and subsequently shape the outcome. Add all of the chapters in part III to your ideas of what might change a mediated narrative, and it is easy to see how a process in one forum might be very different from the process embedded in other forums. Chapters in part III might have included work on the construct of mediator style, but I consciously avoided the topic because of a personal concern that the construct is so complex and unexplored that an entire handbook might be more appropriate. It is a seductive construct that has not been pinned down adequately (perhaps best by Riskin 2003). All of the constructs described in part III could be studied as more fundamental than style – with style probably being a composite of all of these things and much more – such as timing for example. But for the sake of shorthand in this summary, if we were to look at what has been defined as style, one might hypothesize that cases reach mediation from one of several avenues or forums (e.g. court-mandated and mediator-selected, attorney-selected, client-selected, etc.) that predispose mediator and case characteristics. For example, a second set of hypotheses might postulate that fewer facilitative (see Riskin 1996, 2003 for definitions), transformative (see Bush & Folger 1994 for a definition), or narrative (Winslade & Monk 2000) mediators are chosen by attorneys to mediate cases. You might find more evaluative mediators (see Riskin 1996) mediating cases when the assignment/choice originates with an attorney or a higher court. Yet a third set of hypotheses might be that evaluative mediators feel that a settlement suffices, stops the process, so that narration ends with the mediation. Facilitative, transformative, or narrative mediators might assume ongoing conversations about the topics of the mediation and more. Hence, the mediation continues after a settlement. To go further, all of these hypotheses might relate to a case characteristic, namely that a reason or desire exists for a continuing relationship after mediation.

Second, Saposnek, in chapter 12, describes some power dynamics at work when people are experiencing significant emotional turmoil. His descriptions evolve out of divorce situations, but they might just as easily apply to any deep-rooted identity dispute. Consider that mediators are typically trained to balance power, working under an untested assumption that self-determination and just outcomes emerge during problem-solving characterized by a "level playing field" – a clear T_m to $T_{1\&2}$ hypothesis to be tested. Saposnek also highlights the influence of constituents and external advocates – raised earlier in Rubin and Brown (1975) for experimental studies and not fully developed in the model or in the field. A testable hypothesis might be something to the effect that the greater the emotional distress of any participant the greater the probability that he or she clings to external advocates for support and nurturance, and thus places a great deal of salience on what would please these external participants. Scholars could tackle the idea, but so could practitioners. In fact, Zumeta (chapter 21), encourages trainers and researchers to collaborate in an exploration and fine-tune both our understanding and the sophistication of training.

BOUNDARIES TURN GRAY

Compare the ideas presented in chapters 3 through 7 to those in chapters 8 through 13. The ideas are not mutually exclusive. Taken in their totality, understanding contextual framing adds to an understanding of internal dynamics, and vice versa. Even as we fully recognize the power of specific internal dynamics such as framing, facework, or emotions, if we step into a narrative frame and pay attention to language and stories, it becomes impossible to dismiss any one dynamic as irrelevant or not important. It is also hard to discount the many facets of context because they shape where a narrative starts while giving clues about the progression of a narrative. Look at Umbreit and Coates (chapter 7), who suggest that a restorative frame of reference positions mediators to avoid controlling the flow of a mediation. But is that really possible? People – mediators and other participants – engaged in a fight consciously or not select what they say. The result is that some ideas and words are privileged over other words and ideas (Cobb 1993, 1994). Depending on the forcefulness of a person's words and inflection, selective privileging may or may not be a soft form of control. But even a soft form shapes a mediation. So, boundaries begin to blur, the reductionistic comforts of binary thinking become too confining, and the profound and exciting complexities come alive. Deutsch (chapter 17) skillfully transcends the interpersonal, international, dyadic, and large-group context and literatures. He shows the value of understanding how these seemingly disparate contexts build deeper understanding where scholars and practitioners are conversant with several contexts of practice and literature. The chapter goes below the surface of T_0 to explore how participant histories contribute to immediate characteristics of a conflict. He implies a hypothesis: if an intervention creates an atmosphere of "transcendental eloquence," the potential for creative cooperative problem-solving emerges (i.e., a clear T_0–T_m–T_1 connection using the time frame suggested by the model in chapter 2). Deutsch goes on to suggest that repeat behaviors help establish changed attitudes which, in turn, support repeat behaviors, thus opening up research and possible new texts for training that challenge scholars and mediators to assess how immediate success at T_1 impacts the long-term cessation of conflict at T_2. So, a subtle suggestion coming from Deutsch is that the end of a mediation may not be an agreement or settlement at one point in time. There is life after a mediation, and are we implying that mediators consciously raise questions about possible scenarios outside the box of their face-to-face work with clients? What are the implications for training, practice, and research?

FINAL THOUGHTS

Voice is given to so many ideas in this handbook, and yet so many are silent. I mentioned the construct of style as being one. Turning points and timing are others, and I am sure there are so many more. The reflexive intent of the model in chapter 2 and of mediation are noted throughout the text, but the full ramifications are open to deep exploration. So this handbook offers ideas, and hopefully opens doors. It is not the beginning of a literature, but it falls somewhere after creation and before deeper understanding. There is much to be done, and the potential is more exciting today than ever before.

REFERENCES

Bush, R. A. B. & Folger, J. P. (1994) *The Promise of Mediation.* Jossey-Bass, San Francisco.

Cobb, S. (1993) Empowerment and mediation: a narrative perspective. *Negotiation Journal* 8(3, July), 245–259.

Cobb, S. (1994) A narrative perspective on mediation: toward the materialization of the "storytelling" metaphor. In J. P. Folger & T. S. Jones (eds.), *New Directions in Mediation: Communication Research and Perspectives.* Sage, Thousand Oaks, pp. 48–63.

Mayer, B. S. (2004) *Beyond Neutrality: Confronting the Crisis in Conflict Resolution.* Jossey-Bass, San Francisco.

Riskin, L. L. (1996) Understanding mediators' orientations, strategies, and techniques: a grid for the perplexed. *Harvard Negotiation Law Review* 7(Spring), 1–34.

Riskin, L. L. (2003) Decision making in mediation: the new old grid and the new grid system. *Notre Dame Law Review* 79, 1–53.

Rubin, J. Z. & Brown, B. R. (1975) *The Social Psychology of Bargaining and Negotiation.* Academic, New York.

Winslade, J. & Monk, G. (2000) *Narrative Mediation.* Jossey-Bass, San Francisco.

Index of Citations

General Index

able to talk about perceptions and feelings, 32, 33 (figure 2.3), 35 (table 2.2), 37; emotion in mediation process, 286–7; procedural justice, 252; training perspective, 414, 416, 418

active negotiation, 33 (figure 2.3), 34, 35 (table 2.2), 42; in family mediation, 115; justice and the mediation process, 252

active participation, 33 (figure 2.3), 34, 35 (table 2.2), 39; workplace mediation research, 161

acts, 233–4 (figure 10.3), 235 (table 10.1), 236 (table 10.2), 242

adjudication frame, 203–4

advice, expert, 405

advocate, leader as, 376

affect, 407; negative, 408

affiliation, 318

agreement, authorship of, 377

agreement reached, 45 (figure 2.4), 46 (table 2.3), 50–1; measurement of success, 382–3

allocation of resources, 257

American Bar Association Section of Dispute Resolution, 419

analyst, leader as, 375, 377

anger, 130, 288–90, 295

antecedent characteristics, role in mediation, 129

antecedent conditions, 25 (figure 2.2); family mediation, 103, 120–1; justice and, 250–1; restorative justice, 178; training, 413, 417–18

antecedents, 182–3

anxiety about a crime, reduced, 45 (figure 2.4), 47 (table 2.3), 50; enhancing justice for outcomes, 256; see also fear

appeals to political action frame, 204

arbitration, 334–5

architect, leader as, 375, 377

arena for negotiation, 377

artistry, 383

Association for Conflict Resolution, 418

attorneys, 89–90; actions, 136

auspices, 182

authority decides after consultation frame, 205–6

authorship of agreement, 377

autonomy, 318

barriers to resolution of charge, 163–5 (table 6.8)

BATNA (best alternative to a negotiated agreement), 198, 210

Begin, Menachem, 379

behavior, 407

behavioral exchange therapy, 407, 409

bias suppression, 257

Bin Laden, Osama, 357

California Department of Fair Employment and Housing (CDFEH), 173n